Between the Kola Forest and the Salty Sea

A History of the Liberian People Before 1800

Carl Patrick Burrowes, Ph. D.

Unabridged 1st Edition

The lessons offered by *Between the KolaForest and Salty Sea* has to be passed along to our youth, our future. The narrative of our history has always started from the arrival of the settlers, ignoring the rich, long legacies of generations before. Our youth are in desperate need of a "new" reality, one that embraces all and perhaps that will begin to level the playing field in their identity of self - which in turn will help erase some of the "isms" which has blinded their value in society.
— *Miatta "Peeko" Ashley, artist and activist*

With *Between the Kola Forest and the Salty Sea* Dr. Burrowes has filled a significant void in the known history of the West African nation of Liberia. Ironically, because of the rigorous and thorough nature of this work which combs various sources from archaeology, linguistics, and anthropology, Burrowes makes the case that indeed most nations are undoubtedly formed by the migration patterns of diverse peoples with various social, religious and economic motivations. This seminal work suggests that in forging a national identity people should understand their ancient past and acknowledge the choices that their ancestors made in becoming a part of a community within their eventual homeland. For a country still recovering from violent civil conflict this may be the greatest contribution a historian can offer. This is a must read not only for academics and scholars worldwide; it is a story that the Liberian people need to hear.
— *Dawn Cooper-Barnes, Executive Director,*
Coca-Cola Institute for Innovation, A. M. E. University

Prior to reading *Between the Kola Forest and the Salty Sea*, I had not had the opportunity of coming across any work that dealt so thoroughly with how the various people of Liberia are interrelated and interconnected as Dr. Burrowes has recorded.

This book should form part of the curricula of Liberian social studies for every Liberian student. The perspective this book offers is especially needed after the devastating and senseless civil strife that engulfed our country for a little over 15 years and destroyed almost every fabric of the educational system of the country.
— *Tolo Bonah Corfah, Educator*

Dr. Burrowes' work gives us insight into the depth of our history and origins in ways beyond comparison. It makes us realize where we are from and that we all belong here. Definitely a pleasurable read, which I recommend for any inquiring mind.
— *Richelieu Lomax, International Litigation Analyst*

Between the Kola Forest and the Salty Sea packs a heavy punch! Its strength lies in the narratives derived from volumes of archival material, primary and second sources. The language is accessible throughout and lyrical/poetic in many instances. The histories Burrowes conveys are beautifully interwoven, and he argues convincingly that pre-settler Liberia was a by-product of broader political, economic, social, and ecological developments.

— *Dr. Robtel N. Paley, Author and Scholar*

Prof. Carl Patrick Burrowes has written a masterpiece. This is the book I have been looking for most of my life. I salute him and commend him for this most seminal contribution to the literature. Yet this is more than just an important contribution to the academy.

Prof. Burrowes' comprehensive history is the most significant contribution to the Liberian national and Pan-Africanist dialogue in a generation or two. I would not be leaning towards hyperbole if I classify this immediately with the literary contributions of my hero E.W Blyden. Why? Because finally, through this book we have a deeply researched and cogently argued narrative that through a very "longue duree" approach that situates the political, economic history, societal and cultural dynamics of the peoples and places in the area that has become the modern-day polity of "Liberia" within the times series context and realities of the rest of the region.

Burrowes has shown us all the connectivity between the dynamics of events within the Liberian space and Africa as a whole. He has shown us the ocean, when for too long we have only seen the waves before us. In that regard, it is also a deeply political and transformative contribution to our discourse on how Liberia is to progress, based on a fuller knowledge of the forces that have manifested over the past 400 plus years in what has since 1822 become the modern republican polity.

This is not just history. It is my story, it is our story. It is a book that must be taught in universities, schools, at Liberia's foreign service training centre and further afield. This matters today more than ever before because, as the great Southern American scribe William Faulker once wrote: "The past is never dead. It's not even past."

— *Max Bankole Jarrett, Member of the Advisory Board of Africa 2.0 and Former Presenter and Senior Producer/Broadcast Journalist at BBC World Service*

The Honorable Marcus Garvey said, "A people without the knowledge of their history, origin and culture is like a tree without roots" Dr. Burrowes has replanted Liberia into the soil of African history by smelting this book like a Kissi blacksmith who smelts iron to make a currency. This book is rich with historical, theological, political and economic realities of Liberia that we must read.

Very few authors have presented historical details about Liberia before 1822 and this book set the standard for younger Liberians and Africans to research and rewrite our history. Malcolm X said "Of all our studies, history is best qualified to reward our research," and Dr. Burrowes has excellently researched and brought the past into the future.
— *Capt. Emmanuel G. Woods, Chaplain U. S. Army*

Between the Kola Forest and the Salty Sea places the history of Liberia in proper perspective by providing a seamless narrative of how the peoples of this country migrated to what is referred to today as Liberia. This work debunks the longstanding myth that the history of this country started from 1822. In so doing, it has radically shifted the paradigm.

On the contrary, the book provides a narrative of the history as it has unfolded over the past centuries and points out that while the country's relationship with the rest of the world started earlier. The history of Liberia is a history of African peoples migrating from different parts of the continent to settle where we are today. In this light, it is a mosaic of or melting pot for African peoples arriving from different parts of the world to establish a single whole called Liberia.

Burrowes presents telling details coupled with rigorous analysis. He has provided considerable knowledge of the country's past in a lucid way; this is a magnificent scholarly achievement.

I recommend this for university students studying Liberian society and for those interested in knowing Liberia, especially at a time when the country is emerging from the ashes of a senseless war and seeking a better path to the future. It is a must read. I have learned a lot from this work. Cannot wait to see it on the shelves of libraries and of bookstores.
— *Thomas Jaye, Deputy Director for Research, Department of Graduate Studies and Research, Kofi Annan International Peacekeeping Training Centre (KAIPTC)*

Copyright 2016 by Carl Patrick Burrowes
All rights reserved

Maps by Çhonsee, visual artist, independent curator and designer

No part of this book may be reproduced in any form or by any electronic or mechanical means including information storage and retrieval systems, without permission in writing from the author. The only exception is by a reviewer, who may quote short excerpts in a review.

Published by Know Your Self Press, Bomi County, Republic of Liberia
Printed by CreateSpace, Charleston, South Carolina, USA

First Printing: December 2016
ISBN-9780998390505

The author is available for public discussions of the book. To arrange a talk, contact kolaforest@me.com or patrickburrowes via Skype.

Acknowledgment xxiii

Preface xxvii

Introduction 1
    Sons of Ham and Headless People 6
    Eurocentrism and Ancient Egypt 8
    The New Hamites: Fulas and Mandingos 9
    An African Perspective on History 10
    Language and Eurocentrism in African History 14
    Eurocentrism in Liberian Studies 16
    A New Total History 18

The Eden of West Africa 27
    Niger-Congo Languages 33
    Land, Clan and Gender 50
    Sea Salt, Kola Seeds and Malagueta Spice 54
    Shifting Winds, Ocean Currents and Natural Harbors 57
    Taa's Town, Pottery and the Long-Distance Salt Trade 59
    Stone Carvings as Evidence of Iron-Smelting 60

The Way of the Ancestors 71
    The Energy in All Things 73
    Masquerades as Homes to Abstract Powers 74
    Ancestor Veneration, Not Worship 76
    Shrines and Sacraments 78
    Diviners, Prophets and Other Religious Authorities 80
    Blacksmiths, Hunters and the Control of Life-force 82
    Wisdom in Proverbs and Visual Signs 84
    Sociopaths as Sources of Evil 85
    West African Conception of Time 87

Egypt and Religions of the Book 95
    The Mediterranean World 102
    Lost Tribes of Israel? 104
    Christianity's Refuge in North Africa 105
    Islam - Habash to Südan 108

The Rise of Empires 115
    International Trade 116
    Mande Speakers along the Niger 120
    Clans Change to Castes 122
    Tributary States and Empires 123
    The Advantages of Writing 125
    Conversions to Islam 126
    The Ghana and Mali Empires 128
    Succession Fights and Migrations 129

Down from the Niger 139
    Arrival of Southeast and Southwest Mande Speakers 141
    Vai, Dama, Kono 143
    Southwest Mande Speakers 146
    Southeast Mande Speakers 147
    People of the Poro and Sande 150
    The Dark Side of Trade 151

The World Turned Upside Down 159
    The Persistent Presence of Portuguese 161
    Grains, God and Gold 162
    A Napoleon Complex 165
    Columbus, Spain and the New World 165
    Early European Accounts 166
    Gold from Coya 167

More Slaves for More Weapons and Horses	168
The Songhai Empire and Expansion of Islam	169

Dispersal of the Malinké 177
    The Mane Conquest of the Sierra Leone Peninsula 179
    Making Sense of the Invasion 180
    The Quoia Invasion 182
    Interpreting the Quoja Invasion 183
    Emergence of Mende, Disappearance of Dama 188
    A Movement that Shook the Entire Region 189

Into the Forest 195
    Movement from Man 196
    Migration into Western Liberia 197
    The Loma and the Kokologi Agreement 201
    Kpelle and Ma Interactions 202
    Dispersal from Mt. Gedeh 204
    Unique Features of the Southeast Region 209

"They work excellent well in Iron" 217
    The French and English Enter the West African Trade 221
    Local Farming and Foods 225
    Nicolas Villault and the Voyage of the Europa 227
    Intimacy and a Unique Handshake 231

Two-Story Huts & Sugar-Loaf Baskets 239
    William Bosman on the Sexual Habits of Local Women 240
    Wild Men, Fruitful Women and a Funeral 243
    Amsterdam's Decline, England's Rise 246
    Jean Barbot Visits Cape Mount and the Malagueta Coast 248
    Scarification and Traditional Religion at Sestros 251

- Surveyor William Smith and the Soundings of the Rivers ... 253

Lamentations and Chants of Grief ... 259
- British Interpolers and French Adventurers ... 270
- Guns, Rum and Rebellion ... 272
- A Fisher of Men ... 276
- African Resistance to Slavery ... 279

Crawling Ahead, Falling Behind ... 291
- Cities: Seats of the Good Life? ... 293
- "Hungry Times," Smallpox and the Plague ... 294
- Human Labor and Other Sources of Energy ... 295
- Farming and Foods ... 296
- Meat and Other Sources of Protein ... 297
- Clothes, Furniture and Dishes ... 298
- Mud and Wood Dwellings ... 300
- Civility and Sexual Mores ... 301
- Transportation ... 302
- Making Things ... 303
- Markets, Money and Monopolies ... 304
- How Europe Crawled Ahead of Africa ... 307

A New World Order ... 317
- Elephants and Leopards ... 318
- From Calicos and Batiks to "African" Fabrics ... 319
- Brazil's Gifts of Domboy and Gbassajamba ... 320
- From Palmwine to Brandy and Rum ... 322

Conclusion ... 331
- Local Impact of the Slave Trade ... 323
- Migration from the Niger ... 330
- The Problem of "Purity" ... 332

    The Lingering Legacy of de Sintra 333

    Toward the Future 335

Front Matter

Table of Figures

Figure 1. Niger-Congo Language Families in Liberia 5
Figure 2. Blemmyae People of Aethiopia 6
Figure 3. Words Used to Frame Africans Negatively 12
Figure 4. Rock painting, cattle scene, Tassili, southern Algeria, 5000-2000 BC 31
Figure 5. Tracking languages 33
Figure 6. Niger-Congo Language Family Tree 34
Figure 7. Kru languages & cultures 35
Figure 8. Basenji dog in Ancient Egypt and present day 36
Figure 9. African names for months 37
Figure 10. Atlantic languages 46
Figure 11. Kru languages, distribution and number of speakers 50
Figure 12. Kola seeds and malagueta spice 54
Figure 13. "Popo" beads 57
Figure 14. "Iron" in local languages 58
Figure 15. Kissi pomtan stone sculpture 60
Figure 16. Kru iron money 62
Figure 17. Kissi "pennies" 62
Figure 18. "God" in local languages 72
Figure 19. Masked figure, rock painting, Tassili, southern Algeria, 8000-5000 BC 82
Figure 20. Dan Mask with cowrie shells and sacred red 84
Figure 21. Major constellations 86
Figure 22. The night sky in African mythology 88
Figure 23. Akan "Akuaba" fertility doll (left) and two Egyptian Ankhs 96
Figure 24. Religion in Ancient Egypt & West Africa 98
Figure 25. Ancient Egypt & the Old Testament 100
Figure 26. Ouroboros, Ancient Egyptian symbol of infinity 101
Figure 27. Egyptian religion & the New Testament 104
Figure 28. The Islamic calendar 106
Figure 29. Mansa Musa of Mali 130
Figure 30. Great Mosque of Timbuktu 131
Figure 31. Portuguese caravel, based on the Arab dhow 160
Figure 32. Portuguese words in Liberia 162
Figure 33. Kola plant & seeds 167
Figure 34. Arabic influences on Vai words for weekdays 186
Figure 35. Impact of Kru Cultures 204
Figure 36. Coat of Arms of John Hawkins, slave trader 220
Figure 37. Negro-Houses, Cape Mesurado c. 1745-1747 222
Figure 38. Popular foreign goods from Sierra Leone to the Gold Coast, 1558 223
Figure 39. Welcoming Falam Boure 229

Figure 40. "Bridge in the Quoja's Country" c. 1745-1747 232
Figure 41. Canoes, paddles and other objects along the Kru Coast 240
Figure 42. African slave merchant 260
Figure 43. Slave deck, "Wildfire," Key West, Florida, 1860 261
Figure 44. West African slave market 263
Figure 45. Slave exports by regions 264
Figure 46. Trans-Atlantic Slave Trade, 1514-1865 265
Figure 47. Windward Coast slave trade, 1659-1840 267
Figure 48. Windward Coast slave disembarkation by region 269
Figure 49. Enslaved Africans being loaded into hold of slave ship 270
Figure 50. Slaves embarked from Grand Bassa on the Neuva Isabel, 1830 273
Figure 51. Slaves embarked from Grand Bassa on the Neuva Isabel, 1830 (continued) 274
Figure 52. Slaves embarked from St. Paul's River, 1823 277
Figure 53. Slaves embarked from St. Paul's River, 1813 (continued) 279
Figure 54. Enslaved Africans in hold of slave ship, 1817 280
Figure 55. Antislavery actions on the Windward Coast 281
Figure 56. Antislavery actions on the Windward Coast (continued) 283

Table of Maps

Map 1. Dispersal of West Africans c. 2500 BC 28
Map 2. Climate and vegetation in Africa after 2000 BC 30
Map 3. Spread of iron smelting in Africa 38
Map 4. Location of Atlantic languages 48
Map 5. Route of Jesus and his parents through Egypt 103
Map 6. The spread of Islam in the 7th and 8th centuries 107
Map 7. Rainfall patterns & ecological zones c. 700-1630 AD 119
Map 8. Routes and entrepôts of commerce in Africa c. 1000 BC 122
Map 9. Manding heartland & areas where Mande languages are spoken 125
Map 10. Empires of Ghana, Mali & Songhai 129
Map 11. Location of Soso & Jalonke 131
Map 12. Nzérékoré district, Guinea, showing earlier location of Southwest Mande groups 144
Map 13. Liberian languages and ethnic groups 147
Map 14. Groups near Cape Mount mention by Olfert Dapper c. 1668 186
Map 15. Mande penetration toward Gold Coast 189
Map 16. Languages in Mano River Region 191
Map 17. Main historical trade route in Liberia 201
Map 18. Movement of Kpelle, Kono & Ma in Guinea 202
Map 19. Kru languages of Liberia & Côte d'Ivoire 211
Map 20. Spread of Poro Society and Dan style masks 212

Credit for Illustrations

Figure 2. Blemmyae people of Aethiopia, p. 6, from Hartmann Schedel, *Nuremberg Chronicle*, 1493

Map 1. Dispersal of West Africans c. 2500 BC, p. 28, from Albert M. Craig et at, "Africa early history to 1000 CE," *The Heritage of World Civilizations* (New York: Pearson HigherEd, 2012), p. 127

Map 2. Climate and vegetation in Africa after 2000 BC, p. 30, from Christopher Ehret, *The Civilizations of Africa: A History to 1800* (Charlottesville: University of Virginia Press, 2002), p. 108

Figure 4. Rock painting, cattle scene, Tassili, Algeria, 5000-2000 BC, p. 31, from algerieterredafrique.blogspot.com/2012/07/lalgerie-dans-la-prehistoire.html

Figure 6. Niger-Congo Language Family Tree, p. 34, David J. Dwyer, "The place of Mande in Niger-Congo" (pp. 27-65) in Ian Maddieson and Thomas Hinnebusch, eds., *Language History and Linguistic Description in Africa* (Trenton, NJ: Africa World Press, 1998), p. 29.

Figure 8. Basenji dog in Ancient Egypt and present-day, p. 36, from Chatsworth House Derbyshire Limestone Stele dating from 1900 BC and showing Renu and Dedet with basenji type dog under their chair, and www.animals-universe.info/basenji/2443

Map 3. Spread of iron smelting in Africa, p. 38, from Christopher Ehret, *The Civilizations of Africa: A History to 1800* (Charlottesville: University of Virginia Press, 2002), p. 163

Map 4. Location of Atlantic languages, p. 48, from W. A. A. Wilson, "Atlantic," in John Bendor-Samuel, *The Niger-Congo Languages* (Lanham: University Press of America), p. 82

Figure 11. Kru languages, distribution and number of speakers, p. 50, from Lynell Marchese, "Kru," in John Bendor-Samuel, *The Niger-Congo Languages* (Lanham: University Press of America, 1989), p. 126.

Figure 12. Kola seeds, p. 54, from http://www.tradewindsfruit.com/content/cola-nut.htm, and Malagueta Spice, photo by Inna Moody at www.flickr.com/photos/moodyworld/252197885

Figure 14. "Iron" in local languages, p. 58, from Sigismund Wilhelm Koelle, *Polyglotta Africana*. Edited with an introduction by P. E. H. Hair and David Dalby (Graz, Austria: Akademische Druck-U. Verlagsanstalt, 1963; reprint of 1854 edition, p. 82

Figure 15. Kissi pomtan stone sculpture, p. 60, from http://www.bwoom-gallery.com/Kissi%20Nomoli%20Figur%2065101.html

Figure 16. Kru iron money, p. 62, from www.liberiapastandpresent.org/culture2.htm

Figure 18. "God" in Local Languages, p. 72, from Sigismund Wilhelm Koelle, *Polyglotta Africana*. Edited with an introduction by P. E. H. Hair and David Dalby (Graz, Austria: Akademische Druck-U. Verlagsanstalt, 1963; reprint of 1854 edition, p. 74; E. Dora Earthy, "The Impact of Mohammedanism on paganism in the Liberian hinterland," *Numen*, Vol. 2, Fasc. 3 (Sept. 1955): 206-216

Figure 19. Masked figure, rock painting, Tassili, Southern Algeria, 8000-5000 BC, p. 82, from http://ponteoculta.blogspot.com/2016-06-01-archive.html

Figure 20. Dan mask with cowrie shells and sacred red, p. 84, from africadirect.com

Figure 21. Major constellations, p. 86, from George Schwab, *Tribes of the Liberian Hinterlands* (Cambridge, Mass.: Peabody Museum of Archeology and Ethnology, 1947), p. 67

Figure 22. The night sky in African Mythology, p. 88, from Kevin Cuff & Alan Gould, *A Collection of Curricula for the STARLAB African Mythology Cylinder* (Somerville, MA: Learning Technologies, 2005), p. 18

Figure 23. Akan "Akuaba" fertility doll (on the left), and Egyptian Ankh, p. 96, from https://www.novica.com/itemdetail/?pid=162496, and https://plus.google.com/photos/102949872868318346061/albums/6303152192849349681?authkey=CJ-B9dCug9Xt9QE&sqi=107936871396795767208&sqsi=31dabb23-7a18-4d5b-84ff-db4bf0c71d84

Figure 24. Religion in Ancient Egypt & West Africa, p. 98, from Ernest Alfred Wallis Budge, *Osiris and the Egyptian Resurrection* (New York: G. P. Putnam's Sons, 1861)

Figure 25. Ancient Egypt & the Old Testament, p. 100, from Samuel Sharpe, *Egyptian Mythology and Egyptian Christianity, with Their Influence on the Opinions of Modern Christianity* (London: Carter & Col, 1896).

Figure 26. Ouroboros, Egyptian symbol of infinity, p. 101, object from Early Christian and Byzentine Art, Baltimore Museum of Art, Baltimore, image from https://commons.wikimedia.org/wiki/File:Egyptian_-_Gnostic_Gem_with_Scarab_-_Walters_42872.jpg#

Map 5. Route of Jesus and his parents through Egypt, p. 103, from Christiane Desroches Noblecourt, *Gifts from the Pharaohs: How Egyptian Civilization Shaped the Modern World* (Paris: Flammarion, 2007), p. 264

Figure 27. Egyptian Religion & the New Testament, p. 104, from Samuel Sharpe, *Egyptian Mythology and Egyptian Christianity, with Their Influence on the Opinions of Modern Christianity* (London: Carter & Col, 1896), p. 14

Map 6. The Spread of Islam in the 7th and 8th Centuries, p. 107, from G. S. P. Freeman-Grenville, *The New Atlas of African History* (New York: Simon & Schuster, 1991), p. 15

Map 7. Rainfall patterns and ecological zones, ca. 700-1630 AD, p. 117, from George E. Brooks, "Ecological perspectives on Mande population movements, commercial networks, and settlement patterns from the Atlantic West Phase (ca. 5500-2500 B. C.) to the present," *History in Africa*, 16 (1989): 23-40, p. 25

Map 8. Routes and entrepots of commerce in Africa c. 1000 BC, p. 120, from Christopher Ehret, *The Civilizations of Africa: A History to 1800* (Charlottesville: University of Virginia Press, 2002), p. 166 58

Map 9. Manding heartland and areas where Mande languages are spoken, p. 123, from David Dalby, "Distribution and nomenclature of the Manding people and their language," in Carleton T. Hodge, ed., Papers on the Manding (Bloomington: Indiana University, 1971), p. 9.

Map 10. West Africa showing empires of Ghana, Mali and Songhai, p. 127, from https://edu.hstry.co/timeline/ancient-west-african-kingdoms-c61360c3-6c48-47b2-a990-af141a0886c7

Map 11. Location of Susu and Jalonke, p. 129, from Stephen Bühnen, "In quest of Susu," *History in Africa*, Vol. 21 (1994): 1-47, p. 25

Figure 29. Mansa Musa of Mali, p. 132, from a Catalan atlas of the known world c. 1375; object is housed at Bibliothéque nationale de France, image retrieved from http://www.nytimes.com/2012/04/19/arts/design/the-great-mosque-in-djenne-mali.html

Map 12. Nzérékoré district, Republic of Guinea, p. 142, from Jacques Germain, *Guinée: Peuples de la Forêt* (Paris: Académie des Sciences d'Outre-Mer, 1984), pp. 100-101

Map 13. Liberian languages and ethnic groups, p. 145, from Tom W. Shick, *Behold the Promised Land: A History of Afro-American Settler Society in Nineteenth-Century Liberia*. Baltimore: Johns Hopkins University Press, 1980

Figure 31. Portuguese caravel, based on the Arab dhow, p. 162, from http://www.causa-merita.com/descob_embarc_1_i.htm

Figure 32. Portuguese words in Liberia, p. 164, from A. T. von S. Bradshaw, "Vestiges of Portuguese in the languages of Sierra Leone," *Sierra Leone Language Review*, Vol. 4 (1965), pp. 5-37

Figure 33. Kola plant and seed, p. 169, from Gustav Pabst (ed.): *Köhler's Medizinal-Pflanzen in naturgetreuen Abbildungen mit kurz erläuterndem Texte* Gera-Untermhaus (Germany, 1887)

Map 14. Groups near Cape Mount mentioned by Olfert Dapper, p. 184, from Adam Jones, "The Kquoja Kingdom: A forest stte in seventeenth century West Africa," *Paideuma*, 29 (1983), p. 37

Figure 34. Arabic Influences on Vai Words for Weekdays, p. 188, from H. Boikai Freeman, "The Vai and their kinfolk," *Negro History Bulletin*, 16, 3 (Dec. 1, 1952): 51-64

Map 15. Mande penetration toward Gold Coast, p. 187, from Ivor Wilks, "The northern factor in Ashanti history: Begho and the Mande," *Journal of African History*, 11, 1 (1961), p. 27

Map 16. Languages in Mano River Region, p. 189, from Jacques Germain, *Guinée: Peuples de la Forêt* (Paris: Académie des Sciences d'Outre-Mer, 1984), pp. 44-45

Map 17. Main historic trade routes in Liberia area, p. 199, from George W. Harley, "Roads and trails in Liberia," *Geographical Review*, Vol. 29 (July 1939), p.

Map 18. Movement of Kpelle, Kono and Ma in Guinea, p. 200, from Jacques Germain, *Guinée: Peuples de la Forêt* (Paris: Académie des Sciences d'Outre-Mer, 1984), pp. 76-77.

Map 19. Kru languages of Liberia & Côte d'Ivoire, p. 206, from Lynell Marchese, "Kru" (pp. 119-139) in John Bendor-Samuel, *The Niger-Congo Languages* (Lanham: University Press of America, 1989).

Map 20. Spread of Poro society and Dan style masks, p. 209, from George E. Brooks, *Western Africa to c. 1860 AD: A Provisional Historical Scheme Based on Climate Periods* (Bloomington: Indiana University, 1985), p. xxv; credited to William Siegmann

Figure 36. Coat of Arms of John Hawkins featured a lion for Sierra Leone and a bound African, p. 222, from Sir John Hawkins Knight, The Canton geven by Rob[er]t Clar[enceux King of Arms] 1568, National Archives, United Kingdom

Figure 37. Negro-Houses at Cape Mesurado c. 1745-1747, p. 224, from Thomas Astley, ed., A New General Collection of Voyages and Travels (London: 1745-47), Vol. 2, plate 51, facing p. 527, image available from http://slaveryimages.org/details.php?categorynum=2&categoryName=Pre-Colonial%20Africa:%20Society,%20Polity,%20Culture&theRecord=10&recordCount=261

Figure 38. Popular foreign goods most requested from Sierra Leone to the Gold Coast, p. 225, from William Towerson, "Third Voyage in Guinea in 1558"

Figure 39. Welcoming Falam Boure, p. 231, Sieur de Bellefond Nicolas Villault, "A relation of the coast of Africa called Guinea," in John Green, *A New General Collection of Voyages and Travels*, Vol. 2 (London: Thomas Astley, 1745-47), p. 56

Figure 40. Bridge in the Quoja's Country, c. 1745-1747, p. 234, from Thomas Astley, ed., *A New General Collection of Voyages and Travels* (London, 1745-47), vol. 2, plate 57, facing p. 537, image available from http://slaveryimages.org/details.php?categorynum=2&categoryName=Pre-Colonial%20Africa:%20Society,%20Polity,%20Culture&theRecord=11&recordCount=261

Figure 42. African merchant selling slaves to a European, p. 262, from Isabelle Aguet, *A Pictorial History of the Slave Trade* (Geneva: Editions Minerva, 1971), plate 3, p. 18; from Hull Museums, no date, original source not identified

Figure 43. The slave deck of the Bark "Wildfire," brought into Key West on April 30, 1860, a daguerreotype, p. 263, from *Harper's Weekly* magazine, June 2, 1860

Figure 44. West Africa slave market, p. 265, from Richard Drake, *Revelations of a Slave Smuggler* (New York, 1860), opposite title page

Figure 45. Slave export by regions, p. 266, from slavevoyages.org

Figure 46. Trans-Atlantic slave trade, 1514-1866 AD, p. 267, from slavevoyages.org

Figure 47. Windward Coast Slave Trade, 1659-1840 AD, p. 269, from slavevoyages.org

Figure 48. Windward Coast Slaves Disembarkation by Region, p. 271, from slavevoyages.org

Figure 49. Enslaved Africans Being Loaded into Hold of Slave Ship, p. 272, from J. F. Ade Ajayi and Michael Crowder (eds.), *Historical Atlas of Africa* (Harlow, Essex, England, 1985), chap. 42; original source not identified

Figures 50-51. Slaves embarked from Grand Bassa on the *Nueva Isabel* in 1830, pp. 275, 276, from slavevoyages.org

Figures 52-53. Names and ages of slaves embarked from St. Paul's River on an unidentified ship, 1813, pp. 279, 281, from slavevoyages.org

Figure 54. Enslaved Africans in Hold of Slave Ship, 1827, p. 282, from Johann Moritz Rugendas, Voyage Pittoresque dans le Bresil. Traduit de l'Allemand (Paris, 1835; also published in same year in German)

Figures 55-56. Antislavery Actions on the Windward Coast, pp. 283, 285, from slavevoyages.org

DEDICATION

Dr. Mary Antoinette Brown-Sherman (1926-2004),
    heralded but rarely heeded

Dr. Warren L. d'Azevedo (1920-2014),
    seerer and master weaver

Dr. Walter A. Rodney (1942-1980), manja-ding (master star),
    illuminating our moonless nights

Acknowledgment

This history of Liberians has traveled a circuitous route from conception to finished book. As I moved toward the final publication stage, I found myself at a crossroad, facing two sharply different paths.

One promised a smooth, easy ride, along a highway paved with funds from a non-Liberia organization or government. Many friends urged me to take that route. Their recommendations were in keeping with the dependence mentality that permeates contemporary Liberia.

In the current context, "foreign partners" are treated like "sugar daddies." Many Liberian civil society groups are so busy chasing funds from external donors, they have abandoned any focus on genuinely organic local concerns. The charge toward dependency has been led by many Liberian government officials who see outsourcing as the solution to every problem, from fighting Ebola to public education to presentation of the country's history. Many foreign governments and charitable groups privately criticize the begging and perpetually outstretched hands of locals but do little to challenge the habit.

All parties involved in this debilitating culture excuse their behavior as an unavoidable short-term evil in the service of Liberia's long-term recovery from war. But that argument is undermined by the example of Rwanda, which also underwent a devastating war. The Rwanda government has famously eschewed aid in favor of trade, yet the country has recovered faster than Liberia – and is farther along the path toward sustained development.

Had I taken the dependency highway, this book might have been slicker and shinier, but at what price? Loss of authenticity? Compromised integrity? The road I eventually took was riskier and longer, yet much more rewarding.

I opted to fund publication of the book by what is commonly called crowdsourcing using the Kickstarter online platform. I launched a campaign seeking underwriting from multiple donors willing to receive copies of the book in exchange. The response was positively overwhelming. As the end of a one-month campaign, over 125 people gave $7,832 in increments of levels of $25, $100, $250 and $1,000.

They willingly invested in a history project based only on a relatively brief description. While some gave based on their personal relationship with me, many donors were willing to risk their hard-earned funds to help bring into fruition a much needed history of the Liberian people before 1800.

Among those who contributed were some of my former students, including

Chetachi Egwu, Viola Forbin, Keary Horner, and Matthew Toth. Another noteworthy donor is a former Morgan State University colleague, Dr. Umaru Bah. However, the majority of donations came from Liberians.

Silver-level donors were: Sara Lauring Horton, Juliet Allen, Kahnma K., Shon, Joel Young, Elizabeth Sherman, Muna Findley, Roberta Davies-Rashid, Marj, Trypetus Padmore, Jemah Parker, Rev. Madia L. Brumskine, Siafa Sherman, Alonso Munyeneh, Stevie Railey, Glendy Junius-Reeves, Barbra Cooper, Emmanuel Korhone, Mona Browne, St. Tomalin N. George, Williamena Dahn, Grace, Dolly Williams, Jande Freeman-Brewer, J. Dwalo Beysolow, Sayku Kromah, Gledy Badio Wariebi, St. Clare D. Avery, Dawn Cooper Barnes, Marica Cox Mitchell, Andrew Firestone, Kolu Zigbi, Max Jarrett, Jimmy Pierre, Nadine Goff, Masnoh Wilson, Vel Mensah, Jesse R. Cooper, AmiCietta Clarke, Althea Mark, Sannah Ziama, Armah Comehn, Nora P. Findley, Cassandra Mark-Thieson, Vickie Ward, Solomon Vincent, Jacqueline Anderson, Bior Bropleh, Dawn Padmore, Dr. R. Zarwulugbo Liberty, Teta, Ayele, Joel Freeman, Michel Dioubate, Stephanie C. Horton, Nazerene Tubman, Janine Stegall, Steven Keller, Williette Freeman, Charles E. King, W. Weefur, Maya Atta, Leon, Pia Brown, Edward Sharpe and Charles King.

Gold-level donors included: Archie Wilson, Thelma Dahn-Debrah, Ruby M. Harmon, Michael Sayeh, Eugenia Burphy, Emmanuel Woods, Richelieu Lomax, Manfred & Lynn Makor, Varfee Siryon Jr., Phemie, Sally Orme, Toniah Y. Sandimanie, Anastasia Simmonds, Amani Emmanuel Jude, Musu Stewart, Roland Shaw, Vera Duche, Carnley Norman, Arthur & Pairlene Padmore, Elijah Barnard, Precious Smith, Ernest Bruce, Josephine Barnes, Helena Heyward, Richard A. Ellis, Lydia Daniels, Fonati Collins, Earl Burrowes Sr., Augusto Macedo, Seward B. Cooper, Marie-Claire Brown, Clarissa Blegay, Wil Bako Freeman, Chris E. Dennis, Peter Gerhardt, Diayouga Peabody, Seth Edwards, Musumani Woods, Marlene Vasilic and I. Vah Tukpah.

Platinum-level backers were: Amb. C. William Allen, Tiana Sherman Kesselly, Soniia David, Harry B. & Anna C. Harris, Angie Lavela Von Ballmoos and Jeanine Milly Cooper.

Above all, diamond-level support was provided by Frances C. Wilson, president, and Lorraine Johnson, vice president, of the "Those of Us" social club.

The leading role of politically diverse Liberians in funding this history of Liberians is as it should be. After all, an American history funded by the Chinese, Russian or Canadian government would be viewed skeptically by Americans. Liberians should expect no less. No people can expect to get a full history of their ancestors' trials and triumphs until they are prepared to write, pay for and ultimately *read* that history.

I extend my sincere and heartfelt thanks to all who contributed. Without your support, this project might have been delayed or deformed. More importantly, your collective contributions have taken Liberians away from being perennial beggars for handouts to playing a more active role in shaping our history. I hope the stories of our ancestors' creativity and original accomplishments told in this book will further that trend.

In an increasingly interconnected world, no nation can realistically expect to "go it alone." Instead, each should be engaged in actively shaping its own destiny. In multinational collaborations, that requires all parties to have "skin in the game." At the very least, each should bring an investment of sweat and intellectual equity. The payoff is immaterial but priceless: a dignity that stems from self-respect.

Preface

> Breathes there the man, with soul so dead,
>
> Who never to himself hath said,
>
> This is my own, my native land?
>
> — Sir Walter Scott

I have published a couple of books and many scholarly articles. But, nothing I have ever written is as important as this book.

Between the Kola Forest and the Salty Sea is intended as my contribution to Liberia's recovery from decades of war. Many people will dismiss a history book as insignificant in a country with 60.5 percent of the people working in the "informal sector." Much higher on their list of priorities are foreign troops, bridges, roads, fiber optic cables and a laundry list of other inputs.

While not denying the importance of all those factors, I view long-term peace and stability as impossible unless Liberians develop a new, more fully embracing understanding of themselves. And, that can only come from the humanities. That means capturing our cadences in poetry, film, drama and song. But, mainly drawing upon the past to inform our steps forward.

This book has also taken longer to envision, research and write than all my other writings combined. In short, it has taken a lifetime.

It began in the 1950s in Monrovia, Liberia, where I was born to Jamaican parents. They could have emigrated to New York or London, as many Jamaicans did after World War Two. But, my father opted for Liberia instead, influenced by the Africa-first ideas of Jamaica's illustrious Marcus Garvey.

I grew up on Bushrod Island, surrounded by the constant aroma of coffee from a roasting business operated by my parents. Our home stood in the shade of an awe-inspiring silk-cotton tree, which was inhabited by bats and (according to neighbors) a colony of ghosts. The shorter trees in the yard yielded mangoes, guavas, soursop, breadfruits, pawpaws and bananas.

With television unavailable in Liberia until the 1960s, my childhood was filled with legends of frightful supernatural creatures and Spider the trickster. In addition, I recall the sounds of radio, especially the hourly newscast on BBC, music shows on ELBC, and the scary Old Testament stories of a vengeful Yahweh on ELWA. From this environment, I gained an early interest in storytelling and oral history.

Bushrod Island in the 1950s was what people today would call multi-cultural. Our nearest neighbor to the right were relatives of opposition leader Dihdwo Twe, then in exile in Sierra Leone. Beyond their home laid Twe's abandoned rubber farm, which was reportedly haunted by ritualistic killers known as "heartmen." To our left was New Kru Town, the largest nearby community. Getting there involved a 15-minute walk past a compound of Vai-speaking Muslims, a household headed by a Gola father, an Ashanti family and various others.

Hours spent with neighborhood friends fishing in Stockton Creek, hunting birds with slingshots and playing soccer led me to see Liberia as a quilt woven from many cultures. That insight would deepen during my years at St. Patrick's High School, which drew students from all parts of Liberia and diverse economic backgrounds.

Getting to St. Patrick's, on the opposite side of Monrovia, required taking "holeh, holeh" buses, crowded with fellow passengers from all walks of life. My route involved stops at Point Four, Logan Town, Free Port, Clara Town, Vai Town and Waterside Market, before heading uptown to the fancy shops, government offices and cinemas on Broad Street. Those years planted the seeds that germinated into this book.

Another catalyst was a loosely-bound mimeographed book that my father brought home. Titled *Legends of Liberia*, it contained over 100 trickster stories, historical accounts and other folktales. Although each chapter in the book consisted of stories from a separate "tribe," I noticed common themes and characters. This led me to begin comparing and synthesizing various genres of tales.

For example, Spider the trickster was not only common to all Liberian groups, I knew from my parents that Jamaicans, too, told stories about the same rascal, whom they called Anansi. Funny as it may sound, it was actually Spider who first led me to a pan-African consciousness — the realization that African people, despite their diversity, share certain underlying similarities!

A book given to me by one of my high school teachers pushed me deeper. It told the life story of Edward Wilmot Blyden, a Liberian journalist and clergyman who lived about a hundred years before. Blyden argued that Africans share a deep, long and glorious past. At a time when white supremacy was widely accepted, he rejected the idea that blacks were inferior to whites or any other people.

Blyden's book changed me in three fundamental ways: I wanted to become a writer. I began reading deeply and widely in African history. And I decided to use my study and writing of history to help undo centuries of lies and misinformation that fueled a collective sense of black inferiority.

For college, I wound my way to Howard University, then the most dynamic and prestigious black university in the United States, if not the world. I was fortunate to study writing and investigative reporting under luminaries like Samuel Yette, who had covered the Civil Rights Movement with his camera and pen, and Wallace Terry, a former war correspondent in Vietnam. From the works and lectures of C. L. R. James and Walter Rodney I learned that history is made as much by those who till the rice fields as by merchants and monarchs.

There were workshops and interactions with leading black thinkers, including poet Leon Damas (a collaborator with Léopold Senghor in the Negritude Movement that began the 1930s) and writer Haki Madhubuti (a major contributor to the Black Arts Movement of the 1960s). From them I learned that life without myths and music is dry rice without "soup."

Outside of class, I spent countless hours reading the works of W. E. B. DuBois, Carter G. Woodson, Kwame Nkrumah and others who had followed Blyden in challenging the myth of white supremacy and documenting black history. I left Howard committed to writing about blacks with the clarity of Yette, the power of Rodney and the beauty of Madhubuti.

From the warmth of Howard, my journey curved to the wintry cold of UpState New York. At Syracuse University, communication historian Cathy Covert taught me the value of "history from the bottom up." While earning a master's degree, I worked with Laubach Literacy International, where I was reminded daily of the hardships faced by people who cannot read or write. In addition, my male-chauvinist assumptions and behaviors were being challenged by several female friends, including my girlfriend at the time; through them I was introduced to history written from women's perspective.

Together, these experiences deepened my commitment to documenting the stories of people who are traditionally ignored, marginalized and overlooked.

My interest in the history of Liberians took an academic turn in the late 1970s, when I encountered the writings of Dr. Mary Antoinette Brown-Sherman. Her work on the role of the Poro Society in education inspired my interest in African institutions. A devotee of Blyden, she encouraged Liberian scholars to build upon local traditions.

During this period, I also "discovered" the writings of two other important scholars. Dr. Walter A. Rodney, who harnessed his clear-eyed analysis and passion toward building a better world. And, Warren L. d'Azevedo, whose sharp critiques offered an alternative to the stale mainstream scholarship on Liberia. Without the influence of Brown-Sherman, Rodney and d'Azevedo, this book would not have been possible, so for that reason it is dedicated to them.

An important non-academic influence on this book came from my years of activism geared towards securing "rights and rice" for people of African descent. My commitment to an African perspective in scholarship was deepened through my experience with the Africa Youth Movement for Liberation and Unity (AYMLU) in the United States, and later in Liberia with the Movement for Justice in Africa (MOJA).

As with any mass movement, MOJA attracted people with a variety of interests and motives. Some MOJA critics have tried to discredit the group's motives by citing a few former members who turned out to be crooks and "gravy seekers."

But, I have lived long enough to see many goals of AYMLU and MOJA come to pass: freedom for Cape Verde, Guinea Bissau, Angola and Mozambique; the end of Apartheid in South Africa and Namibia, culminating in Nelson Mandela walking from prison to the presidency; democracy in Liberia, with the election of a woman as president, no less; and the expansion of rights for African-Americans, resulting in the election of a black U. S. president. Those results are now embraced by many close friends and relatives who once dismissed my activism as "idealistic" at best and "radical" at worst.

After 1980, I put aside activism to focus on my scholarship. But, I remain inspired by the countless "pure hearted" young MOJA activists who sacrificed personal gains to win societal improvements. Efforts like theirs have encouraged me to produce scholarship that is "relevant" to pressing current concerns.

I am deeply grateful to many who helped along the way. My friend Bloh Sayeh kept a very rough earlier version of this manuscript that I had left in Liberia, which she safely delivered several years later. My children – Kassahun, Hyacinth and Kadallah – all provided suggestions and support that helped to nudge me forward.

I am deeply indebted to several readers who saved me from many errors of omission and commission, namely Dawn Cooper-Barnes, Herbert Brewer, Flomo Kokolo, Dougbeh Nyan, Richleau Lomax, and Christopher J. Nippy. I am especially thankful for early encouragement and detailed comments offered by Mrs. Izetta Cooper, the "dean" of Liberian humanities and arts.

Along the way, I read hundreds of books at scores of libraries and major research centers in London, Paris and across the United States. Key facilities include the Schomburg Center for Research in Black Culture in Harlem, New York; the Library of Congress, Washington, DC; and the Moorland-Spingard Center at Howard University, Washington, DC.

Fortunately, many of my research trips were paid for by the universities where I have taught. I gratefully offer a public "thank you" for support I received from Cal State Fullerton, Marshall University, Howard University and Penn State Harrisburg. I also bought hundreds of books and photocopied thousands of articles from diverse journals to gather the facts and accounts presented here.

Most of what I have published in the past was written for other scholars. But, *Between the Kola Forest and the Salty Sea* is different. It is my own kola offering to the ancestors. Not just my father, who was laid to rest in Bomi County. But, to all of them — from Lofa to Maryland, Cape Mount to Grand Gedeh.

The book illustrates what is possible when African history is written from an Africanist perspective. I think many open-minded non-Africans will find it intellectually rewarding. However, my core audience is West Africans, especially Liberians, Sierra Leoneans and Guineans under 40. Among them, there is hunger for knowledge of all kind. A hunger especially for scholarship that does not advance a narrow political or ethnic agenda. A hunger for answers to the deep questions of "who am I" and "who are we." I hope this book helps them to answer those questions.

This book is offered as the first comment in what I hope will become a broad conversation. In that spirit, I invite readers to contact me at kolaforest@mac.com with criticisms, suggestions and other comments.

Given the many deep divisions in Liberia today, some people will insist that I am simply not the right person to write this book. One person told me that a history of the Liberian people should be prepared by the government of Liberia, not an individual. I suspect more than one person feels that way.

To them I say, take a critical look at the various history books produced by different Liberian administrations and government officials over the years. Each of those books — from Abayomi Kargna through Ernest J. Yancy to A. Doris Banks Henries — went out of fashion with the administration that produced it. Government contracts awarded on a non-competitive basis never produce the best works. That process usually produces "lap dog" scholarship. Far better, as the Chinese say, "to let a hundred flowers blossom and a hundred schools of thought contend."

After the book was completed, a close friend warned me that critics would reject it because I am not of indigenous background. Obviously, I do not accept the assumption that the value of a book is somehow determined by its author's ethnicity or biological characteristics.[1] In my view, writing a book is like cooking: It take years of training, some passion, the right ingredients and a lot of patience.

Like many Liberians, I grew up thinking only Kru women made great palm butter. But, two experiences forever changed my mind. The first was tasting an insipid broth of watery palm oil thrown together by a Kru woman who obviously lacked cooking experience. The other was a memorable palm butter prepared by a male chef who wasn't Kru.

I offer *Between the Kola Forest and the Salty Sea* to you in that spirit. Taste it for yourself, and see.

---

[1] For a short refutation of the current tendency to conflate the ethnicities of authors with their perspectives, see Pelka Masonen, *The Negroland Revisited: Discovery and Invention of the Sudanese Middle Ages* (Helsinki: Academia Scientiarum Fennica, 2000), pp. 60-61.

Introduction

> "...the colonizers sought to enslave the African mind and to destroy the African soul. They sought to oblige us to accept that as African we had contributed nothing to human civilization except as beasts of burden."
>
> — Thabo Mbeki

Liberians display a deep and abiding preoccupation with "history."

In rural communities, elders derive their authority, in part, from their command of history. No urban funeral is complete without a reading of the departed person's life sketch or, better yet, an *Official Gazette* prepared by the Ministry of Foreign Affairs.

At pubic gatherings, it is common to hear one speaker after another buttress political arguments with historical facts and stories. When friends meet informally, whether over a bowl of fufu or bottles of beer, some of the most heated arguments are often about the past.

In these situations, people usually follow a pattern: They present "history" orally and from memory; some even argue that oral traditions are the only valid means for accessing the past. Stories about the past are often not questioned if told by a loved one (e.g., "It's true because it came from my grandmother") or someone of high status (e.g., "It must be true because Shad [Tubman] said so.").[1]

When it comes to the histories of "tribes," people often assert that members of a group have greater authority to speak about its history. They assume that each group has only one homogeneous tradition, which frequently leads to the stories of women and other powerless members being discounted. Some stories are presented as simple morality tales, with members on one group being all-good while non-members are evil incarnate.

Given this fascination with history, Liberians have long thirsted for an integrated record of our past, but that interest has been frustrated by several obstacles. First, many have sought a history exactly like the United States, Britain or France, laced with the exact dates on which generals and kings carried out great deeds. But, such accounts rely on the existence of troves of written sources that simply do not exist for societies without long traditions of literacy. What is required instead is a different type of history fashioned from a wide range of sources, not just oral traditions.

For people who are trained to write about the past, history is more than just "stories;" it is "organized knowledge."[2] In order to *organize* knowledge of the past, historians must draw evidence from a variety of sources.

A major obstacle to unravelling the story of Liberians has been a lack of needed materials. Until the 1950s, African history was "seriously neglected." What little existed was focused on North Africa.[3] The writing of West Africa history in particular was stymied by an entrenched division between research on coastal societies on the one hand and those of the interior on the other. In addition, a 20-year ban on ethnohistorical research imposed by the government of Guinea impeded the collection of oral traditions related to migrations from Guinea to Liberia of Loma, Bandi, Kissi, Kpelle, Ma and Dan groups.[4]

But since the 1950s much-needed materials have been steadily accumulating from disparate quarters. Beginning drip by drip and then building into a stream, necessary evidence has flowed in from various academic fields.[5]

The contribution of archaeology has been to uncover artifacts and debris, usually buried under layers of soil. Those items are then scientifically tested to determine where and when they were created. At a basic level, ancient materials are examined with magnifying glasses to observe details unavailable to the naked eye.

A slightly more advanced test involves using radiography to detect hidden objects without damaging or disturbing them. Similarly, small samples of materials may be tested with chemicals to determine if they contain specific percentages of metals, for example.

At a much more sophisticated level, some items may be heated to release radioactive elements, which facilitates dating.[6] Historian T. Obenga called the application of radiocarbon dating in the context of archaeology "the most decisive methodological advance" in the recovery of the unwritten past.[7]

Also useful to historians of Africa are works by anthropologists. Those are scholars who study rituals, practices and other forms of culture that are passed from one generation to another. At best, their studies portray how people view the mental and social world in which they live. They document the invisible structures created by cultures.[8]

When anthropology began in the 1800s, the founders were concerned with broad cultural patterns and how specific traits were passed from one region to another. While some anthropologists maintain an interest in broad patterns, especially on a regional level,[9] most working in Liberia have focused on "localized traditions,"[10] with each culture "conceived as an integrated and bounded system, set off against other equally bounded systems."[11]

As a result, the story of the Liberian people is often presented as a story of balls crashing against each other on a pool table.[12] In the hands of a skillful player, one ball could be used in tandem with others to reach a goal. But, in the context of Liberia, fate is presented as an inept and cruel pool shark, pitting parochial and unchanging "tribes" against each other in a timeless tragedy. This zero-sum view of history has become more entrenched as a consequence of our recent wars.

Using data from these studies, many well-intentioned amateur historians have charged down a blind alley guided by the assumption that each contemporary ethnic community descended from a homogenous timeless stock. But that fallacy has been discredited by linguists and historians.[13]

Informed in part by the work of anthropologists, the government of Liberia recognizes 16 local ethnic groups (often referred to as "tribes"): Bandi, Bassa Dan (also Gio), Dei, Glebo (also Grebo), Gola, Kpelle, Klao, Kuwaa (Belle), Loma, Ma (also Mano), Malinké (Mandingo), Mende, Vai and Wee (Krahn and Sapo).

That number could change as large numbers of Liberians move from rural areas to Monrovia and other urban centers. In addition, the competition for resources might cause some groups to merge or splinter.

Woven throughout this book are other forms of evidence derived from linguistics, the study of languages. Although early European visitors collected short lists of words in local languages from as early as 1440, the systematic study of West African languages dates to 1854 with the publication of *Polyglotta Africana* by German missionary Sigismund Koelle, who collected and compared nearly 300 words from each of over 190 West African languages.

The systematic classification of African languages advanced in the 1950s and 1960s as Joseph H. Greenberg proposed a scheme that grouped more than a thousand languages from throughout the continent into four families or phyla: Khosian, Nilo-Saharan, Afro-Asiatic, and Niger-Congo.[14]

Among linguists there has long been a general agreement that all African languages commonly spoken in Liberia belong to the Niger-Congo family. But, their understanding of each language and its relationship to others has changed (and probably will continue to change) with new research.

Beginning in 1966, linguists grouped Liberian languages into four language clusters: Mande-tan, Mande-fu, Mel and Kwa. Based on further refinement and a deeper understanding of language relationships, those groupings have been reconfigured. The most radical change resulted in Bassa, Krahn, Klao (widely called "Kru"), Kuwaa and Sapo being classified as Kru, together with related languages in Côte d'Ivoire and Burkina Faso. The Kru family is now regarded as distinct from Kwa.

In addition, Mande-tan is now called northern Mande, and Mande-fu has been split into southwestern Mande and southeastern Mande. Mel is now simply Atlantic (in recognition of the position of those languages mainly along the ocean coast).

Shared patterns among Mande languages like Loma, Kpelle, Mandingo, and Vai include the common use of "fela" or "fele" as the root word for "two;" those languages plus Bandi and Mende share "sawa," "saba" or "sa" for "three" and "nani" for "four." On the other hand, Kru languages like Bassa, Dei, Gbe, Glebo, and Klao share "sõ" as the root for "two" and "ta" for "three." Those languages, with Sikón, share "zyi" or "hyi" as the root for "four."[15]

Linguists have contributed to the writing of African history in three ways: First, they have used shared elements of current languages to reconstruct sounds, words or rules from their common past. In this method, known as historical comparative linguistics, if words and their meanings in two languages differ in a consistent and patterned way, the languages are held to be related. Excluded from consideration are words in the two languages that are similar in sound but differ radically in meaning.

Another approach, known as contact studies, looks at how languages have influenced each other through the distribution of loan words, especially for high value goods.[16] One contact study done by linguist Holma Pasch used words for maize in languages all over the continent to trace the spread of maize from North Africa to the Nile and then westward in the savannah then south from Lake Chad.[17]

A third approach, glottochronology, dates the lexical development of a language based on its basic vocabulary (e.g., numbers from one to five), its cultural vocabulary (e.g., philosophical concepts) and the rate at which these vocabularies have changed over time. Practitioners of glottochronology believe that basic vocabularies change at a constant rate in all languages, somewhere between 81 and 85 percent every 1000 years.[18]

Of course, this book draws on oral traditions since stories about West Africa's past are mainly memorized and spoken, not written down. Prior to the 1960s, however, African oral transitions were not carefully collected or preserved or used. Instead, they were widely disparaged, discounted or dismissed as "myths" by Westerners and educated Africans. This is regrettable because among the treasure trove of African historical narratives are some that may be as wondrous as such "classical" Greek oral traditions as the *Iliad* and *Odyssey*.[19]

Fortunately, recent historians have developed rules for separating the "rice grains" from the "shaft" among oral accounts of the past. These stories tend to follow a formula: They often measure time in generations and lists of important figures. They focus on major traumatic disruptions, like wars. And, disruptions are usually caused by "evil forces," some being invisible and magical. Stories tend to be mystical if they "describe the origin, and consequently the essence, of a people, its reason for existence."[20]

But, as with other sources, oral traditions have their limitations, too. In Liberia they tend to go back only three generations or so because most local cultures lack specialists charged with memorizing history. When groups move, later generations are likely to mix up details told to them about a "homeland" they have never seen. In addition, "praise singers" are known to change their tune to please current patrons, while downplaying the good deeds of those who have fallen out of favor.

In short, memory and stories transmitted orally are malleable: The tales people recall about a marriage tend to be bleak after a divorce, for example, as opposed to the stories told at the 25th anniversary celebration.

Organizing knowledge involves more than assembling multiple sources. Historians must ask critical questions about each one: Is it authentic? Is it original? Is it reliable? Is it typical? Who created it? When and where and why was it created? Their goal is to "choose *reliable* sources, to read them *reliably*, and to put them together in ways that provide *reliable* narratives about the past."[21]

This means historians cannot simply *assume* that sources are telling the truth. The challenge can be illustrated by examining the propagandistic claims — and counterclaims — of various European powers regarding whose explorers were the first to "discover" various sections of the West African coastline. For a while, the French maintained that sailors from the port of Dieppe had reached the Kru Coast

Figure 1. Niger-Congo Language Families in Liberia

Atlantic	Kru	Northern Mande	Southwest Mande
Gola	Bassa	Malinké (Mandingo)	Bandi
Kissi	Dei	Vai	Dan (also Gio)
	Glebo (also Grebo)		Kpelle
	Klao		Loma
	Kuwaa (Belle)		Ma (Mano)
	Wee (Krahn and Sapo)		Mende

before the Portuguese.

The claim that sailors from Dieppe in the 1200s established a post at Grand Cess (called "Little Dieppe" by the French) was first published by *French* nobleman Sieur de Bellefond Nicolas Villault and was copied by Jean Barbot, a *French* Protestant living in exile in England, in a first draft of his manuscript on West Africa.[22] But, unlike the extensive contemporaneous records documenting Pedro de Cintra's visit in 1462, French claims consist of assertions made centuries after by people who did not observe or participate in the "discovery."[23]

Such improbable claims have clouded the history of the area known as Liberia. But, outright liars aren't the only ones who can distort stories of the past. In fact, the greatest distortions are caused by less visible but deadly forces: the powers that be.

Those in power often twist stories to their liking in several ways. On the one hand, they carefully preserve stories about their political and cultural ancestors. They also offer rewards for stories about their ancestors, especially those filled with praise. In addition, they pay to have those stories told through school books, movies, television shows, magazine articles and other media — over and over again.[24]

Figure 2. Blemmyae People of Aethiopia

From Hartmann Schedel
Nuremberg Chronicle, 1493

On the other hand, those who hold power do all they can to erase their ancestors' enemies from history. If that fails, the next step is to make sure those foes are maligned and marginalized. Given this dynamic, it is not enough for historians to use multiple sources and to make sure their evidence is reliable: They must be willing to confront the distorting influence of power.[25]

Sons of Ham and Headless People

Besides a longstanding lack of evidence, the writing of a suitable history has been blocked by a crippling perspective: racism, which is called Eurocentrism when manifest in scholarship. Eurocentrism "sanitizes Western history while patronizing and even demonizing the non-West." It presents the West "in terms of its noblest achievements — science, progress, humanism — but of the non-West in terms of its deficiencies, real or imagined."[26]

To understand African history, one must first understand the history of history itself. In other words, one must understand how Westerners laid the foundation for the writing of history, including the history of Africans. Not surprisingly, that history featured whites as the heroes, the movers-and-shakers, the saviors, with blacks as their opposites.[27]

Ironically, the early building blocks for Eurocentrism were provided by Arabs, non-Europeans themselves who had close contacts with Africans long before whites. For early Arab traders, a major motivation for venturing beyond the Sahara was the pursuit of slaves, which they justified by selective use of Islam, fairy tales portraying black men as demons, popular literature depicting Africans as lazy, smelly, stupid and lecherous, and a racist interpretation of the Biblical story of Ham, a son of Noah.

The legend of Ham was taken from the Book of Psalm, lxxviii, 51; cv, 23; cvi, 22. Those passages refer to the land of "Ham," an Anglicization of the Hebrew word *Kham*, which itself was derived from the Egyptian word *Kmt*, meaning "the Black Land" or northern Egypt.

According to the Biblical story, Noah laid naked in his tent after getting drunk. Upon discovering his father nude, Ham told his two older brothers, Shem and Japheth. They walked backward into the tent, so as not to see Noah's naked body, then covered him. After waking up and learning what had happened, the father reportedly placed a curse on Ham's son, Canaan, making his descendants forever servants of Shem's and Japheth's descendants.[28]

In the original version of the story, the curse fell on Canaan, but not Ham's other son, Kush, who was first identified by Jews and Christians as the ancestors of blacks. In Arab versions of the story, they cast themselves as the children of Shem, with Turks and Slavs as descendants of Japheth. Meanwhile, Ham was portrayed as the ancestor of blacks and, sometimes, Copts, Berbers and the Sindh of India.[29]

Early writings by both Arab and Persian Muslims depicted blacks as "stupid, untruthful, vicious, sexually unbridled, ugly and distorted, excessively merry, and easily affected by music and drink." Some Persian writers went even further, portraying Africans as "cannibals, infidels, enemies of God and Islam, who attack and attempt to occupy Muslim lands." Their view was, "The killing of a single black is penance for a lifetime of sin."[30]

Informed in part by earlier Arab sources, Europeans arrived in Africa with preconceived notions of blacks, some of whom reportedly had eyes in their chests. Where Arabs had seen two sharply contrasting types of societies — Muslim vs. pagan, Europeans arrayed the cultures of the world hierarchically with theirs at the apex of a multitiered pyramid and those of Africa often placed one step above apes.

Between 1514 and 1866, Europeans and their descendants removed at least 10 million Africans to work as slaves on mines and plantations in the Americas. As whites were engaged in unspeakable acts of evil never before seen in history, they were creating endless stories that featured themselves as "saviors" and blacks as "less than human," in an effort to sanitize their crimes.

As explained by sociologist St. Clair Drake, these racist stories directed the "most sustained and severe ... assaults upon [the] bodies and psyches" of black people, both those living in Africa and in the Americas. These accounts portrayed blacks as *inherently* inferior and ugly. By the late 1800s, the idea was deeply rooted in Western culture and scholarship, including historical writing, that black skin, thick lips, flat noses and tightly curled hair were signs of childish thinking and belief in "superstitions."[31]

An important exponent of racism was Thomas Jefferson, slaveholder and author of the American Declaration of Independence. In an influential book first published in 1785, he advanced the opinion that "blacks, whether originally a distinct race, or made distinct by time and circumstances, are inferior to the whites in the endowments both of body and mind."[32]

Racist ideas were propagated even by Voltaire, a leader of the Western enlightenment. He wrote that the whites were "superior to these Negroes, as the Negroes are to the apes, as the apes to the oysters."[33]

Another important proponent of racism was Edward Long, an English slave-owner and defender of African enslavement. In his *History of Jamaica* published in 1774, he wrote that Africans were a "brutish, ignorant, idle, crafty, treacherous, bloody, thievish, mistrustful, and superstitious people: with "a covering of wool, like the bestial fleece, instead of hair." He went on to characterize blacks as having a "bestial and fetid smell" and inferior "faculties of mind."[34]

If these were the ideas of "enlightened" Westerners about blacks, those held by "unenlightened" whites were likely not better and were probably much worse.

As the slave trade intensified, the insidious "Hamitic theory" gained wide acceptance among intellectuals in Europe and the Americas.[35]

Eurocentrism and Ancient Egypt

The secure, comforting Eurocentric edifice was shaken in 1798, when Napoleon Bonaparte invaded Egypt and had tons of Ancient Egyptian artifacts taken to France. With these discoveries, white scholars found themselves forced to choose between three conclusions: Some who viewed Ancient Egypt as African dismissed its accomplishments as inconsequential. But continuous discoveries of gold-filled tombs and awe-inspiring pyramids made that option untenable.[36]

To conclude that Ancient Egypt was African and highly "civilized" would have undermined white supremacy, so it was deemed unacceptable by most. This led the majority of Eurocentric scholars to forge a third option: That Ancient Egypt was more closely aligned with the West than to Africa.

This conclusion defied logic, history and geography, nonetheless it would dominate the stories about Egypt constructed by Western historians.[37] At stake was more than the cultural and ethnic identity of Egypt. Of equal or greater consequence was any influence Egypt might have exerted on Greece, Europe's fabled cradle.

Accepting that Egypt was African would have meant acknowledging the unthinkable: That blacks — now disempowered, denigrated and despised —had influenced European "civilization."[38]

Because North Africans today identify themselves as "Arab" and dark-skinned North Africans are marginalized, a lot of people assume — including many Liberians — that things were always so. But, that conclusion ignores history: The Arab invasion of 639 A. D. changed the face of North Africa, just as the Americas were transformed by the European conquest that followed Christopher Columbus's voyage of 1492 A. D.[39]

Religious teachings, too, have pushed many Africans to reject Ancient Egypt. Both the Bible and the Koran present the land of the Pharaohs as oppressive and pagan to the extreme. For this reason, many African Christian and Muslims see nothing in Ancient Egypt worthy of study and certainly nothing worth emulating.[40]

By the 1840s, the idea that black people were inferior to whites in every way — culturally, intellectually and biologically — dominated Western thought, including the writing of history. Among whites, the blond, blue-eyed "Aryans" were deemed to be superior to all others.[41]

The New Hamites: Fulas and Mandingos

But, just as the notion of Ancient Egypt as a non-African civilization was gaining acceptance in the early 1800s, Eurocentrism received another significant shock. This second challenge came when Westerns encountered the declining West African empires of the Sahel. Around this time, they were also discovering a trove of Arabic manuscripts that described the even greater splendor of those empires centuries earlier.

Unlike Egypt, these "civilized" societies laid in the heart of black Africa. To explain this anomaly, Eurocentric and Arab scholars first assigned credit for any consequential knowledge and achievements in West Africa to outsiders. Failing to produce evidence of white civilizers, they inverted the Hamitic myth.

By the early 1900s, the Hamitic label was applied to certain groups of blacks, who were regarded as superior to the rest. This "new" perspective was advanced by anthropologist Charles E. Seligman, who wrote, "The civilizations of Africa are the civilizations of the Hamites, its history, the record of these peoples and of their interactions with the two other African stocks, the Negro and the Bushmen."[42] Linguist Carl Meinhof captured the new Hamitic myth best when he argued that "in the course of history one phenomenon has constantly recurred, namely that the Hamitic peoples have subjugated and ruled over the black-skinned peoples."[43]

Based on this scheme, Fulfunde (the language of the Fulani) was once classified as "Hamitic" based, not on the principles of linguistics, but because the Fulani pastoralist were assumed to be racially different from other West Africans and culturally superior.[44]

Thus, a new theory of the Hamitic race emerged. This one pits the "primitive" people of the West African forest against the "civilized" Northern Mande-speakers of the Sahel, also known as Malinké and Mandingo.[45] In the absence of evidence, many scholars simply assume that iron smelting, blacksmithing and even the Poro Society diffused from Northern Mande groups to all others.[46]

But, iron-working just as likely spread to the area of Liberia from Nok, Nigeria, a center of metal smelting on an industrial scale. Furthermore, Poro was strongest among non-Northern Mande groups[47] and its sites and rituals faced long-term denigration from Islamized Malinké.

Many scholars fall into using the rich oral traditions of Mande speakers uncritically, resulting in the construction of a Mande-centric history of the region. They are like the proverbial man who lost his key in a dark spot but went looking for it a mile away under a street light only because "that's where the light is."

This privileging of one language group over others stems in part from the high regard some scholars have for the savannah empires of the African Middle Ages and the role Mande-speakers played in them.

But, as noted by historian Philip D. Curtin, "empires are often cruel and unpleasant institutions and are not necessarily a sign of political progress." He added, "Africa's great achievement in law and politics was probably the stateless society, based on cooperation rather than coercion."[48]

The West would only recoil from blatant racism around 1940, after the Germany Nazis had murdered over 13 million Jews, Gypsies, Eastern Europeans and others in an attempt to purify the "white race."[49]

Two social movements after World War Two drove racism underground, where it operates under new guises in more subtle forms. One type, called "modernization theory" now promises to make Africans "modern" where older forms of racism had sought to make them "civilized." It aims to turn "traditional" or "underdeveloped" societies into "modern or "developed" ones.

It has failed repeatedly over 50 years because it largely ignores relations among the people in African societies. It also pretends that Western societies became "modern" exclusively through their own efforts, refusing to acknowledge how removal of 10 millions of Africans through the slave trade helped to underdevelop African societies and to develop the West.[50]

Thus, racism remains deeply woven into the fabric of Western thought, based on hundreds of years of scholarship that shape what everybody "knows" about blacks. Now that racism has become institutionalized, people of color can be automatically subordinated, controlled and discriminated against. Even without deliberate intent, by Africans themselves.[51]

An African Perspective on History

Just as West African farmers burn a field to clear it of weeds, fell trees and bush, anyone writing African history must first tackle the long, poisoned legacy of

Eurocentrism. Inspired by the movements for African independence and African-American civil rights, a determined group of scholars of all races have sought since the 1950s to up root racism from scholarship. Their efforts have produced a revolution in how history is written, but their works remain unknown to most non-scholars,[52] including many Liberians.

This book is written from an Africanist perspective, that is, "reality as perceived, conceptualized, and evaluated by individuals who are stigmatized and discriminated against" because they are descended from the people of that long despised and disparaged continent.[53]

It is a "partial perspective," as explained by Karl Mannheim in *Ideology and Utopia*, a thesis on the sociology of knowledge. He noted, "perspective signifies the manner in which one views an object, what one perceives in it, and how one construes it in his thinking ... not only do the concepts in their concrete contents diverge from one another in accordance with differing social positions, but the basic categories of thought may likewise differ."[54]

Scholars employing an African perspective are relatively few and underfunded, but they have deepened public understanding and appreciation of African history. They have exposed Eurocentric biases and stereotypes, both conscious and unconscious. In the process, they have highlighted some people and events that were wrongly overlooked. Like David battling Goliath, they have helped produce a more accurate record based more on evidence than speculation.[55]

Some of the first scholars to refute racism in writing were those from Timbuctu, one of West Africa's earliest centers of learning founded in the early 1100s A. D. Notable among them was Ahmad Baba (1556-1627), a Malian jurist. Baba received an inquiry from Muslims at the oasis of Tuat, a major center of the slave trade, that sought to justify black enslavement on the basis of the so-called Hamitic curse. In response, he dismissed the myth as blasphemous.[56]

The second significant wave of Africa-centered historical arguments was produced by literate blacks in the New World. They used their knowledge of the Bible to dispute claims that Africans were always slaves, just as Baba had countered Arab racism using the Koran. They frequently cited favorable mentions of Ethiopia and Egypt in the Bible, knowing that both places were in Africa.[57]

They often cited the Book of Genesis, 2, xiiv, which placed the Garden of Eden near a river of Ethiopia called Gihon. Another frequently cited passage, taken from Psalm 68, xxxi, predicted, "Princes shall come out of Egypt; Ethiopia shall soon stretch out her hands unto God." In response to claims that Africans were inherently ugly, African vindicators countered by quoting Song of Solomon, 1, v, "I am black, but comely, O ye daughters of Jerusalem, as the tents of Kedar, as the curtains of Solomon."[58]

Among key black vindicators of the early 1800s were several founders of the Liberian nation. In a speech given in 1845, Liberia's first president Joseph Jenkins

Roberts attacked the notion that "the African race is but a little removed from the brute creation — only an intermediate link between the man and the Orang-Outang — and not formed by the Almighty to attain the same powers of intellect, with which the white man is endowed."[59]

In arguing this point, Roberts placed himself in collision with Thomas Jefferson, the man most responsible for linking the African to the Orang-Outang in the American imagination. Roberts showed no deference, although Jefferson was a former governor of Virginia, a former president of America and an early supporter of colonization.

Black vindicators began citing Egypt more frequently in the early 1800s, after the works of French ethnographers on Ancient Egypt became well known to the public.[60] One of the first Western scholars to assert that the ancient Egyptians were "true Negroes of the same type as all native-born Africans" was nineteenth century orientalist Count Constantin de Volney (1757-1820), who visited Egypt between 1783 and 1785.[61]

John B. Russwurm, founder of the *Liberia Herald* newspaper, repeatedly ar-

Figure 3. Words Used to Frame Africans Negatively

Chief	This label is used indiscriminately for any African and Native American ruler. It is applied to democrats, monarchs and war lords, so it lacks precision. Some "chiefs" govern societies of a few hundred people, others ruler over millions.
Country Devil	"Country" connotes rural but also "bush" and backward. "Devil" is derived from the most powerful spirit of evil in Christianity, Judaism, and Islam. He is often represented as the ruler of hell.
Fetish	When applied to Africans, this term suggests an object of irrational reverence or obsessive devotion used in a "cult."
Spirit	Used in the context of Africa, it suggests a malevolent being that enters and possesses a human being.
Tribe	Another label applied indiscriminately to African and Native American ethnic groups, regardless of size. It was originally the system of government among the people of ancient Rome.
Witchcraft	This word connotes the use of magical powers obtained from evil spirits or communication with the Devil. It is usually applied to all sacraments and rites of African traditional religion.

gued that ancient Egypt laid the foundation for Western "civilization." Inspired by a visit to an exhibition of Egyptian mummies in 1827, he wrote a sweeping historical analyses titled "On the Mutability of Human Affairs." Russwurm reported being moved to tears "over the fallen state of *my* people." He referred to himself as a "descendent of Cush," the Biblical name for a country in the Horn of Africa.[62]

Russwurm cited Herodotus, the Greek "father of history," who described the Egyptians as having "black skin and frizzled hair." He used Herodotus to anchor his claim of a link between ancient Egypt and descendants of black Africa like himself. While "(m)ankind generally" has been unwilling to acknowledge this link, he said, it is widely recognized that "all nations are indebted to the Egyptians for the introduction of the arts and sciences."

In a similar vein, Hilary Teage — Russwurm's former assistant at the *Herald* and the author of Liberia's Declaration of Independence — portrayed Liberians as heirs to the legacy of Ancient Egypt. In a poem titled "Land of the Mighty Dead," published in 1842,[63] he argued:

> Land of the mighty dead!
> Here science once displayed,
> And art, their charms;
> Here awful Pharaohs swayed
> Great nations who obeyed,
> Here distant monarchs laid
> Their vanquished arms.
>
> They hold us in survey,
> They cheer us on our way
> They loud proclaim—
> From Pyramidal hall—
> From Carnac's sculptured wall—
> From Thebes they loudly call—
> Retake your fame!

That poem was recited by Edward Wilmot Blyden, Teage's former private secretary, upon visiting the pyramids of Egypt in 1866.[64]

In 1863, Roberts and others of his generation created Liberia College (now the University of Liberia) to pass their African perspective on knowledge to future generations. However, that institution has often strayed from that mission.

Assertions of a link between Ancient Egypt and the rest of Africa were initially limited to a few voices crying out in the wilderness. But today three key points are accepted by the best scholars of Ancient Egypt. First, the people of the Nile Valley were mostly blacks, including the Egyptians, Nubians, Abyssinians and the ancestors of present-day Uganda. Second, the culture of Egypt was just one stream of Africa-wide beliefs, rituals and practices. Third, the religious system and ethics of the

Nile Valley reflected "a common core of African beliefs and practices that were widespread south and east of Egypt."[65]

The quest for an Africa-centered history reached a new height in 1947, when scholars of African descent based in Paris founded the Sociéte Africaine de Culture and its journal *Présence Africaine*.[66] Since then, historians of African descent, with crucial assistance from Western colleagues willing to challenge the Eurocentrism of their own societies, have upended one erroneous assumption after another.

Since the 1950s, Africa-centered scholars have uncovered broad patterns among African cultures. Notable among them was historian Chekh Anta Diop, who argued that similarities in art, architecture, musical instruments, and circumcision rites outweighed superficial differences.[67]

In a similar vein, sociologist Jacques Maquet coined the word "Africanity." It referred to "a certain common quality," which is more noticeable by "foreigners and by Africans, who, after some time away from Africa, visit some region of Africa other than that in which they had previously lived." Africanity involved the gathering of "actual cultures" into a "few large groups: civilizations."

For Maquet, these civilizations are "cultural units, but, unlike cultures, they are not realities of which their members are directly aware." In his view, that "certain quality" of cultural unity can be confirmed by "careful examination of specific cultural phenomenon."[68]

The search for commonality among Africa culture is similar to what European folklorists and other scholars did for their cultures in the nineteenth-century.

Scholars like Diop, Maquet and political scientist Ali Mazuri credited migrations and traders with spreading across the continent common cultural elements, such as musical instruments and the counting game played with beans or stones known generally as Mankala.

As noted by folklorist Harold Courlander, "River highways and camel caravans have carried not only men and goods, but information, traditions, tales and beliefs."[69] For the people of West Africa, including Liberia, that underlying unity can be traced to their shared roots in the Niger-Congo language phylum.

Language and Eurocentrism in African History

The argument that power affects how history is written may seem abstract. But it is distilled in the words used repeatedly to describe any group of people. These words may be full of praise, neutral or insulting. In Eurocentric history, the West, its "civilization" and religion are usually described using positive words associated with beauty, truth and good. On the other hand, Africans, their "tribal cultures" and "pagan superstitions" are framed negatively.

Since the 1970s, historians have paid closer attention to the denotation and connotation of often used words. After all, words are the building blocks of history, and facts are colored by the words used to express them.

If the words used to describe a group of people have the same connotation — positive, neutral or negative, historians call that a "discourse." Each discourse consists of "speech, thought, and action that constitute knowledge — that make knowledge. According to this kind of theory, no 'facts' exist independently of the thought-world that makes a given fact knowable."[70]

The African perspective is but one of many new approaches to writing history that erupted in the 1970s. Others include history from women and workers perspectives.[71] These various approaches were "directed not just at recovering the history of those whom traditional history writing had ignored ... but at demonstrating that their roles in historical change had been profound." The new perspectives seek to uncover "the historical circumstances in which [disempowered people] had been able to take control of their lives."[72]

Among the terms once used regularly in reference to non-Europeans are "savages," "primitives" and "uncivilized." Of course, these terms have no objective meaning. They usually mean behaving "in a violent, disorderly manner" and acting "without the restraint of law or custom."

By that definition, linguist Christopher Ehret noted, "uncivilized" would be applicable to "Europeans of the twentieth century, with their recurrent descents into genocide and pogroms, and those southern white folk of the early decades of the century who lynched black folk."[73]

Many of the words used to describe black people in particular reflect the Western worldview of the 1600s, when Europeans first encountered Africans on a large scale. One such word, "tribe," was originally a system of organization among the Romans. Europeans of the Middle Ages applied the word to people they perceived as "backward," as if those people were stuck in a time wrap from 1400 years before.

Over time, the term came to be applied to a wide-range of people with diverse systems of organization whose only similarity was being at the periphery of a large empire. On the other hand, those at the core of empires are labeled "nations."[74] "Tribe" is now applied uncritically by Africans to describe themselves.

In the past, Africanist historians paid little attention, if any at all, to the ideas and values and motivations of Africans and their descendants around the world. Meanwhile, they would portray the innermost thoughts and feelings of Europeans, using well preserved written diaries and journals. As a result, blacks are presented as victims or pawns of intelligent, self-directed whites.

Because early Africans left few written journals and dairies, one way to unlock their ideas is to understand their religion. Unfortunately, traditional religion is *the* aspect of African culture most demeaned by early non-African visitors, both Arab and European.[75] It is denigrated by the use of terms like "spirit possession," "country devil," "devil worship," "demonic," "secret society," and "witchcraft."[76]

"Witch," and others words like it, were used to describe non-Christians in Europe, when Westerns first met Africans. Between 150 A.D. and 1750 A. D., for example, some 100,000 to 200,000 people in Europe were tried as "witches" and between 50,000 and 100,000 were executed.[77] Western writers now rarely use such terms to describe non-Christians in their midst, but that discourse continues to be applied to Africa. As a result, the West has projected its dark side onto Africans, producing an "othering" of Africa and its people.

To take just one other example, the term "fetish" is regularly applied to African ritual objects, especially statues. It was apparently derived from the Portuguese word *fetiçao* (meaning "false"). As used by early Portuguese visitors to West Africa, it implied that these objects were "false gods," but Africans never considered their carvings to be gods.[78]

Eurocentrism in Liberian Studies

The writing of Liberian history has remained stymied in Eurocentrism while an alternative African perspective laid unexplored. In Liberian studies, it continues to be widely assumed that the West and its values are superior, ethnic groups are inherently incompatible, and group identities are unchanging.

Eurocentrism in Liberian studies is evident in the continued classification of the Gola and Kru-speaking people as "hunters and gathers."[79] That label implies placement at the lower rung of an evolutionary chain with a corresponding lack of "civilization." But, many transnational corporations today are dependent on "hunting and gathering" timber and seafood from around the world. Why, then, are they considered more civilized that the Gola who trafficked in kola from the forest and the Kru who harvested fish from the ocean?

Despite evidence of local agriculture, pottery and iron smelting, the presence of hunting is used by Eurocentric scholars to suggest that some people living in the area of Liberia before 1820 were stuck at a "primitive" stage. However, it is clear that hunting persisted in many parts of West Africa because wild game was plentiful and the presence of the Tsetse fly inhibited the keeping of livestock. What is more, the devastating impact of slave-trading actively fueled underdevelopment.[80]

Also alive and well in Liberian studies is the myth of the Hamitic race. It was advanced by British colonial officer and historian Harry Johnston in his book, *Liberia*, where he presented the "semi-Caucasian" Fula as the embodiment of the Hamitic race.[81] Johnson's writings continue to be widely cited without a critical examination of this and other questionable assumptions.

Even more pronounced among scholars of Liberia is a romanticization of the Northern Mande role in West Africa. This view dates back to nineteenth-century scholar Edward Wilmot Blyden. A professor at Liberia College, he sought to endow a "Mary Kingsley Scholarship of Arabic, Mandingo or Vey [Vai]" at Liberia College, for instance, but not of Gola, Dei or any other non-Mande languages.

Blyden's belief in Mandingo superiority was reinforced by his equally naive view of Islam and the Arab invasion that implanted it in Africa. In *Christianity, Islam and the Negro*, his largest work, he transformed the Arab invasion to a gentle influence that "met the Negro in his own home, was a healthy amalgamation, and not an absorption or undue repression."[82]

Blyden also argued that "Islam, in contrast to Christianity, is an 'African religion' or has been more in tune with the African personality and heritage than its Western-Christian rival."[83]

To Blyden, who was a Presbyterian cleric, Islam might have seemed to fit well with African culture. But, that was only because he was not a practicing Muslim. Many Islamic requirements clash with traditional practices, including its prohibitions on alcohol, realistic sculptures of people, certain types of music, and public displays of female breasts.[84] Adhering to Islam isn't easy because a believer happens to be African; it requires discipline and submission of all Muslims.

In addition to racist assumptions, certain local attitudes have inhibited research on traditional religious ideas and practices. On the one hand, many Liberian scholars have imbibed a Western secular bias — line, hook and sinker. As a result, they give little or no attention to religion in their writings, despite its importance in the lives of Liberians.

On the other hand, many Liberian ethnic chauvinists (so-called "tribalists") and American anthropologists have insisted that traditional religious ideas and rituals be studied in isolation from broader patterns. This approach is so focused on the trees it misses the woods.

The gathering of useful evidence on the history of local groups has been impeded, too, by the impact of indigenous Africa power structures on ethnic names. For example, the name Kran is thought to be derived from Kuraan, which is the Dan and Ma name for the Wee. The names Sapo and Tchien (also Kie) have become entrenched as the equivalent of ethnic groups, but the former originally applied to a cluster of seven Wee clans and the latter was just the name of one clan.[85]

Complicating matters further, members of some groups live in other countries, where they have been given different names. In Guinea, the Loma are officially known as *Toma*, the name given to them by Malinké speakers. To add insult to injury, many original Loma, Kpelle and Ma names for towns in Guinea have been replaced with Malinké names.[86]

Similarly, the Dan people have come to be known in many parts of West Africa as *Gio*, apparently derived from the Northern Mande *gyo-la* (meaning "the land of slaves captured through warfare"). In Côte d'Ivoire, they are known as Yacouba, a name originally applied by Northern Mande-speakers to all kola traders from the forest belt, including the Kpelle, the Mano and the Dan.

The people in Liberia and Côte d'Ivoire who call themselves Wee, such as the

Krahn and Sapo, are labeled in many French text as Guéré or N'Guéré. That label is derived from the Malinké term *gere* or *ge*, which connotes "uncivilized" or "crude" and was disparagingly applied to all groups living near the forest.⁸⁷

A New Total History

Liberians today face a critical choice: continue to accept history as filtered through the lens of others or, as much as possible, employ a framework rooted in the perspective of their ancestors. *Between the Kola Forest and the Salty Sea* is a step in a new direction.

Given the centuries-long negative framing of all-things African, recovering African history requires a rebirth. A renaissance of new words, new language, new thinking. To grasp African history, especially the history of Liberians, you must be prepared to give up on many false assumptions. You must also be willing to use new words to describe blacks and African culture instead of negative language.

The book was composed using evidence from oral traditions, archaeological digs, historical linguistics, studies of cultural patterns embedded in masks and other forms of material culture, regional and continental histories that provide essential context, and even biological anthropology.

The chapters of the book focus on specific periods, but they overlap in some cases: The Eden of West Africa, c. 9000-2500 BC; Land of Sea Salt, Kola and Canoes, c. 300 BC - 700 AD; The Way of the Ancestors, from 2500 BC; Egypt and Religions of the Book, 1413 BC-800 AD; The Rise of Empires, c. 700-1100 AD; Down from the Niger, 1076-1461; The World Turned Upside Down, c. 1462-1580 AD; Dispersal of the Malinké, 1550-1670; Into the Forest, 1560-1668; "They work excellent well in Iron," c. 1500-1630; Two-Story Huts and Sugar-Loaf Baskets, 1554-1727; Lamentations and Chants of Grief," c. 1630-1800; Guns, Rum and Rebellions, 1666-1822; Crawling Ahead, Falling Behind, 1462-1822; A New World Order, from 1600.⁸⁸

Those time periods (around which the chapters are structured) were identified by historian George E. Brooks, using climate patterns. He argued convincingly that many historical developments were shaped by "changes in rainfall patterns and ecological conditions." Examples include the diffusion of foodstuff and domesticated animals, movements of language groups, the exploitation of resources, the growth and placement of trade routes, and techniques of state-building and warfare.

The first chapter relies heavily on archeological findings, especially scientifically dated remains of ancient people, as well as their pottery, tools and other cultural effects. In the absence of ancient written records, historians of West Africa must begin with the large-scale shaping forces like climate and geography because factors like drought and flooding often determined where people lived and when they moved.

When the current names of ethnic groups are used in the text it does not mean that those groups existed in their current form back then. I have occasionally used the current name, for example "Mano," to avoid using the lengthy "ancestors of the Mano" or the awkward "proto-Mano" or "pre-Mano."

Between the Kola Forest and the Salty Sea draws upon evidence from a range of academic disciplines painstakingly collected and synthesized over the course of about 30 years. It is an attempt to answer the call by historian Joseph Ki-Zerbo for a new total history, "history apprehended at all levels and in all dimensions and by means of all the tools of investigation available."[89]

This is not just a history of names and dates. It tries to answer the more important questions of *how* and *why*. The approach adopted here situates the history of the Liberia area in "larger transregional, transcultural and global contexts."[90]

Historians must balance two sides of a see-saw: First, recapture the textile and color of people's lives in the past. But also important, show the relevance of their stories to the present.[91] Give more weight to one side, and the other will not touch the ground. I have tried to achieve relevance not just in the themes of this book, but also in being faithful to the *way* history is retold in African cultures.

While a lack of evidence has slowed research on Liberians before 1820, so too has a sense of "shame." The use of words like "fetish," "witch," "country devil" and countless others keep African culture trapped in a language web that portrays it as "strange," "weird," even "evil." Instead of challenging this negative discourse, some Western-educated Africans argue for their continued use of those demeaning words because they are widely used by uneducated Africans.

To break out of a patronizing Eurocentric discourse, I have deliberately used more neutral words to describe African culture throughout this book. I use ethnic group (not "tribe"), energy or power (not "spirit"), ruler (not "chief" or "king").[92]

In truth, uneducated Africans copied those pejorative words from their educated brethren of an earlier era who copied them from Western missionaries and "scholars." In the United States, the power of the Eurocentric discourse is evident in the use of "nigger" by black youths to describe each other. Instead of "blaming the victims," elite Africans must accept responsibility for fixing the problem, since we helped to legitimize this language of racial inferiority.

An unfounded "embarrassment" stems mainly from the way our history has been portrayed by *Arab* Muslims and *European* Christians. The result is an estrangement from our history, an alienation often accepted as the price for being true Muslims or Christians. If Arabs and white Christians lived by that standard, they would reject pagan traditions that have been incorporated into their contemporary cultures. Instead, they celebrate the pre-Christian cultures of Arabia, Greece and Rome.[93]

In the battle against Eurocentrism, Africa-centered historians can neither ignore nor bend counter evidence. On the contrary, doing so deceives their readers, dishonors their ancestors, and diminishes their own reputations. Instead, such writing must involve a constant conversation between the perspective and the evidence.[94]

Between the Kola Forest and the Salty Sea seeks to rescue Liberian history from the clutches of both ethnic particularism and Eurocentrism. It is rooted in a view that ethnic groups and polities are dynamic, not frozen. It assumes that relationships between groups throughout history are characterized, not just by conflicts, but also by cooperation. The book presents, not only the history of Liberians, but presents that story in connection with the rest of Africa and larger trends in the world.

1. "It must be true because Shad [Tubman] said so" is a translation into standard English of a lyrics from a Liberian political campaign song from the 1950s for Pres. William V. S. Tubman. The original words said, "I hope it nah [not] so-so, so-so lies, Shad say so." The song used an abbreviation of Tubman's middle name as a sign of endearment.

2. Raymond Williams, *Keywords: A Vocabulary of Culture and Society* (New York: Oxford University Press, 1983), p. 146; Michel-Rolph Trouillot, *Silencing the Past: Power and the Production of History* (Boston: Beacon Press, 1995), p. 2.

3. P. D. Curtin, "Recent trends in African historiography and their contribution to history in general" (pp. 54-71), *General History of Africa*, Vol. I: Methodology and African Prehistory (Berkeley: University of California Press, 1981), especially pp. 54, 66.

4. Yves Person, "Ethnic movements and acculturation in Upper Guinea since the fifteenth century," *African Historical Studies*, IV, 3 (1971): 669-689, especially p. 669; Andreas W. Massing, "The Mane, the decline of Mali and Mandinka expansion towards the South Windward Coast," *Cahiers d'Études africaines*, 97, 26 (1985): 21-55, especially p. 22.

5. Daniel F. McCall, *Africa in Time-Perspective: A Discussion of Historical Reconstruction from Unwritten Sources* (New York: Oxford University Press, 1969), p. 146.

6. Z. Iskander, "African archeology and its techniques including dating techniques" (pp. 206-232), *General History of Africa*, Vol. I: Methodology and African Prehistory (Berkeley: University of California Press, 1981), especially pp. 206-213; J. R. Gray, "Dating the African past" (pp. 41-46), in J. D. Fage and R. A. Oliver, eds., *Papers in African Prehistory* (London: Cambridge University Press, 1974); Andah Bassey, Alex Okpoko, Thurstan Shaw and Paul Sinclair, eds., *The Archaeology of Africa: Food, Metals and Towns* (London: Routledge, 2001).

7. T. Obenga, "Sources and specific techniques used in African history: A general outline" (pp. 72-86), *General History of Africa*, Vol. I: Methodology and African Prehistory (Berkeley: University of California Press, 1981), p. 73.

8. Howell and Prevenier, 2001, p. 116.

9. Paul Bohannan and Mark Glazer, eds., *Highpoints in Anthropology* (New York: Alfred A. Knopf, 1973), especially pp. 3-63, which presents excerpts from early anthropology texts by Herbert Spencer, Lewis Henry Morgan and Edward Burnett Tylor. For examples of this regional approach, see: Warren L. d'Azevedo, "Some historical problems in the delineation of a Central West Atlantic Region," Annals of the New York Academy of Science. Vol. 96 (January 1962): 512-538; George P. Murdock, *Africa: Its Peoples and their Culture* (New York: McGraw-Hill, 1959); Adam Kuper, *Wives for Cattle: Bridewealth and Marriage in Southern Africa* (London: Routledge & Kegan Paul, 1982); Michael Rowlands, "The unity of Africa" (pp. 39-54), in David O'Connor and Andrew Reid, eds., *Ancient Egypt in Africa* (Walnut Creek, Calif.: Left Coast Press, 2003), p. 40.

10. Rowlands, 2003, p. 40.

11. Eric R. Wolf, *Europe and the People Without History* (Berkeley: University of California Press, 1982), p. 4.

12. Wolf, 1982, p. 6. A view of Liberian ethnicities as incommensurate is enshrined in anthropological writings, with titles like "The Conflict of Cultures," "The Settler-African conflicts" and "The Dual Legacy." See also J. Gus Liebenow, *Liberia: The Evolution of Privilege* (Ithaca: Cornell University Press, 1969); although not an anthropological study, it is noteworthy because of its impact on Liberian studies broadly.

13. Warren L. d'Azevedo, "Tribe and chiefdom on the Windward Coast," *Liberian Studies Journal*, Vol. 14, Issue 2 (1989): 90-116; M. E. Kropp Dakubu, "Linguistics & history in West Africa" (pp. 52-72), in Emmanuel Kwame Akeyampong (ed.), *Themes in West Africa's History* (London: James Currey, 2006), especially pp. 53-54, 60; e. g., see "Kemit - The Egyptian Origins of the Bassa of Liberia," accessed Feb. 20, 2014, 3:21 pm, http://www.peuplesawa.com/fr/bnlogik.php?bnid=265&bnk=&bnrub=&sites=280

14. P. E. H. Hair, "Ethnolinguistic continuity on the Guinea Coast," *Journal of African History*, VIII, 2 (1967): 247-268; Kropp Dakubu, 2006, p. 61; J. M. Stewart, "Kwa" pp. 217-245), in John Bendor Samuel (ed.), *The Niger-Congo Languages* (Lanham, MD: University Press of American, 1989); W. A. A. Wilson, "Atlantic" (pp. 81-104), in John Bender Samuel (ed.), *The Niger-Congo Languages* (Lanham, MD: University Press of American, 1989).

15. Frederick William Hugh Migeod, *The Languages of West Africa*, Vol. 1 (Freeport, N. Y.: Books for Libraries Press, 1972; reprint of 1911-13 edition), pp. 154-157.

16. Kropp Dakubu, 2006, pp. 57-58; Derek Nurse, "The contribution of linguistics to the study of history in Africa," *Journal of African History* 38 (1997), pp. 177-218; David Dalby (ed.), *Language and History in Africa* (London: Frank Cass & Co., 1970).

17. Holma Pasch, "Zur geschichte der verbreitung des maises in Afrika," *Sprache und Gershichte in Afrika* 5 (1983), pp. 177-218.

18. P. Diagne, "History and linguistics" (pp. 234-270), *General History of Africa*, Vol. I: Methodology and African Prehistory (Berkeley: University of California Press, 1981), pp. 237-238.

19. For a collection of some African epics, see John William Johnson, Thomas A. Hale and Stephen Paterson Belcher, eds., *Oral Epics from Africa: Vibrant Voices from a Vast Continent* (Bloomington: Indiana University Press, 1997).

20. Jan Vansina, "Oral tradition and its methodology" (pp. 142-165), *General History of Africa*, Vol. I: Methodology and African Prehistory (Berkeley: University of California Press, 1981), pp. 156-157.

21. Howell and Prevenier, 2001, pp. 1-2.

22. Sieur de Bellefond Nicolas Villault, *A Relation of the Coasts of Africk called Guinee* (London: John Starkey, 1670), p. 130; P. E. Hair, Adam Jones and Robin Law, eds., *Barbot on Guinea: The Writings of Jean Barbot on West Africa 1678-1712* (London: The Hakluyt Society, 1992), Letter 19, p. 242, 254 n. 31. On the myth of a French presence in West Africa before the Portuguese, see Masonen, 2000, pp. 38-51.

23. Hair, Jones and Law, 1992, p. xii, Letter 113, pp. 7-9; Barbot, 1732, pp. 9-11; Adam Jones, *Zur Quellenproblemmatik der Geschichte Westafrika, 1450-1900* (Stuttgard: Franz Steiner, 1990), pp. 55-58.

24. Trouillot, 1995, p. 29; Curtin, 1981.

25. Trouillot, 1995, p. 26; Michel Foucault, *Power/Knowledge: Selected Interviews & Other Writings, 1972-1977*, edited by Colin Gordon (New York: Pantheon Books, 1980).

26. Ella Shohat and Robert Stam, *Unthinking Eurocentrism: Multiculturalism and the Media* (New York: Routledge, 2001), p. 3; also Howell and Prevenier, 2001, p. 10; Curtin, 1981, p. 54; J. M. Blaut, "Fourteen Ninety-two" (pp. 1-63), in J. M. Blaut, ed., *1492: The Debate on Colonialism, Eurocentrism and History* (Trenton, NJ: Africa World Press, 1992); Immanuel Wallerstein, "Eurocentrism and its avatars: The dilemmas of social science" (pp. 168-184), in Immanuel Wallerstein, *The End of the World as We Know It: Social Science for the Twenty-First Century* (Minneapolis, MN: University of Minnesota Press, 1999.

27. O'Connor and Reid, 2003, p. 3; V. Y. Mudimbé, *The Invention of Africa: Gnosis, Philosophy, and the Order of Knowledge* (Bloomington: Indiana University Press, 1988); Thomas C. Holt, "Explaining racism in American history" (pp. 107-119), in Anthony Molho and Gordon S. Wood, eds., *Imagined Histories: American Historians Interpret the Past* (Princeton, NJ: Princeton University Press, 1998.

28. John Alembillah Azumah, The Legacy of Arab-Islam in Africa: A Quest for Inter-religious Dialogue (Oxford: Oneworld, 2011), p. 128.

29. Azumah, 2001, p. 129; Lewis, 1990, pp. 44-45.

30. Azumah, 2001, p. 134.

31. St. Clair Drake, *Black Folk Here and There* (Los Angeles: Center for Afro-American Studies, University of California, Los Angeles, 1998), pp. 23, 120, 26, 13.

32. Thomas Jefferson, *The Portable Thomas Jefferson*, edited by Merrill D. Peterson (New York: Penguin, 1986), pp. 185-188.

33. Voltaire, *Traité de métaphysique* (Editions la Bibliothéque Digitale, 2013), p. 29.

34. Edward Long, *History of Jamaica* (London: T. Lowndes,1774), pp. 352-354.

35. For critiques of the Hamitic myth, see Diagne, 1981, p. 245 n. 37; J. D. Fage, "The development of African historiography" (pp. 25-42), *General History of Africa*, Vol. I: Methodology and African Prehistory (Berkeley: University of California Press, 1981), pp. 35-37; D. Olderagge, "Migrations and ethnic linguistic differentiation" (pp. 271-286), *General History of Africa*, Vol. I: Methodology and African Prehistory (Berkeley: University of California Press, 1981), p. 273; Wyatt MacGaffey, "Concepts of race in the historiography of Northeast Africa" (pp. 99-115), in J. D. Fage and R. A. Oliver, eds., *Papers in African Prehistory* (London: Cambridge University Press, 1974), pp. 101-105; William McKee Evans, "From the land of Canaan to the land of Guinea: The strange odyssey of the 'Sons of Ham," *American Historical Review*, LXXXV (1980): 15-43; Masonen, 2000, p. 126.

36. Paul Strathern, *Napoleon in Egypt* (New York: Bantam, 2008).

37. Andrew Reid, "Ancient Egypt and the source of the Nile" (pp. 55-76), in David o'Connor and Andrew Reid, eds., *Ancient Egypt in Africa* (Walnut Creek, Calif.: Left Coast Press, 2003), p. 55; David O'Connor and Andrew Reid, "Introduction — Locating Ancient Egypt in Africa: Modern theories, past realities" (pp. 1-21), in O'Connor and Reid, 2003, p. 1, 4; Martin Bernal, "Afrocentrism and historical models for the foundation of Ancient Greece" (pp. 23-38), in O'Connor and Reid, 2003, p. 23, 28.

38. Bernal, 2003, p. 23; O'Connor and Reid, 2003, p. 11.

39. Blaut, 1992.

40. O'Connor and Reid, 2003, pp. 2, 9; Drake, 1998, pp. 131-132.

41. Drake, 1998, pp. 20-23.

42. Charles E. Seligman, *The Races of Africa* (London: Butterworth, 1930), pp. 96.

43. Carl Meinhof, *Die Sprachen der Hamiten* (Hamburg: Frederichsen, 1912).

44. For the impact of the Hamitic myth on linguistics, see Joseph H. Greenberg, *Languages of Africa* (Bloomington, IN: Indiana University Press, 1966), p. 24, and W. A. A. Wilson, "Atlantic" (pp. 81-164, especially pp. 83-85), in John Bendor-Samuels, ed. *The Niger-Congo Languages* (Lanham: University Press of America, 1989). For its influence on the writing of African history, see Joseph H. Greenberg, "The Negro kingdoms of the Sudan," *Transactions of the New York Academy of Sciences*, Series II, Vol. 11, No. 4 (February, 1949), pp. 126-135; St. Clair Drake, "The responsibility of men of culture for destroying the 'hamitic myth'," *Presencé Africaine*, special issue (English language version), No. 24-25 (1959), pp. 226-243; MacGaffey, 1966, pp. 4, 6-9; Edith R. Sauders, "The hamitic hypothesis: Its origin and functions in time perspective," *Journal of African History*, Vol. 10, Issue 4 (1969): 521-532; Joseph Harris, *Africans and Their History* (New York: Mentor, 1972), pp. 21-24; Philip Curtin, Steven Feierman, Leonard Thompson, and Jan Vansina, *African History* (Boston: Little, Brown & Company, 1978), pp. 121, 168-169; Drake, 1998, p. 127; Ray, 1976, p. 11.

45. Migeod, 1972, p. 31.

46. e. g., Massing, 1985, pp. 24-25.

47. e.g., Brooks, 1985, pp. 133-134.

48. Curtin, 1981, p. 58.

49. Drake, 1998, pp. 20-23.

50. Wolf, 1982, p. 13; A. Temu and B. Swai, *Historians and Africanist History: A Critique* (London: Zed Press, 1981), p. 9.

51. Drake, 1998, pp. 34, 135.

52. Curtin, 1981, p. 55.

53. Curtin, 1981, p. 54.

54. Karl Mannheim, *Ideology and Utopia: An Introduction to the Sociology of Knowledge* (New York: Harcourt, Brace and Col, 1936), pp. 244, 246.

55. Drake, 1998, pp. 2, 4, 32. According to an assessment done in 2000, less than 10 percent of African history articles in two leading journals were written by African scholars living on the continent; see Masonen, 2000, p. 57.

56. Lewis, 1990, p. 57; Nehemia Levtzion, "The early states of the Western Sudan to 1500" (pp. 120-157), in J. F. Ade Ajayi and Michael Crowder, *History of West Africa*, Vol. I (New York: Columbia University Press, 1972), especially p. 140; Marq de Villiers and Shiela Hirtle, *Timbuktu: The Sahara's Fabled City of Gold* (New York: Walker & Company, 2007).

57. Drake, 1998, p. 32, 131.

58. Drake, 1998, p. 131.

59. Taken from *Liberia Herald*, Vol. XIV, No. 2, Oct. 5, 1845, pp. 6 (front page) through p. 7, a reprint from the rival *African Luminary*. The text was prefaced by the following: "The following address was delivered before the Liberia Lyceum in this town, by Governor Roberts, on the evening of the 6th August, to a crowded audience of our citizens of both sexes. The pleasure with which it was listened to may be estimated from the character of the production, and the interest all felt in the discussion of the subject. We really began to feel as if philosophers and sages may have been mistaken in referring to us as a race, constitutional, and consequently, irremediable impotent in intellect and that after all, there was some hope in our case, we might be like the other races God has made."

60. Drake, 1998, p. 131.

61. Drake, 1998, p. 133.

62. "On the Mutability of Human Affairs," *Freedom's Journal*, April 6, 1827, 15; "On the Mutability of Human Affairs (Continued)," *Freedom's Journal*, April 20, 1827, 3. Other *Journal* articles valorizing ancient Egypt include "For the Freedom's Journal," *Freedom's Journal*, August 24, 1827, 94.

63. *Liberia Herald*, 23 December 1842, p. 8.

64. For Blyden's invocation of Teage's poem, "Land of the Mighty Dead," during a visit to the pyramids in Egypt, see Ruth Holden, *Blyden of Liberia: An Account of the Life and Labors of Edward Wilmot Blyden, L.L.D., as recorded n letters and in print* (New York: Vantage Press, 1966), 141.

65. Drake, 1998, p. 142.

66. Fage, 1981, p. 40.

67. Ali A. Mazrui, *The Africans: A Triple Heritage* (Boston: Little, Brown and Company, 1986); Cheikh Anta Diop, *The Cultural Unity of Black Africa* (London: Karnak House, 1989), p. 1; and Cheikh Anta Diop, *Civilization or Barbarism: An Authentic Anthropology* (New York: Lawrence Hill, 1991), p. 15; also Elliott P. Skinner, "The African presence: In defense of Africanity," in William G. Martin and Michael O. West, *Out of One, Many Africas* (Urbana: University of Illinois Press, 1999), pp. 62-82; O'Connor and Reid, 2003, p. 7.

68. Jacques Maquet, *Africanity: The Cultural Unity of Black Africa* (New York: Oxford University Press, 1972), pp. 3, 5, 9, 10; also Molefi Kete Asante, *The Afrocentric Idea* (Philadelphia: Temple University Press, 1998); Molefi Kete Asante, *Afrocentricity: The Theory of Social Change* (Buffalo, New York: Amulefi Publishing Co, 1980).

69. Harold Courlander, *A Treasury of African Folklore: The Oral Literature, Traditions, Myths, Legends, Epics, Tales, Recollections, Wisdom, Sayings, and Humor of Africa* (New York: Crown Publishers, 1975), p. 2; also Toyin Falola, The Power of African Cultures (Rochester: University of Rochester Press, 2003), pp. 55-56; Ki-Zerbo, 1981, pp. 19, 21; Curtin, 1981, p. 67.

70. Howell and Prevenier, 2001, p. 108, also 99, 101; Foucault, 1980; Dorothy Ross, "The new and newer histories: Social theory and historiography in an American key" (pp. 85-106), in Molho and Wood, 1998, especially pp. 97-106.

71. Linda Kerber, "Gender," in Molho and Wood, 1998, pp. 41-58; e.g., E. P. Thompson, *The Making of the English Working Class* (New York: Vintage Books, 1966).

72. Howell and Prevenier, 2001, p. 113, also 15.

73. Christopher Ehret, *The Civilizations of Africa: A History to 1800* (Charlottesville: University of Virginia Press, 2002), pp. 4-5.

74. Robert J. Gregory, "Tribes and tribal: Origin, use, and the future of the concept," *Studies of Tribes and Tribals*, Vol. 1, No. 1 (2003): 1-5.

75. Ladislas Segy, *African Sculpture Speaks* (New York: Hill and Wang, 1969, pp. 26-27. For examples of early references to "witchcraft," "devil worship" and other derogatory terms applied to African traditional religious practices, see Abū 'Ubayd 'Abd Allāh ibn 'Abd al-'Azīz al-Bakrī, Kitāb al-Masālik wa-al-Mamālik, in N. Levtzion and J. F. P. Hopkins, eds., *Corpus of Early Arabic Sources for West African History* (Princeton: Markus Wiener Publishers, 2011), p. 80; Yāqūt ibn-'Abdullah al-Rūmī al-Hamawī (writing c. 1212-1229) Kitāb mu'jam al-buldān, in N. Levtzion and J. F. P. Hopkins, eds., *Corpus of Early Arabic Sources for West African History* (Princeton: Markus Wiener Publishers, 2011), p. 168; Abu Al-fida' Isma'il Ibn 'ali ibn Mahmud Al-malik Al-mu'ayyad 'imad Ad-din (writing c. 1321) 'Tarikhu 'al-Mukhtasar fi Akhbar al-Bashar in N. Levtzion and J. F. P. Hopkins, eds., *Corpus of Early Arabic Sources for West African History* (Princeton: Markus Wiener Publishers, 2011), p. 203; J. W. Lugenbeel, "Native Africans in Liberia — Their customs and superstitions," *African Repository*, January 1852, pp. 13-17; February 1852, pp. 53-55; June 1852, pp. 171-174; July 1852, pp. 212-214; October 1852, pp. 310-315; Benjamin L. Ray, *African Religions: Symbol, Ritual, and Community* (Englewoods Cliffs, NJ: Prentice-Hall, 1976), p. 5.

76. For a discussion of the use of "devil" in reference to Poro ritual performers, see Beryll Larry Bellman, *The Language of Secrecy: Symbols and Metaphors in Poro Ritual* (New Brunswick: Rutgers University Press, 1984), p. 145.

77. John Demos, *The Enemy Within: 2,000 Years of Witch-hunting in the Western World* (New York: Viking, 2008), pp. 38-39.

78. Segy 1969, p. 10; Rosalind I. J. Hackett, *Art and Religion in Africa* (New York: Cassell, 1996), pp. 1-21; E. A. Wallis Budge, *Osiris & the Egyptian Resurrection* (New York: Dover, 1973), p. 274.

79. e. g., Sven E. Holsoe, The Cassava Leaf Eating People: An ethno-historical study of the Vai people with particular emphasis on the Tewo chiefdom. Ph. D. dissertation, Boston University, 1967, p. 2.

80. Walter Rodney, *How Europe Underdeveloped Africa* (Washington, DC: Howard University Press, 1974); Samir Amin, "Underdevelopment and dependence in Africa: Historical origin," *Journal of Peace Research*, 9 (June 1972): 105-119.

81. Harry H. Johnston, *Liberia* (London: Hutchinson & Co., 1906), p. 14.

82. E. W. Blyden, *Christianity, Islam and the Negro Race* (Edinburgh: Edinburgh University, 1967, pp. 11-12.

83. Azumah, 2011, p. 4.

84. King, 1986, p. 88.

85. Andreas W. Massing, "Economic Development in the Kru Culture Area." Ph. D. dissertation, Indiana University, 1977, p. 27; Sven E. Holsoe and Joseph J. Lauer, "Who are the Kran/Guéré and the Gio/Yacouba? Ethnic identifications along the Liberia-Ivory Coast border," *African Studies Review*, Vol. XIX, No. 1 (April 1976): 139-149, especially pp. 143, 145.

86. Facinet Béavogui, *Les Toma (Guineé et Liberia) au temps des négriers et de la colonization from gaise* (Paris: L'Hamattan, 2001), p. 25.

87. Holsoe and Lauer, 1976, pp. 141, 144. Alternative names for the two ethnic groups mentioned here include *Gio* (also *Dioula, Gyo, Gyola, Guiola* and *Guio*), which is derived from *gyo-lo* (also *dyo-la* or *jo-la*), and *Yacouba* (also *Diafoba, Diabouba* and *Yabouba*).

88. George E. Brooks, *Western Africa to c. 1860 A. D.: A Provisional Historical Schema Based on Climate Periods* (Bloomington: African Studies Program, Indiana University, 1985), p. xi.

89. J. Ki-Zerbo, "General introduction" (pp. 1-24), *General History of Africa*, Vol. I: Methodology and African Prehistory (Berkeley: University of California Press, 1981), p. 23.

90. Jerry H. Bentley, "The task of world history" (pp. 19-35), in Jerry H. Bentley, ed., *The Oxford Handbook of World History* (Oxford: Oxford University Press, 2013), p. 12; also Dunn, 1972, p. xvi. Dunn notes, "A view that excludes the linkage between metropolis and colony by choosing one perspective and ignoring the other is necessarily incomplete." He was speaking about the English Caribbean in particular, but his point applies to all societies locked in semi-colonial relationships.

91. Alan L. Karras, "The Atlantic Ocean Basin" (pp. 529-545), in Jerry H. Bentley, ed., *The Oxford Handbook of World History* (Oxford: Oxford University Press, 2013), p. 529.

92. Many contemporary Liberians have embraced the use of "king" or "queen" to describe early traditional rulers. This is a classic example of "we too-ism," an uncritical acceptance of European cultural features as universal ideals. In reality, "king" and "queen" designate absolute rulers in a system where power is transmitted intergenerationally. That was rarely the case in Africa, even within the Sahelian empires of West Africa. In reference to the Dei, Gola and Vai specifically, it was noted, "the principal rulers ... attained their positions either by means of conquest or by preference of the governed;" see James K. Ballah, *The Tribes of the Western Province and the Denwoin People* (Monrovia: Bureau of Folkways, Interior Department, 1955), p. 6.

93. Azumah, 2001; Bart D. Ehrman, *The New Testament: A Historical Introduction to the Early Christian Writings* (Oxford: Oxford University Press, 2008).

94. Temu and Swai, 1981, p. 13.

Chapter 1
The Eden of West Africa

> "Any writer who attempts to recall from obscurity and oblivion the past ages of an illiterate nation, and to lay before the public even the most elementary sketch of its history, will probably have to contend against the strong prejudices of numerous critics, who are accustomed to refuse belief to whatever is incapable of bearing the strictest inquiry."
>
> — Heinrich Barth, German explorer[1]

The story of the Liberian people does not begin in America, as portrayed in many history books, nor in the rain forest of present-day Liberia, as many people would assume.

The story began about 1.5 million years ago in East Africa, where the oldest human bones have been found. From there, early people migrated to Asia, then to various corners of the world. In short, Africa is the ancestral home of people all over the world, including those living in China, Europe and America.[2]

The story shifted about 60,000 years ago. By then, people were living in West Africa and making a variety of simple tools.[3]

As with other West Africans, the ancestors of most Liberians originated 2000 miles to the north, in the part of Africa called the Sahara. Here, West Africans developed, on their own, some of the world's first systems of farming, working with metals, and trading.

The history of West Africa was shaped by its people, but also by the environment. The region covers about 2.4 million square miles. Imagine the United States, east of the Rocky Mountains. It extends from about 5° to 25° north latitude and from 17° west to 15° east longitudes.

An ancient block of rock runs from Sierra Leone through Guinea and Liberia to Burkina Faso and Ghana. Water gushing from deep in the ground sometimes brings gold, diamonds, iron-ore, chrome and other minerals to surface rivers and streams.[4]

West Africa is hot, averaging 87° Fahrenheit. Two large masses of air blow this heat across the region. Starting from the Sahara, the Harmattan blows warm, dry and dusty air over the entire region at its peak in January.

During the Harmattan, as noted by a nineteenth-century resident of Liberia, "the leaves and covers of books sometimes curl, as if they had been placed near a fire;

the seams of furniture, and of wooden vessels, sometimes open considerable, and the skin of persons sometimes feels peculiarly dry and unpleasant, in consequence of the rapid evaporation of both the sensible and insensible perspiration." The Gola call this first month *Waaduugbee* for "big dew moon" [5]

The other air mass begins over the southern Atlantic Ocean and blows inland from January to July. It brings rains of 50 inches to 100 inches along the coast but tapers off to less than 10 inches at the edge of the Sahara.

Two sharply different seasons affect the northern-most section of West Africa. A severe dry from November to March alternates with a compact wet from June to October.

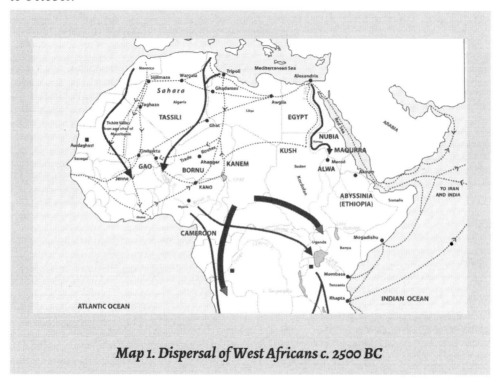

Map 1. Dispersal of West Africans c. 2500 BC

Three-quarters of West Africa is covered by grasslands and dotted with deciduous trees of 164 feet in height. This area is immediately south of the Sahara. For that reason, it is called the Sahel, meaning "the shore" of the desert.

Farther north, the rough, broken southern portion of the grassland gives way to an open plateau. The dominant feature of this section is the Niger, Africa's third longest river.[6]

Sahara. The name is taken from the Arabic word for desert — "Sahra."

The first use of that name has been traced to Egyptian historian Ibn Abd-al-Hakam (d. 871), writing in the ninth century.[7]

In reality, the Sahara is composed of many separate deserts and, before the

Arabic label was applied to the whole region, local people had different names for each section of the great sand sea.

The desert is desolate: It looks like the floor of the Atlantic Ocean if all the water dried up. Picture hills of solid rock, miles upon miles of gravel, and soil soaked in salt. Shifting among these is a sea of sand sometimes swirling up 600 feet — as high as six of Monrovia's highest hotel, the Ducor Palace Hotel, stacked on top of each other![8]

Towering over this bleak sand-scape are three mountains: the Aïr in northern Nigeria at 6,000 feet, the Ahaggar in Algeria rise at 9,000 feet, and the Tibesti in northern Chad at 11,302 feet (almost twice the height of Mount Nimba in northern Liberia).[9]

The dry, salty soil supports few plants. One notable exception is the date palm, for which the region is famous. The few creatures that thrive here are often tough and mean: mainly reptiles and scorpions.[10]

Living things, including people, lizards and date palm trees, tend to cluster around the desert's widely scattered pools of water. These fountains, called oases, form when water from deep below is pushed up to the surface through cracks in the rocks.[11]

These oases are mere drips from vast oceans of pure water that lay beneath the Sahara's surface.[12] Under Algeria, Libya and Tunisia is one body of water as large as France.

But, not all the surface water is suitable for drinking or nurturing plants. A lake called Chott el-Djerid stretches for 2,500 square miles, but it is so salty the surface shines white.[13]

The desert is vast — three-and a half million miles stretching from the Atlantic Ocean in the west to the Red Sea in the east.

Think France, Germany and Spain combined, filling into the desert with space left over. Or, the entire United States, including Hawaii and Alaska.[14]

There are 64 countries in Africa, and 11 of them share this one desert: Mauritania, Western Sahara, Morocco, Mali, Algeria, Tunisia, Chad, Niger, Libya, Egypt, and Sudan.[15]

Every year, millions of birds try to escape the harsh winters of Europe by migrating to Liberia and other parts of West Africa. But, many perish in the desert as they attempt to cross due to heat, thirst and exhaustion.[16] For countless animals and travelers who don't know their way, the Sahara is the proverbial Valley of the

Shadow of Death.

Millions of years ago, this vast land was covered with water and teeming with life. Panoramic pictures taken by NASA satellites in 1981 revealed many, many dried channels where rivers once flowed.[17]

Archaeologists digging 100 miles west of Cairo discovered the remains of whales scattered over 100 square miles of the desert floor. In a section of central Niger called "the place the camels fear to go," French scientists found the bones of extinct super-crocodiles with jaws six feet long.[18]

The Sahara back then looked like Lofa County must have been 200 years ago.

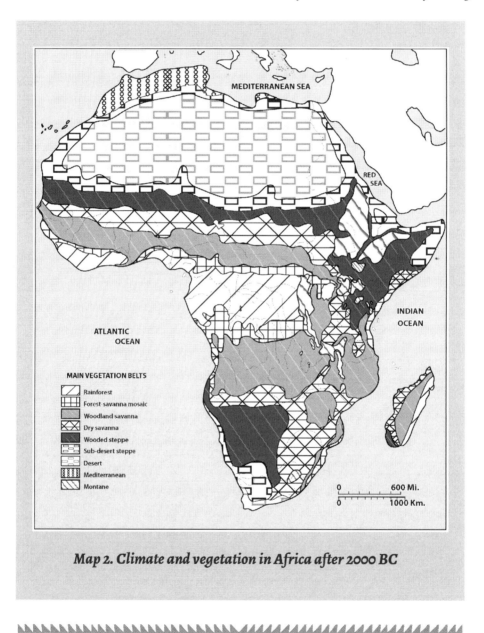

Map 2. Climate and vegetation in Africa after 2000 BC

The now barren Aïr, Ahaggar and Tibesti were covered in trees. Animals sheltered beneath them, feasting on the oaks, pines, olives and walnuts that fell from their branches. Lions preyed on giraffes, gazelles and even elephants that grazed the grass fields. The region's many freshwater lakes and rivers supported hippopotamus, crocodiles and various types of fish.[19]

How do we know this?

Archaeologists digging in the desert have found bones of fish, skeletons of animals and dried tree trucks. Deep beneath the sands, they have also discovered evidence of ancient people: bones, tools and art.

A major breakthrough came in 2000 at Govero, Niger, when archaeologists found the Sahara's largest and oldest graveyard. The 200 graves held skeletons, jewelry and other handmade objects. These suggest a continuity with current African funeral rites. Based on the age of the grave objects, scientists determined that people living in the area had used the same graveyard for over 5,000 years.[20]

Figure 4. Rock painting, cattle scene Tassili, Algeria, 5000-2000 BC

More dramatic and revealing than the graves are the over 30,000 drawings and paintings on rocks found throughout the Sahara. Over and over, rock paintings show people herding cows, sometimes dancing with masks, but mostly hunting with rocks, bows and clubs. Less common are images of plants or people fighting.[21]

Several art forms found in West Africa today date to the earliest days of Niger-Congo cultures. Among these are weaving, polyrhythmic music, hair braiding and wood carving, notably figure sculpture, masks and drums.[22] The earliest cloth-making tradition consisted of bark cloth, made by pounding sheets of bark striped from trees.

By 6000 BC, however, these communities had developed a range of skilled weaving activities. Products included baskets, mats for sleeping and raffia cloth (fashioned from raffia palm fibers).[23]

Across Niger-Congo cultures, both music and dance were more polyrhythmic and percussive than in other cultures of Africa. Typically, musical performances featured interweaving rhythms that were produced using "drums of different pitches beaten simultaneously."

This tradition came to be augmented by the addition of the thumb piano, with iron prongs, invented in southern Africa, and the xylophone, which spread from Southeast Asia, reaching the forested region of West Africa around 400 AD. Usually driven by drumming, dance performances featured multiple body parts, not just the feet, engaged in energetic movements.[24]

Besides their beauty, the rock paintings reveal an important truth: West Africans produced art and talented artists as early as 12,000 BC. Images of masked dancers and jewelry buried in graves underscore another key fact: They possessed rituals and, perhaps, religious ideas about life after death.[25]

Some of the oldest paintings show full-size elephants, crocodiles and rhinoceroses, animals that no longer live in the area. These large animals disappear as subjects in rock art after 3,000 B. C., when the Sahara turned dry. The later pictures also show less hunting, more herding.[26]

These rock paintings show two groups of people — both dark-skinned — living in the Sahara about 4,000 B. C. Some were undoubtedly among those fled the encroaching desert for refuge along the Nile.[27]

Scientists have found only a small number of human bones throughout the desert from the time when it was green. For that reason, it seems likely only a few thousand people lived there at any one time before 2,000 BC. The location of their bones suggest they stuck close to the lake shores and river banks.[28]

Just as the hunters had moved frequently in pursuit of game, the herders went round and round in search of green pastures. Year after year.

People kept goats and sheep, too, but only cows could travel long distances in search of grass and water.[29] During the dry season, some herders went south to the Niger River, others east toward the Nile, still others high up the then green mountains.[30]

These regular migrations laid the basis for many cultural similarities from the Nile to the Niger: similar fine arrowheads, similar axes for shaping wood, and similar pots shaped like bags for holding milk.[31]

Tools were important, but survival depended even more on knowledge of the environment and social networks.[32] Those ancient tracks linking the Nile to the Atlantic would endure long after the Sahara had changed into a desert.[33]

Living in the desert led people to focus keenly on the often cloudless sky. Unlike the boring, baking and sometimes blinding yellow of the daytime, the night sky teemed with awesome activities and captivating cycles: an ever waning and waxing moon, fearful falling comets, and twinkling stars that appeared to cluster in the shapes of humans and animals.

But, stargazing provided more than entertainment; it held life-saving clues for navigating a landscape devoid of many landmarks, such as tracking direction with help from the North Star. Early West Africans would pass on various festivals and a calendar based on the cycles of the moon to their children's children through countless generations.

> **Figure 5. Tracking languages**
>
> How do scholars trace the birthplace of a language?
>
> First, they find the central block of closest relatives, which very likely constitute the heartland. Next, they try to match this place with known events that would likely have precipitated a migration. To find such occurrences, they study oral traditions, climate changes, and other evidence.
>
> By this method, linguists have traced the roots of the Niger-Congo languages to the Sahara.
>
>

During the wet period, West Africans in the flooded savannah created an aquatic culture, according to historian J. E. G. Sutton. Archaeologists have found fish bones, skeletons of water animals, and carved bones used to harpoon catches. This culture featured a unique style of pottery called "wavy-line" and "dotted-line." These were decorated with the imprints of fish bones and water-shells to look like woven baskets.

The people of this aquatic culture would have become "wedded, psychologically as well as economically, to the waters." While the waters lasted, their culture was economically successful and culturally prestigious.

Bu the rains that renewed life in the Sahara in every year tapered off. This happened little by little, over millions of years.[34] People began herding cows around 6,000 BC, as the drying increased dramatically.

By 5,000 BC West Africans were growing of rice, yams, watermelons and cotton. Some of these crops later spread to the Nile Valley, where cotton in particular proved to be very important.[35]

Niger-Congo Languages

Because the Niger-Congo languages of West Africa derive from a common core, they share similarities despite their diversity.[36]

The Niger-Congo language family is the largest phylum in the world and includes some of the largest in Africa, including Wolof, Fulfulde, Manding, Akan, Yoruba, Lingala, Xhosa and Zulu. Niger-Congo languages cover more of the continent than any other group and are spoken by at least 360 million people.[37]

Atlantic languages split off first from the Niger-Congo root around 6,000 BC.[38] The Kru languages followed 2,000 years later.[39] Another 1,000 years later,

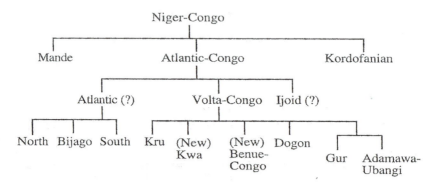

Figure 6. Niger-Congo Language Family Tree

Mande broke off. Around that time, the Sahel was swampy, infested with the Tsetse fly and difficult to inhabit.

The Sahara then was going through the final stage of turning into a desert, and Lake Chad was drying down from 332 m above sea level to its current height of 280 m.

There are several reasons to believe that Kru speakers, as well as some Kwa and Gur groups, were engaged in the early aquatic culture. First, linguists estimate that Kru separated from Niger-Congo around 4000 BC, just as West Africa was beginning to dry down. Second, one Kru language, Seme, is spoken in Burkina Faso, which is thought to be the area from which the language family dispersed down the rivers in a general southward direction. Third, most Kru-speakers are located furthest south, along the rivers, lagoons and Atlantic coast.[40]

According to most recent scientific estimate, Mande languages began in the Southern Sahara, north of 16° latitudes, perhaps even as far as 18°, and between 3° and 12° of Western longitude. After the Sahara turned suddenly dry, Mande speakers moved south to the Sahel around 300 BC. As the Mande developed farming along the Niger, their population grew and their languages splintered further.[41]

Before the breakup of the Niger-Congo family, the ancestors of West Africans and those of today's inhabitants of the Nile probably lived close to each other. This theory is supported by an unusual form of evidence: a fast, fretful-looking and barkless dog found today among the Loma and Kpelle. This unique breed, known as Basenji, was portrayed on ancient Egyptian monuments with

As the Sahara dry period set in, Niger-Congo speakers would have retreated toward the wetter regions in the south. In the process, their language divided into four families: Along the western coast were the ancestors of Atlantic speakers. This family includes the Wolof, who were engaged in swamp rice cultivation, and the Fulani, circulating throughout the region with their cattle, sheep and knowledge of metal-smelting.[42]

In the Sahel were the Mande, conducting long-distance trade and farming fonio and rice. Ancestors of the Kru were apparently engaged in an aquatic culture in the Middle belt, but less is known about this group than the three others. East along the Benue, the Kwa speakers engaged in iron smelting and farming yams.

> **Figure 7. Kru languages & cultures**
>
> Kru is a family of 41 languages spoken mainly in Liberia and Côte d'Ivoire. Linguists who study the relationship of African languages to one another have long struggled with how to classify Kwaa, Dei, Krahn, Sapo, Glebo, Klao, Glebo and Bassa. In 1966, Greenberg tentatively placed them in the Kwa group, which includes Twi.
>
> However, it has now been recognized that these languages share less affinity to the coastal Kwa languages immediately to the east than with Aizi (an isolated language on the Ebrie Lagoon in Côte d'Ivoire) and Siamon (spoken in the Orodara region of Burkina Faso). Approximately eight Kru languages have less than 10,000 speakers, including Kwaa and Dei in Liberia, placing them in danger.
>
>

By 2,300 B. C., the Sahara was so dry, shade trees disappeared. Residents faced a tough choice: move or die.[43]

Those who survived the harrowing exodus naturally sought refuge near large bodies of water: Lake Chad, the Nile and the Niger. Confined to those locations, people took to farming instead of gathering food from the wild. Together with the reliable supply of meat and milk from herding cows, farming boosted the population dramatically.

The sudden drying of the Sahara has recently yielded hidden wealth. By boiling the dead plants and animals underground, the heat has produced vast supplies of gas and oil, especially in Algeria and Libya.[44]

Through the ages, the Sahara has continued to expand and contract with deadly results. When it shrinks, people plant crops and gaze animals at the desert's edge. But, erratic rainfall and overgrazing have repeatedly led to the desert's growth. This cycle has produced devastating famines in the Sahel as recently as 1968, 1974 and 2010.[45]

Life in the Nile Valley

Of the three key bodies of water, the Nile Valley has yielded the most evidence on population growth, so data from there will be used to illustrate how the process unfolded. In 9,000 BC, no more than a thousand people at one time hunted, herded and gathered food along the river banks from present-day Cairo to Khartoum. By 4,000 BC, people had shifted to farming regularly, and each square mile of the river banks supported 30 to 46 people.[46]

With people living longer and having more children, farmers were quickly able to clear eight times more land. Within 400 years, the population increased ten times, to 460 people per square miles. Some of them were now full-time traders and priests. Villages consisted of rectangular mud-brick houses, some enclosed with walls.[47]

Ancient Egyptians called their country *Kmt*, meaning "the black land." Many historians believe the name *Kmt* stems from the color of the Nile Valley's rich, dark soil. The name "Egypt" is derived from the Greek word *Aigyptios*. This term was a corruption of *Hikuptah*, the capital of Egypt, which the Greeks called Memphis.[48]

While Egyptians farmed the moist valley soil, they buried their dead in the desert, facing the rising sun in the east with the vast Sahara at their backs.[49] Engravings estimated to be from 3,500 BC that were recently unearth in the Eastern Sahara show ideas and practices that later flowered in Ancient Egyptian culture.[50]

Ancient Egyptians spoke a language that belongs to the Afrasiatic family (sometimes called "Afrasian"). Linguists believe this family began 15,000 years ago in the area of present-day Ethiopia, Somalia and Eritrea. It includes such current languages as Oromo (of Ethiopia), Tuareg (of the Sahara) and Hausa (of Nigeria).[51]

Egypt's neighbor's were Nubia to the south, Axum to the east (later called Abyssinia) and Libya to the west, all well known trade partners. To classical Greek writers, Nubia was "Ethiopia" and Axum was "Punt" (which sometimes included present-day Somalia and Eritrea).[52]

Figure 8. Basenji dog

It was known in Ancient Egypt as the Pharaoh's favorite dog. It is found among the Loma and Kpelle in Liberia

Egyptian rulers were clearly interested in the rest of Africa because Pharaoh Necho II commissioned Phoenician mariners to sail around the continent, about 2,000 years before Europeans ventured down the coast of West Africa.[53]

African predecessors of ancient Egyptians came from Libya to the west, as well as Nubia and Punt to the south. They were joined by elephants, hippopotami, lions, crocodiles, turtles and all manner of other animals forced there by thirst.[54]

Major landmarks along the Nile are six piles of rocks, called cataracts, that slow the river's flow between present-day Khartoum and Aswad. South of Aswad, the river travels 600 miles without major interruptions before spilling into the Mediterranean Sea. Ancient Egypt thrived mainly on the fertile soil along with strip, as well as the wide rich delta at the mouth of the river.[55]

> **Figure 9. African names for months**
>
> The Gola name for the first month of the year, like the names of months in many local languages, reflects knowledge of the climate and natural environment.
>
> In contrast, January — the English name for that month — is the name of a pagan Roman god. Yet, it is African cultures that have been dismissed as rooted in "superstitions." And, as a result, it is their knowledge of climate and the environment — as embedded in traditional calendars — that is at risk of being lost.
>
>

Sometime around 3,200 BC, the previously separate cities and regions of the Nile Valley were brought under one government. Taxes from farmers and income from gold and other natural resources supported full-time soldiers, priests and scribes. The government was headed by a pharaoh, and power passed down within the pharaoh's family. This system lasted for more than 3,000 years, with occasional interruptions due to external conquerors or internal revolts.[56]

The cultures and empires that developed along the Niger and Nile were both controlled by rulers who were assisted by full-time priests.[57]

Like the Nile, the Niger, too, saved the original people of the Sahara from likely extinction. Along with life-giving water, it provided rich soil for farming, moist grass for cows to graze, hard trees for canoes, plus a variety of fish, game and birds for food.[58] But, what the Niger gives in times of normal flow, like the Nile, it takes away in times of flooding.[59]

Centers of Cultivation and Iron Smelting

West Africa underwent a quiet revolution around 8,000 BC. It occurred, thanks to three major changes. First, people shifted from gathering wild food to farming. In addition to hunting for meat, they domesticated animals like sheep

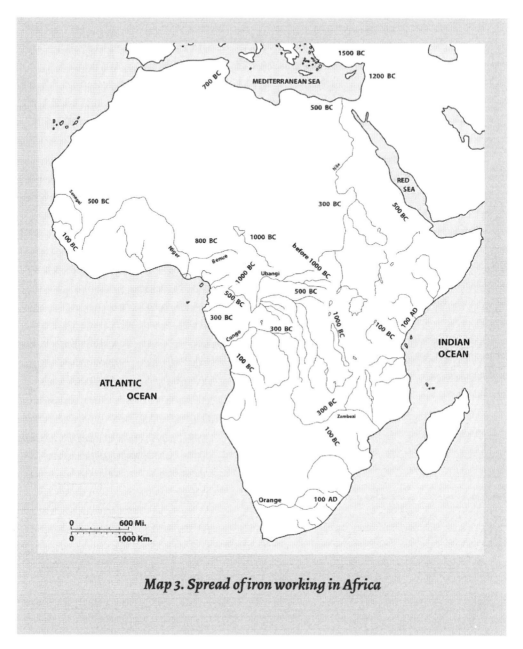

Map 3. Spread of iron working in Africa

goats and cows. In place of tools carved from stones, they learned to make stronger ones from melted metals, especially iron. These changes were indigenous, not imported.[60]

Together, the three innovations changed life dramatically. People were better able to control their food supply. They also increased the amount of food produced. As a result, the population of West Africa grew quickly. As people moved in search of new farmlands, pastures and mines, languages splintered.

The shift toward farming, herding and smelting occurred in three locations: One was Northern Nigeria, the apparent disbursal-point of Kwa-speakers. Another was the Niger River, heartland of the Mande language group. The third was southern Mauritania, home of Atlantic cultures.

Trading between fishing folk, farmers or herders helped forge the underlying cultural and linguistic unity of West Africa.[61] Because some regions produced goods that others didn't have, trade developed between different areas: Kola went from one place in exchange for salt as rice was traded for iron.

The revolution began when groups in the woodland savanna region shifted from gathering to growing several types of African yams (genus *Dioscorea*). Just by selecting those that were most beneficial and neglecting those that proved harmful, they helped nurture into existence two types of yam: white and yellow.

These plants yielded both edible greens and large, fleshy underground sections of their stems known as tubers. Increased food productivity fueled a population increase. Within 4,000 years, those two yams had become staple food crops.[62]

By 3,500 BC, stone tools were being used in southern Côte d'Ivoire, probably to clear trees for planting yams and other food stuff.[63] Within 500 years, farmers in the region were keeping guinea fowl and growing okra, black-eye peas and African groundnuts. They soon began tending kola trees.

A major breakthrough came when West Africans learned to harvest oil and raffia palm trees. The first yields cooking oil and palm wine, the second provides raffia fiber and another kind of palm wine.

Before 1,000 BC, sub-Saharan Africa as a whole held less than 10 million people. Imagine three times the population of present-day Liberia spread over the entire sub-continent. At the time, West Africans numbered approximately 2 people per square mile.[64]

In Africa, iron smelting seems to have developed around 1000 BC in the area of Central African Republic. From there it spread east to the Great Lakes region and west toward northern Nigeria. Then it diffused along the Atlantic until becoming established in the Liberia area.

By 200 BC, Nok in Nigeria and Jenne-jeno in Mali were producing iron on an industrial scale, not just by individual artisans.[65] Iron tools allowed the clearing of more land with a consequent boost in population. By 1000 BC, the first large communities began to form in the forest belt, thanks to yam farming and iron smelting.[66]

Another site of innovation was the Middle Niger floodplain, where the river flows through grasslands and scrubs. By 9,000 BC, people there had developed a tradition of pottery making and grinding stones for processing wild cereals.[67] Within another 2,000 years, shepherds living between 20° and 24° were herding local cattle, as well as imported sheep and goat.[68] This shift is documented both by cattle remains and rock paintings.

By 4000 BC, Niger-Congo speakers in the savannah were living in settled communities, some of whom fished (using baskets and hooks fashioned from bones and shells).

As West Africa entered a period of less rainfall around 3,500 BC, farmers near present-day Bamako began growing African rice (*Oryza glaberrima*). They soon began using iron tools and farming fonio, bottle gourd and watermelon.[69] Within 500 years, they had coaxed into existence several beneficial forms of millet, sorghum and rice.

From that inland delta area, rice farming spread south, along the tributaries of the Niger and coastal river deltas.

A third point of innovation was Mauritania. Here is where Fula cattle-herders emerged about 3,000 BC. Here, too, the farming of pearl millet (also called "bulrush") led to sedentary occupations and larger settlements. Around 700 AD, Serer-speakers and Fula shepherds began moving south toward the Senegal Valley.

Each year, the herders migrated with their livestock according to the seasons. They went north to the Sahel when the rains began, then during the dries they traveled south to let their animals graze in the savannah after local farmers had harvested their crops. In the process, they formed a symbiotic relationship with local farming communities, providing fertilizing manure, as well as exchanging milk and butter for crops.[70]

This expansion probably followed the general pattern of herders, which involves some youths branching out to graze their animals in fresh pastures. By 1,300 BC, Fula communities were especially pronounced in the Futa Toro region of Guinea.[71]

A major consequence of the farming, herding and smelting revolution was a constant southward movement of people toward the forest. That's one reason West African oral traditions are filled with stories of migration. This population movement was once taken as proof that Africans were "primitive." But, if European and Asians at the time moved less, it was simply because they faced different conditions, not evidence of their "superiority."

Like people elsewhere, early Africans sometimes moved due to droughts, conflicts with other groups and epidemics.[72] These migrations were easy, thanks to the river and the flat land. But, West Africa's mobility was driven mainly by population growth due to farming, herding and the use of iron tools. Besides the Nile and the Niger, Africa had few areas that were naturally irrigated and fertilized through annual flooding.

So, population growth drove a search for unclaimed land, which was more available in West Africa than in Asia and especially Europe. Plentiful land allowed West Africans to develop a system of rotating farms. They left previously farmed land to rest and become re-fertilized by wild plants before using it again.[73]

In short, early West African migrations stemmed from technological advancement, not stagnation.

1. Heinrich Barth, *Travels and Discoveries in North and Central Africa*, Vol. II (London: Frank Cass & Co., 1965), p. 15.
2. Drake, 1998, p. 122; Ehret, 2002, pp. 17-25; James L. Newman, *The Peopling of Africa: A Geographic Interpretation* (New Haven: Yale University Press, 1995), pp. 11-21; J. Desmond Clark, *The Prehistory of Africa* (London: Thames and Hudson, 1970), pp. 76-104; Christopher Ehret, "Africa in world history: The long, long view" (pp. 455-474), in Jerry H. Bentley, ed., *The Oxford Handbook of World History* (Oxford: Oxford University Press, 2013), p. 455.
3. Drake, 1998, p. 122; Ehret, 2002, pp. 17-25; Newman, 1995, pp. 11-21; Clark, 1970, pp. 76-104.
4. Akin Mabogunje, "The land and peoples of West Africa" (pp. 1-32), in J. F. Ade Ajayi and Michael Crowder, *History of West Africa*, Vol. I (New York: Columbia University Press, 1972), especially p. 11.
5. Lugenbeel, 1853, p. 6; Johnson, 1961, p. 81.
6. John Hunwick, *West Africa, Islam and the Arab World: Studies in Honor of Basil Davidson* (Princeton: Markus Wiener Publishers, 2006), p. 7.
7. Brian Fagan, *The Long Summer: How Climate Changed Civilization* (New York: Basic Books, 2004), p. 148; Lamonn Gearon, *The Sahara: A Cultural History* (New York: Oxford University Press, 2011), p. xii.
8. Fagan, 2004, p. 148.
9. Gearon, 2011, p. xvi.
10. Fagan, 2004, pp. 148, 150; Gearon, 2011, pp. xv, xvi, xvii, xx.
11. Gearon, 2011, pp. xv, xvii.
12. Fagan, 2004, p. 148.
13. Gearon, 2011, p. xvii.
14. Gearon, 2011, p. xii.
15. Gearon, 2011, p. xi. There are 64 African countries, consisting of 54 sovereign states and 10 non-sovereign territories.
16. Gearon, 2011, p. xix.
17. Gearon, 2011, pp. 3, xiii; Mabogunje, 1972, pp. 5-6, 11, 27; Levtzion, 1972, p. 120; Hunwick, 2006 p. 13.
18. Gearon, 2011, pp. 3, 6.
19. Gearon, 2011, p. 7; Fagan, 2004, p. 151.
20. Gearon, 2011, p. 8.
21. Fagan, 2004, p. 152; Gearon, 2011, pp. 11, 13.
22. Ehret, 2002, p. 47.
23. Ehret, 2002, p. 47.
24. Ehret, 2002, pp. 48-49, 191, especially p. 48.
25. Gearon, 2011, pp. 6, 11.
26. Gearon, 2011, p. 11; Fagan, 2004, p. 152.
27. Drake, 1998, pp. 164-165.

28. Fagan, 2004, pp. 152, 148.

29. Fagan, 2004, p. 155.

30. Fagan, 2004, pp. 154, 157, 159.

31. Fagan, 2004, p. 159; Ehret, 2002, pp. 3, 26, 35; S. K. McIntosh, "Archaeology of Holocene West Africa, 12,000-1,000 BP" (pp. 11-32), in Emmanuel Kwame Akeyampong (ed.), *Themes in West Africa's History* (London: James Currey, 2006), pp. 15-16.

32. Fagan, 2004, p. 159.

33. Gearon, 2011, p. 33; Fagan, 2004, p. 162.

34. Fagan, 2004, pp. 150-151.

35. Drake, 1998, pp. 127, 155; George P. Murdock, *Africa: Its Peoples and Their Culture History* (New York: McGraw-Hill, 1959); Ehret, 2013, p. 459. According to Ehret, cotton was domesticated separately in Africa, India and the Americas.

36. Webb, 2006, pp. 38-39; Roland Portéres, "Primary cradles of agriculture in the African continent" (pp. 43-58), in J. D. Fage and R. A. Oliver, eds., *Papers in African Prehistory* (London: Cambridge University Press, 1974).

37. Kay Williamson and Roger Blench, "Niger-Congo" (pp. 11-42), in Bernd Heine and Derek Nurse, eds., *African Languages: An Introduction* (Cambridge: Cambridge University Press, 2000), p. 11.

38. Brooks, 1985, p. 12.

39. R. Blench, *Archeology, Language, and the African Past* (Lanham: Rowman Altamira, 2006), p. 133.

40. William Y. Adams, "The coming of Nubian speakers to the Nile Valley" (pp. 11-38) in Christopher Ehret and Merick Posnansky, eds., *The Archaeological and Linguistic Reconstruction of African History* (Berkeley: University of California Press, 1982), pp. 12-13.

41. Vydrine, 2009, pp.109, 112-116; also Brooks, 1989, p. 30.

42. J. E. G. Sutton, "The aquatic civilization of Middle Africa," *Journal of African History*, Vol. 15, No. 4 (1974): 527-546, especially pp. 529, 535, 539.

43. Gearon, 2011, p. 10; Fagan, 2004, pp. 157-158; Drake, 1998, p. 129.

44. Gearon, 2001, pp. xviii, 52.

45. Fagan, 2004, p. 150; Wayne T. Brough and Mwangi S. Kimenyi, "Desertification of the Sahel: Exploring the role of property rights," *PERC Report*, Vol. 22, No. 2 (Summer 2004): 15-17.

46. Fagan, 2004, p. 153.

47. Fagan, 2004, pp. 160, 164.

48. Christian Cannuger, *Coptic Egypt: The Christians of the Nile* (New York: Harry N. Abrams, Inc., 2001), p. 11.

49. Gearon, 2011, p. 29; Fagan, 2011, p. 29.

50. Fagan, 2004, p. 162.

51. Ehert, 1991.

52. O'Connor and Reid, 2003, p. 12; Drake, 1998, p. 147.

53. O'Connor and Reid, 2003, p. 17.

54. Ernest Alfred Wallis Budge, *A History of Egypt from the end of the Neolithic period to the death of Cleopatra VII, B. C. 30*, Vol. I: Egypt in the Neolithic and Archaic Period (London: Kegan Paul, Trench Trübner & Co., 1904), pp. iii, 37-39, 46, 60.
55. Drake, 1998, p. 147.
56. Drake, 1998, p. 143.
57. Drake, 1998, p. 129; Hunwick, 2006, p. 8.
58. De Gramont, 1975, p. 26; Gearon, 2011, p. xiv.
59. De Gramont, 1975, p. 26.
60. Ehret, 2002, p. 45.
61. Ehret, 2002, pp. 44, 82-83; James L. A. Webb, Jr., Economy & culture in West Africa" (pp. 33-51), in Emmanuel Kwame Akeyampong (ed.), *Themes in West Africa's History* (London: James Currey, 2006), especially p. 34; also Diop, 1989; Diop, 1991; Marquet, 1972.
62. Webb, 2006, pp. 33-39.
63. Ehret, 2002, pp. 27, 139; McIntosh, 2006, pp. 17-24, 26.
64. Posnansky, 1992, pp. 726-727.
65. Ismail Rashid., "Class, caste & social inequality in West African history" (pp. 118-140), in Emmanuel Kwame Akeyampong (ed.), *Themes in West Africa's History* (London: James Currey, 2006), especially p. 121.
66. Webb, 2006, p. 41.
67. Ehret, 2002, pp. 28, 35, 44, 82-83; McIntosh, 2006, pp. 15-16.
68. Webb, 2006, p. 40.
69. Ehret, 2002, pp. 27, 139; McIntosh, 2006, pp. 17-24, 26.
70. Mabogunje, 1972, p. 26.
71. Jan Vansina, "Population movements and the emergence of new socio-political forms in Africa," *General History of Africa: Africa from the Sixteenth to the Eighteenth Century*, Vol. V. Berkeley: University of California Press, 1992), pp. 25-38, especially p. 29.
72. Vansina, 1992, pp. 25, 27.
73. Wright, 1999, pp. 419-426.

Chapter 2
Land of Kola, Canoes & Salt

The first signs that people were living in the area of Liberia are mainly from 410 AD to 1085 AD. These include tools for cooking, smelting iron and boiling salt. There were all collected by archaeologists in the 1970s and dated using advanced scientific tests.

The items from 410 BC are charcoal, stone tools, pieces of clay pots and oil-palm kernels.[1] These were found in a rock shelter near Sanniquellie. So far, nothing else from that early has been found.

The largest collection of items left behind by early people in the region are from Sierra Leone, near the present-day towns of Kamabai, Yagala, Tengama, Koidu and Bo. Included are stone tools, a mound for casting brass, and left-overs from iron smelting — all dating between 500 and 900 AD.[2]

Among those items, the most interesting pieces are broken pots from around 760 AD that were found in a rock shelter near Kamabai. These are remarkable because they match the "wavy-line" pottery style used by an aquatic culture near Lake Chad before 2,500 BC. Although the areas are 1,790 miles apart, they were apparently in contact.[3]

Small pieces of broken pots may seem like trash, but they unlocked a key finding: People in the area of Liberia were living settled lives by 760 BC.

How do we know this? First, groups that lived by hunting and gathering had little need for containers. Second, clay pots would have been too fragile for wandering groups to carry around.

Fewer items left over by early people have been found in Liberia. Those items were discarded in obscure places, but they yield important facts about the people who left them.

One group, dating from 450 AD, was found between Bolahun and Kolahun near the Kaihar River. In a shelter cut into a rock, people left stone tools, the base of a large pot, charcoal and charred palm-oil.[4]

Another set of items from 900 to 1085 AD were recovered on the Atlantic coast just west of the Po River mouth. Included were elaborate pottery and items that had apparently been used to distill salt from sea water by boiling.[5] In addition, ancient but undated iron-smelting sites were uncovered in Grand Gedeh.

There is no direct evidence linking any of these sites to a specific language group. However, it is very likely that the items from Bolahun and Sierra Leone were left by Atlantic-speakers.

Atlantic groups spread from a base in Mauritania, around 6,000 BC down the coast through Senegal and Gambia before entering Guinea, Sierra Leone and Liberia. From Senegal, Fula split from Wolof and Serer (its two closest relatives) and spread westward.[6] Despite vast variations in vocabularies, Atlantic languages share similar sound-systems, grammars and semantics.[7]

The origin stories of Atlantic groups lack any reference to water travel. This suggests they came by land rather than sea. When they arrived, vast sections of the Liberian and Sierra Leone interior were uninhabited forest. Wild game was plentiful, including hippopotamus, elephant and water buffalo.

> ### Figure 10. Atlantic languages
>
> Atlantic is a family of 65 languages, at least 13 of which have less than 10,000 speakers. Some of these languages, like Gola (Liberia) and Kissi (Sierra Leone, Liberia and Guinea), are surrounded by Mande speakers, resulting in some shifting to the languages of their neighbors.
>
> The Kissi language is classified with the Atlantic family, but the people share historical ties to the Malinké, especially those living in Guinea.
>
> Smaller languages in this family are especially vulnerable because Atlantic speakers have generally lived in hamlets, not large compact towns. languages are very diverse, which makes uncovering patterns among them very difficult.
>
>

According to linguistic evidence, Atlantic-speakers were the earliest Niger-Congo groups implanted in southern Senegambia, Guinea and Sierra Leone.[8] Their location relative to their homeland in Mauritania suggest they entered from the northwest. The Bullum, Krim, Kissi and Gola formed the southern-most vanguard along the coast of Sierra Leone.[9]

Various oral traditions from western Liberia credit the Gola with being the first Atlantic group to settle that region. According to Gola oral traditions, they were initially a small isolated group living in a homeland called Mana in the northwestern mountains of Liberia.[10]

Although the Kissi and Gola speakers are only 80 miles apart today, their languages are markedly different, suggesting that linguistic separation occurred centuries ago, long before their arrival in the forest region.[11]

At first, Atlantic groups apparently settled along the northern edge of the forest, while Kru-speakers occupied the mangrove fringe along the coast. About that time, the Mande were moving west from Lake Chad toward the Niger bend.[12]

According to linguistic evidence, the Kru language separated from the Niger-Congo root sometime around 4,000 BC. That was probably the beginning of the Kru long trek south.

The Kru apparently came along the Camoe River to the edge of the forest. At that time, territories to the east were occupied by large numbers of Gur and Kwa groups. Veering west, they dispersed into the Nzo Valley.

Kru groups continued migrating further west, with some settling north of Gedeh, Bong and Nimba mountains, while others followed the rivers down to the coast. Specifically, some ancestors of the Klao seem to have followed the Cestros River, and the Dei ventured down along the St. Paul.

Taken together, the oral traditions of various groups, the linguistic evidence, and the dated palm oil and other items from Kolahun all point to one logical conclusion: the Atlantic speakers, probably ancestors of the Gola and Kissi, were in Liberia by 450 BC.

It is also likely that items discovered at Sanniquellie, Grand Gedeh and the Po River were left by Kru groups.[13]

The Dei and Settra Kru all share oral traditions of previously living in close association with Mande-speakers further north.[14] Oral traditions of various Mande groups acknowledge that their ancestors met Kru speakers in Liberia. The language map of the region suggests they migrated from the Niger via the major rivers to the northern savannah region of Côte d'Ivoire.

According to oral traditions of various Kru groups (including the Killipo), they moved south and west toward Grand Gedeh, before pushing toward the coast. The focal point of those migrations was Mt. Gedeh (also called Mt. Niété).[15] The Dei, Kabor and Gbeta have all been acknowledged as the vanguard by other Kru speakers.[16]

Taken together, the linguistic evidence, various oral traditions and the dated pottery from the Po River support one conclusion: That Kru speakers were living in Liberia by 990 AD. They were very likely the ancestors of the Dei and the Klao, especially the Kabor and Gbeta.

The ancestors of Kru speakers probably left the palm kernels and tools near Sanniquellie around 410 BC, before fragmenting. They were also very likely responsible for the undated iron-smelting items at Mt. Gedeh. But, the salt-making tools at the Po River were almost certainly left specifically by ancestors of the Dei.

Both the Kru and Atlantic speakers say they met people here whom they describe as Pygmies.[17] Well into the twentieth century, a British colonial officer for the Gold Coast, Frederick W. H. Migeod, claimed to have "personal knowledge" that "dwarfs" existed in areas occupied by the Mende and the Kru.[18]

This is possible, given the presence of Pygmies in Africa's other major forest belt, the Congo. Plus, Liberia is home to many pygmy animal species, including hippopotamus and antelope.

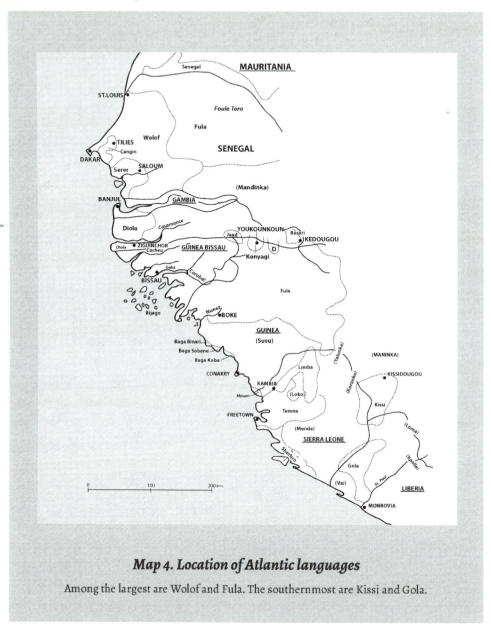

Map 4. Location of Atlantic languages

Among the largest are Wolof and Fula. The southernmost are Kissi and Gola.

If there were Pygmies, their numbers soon dwindled, as they were overrun or absorbed by Kru and Atlantic groups. Pygmies or not, any earlier inhabitants must have been few because very little of the forest had been cleared.

The movement of Atlantic and Kru groups into the the Liberia area was the harvest of fruits planted many generations before. In areas where people farmed,

Land of Kola, Canoes & Salt

herded and smelted iron, their [...]
for new lands. Centuries after Atlant[...]
ers migrated from near southern Nigeri[...]

Challenges of the Forest

For the ancestors of the Gola, the Kissi, the [...] savannah was tough, but settling in the forest belt was tou[gh...] the forest is sparsely populated, including Liberia.[20]

A sign that some ethnic groups are relatively recent to th[e...] their fear of the forest. Among the scariest characters in local folkta[les...] spirits, known as *lausing* in Kpelle, for instance. The heroic role of hunters [in] founding tales also reflects anxieties about the forest, inhabited by bush cows, [ele]phants and leopards when the first ancestors of Liberians arrived.

The forest is hard to cross and to clear for farming. Historian Ivor Wilks estimated that one person using traditional tools would take 500 days to clear 2.5 acres of forest. On average, this would yield about 1,400 tons of plant material.[21]

Iron is present in the soil along the northern edge of the forest belt. If exposed to rain for awhile, the iron-laced soil turns hard and infertile. It forms reddish pebbles or even blocks as thick as 30 feet. This condition is called *ferruginous laterite*.[22]

Worse still, the forest belt teemed with significant risks to human life. Threats included leopards, bush cows and other predatory animals. In addition, the Tsetse fly still infests people and cow with African sleeping sickness. Measured in aches, fevers and deaths, perhaps the worst of all are blood-sucking mosquitos that serve as vectors for Plasmodium that causes potentially fatal malaria.

Initially, *vivax* malaria caused widespread debilitation throughout West Africa. But, after 50,000 BC, the disease nearly disappeared because people developed a natural immunity. It was replaced by a second strain called *falciparum*. While some West Africans developed an immunity known as sickle-cell, a few carry a defective form called sickle-cell anemia that causes severe pain and sometimes death.[23]

The forest belt includes a thin strip of mangrove and fresh water swamp along the coast. The forest proper begins slightly further inland. It consists of trees 200 ft. in height and three feet in girth.

From Sierra Leone in the west to Cameroon in the east, the forest extends 200 miles inland, except for a stretch of grassland that extends to the coast in modern Ghana.[24]

One group of forest trees shed some or all of their leaves in the course of a year; these are called *semi-deciduous*. Another group, the *evergreens*, keep the leaves yearround. These trees grow in areas with the highest rainfall; they cover a third or more of Liberia.

the rains are
July and from
r. During this
night than dur-
son, pedestrians
ll often dash be-
pours. Rains usu-
ain, off-again until

the rain falls heavy in
ts are plentiful. Areas
e fewer plants.
eavy rainfall provides
much of a good thing.
s and mangrove swamps
ig. Torrents of water wash
m the soil, resulting in less
plants.[26]

vember is the beginning of
The Gola call this month *Bobo*,
during which the swamp mud
begins to get hard." During this period, blistering sunshine is softened by a cooling sea breeze along the coast from 1 p.m. to 10 p.m. Between 1 a.m. and 10 a.m., a counter wind blows from the interior. During the windless hours around midnight and noon, the air is dry, hot and still.[27]

December stands out, as noted by a nineteenth-century observer, because the "sun usually rises with brilliancy and beauty; and the hills and groves, teeming with the verdure of perpetual spring, are enriched by the mingled melody of a thousand songsters."[28]

Land, Clan and Gender

After 6000 BC, villages in the rain forest area were generally arrayed

Western Kru		
Grebo complex		
Ivorian		28,000
Tepo-Plapo, Pie		
Liberian		120,000
Wedebo, Glebo, Jabo, Gedebo, Nitiabo, Fopo, Chedepo		
Oubi-Glio		
Guere (Wee) complex		303,000+
Nyabwa-Nyedebwa		
Wobe		
Guere-Krahn		
Konobo		
Bassa		214,000
Gbii		
Dewoin (Dey)		5,000
Klao		120,000
Kuwaa		7,000
Azizi		
Seme		

along both sides of a single road or along the banks of a river. Houses were typically rectangular in shape, with ridge roofs made with woven palm matting.[29] This style would be retained by Kru-speakers in southeastern Liberia, but over time Mande and Atlantic groups switched to round buildings.

One characteristic of Niger-Congo societies from their earliest days was their organization on the basis of clans, family groupings that formed the outer limit of social and political structuring. Each clan (or specific lineage within a clan) typically lived in a village of 100-200 residents.

During this period, life was precarious, not just in this region. Folktales from around the world show that food shortages were common, bad weather or a "swarm of locust" could easily lead to famine. Given such threats, people had to address two major priorities: How to provide their basic necessities, mainly tools, food, shelter and clothing. And, how to keep family and community life going, mainly by having children. In short, how to ensure production and reproduction.[30]

Initially, small-scale settlements in the edge of the forest were facilitated by stone tools and controlled burning, but timber-clearing on a scale needed for rice farming and durable housing required the use of iron tools. It is certain that large-scale settlements in the area of Liberia could only have been possible after iron tools became available around 100 BC.[31]

For farming communities, successful production depended mainly on the proper allocation of land and labor.[32] Community leaders addressed production needs largely by enforcing internal rules on local people. It helped if they were on good terms with neighbors in case extra hands were needed to respond quickly to a disaster or an unusually bountiful harvest.

For successful reproduction, however, compact villages had to maintain good relations with outsiders to avoid incest, a major taboo. Rules were enforced to ensure that one village did not gain at the expense of the other.[33] In addition, elders from each community kept a mental balance "sheet" of how many women from their town married how many men from another. The goal was to maintain a fair and balanced exchange.

Success was not automatic in either realm. It required strategizing and negotiating. And success was never permanent. Each delayed rainfall, each new disease, each insect infestation brought the danger of extinction.

This meant strategizing and negotiating were ongoing — year after year, new moon after new moon, day by day.

Many Liberian folktales recount frequent "hungry times" and migration due to famine.[34] These attest to failed production strategies. Perhaps an equal, if not larger, number of tales tell of tensions and even scrimmages between communities over "women."[35] Those highlight breakdowns in exchanges required by each community to maintain its reproduction.

In Niger-Congo societies, tasks and responsibilities were often assigned by sex and age, based on an idealized complementarity.[36] Too often these distinctions are inaccurately equated to patriarchy in Western culture by well intentioned but uninformed advocates of women's rights.

Even in societies where men exercised public leadership, women — especially after menopause — were viewed as having sacred power that was "parallel, complementary and sometimes superior."[37] Some West African cultures cast women as more effective conduits to God, the ancestors and the life-force.[38]

Even the natural world was inscribed with gender codes. Because the sun is born in the east, that direction was associated with women, who gave birth. As the direction of the sun's death, west was linked to men. In keeping with this code, villages were laid out, whenever possible, so "female" gardens were in the east and male Poro groves in the west.[39]

In West Africa, both production and reproduction were managed using kinship rules. In other words, kinship determined who was obligated to feed you as a child, who you could marry, who had first claims on your loyalty, time and labor.

While kinship was used similarly in many cultures, the specific rules differed. In West Africa, for example, you might owe a greater obligation to your maternal uncle than to your father. Persons defined as "brothers" here would be classed as "cousins" in the West.

Unlike some other cultures also, West Africa applied the language of kinship to many different domain. For instance, "brother" was used by some cultures to describe a close business partner. A political or religious leader might be called "father."[40] But, such references were metaphorical.

In practice, kinship rules were strictly applied only within families — relations between spouses, between parents and children, between siblings.[41] Kinship labels carried looser obligations and claims when extended to people in your neighborhood or social network.[42]

As summarized by anthropologist Eric Wolf, "Kinship thus involves (a) symbolic constructs ('filiation/marriage; consanguinity/affinity') that (b) continually place actors, born and recruited, (c) into social relations, with one another. These social relations (d) commit people in variable ways to call on the share of social labor carried by each in order to (e) effect the necessary transformation of nature."[43]

Among other purposes, the kinship system served to mobilize people and channel their labor toward production and reproduction. Through the kinship system, those who first invested labor in the land reaped returns from latecomers. After all, forest land was turned into farm land only through hard, strenuous, exertion.[44]

On one level, the family whose ancestors first "discovered" or worked the land held it as a sacred trust. The oldest town of this family usually served as the "capital" of the community.[45]

Consequently, newcomers or "strangers" earned a place in the community by providing gifts or sweat equity to the first family. Presents ranged from a one-time gift of a gown made from home-spun cotton among the Dan to an annual fee in crops and game among the densely populated Kpelle. For several generations, the descendants of such a settler would continue to be called "strangers."[46]

Within families, elders controlled shelter, seeds and marriageable women, by virtue of their lifetime expended in building the community and working the land. In turn, junior family members and dependents owed them deference, respect and labor.[47]

The elders also controlled how the community reproduced itself. First, they decided who from outside was permitted to marry their eligible daughters. Second, they could provide or withhold the resources their sons needed in order to get married. But more important, the elders were the main beneficiaries of a marriage system that allowed each man to have more than one wife.[48]

Thus, the various kin relations were arrayed in a hierarchy: at the top were the elder with longstanding ties to the community and at the base, young men, strangers and women of reproductive age.[49]

Kinship groups organized themselves into clans, giving authority to a ruler from the landholding lineage, who generally adjudicated internal disputes, allocated residential and farm land controlled by the clan, presided over ceremonies, and represented the clan in dealings with other groups.[50]

As with any hierarchy, the kinship system generated its own tensions between the rulers and the ruled. Tensions erupted, not just between elders and young men.[51] As portrayed in many folktales, tensions also pitted junior brothers against their seniors and junior wives against their senior.[52]

In small villages, tensions were harder to manage than in large towns. When they boiled over, young men often left, cleared fresh land and started new villages.

Despite language differences, Atlantic groups in northeast Liberia and Kru groups on the coast organized based on kinship hierarchies. Although living in widely separated parts of the territory, ancestors of the Kissi, Gola, Dei and Kru developed similar patterns of small, scattered villages.[53]

This pattern stemmed from the basic dynamic of the system — junior members of communities struck out when conflicts erupted over seeds, shelter and sexual partners. This is one of many ways in which "obvious" differences in language masked fundamental similarities in how people organized themselves. As villages became separated by distances and time, new clan and ethnic identities emerged.

An ethnic group is defined, following anthropologist Warren L. d'Azevedo, as a "persistent and distinctive" unit "identifiable by language, a relatively firm and commonly recognized territory, a name, a consciousness of kind, and a peculiar configuration of details in customs which are nonetheless significant marks of affiliation, regardless of wider regional regularities that might override them" (such as confederation or empire).[54]

As noted by d'Azevedo, "To think of one's self as a Gola, a Kpelle or a Mende is to some extent a matter of choice, but the basis of validation is intricate and far from arbitrary. It is possible, for example, for a Kpelle man or woman to 'become' a Gola. The very first requirement is language competency and permanent residence in a Gola community. But it is not enough that such a person be incorporated into a system of relations through marriage, land use, and participation in village administrative councils. He must demonstrate his absolute loyalty to 'Gola-ness' by applying himself diligently to learning the style of Gola behavior, by identifying with a vague but highly potent sense of Gola heritage, and by instilling this consciousness in his children."[55]

Figure 12. Kola seeds & malagueta

Top: Kola seeds in pink
Bottom: Dried malagueta spice

Given the element of choice inherent in ethnic identity, which is affected by power relations, it is simply unrealistic for historians to rummage through records hoping to uncover the ethnic groups of today living under the identical names and with the same characteristics in the past.

In this context, people apparently identified more on the basis of kinship, class, village, political unit and occupational status than ethnicity or language. And, as noted by Donald R. Wright, "one's ethnicity seems to have been more a matter of cultural lifestyle than of parentage or ancestry."[56] Historian Allen M. Howard made a similar point, arguing "ethnic boundaries were fluid, that communities ... were created, dissolved, arranged, and recreated over time, and that symbols and institutions were invented."[57] Historian Paul Nugent is more emphatic; he noted, "Ethnicity as we think of it — a clear identity with, and strong loyalties to, an ethnic group — almost certainly did not exist in precolonial Africa."[58]

Sea Salt, Kola Seeds and Malagueta Spice

Four products of the forest dramatically affected the history of West Africa: kola seeds, malagueta spice, salt and iron. They influenced the opening and closing of trade routes, the migration of language groups, even the rise and fall of empires.[59] Historian George E. Brooks linked Kru westward movement to the trade in malagueta spice, salt, kola, iron, cloth and other products.[60]

As early as the 1200s AD, an unnamed seed from Africa, whose description seemed to fit the kola, was present in markets along the Mediterranean.[61]

The large kola tree bears pods with about six seeds that falls to the ground when ripe year round. Although kola now grows in Central Africa, as far east as the Congo river, it originated in the West African forest. Of the more than 40 types of kola, only four were widely traded. Of these, the most valued (and apparently first commercialized) was *Cola nitida*.

Cola nitida grows between 6° and 8° N from the Upper Guinea to the Volta River. But, it is commonly found in the forest in the region of Sierra Leone, Liberia and Guinea, between 150 to 300 kilometers from the coast.

Although some kola trees grow further north, they tend to be eaten locally because they are too small to be traded.[62] For these reasons, it is likely that groups living near the forest developed a brisk northward trade in kola nuts from the region known as the Gola forest.

The most widely sold varieties of kola are now known to contain large amounts of caffeine, which stimulates the central nervous system. Also present are smaller amounts of three other stimulants: kolatin (for the heart), theobromine (for the skeletal muscles) and glucose (for the body as a whole).[63] These same ingredients have made cola a popular ingredient in soft drinks around the world.

Kola was the ultimate social lubricant among widely scattered West Africans groups speaking vastly different languages. It was used in divination, given to guests as a sign of hospitality, offered to strangers as an indication of a "clean heart," and presented to the ancestors in remembrance. Kola also supplied a yellow-brown dye that was used to color textiles.[64]

Kola nuts deteriorate rapidly, so fresh supplies had to be transported to the savannah continuously. By 1332, according to Ibn al-Mukhtar, the Mali Empire during the reign of Kankan Musa was the site of a booming kola trade. That level of demand shows that kola was already well integrated into cultures extending from the forest to the Sahel.[65]

Kola was to West Africa what tea was to Asia and coffee was to the Middle East.

So, who began exporting kola from the forest? No written sources link the early trade to any specific ethnic group, but the terms for kola are identical to the name of only two languages — Gola, an Atlantic group, and Guro, a Mande language.[66]

In Mande languages from the Atlantic Ocean to Lake Chad, as well as in Atlantic languages other than Temne and Gola, the word for kola is a variant of *goro* or *woro*, suggesting the Guro were the main conduit for diffusion of the commodity throughout the grasslands and the Sahel. Probably in recognition of the Guro's role in kola trading, the area just to the north of where they live is called Worodugu, meaning "Kola nut" (*woro*) and "land" (*dugu*) in Malinké.[67]

But, several other factors point specifically to the Gola. The land first settled by the Gola produced the most desirable kola. Among the Temne (neighbors of the Gola who also speak an Atlantic language), the word for kola is *kola* or *tola*, and kola trees are known as *nola* or *yola*.[68]

Furthermore, it is possible that *goro* was derived from Gola because both "l" and "r" are often interchangeable in Mande languages, as well as a shift from "g" to "w." Also, there are Guro oral traditions claiming they moved south from the savannah in search of kola.[69] If that is the case, the nuts had already been commodified by people living in the kola forests, very likely the Gola.

Like kola, malagueta spice was known early in Europe. By 1214 AD, it was listed among a variety of fruits, flowers, perfumes and spices available at a festival in Treviso in Northern Italy. Due to its purported medicinal properties, it was prescribed by doctors in a wide area, including Nicosia, Rome, Lyon and Myddvai, Wales.[70]

One known route of malagueta distribution into Europe was from the harbor of Mud'barca near Tripoli across the Mediterranean Sea to Italy. It was also traded in Malaga, Portugal, which suggests there was another shipping route across the Western extreme end of the Mediterranean.[71]

The spice bush grows erect, has many branches and is sometimes woody at the base. The berries are small, narrow and extremely pungent. They grow in clusters of two or more per node and turn from green to yellow to red as they ripen.

The harvesting of berries begins one to two months after planting and continues for three to five months, at one to two week intervals. After the berries are collected, they are dried for one to two weeks in the sun. Yields vary between 1900 lb/ha when grown singly and 800 pounds per hectare (lb/ha) – if grown with other crops, as was usually the case.

Malagueta plants do survive with minimal cultivation, but crop yield was low. They are sensitive to water-logging and require weeding and occasional fertilization, even if only with wood ash.[72]

No doubt people in other parts of West Africa desired kola and even as far as southern Europe they liked malagueta spice. But, people in the Sahel absolutely needed one other product of the Liberia area: salt.

While kola and malagueta were merely desirable, salt was essential for human survival. Deprived of salt for a long time, people will suffer shock, coma and death.[73]

Fortunately for the people living in the coastal area that is now Liberia, an unlimited salt supply was available to them from the ocean. Meanwhile people along the Niger and further north faced a chronic shortage. This imbalance between coastal supply and northern demand led to a significant trade.[74]

Salt was extremely scarce and valuable in the savannah. As noted by Ibn Hawqal, a visitor from Mesopotamia in 951 A. D., one load sold "in the interior and more remote parts of the land of the Sudan, may fetch between 200 and 300 dinars." That sum would have supported 10 middle-class Middle Eastern families for a year during that period.[75]

Who in the forest region of Liberia were trading these commodities?

As with kola, written records do not link salt or malagueta spice to any specific ethnic group. However, oral traditions from Western Liberia point unanimously to the Dei as the first salt producers on the coast. The ancestors of the Klao likely participated too, given their ocean-centered economy. They were almost certainly the exporters of malagueta.

Shifting Winds, Ocean Currents and Natural Harbors

Some of the earliest Kru-speakers apparently traveled along the coast by water, relying on maritime prowess developed on the Niger and adopted for use along the Atlantic Ocean.

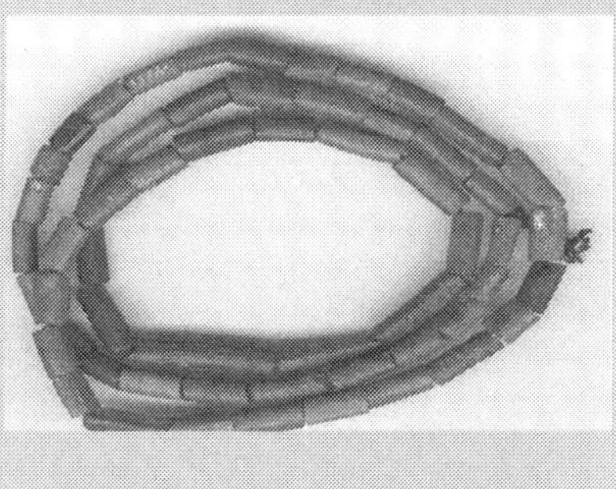

Canoes plied most of the lagoons and navigable rivers throughout the region. But, only communities at three points along the coast were renown for regularly navigating and fishing the Atlantic. Their skill and knowledge reflected a remarkable adaptation of in-land maritime culture to the much more challenging conditions of the ocean.[76]

One Wolof-speaking group lived at the mouth of the Senegal River. Another was the Klao of southeastern Liberia.

The most expert of all were the Fanti communities of the Gold Coast. Fanti fishermen from Mina, Axim and Winneba reportedly paddled as far as Angola against prevailing current and wind.[77] The fact that "Aggrey" beads from the Gold Coast were popular among the Klao, but not in the rest of the Liberia area, points to a likely link between those two fishing communities.[78]

Figure 13. "Popo" beads

They once were popular on the Kru Coast, suggesting a possible link to the "Gold Coast."

Given a shortage of livestock and large wild game near the coast, fish and other seafood filled a critical void. Besides fishing, canoes were used for carrying goods along the coast and up navigable rivers. Notable trade items included salt and dried fish produced by fishing communities.[79]

West Africa coastal fishing folks apparently relied exclusively on canoes. These are boats carved from tree trunks that are pointed at both ends and propelled by paddles. In contrast, boats along the Nile were made from papyrus and those of Lake Chad from reed. According to historian Robert Smith, boats made of bark were not likely in this region because forest trees have thin barks.[80]

Each canoe was made from a single tree truck that was hallowed out using an iron tool to a thickness of about two inches on the bottom and an inch on the side. Straw was then burnt in the hallow to protect the boat from insect infestation and to release a tar-like sealant from within the wood. Softer woods were preferred, especially for larger boats, such as the silk cotton tree (*Ceiba pentandra*).[81]

Carving was the work of specialists who generally lived near the forest where the trees were felled and fashioned. Lagoon canoes usually lasted two to tree years. The costlier sea-faring boats lasted up to 15 years, with careful maintenance and patching.[82]

Fishing communities possessed specialized knowledge and many land-based skills. These included carving, iron-smelting, and smithing of metal tools. Interior towns generally carved canoes, while fishing, rowing and navigation were confined to communities directly on the coast.[83]

Coastal fishing communities also possessed a sophisticated understanding of seasonal ocean currents, wind patterns and the habits of various seafoods.

For example, two strong currents flow in opposite directions along the Liberian coast. Closest to the coast and running parallel to it is the Guinea current. It flows in a southeastern direction from Sierra Leone to Gabon at an average 0.75 knots during the dry season and 2.0 knots during the rains.[84]

Figure 14. "Iron" in local languages

Bandi, *kólui*
Bassa, *ne*
Dan, *píe*
Dei, *wúlie*
Gbese, *kóli*
Grebo, *plé and pléde*
Gbe, *néte*
Krahn, *bagela*
Kissi, *kílende, pl. kílendon*
Loma, *kolu*
Ma, *pékúru*
Maninké, *nére*
Mende, *kóru*
Vai, *kúndu*

Between Tabou and Abidjan along the Côte d'Ivoire coast, a break in this current required canoers to propel their vessels solely by paddling.[85]

Further from the coast, a parallel current runs in the opposite direction. The opposing flow of these two main currents meant that canoers wishing to travel in a southwestern direction had to paddle forcefully through the first in order to reach the second.[86]

Although local fishing communities did not rely on sails, wind conditions were important given their impact on the ocean waves and swells. Because the land heats faster than the ocean in the morning, a southwestern or western breeze from the ocean runs from late morning until about 9 p.m. As the land also cools faster at night, the wind reverses course, blowing from the east or southeast from midnight to early morning.[87]

Along with the currents, the daily and seasonal rhythm of the wind helped dictate where fishermen sought their catch.

Through trial and error, fishing folk learned to place their communities near three beneficial natural features. First, bays provided natural harbors and generally supported reefs. Second, towns were also located near drinking water sources, such as creeks or rivers running to the ocean. Third, lagoons usually provided the added benefit of a plentiful supply of freshwater fish.[88]

Tad's Town, Pottery and the Long-Distance Salt Trade

According to a Dei founding legend told by Gbii Woso, a descendent of the landholding lineage, the group descended from the marriage of a father, Zie, who emerged from the water, and Dewulo, a mother who previously lived with her parents in a cave.

As expressions of their mutual affection, Zie gave Dewulo a silver coin and she gave him a gold ring. Zie's dowry for Dewulo was a carved iron drum decorated with brass and copper, which fell from the sky near the town of Millsburg, then called Dalon.

After the original drum disappeared, leaders of the Poro power association created a replica in wood, called *foivo*, which is the chief musical instrument in all Dei higher-level ceremonies of the Poro power association.[89]

Putting aside the fantastic elements that accrue to such stories retold over centuries, the legend offers several intriguing clues regarding the origin of the Dei. First, it traces their origin to the mixing of a local woman (or, more probably, women) and a maritime man (or men), who apparently arrived from up north via the St. Paul River. Second, it points to knowledge of metal smelting as central to the identity of the new people that emerged.[90]

The exchanged items were probably different in earlier versions of the story, but was updated to a ring and a coin to suit recent audiences. Third, the multiple metals used in making the dowry drum, as well as its elaborate decoration, suggest the men who descended from north brought a knowledge of metal working.

Dei oral traditions cite a town called Kambai Bli (on the current road to Bomi Hills) as one of their oldest and most economically important. This town was the site of a large clay pit for producing pottery products that attracted buyers from afar.[91] However, far more important was the production of salt from sea water for sale to northern markets.

According to Dei oral traditions, it was principally their wealth from salt boiling that attracted other groups to join them.[92] Important salt boiling towns were located along the beach from the mouth of the St. Paul to Cape Mount. They included Duojena, Dugbei, Gakpoja and Mbaanwoin.[93]

The Dei also claim that Bopolu was founded by their ancestors as a trade town where their salt was exchanged for products from the north. Originally called Taabli ("Taa's town"), it became a regular stop for trade caravans from elsewhere in West Africa. The town was far from their home near the coast, so the name was changed to Bopolu because people kept complaining "bo po mole" (meaning "only foot will put you there").[94]

Bopolu was just one of many such towns established by people in the forest and woodlands just for trading. Located miles away from their homes, workshops and raw materials, these towns provided a place to meet with visiting traders without allowing outsiders access to the sources of their resources.

As is still done by companies around the world, local producers went to great lengths to protect their trade secrets. For example, a Dei ruler named Duwan reportedly made the Gola pay to taste salt water — although his mother was Gola![95]

Stone Carvings as Evidence of Iron-Smelting

It is likely that Atlantic groups brought rice farming with them to the Liberia-area. In particular, the Kissi have been called "the rice people" because they grow so much of it.[96]

Rice had an advantage over tubers because it has a long shelf life. Today, the rice belt of West Africa overlaps mainly with the area inhabited by Atlantic-speakers.

Unlike forest-margin crops, rice was cultivated seasonally and limited to the coast and the forest west of the St. John River. By 1687 rice and millet were reportedly grown as far east as Grouwa. In those areas where swamp rice was planted, it was possible to reap thre e harvests a year.[97]

The clearing of the fields – done with cutlasses and axes – would begin as the dry season came to an end, in January. Later, the dried trees and bushes were burnt. Farmers covered seeds and removed weeds simultaneously, using short handled hoes.

When the rice ripened in November, it was harvested, usually with knives, and stored away in small farm silos.

Figure 15. Kissi pomtan stone sculpture

Unlike tuber cultivation, rice farming was "extensive" agriculture requiring a great deal of labor input. Field clearing in this forested zone required large numbers of able-bodied people. Similarly, harvesting demanded the participation of several families, since it was a race against the birds and wild animals.

The tasks of rice farming were divided according to age and sex. Adult men were responsible for field clearing. The task of driving away pests with sling-shots, rocks and musical instruments fell largely on young boys. Women were charged with planting, weeding, harvesting, hulling, smoking and, finally, cooking the rice. Others would help if there was a shortage of hands.[98]

The Atlantic language stems for rice –*malo* and *maro* (or *mààlón* in Kissi) – are similar to the Mande stem for rice, *màlo*.[99] This means the languages might have shared a common root before they separated. Or, the crop was transmitted from one of these language groups to the other at an early state in their development, along with the word for it. In short, there is no reason to assume that rice diffused from Mande-speakers to Atlantic groups because the linguistic evidence is inconclusive.

Scholars blinded by Eurocentrism and Malinké myths have long dismissed the Gola, the Kissi and Kru-speakers as "primitives" or "hunters and gatherers." In their view, knowledge of rice farming, along with iron-smelting were brought to the forest region by the more "civilized" Malinké.

But, their claims are undermined by stone statutes that were carved using iron tools long before Mande-speakers arrived. They have been found buried in scattered fields through the border region of Liberia, Sierra Leone and Guinea.

So, who carved these mysterious sculptures?

All signs point to Atlantic speakers, notably ancestors of the Kissi and Temne. First, the figures have been found in areas that either are or previously were occupied by them. According to the Kono, who possibly came as early as the ninth century, the figures predated their arrival in the area. Among the Kissi, it is widely believed that the figures were left by *their* ancestors from a time out of memory. In contrast, the Mende, who now live in the territory, ascribe the statutes to previous landowners, to whom they are not related.[100]

The stone sculptures found in territory occupied by the Kissi are called *pomtan*, while the Mende refer to those in Sierra Leone as *nomoli*. According to historian B. W. Andah, the *nomoli* and *pomtan* are stylistically different, with the latter being more elaborate.

But, art historian Frederick J. Lamp differs. He argues "stones may be found from distant sites bearing similar style and seeming to come from a single school of carving or perhaps even from the same hand." In other words, the sculptures were the work of itinerant artists or an extensive marketing network.[101]

Nomoli range in color, from nearly white through yellow-brown to dark green. While some of the stone objects are in *chlonteschist* and *amphibolite* and a few in hard rocks like *sandstone*, *doderite* and *granite*, most are of *talc* or *steatite*.[102] According to someone who reportedly observed the excavation of several statutes, many *nomoli* were found attached to the rocks onto which they were carved. This suggest they were first carved in placed, then removed after being completed.

Some stone figures are as long as one foot, most of the *pomtan* type are 3 to 6 inches and the *nomoli* between 6 and 8 inches.

Among both styles, male figures predominate. Some show in detail beads, scarification, hair style and form of head dress, but rarely genitals. The female figures are sometime rendered in a bulbous style.[103]

Many figures feature front teeth filed to sharp points, in keeping with a practice common among the Temne, Bullom, Limba and Kissi. Other widely reproduced features are elaborated plaited hair and scarification. Both of these features art historian Frederick Lamp has linked to a Temne aesthetic based on the patterning of planted fields. Some designs are very similar to some Kissi wood carvings, suggesting they are culturally linked.[104]

Figure 16. Kru iron money

Andah cites three factors to explain why the stone-carving tradition must have originated locally: First, the sculptures are plentiful. Second, they were widely distributed. And finally, they were fashioned from relatively hard and heavy materials, rather than more portable materials like clay. In addition, he noted, the stone-carving traditions in the region were all located in southern West Africa, suggesting local diffusion. They existed in parts of Guinea, Esie in Yorubaland and among the Ekos of Cross River.[105]

The presence of these stone sculpture point to an early iron-working tradition among Atlantic groups. First, most figures were carved from stones that contain a high percentage of iron and some from granite and other hard stones.[106] That would have required iron tools. Second, some carvings depict axes and spears, suggesting the presence of iron implements in local cultures. Third, blacksmiths in this region, not only made iron tools; they also did wood carvings. For that reason, blacksmiths probably carved the stone sculptures as well. Fourth, blacksmiths usually traveled from town to town selling their wares, which would explain the broad distribution of specific *nomoli* and *pomtan* styles.

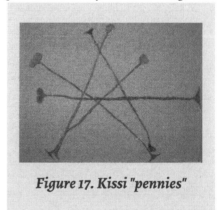

Figure 17. Kissi "pennies"

Several factors suggest the Kissi were involved in iron working from an early date. They have lived atop rich iron deposits for centuries. More significantly, smelted iron functioned as a currency in their region, which is unlikely to have developed if they were not better smelters than their neighbors. Circulating throughout the savannah and forest were small hoe-shaped implements called *geze* that served as a currency in the kolaproducing areas west of the Sassandra River in Côte d'Ivoire.[107]

As gold did in other parts of the world, certain commodities came to serve as currencies, if they were produced in surplus in one region and highly valued elsewhere.

Certain features embedded in the carvings hint at the presence of iron tools: First, some figures were carved with what seem to be whips, axe blades, clubs or spears in their right hands.[108] Axe blades and spear heads suggest iron working. Second, the filing of front teeth could not have been with simply stone tools.

This means that iron working probably did not diffuse from Northern Mande to other groups, as widely assumed.[109] Instead, each language group may have developed an early iron-working tradition. None of the words for "iron" in local Atlantic, Kru, Southwestern Mande and Southeastern Mande collected by linguist Sigismund Koelle share a root with *"nere,"* the northern Mande word.[110] Finally, iron smelting very likely originated among non-Mande groups, given the outsider status of iron workers in Northern Mande cultures.

To summarize, the evidence available so far suggests that salt boiling tools from 1085 AD were left by ancestors of the Dei. In addition, the Gola originated kola trade, the Klao the export of malagueta. The latter two groups would have been in place well before 1214 AD, when their commodities became know to southern European writers.

There is no evidence that other Kru-speakers had arrived during this period. Another 200 years would pass before southern Mande speakers migrated from the Niger region. The arrival of the Malinké was still centuries away.

1. John H. Atherton and Milan Kalous, "Nomoli," *Journal of African History* XI, 3 (1970): 303-317, especially p. 309.
2. Andah, 1992, p. 266. For metal smelting traditions in modern Liberia, see Schwab, 1947, pp. 136-146 (Ma, Dan, Sapo, Loma, Bandi, Kpelle).
3. Andah, 1992, p. 266.
4. Sutton, 1974, p. 530.
5. Atherton and Kalous, 1970, p. 309; J. E. G. Sutton, "The Aquatic Civilization of Middle Africa," *Journal of African History* XV, 4 (1974): 527-546, especially p. 530.
6. Blench, 2006, p. 133.
7. Brooks, 1985, p. 12.
8. Ehret, 2002, p. 322.

9. B. W. Andah, "The People of Upper Guinea (Between Côte d'Ivoire and the Casamance)," *General History of Africa: Africa from the Seventh to the Eleventh Century, Vol. III.* Berkeley: University of California Press, 1992), pp. 258-269, especially p. 263.

10. d'Azevedo, 1959, pp. 53-55.

11. George Tucker Childs, *A Grammar of Kisi: A Southern Atlantic Language* (New York: Mouton de Gruyter, 1995), p. 5.

12. Andah, 1992, p. 267; Mabogunje, 1972, p. 61.

13. Siegmann, 1969, p. 8; Creighton Gabel, R. Borden, and Susan White, "Preliminary report on an archeological survey of Liberia," *Liberian Studies Journal* V, 2 (1972-74): 87-105; Creighton Gabel, "Microlithic occurrences in the Republic of Liberia," *West African Journal of Archeology* 6 (1976): 21-33; J. H. Atherlon, "Liberian prehistory," *Liberian Studies Journal*, III, 2 (1970-71), pp. 83-111.

14. Schröder and Seibel, 1974, p. 22.

15. Martin, 1968, p. 48; "Tour two hundred miles interior," *African Repository*, Vol. 45, Vol. 5 (May 1869), pp. 153-154; "Missionary exploration by a native, *African Repository*, Vol. 45, Vol. 10 (October 1869), pp. 308-313.

16. Massing, 1977, p. 62. Thanks to Dr. Dougbeh Nyan for affirming the resonance of this trajectory with Killipo tradition.

17. S. Jangaba M. Johnson, "The Traditions, History and Folklore of the Belle Tribe," *Liberian Studies Journal*, I, 2 (1969), pp. 45-73. On pygmies in this region also see Capitaine Réné Viard, *Les Guérés, peuple de la forêt: Etude d'une sociéte primitive* (Paris: Société d'éditions géographiques, maritmes et colonales, 1934); M. Jacquier, "Note sur l'existence probable de Négrilles dans les forêts vierges de l'ouest de la Côte d'Ivoire," *Bulletin de la Comité d'Études Historiques et Scientifiques d'Afrique Occidentale Française* 18 (1935): 57-61; and Jean Boulnois, *Gnon-Sua: Dieu des Guérés* (Paris: Founier, 1933).

18. Migeod, 1972, p. 8.

19. Drake, 1998, p. 287; Fagan, 2004, p. 150; Catherine Coquery-Vidrovitch, "Research on an African mode of production" (pp. 261-288), in David Seddon (ed.), *Relations of Production: Marxist Approaches to Economic Anthropology* (London: Frank Cass, 1978), pp. 270-271, 277.

20. Mabogunje, 1972, p. 5.

21. Ivor Wilks, "Land, labor, gold, and the first kingdom of Asante: A model of early change" (pp. 41-81), In Ivor Wilks (ed.), *Forests of Gold: Essays on the Akan and the Kingdom of Asante* (Athens, Ohio: Ohio University Press, 1993), pp. 58-59.

22. Mabogunje, 1972, p. 13.

23. James L. A. Webb, Jr., Economy & culture in West Africa" (pp. 33-51), in Emmanuel Kwame Akeyampong (ed.), *Themes in West Africa's History* (London: James Currey, 2006); Frank L. Lambrecht, "Aspects of evolution and ecology of Tsetse flies in prehistorical African environment" (pp. 75-98), in J. D. Fage and R. A. Oliver, eds., *Papers in African Prehistory* (London: Cambridge University Press, 1974). African sleeping sickness is caused by a parasite called Trypanosoma; Plasmodium has several species including falciparum, ovale, knowlesi, vivax and malariae. Thanks to Dr. Dougbeh Nyan for clarifying the science underlying this section.

24. Mabogunje, 1972, p. 3.

25. Mabogunje, 1972, p. 1-2.

26. Massing, 1977, p. 11.

27. James W. Lugenbeel, *Sketches of Liberia: Comprising a Brief Account of the Geography, Climate, Productions, and Diseases of the Republic of Liberia* (Washington: C. Alexander, 1853), p. 10; S. Jangaba M. Johnson, *The Traditional History and Folklore of the Gola Tribe in Liberia, Vol. 1, Traditions* (Monrovia: Bureau of Folklore, 1961), p. 81.

28. Lugenbeel, 1853, p. 13.

29. Ehret, 2002, pp. 45-46.

30. Claude Meillassoux, "The social organization of the peasantry: The economic basis of kinship" (pp. 159-169), in David Seddon (ed.), *Relations of Production: Marxist Approaches to Economic Anthropology* (London: Frank Cass, 1978), pp. 160-161,165.

31. Ehret, 2002, pp. 160-162, 331-334, 340; McIntosh, 2006, p. 28; Francis J. Keuse, *Traditional African Iron Working* (Calgary, Alberta, Canada: University of Calgary, 1983). For a review of iron production and trade in Liberia see Susan L. White, "Iron production and iron trade in northern Liberia: History of a major indigenous technology." Paper presented at the Sixth Annual Conference of the Liberia Studies Conference, Madison, Wisconsin, April 1974.

32. Meillassoux, 1978, p. 160.

33. Meillassoux, 1978, pp. 165-166.

34. "Hungry times" or famines are common in West African folktales. See William Russell Bascom, *African Folktales in the New World* (Bloomington: Indiana University Press, 1976), pp. 206-207; Elphinstone Dayrell, *Folk Stories from Southern Nigeria* (London: Longman, 1910) pp. 86-90; Leo Frobenius, "Die Atlantich Götterlehre," *Atlantis*, 10 (1926): 294-296. In one set of famine tales, Spider and an animal agree to sacrifice one family member each for the other to eat. The dupe fulfills his part of the contract only to find that Spider had reneged.

35. For struggles over women among the Glebo, see Martin, 1968, p. 25.

36. Hackett, 1996 pp. 31-33.

37. Zahan, 2011, p. 19; Harley, 1941, p. 11. In Callava, for example, the male society was open to women over 40 years old; see Martin, 1968, p. 21.

38. MacGaffey, 2011, p. 237.

39. MacGaffey, 2011, p. 235.

40. Wolf, 1982, pp. 89-90; Ismail Rashid, "Class, caste & social inequality in West African history" (pp. 118-139), in C. Conrad, in Emmanuel Kwame Akeyampong (ed.), *Themes in West Africa's History* (London: James Currey, 2006), especially p. 19; Little, 1951, pp. 82-85. As explained by Rashid, kinship in West Africa "expressed a set of affective blood, matrimonial or fictive relations within a family, household, lineage or even an ethnic group. It was usually the prime determinant of a person's social identity. The kinship idiom provided the fundamental basis of social solidarity and succession, definitions of corporate citizenship or outsider status as well as the political unit of competition for power."

41. Wolf, 1982, pp. 89-90.

42. Wolf, 1989, pp. 89-90.

43. Wolf, 1982, p. 91.

44. Wolf, 1982, p. 91; Meillassoux, 1978, p. 160.

45. Horton, 1972, pp. 94-95. For the position entrusted to the first family that settled the land, see Jane J. Martin, The dual legacy: Government authority and mission influence among the Glebo of Eastern Liberia, 1834-1910. Ph. D. dissertation, Boston University, 1968, pp. 16, 22 (Glebo, *wodo baa*); Johnston, 1906, p. 1076 (Glebo, *woraba*); Kenneth Little, *The Mende of Sierra Leone: A West African People in Transition* (Routledge & Kegan Paul, 1967; reprint of 1951 edition), pp. 82-85, 179 (Mende, *ndo-bla*); Andreas W. Massing, "Materials for a history of Western Liberia: The Belle," *Liberian Studies Journal*, III, 1 (1970-71), pp. 183-184, especially p. 195 (Kuwaa); Andreas W. Massing, *The Economic Anthropology of the Kru (West Africa)*. (Wiesbaden: Franz Steiner Verlag GMBH, 1980), pp. 45-48 (Klao); Ronald W. Davis, *Ethnohistorical Studies on the Kru Coast* (Newark, Del.: Liberians Studies Monograph Series No. 5, 1976), pp. 23, 25-26 (Klao, *krogba*). According to Massing (1980), the "owner of the land" office is found among 25 percent of the Kru and 72 percent of the We people. The cause of this discrepancy remains to be investigated.

46. G. E. Currens, "Land, labor and capital in Loma agriculture," in Vernon R. Dorjahn and Barry L. Isaac (eds.), *Essays on the Economic Anthropology of Liberia and Sierrra Leone* (Philadelphia: Institute for Liberian Studies, 1979), p. 82; Warren L. d'Azevedo, *The Gola of Liberia* (New Haven, Conn.: Human Relations Area Files, 1972), p. 434; Bureau of Folkways, *The Tribes of the Western Province and the Denwoin People* (Monrovia: Bureau of Folkways, Interior Department, 1955), p. 64; George Schwab, *Tribes of the Liberian Hinterland*, Peabody Museum Papers, No. 31 (Cambridge, Mass.: Harvard University Press, 1947), pp. 163, 168, 417; Günter Schröder and Dieter Seibel, *Ethnographic Survey of Southeastern Liberia: The Liberian Kran and the Sapo* (Newark, Del.: Liberian Studies Association, 1974), pp. 66 and 70-71; James L. Sibley and Diedrich W. Westermann, *Liberia, Old and New* (Garden City, N.Y.: Doubleday and Doran, 1928), pp. 140-141; and William Siegmann, *Ethnographic Survey of Southern Liberia: Report on the Bassa* (Robertsport: Tubman Center of African Culture, 1969), pp. 12, 24.

47. Meillassoux, 1978, pp. 160-161.

48. Meillassoux, 1978, p. 166.

49. Meillassoux, 1978pp. 161, 163.

50. Ehret, 2002, p. 46.

51. Wolf, 1982, pp. 93-95.

52. Jan Jansen, "The younger brother and the stranger in Mande status discourse." Paper presented at the Third International Conference in Mande Studies, Leiden, March 1995; Charles S. Bird and Martha B. Kendall, "The Mande Hero" (pp. 13-26), in Ivan Karp and Charles S. Bird, eds., *Exploration in African Systems of Thought* (Bloomington: University of Indiana Press, 1980). For examples of tales, see Peter Pinney, *Legends of Liberia* (Tenafly, NJ: SMA Fathers, 2007), especially "The Wrath of Sande-Nyana" (p. 77) and "Why the Sea is Salty" (pp. 107-108).

53. Fernand Braudel, *The Perspective of the World: Civilization & Capitalism, 15th-18th Century*, Vol. 3 (New York: Harper & Row, 1984), p. 261According to historian Braudel, "No human group can live and above all survive to reproduce itself, unless it contains at least four or five hundred individuals."

54. Warren L. d'Azevedo, "The setting of Gola society and culture: Some theoretical implications of variation in time and space," *Kroeber Anthropological Society Papers* 21 (1959): 43-125, especially p. 62; I have substituted "ethnic group" for the word "tribe," which was used in the original.

55. d'Azevedo, 1959, p. 94.

56. Donald R. Wright, "'What do you mean there were no tribes in Africa?': Thoughts on boundaries and related matters in precolonial Africa," *History in Africa*, Vol. 26 (1999): 419-426, especially pp. 418-419; Donald R. Wright, "Thoughts on the Nature of Precolonial Mandinka Polity and Society, Gambia-Guinea-Bissau," (Unpublished paper, 1981 African Studies Association convention), 10; Donald R. Wright, "Beyond migration and conquest: Oral traditions and Mandinka ethnicity in Senegambia," *History in Africa* 12 (1985): 335-348; Brooks, 1985, p. 8; Jean-Loup Amselle, "Anthropology and historicity," *History and Theory*, Vol. 32, No. 4 (Dec. 1993): 12-31. Amselle noted a shift in how ethnicity is conceived by anthropologists — from primodialism to constructivism.

57. Allen M. Howard, "Mande identity formation in the economic and political context of northwest Sierra Leone, 1750-1900, *Paidema*, 46 (2000): 13-35, especially p. 15.

58. Paul Nugent, "Putting the history back into ethnicity: Enslavement, religion, and cultural brokerage in the construction of Mandinka/Jola and Ewe/Agotime identities in West Africa, c. 1650-1930," *Comparative Studies in Society and History*, Vol. 50, No. 4 (Oct. 2008): 921-948. So, how did ethnicity come to be so important in Africa today? Nugent (p. 924) argued, "African interpreters codified and transmitted basic information, while their European counterparts fitted what they heard into their own cognitive grids."

59. Brooks, 1985, p. 15.

60. Brooks, 1985, p. 12.

61. For early references to kola trade, see: P. E. H. Hair, "Ethnolinguistic inventory of the Upper Guinea coast before 1700," *African Languages Review* VI: 32-70; N. Levtzion, *Ancient Ghana and Mali* (London: Methuen, 1973), pp. 181-182; Raymond Mauny, *Tableau géographique de 'Ouest africain au moyen age* (Dakar: IFAN, 1961), p. 249.

62. Lovejoy, 1980, pp. 98, 100-101; Brooks, 1985, p. 16.

63. Lovejoy, 1980, pp. 98.

64. Brooks, 1985, p. 44; Harley, 1941, p. 9. For other dyes, see Schwab and Harley, 1947, p. 127.

65. Lovejoy, 1980, pp. 98.

66. Lovejoy, 1980, p. 98.

67. Lovejoy, 1980, pp. 106-107.

68. Lovejoy, 1980, pp. 107-108.

69. Lovejoy, 1980, pp. 103-108.

70. A. M. Van Harten, "Melegueta pepper," *Economic History* 24 (1970): 208-217, especially pp. 208-209.

71. Van Harten, 1970, pp. 208-209.

72. A. H. Kassam, *Crops of the West African Semi-Arid Tropics* (Hyderabad, India: International Crops Research Institute for the Semi-Arid Tropics, 1976), pp. 85-87, 105, 190; J. W. Purseglove, *Tropical* Crops, Dicotyledons (London: Longman, 1974), p. 527; Jean Barbot, A Description of the Coast of North and South Guinea and of Ethiopia Inferior, Vol. 5, Book II, in Awnsham and John Churchill, Collection of Voyages and Travels (London: Awnsham and John Churchill, 1732), p. 138.

73. Paul E. Lovejoy, *Salt of the Desert Sun: A History of Salt Production and Trade in the Central Sudan* (Cambridge: Cambridge University Press), p. 1.

74. For the exportation of coastal sea salt to the Sahel, see Masonen, 2000, p. 135.

75. Ibn Hawqal (writing c. 988) in Levtzion and Hopkins, 2011, pp. 43-52, especially p. 49.

76. Massing, 1977, pp. 21-25; George E. Brooks, Jr., *The Kru Mariner in the Nineteenth Century* (Newark, Del., Liberian Studies Association in America, 1972), pp. 76-77; Robert Smith, "The canoe in West African history," *Journal of African History*, Vol. II, No. 4 (1970): 515-533, especially p. 522.

77. Smith, 1970, p. 522; also Hair, Jones and Law, 1992, pp. 100-101, 110, n. 4-5.

78. Brooks, 1972, pp. 105-106.

79. Smith, 1970, p. 516-517, 522, 525.

80. Smith, 1970, p. 520.

81. Smith, 1970, pp. 515, 519, 520.

82. Smith, 1970, pp. 515, 519, 520.

83. Massing, 1977, pp. 34-40.

84. Massing, 1977, pp. 21-23.

85. Massing, 1977, pp. 21-31.

86. Massing, 1977, pp. 21-31.

87. Massing, 1977, p. 23

88. Massing, 1977, pp. 22-23, 34-36.

89. Bureau of Folkways, 1955, p. 41.

90. For the use of stereotypes and formulaic elements in oral traditions, see Jan Vansina, *Oral Tradition as History* (Madison, Wisconsin: University of Wisconsin Press, 1985), pp. 88-91, also pp. 12, 21, 28, 47, 50, 52-53, 71, 86, 137, 139-140, 144-146.

91. Bureau of Folkways, 1955, p. 43.

92. Bureau of Folkways, 1955, p. 53.

93. Bureau of Folkways, 1955, p. 50.

94. Bureau of Folkways, 1955, p. 44. As explained by Dr. Dougbeh Nyan, the phonology of "Bopolu" in Grebo is almost identical to Dei; in Grebo "bo" is foot, "po" is put and "lu" is there.

95. Bureau of Folkways, 1955, p. 52.

96. Denise Paulme, *Les gen du riz: Kissi du Haute-Guinée française* (Paris: Librare Plon, 1954).

97. G. P. Mudock, *Africa: Its People and Their Culture History* (New York: McGraw-Hill, 1959), pp. 64, 70, 71; Walter A. Rodney, *A History of the Upper Guinea Coast, 1545-1800* (Oxford: Clarendon Press, 1980), pp. 20-25; Barbot, 1732, p. 118; for contemporary practices, see C. H. Bledsoe, *Women and Marriage in Kpelle Society* (Stanford: Stanford University Press, 1980), p. 31; Benjamin C. Dennis, *The Gbandes: A People of the Liberian Hinterland* (Chicago: Nelson-Hall, 1972), pp. 23-31.

98. Barbot, 1732; W. Bosman, *A New and Accurate Description of the Coast of Guinea* (London: J. Knapton, 1705); J. Smith, *Trade and Travels in the Gulph of Guinea* (London: Webb Millington and Co., 1851).

99. G. Tucker Childs, "Borrowings into Kisi as evidence of Mande expansionism and influence," *Journal of West African Languages* XXIX 2 (2002): 81-120, especially p. 106.

100. Andah, 1992, p. 267.

101. Andah, 1992, p. 266-267; Frederick J. Lamp, "House of Stones: Memorial Art of Fifteenth-Century Sierra Leone," *The Art Bulletin* LXV, 2 (June 1983): 219-237, especially p. 222, 231; Bureau of Folkways, 1955, pp. 20-22.

102. Andah, 1992, p. 266-267.

103. Andah, 1992, p. 267.

104. Andah, 1992, p. 266-267.

105. Andah, 1992, p. 266-267.

106. Atherton and Kalous, 1970, pp. 303, 306.

107. Lovejoy, 1980, p. 112; also see Roland Portères, "La monnaie de fer dan l'Ouest africaine au XXe siècle," *Reserches africaines* 4 (October-December 1960): 3-13; Claude Meillassour, *Anthropologie économique des Gouro de Côte d'Ivoire* (Paris, La Haye: Mouton, 1964), pp. 101-129, 241, 675-678, 686; Yves Person, *Samori: Une Revolution dyulo* (Dakar: l'Institute fondamental d'Afrique noire, 1968), pp. 59, 68, 176, 200, 294, 370, 448-462; Auguste Chevalier and Émile Perrot, *Les Kolatiers et les noix de kola* (Paris: Augustine Challamel, 1911) pp. 448-462; C. Wondji, "The states and cultures of the Upper Guinea coast," *General History of Africa: Africa from the Sixteenth to the Eighteenth Century, Vol. V*. Berkeley: University of California Press, 1992), pp. 38-39, 42-43, 50.

108. Lamp, 1983, pp. 224, 227.

109. Brooks, 1985, pp. 19, 48-50.

110. Sigismund Wilhelm Koelle, *Polyglotta Africana*. Edited with an introduction by P. E. H. Hair and David Dalby (Graz, Austria: Akademische Druck-U. Verlagsanstalt, 1963; reprint of 1854 edition), p. 82.

Chapter 3
The Way of the Ancestors

> Those who are dead are never gone:
>
> they are in the breast of the woman,
>
> they are in the child who is wailing
>
> and in the firebrand that flames.
>
> — Birago Diop, Senegalese poet

Although there are no written records on traditional religion and associated practices before 1100 AD, more indelible forms of evidence were inscribed in the rituals and customs that persist over a thousand years later. Despite linguistic diversity, Niger-Congo cultures share many similarities in rituals, aesthetics and beliefs across widely scattered cultures. Some of these societies have been Muslim for generations, giving confidence that common elements of the traditional religion predate the adoption of Islam and even the split of Niger-Congo into separate languages 5000 years ago.

Most readers are likely to know less about African religious beliefs and practices than they do about Judaism, Christianity, Islam or even Buddhism. For this reason, it is important to understand first what African traditional religion is *not*. It lacks a sense that God is holding people today responsible for something done by their ancestors at the beginning of time. Without "original sin," all people need not be redeemed by any one sacrifice (such as that offered by Jesus).[1]

There was no Torah, Bible or Quran. In the absence of a set "text" to measure disputed claims against, there was less rigidity. There was no universal truth to which others had to be converted.[2]

"Religion." That category did not exist in African languages. The closest concept was "the way of the ancestors."[3]

The way of the ancestors made no distinction between "physical" and "spiritual" or "natural" and "supernatural" realms. For that reason, it had no words equivalent to "spirits," "ghosts," or "supernatural beings." What are usually translated into English as "spirits" would be better described as forces or powers. As envisioned by West Africans, those powers were inherent in the material world, not apart from it.[4]

African religion was not animist because people did not worship their sacred objects and places,[5] any more than Roman Catholics worship their rosaries, relics,

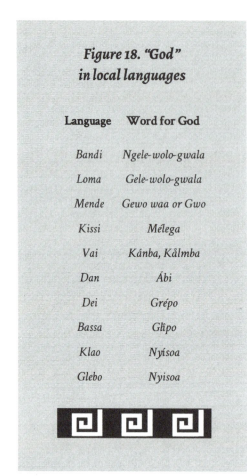

Figure 18. "God" in local languages

Language	Word for God
Bandi	Ngele-wolo-gwala
Loma	Gele-wolo-gwala
Mende	Gewo waa or Gwo
Kissi	Mélega
Vai	Kánba, Kålmba
Dan	Ábi
Dei	Grépo
Bassa	Glĭpo
Klao	Nyísoa
Glebo	Nyisoa

shrines and holy water.

It was not polytheistic because people recognized one Creator, although usually conceived of as inhabiting the sky and distant from human affairs.[6] However, the use of negative language over centuries has obscured even from contemporary Africans the life-affirming essence of traditional religion, concerned as it was mainly with fertility and increase.[7]

In the way of the ancestors, God's name is rarely evoked because of the power it contains. Instead, the Creator is discussed poetically using "nicknames," through parables and by comparison to visible powers.[8] Christians do this when they refer to Jesus as the "Lamb of God" or represent Him on a bumper sticker with the symbol of a fish.[9]

In the way of the ancestors, God is conceived in three distinct ways: as the Creator who disengaged from people's everyday lives; as Judge who supervises people's affairs and intervenes directly; or as Creator and Judge. Overlapping with these is a widespread image of God as Hunter who reaps people's essence at the end of life.[10]

Unlike "religions of the book," the way of the ancestors (especially in the forest belt) lacks an elaborate theory of how the world was created. Most West African cultures explain how the world was created in one of four ways: God thought it, and it came into being; God spoke it into existence; God made it — like an artisan; or God vomited it.

In most of these stories, people originally lived with God, but they fell from the sky or came to be separated from the Creator in some other way. As a result, the world became divided into several opposites: the world of God from the world of people, good from evil, order from disorder.

Other complementary polarities can be seen at traditional funerals: corpses were usually carried feet first, symbolizing the opposite of how people are born.[11] Similarly, the full moon was associated with renewal and rebirth. In contrast, the "dead" moon time was when evil stalked the earth, and innocents stayed home. Among many Mande and Atlantic-speaking groups, the number three is associated

The Way of the Ancestors

with men and four with women; the links of those numbers to genders are reversed among Kru groups.[12]

The Creator is hidden, yet available to those who grasp the meaning of the thunder, the yellow moon or countless other signs. God's will is read, not from a book, but from the living, breathing world.[13]

The Energy in All Things

The highest goal of the way of the ancestors was the preservation of life. This obligation extended to the past — preserving the memory of the ancestors and their rules of behavior. By teaching the ancestor's norms to the children, it reached into the future. The way of the ancestors was focused on the family, but extended outward to the larger community. It applied to the life force in all things — animals, plants, even minerals. Life, here, is conceived as a web.[14]

In African traditional thought, as summarized by religion scholar E. G. Parrinder, "Man beneath the sky lives on the land, not in a void but as a sovereign vital force."[15] As noted by African studies scholar Evan M. Zuesse, "Man is a coworker with God in all the levels of life."[16] People are not given "dominion" to pillage and plunder the earth. Thus, they must allow plants and animals to replenish.

The focus of traditional worship and rituals was life-force, a vital energy that was thought to dwell in all matter.[17] The life force links all things - every word, thought or action, yet is manifest uniquely in each person and domain of nature. Whereas the Creator was associated with the male aspect of the Divine, life-force was often conceptualized as female, especially that within the earth, which was likened to a womb requiring impregnation.[18]

Human well-being was dependent on being in harmony with life force in all its manifestations. Maintaining harmony involved showing respect towards the energy in everything. This was especially critical when people harnessed life-force from the land, rain, minerals, wild game and timber. Some locations, such as bodies of water, ancient trees and mountains, were thought to have more concentrated life energy than others.[19]

These elements were unpredictable so they required offerings. Sacrifices and prayers were required to ensure that soil brought forth crops, clouds showered necessary rain, predatory animals were kept at bay and trees gave lumber without taking lives. Each of these elements required acknowledgment through appropriate rituals, such as libation (often palm wine, liquor or water), prayer and sacrifice (usually a white chicken, red rooster, sheep or goat).

Because life-energy manifested itself uniquely in these elements, its propitiation was the responsibility of certain categories of people with specialized knowledge, including midwives in regards to fertility and often women from the landowning lineage in the case of the soil.[20]

Translating those ideas into Western religious language has been as difficult as trying to fit square pegs into round holes. "Soul" is one of many concepts without direct equivalents in traditional African religion. Instead, many Africans believe that several non-material things inhabit the body until a person dies.[21] In some ways, African ideas on multiple immaterial parts of a person are more akin to Western psychology's theory of the Ego, Id and Supergo.

Among these forces in each person is one often viewed as a person's "double." It is especially vulnerable to attacks by *geniis* and other antisocial powers. Another of a person's invisible forces is closer to what English-speakers call "personality" than to "soul." It is able to travel away from the body at night. While away, this part of a bad person could kill, rape or perform other anti-social actions.[22]

But, God was viewed as the source of all power, including those possessed by minerals, plants, animals and the ancestors. Some powers are so closely fused with the visible form that the two may seem inseparable — fire, rivers and killer animals. But, others are abstract and amorphous; they seem to combine the powers of more than one object. These include "the force of the forest" or "the power of the mountain."[23]

Masquerades as Homes to Abstract Powers

For powers without concrete, specific form, people created "bodies" which they were invited to inhabit. An example is *Gbetu*, a masquerade that performs on certain ritual occasions. All adults know its mask is carved from wood, its covering is woven from raffia, and its movements are enacted by a dancer. But, during performances, it is thought to embody "the force of the forest." To emphasize this transformation, the masquerade usually speaks in a voice that is distinct from the voice of the person within it.[24]

The otherworldly dimension of religious performances was heightened by dancers performing covered entirely in woven fabric and, in some cases, on stills (among the Loma and Dan, for example).[25]

Early evidence of West African masked dancers appear in rock paintings from 8000-5000 BC from Tassili, Southern Algeria.[26]

All masquerades were not of equal power, however. Their gravitas depends in part on the social power of their creators. Truly sacred masquerades are the work of older men with power, especially heads of founding families. In contrast, the masquerades created by women and young men are associated with "play" or entertainment.[27]

This distinction can be seen among the Sapo of southeastern Liberia. The costumed mask of young Sapo men sings and speaks in a strange, funny language that must be translated. This "dressed" daytime entertainment contrasts with the "naked" nighttime mask used by heads of leading families to deliver legal rulings. It appears as a man wearing amulets and a wig whose voice is filtered through a device to disguise it.[28]

Policy-makers, judges, priests and ritual dancers appeared publicly in masks to symbolize their roles as conduits of life force.[29] Much as European judges dressed in robes to project the timelessness, impartiality and anonymity of the law, they wore masks when performing their public ritualistic functions, which distinguished their public roles from their personal identities.

Once the forest power or other abstract force is infused into the masquerade or other object, it's human-made dwelling becomes sacred and metaphorically radioactive. For this reason, masks and other sacred objects are concealed in shrines when not in use. This is done to avoid harming viewers thought to be vulnerable, especially women.[30]

As with masks, Niger-Congo music emphasized "the patterned, rhythmical arrangement of the shapes."[31] As with Westerners at an opera or symphonic performances, African audiences brought knowledge and expectations that enhanced their experience of ritual performances.[32]

The masks and other objects used in rituals usually encompassed items thought to embody rare and significant life-force, including cowrie shells, feathers, leopard skin, the claws of predatory animals and iron.[33] There were masks, mostly in wood and rarely in ivory and fewer still in brass, used in a variety of rites, including earth fertility, funeral, initiation, law enforcement, adjudication, healing, divination and fighting sorcerers.[34]

Of the various abstract, amorphous forces, two were broadly recognized: First, the tradition of creating homes where the force of the forest could dwell and be controlled. Second, the power inherent in large bodies of water. Both are widespread, extending from present-day Sierra Leone to southern Congo.[35]

Water forces were renown for producing good fortune for some people and ill in the lives of others. Properly satiated with sacrifices, they yielded gold, gems, business success, and children. Gifts like creativity, wisdom and healing skills are reserved for acolytes who are said to be taken under water. If offended, however, water energy caused drowning, overturning of boats, childlessness and insanity.[36]

The best known West African water power is Mami Watta. To get her gifts, people are required to abstain from sex or certain foods and drinks. As with all water powers, she can produce good fortune or great ill.[37]

These qualities have remained consistent overtime, but her image has changed. It now consists of many pieces braided together from different cultures. These pieces include the half-fish, half-woman image of the mermaid (derived from fifteenth-century European sailors) and colorful female Indian divinities like Lakshmi (adopted from Gujarati merchants in the early 1900s).[38]

Ritual art can be placed in two groups: the timeless and the time-bound. The first includes carvings and other formal images of deceased rulers and other ancestors. They are designed to set the subjects beyond time; their ritual significance is fixed, so they can be passed from one generation to another. The second group consists of objects used at festivals and other specific times. Faith in their power is dependent on results, such as a successful harvest. If they prove ineffective, they are abandoned.[39]

God is not knowable, in the way of the ancestors, but these forces are. God is remote, but they are ever-present. People need these forces, but they depend on people, too, and use us in turn.[40] They remain latent, until unlocked by people who have the discernment and skills to become partners with God.[41]

The life force within each domain had specific preferences in offerings, including drink, song and rhythm, as well as color and sacrificial animal. Two symbolically significant colors were white (preferred for sacrificial animals because it signified purity) and red (which matched the ultimate signifier of life force - blood - and was often reserved for use by priests).[42]

Through appropriate drumming patterns and dance routines, it was possible to access the life-force in concentrated forms that served to revitalize individuals and communities. The liver of an animal was a supreme offering, based on its centrality to maintaining the flow of life energy. The human liver served in a similar way for individuals and groups intent on harvesting life force for selfish or antisocial purposes.[43]

Whether in minerals, plants or animals, life-force is neither inherently good or evil. It's application depends on the heart of the user — just as nuclear power can be used to generate electricity or to destroy entire cities.

Ancestor Veneration, Not Worship

In the way of the ancestors, death was seen as a change in people's status, not an end to life. The afterlife contrasts with life on earth in being free from violence and in moving more slowly.[44]

Contrary to a popular misconception, not everyone who died was considered a venerated "ancestor." That status was reserved for those who lived upright lives, acquired wisdom, left descendants and lived to a ripe old age. They were usually men, even in matrilineal groups. Excluded from consideration were people killed by lightning, drowning, suicide or strange diseases like smallpox.[45]

In short, an ancestor was someone who obviously enjoyed God's blessings. Such ascended ones were thought to gain both strength and insight after passing into the next phase of life.[46]

Like saints in Catholicism, ancestors were intermediaries between their descendants and God. They helped to safeguard the community and its moral order. The norms or "ways" passed on by them formed the foundation of law, religion and morality. For this reason, they were involved in punishing violators of society's norms. In this way, the living and the ancestors enjoyed a mutual dependence: Each group needed the other to survive.[47]

The ancestors were the main intermediaries between their family members (to whom they had contributed their life force) and the deeper wellspring of unseen vital energy, but they could be responsible for conflicts between lineages.[48]

In the way of the ancestors, the living were required to honor the ancestors for the moral foundation they had laid, for their role in first reclaiming the land and for their continued help. They were offered the first taste of food and a libation at feasts. Before they were consulted they were offered a gift, such as chewed kola or the blood of a freshly killed chicken.[49]

This relationship was often misleadingly called "ancestor worship."[50]

West Africans honored the ancestors in several standard ways. One form was symbolic: It involved placing a small Y-shaped ladder with notched steps near an altar to help them climb to God. A more substantive way of showing respect was by following their upright example. In addition, the ancestors were honored by preserving their memory and passing on their names to descendants.[51]

Libations, however, are the best known way of honoring ancestors in West Africa. Today, people typically offer the first pour of whatever they happen to be drinking, especially expensive, imported liquors. But, traditionally libations were in the form of fresh water, millet flour mixed with water, millet beer or palm wine, all derived from within the region.

Fresh water or millet flour in water was used to "cool" off the ancestors. Alternatively, millet beer or palm wine stimulated them.[52]

Libations by themselves were routine offerings. Sometimes these were supplemented with kola or food. Fixing major transgressions required even more. In such cases, a libation was followed by the sacrifice of a domestic animal. This could range from a white chicken through a sheep or goat to a cow. The bigger the transgression, the bigger the offering.[53]

The ancestors were not passive recipients of libations and other offerings. They brought messages to the living through flashes of insight, creativity and dreams. As a more profound level, they sometimes spoke through persons who become "possessed" while participating in a dance or other ritual.[54]

Keeping obligations to ancestors helped keep living family members together, it was thought. And failing to meet those obligations brought ill fortune.[55]

In the way of the ancestors, many forms of ill-fortune were viewed as the result of angering the ancestors. In a minor case, not naming children after them could result in illness. At the other extreme, incest was thought to produce infertility in the family as well as infertility of the land. In this context, both illness and infertility are seen as punishments for immoral conduct.[56]

Shrines and Sacraments

Unlike Christians, Muslims and members of many other faiths, adherents to the way of the ancestors did not worship in elaborate buildings. Instead, altars and shines were placed outdoors. They were located near awe-inspiring natural formations that brought people into closer communion with God through the powers and wonders of creation. These included water falls, mountains, caves, mysterious rocks and majestic cotton silk-wood trees.[57]

The alchemy that unfolded in these spaces was akin to what went into creation itself, albeit on an infinitely smaller scale.[58] Sometimes objects carved to honor the ancestors or various life-forces were placed in these shrines. Sometimes the carvings themselves functioned as shrines.[59]

One exception to the outdoor-shrine norm was the blacksmith's workshop. It was an argument-free zone. It's sacred status derived from the mastery of dangerous forces required in smithing — fire and molten metal.[60]

The two most common sacraments were animal sacrifices and rites of passage.[61]

The animal-offering ceremony was akin to the Christian communion. But, it was done not just to remove impurity. It called on the Divine to alter people's status in a variety of ways, including restoring health, revealing the future and increasing fertility.[62]

The rite consisted of three phases: First, the officiating person consecrated the occasion. This served to purify the participants, the place and the sacrificial animal.[63]

The second phase was the offering itself. What was dispatched to the world of the unseen was the life-force of the animal, directed on its way by appropriate prayers and songs. Some of its flesh was offered to God, the ancestors or the appropriate life-force, but only symbolically. The rest of the flesh was shared by the participants.[64]

This sanctified meal brought heaven and earth into communion. It marked a renewal of the covenant between the worlds of the seen and the unseen.

The final phase of the offering ceremony was like a benediction; it returned everyone and everything involved to their everyday existence.[65]

Rites of passage consecrated moments of transition in the life of the community. Each rite was organized into three phases: death, rebirth and a period in between when normal life and time were suspended. Except for funerals, the "death" phase in all other rites was symbolic. It emphasized a break with routines of the past, even a renunciation.[66]

Most important was the middle phase, when people were suspended between what they were and what they hoped to become. During this phase, people were encouraged toward moral and cultural renewal through visual symbols, lyrical language and rhythmic music.[67]

These rites were expected to induce multiple shifts in focus — from oneself to the greater whole, from the "secular" (so to speak) to the sacred, from fear of "death" to faith in immortality. At the end of each rite, people were "born again" — infants into the community, children "died" and were "reborn" as adults, a man and a woman became husband and wife, a claimant was invested with authority to rule, and a deceased person was ushered into the land of the ancestors.[68]

Some rites commemorated changes in the natural environment. Key holy days on the liturgical calendar marked the New Year, the annual end of harvest, and seasonal changes. During the New Year event, for example, people could publicly express their grievances and resentments without fear of reprisal, even to the ruler and other authorities.

By throwing out trash that belonged to the old year, people entered the new year unburdened and renewed.[69] This tradition is echoed in the annual Mardi Gras celebration in New Orleans, Carnival in Trinidad and Tobago, and Carnaval in Brazil, all sustained mainly by people of African descent.

These communal religious practices were designed to harness the power inherent in universal energy for the health and well-being of the community. Rituals celebrated the cycles and seasons in nature, such as farming rituals performed before charring the land, after planting and at harvest. Others sought to impose order on disordered life through the enactment of standardized performances.[70]

Another set of rites marked shifts in the lives of people: birth, adulthood, marriage, investiture in political office, and death.[71] Funeral rites aimed to induce the spirit of the deceased to join the ancestors, rather than continuing a restless existence among the living.[72]

How these were organized can be seen in detail by examining the passage from childhood to adulthood. Almost universally, there was a period of formal preparation to mark the passage from childhood that varied from two to three years among the Kpelle, to four among the Gola, or between four and seven years among the Loma.[73]

It began when children were taken to a boarding camp in the "wild" of the bush. Their removal from the ordered village and the bosom of their families marked their "death." Suddenly they were cut off from parents, siblings and other member of their original household, as well as the psychic strings that had anchored them to that old world.[74]

The in-between phase was like the Christian catechism and baptism combined. The sacred authorities taught the children self-mastery through various tests of endurance and deprivations. They redirected the children's focus from the transient to the transcendental, from the obvious world that is available through the senses to the hidden world of powers and cycles.[75]

From early in history, West African cultures apparently circumcised boys as a rite of passage into adulthood.[76] In some, the children underwent scarification.[77]

At the end of the rite, the community hosted a rebirth celebration to welcome the "new adults." In many cultures, the women who completed the passage were smeared in white clay and dressed in special clothing to symbolize their newness.[78]

Of age groupings, there were usually three: adolescents, middle-aged adults and elders. The elders stood between the community and the ancestors. Guided by precedence (distilled as "the way of the ancestors"), they preserved order in all forms — from the moral and political to the cultural. Where the young and inexperienced saw a budding twig here and a hollowed trunk there, the elders were expected to grasp the forest of threats and opportunities. They did not oppose change, as sometimes falsely portrayed by scholars. Instead, they resisted disorder.[79]

In addition to community-wide rites of passage, some cultures maintained parallel institutions of blacksmiths, hunters, midwives, performing artists and other specialists, devoted to maintaining healthful life-force within each of their domains.

Some groups maintained multiple rites of passage for different groups, such as the Leopard Society and Snake Society. These often were communities in crisis or coping with unassimilated immigrants.[80]

Beyond the level of the clan, various Niger-Congo cultures developed institutions to coordinate a broad variety of functions including adjudication, collective defense, preservation of rituals and administration. A useful comparison would be the Catholic Church in Medieval Europe, which operated schools, hospitals and a variety of other institutions, not for their own sake, but ostensibly for keeping society in proper moral balance.

Diviners, Prophets and Other Religious Authorities

In West African cultures, several different religious authorities were entrusted with bridging the worlds of the seen and the unseen. They included priests, prophets, diviners, dancers, carvers, blacksmiths and sacred rulers. People usually specialized in one role or another; most performed their religious duties on a part-time basis, especially in small communities.[81]

Of the various authorities, two were especially common: diviners and people possessed by a life-force from outside themselves.

Diviners all specialized in reading the future of individual clients. But, their methods for tapping the future varied. Some elders and others engaged in divining on a part-time basis. They used a variety of methods, such as divining patterns in randomly tossed cowrie shells, "cutting" sand, reading the entrails of a sacrificed chicken, casting kola and spinning eggs.[82]

Other diviners used wisdom — standing on the knowledge of the ages to see the other side of life's mountains. Still others claimed to serve as channels for truths from the unseen world and dreams. But, the most impressive employed extra-human vision. They usually would establish credibility by revealing to a new client private details about that person's life or recent journey.[83]

Unlike diviners, prophets were leaders of movements, not consultants. They accessed the unseen world without having to read kola, sand, cowries or another other media. They addressed the fate of the community, not individuals.[84]

Possession was more common in sub-Saharan African than anywhere else in the world. It usually occurred at public religious ceremonies when a dancer was captured by a hypnotic rhythm. First, the person would let go of self-consciousness and surrender to the beat. Riding on the back of the rhythm, an external power would seize the dancer. Under its influence, the possessed person would alternatively gasp in ecstasy, fall limp, leap into a flurry of activity, and speak in an otherworldly voice.[85]

Because possessed persons were unaware of their actions, it was usually left to religious authorities to explain what had happened and why. In doing so, they made possession appear to be less threatening, less strange. Rarely, if ever, was possession said to be done by God directly.[86]

Possession most often occurred in highly rigid societies. And most likely, it involved women, enslaved persons, and poor men. To them, possession offered freedom, even if on a temporary basis. Freedom from control by others. Freedom from having to "behave." Freedom to disrupt the status quo. In that moment, the world was overturned: Those from the margins moved to center stage.[87]

To address misfortune or illness, Niger-Congo cultures turned to healers-diviners (derisively labeled "medicine men" by Europeans) who were thought to be skillful in reading people and knowledgable in the healthful (and harmful) properties of organic matter, including certain clays, unusual stones, plants, ointments and gall derived from crocodile and other animals.[88]

The goal was to decrease the destructive use of life force and increase its positive use through protective steps, such as burning appropriate items, especially herbs; wearing specific clothes or masks; marking the body with sacred symbols using clay or white chalk; and wearing charms or amulets.[89]

Healers knew the pharmacological properties of plants, claws, teeth, shells, hides, feathers, eggs and organs of various animals, as well as where they could be acquired. In addition to dispelling illness from individuals, they were expected to use knowledge and skills to benefit the community by drawing rain and encouraging crop growth.[90]

This was also the case with some people, especially proficient artisans and artists, whose disproportionate energies were thought to be innate or shaped through appropriate training and practice. The creativity of artists and artisans were viewed as a potentially dangerous power. For this reason, they were feared and admired at the same time.[91]

As artisans increased in number, they tended to form guilds. These artisan-only groups served their members' interest in several ways: They protected trade secrets, fought for access to markets and limited competition.[92] In the region of Liberia, several groups of artisans apparently formed such guilds, including blacksmiths, hunters, and bridge-builders.[93]

Exemplars of such high energy were given responsibility for specific rituals. They included leatherworkers (charged with life-force from the animals whose skins they treated) and carvers (for harvesting the energy of wood for charms and religious icons).[94]

Blacksmiths, Hunters and the Control of Life-force

Of the specialists capable of controlling life-energy, among the most respected were blacksmiths. They alone knew the alchemy of fire, land, water and forest involved in smelting and iron-working, and could control the powerful, dangerous forces they embodied. Relying on similar knowledge, their wives were generally potters and weavers.[95]

Given their divine knowledge, smiths often monopolized several areas of ritual significance, such as carving masks, preparing amulets, and presiding over circumcisions at ceremonies marking the transition of youth into adulthood. Since few dared challenge their authority, smiths usually mediated disputes within their communities.

Their forges were widely regarded as sacred spaces, their bellows were used for swearing oaths by some groups. In addition, the metal brackets, bells and rings they produced were thought to carry concentrated forms of energy.[96]

Among the Klao, for example, the symbol of office bestowed on the high priest was an iron ring.[97] In traditional religion, even among the Muslim Wolof and Mande groups, iron-smiths were regarded as diviners and priests based on their access to esoteric supernatural knowledge.

Figure 19. Masked figure
Rock painting
Tassili, Southern Algeria,
8000-5000 BC

Archaeological findings of smelting sites and other evidence from around West Africa show that iron diffused across the region between c.300 BC - 700 AD.[98]

Another highly regarded group of specialists were hunters. They were essential to the smooth functioning of their societies in their primary roles as killers of fearful predatory animals and as suppliers of protein in societies lacking large livestock due to the presence of Tsetse flies. They were revered for the energy from the animals they killed that, in turn, could cause their death.

Skillful hunters developed an impressive set of physical skills, which made them quite different from other people. In addition, they learned to control unseen powers in ways that made them very potent and potentially dangerous."[99]

The nature of their work required them to spend days, weeks and sometimes longer periods in the bush, surviving mainly on what was available to them in that environment. In the process, they learned, not just the habits and anatomy of animals, but also the helpful and harmful properties of plants.[100]

During extended sojourns, they sometimes discovered new, more fertile and uninhabited territories, which was critical for societies practicing slash-and-burn agriculture. In short, experienced hunters combined the adventurous personalities of explorers with the most advanced knowledge of zoology and botany, which Mande-speakers called *jiridon* (meaning, "science of the tress").

Historian Patrick R. McNaughton summarized the status of hunters in Mande societies specifically, but his portrait described their place in many other cultures as well. They have "an incredible thirst for adventure, along with the pluck and determination to indulge that thirst and survive. They are also by and large very self-possessed and very self-oriented, features that are both good and threatening to the rest of society."

For all these reasons, hunters stood apart from others, while the rest of society also kept them at a safe social distance. Reinforcing the sense of mystery surrounding them was the unique shirts some wore. These were often roomy to allow air to circulate. The cloth was often mud-dyed or stained with a rust-brown herbal solution.

In contrast to the orderly clothes of others, hunters' shirts embodied the disorder of the bush, with attachments of horns, claws, strips of leather and skin-covered amulets. This attire symbolized both their difference and their embodiment of the life-force of the bush and the animals they had killed.

In Mande societies, hunters were thought to possess *Fadenya* ("father-childness"). This concept derived from the term for siblings of the same father but different mothers, who embodied competitiveness in their attempts to make a name for themselves. *Fadenya* is contrasted to *Badenya* ("mother-childness"), a quality of affectionateness perceived in the relationship of siblings who share the same mother and father.[101]

The center of the way of the ancestors was an ethical system. Adherents were expected to balance personal and community interests; their own aspirations against the ways of the ancestors; and claims of the worlds of the seen with those of the unseen.[102]

The equivalent of a "saint," "fakeer," or "holy person" in the way of the ancestors is not a monk who lived apart from society or renounces "things of the flesh." It was someone who stood in a right relationship with God, with the ancestors, with the living community and with all forces — visible and invisible. Someone who integrated self-control, interpersonal effectiveness and an understanding of timeless truths. Someone who maintained balance in the midst of change.[103]

Such integration was gained through rituals that teach mastery of self and reveal the mystical in the mundane. The rituals would teach, but not everyone would learn.

Wisdom in Proverbs and Visual Signs

Wisdom in West Africa was often transmitted in poetry and proverbs. Those lend themselves to the transmission of wisdom because they are abstract and can be applied to multiple situations. Whether or not they are applied appropriately depends on the skill or "wisdom" of the user.[104]

Because these forms of speech are compressed and lyrical, they are easier to remember. This pattern is evident in the wisdom books of the ancient Israelites, including Proverbs, Ecclesiastics and Psalms, that were transmitted orally before they were written down.

Wisdom was also encoded in visual symbols.[105] These were the stained-glass windows of the way of the ancestors.

Basic building blocks of visual symbols were three key colors. Red was generally reserved for middle-aged men because of its association with blood, vitality, anger, transition and violence.[106] White symbolized wisdom, tranquility innocence, purity, coolant and well-being. It evoked the ancestors, water forces or women, depending on the context. Black suggested raw power, emotion and mystery. It was associated with young men

Figure 20. Dan Mask with cowrie shells and sacred red

and the life-force of the forest.[107]

If a mask or other sculpture was two-toned, this meant it mediated between two worlds.[108]

Other artistic elements were also invested with meaning. A zig-zag pattern usually represented water, both in the sky and on land. A refined, smooth and naturalistic style was often associated with female beauty. Neck rings used on female masks suggested the layering around a caterpillar before it turns into a butterfly or moth. In contrast, maleness was linked to sharp angular style, as well as horns, teeth and unpleasant smell.[109]

In the way of the ancestors, words, too, had tremendous power. In this context, naming a person or thing was not just "a rational, aesthetic, artistic or even creative act." It is supposed to reveal their inherent characteristic, force or power.[110]

Knowledge was the ultimate power or force.[111] While West African societies supported various specialists, they viewed knowledge holistically; it combined what in the West are regarded as distinct disciplines: chemistry and biology, theology and history, poetry and musicology.[112]

But, even in the West, science was not always what it has become. According to science historian Hugh Kearney, it began as a mix of three traditions: organic, magical and mechanistic.

Rooted in what is now called "biology," organic science was focused on living things. It described life in terms of growth and decay. In contrast, magical scientists saw nature as a work of art and God as the master artist. In their view, science was sacred work that unlocked the mysteries of the universe. For mechanical scholars, the world moved in regular and predictable ways, like a machine.[113]

Contrary to common stereotypes, the way of the ancestors was not hostile to science. It used a mix of therapies to treat illnesses, including herbs, counseling and magic. It ascribed ill-health to unseen forces, and this was widely dismissed as spiritual mumbo-jumbo. But, Western science also blames illnesses on forces that are not visible to the naked eye — viruses, germs and toxins.[114]

Because knowledge could be used for good or evil, every precaution was taken to ensure it did not fall into the hands of antisocial people.[115] To illustrate with one example, master drummers are able to induce possession or trace, by getting dancers to stop being self-conscious and surrender to the force of the rhythm.

Sociopaths as Sources of Evil

In the way of the ancestors, the Creator was all good, but not all-powerful. At creation, God had filled the world with wonders and powers, which are morally neutral. There was no Devil, Shatan, or other fallen angel. Evil originated, not with God or nature, but within the unclean hearts of some antisocial men and women.[116]

The way of the ancestors, through its sacraments and rites, tried to ensure that the awesome powers of the universe were channeled to people who would use them for good. Evil people possessed as much knowledge about life-forces — and skill in using them — as religious authorities. But, they used herbalism and iron-smelting for destructive purposes.[117]

What set evil people apart from others was their drive to amass seen and unseen power for selfish reasons.[118]

Their behaviors violated all of the sacred norms. They stared when no one was watching them but became shifty-eyed when observed by others. Their least criminal acts included dancing naked outdoors, digging up graves, and despoiling other people's lands with vomit or feces. At the other end of the wrongdoing spectrum, they killed young people, murdered relatives, ate human flesh, devoured corpses and committed incest.[119]

Evil people left few clues linking them to their crimes because, it was thought, they could fly and walk on their hands.[120]

By attacking norms and taboos, sociopaths risked unleashing concentrated natural powers against the society itself. Through their actions, they threatened to destroy the moral order.[121]

Their personalities were marked by extreme egotism and even narcissism. They were driven above all by unbridled passions — hatred, ambition, acquisitiveness and revenge. Their traits were the least desirable in normal society — pushy, arrogant, sullen, gloomy, covetous, resentful, sneaky and insincere.[122]

Figure 21. Major constellations

"Of more importance to the native farmer than the moons is the position of certain constellations. For the [Bandi], Mano, and Sapo the significant constellation is the Pleiades. The [Dan] watch for ye-negruzengru, which appears to be a combination of the Pleiades and three stars in the constellation of Orion, near his belt.

"Farm cutting must begin when the Pleiades are in the east at sunset. the distance they should be above the horizon varies somewhat in different regions. The [Dan] and Sapo begin cutting as soon as they are showing well in the east; the [Bandi], when they are about halfway between the horizon and the zenith. The [Ma] stated that all clearing, burning, and planting must be done before this constellation has passed the zenith. Otherwise the steady rains will be at hand, and it will be too late to plant."

Their world was the mirror opposite of orderly village life. Their appearance was unappealing, often dirty. They travelled and worked their evil at night, while normal people were asleep. What others discarded, they collected for use in their nefarious rituals — hair, sweat, urine, vomit, and blood.[123]

Yes, they had leaders and meeting[...] cussed the common good in a palava hut nea[...] convened in the branches of tall tress and underw[...] emitted from their mouths and anuses could be see[...] the shore.[124]

They recruited newcomers the way criminal gangs[...] cent person who came seeking a charm would be sworn to sec[...] would be used to commit one antisocial act after another. Once th[...] a relative, the chances of leaving were slim.[125]

Evil people were assumed to be the allies of any creature that ev[...] loathed — deadly insets, bats, owls and predatory animals. They had the[...] was thought, to send their animals on errands, to have sex with them and to c[...] into them.[126]

Sociopaths were capable of wrong-doing not only in the seen world. They also manipulated unseen forces to cause mental illnesses, thefts, business failures, family disputes, loss of affection, ill health, undeserved misfortune and even death.[127]

Using charms, spells and portions [potions?], they could seize the body and mind of others, turning them into instruments of evil. They were also able, it was thought, to drain the life-force from a person's limb, leaving it lifeless with no external signs of harm. Especially targeted were arms, legs and lungs (which immobilized victims) and wombs and penises (essential for lineage reproduction). They were also suspected if a hardworking, thrifty person failed to get rich.[128]

If caught and tried, repentant evil-doers could be ritually cleansed and brought back into society.[129]

Religious authorities usually launched campaigns to uncover sociopaths during times of social tensions. Such investigations were common in small farming communities where people of different backgrounds were recently brought together.

Often it was older brothers and head wives suffering ill fortune who brought charges against younger rivals. Equally vulnerable to being charged were wealthy people, the elderly poor, and young wives from an outside clan who recently married into the community.[130]

West African Conception of Time

In West African life, multiple time frames operated simultaneously, but each was measured differently. In the absence of clocks, none was precise. All however, were cyclical and repetitive.[131]

African thought was rooted in a materialist view of life, grounded in lived experience. As such, its conception of time extended from the present into the past,

ual was determined by natural events (such as the full moon) or major task (time after the harvest, for example). During each ritual, however, the fast pace of everyday life was arrested or at least slowed as participants lost track of time.

These multiple time measures operated like a symphony of drums. Each had a distinct tone and rhythm, but they skillfully played off each other. The time of natural events was like the bass drum, driving the tempo. Atop that was the *fanga* sound of the major task times; it beat out intense, rapid-fire bursts for short periods, with controlled silences between. Those were coupled with the trance-inducing patterns of ritual times. Together, these ordered the steady heart beat of community life.[137]

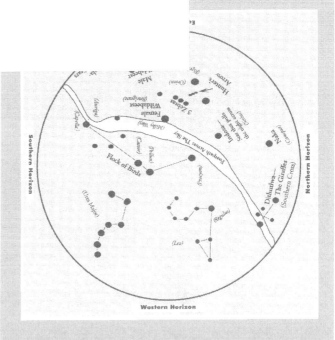

Figure 22. The night sky in African mythology

1. Dominique Zahan, "Some reflections on African spirituality" (pp. 3-25), in Jacob K. Olupona, ed., *African Spirituality: Forms, Meanings and Expression* (New York: The Crossroad Publishing Co., 2011), p. 3.
2. Frankfort, 1948, p. 3, makes a similar claim about Ancient Egyptian religion; Kathleen O'Brien Wicker, "Mami Water in African religion and spirituality" (pp. 198-222) in Jacob K. Olupona, ed., *African Spirituality: Forms, Meanings and Expression* (New York: The Crossroad Publishing Co., 2011), p. 198.
3. Elizabeth Isichei, *The Religious Traditions of Africa: A History* (Westport, Conn.: Praeger, 2004), p. 4.
4. Wyatt MacGaffey, "Art and spirituality" (pp. 223-256), in Jacob K. Olupona, ed., *African Spirituality: Forms, Meanings and Expression* (New York: The Crossroad Publishing Co., 2011), pp. 225-226, citing Oliver de Sandan, 1992, 11; Boubou Hama and J. Ki-Zerbo, "The place of history in African society," (pp. 43-53), in J. Ki-Zerbo, ed., *UNESCO General History of Africa: Methodology and African Prehistory*, Vol. I (Berkeley: University of California Press, 1981, p. 50.
5. Segy, 1969, pp. 20-21.
6. Segy, 1969, pp. 8-9; Hackett, 1996, p. 10; George Schwab, *Tribes of the Liberian Hinterlands* (Cambridge, Mass.: Peabody Museum of Archeology and Ethnology, 1947), pp. 315-318.
7. Ray, 1976, pp. 50, 51.
8. Zahan, 2011, p. 5; George W. Ellis, *Negro Culture in West Africa* (New York: The Neale Publishing Company, 1914), pp. 85-86; George W. Harley, *Notes on the Poro in Liberia* (Cambridge, Mass.: Peabody Museum of American Archaeology and Ethnology, Harvard University, 1941), p. 4; Robert Cameron Mitchell, *African Primal Religions* (Niles, Ill.: Argus Communications, 1977), p. 10. Like many other scholars, Mitchell notes that African traditional religions "are many but one."
9. For a discussion of the lamb symbol in the context of Christianity, see E. A. Wallis Budge, *The Gods of the Egyptians*, Vol. 1 (New York: Dover, 1969), p. 2, n. 1.
10. Zahan, 2011, pp. 5, 7.; Ray, 1976, pp. 50, 53, 64. For explantations of creation among the Ma, Dan, Bandi and Glebo, see Schwab, 1947, pp. 318-219.
11. Zahan, 2011, p. 8, 10; Ray, 1976, pp. 24, 32, 38, 41.
12. Martin, 1968, p. 33, n. 65; Harley, 1941, p. 6. The complimentary structure of gender roles extended to the declaration of war. As noted by Harley, the upper levels of the Poro could decide to declare war without consulting common men, but not without the consent of Sande leaders.
13. Zahan, 2011, p. 5.
14. Theo Sundermeier, *The Individual and Community in African Traditional Religion* (Piscataway, NJ: Transaction Publishers, 1998), pp. 15-22; Evan M. Zuesse, *Ritual Cosmos: The Sanctification of Life in African Religions* (Athen, OH: Ohio University Press, 1979), pp. 3, 7; Noel Q. King, *African Cosmos: An Introduction to Religion in Africa* (Belmont, Calif.: Wadsworth Publishing Co., 1986), p. 4.
15. E. G. Parrinder, *African Traditional Religion* (London: Hutchinson's University Library, 1954), p. 25.

16. Zuesse, 1979, p. 161.

17. Segy, 1969, 1969, pp. 8-9.

18. Segy, 1969, 1969, pp. 26-27; Schwab, 1947, p. 344. Dominique Zahan, *The Religion, Spirituality, and Though of Traditional Africa* (Chicago: The University of Chicago Press, 1979), pp. 23, 25, 94-95. John Leighton Wilson, who served as a Presbyterian missionary in Liberia from 1833 to 1844, found the belief in one Supreme God to be universal in Africa; J. Leighton Wilson, *Western Africa* (New York: Harper and Bros., 1856), p. 209.

19. Zahan, 1979, pp. 27-28; Ellis, 1914, pp. 90-91; Hackett, 1996, p. 149. Writing about the Vai in the early 1900s, Ellis noted sacrifices to the feared alligators, the forces behind lightning and drought, and the fruitful palm trees, especially the dominant one. For early examples of a tree and a rock at the center of rituals, see Al-Mas'udi (MAS), Akubar al-zaman (written late-1000s) in N. Levtzion and J. F. P. Hopkins, eds., *Corpus of Early Arabic Sources for West African History* (Princeton: Markus Wiener Publishers, 2011), pp. 35, 37; this work is one of two modern compilations of Arabic sources widely accepted by scholars around the world; the other is Joseph Cuoq, ed., *Recueil des sources arabes concern ant l'Afrique occidental du VIIIe au XVIe siècle [Bilad al-Sudan]* (Paris: Centre National de la Recherche Scientifique, 1975).

20. On midwives, see James L. Gibbs, Jr., "The Kpelle of Liberia" (pp. 197-240), in James L. Gibbs, Jr., *People of Africa* (New York: Rinehart and Winston, 1965), especially p. 209 (Kpelle); Johnston, 1906, p. 1049 (general); Captain Theophilus Conneau, *A Slaver's Log Book or 20 Years Residence in Africa* (Englewoods Cliff, NJ: Prentice-Hall, 1976), p. 385 (Vai).

21. Ray, 1976, p. 140; Jean-Marie Gibbal, *Genii of the River Niger* (Chicago: University of Chicago Press, 1994), p. 8, n. 10; King, 1986, p. 72; Schwab, 1947, pp. 320-322.

22. Ray, 1976, p. 140; Gibbal, 1994, p. 8, n. 10; King, 1986, p. 72.

23. Sundermeier, 1998, p. 31; Schwab, 1947, p. 344.

24. Ray, 2011, p. 35; Kalu, 2011, p. 55; MacGaffey, 2011, pp. 240, 242, 245-246; Arthur P. Bourgeois, "Masking in sub-Saharan Africa" (pp. 68-70), in Theodore Celenko, ed., *Egypt in Africa* (Indianapolis: Indiana University Press, 1996).

25. Segy, 1969, 1969, p. 13.

26. Segy, 1969, 1969, pp. 44-45; Bourgeois, 1996, p. 69; Arlene Wolinski, "The case for ceremonial masking" (pp. 71-74), in Theodore Celenko, ed., *Egypt in Africa* (Indianapolis: Indiana University Press, 1996); Robert Steven Bianchi, "The case against extensive masking in ancient Egypt" (pp. 75-77), in Theodore Celenko, ed., *Egypt in Africa* (Indianapolis: Indiana University Press, 1996).

27. MacGaffey, 2011, p. 246.

28. MacGaffey, 2011, p. 246.

29. Segy, 1969, 1969, p. 9; Bourgeois, 1996, p. 68.

30. MacGaffey, 2011, pp. 228, 245; Bourgeois, 1996, p. 68.

31. Segy, 1969, 1969, p. 11.

32. Segy, 1969, 1969, p. 12; Bourgeois, 1996, p. 70.

33. Zahan, 1979, p. 86 (cowries); Bourgeois, 1996, pp. 68-69.

34. Segy, 1969, 1969, pp. 25-30, 34-35; Harley, 1941, p. 24; Bourgeois, 1996, pp. 68-69.

35. MacGaffey, 2011, p. 229; O'Brien Wicker, 2011, p. 198-199.

36. O'Brien Wicker, 2011, pp. 198, 207; Schwab, 1947, pp. 337-338, 340-341.
37. O'Brien Wicker, 2011, pp. 198, 207; Schwab, 1947, pp. 337-338.
38. O'Brien Wicker, 2011, pp. 198-200, 202.
39. MacGaffey, 2011, p. 230, citing McLeod, 1976.
40. Ray, 1976, pp. 64.
41. Sundermeier, 1998, p. 31; Ray, 1976, pp. 50, 64; Zahan, 2011, p. 5.
42. For the association of red with ritual sacrifices, see David Conrad, *A State of Intrigue: The Epic of Bamana Segu* (New York: Oxford University Press, 1990), pp. 58, 132, 180.
43. Johnson, 1961, p. 24; Zahan, 1979, pp. 33, 35, 148-150, 152 (blood).
44. Zahan, 2011, pp. 10-11; Chapurukha M. Kusimba, "Ancestor worship and divine kingship in sub-Saharan Africa" (pp. 59-61), in Theodore Celenko, ed., *Egypt in Africa* (Indianapolis: Indiana University Press, 1996).
45. Zahan, 2011, pp. 10-11; Kalu, 2011, p. 57; Kusimba, 1996, pp. 59-60.
46. MacGaffey, 2011, pp. 239.
47. Ogbu U. Kalu, "Ancestral spirituality and society in Africa" (pp. 54-84), in Jacob K. Olupona, ed., *African Spirituality: Forms, Meanings and Expression* (New York: The Crossroad Publishing Co., 2011), p. 54; Ray, 1976, pp. 140, 147; Kusimba, 1996, p. 60.
48. Horton, 1972, p. 107; Kusimba, 1996, p. 60.
49. Kusimba, 1996, pp. 59-60; Schwab, 1947, pp. 324, 327 (offerings of food, water, palm wine, gin; also burial feast among Ma, Dan, Glebo, Sapo); Zahan, 1979, p. 83 (kola); Ellis, 1914, p. 87. Writing about the Vai, Ellis noted the tradition in the early 1900s of taking rice, rum, palm butter and other sustenance to the graves of relatives once or twice a year.
50. Ray, 1976, pp. 140, 147; Sundermeier, 1998, p. 25. For a report of libations being poured to the ancestors dating to 1068 BC, see Abū 'Ubayd 'Abd Allāh ibn 'Abd al-'Azīz al-Bakrī, *Kitāb al-Masālik wa-al-Mamālik*, in N. Levtzion and J. F. P. Hopkins, eds., *Corpus of Early Arabic Sources for West African History* (Princeton: Markus Wiener Publishers, 2011), p. 81.
51. Zahan, 2011, p. 14. Some groups in Liberia converted certain corpses to mummies by smoking them, notably Poro leaders; see Harley, 1941, p. 27.
52. Zahan, 2011, p. 13.
53. Zahan, 2011, pp. 12-13.
54. Westerlund, 2011, p. 167; Schwab, 1947, pp. 322-323.
55. Westerlund, 2011, p. 167.
56. Ray, 1976, p. 150; Westerlund, 2011, p. 166; MacGaffey, 2011, pp. 239. For the existence of bad ancestors, see Schwab, 1947, pp. 324-325.
57. Zahan, 2011, pp. 15, 17; Benjamin Ray, "African shrines as channels of communication" (pp. 26-37), in Jacob K. Olupona, ed., *African Spirituality: Forms, Meanings and Expression* (New York: The Crossroad Publishing Co., 2011), pp. 26, 31, 34. Among the Glebo, for example, there is a sacred rock between Bigtown at Cape Palmas and Half Graway; Martin, 1968, p. 25.
58. Zahan, 2011, pp. 18-19.
59. Ray, 2011, p. 34.

60. Zahan, 2011, pp. 18-19.
61. Ray, 1976, pp. 65, 78; King, 1986, pp. 65, 70.
62. Ray, 1976, p. 78.
63. Ray, 1976, pp. 78-79; King, 1986, pp. 65, 70.
64. Ray, 1976, pp. 78-79; King, 1986, pp. 65, 70.
65. Ray, 1976, pp. 78-79; King, 1986, pp. 65, 70.
66. Ray, 1976, p. 91; MacGaffey, 2011, p. 233; Segy, 1969, 1969, pp. 29, 17.
67. Ray, 1976, p. 91; MacGaffey, 2011, p. 233.
68. Ray, 1976, p. 91; Zuese, 1979, p. 152; Zahan, 2011, p. 21.
69. Ray, 1976, pp. 91, 97.
70. Segy, 1969, 1969, pp. 8-9.
71. Ray, 1976, p. 91.
72. Segy, 1969, 1969, p. 26; Zahan, 1979, pp. 47, 50-51.
73. Ehret, 2002, p. 46. For age-set patterns among groups in Liberia, see: Bureau of Folkways, 1955, pp. 18, 25, 28; Little, 1951, pp. 113-139; Etta Becker-Donna, *Hinterland Liberia* (London: Blackie & Son, 1939), p. 62; Johnson, 1961, pp. 1-23; Thomas E. Hayden, "A description of the 1970 Grand Cess Bo," *Liberian Studies Journal*, IV, 26 (1971-1972): 183-188; Beryl Larry Bellman, *The Language of Secrecy: Symbols and Metaphors in Poro Rituals* (New Brunswick: Rutgers University Press, 1984), pp. 13-18; F. W. Butt-Thompson, *West African Secret Societies* (London: Witherby, 1929). For age-set patterns more broadly, see Anne Foner and David Kertzer, "Transition over the life course: Lessons from age-set societies," *American Journal of Sociology*, Vol. 83, No. 5 (March 1978): 1081-1104; S. N. Eisenstadt, "African age groups: A comparative study," *Africa: Journal of the International African Institute*, Vol. 24, No. 2 (April 1954): 100-113.
74. Zuese, 1979, p. 146; Harley, 1941, p. 13; Bellman, 1984, pp. 13-18; Butt-Thompson, 1929. As noted by Rashid (2006, p. 11), "the initiation into, and membership of 'secret' societies based on age-sets, religious beliefs, gender, profession, and even wealth, gave individuals broader social identities and created communal solidarity beyond the kinship group."
75. Zahan, 2011, p. 21; Zuese, 1979, pp. 146, 152.
76. Ehret, 2002, p. 46.
77. Chike C. Aniakor, "Body art in Africa: Painting, tattooing, and scarification" (pp. 78-80), Theodore Celenko, ed., *Egypt in Africa* (Indianapolis: Indiana University Press, 1996). Compare to Robert Steven Bianchi, "Tattooing and skin painting in the Ancient Nile Valley" (pp. 81-83), Theodore Celenko, ed., *Egypt in Africa* (Indianapolis: Indiana University Press, 1996).
78. MacGaffey, 2011, p. 233.
79. Zuese, 1979, p. 163; MacGaffey, 2011, p. 241; King, 1986, p. 59.
80. Zuesse, 1979, p. 233.
81. Ray, 1976, pp. 17, 103; Schwab, 1947, pp. 129-130 (wood carvers).
82. Zuesse, 1979, p. 206; Ray, 1976, p. 111; Harley, 1941, p. 21.
83. Zuesse, 1979, pp. 206, 212-213, 218; Schwab, 1947, pp. 322-323.
84. Ray, 1976, p. 111.

85. King, 1986, p. 60; Zuesse, 1979, p. 187.
86. Ray, 1976, p. 111; Zahan, 2011, p. 4; Schwab, 1947, p. 336.
87. Zuesse, 1979, pp. 186-187.
88. Ehret, 2002, pp. 49-51; Zahan, 1979, pp. 24, 78-79, 129; Harley, 1941, pp. 10, 20, 21.
89. Robin Horton, "Stateless societies in the history of West Africa" (pp. 78-119), in J. F. Ade Ajayi and Michael Crowder, *History of West Africa*, Vol. I (New York: Columbia University Press, 1972), especially pp. 84-85, 94-95, 97, 106-107; Hackett, 1996, p. 135; Harley, 1941, p. 14. For the theory of medicine in Liberian cultures, see Schwab, 1947, pp. 357-359. For medical practices among the Kpelle, see Kenneth G. Orr, "Field notes on tribal medical practices in Central Liberia," *Liberian Studies Journal*, Vol. 1, No. 1 (1968): 20-41. A broad study (based on field study of Ma practices as well as a review of the literature of African medical knowledge) is George W. Harley, *Native African Medicine* (Cambridge, Mass.: Harvard University Press, 1941).
90. Horton, 1972, especially pp. 84-85, 94-95, 97, 106-107; Hackett, 1996, p. 135; Harley, 1941, p. 14; Davies, 1977, p. 24 (Klao); Schwab, 1947, p. 374-378 (Ma, Dan, Glebo); Johnston, 1906, p. 1068 (Glebo).
91. MacGaffey, 2011, pp. 250-251; Harley, 1941, pp. 22-24.
92. Braudel, Vol. 2, 1982, pp. 314-316.
93. Harley, 1941, p. 26.
94. Zahan, 1979, pp. 27, 34 (chicken), pp. 16, 24-26, 83, 128 (rain), pp. 15, 128, 150 (hunters); also Bureau of Folkways, 1955, p. 11; Hackett, 1996, p. 120.
95. Dennis, 1972, pp. 193-195 (Bandi); Schröder and Seibel, 1974, pp. 143-144 (Wee); Schwab, 1947, pp. 121-136, 145, 199 (Ma, Dan, Sapo, Loma, Bandi).
96. Willi Schulze, "Early iron smelting among the Northern Kpelle," *Liberian Studies Journal* III (1970-71): 113-127, especially p. 126; Zahan, 1979, pp. 29-30, 121, 123; Hackett, 1996, pp. 27-31. For the status of blacksmiths as mediating outsiders, see Horton, 1972, p. 109.
97. Massing, 1980, p. 63.
98. Brooks, 1985, pp. 48-49.
99. McNaughton, 1982, pp. 54-58, 91; also Warren L. d'Azevedo, *The Gola of Liberia* (New Haven, Conn.: Human Relations Area Files, 1972), p. 427.
100. Patrick R. McNaughton, "The shirts that Mande hunters wear," *African Arts*, 15, 3 (1982), p. 54.
101. McNaughton, 1982, pp. 54-58, 91; Jansen, 1995, p. 10.
102. Ray, 1976, p. 132.
103. Zuesse, 1979, pp. 7-8.
104. Bellman, *The Language of Secrecy: Symbols and Metaphors in Poro Rituals* (New Brunswick: Rutgers University Press, 1984), pp. 13-18.
105. Zuesse, 1979, p. 139; Chapurukha M. Kusimba, "Animal deities and symbols in Africa" (pp. 62-65), Theodore Celenko, ed., *Egypt in Africa* (Indianapolis: Indiana University Press, 1996). For religious symbolism generally, see Victor Turner, *The Forest of Symbols: Aspects of Ndembu Ritual* (Ithaca: Cornell University Press, 1967).
106. MacGaffey, 2011, pp. 233, 236-237.

107. MacGaffey, 2011, pp. 233, 236-237.
108. MacGaffey, 2011, p. 233.
109. MacGaffey, 2011, pp. 233, 235-237, 242.
110. Sundermeier, 1998, p. 22; Schwab, 1947, p. 344.
111. MacGaffey, 2011, p. 250.
112. MacGaffey, 2011, p. 226; David Westerlund, "Spiritual beings as agents of illness" (pp. 152-175), in Jacob K. Olupona, ed., *African Spirituality: Forms, Meanings and Expression* (New York: The Crossroad Publishing Co., 2011), p. 152.
113. Hugh Kearney, *Science and Change, 1500-1700* (New York: McGraw Hill, 1971), pp. 22-25.
114. MacGaffey, 2011, p. 226; Zuesse, 1979, p. 238; Harley, 1941, p. 20.
115. MacGaffey, 2011, p. 250.
116. Ray, 1976, p. 150; Schwab, 1947, pp. 319-320, 326. In Ma culture, Schwab (1947, p. 316) noted the concept of a "Bad One" or devil, but this might have been due to Islamic or Christian influence.
117. Zuesse, 1979, pp. 168, 223, 228; Boudillon, 2011, pp. 178-179; Ehret, 2002, pp. 49-51; Zahan, 1979, p. 102; Schwab, 1947, pp. 378-382.
118. Zuesse, 1979, p. 226; Ray, 1976, p. 150; Bourdillon, 2011, p. 176-177, 179; Schwab, 1947, pp. 325-327.
119. Zuesse, 1979, p. 226; Ray, 1976, p. 150; Bourdillon, 2011, p. 176-177, 179; Schwab, 1947, pp. 331-333.
120. Ray, 1976, p. 150.
121. Zuesse, 1979, pp. 226-227.
122. Zuesse, 1979, pp. 168, 178, 226-228, 234.
123. Ray, 1976, p. 150; Zuesse, 1979, p. 230
124. King, 1986, p. 72; Schwab, 1947, p. 335.
125. Bourdillon, 2011, p. 191.
126. Zuesse, 1979, p. 225-226; King, 1986, p. 72; Schwab, 1947, p. 325 (owls).
127. Ray, 1976, p. 157; Bourdillon, 2011, p. 179; O'Brien Wicker, 2011, 206.
128. King, 1986, p. 72; Zuesse, 1979, pp. 224-225; Bourdillon, 2011, p. 179; Schwab, 1947, pp. 332-334.
129. Bourdillon, 2011, p. 177.
130. Bouirdillon, 2011, p. 182, 185, 190; Zuesse, 1979, p. 226.
131. Zahan, 2011, p. 3; Ray, 1976, p. 41.
132. John S. Mbiti, *Concepts of God in Africa* (New York: Praeger, 1970); Ray, 1976, pp. 41.
133. Ray, 1976, p. 40.
134. Sundermeier, 1998, p. 25.
135. Sundermeier, 1998, p. 25; Ray, 1976, p. 41.
136. Sundermeier, 1998, p. 25; Ray, 1976, p. 41.
137. Hamas and Zerbo, 1981, p. 94.

Chapter 4
Egypt and Religions of the Book

"The body is the house of God."

That is why it is said: "Man, know thyself."

– Ancient Egyptian maxim

The way of the ancestors left no written records, but it apparently influenced religion in ancient Egypt, which did leave extensive inscriptions. Those records show striking similarities between ideas and practices of Egypt and contemporary West Africa.

For over a hundred years, most Western Egyptologists credited ancient Egyptian religion to invaders from the Middle Eastern or Mediterranean world. But, E. A. Wallis Budge broke with that consensus in 1911.[1]

Budge's conclusions drew on multiple sources: his experience as keeper of the Egyptian and Assyrian Antiquities in the British Museum; a scientific examination of mummies; historical and geographical evidence taken from hieroglyphic inscriptions; a study of ancient Egyptian language, as conveyed in hieroglyphic texts; claims of ancient Greek and Roman chroniclers; and impressions of contemporary African cultures derived from living in Egypt and Sudan.[2]

The roots of Egyptian religion, Budge argued, laid deep in Africa. He found parallels in parts of Africa with no known Egyptian influence. For that reason, he concluded, the similarities did not flow from the Nile. Instead, it came from a common source in Africa, which predated ancient Egypt.[3]

Many early European Egyptologists lacked Budge's in-depth experience with other parts of Africa that made his comparisons possible. Because Greek and Roman writers were ignorant of African culture, Budge argued, they produced analyses of Egyptian religion that "border on the ridiculous." Recent Egyptologists without a familiarity with black Africa only added to the confusion.[4]

Many recent scholars have followed Budge's lead.[5] According to historian Basil Davidson, Egyptians viewed the lands to their south and west as homes of their divinities and ancestors.[6] Archeologist Thurston Shaw concluded, "early African social customs and religious beliefs were the root and foundation of the ancient Egyptian way of life."[7]

Ancient Egyptian cultural traits that have been traced to African roots include Saharan rock painting motifs in pharaonic art, Saharan pottery, royal incest, mummies, and language.[8]

Ancient Egyptian ideas about the afterlife are preserved in three collections of funeral texts; the Pyramid texts (after 2400 BC), the Coffin texts (after 2000 BC) and the Spells for Going Forth by Day (after 1500 BC). The first set was recorded inside the tombs of the pharaohs. They consist of hymns, prayers and spells intended to protect the royal family in the heavenly realm.

The Coffin text were similar to those buried in the pyramids, but were placed in the graves of commoners instead. They offered the deceased guidance through a maze of judgments in the underworld. The third collection was inscribed on sheets of papyrus. It consisted of over 190 spells that were used for more than 1,000 years. They are often called The Egyptian Book of the Dead, but the Egyptians called them the Spells for Going Forth by Day.[9]

These three collections provide a baseline to which widespread African traditional religious ideas can be compared.

Egyptian ideas about how the world began were similar to those in West Africa. According to the theology taught at Memphis, Egypt's capital, the Creator first thought everything "in his heart." Then God spoke everything into existence.[10]

Figure 23. Akan "Akuaba" fertility doll (left) and Egyptian Ankh

As in traditional African religion, ancient Egyptians viewed the Creator as detached from people's daily affairs. Instead, their lives were more directly impacted by the energy God had invested in objects, plants, animals and other people.[11] In short, both religions were a mixture of "magic and materialism."[12]

Both religious traditions conceived of God as all good but not necessarily all powerful. Evil, illness and misfortune were seen as emanating from powers other than God, the source of evil being personified as Seth in ancient Egypt. Thus, these traditions avoided the difficulty Christianity faces in explaining why an all-good and all-powerful God permits bad things to happen to good people.[13]

Most people today think ancient Egyptian religion was centered around Ra, God as symbolized by the sun. But according to Budge, that was a cult of the elite. In contrast, most Egyptians worshipped Osiris, God as symbolized by the moon. As in many African cultures, the most important festivals in early Egypt marked the first and fifteenth days of the lunar cycle.[14]

Osiris's chin sported a plaited beard and his crown featured feathers and horns, which Budge noted, resembled the appearance of many African rulers. His body was often painted white, as if covered in the clay used in the initiation rituals of many West African cultures.[15]

In Budge's view, Egyptians originally saw Osiris as a venerated ancestor, who later evolved to be seen as part-God, part-man. His origin as a man who rose from death to divinity gave Egyptians hope that they, too, could achieve resurrection and immortality.[16]

The ancients both in Egypt and other parts of Africa buried slaves and favorite wives with rulers. But after worship of Osiris took hold, followers were allowed to bury statutes of dependents instead, ending the need for blood sacrifices.[17]

Budge noted that criminal suspects in West Africa declared their innocence before undergoing trial by *sassywood*, that is, drinking a decoction to determine guilt or innocence. He compared that ritual to the ancient Egyptian belief that the deceased professed innocence before having his heart weighed in the afterlife.[18]

Egypt developed the first known ethical code called *Maat*, reflected in the Spells for Going Forth by Day. These precepts were stated as "general principles whose application depends upon circumstances and reason." They provided "limits on behavior" that "were essential to governing a complex" agricultural society.[19]

For almost 3,000 years, the people in each city and region of ancient Egypt maintained a distinct religious tradition. Although their rituals, totemic animals and names of God differed, the traditions share many underlying similarities.[20] As in West Africa, people in different parts of Egypt conceived of God differently, and none of them was regarded as true or false.[21]

But around 1375 BC, a recently installed pharaoh imposed a unified worship of one God, Aten. Overturning centuries-old traditions, Amenhotep IV declared all other religions to be "false," abolished their priesthoods and defunded their temples. He even changed his name to Akhenaten (probably "servant of the Aten"). In the most radical move of all, he jettisoned belief in the afterlife and God's weighing of hearts, knocking out the pillars on which morality rested.[22]

A hymn composed for Aten contained many passages that are echoed in the Old Testament Book of Psalms. One passages reads: "The earth grows bright when you arise in the horizon, ... the Two Lands [Egypt] make festival. Awakened, they stand at your feet, for you have raised them up. The entire land goes about its work." The psalmist wrote, "The sun ariseth, they gather themselves together, and lay them

> **Figure 24. Religion in Ancient Egypt & West Africa**
>
> Egyptologist E. A. Wallis Budge identified many similarities in religious ideas and practices:
>
> - dancing as a form of religious expression
> - circumcision
> - the ascension of rulers to divinity after death
> - elaborate burial ceremonies for rulers, who were expected to provide protection for the community from their place in the hereafter
> - a tradition of second burial for bones after the decay of the flesh
> - attachment of pygmies to the courts of rulers
> - wearing of amulets as protection from evil but never as objects of worship
> - ritual cannibalism (until Osiris priest ordered its end in ancient Egypt)
> - the concept of God as jealous and demanding of respect
> - providing beds for the "souls" of the dead
> - the view of a person's blood as synonymous with his/her life-force
> - the association of beetles and frogs with fertility, renewal and even reincarnation.
> - sacrifices to the ancestors who were thought to consume the energy of the offerings, not the objects themselves
> - atonement for sins by offering gifts and sacrifices to God, not mere prayers or petitions for grace
>
>

down in their dens. Man goeth forth unto his work and to his labour until the evening."[23]

Akhanaten's new religion was largely ignored by the masses. His death in 1367 BC led to a religious counter-revolution: His buildings were destroyed, his name erased from monuments and his reforms cancelled. Within two generations, the old local traditions were flourishing with state funding.[24]

African religious ideas and rituals, whether as practiced in ancient Egypt or the rest of continent, are regularly presented as the opposite of Western religions. In truth, Africa was the womb that nurtured the Abrahamic religions, beginning with Judaism.

In the earliest days of Judaism, the Israelites were shepherds who saw their way of life as morally superior to farming. That view is documented in the story of brothers Cain and Abel in the Book of Genesis. Cain, the one murdered by his brother, was an innocent shepherd. In contrast, Abel's descendants were associated with farming, musical instruments, iron smelting and city life.[25]

The influence of Nile civilization on Judaism dates at least to 1413 BC, approximately the time when Joseph was sold into Egyptian slavery by his brothers. In the search for Joseph, Jacob directed Judah to Goshen, which is given as "Pethum" in early non-English versions of Genesis, XLVI. Ties between Judea and Egypt — then the dominant Mediterranean power — deepened during the days of King Solomon.[26]

During Solomon's reign, Israel's link to Africa expanded beyond Egypt. As is well known, Queen Makeda of Ethiopia (widely called the Queen of Sheba) journeyed to Jerusalem, drawn by the king's legendary wisdom. According to Ethiopian traditions, Makeda and Solomon had an affair, which produced a son, Menelik. During a subsequent visit to Jerusalem, the son reportedly spirited the Ark of the Covenant away to a secret location in the Ethiopian Highlands.[27]

After Solomon's death, the Israelites split into two, and the Southern Kingdom formed an alliance with Egypt. During this period of disunity, King Sargon of Mesopotamia invaded. Between 722 and 715 BC, he deported almost 30,000 Jews and replaced them with people from elsewhere in the region. Due to Sargon's actions, people began referring to "the Lost Tribes of Israel," and the Kingdom of Israel disappeared from history.[28]

The story of Moses and the Jewish exodus from the land of pharaohs is well known. As recounted in Exodus, XII, 51, "And it came to pass the selfsame day, that the Lord did bring the children of Israel out of the land of Egypt by their armies." Archeologists have traced their point of departure to Pethum, a fortified military granary built during the reign of Rameses II (1300-1250 BC). And scholars have dated the exodus to approximately 1336 B.C.[29]

An interesting story about Moses is not including in the Old Testament, but is recounted in the Talmud, the collection of Jewish laws and legends compiled in the early centuries AD. According to the Talmud, Moses once lived in Ethiopia, where he fought gallantly for the king against a usurper. When the king died, Moses was appointed to the throne and married the widowed queen.[30]

The book of Job reveals an intimate familiarity with Egyptian civilization, as evident in the claim that earthly kings and counsellors had built monuments to themselves in the desert. In the Hebrew version, the book describes spiritual beings in the form of humans "who are born beneath the waters, and are the inhabitants thereof." This belief is common in West Africa, notably among the Bassa, among whom these creatures are called *Neegee*.[31]

Moses brought into Judaism the monotheism of Akenaten with the distinction between true and false religion.[32] Like Akenaten, Moses claimed God had commanded him to found a new religion. Just as Akhenaten alone spoke to Aten, Moses alone spoke to Yahweh.[33]

Regarding morality, historian Richard A. Gabriel noted, the Mosaic Code, enshrined in the Ten Commandments, is "not ethics in the proper sense of the term insofar as it removes from the individual any need or requirement to freely decide how to behave by reasoning through the connection between precept and circumstances in which the ethical precept must be applied." The Commandments are "absolute, unconditional, and categorical."[34]

> ### Figure 25. Ancient Egypt & the Old Testament
>
> Unitarian reverend and Egyptologist Samuel Sharpe traced the following elements in the Old Testament to ancient Egyptian religion:
>
> - the Almighty forming the world by dividing the land from the water (Genesis, I, 9)
> - the Garden of Eden that was watered without rain, an apparent reference to the Nile (Genesis, II, 5-10)
> - the Serpent that tempted Eve and the later holy war against it (Genesis, III, 1-15)
> - the Cherubims with drawn sword standing east of Eden (Genesis, III, 24)
> - the breastplate of the Jewish high priest (Exodus XXVIII, 16)
> - the staff topped by a brazen Serpent made by Moses was a replica of the Pharoah's symbol of authority (II Kings, 18: 3-4)
> - the brazen Serpent that the people of Jerusalem maintained until the time of Hezekiah (2 Kings XVIII, 4)
> - the calves worshipped at Dan and Bethel (1 Kings XII, 28)
> - divination cups, as used by Joseph (Genesis, XLIV, 5)
> -
>
>

One fundamental African religious belief was not borrowed by Judaism: life after death.[35] The afterlife has long been a central focus of African cosmology, as can be seen in the mummies and pyramids of ancient Egypt. Underlying those monuments were very elaborate ideas about what happens to people after death.[36]

As in the way of the ancestors, Egyptians believed that several non-material things inhabit the body. These non-physical aspects of a person included the *sahu*, the *ka*, the *ba*, the *khaibit*, the *khi* and the *sekhem*.[37]

When a person died, their community conducted prayers and ceremonies to change the body into a non-physical copy called a *sahu*. This "lasting and incorruptible" copy could join God. But, such a change was only possible for people who were righteous.[38]

The *ka* could be translated as "life-force." It combines what English-speakers call a person's "conscience" and "character." In the Coptic language (which descended from ancient Egyptian), it is synonymous with "image, genius, double, character, disposition and mental attributes." The *ka* lived in the heart while a person is alive, but it was liberated at death to move freely on earth and to join God." After death, it derived sustenance from the "life-force" of sacrifices and offerings made by the community, like the *ba* and *khaibit*.[39]

The *ba* is best translated as the "sublime" or the "noble" part of a person, but English-speakers often simplify it as "heart-soul" or "double." It was depicted as a bird with a human head. If properly fed by the descendants of the deceased, it would live forever. Immediately after death, it returned to converse with the body, but it ultimately joined God in the afterlife.[40]

The *khaibit* was the "shade" or "shadow" of a person. It had the ability to detach from the body and travel freely. The *khu* has often been translated as "shining one," "glorious," and "intelligence." It is eternal and joins God immediately after the body's death.

The *sekhem* can be translated as "vital part." It is synonymous with a person's real name or true identity, which often was not known to others. According to ancient Egyptians, all of these non-physical parts of a person joined to form his or her Osiris in the afterlife.[41]

Figure 26. Ouroboros, Egyptian symbol of infinity

The snake swallowing its tale also appears in West African art.

The Egyptian conception of time was strikingly similar to the traditional view of time in West Africa. For Egyptians, time was cyclical. This conclusion was deduced from the alternating seasons, the annual flooding of the Nile and the recurring patterns made by stars in the heavens. Their cyclical concept was represented by Ouroboros, a snake shown swallowing its own tail. This symbol of infinity is present in many West African cultures.[42]

As among West Africans, Egyptians treated illness using psychological suggestion, mixed with spells, prayers and charms, as well as cures derived from minerals, plants and animals.[43]

Long after Akenaten's religious revolution was reversed in Egypt, its legacy lingers in Judaism, Christianity and Islam. Centuries after Akenaten's passing these religions – especially the last two – would have their own very different impact on Egypt and the rest of Africa.

The Mediterranean World

West Africa regularly drew traders from throughout the Mediterranean world, the Middle East and even Asia. As powerful governments emerged along the Mediterranean, each sought to capture the valuable West African trade. Some succeeded by seizing key northern ports or occupying the northern section of the region. But the Sahara repeatedly blocked them from penetrating farther.[44]
As early as 1,500 BC, the North African trade attracted a mysterious groups of settlers from outside. No one knows where they originated or what they called themselves. The Greeks called them Garamantes, the name they are now known by. They moved from the coast into the Sahara, where they built a creative watering system. Using this system, they were able to farm in the desert for centuries.

The Garamantes also built a trade network that dominated the eastern half of Sahara. They sold Mediterranean goods south in exchange for salt, gold, gems and slaves.[45]

The first recorded incursion into northern West Africa was by Phoenicians. Based in present-day Lebanon and Syria, they dominated sailing and trading along the Mediterranean. By 600 BC, they firmly controlled North Africa.

Phoenicians planted a string of small trading colonies along the North African coast. These included Utica, Leptis Magna (Lebda), Lixus in Morocco, Mogador, Cap Bon in Tunisia, and, most notably, Carthage (from the Phoenician "*Kart Hadasht*, meaning "New City").
Phoenician trade towns in North Africa signaled a new phase in Mediterranean trade.[46] In the past, prices had been set mainly by the more or less organic give and take between individual traders and buyers. In its place, the Phoenicians created something akin to a modern multinational corporation with price-fixing ability based on control over the entire distribution process.

Carthage emerged as a formidable power based on the Phoenician's dominance of the sea route to Spain and the desert route to the Sahara. It's imports from south of the Sahara included textile, slaves and gold, which were exchanged for cheap foreign manufactured goods. Fattened by this trade, the city grew to 400,000

Egypt and Religions of the Book

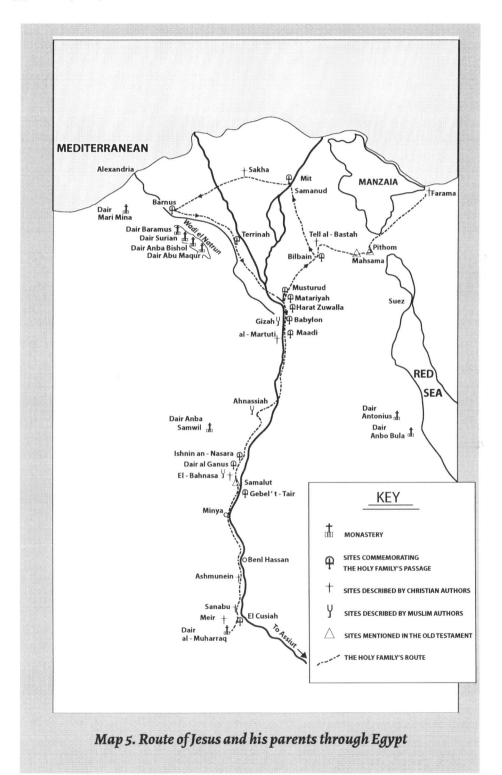

Map 5. Route of Jesus and his parents through Egypt

residents, including mercenary troops from Mauritania, Morocco and Algeria.[47] The Phoenicians would be followed by other foreign powers, attracted by the region's wealth and strategic importance.

Between 336 and 272 BC, Alexander the Greek created an empire that encompassed the once mighty kingdoms of Egypt and Persia and extended as far east as India. But, Phoenician North Africa managed to remain outside his orbit. Another formidable military power in the western Mediterranean, centered in Rome, had also maintained its independence.

After Alexander's death in 272 BC, his empire fractured. The Romans stepped into the power vacuum and seized the Mediterranean section of Alexander's former empire bit by bit. In 146 BC, they sacked Carthage and took control of what had been Phoenician North Africa.[48] From then, Rome was sustained by wheat from Egypt and the rest of North Africa.[49]

Lost Tribes of Israel?

West Africa's growing wealth and renown soon attracted a diverse mix of foreign traders and thrill-seekers. That group included a smattering of Jews, mainly merchants and artisans. Although few in number, they arrived cloaked in romance and legend, given their "religion of the book."[50]

After Egypt, Ethiopia was the second place in Africa that received large numbers of Jews. According to the *Kebra Nagast*, a book chronicling the history of Ethiopian rulers, Menelik I was the son of Jewish King Solomon (reign 970 to 931 BC), conceived while his mother, the legendary Queen of Sheba, was visiting Jerusalem. Her visit spurred some Jews to settle in Ethiopia, where they were called Falasha.[51]

By 100 A. D., Jews were in other parts of Africa, according to reports by Roman historian Tacitus and such Arab writers as Ali al-Mas'udi

Figure 27. Egyptian religion & the New Testament

Several doctrines of ancient Egyptian religion have parallels in modern Christianity. These include the Trinity of God, atonement through suffering, and the twoness of Christ.

The first of these holds that God is made up of three persons who created and govern the world.

The second insists that winning the favor of God requires a sacrifice of blood, which was fulfilled by four divine mediators (in Egyptian religion) or Christ (in the context of Christianity).

The third asserts that God once lived on earth in human form before ascending *back to heaven.*

(896-956), Abu al-Hasan Ali ibn al-Husayn ibn Ahmal al-Biruni (73-1048) and Muhammad al-Idrisi (1099-1165 or 1160).[52]

When did Jews arrive in West Africa, from where and why?

These questions gave rise to wild rumors and speculation. Some said they came from Crete, others said Egypt, but the most popular home cited was Ethiopia.

Jewish artisans and merchants involved in the West African trade maintained an outpost at Tafilalt in the Moroccan desert until 1050 A. D., when they were expelled.[53] In *Description of Africa*, written 1528-1529, Arab historian and geographer Leo Africanus reported seeing several individual Jews throughout the Mali empire. He also reported the presence of a warrior ethnic group in the Atlas Mountain that claimed descent from King David.[54]

Regional oral traditions abound with claims of ties to Jews, fueled in part by two elements from the Old Testament. Often cited as "proof" are similarities between ancient Jewish customs and some in West Africa, including circumcision, purification rituals, burnt offerings and blood sacrifices.

Early Jewish residents of West Africa left Hebrew inscriptions across the desert, especially on graves. These gave rise to a legend that the Berber, Tuareg and other North Africans were "lost tribes of Israel." According to the Book of Exodus, Jews initially belonged to 12 tribes, each descended from a son of the patriarch Jacob. Several of the northern tribes scattered from their homeland after 721 B.C.[55]

But, the idea that a few, far outnumbered, Jews would have impacted widely scattered cultures through the region seems implausible. A more logical explanation is often overlooked: That Jewish culture absorbed African elements during the centuries-long sojourn of the Hebrews in Egypt.

Judaism cast the Israelites as the chosen people of Yahweh, the one true God, but Jews showed little interest in converting Africans, whether through persuasion or force.[56] That would not be the case with other major religions that followed.

Christianity's Refuge in North Africa

When Christianity arrived in Egypt around 30 BC, Ancient Egyptian religion was alive and well throughout the Mediterranean world. Central to the religion were Orisis, his wife Isis and their son Horus. From 700 BC, Egyptian worship came to focus on Isis.[57]

After Rome incorporated Egypt as a province, some people throughout the empire adopted Egyptian religion. Its age gave it prestige. Shrines to Iris were erected, not just in Italy, but as far away as Spain and Gaul (now France).[58]

Many adherents to Egyptian religion found Christianity appealing for two reasons: First, there were many references to Egypt throughout the Bible, suggesting it had a special place in God's design: The Israelites, including Abraham, had sheltered there; Joseph had served as the Pharaoh's minister; and Moses had "trained in all the wisdom of the Egyptians."[59]

More important still, Egypt had given refuge to the baby Jesus and his parents from persecution by Herod, king of Judea.[60]

In addition, adherents to Egyptian religion heard echoes of Osiris, Isis and Horus in the Biblical story of God the Father, Mary and Jesus.[61] As people who previously venerated Isis became Christians, many of them brought statutes of her holding Horus into the churches to represent Mary and the infant Jesus.[62] Some of these statutes came be called "Black Madonnas" because Isis was often portrayed with dark skin.

Figure 28. The Islamic calendar

"The Muslim year is divided into twelve lunar months of 29 or 30 days The each. year is approximately 354 days long, that is, ten or eleven days shorter than a solar year. Consequently, dates of the Islamic calendar have no fixed relationship either to dates of the Gregorian (Western) calendar or to seasons of the year."

"The base-year of the Islamic calendar is 622 A. D., when the Prophet Muhammad and his followers made the *hijra*, or 'migration,' from Mecca to Medina."

Egypt was the first country to convert *en masse* to Christianity.[63] The man who brought the new religion to Egypt was perfect for the job; he was both a native North African and a former close associate of Jesus.

The apostle Mark (also called John Mark) was born in Cyrene to Jewish parents. His family moved to Palestine just as Jesus was beginning his ministry.[64]

Mark's mother opened her home to Jesus and his disciples for daily prayers. According to Acts, 1: 1-47, the Holy Spirit visited the disciples here after Jesus had ascended into heaven.[65]

Mark preached at Alexandria between 43 and 48 AD before moving to Rome, the capital of the empire. In 64 AD, the apostle Peter was killed in Rome, and Mark returned to Alexandria to revise his Gospel. He was lynched there about four years later.[66] Christians often depict St. Mark with a lion in the desert, to reflect his link to North Africa.

Thanks to the foundation laid by Mark, Christianity spread from Alexandria across North Africa. It was implanted in the Sahara before putting down roots in either Greece or Rome. When the new religion was being persecuted by the imperial powers of the Mediterranean, it found refuge among the Egyptians, Berbers, Libyans and Numidians.[67]

When Christians arrived in North Africa, they first focused on converting

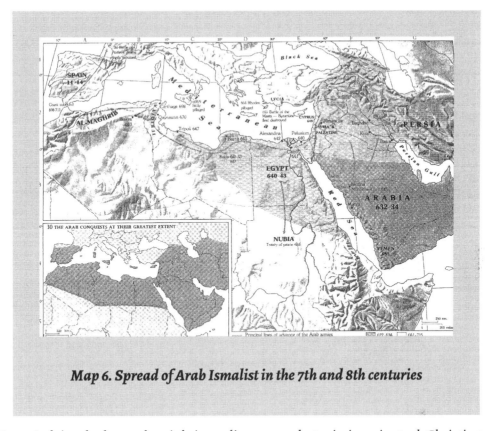

Map 6. Spread of Arab Ismalist in the 7th and 8th centuries

Jews. Judaism had stayed mainly in trading towns, but missionaries took Christianity into the countryside.[68]

Several North Africans played key roles in developing early Christianity.

St. Anthony, an Egyptian, was the first Christian to isolate himself in the Sahara for prayer and meditation. From his home in Alexandria, he moved sixty miles west to Nitra (present-day Wdi Natrun), where he stayed for 13 years.[69]

Another was Tertullian (160-c. 220 AD), a Berber from Tunisia. His contributions to Christianity include such central ideas as the trinity (three persons in one God), the twoness of Christ (human and divine) and the division of scripture into two testaments, old and new.[70]

The best remembered is undoubtedly St. Augustine (354-430 AD), a Numidian Berber from Algeria. He was ordained against his will but on the insistence of the church in Hippo. Within 10 years, he was elevated to bishop.[71]

His most popular book, *The Confessions*, is often cited as the first modern autobiography. He wrote over 100 works, including sermons and Biblical commentaries. His ideas dominated Christian Europe for over 1,000 years.[72]

During the first 400 years of Christianity, Alexandria was its seat. This was evident in 431 AD, when church leaders from various countries gathered at Ephesus.

The pope of Alexandria was able to impose Egyptian interpretations of key doctrines, with backing from the bishops of Asia.[73]

Egyptian contributions to early Christianity included using monks to spread the gospel, giving Mary the title of "Mother of God, and calling church leaders "father" (reflected in the Catholic use of pope, which means "papa").[74] Egyptian church leaders passed office from uncle to nephew, in keeping with a widespread African tradition.[75]

Egyptian missionaries were responsible for spreading Christianity to Nubia and Axum (then Ethiopia), where it was quickly adopted and remained entrenched for centuries. After Egypt, Ethiopia was the second country in the world to adopt Christianity *en masse*.[76] Christians based in Rome and Constantinople would later use the political power of their empires to marginalize the Coptic churches of Egypt and Ethiopia.

Islam - Habash to Sūdan

Of the three "religions of the book," Islam would have the biggest influence in West Africa.

As with Christianity, Islam, too, first found refuge in Africa from persecution elsewhere. Facing attacks from Arab non-believers, the Prophet Muhammad advised some of his followers to seek haven in Ethiopia, which he regarded as "friendly."

As expected, they were received kindly, in keeping with a prevailing African standard of hospitality. More than etiquette, it had the force of law and religious obligation. It imposed mutual obligations on host societies and visitors.

One of the refugees, who later married the Prophet, reported, "When we reached Abyssinia the Negus [the king] gave us a kind reception. We safely practiced our religion, and we worshipped God, and suffered no wrong in word or deed."[77]

In addition, several early Muslim leaders were descendants of Africa.

The Caliph 'Umar had an Ethiopian grandmother. So did 'Amr ibn al-'As, an architect of the Arab empire and the conqueror of Egypt. The most famous was Bilal ibn Rabah, Islam's first muezzin, the person who calls Muslims to prayer.[78]

The Prophet Muhammad died in 632 AD, and within four years, Islam had spread Saudi Arabia to Syria, Lebanon and Palestine. In 638 AD, Arab crusaders crossed the Gaza Strip into Egypt.

Egyptian Christians and their allies offered little resistance because they were divided over interpretations of their faith. Egypt surrendered within six years.[79] After Egypt was conquered, it was ruled mainly from Damascus or Baghdad.[80]

As Christianity had done, Islam spread from Egypt to North Africa.[81]

Egypt and Religions of the Book

Within three years, Arabs had conquered North Africa and planted a military capital in Tunisia, then known as Ifriqiya. Their army kept expanding by converting and absorbing conquered people.[82]

The rest of North Africa did not fall as quickly as Egypt. The most serious resistance was actually led by a mysterious woman named al-Kahina. Some claimed she was a Jew; others, a Christian; still others, a witch. Although outnumbered and out gunned, she inspired other Berber to resist. Fighting continued until 1200 AD.[83]

By 800 AD, Arabs controlled North Africa, from the Red Sea to the Atlantic. Their territory stretched about 150 miles from the Mediterranean Sea toward the Sahara.[84]

At first, the new rulers extended protections to Christians that were denied adherents to the way of the ancestors. But, those protections were removed over time. As a result, Christianity was nearly erased from North Africa, outside of Egypt.[85]

Unlike the Phoenicians and Romans, the Arab invaders totally changed the North African cultural landscape. They viewed Islam as inseparable from Arab culture, so they also imposed their language and lifestyle.[86]

As Arab crusaders spread across North Africa and the Mediterranean, they carried several Asian crops, including plantain, mango, eggplant, citrus fruits and sugar cane.[87]

The Arab conquests created something new in the world. It forged a *caliph* or world government that stretched from Spain through North Africa, down the East African coast, and across to China. No empires had covered that much of the world. And none had imposed one religion throughout its territory.

It also created a world economy centered around key cities in the Arabia, like Baghdad and Cairo. Historian Fernand Braudel identified several rules that govern the behavior of a world economy: It has three zones — a developed core, a somewhat developed middle, and a large undeveloped periphery. It has "an urban center of gravity, a city." Concentrated in the city are power, population and prosperity. In contrast, the periphery is an area of very little economic activity.[88]

Even more, Islam required every adult Muslim to visit holy sites in Saudi Arabia at least once. This pilgrimage, known as the *hajj*, helped bind Muslims of diverse backgrounds — Africans, Europeans, Indians and Chinese.[89]

Arabs mainly used two words to refer to Africans: *Habash* and *Sūdan*. Habash was derived from *Habashat*, the section of Ethiopia that gave refuge to the Prophet Muhammad's followers. The term is generally applied to Ethiopians and their immediate neighbors. Sūdan means "black" in Arabic. It was applied to West Africans and the people living above Egypt, as well as to their lands.[90]

Once neutral in meaning, both words took on negative associations as Arabs brought more and more Africans as slaves to live in their midst.[91]

Negative images of Africans began circulating among Arabs by 700 AD. Around that time, *The Thousand and One Nights* was translated from Persian into Arabic. The stories featured blacks frequently as slaves, cooks, porters and other servile roles. In one especially vile story, a Persian king returns home unexpectedly and meets his wife in bed with a black slave. He promptly runs a sword through both.[92]

Most Arab geographers depicted Africans as primitives — nude, pagan cannibals. One of the most enlightened, Ibn Khaldun, wrote that blacks are the "only humans who are closer to dumb animals than to rational beings." They recorded few details on West African life. They focused instead on trade routes and goods. Their lack of interest stemmed in part from an assumption of African religious inferiority.[93]

---

1. Frazer, 1914, p. 161; Reid, 2003, p. 69.

2. Budge, 1904, p. 2.

3. Ernest Alfred Wallis Budge, *Osiris and the Egyptian Resurrection* (New York: G. P. Putnam's Sons, 1861), pp. xvii, 17, 30; S. O. Y. Keita and A. J. Boyce, "The geographical origins and population relationships of early ancient Egyptians" (pp. 23-24), in Theodore Colenko (compiler), *Egypt in Africa*, pp. 25-27 (Indianapolis: Indianapolis Museum of Art and Indiana University Press, 1996.

4. Budge, 1861, p. 22; also Frankfort, 1948, p. 70; Wengrow, 2003; O'Connor and Reid, 2003, p. 11,18, 21.

5. e.g., Sergio Donadoni, "Remarks about Egyptian connections of the Sahara Rock Sherlter art," in L. P. Garcia and E. R. Perello (eds.), *Prehistoric Art of the Western Mediterranean and the Sahara*, pp. 185-90 (Hawthorne, NY: Aldire, 1964; Christopher Ehert, "Ancient Egyptian as an African language, Egypt as an African culture," in Theodore Colenko (compiler), *Egypt in Africa*, pp. 25-27 (Indianapolis: Indianapolis Museum of Art and Indiana University Press, 1996; and Henri Franfort, *The Birth of Civilization in the Near East* (Garden City, NY: Doubleday, 1956), pp. 39-40.

6. Basil Davidson, *The Lost Cities of Africa* (Boston: Atlantic-Little, Brown and Company, 1970), p. 63.

7. Thurston Shaw, "Changes in African archaeology in the last forty years" (pp. 156-168), in Christopher Fyfe, ed., *African Studies Since 1945: A Tribute to Basil Davidson* (London: Longman, 1976), p. 392; Shomaka O. Y. Keita, "Royal incest and diffusion in Africa," *American Ethnologist*, Vol. 8, No. 2 (May 1981): 392-393. Keita has argued, "The most parsimonious explanation for cultural similarities between various African societies, through time and space, is that they shared common-root cultural elements and were 'preadapted' and predisposed to similar ethos and institutions that were evolving in parallel fashion. Egypt's neolithic womb was African."

8. Mohamed Sahnouni, "Saharan rock art" (pp. 28-30), in Theodore Colenko (compiler), *Egypt in Africa*, pp. 25-27 (Indianapolis: Indianapolis Museum of Art and Indiana University Press, 1996; F. Mori, "Some aspects of the rock art of the Acaces (Fessan Sahara) and data concerning it" (pp. 225-252), in L. P. Garcia and E. R. Perello, eds., *Prehistoric Art of the Western Mediterranean and the Sahara* (Hawthorne, NY: Aldine, 1964), pp. 243-244; Colin Flight, "A survey of recent results in the radiocarbon dating chronology of Northern and Western Africa, *Journal of African History*, 14: 531-554; Donadoni, 1964, pp. 185-188; UNESCO, "The peopling of Ancient Egypt and the deciphering of the Merotic script," UNESCO Document SHC-73/Conf. 812/4 (Paris: UNESCO, 1974).

9. Geraldine Pinch, *Egyptian Mythology: A Guide to the Gods, Goddesses, and Traditions of Ancient Egypt* (New York: Oxford University Press, 2002), pp. 9, 13, 26; Frankfort, 1948, p. 59; Budge, 1969.

10. Frankfort, 1948, p. 23.

11. Budge, 1861, pp. xviv-xxvi.

12. Budge, 1861, pp. 17.

13. Budge, 1861, p. 378; compare to the concept of the divinity among Liberian ethnic groups in Schwab, 1947, pp. 315-319.

14. Budge, 1861, pp. xv, 390.

15. Budge, 1861, pp. 320, 322, 324.

16. Budge, 1861, pp. xix, 17, 22, 30.

17. Budge, 1861, pp. xii-xxiii.

18. Budge, 1861, pp. 318, 340; see Schwab, 1947, pp. 327-331, for concepts of the afterlife among Liberian ethnic groups that echo ancient Egyptian ideas, including judgment by God's messenger (Loma, Sapo) and crossing a big water (Loma, Bandi, Kpelle, Sapo, Glebo).

19. Gabriel, 2002, p. 86; Maulana Karenga, *Maat: The Moral Ideal in Ancient Egypt* (Los Angeles: University of Sankore Press, 2006).

20. Frankfort, 1948, p. 107.

21. Gabriel, 2002, p. 87; Frankfort, 1948, p. 117.

22. Rosalie David, *Religion and Magic in Ancient Egypt* (London: Penguin, 2002), pp. 212-223; Lionel Casson, *Everyday Life in Ancient Egypt* (Baltimore: Johns Hopkins University Press, 2001), pp. 100-113.

23. David, 2002, pp. 228-229; Psalm, 104: 22-23.

24. David, 2002, pp. 238, 393; Ahmed Osman, *Moses and Akhenaten: The Secret History of Egypt at the Time of the Exodus* (Rochester, Vermont: Bear & Company, 2002), p. 67.

25. Drake, 1998, p. 169. For the existence of a herding way of life in the ancient world, from the Sahara through Iran and Turkestan into Mongolia, see Wolf, 1982, p. 25. The view that the Old Testament presents a shepherd way of life as heroic and morally superior to the life of farmers is from Yoram Hazony, *The Philosophy of the Hebrew Scripture* (Cambridge: Cambridge University Press, 2012).

26. Samuel Sharpe, *Egyptian Mythology and Egyptian Christianity, with Their Influence on the Opinions of Modern Christianity* (London: Carter & Col, 1896), pp. 31; Job, III, 14; Egypt Exploration Fund, 1894, p 7; Osman, 2002, p. 105; Drake, 1998, p. 228.

27. Drake, 1998, p. 232; Tudor Parfitt, *The Lost Ark of the Covenant: Solving the 2,500 Year Old Mystery of the Fabled Biblical Ark* (New York: HarperCollins, 2008); E. A. Wallis Budge, *The Kebra Nagast: The Queen of Sheba and Her Only Son Menyelek* (Oxford: Oxford University Press, 1922).

28. Drake, 1998, pp. 233, 236-237.

29. Egypt Exploration Fund, 1894, p. 7; Osman, 2002, p. 105.

30. Osman, 2002, pp. 22-23.

31. Sharpe, 1896, p. 71; Job, III, 14; Job, XXVI, 5;

32. Richard A. Gabriel, *Gods of Our Fathers: The Memory of Egypt in Judaism and Christianity* (Westport, Conn.: Greenwood, 2002, p. 89.

33. Gabriel, 2002, p. 92.

34. Gabriel, 2002, p. 86.

35. Sharpe, 1896, p. 57.

36. Cannuger, 2001, p. 12.

37. Ernest Alfred Wallis Budge, *The Book of the Dead* (New York: Bell Publishing Company, 1960), pp. 70-71; compare to concepts of the "soul" among Liberian ethnic groups in Schwab, 1947, pp. 320-327.

38. Budge, 1960, pp. 70-71.

39. Budge, 1960, pp. 74-75, 78-79.

40. Budge, 1960, pp. 76-78.

41. Budge, 1960, pp. 78-82.

42. Pinch, 2002, pp. 57, 90; Frankfort, 1948, pp. viii, 13.

43. Lionel Casson, *Everyday Life in Ancient Egypt* (Baltimore: Johns Hopkins University Press, 2001), p. 62.

44. Gearon, 2011, p. 39; John Obert Voll, "The Middle East in world history" (pp. 437-454), in Jerry H. Bentley, ed., *The Oxford Handbook of World History* (Oxford: Oxford University Press, 2013), p. 438; David Abulafia, "Mediterranean history" (pp. 493-507), in Jerry H. Bentley, ed., *The Oxford Handbook of World History* (Oxford: Oxford University Press, 2013), p. 493. Following Abulafia, the Mediterranean is defined here as "That sea, the islands within it, and the lands that border it," especially "those areas where daily life is bound up in some way with the Mediterranean Sea."

45. Gearon, 2011, pp. 41-42.

46. Abulafia, 2013, p. 501. As noted by Abulafia, these towns were not *colonies* (with control from a distance), but daughter settlements.

47. B. H. Warmington, "The Carthaginian period" (pp. 441-464), in G. Makhtor, ed., *UNESCO General History of Africa II: Ancient Civilizations of Africa* (Berkeley: University of California Press, 1981).
48. A. Mahjoubi, "The Roman and post-Roman period in North Africa" (pp. 465-510), in G. Makhtor, ed., *UNESCO General History of Africa II: Ancient Civilizations* (Berkeley: University of California Press, 1981).
49. Abulafia, 2013, p. 502.
50. I use the terms Judaism, Christianity and Islam to describe these religions as they were *practiced*, not as prescribed in their respective scriptures.
51. Tudor Parfitt, *Black Jews in Africa and the Americas* (Cambridge: Harvard University Press, 2013), pp. 13-18; Jacob S. Dorman, *Chosen People: The Rise of American Black Israelite Religion* (Oxford: Oxford University Press, 2013, p.136.
52. Parfitt, 2013, pp. 13-18, 22-23; Dorman, 2013, p. 56.
53. Parfitt, 2013, pp. 21; Dorman, 2013, pp. 56.
54. Parfitt, 2013, pp. 22-23; Leo Africanus, *The History and Description of Africa*. Book I (London: Haklut Society, 1896), pp. 202, Edward William Bovill, *The Golden Trade of the Moors* (Princeton: Markus Wiener Publishers, 2008), pp. 49-50.
55. Parfitt, 2013, pp. 36-49; Dorman, 2013, pp. 56-57; e.g., Olaudah Equiano, *Interesting Narrative of the Life of Olaudah Equiano, or Gustavus Vassa, the African* (London: by the author, 1789), pp. 19-21; Gearon, 2011, p. 50.
56. Gearon, 2011, p. 50.
57. Cannuger, 2001, p. 13.
58. Drake, 1998, p. 171; Casson, 2001, p. 89.
59. Acts, 7:22.
60. Isaiah, 19:21; Matthew, 2: 13-20; Cannuger, 2001, p. 15.
61. Cannuger, 2001, p. 14.
62. Cannuger, 2001, p. 14; Frank J. Yurco, "Mother and child imagery in Egypt and its influence on Christianity" (pp. 43-45), in Theodore Colenko (compiler), *Egypt in Africa*, pp. 25-27 (Indianapolis: Indianapolis Museum of Art and Indiana University Press, 1996.
63. King, 1986, p. 75.
64. Cannuger, 2001, p. 114.
65. Cannuger, 2001, p. 114.
66. Cannuger, 2001, p. 16.
67. Gearon, 2011, p. 52.
68. Gearon, 2011, p. 50.
69. Gearon, 2011, pp. 52-53.
70. Gearon, 2011, p. 51.
71. Gearon, 2011, p 51-52.
72. Gearon, 2011, p. 52.

73. King, 1986, p. 76.
74. King, 1986, pp. 76-78; Cannuger, 2001, p. 118.
75. King, 1986, p. 76.
76. King, 1986, p. 77; Drake, 1998, p. 295.
77. Azumah, 2001, p. 39.
78. Lewis, 1990, p. 25.
79. Azumah, 2001, p. 25; Gearson, 2011, p. 58; Azumah, 2001, p. 25.
80. Pinch, 2002, p. 46.
81. King, 1986, p. 83.
82. Lewis, 1990, p. 62; Gearon, 2011, p. 57.
83. Gearon, 2011, p. 60; Azumah, 2001, p. 25.
84. Hunwick, 2006, pp. 53-55; King, 1986, p. 86.
85. Gearon, 2011, pp. 58, 61.
86. Gearon, 2011, p. 57.
87. Sidney W. Mintz, *Sweetness and Power: The Place of Sugar in Modern History* (New York: Viking, 1985), p. 25
88. Bruadel, Vol. 3, 1984, pp. 21-88, especially pp. 27, 31.
89. Bernard Lewis, *Race and Slavery in the Middle East: An Historical Enquiry* (New York: Oxford University Press, 1990), p. 18.
90. Lewis, 1990, pp. 17, 50; Stuart Munro-Hay, *Ethiopia, the Unknown Land: A Cultural and Historical Guide* (New York: I. B. Tauris, 2002, p. 19.).
91. Lewis, 1990, p. 50; Munro-Hay, 2002, p. 19.
92. Lewis, 1990, p. 52.
93. Masonen, 2000, pp. 189-190, especially 190, n. 134.

Chapter 5
The Rise of Empires

> Who built the seven gates of Thebes?
>
> The books are filled with names of kings.
>
> Was it the kings who hauled the craggy blocks of stone?
>
> — Bertolt Brecht

After 1000 AD, traders from the Sahel began frequent visits to trade towns in the south.[1] According to historian George E. Brooks, trade links between Kru and Southeastern Mande groups in the area of Côte d'Ivoire probably began during the wet period of 700 to 1100 BC.[2] Around this time the narrow horizontal loom used by male weavers to produce cotton cloth spread throughout West Africa, probably by itinerant weavers and traders.[3]

By the 1200s AD, salt, malagueta spice and kola from the area of Liberia were being traded in communities along the Niger River. Malagueta and kola lose their flavor quickly, so fresh shipments had to be sent on a regular basis. The trade was vigorous enough that some spice was reaching Europe by 1214 AD.

West African societies appeared self-contained because they produced their basic necessities. But, even in this early period, they were tied together by trade with distant markets.[4]

At the west end, one trade route ran from Senegal through southern Mauritania to Sijilmasa in present-day Morocco.

Meanwhile, seafaring groups along the Atlantic ferried goods to the mouths of navigable rivers.[5]

A central route went from Kwakaw up to Tahart in Algeria.

In the east, a track connected Lake Chad located between Niger, Nigeria, Chad and Cameroon to Jabal Nafusa in present-day Libya.

A horizontal route ran from the Niger through the Aïr Mountain to Cairo, Egypt, which was a major stop for Muslim pilgrims *en route* to Mecca.[6]

This network was probably connected to an early route that ran from the mouth of the St. Paul River through Bopolu (both in what is now Liberia) to Musadu (a town in present-day Guinea currently called Beyla), then up to the Niger River.[7]

Long-distance trading throughout West Africa was aided by a well known African standard of hospitality. On the one hand, land-holding groups were expected to provide food, board and security for "strangers." Beneficiaries included hunters, herders, traders, itinerant artists and refugees. In return, visitors were bound to show respect for local traditions, offer presents, pay tariffs, and share profits with local leaders.[8] If they stayed long, they were expected to help with collective work projects.

In West Africa, goods were carried by different means depending on the terrain:

In the forest, groups of 500 to 1,000 merchants and porters were common because there were no beasts of burden.

In the savannah, merchants relied on donkeys and typically travelled together in groups ranging from several hundred to several thousand.

After 600 BC, camel caravans in the Sahara commonly consisted of 3,000 animals, but some exceeded 20,000.

Although caravans travelled up to 621 miles through dangerous terrain, profits of up to seven times the investments were possible.[9]

International Trade

Camels were probably first brought to North Africa in 600 BC, when the Assyrians invaded Egypt. Within 300 years, the animals multiplied and were carried west into the Sahara. By 100 BC, they had replaced the oxen and horses once used to cross the desert.[10]

When it comes to desert travel, camels have several advantages over other pack animals.[11] Camels don't require water often because they rarely break a sweat under 106 degrees F. As a result, they can go 10 days or more without drinking. They can carry 330 lb. — twice as much as oxen. Plus, they don't need carts. Their long legs give them the ability to go farther and faster.[12]

But, camel-keeping remained confined to the desert because the animals are especially prone to African sleeping sickness.[13]

The Arab traders who first crossed the desert using camels were soon joined by Muslim cleric and scholars.

Given the dangers of the desert, camel caravans stuck to a precise and rigid pattern: They set out at late dawn but stopped before noon, as the ground was getting unbearably hot. At this point, people tied the camels, unpacked their loads, and stretched out cloth covers for shade. At sun set, they decamped and marched until midnight. Even a slight shift from this routine could lead to death.[14]

Between c. 700 AD and 1100 AD, West Africa entered a period of greater rainfall than it had experienced in the preceding one thousand years. As a result, rivers and other waterways grew fully, higher and wider. This expansion facilitated long-distance water travel, while supporting an increased stock and variety of seafoods.[15]

The Rise of Empires

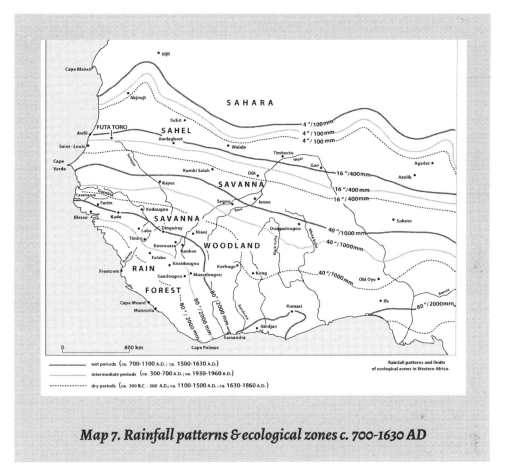

Map 7. Rainfall patterns & ecological zones c. 700-1630 AD

Thanks to increased rains, the forest expanded approximately 310 miles north to claim areas previously held by woodland-savannah, the savannah claimed territory once occupied by the Sahel, which encroached on what was the desert.[16]

One result of the international trade network was the importation of cowry shells from the Indian Ocean, where they functioned as currency. By 1300 AD, cowries were firmly incorporated into local cultures as decoration, currency and tools of divination.

And 300 years later, several supplemental imported foods were available in West Africa, including bananas and plantains from the Indian Ocean, as well as chicken (first domesticated in India).[17]

Other items traded south from Europe and North Africa included one necessity: rock salt. Most were luxury items like brass vessels, glassware, tailored clothes, beads, mirrors, perfumes and paper. More ominous were such implements of war as horses (which arrived around 300 BC), swords and chain mail.[18]

In exchange, Africa sent mainly ivory, gold and slaves. Demand for West African gold and other goods increased dramatically in 632 AD, when Arabs pushed across North Africa into Spain. It expanded again in the 1200s. As early as the 1100s, West African cotton cloth was being sold in Europe. Based apparently on *barinkan*, the Mande word for "garment," this textile came to be known as *barrakan* in Arabic, as well as *barra cana*, *bucaranum* and *boqueranus* in Europe.[19]

Before the Arab invasion, slavery hardly existed in West Africa. The few slaves were usually people convicted of crimes, seized for unpaid debts or captured in battles. A few black slaves were first reported in North Africa around 202 BC, after the Roman conquest.[20]

Slave taking escalated in the 800s AD after Muslims seized Egypt and subdued Nubia. They then signed a *baqt* (meaning "contract") with Nubia requiring delivery of 360 slaves per year. This agreement remained in force for five centuries. It was the first ominous sign of things to come.[21]

In Arabia, some large groups of enslaved black men were used to drain marshes and dig mines. Others were employed on large sugar cane plantations along the Mediterranean.[22]

Sugar cane apparently began its climb to world domination in humble New Guinea. Around 4000 BC, it spread to the Philippines, India and possibly Indonesia. From India, it diffused through Arabia to Europe.[23]

The crop demands a lot more labor than most others. That was especially true during a period when many machines had not been developed to help.[24]

Arabs had pioneered the growing of sugar on plantations in the area of Lebanon. They were joined by Europeans after 1123, when crusaders invaded the region seeking to wrest control of Christian holy sites from Muslims. From the Lebanon area, sugar plantations spread to Cyprus, Sicily, Morocco and Spain. Some were financed by the merchants of Genoa.[25]

Africans on these plantations were far unnumbered by slaves from elsewhere, including Europe. But, it was the start of enslaved Africans being used on European plantations.[26]

Between 700 and 1900 AD, more than nine million West Africans were sold into Mediterranean slavery.[27]

Ibn Battuta saw the hand of God in the enslavement of non-Arabs. Writing about Turkish slaves, he wrote, "loyal helpers, who were brought ... to the House of Islam under the rule of slavery, which hides in itself a divine blessing. By means of slavery, they learn glory and blessing and are exposed to divine providence."[28] This twisted religious justification for the enslavement of others would be echoed 350 years later by Christian theologians in the context of the American slave system.[29]

Prestige, knowledge and some profits from the long-distance trade were channeled into supporting vast administrative and military infrastructures of successive empires in the Sahel, the most celebrated being Ghana (c. 800-1240 AD), Mali (1240-1464 AD) and Songhai (1464-1591 AD).

The first reference to a West African place called "Ghana" in European sources dates to around 1141 AD. Around 1150, for what was apparently the first time, Arab writer al-Zuhri applied the name Janawa to a section of West Africa. That Arabic word was apparently the source of "Guinea," the European name for the coastal part of West Africa.[30]

Their administrative centers and the bulk of military forces were usually located near the gold fields, which supplied a major share of their wealth and prestige.[31]

Merchants in West Africa were content with leaving expensive and labor-intensive deep-earth mining in the hands of the state. Their profits came from trading the recovered ore.

From the rise of the first of these empires until the European seizure of the Americas, the Sahel was the major supplier of gold to both Europe and the Muslim world.[32] To facilitate large-scale trading, several items functioned as currencies in West Africa. These included sorghum, cowrie shells, gold, salt, strips of cloth, iron bars, copper, silver and kola.[33] But, these served less as all-purpose money and more as units of accounting for measuring the value of one commodity against others.[34]

West African gold laid at the base of the early European currency system. On the one hand, much of the gold imported into Spain by the Almoravids was derived from West African mines. On the other hand, the first Castilian gold coins minted in 1173 copied the Almoravid *dinars*, even to the point of including Arabic inscriptions.[35]

For centuries, West Africa simultaneously dazzled Arab and European traders yet kept them confined to the desert edge. They were drawn by the spectacular rumors of limitless gold. But they were kept at arm's length by local rulers and killer illnesses.[36]

The people of southern European cities, especially traders, held a longstanding interest in West Africa. This is not surprising since both regions were part of a trading circuit centered in the Middle East. The West African trade was so important, people along the Mediterranean began collecting intelligence early that would allow them to draw maps of the region.

A Genoa mapmaker who died around 1330 produced the oldest surviving map of the West African interior. A "Laurentian world map" from about 1351 accurately depicts the shape of Africa. In the 1350s, an anonymous Franciscan friar published a book in Spanish titled *Libro del Conosçimiento* ("Book of the Knowledge of All the World") that indicated knowledge of Madeira and the Azores. Several more detailed maps were produced later in Majorca. Spanish mapmakers very likely derived some of their information from Castilian and Catalan mercenaries who had fought for North African Muslim rulers.[37]

As the Garamantes had in the eastern desert, Mande-speakers dominated trade in West Africa. Linguists estimate that Mande languages began in the Southern Sahara, north of 16° latitude, perhaps even as far as 18°, and between 3° and 12° of Western longitude. Around 300 BC, Mande speakers moved south to the Sahel and developed farming along the Niger.[38]

Mande Speakers along the Niger

The original Mande language probably separated into Northern, Southwestern and Southeastern branches between 1100 and 1500 AD. During this period, West Africa was experiencing a dry period that probably caused people to scatter in search of water and fertile land.[39] As their population grew, their languages splintered further.[40]

The northern Mande speakers split into four major groups based on religion and region, all mutually intelligible. Those at the core of Mali who converted to Islam are known as Malinké. Others who held on to the way of the ancestors for longer are classified by location: Soso in Senegambia, Guinea and Sierra Leone, Soninké in the Upper Niger, Upper Guinea and southern Senegambia; and Bambara in the east (the people call themselves "Bamana"). A branch of Mande straddles southern Mali and northeastern Guinea.[41]

Other Mande languages are divided into four branches: the Southern (Dan, Guro, Yaouré, Tura, Ma, Mwan, Wan, Beng, Gban and Gbin); the Eastern (San, Sane, Bisa, Boko, Bokobaru, Busa, Kyanga, and Shanga); the Soso and Jalonke; and the Southwest Mande.[42]

The Mandekan branch of Mande apparently developed around the Bambuk

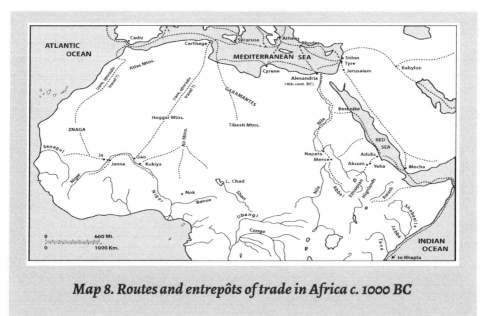

Map 8. Routes and entrepôts of trade in Africa c. 1000 BC

and Bouré goldfields.[43]

Mande merchants were drawn mainly from the Dyula, Jakhanke and Soninké castes of the Malinké group.[44]

Dyula merchants in particular were critical to these exchanges with the forest areas, including Liberia. At considerable risk, they established outposts at Cape Mount, Côte d'Ivoire, and present-day Ghana. Their long-distance trading fueled unprecedented prosperity in their Niger homeland. Over time, some of that wealth was directed towards controlling West African commerce with the Mediterranean world and the Middle East.[45]

The Nile is today the only river running north-south through the Sahara.[46] There once were at least three others.

One started as trickles in the mountains near the border of present-day Sierra Leone, Liberia and Guinea. But, it gained enough force to cut a channel through granite before flowing north pass Timbuctu to empty into the Juf lake near the Taodenni salt mines. Another began in the Ahaggar mountains of North African and flowed south through present-day Nigeria into the Gulf of Guinea.[47]

As the Sahara dried out, however, the northern portions of both rivers evaporated. This caused the river flowing from the Futa Jalon to veer east near Faranah until it was captured by the southern half of the other river.[48]

The people of Mali today call what's left of the north-bound river the Joliba and the southbound fragment of the other one the Quorra.[49]

What began as two separate rivers joined to become the Niger. This 2,600 mile artery runs through the heart of West Africa, linking present-day Guinea, Mali, Niger, Benin and Nigeria.[50]

Around Bamako, the river turns flabby, flat and lazy, meandering into lakes, creeks and marshes. Here, the river is plied by fishing folk called Bozos, who use poisoned spears to hunt hippopotamus. Some anthropologists believe they migrated from the Nile to the Niger 5,000 years ago.[51]

From Timbuctu, the river becomes leaner and meaner for a trek through the desert. After traveling 300 miles east, it veers sharply south toward Gao.[52] Like Timbuctu, this town began as a place where people of the desert and those of the Sahel met to trade.[53]

After Gao, the river zigzags through lush vegetation, its banks lined with lounging hippopotamus, vicious alligators and chattering monkeys.[54] South of Nok, Nigeria, the Benue River empties into the Niger, broadening it up to 10 miles across.[55]

Having coursed along the West African plateau for all its journey so far, the Niger suddenly drops 2,000 feet before cutting through the forest, spilling across the wide delta, then emptying into the Atlantic.[56]

The locations where trade routes intersected, like Jenne, were the homes of the merchants who organized the trade and profited the most. People at the end of the routes also benefited, not just from access to foreign goods, but also from the ideas and information that flowed along with goods.[57]

Clans Change to Castes

At least until 1063 AD, Niger-Congo societies — especially Mande and Atlantic groups— were matrilineal, transmitting office and property through one's mother or the brother of one's mother. A would-be groom was expected to work for his prospective in-laws before marriage and to move into their village thereafter.[58]

Remnants of the earlier pattern linger among the Akan of modern Ghana, whose Queen Mother serves as the fulcrum for the intergenerational transmission of hereditary office.[59]

But, most Niger-Congo communities shifted to patriliny, that is, the transfer of power and goods through one's father. Two factors probably contributed: First, patriarchal Arab influences. Second, reliance on coercion and mainly male warriors for allocating power and property in the empires.

Even in Niger-Congo communities where the change-over seemed more definitive (including parts of Liberia), women continued to hold political office, engage in full-time trading and possess wealth independent of their husbands,[60] unlike women in many parts of Europe and the Middle East.

Initially, Mande speakers organized themselves according to the kinship system, as had the Gola, Kissi, Dei, Klao and other forest groups. That system had assigned political and sacred power to elders from the family that first claimed the land. But, that arrangement had lost its logic in a context where land had suddenly and dramatically lost its value.

Land was no longer the main source of wealth. It was not even necessary for creating wealth. Traders never had to farm to eat; they could just buy all of life's necessities and many foreign luxuries, too.

Large-scale trading shattered what had been a community of more or less equal families, all engaged in farming. In its place a hierarchy was created at least by 1351 A. D., with each family's position based on its specialization.[61]

The leading men, mainly traders, forged ties across the region. Historian Allen M. Howard described the process in Sierra Leone, but it probably applied more broadly. They "arranged kin, marital, political and commercial alliances with their counterparts throughout the region and beyond. young men and women were sent to other households for training or, especially in the case of women, for marriage."[62]

The vast mass of farmers occupied the middle position. Among the Mande, Wolof and Soninké, non-farming families were assigned to castes, rigid occupational groups that transmitted their skills from parents to children. Those castes in-

The Rise of Empires 123

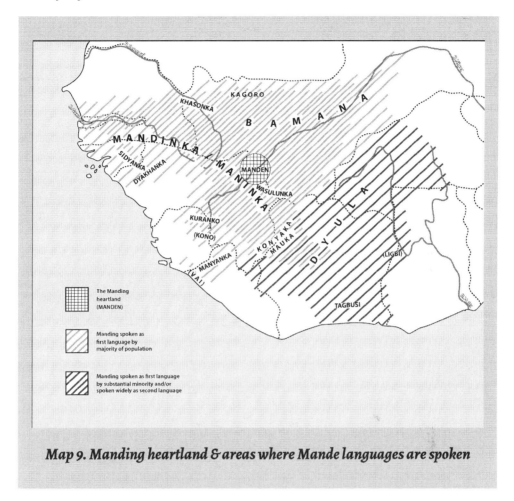

Map 9. Manding heartland & areas where Mande languages are spoken

cluded metal smiths, potters, leatherworkers, iron smelters, and professional entertainers (widely known as griots, who were purveyors of official history.) [63]

Tributary States and Empires

At the top of the pyramid was the ruler with near absolute political power. Of course, traders occupied a position near the top. Like the political ruler, merchants, too, relied on slaves to grow their food, cook and provide other services. Other castes like blacksmiths were near the bottom and barred from marrying outside their group. As a result, members of lower castes became permanent "outsiders."[64]

Atop the splinters of the old system, a new basis was created for assigning political power. It all came down to military might. Force operated at two levels: Within Niger societies, political disputes were increasingly settled using arms.

Power went to the best military strategist and mobilizer. A similar process was unfolding elsewhere, notably in Greece and Rome.

To secure wealth that laid outside, Sahelian societies came to rely on large full-time armies.[65] Force became the basis of a new administrative structure commonly called the tributary state.[66]

But, all tributary states did not operate by the same rules. In many parts of Europe, nobles used the state to seize land from farmers, who then had to work for them. In China and Egypt, farmers were forced to work on large-scale public projects like the Great Wall or the pyramids.[67]

Along the Niger, however, farmers were neither compelled to leave their land nor perform major projects. Instead, the state used its vast army to acquire slaves and wealth from beyond its borders.[68] The horses in military calvary provided significant psychological superiority, a boost in speed of travel, and an increase in distance travelled. The camel conferred advantages in trading over societies relying on human porters.[69]

As in other regions of the world, trade in West Africa was characterized by competition and profit seeking. But, the entrenched cultures and kinship relations of the area muted the dictates of supply and demand. For example, capital remained embedded in families and rarely flowed purely on the basis of opportunity. Traders drew heavily from different ethnic ties. As a result, rivalries between different traders often pitted their ethnic groups in raids, reprisals and outright war.[70]

But, societies in the Sahel went beyond the development of states to become empires. As noted by historian Allen M. Howard, "Some had known boundaries, but in other cases they were spheres of authority and influence that waxed and waned in size, depending on resources, allegiances, and the strength of supporting networks."[71]

Each empire combined many cultures and political units but they shared one economy. The various groups relied on goods and services from the others, although one cultural and political unit received most of the benefits.[72]

The Manding language probably began its spread by serving as a trade language. Trade languages become simplified overtime which would have helped them to spread further.[73] This resulted in a hierarchy. Marginalized groups would use the dominant language to access wider knowledge and privileged channels of communication. As a result, the dominant language would expand at the expense of the others.[74]

What began as ethnic units of several thousand people expanded into nations of millions. This process occurred with Latin in the Roman Empire, Han in China (206 BC-220 AD), Arabic in North Africa (from 600 AD), and Spanish in Latin America (from 1492). In Africa, this process was at work within states linked to Mande, Fulani, Hausa, Yoruba, Amharic, and Bantu.[75]

The Advantages of Writing

Within each Sahelian empire, the rulers enjoyed military and logistical advantages over other groups because of their access to horses and advanced technologies, use of written communication, and knowledge of an international language (Arabic).

Arabic was an international language and it was written. By using Arabic, Sahelian empires could access the world's acquired knowledge in books, keep permanent records and send messages halfway around the world. These were decisive advantages over forest societies. As was the case in ancient Egypt, the introduction of writing qualitatively extended the capacity of the state.[76]

Being able to write in Arabic also gave advantages to Muslim individuals. Some taught Arabic and the Quran to Muslim youth. Their students called them *Karamoko* (from the Arabic *qara'a*, meaning "to read") and treated them with reverence.[77]

Traders often learned enough to keep their books. Clerics served as secretaries to traditional rulers. They also used Arabic script for divining and preparing amulets. Among non-readers in traditional societies, Muslim writers and writing were viewed with awe.[78]

Arab culture had a equally profound impact on trade: It introduced standardized currencies. Its use of weights and measures helped to stabilize rates of exchange.[79]

North African Muslims quickly emerged as major contributors to Islamic thought. They developed two of the leading approaches to Islamic law: the Sahf'ite and the Malikite. These schools trained many of the earliest West African Islamic jurists.[80]

Out of Muslim North Africa emerged two of the world's most renown scholars. One was Muhammad Ibn Battuta of Tangier (1304-1369), who travelled throughout the Islamic world, from Spain to China. After settling back in Morocco, he wrote *Rihla* or *Book of Travels*, an engaging and informative account of his many journeys.[81]

Another was Rahman Ibn Khaldun of Tunis (1332-1406 AD), whose best known book is *Introduction to World History*. His contributions enriched the fields of economics, geography and history.[82]

The most influential figure was undoubtedly Abd Allah b. Yasin (d.1059), a Moroccan. The son of a Berber mother, he felt North Africans were merely paying lip service to Islam in the 1000s AD. In disgust, he and his followers retreated to a monastery ("ribat" in Arabic) to fortify themselves. Emerging from their retreat, these "Almoravids" (meaning, "men of the ribat") sallied forth to spread reform the Sahara, North Africa and Spain.[83] A "considerable number" of West African troops were among the Almoravid conquerers of Spain.[84]

Some of Almoravid troops later entered the Sahel, plundered, imposed tribute and forced some Mande-speakers to convert. In the process they weakened the

Ghana empire.[85]

Beginning around 1,000 AD, some traders from Berber Muslim communities moved south. In the Sahel, they served as agents and hosts for other Muslim traders. Together, Muslim Malinké and Muslim Berber traders forged a West African link to a Muslim trading chain that ran as far east as China.[86]

The main variant of Islam law promoted by the Almoravids was the Malik school (madh'hab), which remains dominant in West Africa.[87]

Malinké traders began converting to Islam around 1000 AD. Muslim status opened up a new world of options: worldwide trading partners, contracts based on Islamic law, and trust anchored in share values, not just personal reputation.[88]

Conversions to Islam

Soon after 1000 AD, some Sahelian political leaders and most traders had converte d to this new "religion of the book." As some rulers and traders converted to Islam, they learned Arabic to read the Qur'an, before adopting it as their language for writing.[89] T hey were able to exploit the scribal advantages it offered for record-keeping and trans-national communications.[90]

Conversions were impeded by deep differences between Islam and African traditional values. For example, religions that originated in the Middle East — including Islam and Christianity — viewed the body as sinful, especia lly the female body. In contrast, West African generally saw nothing morally wrong with sexually suggestive dance, women appearing bare-chested in public, or phallic and fertility symbols in art.[91]

Conversion was even more complicated for rulers, if most of their constituents were traditionalists. Like politicians in other eras, many tried having it both ways: They attended Friday prayers with Muslim traders and advisors, who provided strategic support. But, they also presided at traditional ceremonies with the mass of tax payers.[92]

This religious duality was still in evidence in 1352, when Moroccan traveller and memoirist Ibn Battuta noted that on festival day in Mali, the mosque was crowded in the morning with people all dressed in white, but the afternoon festivities featured the dyeli (Griots) performing traditional rites while wearing bird masks and garments of feathers.[93]

When "conversion" occurred, it was usually partial. Many who embraced Islamic prayer preferred local laws and political arrangements to Islamic ones. Some joined worship of Allah to ancestor veneration and local divination. Some adopted Muslim dress more as a sign of high status than religious affiliation.[94]

This halting conversion process occurred with commoners as well as rulers and other leading men. In 1351, about 50 years after Malian leaders had adopted Islam, geographer Ibn Battuta noted that sexual segregation was not being strictly enforced. Visiting the home of a *qadi*, he was shocked to find the judge casually chatting with a beautiful young woman. When Battuta expressed reluctancy about joining them, he was even more disappointed when the *qadi* said it was okay because the woman was his "friend."[95]

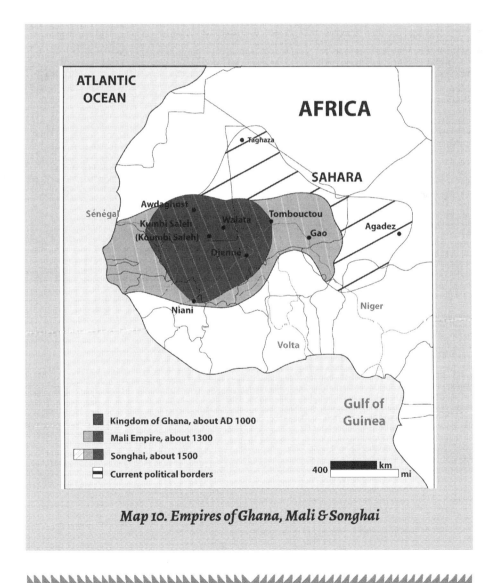

Map 10. Empires of Ghana, Mali & Songhai

The Ghana and Mali Empires

The first significant West African empire, ancient Ghana (c. 830-c. 1235 AD), was created by the Soninké (then known as the Wagadu), who inhabited Awkar and Hodh. It controlled a vast 100,000-square mile region between Senegal and Niger. The empire encompassed a diverse mix of Mande languages, with the Soninké at the core.

Ghana reigned as the import-and-export center for West Africa salt for 400 years. It exercised tight controls over information regarding the sources of its imports, including those from the forest.[96]

As early as 700 AD, Muslim Berbers from the north emerged as major traders in Ghana. They came to occupy a separate town next to the traditional capital.[97]

But, several factors contributed to Ghana's decline around 1235 AD: Its rulers and traders had focused on trade with western North Africa, especially Morocco. Meanwhile, an alternative route had developed outside the ambit of the empire that was diverting trade toward Egypt and beyond. More dramatic was a seven-year drought that dispersed the Soninké across a swath of West Africa, from Gambia to Songhai. Finally, the Almoravids of Morocco attacked in 1076-77 AD, hastening the empire's decline.[98]

Following this invasion, Islamic purists influenced by the Almoravids disbursed into the forest belt.[99] The fall of the Ghana empire also led to major political realignments in the Sahel. First, it resulted in a dispersal of some Wangara, an ethnic group formerly near the center of the empire. The main participants were from the Dyula (also Juula) caste, whose members were mainly traders.

Historian Andreas W. Massing proposed that "Wakoré/Wangara were Soninké clans specialized in trade, Islamic scholarship and law who emigrated in the 14th-15th centuries from the Awkar, now on Mauritanian territory, into the Mali provinces of Mema, Beledugu, Zaza, Bendugu, Manina?, and further East and South, perhaps founding such towns as Odienne, Koro, Boron and Kong."[100]

The best known Dyula diasporas were established near gold fields — at Borré in present-day Guinea and among the Akan in present-day Ghana.[101] This suggest early Dyula traders were primarily seeking gold. They may also have had an advanced understanding of how and where to find it.[102]

Being from the Ghana empire, they were ideally positioned to serve as middlemen — between the gold producers of the forest belt whose value of gold was apparently lower than the ore's price on the world market. Those early Dyula communities could best be described as diaspora, in other words, new settlements that are geographically discontinuous from the territory of their parent stock.[103]

Succession Fights and Migrations

Several contenders formerly at the edge of Ghana sought to fill the void. These were battles over more than ethnicity. The contenders may not have known it, but the outcome of their fight would determine the religious and economic future of the region.

Kémoko Kanté forged one major political unit that was rooted in the ethnic

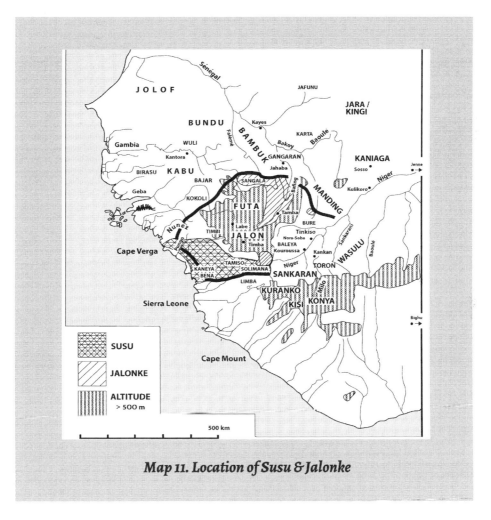

Map 11. Location of Susu & Jalonke

group known as Soso (also "Susu" and "Soosoo"). It rose from a province of the Ghana empire to dominate West Africa. When Kanté died in 1200 AD, he was succeeded by his son, Sumaoro Kanté (or Sumanguro). During Sumaoro's tenure the balafone (xylophone) was adopted.[104] With support from the nearby Kaniaga, this new Soso kingdom dominated the region for a few decades by suppressing its rivals.[105]

Historian Stephen Bühnen argued that the Soso and Jalonke are branches of the same ethnic group. The first lived closer to the Atlantic Ocean while the second lived in the mountain region of the Futa Jalon.[106] "Jalonke" is a northern Mande word for "people from Jalon," while "Futa Jalon" is Fula for "Jalo land."[107]

The Soso and Jalonke were at the core of a political unit that existed for centuries, but changed names over the years. It was called Do in the 1000s and 1100s AD, Susu from the 1300s, Jalo/Concho in the 1500s, and Sankaran in the 1600s.[108] They were spread from the southern loop of the Black Volta River in the east to the forest belt of Guinea and Sierra Leone.[109] Areas occupied by Soso and Jalonke today cover half of present-day Guinea, along with small parts of Sierra Leone, Senegal and Mali.[110]

Among the Malinké, a large rival political unit emerged. Some people called it "Mande," others "Malal," still others "Mali." One Mande challenger, Dankaran Tuman (c. 1200-1235 AD), fled south after being defeated. Accompanied by his troops, dependents and loyalists, he settled in the area around Kissidugu in present-day Guinea.[111]

By the early 1230s, the battle lines were drawn. For Sumaoro, the battle

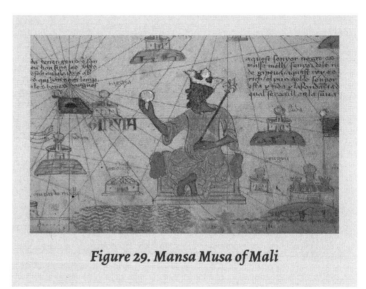

Figure 29. Mansa Musa of Mali

was over more than kinship. He was vehemently opposed to Islam and the trade in enslaved Africans. He drew support from the blacksmiths and others with ritual standing in the traditional religion.[112]

It is not known if Tuman and his followers were Muslim, but Sumaoro's next major Mande challenger certainly was. That foe was Tuman's younger brother Sogolon Diata (commonly known as "Sundiata" or "Sunjata"), whose family had converted to Islam early. Tuman's mother was Tasuma Berette, while Sundiata was the son of Sogolon Kejugu, Farako Makan Kunkenyi's second wife. In epics glorifying Sundiata, his older brother Tuman is portrayed as a coward who fled Sumaoro.[113]

Using kinship symbols and language, Sundiata united the Mande against the Soso kingdom. His mother was reportedly from Soso, so the fight must have been emotionally wrenching. His support was anchored in two of the largest Malinké political units — Mali and Kangaba. His supporters included some wealthy merchants who had apparently developed alternative trade routes in the shadow of the old empire. In Malinké oral tradition, Sumaoro was portrayed as a sorcerer and oppressor.[114]

Sumaoro's defeat by Sundiata in 1235 AD was momentous. Some surviving Soso fled *en masse* from the Beledougou region of Mali (near Segou) into the Futa Jallon and around Farana. Meanwhile, Sundiata formed a pact at Kurukanfuga among the leading families among his ethnic group.[115]

Figure 30. Great Mosque of Timbuktu

Reportedly built under the supervision of
Abu Ishaq al-Sahili of Andalusia

This agreement united the Malinké around the Mali province and launched it into an empire.[116] After Sundiata's victory, Soso became a core but subjugated province of Mali. The empire also included the remnant of Ghana in the north; it was also called Jara and Mema by different authors. There was Jolof in the far west.[117]

Sundiata began by seizing control of a trade route running though Adagh (also Adrar des Ifoghas) and Hoggar. He then moved his capital south to Niani, far from the nomadic marauders from the Sahara. This town was also close to the sources of such all-important resources as gold, ivory, palm oil and salt.[118]

According to oral tradition, Sundiata married a daughter of Ghana's last ruler, Manga Diabé. Within Mali, he suppressed the blacksmiths and other castes that had supported Sumaoro.[119]

During a 25-year reign, Sundiata consolidated a new empire, Mali, that was larger and even more prosperous than Ghana. The empire increasingly drew salt supplies from the Atlantic coast to its south and less from traditional suppliers in the Sahara.[120]

Around 1250 AD, Mali took control of Timbuktu, a town established by the Sanhaja Berber. A Great Mosque commissioned by Mansa Musa was reportedly built by Andalusian Abu Ishaq al-Sahili. Over the next century the town blossomed into a commercial center and an internationally renown seat of Islamic learning.[121]

Within 100 years, increasing quantities of gold from the Akan forest were being channelled through Jenne, then on to Europe and the Arab world.[122]

After Sundiata's death in 1250, Mali was led by a series of lesser lights until the emergence in 1317 of Mansa Kanka Musa, Sundiata's nephew, who reigned until 1332.[123]

In 1326, Mali achieved notoriety in the Mediterranean world when Mansa Musa undertook his first *hajj*. He crossed the Sahara with 100 camels loaded with gold ore. His traveling party included thousands of slaves, soldiers, officials and wives. The entourage spent so freely in the bazaars of Cairo, the value of gold fell in Egypt.[124]

Another Mansa of Mali, Abu Bakr the Second, reportedly set out to cross the Atlantic in 1311, leading a fleet of well-stocked boats. They entered the Canaries current, "a river with a powerful current," that sweeps towards the Americas.[125]

Mainly due to gold exports, Mali reached its peak of power and grandeur between 1350 and 1450 AD. During that period, European and Arab markets pushed gold demand and prices high. Mali responded by increasing production and supplying almost two-thirds of the world's supply.[126]

This trade came to be known in Europe as "the Golden Trade of the Moors." Moor is derived from the Greek word, "μαυρο" or "mavro" which literally means "black, blackened or charred." Some Greeks still use the term as a negative word for Africans.[127]

The total population of Mali is not known, but just one district, Jenne, reportedly contained 7,071 villages around 1337 AD. The capital, Niani, had 100,000 inhabitants, and its army 100,000 soldiers.[128]

At Mali's height, the empire was 1,200 miles wide. It encompassed parts of the Sahara, the Sahel, the savannah, and the coast between the Gambia and Rio Grande river. Along with a farming majority, its diverse population included Mesufa nomads, Fulani cattle herders, and fishing communities among the Beafada, Balante, Diola, Felupe and Bainuke.[129]

Along the western edge, the northern-most town was Sijilmasa, eight days from Fez by camel. In 1351 AD, its residents included Muhammad al-Bushi, who had family in China.[130]

On the eastern end, the main trade route went through the salt-mining town Taghaza, which had a mosque built entirely from salt! Almost 500 miles away was most northern town, Walata.[131]

1. Brooks, 1985, p. 14. Brooks credits Sahelian traders with founding these commercial centers, but the evidence presented in Chapter 2 of this book suggests they pre-dated Mande involvement.
2. Brooks, 1989, p. 31. I have substituted "Kru" where Brooks used "Kwa" because the languages that were considered "Kwa" when Brooks was writing have been reclassified as as "Kru."
3. Brooks, 1985, p. 44. For a summary of the European literature on early trans-Saharan contacts, see Masonen, 2000, pp. 63-64; Schwab, 1947, pp. 121-136, 145, 199 (Ma, Dan, Sapo, Loma, Bandi).
4. Coquery-Vidrovitch, 1978, pp. 271, 276.
5. Brooks, 1985, p. 5.
6. Hunwick, 2006, p. 15.
7. d'Azevedo, 1959, p. 54.
8. Brooks, 1985, pp. 46-47.
9. Catherine Coquery-Vidrovitch and Paul E. Lovejoy, "Introduction" (pp. 9-24), in Catherine Coquery-Vidrovitch and Paul E. Lovejoy (eds.), *The Workers of African Trade* (Beverly Hills: Sage, 1985), pp. 9-11, 13; I. Hrbek, ed., *General History of Africa, III: Africa from the Seventh to the Eleventh Century* (Berkeley: University of California Press, 1992), p. 350; Brooks, 1985, p. 28.
10. Gearon, 2011, p. 47.
11. Webb, 2006, p. 43; Levtzion, 1972, p. 120; Moseley, 1992, p. 527.
12. Ross E. Dunn, *The Adventures of Ibn Battuta: A Muslim Traveler of the Fourteenth Century* (Berkeley: University of California Press, 2012), p. 291; Gearon, 2011, p. 46.
13. Brooks, 1985, p. 28.
14. Dunn, 2012, pp. 296-297, quoting the twelfth-century geographer al-Idrisi.
15. Brook, 1985, p. 32.
16. Brook, 1985, p. 32.
17. Ehret, 2002, pp. 313, 338; for cowry shells in divination, see McNaughton, 1988, pp. 53-54.
18. Hunwick, 2006, p. 16; Wolf, 1982, p. 39; Moseley, 1992, pp. 523-527; J. R. McNeil, "Biological exchanges in world history" (pp. 325-344), in Jerry H. Bentley, ed., *The Oxford Handbook of World History* (Oxford: Oxford University Press, 2013), p. 331.
19. Dunn, 2012, p. 291; Wallerstein, Vol. 1, 1974, p. 39; Masonen, 2000, p. 123, n. 1.
20. Paul E. Lovejoy, *Transformations in Slavery* (Cambridge: Cambridge University, 1983), p. 20; also Walter Rodney, "Slavery and other forms of social oppression on the Upper Guinea Coast in the context of the Atlantic slave trade" (pp. 61-73), in J. E. Inikori, ed., *Forced Migration: The Impact of Export Slave Trade on African Societies* (New York: Africana Publishing Co., 1982); Azumah, 2001, p. 115.
21. Azumah, 2001, p. 122.
22. Lewis, 1990, pp. 14, 56; Azumah, 2001, p. 159; Philip D. Curtin, *The Rise and Fall of the Plantation Complex: Essays in Atlantic History* (Cambridge: Cambridge University Press, 1990), pp. 3-5.
23. Mintz, 1985, pp. 19-21, 23-24.
24. Lewis, 1990, pp. 14, 56; Azumah, 2001, p. 159; Curtin, 1990, pp. 3-5.
25. Felipe Fernández-Armesto and Benjamin Sacks, "The global exchange of food and drugs" (pp. 127-144), in Frank Trentmann, ed., *The Oxford Handbook of the History of Consumption* (Oxford: Oxford University Press, 2013), p. 135; J. R. McNeil, "Biological exchanges in world history" (pp. 325-344), in Jerry H. Bentley, ed., *The Oxford Handbook of World History* (Oxford: Oxford University Press, 2013), p. 330; Abulafia, 2013, p. 504; Mintz, 1985, pp. 27-28, 98.

26. Curtin, 1990, pp. 16-19.
27. Masonen, 2000, p. 136, n. 77; Claude Meillassoux, "The role of slavery in the economic and social history of Sahelo-Sudanic Africa," in J. E. Inikori, ed., *Forced Migration: The Impact of Export Slave Trade on African Societies* (New York: Africana Publishing Co., 1982): 74-99.
28. Lewis, 1990, p. 65.
29. Azumah, 2001, p. 127; Larry E. Tise, *Proslavery: A History of the Defense of Slavery in America, 1701-1840* (Athens: the University of Georgia Press, 1987), pp. 97-123.
30. Masonen, 2000, pp. 70, 102.
31. Webb, 2006, p. 43.
32. Levtzion, 1972, p. 148; Katherine P. Moseley, "Caravel and caravan: West Africa and the World-Economies ca. 900-1900 AD," *Review*, Vol. 15, No. 3 (Summer 1992): 523-555, especially p. 533.
33. Shams al-Din Abu 'Abdallah Muhammad ibn 'Abdallah ibn Muhammad ibn Ibrahim ibn Muhammad ibn Ibrahim ibn Yusuf al-Lawati al-Tanji Ibn Battuta, *Tuḥfat al-nuẓẓār fī gharā'ib al-amṣār wa-'ajā'ib al-asfār*, often shortened to *Rihla* or "The Journey" (pp. 281-304), in Levtzion and Hopkins, 2011, especially pp. 301-302 (gold, copper); Aḥmad ibn Yaḥyá Ibn Faḍl Allāh al-'Umarī, *Masālik al-abṣār fī mamālik al-amṣār*, Vol. 1 (pp. 254-278), in Levtzion and Hopkins, 2011, especially p. 260 (cloth, cowries, beads, copper, silver); Abū 'Ubayd 'Abd Allāh ibn 'Abd al-'Azīz Bakrī, *Kitāb al-Masālik wa'l-mamālik* (pp. 63-87), in Levtzion and Hopkins, 2011, especially pp. 78 (sorghum, salt, copper, cloth) and 87 (salt).
34. B. Marie Perinbam, "Social relations in the trans-Saharan and Western Sudanese trade: An overview," *Comparative Studies in Society and History*, 15, 4 (Sep. 1973): 416-436; Stewart, 1979 p. 294 (cowries as currency); Marion Johnson, "The cowrie currencies of West Africa, Part 1," *Journal of African History*, XI (1970): 17-49; Marion Johnson, "The cowrie currencies of West Africa, Part 2," *Journal of African History*, XI (1970): 331-353; M. Hisketh, "Materials relating to the cowrie currencies of the Western Sudan, Part 2," *Bulletin of the School of Oriental and African Studies*, XXIX (1966): 339-366; Marion Johnson, "The nineteenth-century gold 'Mithqal.' in West and North Africa," *Journal of African History*, IX (1968): 547-569; Raymond Mauny, *Tableau géographique de l'Ouest africain au Moyen Age, d'après les sources écrites, la tradition et l'archéologie* (Dakar, Institut français d'Afrique noire, 1961).
35. Masonen, 2000, p. 69.
36. Masonen, 2000, pp. 89-92, especially p. 89, n. 122.
37. Masonen, 2000, pp. 81, 83, 99, 207.
38. Valentine Vydrin, "On the problem of the proto-Mande homeland," *Journal of Language Relationship*, 2009: 107-142, especially pp.109, 112-116; Marjorie Helen Stewart, "The role of the Manding in the hinterland trade of the Western Sudan: A linguistic and cultural analysis," *Bulletin de l'Institute francais d'Afrique noire*, Série B, 2 (1979): 218-302, especially p. 282.
39. George E. Brooks, "Ecological perspectives on Mande population movements, commercial networks, and settlement patterns from the Atlantic West Phase (ca. 5500-2500 B. C.) to the present," *History in Africa*, 16 (1989): 23-40, especially p. 30.
40. Vydrine, 2009, pp.109, 112-116.
41. David C. Conrad, "Oral tradition & perceptions of history from the Manding peoples of West Africa" (pp. 73-96), in Emmanuel Kwame Akeyampong (ed.), *Themes in West Africa's History* (London: James Currey, 2006), especially p. 73, n. 1, p. 84; Stephen Bühnen, "In quest of Susu," *History in Africa*, Vol. 21 (1994): 1-47, especially p. 26.
42. Vydrin, 2009, pp. 107, 112-116. In contrast, the separation of Northern Mande from Southwestern Mande is dated to after 500 AD in Dwyer, 2005, p. 15.
43. Brooks, 1989, p. 32.

44. Azumah, 2001, p. 26; Marjorie H. Stewart, "The role of the Manding in the hinterland trade of the Western Sudan: A linguistic and cultural analysis," *Bulletin de l'Institut fondamental d'Afrique noire*. Serie B, Sciences humaines. 41 (2) avril 1979: 281-302, especially pp. 285-287.
45. Azumah, 2001, p. 26; Stewart, 1979, pp. 285-287.
46. Fagan, 2004, p. 152.
47. Sanche de Gramont, *The Strong Brown God: The Story of the Niger River* (Boston: Houghton Mifflin, 1975), pp. 26-28.
48. De Gramont, 1975, p. 27.
49. De Gramont, 1975, pp. 27-29.
50. De Gramont, 1975, p. 27.
51. De Gramont, 1975, pp. 30-31.
52. De Gramont, 1975, pp. 29, 33-34.
53. De Gramont, 1975, pp. 33-34.
54. De Gramont, 1975, p. 34.
55. De Gramont, 1975, p. 35.
56. De Gramont, 1975, p. 35; Gearon, 2011, p. 29.
57. Ehret, 2002, pp. 164-167, p. 327.
58. Ehret, 2002, p. 46; Levtzion, 1972, p. 126; Brooks, 1985, p. 109. Harley (1941, p. 11) speculates that the female face of the main Poro mask is "a relic of the earth mother idea."
59. Ivor Wilks, *Forests of Gold: Essays on the Akan and the Kingdom of Asante* (Athens: Ohio University Press, 1993), pp. 66-72. In Grand Cess, land is still sometimes matrilineally inherited; see Martin, 1968, p. 12. For matrilateral ideology among the Loma, see Højbjerg, 2007, p. 91.
60. Ehret, 2002, pp. 44-45; Mabogunje, 1971, pp. 24-25; Migeod, 1972 (regarding the Mende) and Sibley and Westermann, 1928, pp. 114-116 (on the Kpelle).
61. Coquery-Vidrovitch, 1978, p. 278; Jean Suret-Canale, "Traditional societies in tropical Africa and the concept of the 'Asiatic mode of production': Marxism and the study of African societies (pp. 1-24), in Jean Suret-Canale, *Essays on African History: From the Slave Trade to Neocolonialism* (Trenton, N.J.: Africa World Press, 1988.
62. Howard, 2000, p. 20. Fernand Braudel, *The Wheels of Commerce: Civilization & Capitalism 15th-18th Century*, Vol 2 (New York: Harper & Row, 1982), pp. 148-153, 437) describes collaborations within trading families and competition between networks in Europe that were strikingly similar to processes in West Africa.
63. David C. Conrad, "Oral tradition & perceptions of history from the Manding peoples of West Africa" (pp. 73-96), in Emmanuel Kwame Akeyampong (ed.), *Themes in West Africa's History* (London: James Currey, 2006), especially p. 76; Rashid, 2006, p. 121; David C. Conrad and Barbara E. Frank (eds.), *Status and Identity in West Africa: Nyamakalaw of Mande* (Bloomington, IN: Indiana University Press, 1995).
64. Wolf, 1982, p. 98.
65. Wolf, 1982, p. 80.
66. Wolf, 1982, pp. 79-81, 99; Samir Amin, *Unequal Development* (New York: Monthly Review Press, 1976), pp. 13-58; Moseley, 1992, p. 527.
67. Wittfogel, 1931; Wolf, 1982, p. 80; Coquery-Vidrovitch, 1978, p. 270.
68. Coquery-Vidrovitch, 1978, p. 277; Dunn, 2012, p. 292; Amselle, 1993, p. 24. According to Amselle, "state and segmentary societies, far from corresponding to two types of societies, are nothing but the two poles of an oscillating process."

69. F. de Medeiros, "The People of the Sudan: Population movements," *General History of Africa: Africa from the Seventh to the Eleventh Century*, Vol. III. Berkeley: University of California Press, 1992), pp. 63-74, especially p. 70; Moseley, 1992, p. 529. Ehret (2013, p. 454) dates the arrival of horse in the Niger delta to the 1000s.
70. B. Marie Perinbam, "Social relations in the trans-Saharan and Western Sudanese trade: An overview," *Comparative Studies in Society and History*, 15, 4 (Sep. 1973): 416-436; Stephen Bühnen, "Brothers, chiefdoms, and empires: On Jan Jansen's 'The representation of status in Mande'," *History in Africa*, Vol. 23 (1996): 111-120, especially pp. 112-113. Bühnen notes that power in the context of the Mande empire continued to be expressed in kinship language.
71. Howard, 2000, p. 21.
72. Immanuel Wallerstein, *The Capitalist World-Economy* (New York: Cambridge University Press, 1979), p. 5.
73. Charles S. Bird, "The development of Mandekan (Manding): A study of the role of extra-linguistic factors in linguistic change" (pp. 146-159), in David Dalby, *Language and History in Africa* (New York: Africana Publishing Corp., 1970), especially pp. 153-154; Stewart, 1979, pp. 285-286.
74. Pierre Achard, "The development of language empires," in Ulrich Ammon, Norbert Dittmar, Klaus J. Mattheier, eds., *Sociolinguistics: An International Handbook of the Science of Language and Society* (New York: Walter de Gruyter, 1988): 1541-1551; Bühnen, 1994, p. 22.
75. Rainer Enrique Hamel, "Language empires, linguistic imperialism, and the future of global language," Universidad Autónoma Metropolitana, Department of Anthropology, México, 2005, pp. 1-41.
76. Harold A. Innis, *Empire and Communications* (Oxford: The Clarendon Press, 1950), pp. 13-29.
77. King, 1986, p. 89.
78. Azumah, 2001, pp. 28, 31.
79. Parinbam, 1973, p. 426.
80. Gearson, 2011, p. 58.
81. Dunn, 2012, p. xiii.
82. King, 1996, p. 83.
83. King, 1986, p. 85; Azumah, 2001, p. 25.
84. Masonen, 2000, p. 67.
85. Azumah, 2001, p. 69.
86. Dunn, 2012, p. 293.
87. Hunwick, 2006, p. 18.
88. Dunn, 2012, pp. 293-294.
89. Hunwick, 2006, pp. 25, 55.
90. María Rosa Menocal, *Ornament of the World: How Muslims, Jews, and Christians Created a Culture of Tolerance in Medieval Spain*. New York: Little, Brown & Company, 2002, pp. 17-49; Ehret, 2002, pp. 168-169, 314-315; Levtzion, 1972, pp. 124, 143.

91. Zuesse, 1979, p. 142; Fuad I. Khuri, *The Body in Islamic Culture* (London: Saqi, 2001), especially pp. 35-48; William Loader, *Sexuality and the Jesus Tradition* (Grand Rapids, MI: William B. Eerdmanns, 2005), especially p. 34; Asma Barlas, "Islam and Body Politics: Inscribing (Im)morality," Conference on Religion and Politics of the Body, Nordic Society for Philosophy of Religion, University of Iceland, Reykajarik, June 26-28, 2009. As Barlas notes (pp. 2-6), the *Qu'ran* established notions of modesty and purity for both men and women. It also urged Muslim women to veil only when going among non-Muslim men. Later explanations of the Qu'ran by scholars from the 1200s AD depicted women as "evil temptresses" and their entire bodies as unclean.
92. Dunn, 2012, p. 294; Nehemia Levtzion, "The early states of the Western Sudan to 1500" (pp. 120-157), in J. F. Ade Ajayi and Michael Crowder, *History of West Africa*, Vol. I (New York: Columbia University Press, 1972), especially pp. 153, 155.
93. Levtzion, 1972, p. 156.
94. Azumah, 2001, p. 60; King, 1986, p. 87.
95. King, 1986, p. 87; Dunn, 2012, pp. 299-300.
96. Medeiros, 1992, p. 72.
97. Azumah, 2001, p. 26; King, 1986, p. 85.
98. Medeiros, 1992, p. 69; Levtzion, 1972, p. 131; Brooks, 1985, pp. 97, 110, 119.
99. King, 1986, p. 85.
100. Andreas W. Massing, "The Wangara, an old Soninké diaspora in West Africa?" *Cahiers d'etudes africains*, 158, XL-2 (2000): 218-308, especially p. 289.
101. Niane, 1985, p. 69.
102. Niane, 1992, p. 50; Brooks, 1985, p. 41.
103. Vansina, 1992, p. 30.
104. Roger Blench, "Evidence for the Indonesian origins of certain elements of African culture: A review, with special reference to the argument of A. M. Jones," *African Music*, Vol. 6, No. 2 (1982): 81-93. Blench questions the claim of some scholars that the West African xylophone originated in Indonesia.
105. N. D. Niane, "Mali and the second Mande expansion," *General History of Africa: Africa from the Seventh to the Eleventh Century, Vol. IV*. Berkeley: University of California Press, 1992), pp. 50-69, especially p. 50-52; Levtzion, 1972, p. 131; R. Cornevin. *Histoire des peuples d'Afrique noire* (Paris: Berger-Levrault, 1960), pp. 268, 274, 348-349; Bühnen, pp. 1, 6.
106. Bühnen, 1994, pp. 27, 34-35.
107. Bühnen, 1994, pp. 20-24.
108. Bühnen, 1994, pp. 27, 34-35.
109. Bühnen, 1994, pp. 27, 34-35.
110. Bühnen, 1994, pp. 1, 6, 24.
111. Niane, 1992, pp. 50-52; Levtzion, 1972, p. 131; Cornevin. 1960, pp. 268, 274, 348-349.
112. Niane, 1992, pp. 50-69, especially p. 50-52; Levtzion, 1972, p. 131; Cornevin. 1960, pp. 268, 274, 348-349.
113. Jan Jensen, "The representation of status in Mande: Did the Mali Empire still exist in the nineteenth century?" *Africa in History*, 23 (1996): 87-109, especially p. 96.
114. Dunn, 2012, p. 294; Bühnen, 1994, p. 11; David C. Conrad, *Sundiatta: A West African Epic of the Mande People* (Indianapolis: Hackett, 2004), especially pp. xx, xxix-xxx, 118-122.

[115]. Wondji, 1992, pp. 187-203, especially p. 189; Masonen, 2000, p. 108; Emmanuel Kwaku Akyeampong, Henry Louis Gates and Steven J. Niven, *Dictionary of African Biography*, Vol. 6 (Oxford: Oxford University Press, 2012), p. 291. The leading clans were Traore, Kone, Kamara, Keita, and Konate; see Stewart, 1979, p. 287.

[116]. Wondji, 1992, pp. 187-203, especially p. 189; Akyeampong, Gates and Niven, 2012, p. 291.

[117]. Bühnen, 1994, p. 5; also Bühnen, 1996, p. 115.

[118]. Medeiros, 1992, p. 74.

[119]. Rashid, 2006, p. 121; Masonen, 2000, p. 109; Tal Tamari, "The development of caste systems in West Africa," *Journal of African History* 32 (2), pp. 221-250.

[120]. Massing, 1985, p. 41.

[121]. Levtzion, 1972, p. 140; Hunwick, 2006, pp. 25, 32; King, 1986, p. 85. For a skeptical view of Al-Sahili's reported work as an architect, see Masonen, 2000, pp. 212-213.

[122]. Levtzion, 1972, p. 149.

[123]. Niane, 1985, p. 57.

[124]. Dunn, 2012, p. 290.

[125]. Ibn Fadl Allah al-'Umari, *Masalik al-absar fi mamalik al-ansar*, in N. Levtzion and J. F. P. Hopkins, eds., *Corpus of Early Arabic Sources for West African History* (Princeton: Markus Wiener Publishers, 2011), pp. 270-271, 268-269.

[126]. Dunn, 2012, p. 292; Hopkins, 1973, p. 82; Wolf, 1982, p. 40.

[127]. Dunn, 2012, p. 292; Hopkins, 1973, p. 82; Wolf, 1982, p. 40.

[128]. Niane, 1985, p. 64. The year 1337 AD is when al-'Umari's work was published.

[129]. Dunn, 2012, p. 292; Niane, 1985, p.62-63; Medeiros, 1992, pp. 67-68.

[130]. Dunn, 2012, p. 296.

[131]. Dunn, 2012, pp. 297-299.

Chapter 6
Down from the Niger

> When elephants fight, the grass gets trampled.
>
> – *African proverb*

As early as 1000 AD, West Africa formed an integrated social system. Each empire combined many cultures and political units, but they shared one economy. The various groups relied on goods and services from the others, although one cultural and political unit received most of the benefits.[1] At first, the Soninké were at the core. They lost out to the Soso, who were replaced by the Malinké.

Regional tribute-taking and trading produced tensions within Niger empires that had to be carefully managed by the rulers. State administrators provided protection to traders in exchange for loyalty and taxes. But, they had to prevent price-gorging by merchants in order to keep local farmers happy. A loss of support from traders was apparently one factor that led to the overthrow of Soso ruler Sumaoro Kante.[2]

Of greater consequence were conflicts that repeatedly erupted in "royal" families or among military officers over the transfer of power. Sons, nephews and generals who felt cheated would rebel. Each contender would mobilize a section of the population and of the massive army using kinship language.[3]

Such grabs for power often led to widespread fighting and, ultimately, massive migrations. That was the case when Dankaran Tuman, a Malinké aspirant challenged Sumaoro. Losers who survived often fled, as Dankaran did, taking loyalist soldiers and their families, together with villagers who had backed the "wrong" side.[4]

But, Sahelian migrants were also pulled toward the forest by the presence of salt, kola, iron ore and other resources nearer the coast.[5] Such movement were common elsewhere. As noted by historian Dirk Hoerder, "The history of humanity is a history of migration."[6]

Early Mande migrations occurred in three stages, each involving more people than the previous one.

The first recorded migration occurred around 1076. Merchants established diasporas near key sources of important goods in an effort to better control the trade and maximize profits. These settlements were generally by small groups who may have contributed cultural elements but adopted the languages of their "landlords."[7]

Several factors spurred other migrations. Crucial to iron smelting along the

Niger were specific species of hardwoods harvested by smiths for charcoal. These grew in greater profusion in the forest belt, which fueled a gradual movement of smelters and smiths southward in search of virgin woods.[8]

In addition, Mande speakers would likely have turned to iron smelting sites further south, as initial iron sources along the Niger were exhausted. Early possible targets of such migrations were sites in Côte d'Ivoire dating to 400-600 BC[9] and others in Putu, Liberia, which remain undated but are apparently ancient.[10]

A bigger factor was a seven-year drought that began around 1100 in the Soninké heartland. It caused their dispersal across a swath of West Africa, from Gambia to Songhai. Their migration intensified after the Almoravids of Morocco attacked Ghana in 1076-77, hastening the empire's decline.[11]

The main Soninké emigrants to the forest region were from Kankaba. They were mainly traders from the Dyula (also Juula) caste. They were the first northern Mande speakers many non-Mande groups encountered. As a result, many non-Mande groups throughout the forest belt still refer to all Mande traders as "Dyula."

This label is inaccurate because not all Dyula were traders. Some farmed, others weaved, still others engaged in Islamic proselytizing. But, it was grounded in history: The Dyula were the first Mande-speakers to trade with many of these groups.

The collapse of Ghana led to major power struggles and additional migrations. Sometime between 1200 and 1235, Sumaoro Kanté of the Soso Kingdom crushed a Malinké challenger, Dankaran Tuman. After being defeated, Dankaran fled to Kissidugu in present-day Guinea, with his Mande troops, dependents and loyalists.[12]

Among their likely descendants are the Manya of Guinea, the Malinké group that has apparently lived longest along the forest rim. They have been neighbors and sometimes allies of the Loma for centuries. Historian Yves Person called them "bush Mandingo."[13]

According to anthropologist Christian Kondt Højbjorg, "The origin of the Loma is unequivocally closely associated with [Malinké] sub-groups, especially the Konianké.[14]

A third set of Mande immigrants came after Sumaoro's defeat in 1235 by Sundita Keita of Mali. It included a large number of Soso and allied groups who fled *en masse* from the Beledougou region of Mali (near Segou) into the Futa Jallon and around Farana.[15]

This last group was fleeing more than ethnic persecution. Their side had fought against the growing slave trade and in defense of traditional religion. Losers included Mande backers of Sumaoro, such as blacksmiths and others with ritual standing.[16] They lost to a new regime centered in Mali that was committed to Islam and the growing trade in enslaved Africans.[17]

Each group probably migrated for multiple reasons. For example, Soso would likely not have come south if there were not people living there and valuable resources. Similarly, southeast Mande groups came, not only to escape religious persecution, but also to exploit kola.

Migrations caused by power struggles were not like earlier diasporas of traders, weavers and blacksmiths. These were abrupt and permanent relocations involving journeys of more than a year by entire groups — men, women and children carrying as many of their belongings as they could over long distances.[18]

Like immigrants elsewhere, those who relocated south forged relations with local people while keeping some ties with their homelands.[19] Local communities would likely have recognized the newcomers' leader as spokespeople for the group with responsibility for their behavior.[20]

Arrival of Southeast and Southwest Mande Speakers

Several ethnic groups now in Liberia originated in those migrations: the Vai, Kpelle, Loma, Bandi, and Mende. The Vai location nearest the coast suggest their ancestors came first, followed by the others.

They would likely have followed several routes that linked the Niger to the salt-producing coast as well as the kola forest of Sierra Leone and Liberia. All of those routes passed through Kankan, which was the main transit point for the flow of goods between the Buré gold-working region and forest societies on the one hand and the Sahel on the other.[21]

One route went from the Niger through Kankan to the Sierra Leone peninsula.[22] The Dyula ancestors of the Vai ethnic group apparently took this route to the Sierra Leone peninsula before slowly gravitating toward Cape Mount.

A second path ran from Kankan to Musadu to Bopolu to Jondu to Gowolo to Gowolonamalo to Cape Mount.[23] This route was taken by the southwest Mande part of the way, but they stopped around Musadu.

Still another route began near Kankan went down to the Milo River then to Makona.[24] The Soso apparently arrived by this route and occupied land in the grasslands of northern Guinea.

As the southwest Mande were moving from the north, some southeast Mande speakers were approaching from the east, following the Sassandra River. They eventually met around Nzerekore, Guinea. As a result of this process, the Kpelle (southwest Mande speakers) and Ma (a southeast Mande group) are next to each other today.[25]

Speakers of both southeast and southwest Mande had probably migrated slowly, exploring through trial-and-error different soil types and resources along the way. It seems by no means arbitrary that they settled on some of the best soil in the region, atop deposits of iron and gold and near the forest sources of kola.

Oral traditions from the Sahel provide the departure dates of Dankaran and the Soso. But, oral traditions from the forest region provide no dates for when groups arrived.

Fortunately, linguistic evidence offers a hint. A major split in southwest Mande is between Loma and Kpelle, on the one hand, and Bandi, Loko and Mende, on the other. Linguists have found that Bandi, Loko and Mende share a closer historical affinity to Soso, than Soso does to Malinké.[26]

This suggests one of two options: Similarities between Soso and some southwest Mande languages developed from them living near each other in Guinea.

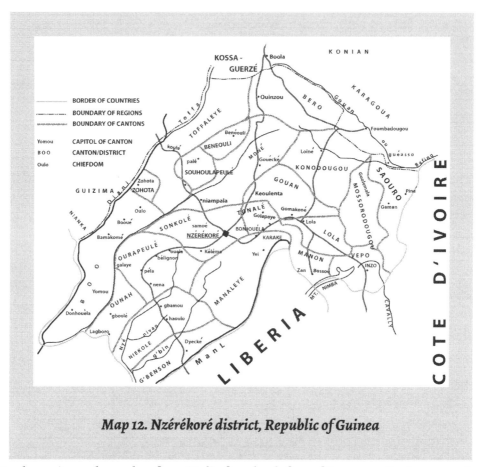

Map 12. Nzérékoré district, Republic of Guinea

Or, they migrated together from Mali after the defeat of Sumaoro. In that case, the Loma may have descended from Dankaran loyalists.

Living in the Guinea highlands were the Kissi and Gola, along the western rim of the Liberian forest. Along the eastern edge of the forest were Kru speakers.

When the Southwest Mande groups arrived, the Gola were apparently confined mainly to the Komgba Mountain. The Kissi were dispersed through territory now occupied by the Kono and Loma in Guinea and the Bandi and Mende in Liberia and Sierra Leone.

Several facts point in that direction: Many towns in the area still bear Kissi names, although they are occupied by different ethnic groups. In addition, *pontan* stone sculptures continue to be unearth throughout the territory. The Kono, Loma, Bandi and Mende living there claim no connections to those sculptures, but the Kissi do.

Although the oral traditions of various groups recount historical events from their narrow perspective, taken together they support each other in depicting a very broad pattern of migrations and later interactions.

Vai, Dama, Kono

The first Mande group to arrive were the Dyula, who left the Sahel around 1076.[27] They settled in a corridor along eastern Sierra Leone, western Liberia and southern Guinea. The belt of Dyula immigrants splintered into three groups: the Kono in the north, the Dama in the middle and the Vai on the coast.[28]

How do we know this?

Linguistic analysis shows that Kono, Dama and Vai of Liberia/Sierra Leone are archaic forms of Dyula.[29] So, too, are Kuranko (Sierra Leone) and Kakabe, Lele and Mogofin (Guinea).[30] Other archaic forms of Dyula are spoken by the Ligbi of eastern Côte d'Ivoire/Burkina Faso and western Ghana.[31]

The Dyula call themselves Dyulanke, but the Guro of present-day Ghana call them Va,[32] which sounds intriguingly similar to the name of their kindred further west in Sierra Leone/Liberia.

Further support is provided by oral traditions: The Vai say their ancestors were drawn to this area by the Gola salt trade.[33] According to the Dei, the Vai first entered Gola territory, but the Gola pushed them toward the coast near the Dei.[34] In addition, the Gola cite the Dei and Vai as their earliest neighbors. Finally, various Mande groups in western Liberia all say they were preceded by the Vai.

Oral traditions of the Vai, Gola and Dei of Liberia point to intermarriages being common between the three groups.[35] But, the Dyula language could only have survived if the first group of Soninké immigrants had included a large number of women. After all, it is mainly women who pass the "mother tongue" from one generation to another.

However, the linguistic evidence is not fully supported by four Vai oral traditions. Those stories date the group's arrival to several hundreds of years after the Dyula dispersion. They also link Vai ancestry to groups other than the Dyula. Furthermore, they seem to contradict each other. Finally, one oral tradition gives many details but several of them seem implausible.

The four oral traditions agree on one point: the Vai founders were men, at least the ones "worthy" of being remembered.[36]

Beyond that there are many differences. One story suggests the Vai emerged from among supporters of Sumanguro defeated by Sundiata in 1235.[37] Those refugees reportedly went to Musadu in Guinea before disbursing to establish various towns.[38]

Another tradition traced the group's origin to an expedition sent by the Mali empire in 1300 AD. A third claims the Vai descended from the son of a Malinké ruler who was expelled from Musadu at an unknown date.[39] A fourth points to the Kamara family from Mali, who arrived around 1550.[40]

These claims are not mutually exclusive. After all, the group now known as Vai may have received multiple waves of northern Mande immigrants over centuries. In that case, each of these traditions might recall a separate infusion.

But, these traditions seem to contradict the linguistic evidence in two important respects: they credit Vai origin to founders who were not Dyula and who were all men.

How can these differences be explained? It is possible that, in emphasizing the heroic roles of soldiers and rulers, the Vai oral traditions effaced female immigrants. Similarly, more recent Malinké movements might have been retained at the expense of older Dyula ones.

In that case, the two types of evidence would not be contradictory. They simply refer to different events: The linguistic evidence probably applies to the Vai's origin, while the oral traditions refer to later additions.

One Vai oral tradition is especially rich in details, but many of them are difficult to corroborate. It recalled a northern Mande ruler, Kamala Ba Jomani, whose hunters returned from an expedition with a report of having reached the ocean in eastern Sierra Leone. They also brought back salt bought from the Gola.

In reaction, Jomali called up hundreds of foot soldiers, along with dozens of horsemen, from the 12 provinces of the Mali Empire for an expedition to implant a colony on the coast. Every 14 days a group consisting of 10 calvary and 100 men on foot were sent.

After traveling for several weeks, the expedition settled in the forest near the Kambo Mountains. Years later, a messenger arrived with orders that they continue the quest. The ruler's brother, Ngolo; his son, also named Jomali; and their cousin Kia Tamba pushed on with their troops.

Upon leaving, one of them reportedly said, *N kono, in be taa vai* (meaning, "you remain behind, I am going on"). This quote is cited as the basis for the names of the two northern Mande groups in the region, the Kono ("those left behind") and the Vai ("those who forged ahead").

Down From the Niger

The younger Jomali was the first to reach the beach near Kasse, about 100 miles north of Koi-Je. At that point, his praise singer reportedly exclaimed *mansa goi* (meaning, "you are indeed a king"). This is cited as the root of the family name Massaquoi and the basis of their claim to being the founding lineage of the Vai.[41]

It is likely that the "every 14 days" and "10 calvary and 100 men" in this story were used metaphorically, to aid recall. A similar use of numbers occurs in the Bible when reference is made to "40 days and 40 nights." In earlier times, such numbers simply meant "many" or "a lot."

The tradition points to salt as the reason ancestors of the Vai were attracted to the area. That makes sense, given the shortage of salt in the Sahel. But, it seems implausible that the empire would have launched a massive military expedition to secure one salt supply, when many other sources were available nearer to Mali.

Furthermore, the rulers of Mali had learned that force sometimes produced unwanted effects. As Mansa Musa explained in 1326, miners in the Buré gold fields

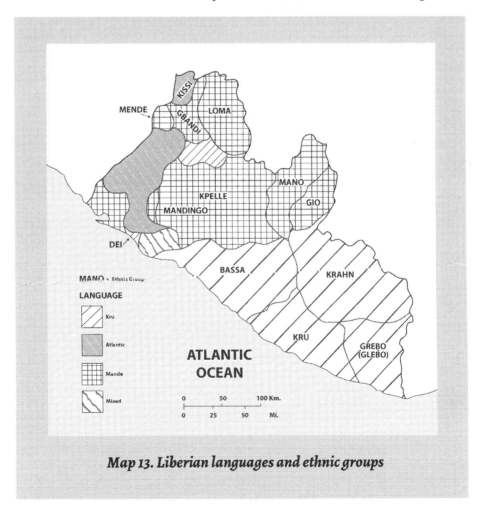

Map 13. *Liberian languages and ethnic groups*

produced more when subjected to less direct control. If Malian rulers were treating gold producers lightly, sending troops to secure a salt source seems excessive.

Another detail in the story is also challenging. According to Momolu Massaquoi, the source of this tradition, these events occurred around 1300, based on the Kpato trees that were specifically planted upon their arrival.[42] But, this date does not fit with any known development in the Sahel that might have led to such an expedition.

One Vai custom suggests that the culture had an archaic origin, dating back possibly to the Dyula dispersion. Among them, a practice of burying slaves with rulers persisted until 1678. This custom was once common elsewhere in Africa. But, it was ended in ancient Egypt by the Osiris priesthood and in Sahelian empires by 1352 AD under Muslim rulers.[43]

Taken together with what is known about Dyula settlement in other parts of the forest region, the first migration by ancestors of the Vai to the coast likely occurred c. 1077 AD.[44] They were possibly supplemented by other immigrants after 1235 and again around 1550.

Southwest Mande Speakers

Long before southwest Mande groups arrived in the area of Liberia, they shared a common language and perhaps a common name. That collective name was probably Bandi (or a word close to it). Linguist Kirill Babaev has identified remnants of that name in various forms among many of the offshoot groups.

Babaev points to the following facts: First, there is the name Bandi, which is applied to one Liberian ethnic group. Second, the Limba in Sierra Leone call the neighboring Loko *Wu-bandi* and their language *Hu-bandi*. Third, several Loma dialects have names with echoes of the word, such as *Bandi*, *Gbunde*, *Bunde* and *Bode*.

In addition, the northern most dialect of Kpelle is called *Gbanli-woo* (meaning, "language of the Gbali). According to Babaev, the difference in final consonant stems from the widespread use of a soft "l" in Kpelle where a strong "d" is used in Bandi.[45]

The current names of other southwest Mande ethnic groups and their dialects were assigned based on where each settled, Babeav argues. Examples include *Loko* (meaning "river mouth land") and *Hasa-la* (a subgroup of the Bandi whose name means "the rocky place"). Several dialects of Loma have names that match their locations, such as *Nini-bu* ("under the shade"), *Gizi-ma* ("on the mountain"), *Zie-ma* ("on the water"), and *Bulu-ye-ma* ("on the saltwater").

One exception to this naming pattern is the ethnic group called Mende. According to Babaev, its name is derived from *man-da* (meaning "lord" or "lordship" in Mande).[46]

David Dwyer posits *the* major split within southwest Mande to be between

Kpelle and the other languages. However, Loma is the most distinct.[47] Loko, Bandi and Mende could be considered distinct dialects of the same language.[48]

One Loma oral tradition claims that the group's name is derived from the Mandinké word for "joiner" and was applied to them because they choose to be initiated into the Poro.[49] But, historian Joseph Gjuilavogui linked "Loma" to where the group's ancestors first lived when they came to the area. The name, he says, is a contraction of "Löwöma Vhéati," the name for the headwaters of the St. Paul's River northeast of Beyla.[50]

By all these accounts, Loma group identity emerged after 1235 AD, when southwest Mande groups began settling along the rim of the forest, not earlier.

So, where and when did Kpelle identity emerge?

One Kpelle oral tradition traces the group back to "Gbanhana." That town still exists in Mali, where it is known as Mahana.

Another tradition holds that the group's first ancestor, a hunter named Niama, descended from the iron-bearing Simandou Mountain between Beyla and Boola in the Savannah region of Guinea.[51]

Taken together, those two stories point to the formation of Kpelle identity along the Mali-Guinea border. That location coincides with the route taken by Dankaran Tuman's allies after his defeat in 1235 AD.

When Niama descended, the entire area around Nzerekore was occupied by Kru-speaking people from the Wee group. After marrying a woman from among them named Gama, he left, taking his wife and children northward.[52]

The first Kpelle migration from Beyla to the forest region was led by the Tohoma Téa clan. They reportedly settled among the Ma in a town called *Guiépa* (in Mano) and *Guiéta* (in Kpelle).[53]

Once in kola territory, all of the southwest Mande groups began taking care of kola trees in cleared patches of forest near their villages. Both Loma and Kpelle staked claims to kola trees using straw, pieces of calabash stuffed with cotton and other talisman.[54]

Southeast Mande Speakers

Linguistic research shows that the southeast Mande languages in present-day Liberia, namely, Dan and Ma, are related to a number of small isolated languages in Burkina Faso, northern Benin and Western Nigeria (e.g., Busa, Bisa and Samo). In contrast, the Ma and Dan share less in common with neighboring southwest Mande and northern Mande languages (e.g., Malinké, Vai and Kono).[55]

The ancestors of the Dan, Ma and Guro probably once lived in the area of Burkina Faso inhabited today by the Bobofing, who speak a related southeast Mande language. After the southeast Mande language splintered, the Bisa and Mossi-Dagomba remained in place, while related groups moved in a southwest direction. One exception was the Busa in Nigeria, who (according to oral tradition) went southeast.

Although the Kpelle and Ma approached the forest rim from different directions, their origin stories are similar in important respects. According to the Ma, their first ancestor named Dané descended from a mountain. The mountain is called Sango in some accounts, Kohiré in others.[56]

After descending, Dané founded the town called Karana, from which all Ma dispersed.[57] Many then settled around Nzerekore, where they mixed with the region's Kru-speaking inhabitants.[58]

The stories don't refer to the ethnicity of Dané's wife, but they go on to recount how one of his descendants encountered the Kru-speaking Wee (in some versions) or the Dan (in others).

At least one oral tradition holds that a union between ancestors of the Ma and an unnamed group produced the Guinea Kono.[59]

The Dan, too, trace their origin to a first ancestor, Dio or Guio, descended from a mountain called Gouin near Touba, Côte d'Ivoire.[60]

The various oral traditions of the Kpelle, Loma, Ma and Dan help identify their approximate locations after leaving the savannah and the directions of their subsequent movements. The stories also highlight the fact that Kru speakers preceded Mande groups into the region near the forest. Although speaking different languages, these groups intermarried and forged other mutually beneficial relationships.

Most Loma oral traditions point to the Konian in the Beyla region in southeast Guinea as a former residence. They were apparently displaced from the area by the Konianké. The Lulama district in Guinea is the area with the fewest non-Loma residents. As a result, it is considered the most authentic.[61]

According to oral traditions, their founder was Bako Massa Traore. He reportedly came from Ségazou, which is identified with Sikasso in present-day southern Mali. Traore is the Bamara and Mandingo clan that has the dog as it's totem. That is the totem of the Guilavogui, the leading Loma clan in the area.[62]

People in Wotoumé district cite Woko Soroqui from the horse clan as their founder. His father, Fasouma Bongo, was reportedly a Malinké from Mani near Kerouané.[63]

Oral traditions of the Wubomai Loma trace their origin to Fala Wubo, son of a Malinké father and a Kissi mother who joined the Poro. Fala's brother, Seimavileh, did not join; he is considered the founder of the Malinké community in Wonnegomai.[64]

According to one Loma oral tradition, the group descended from a Kissi woman named Kumba, making the two groups "uncle" and "nephew." For that reason, the Loma exploring party into Liberia choose territory near the Kissi.⁶⁵ This relationship suggests a longterm symbiotic connection between a Mande group of mainly men who married Kissi women (or whose male leaders did).

Loma is the name used for itself by the group, but it is known as *Toma* in Malinké and Dan, *Twaan* in Kpelle and Ma, *Kénia* by the Kissi of Gueckédou, *Gbalawi* by the Bandi, *Bouse* by the Mende and *Gboande* by the Gola.⁶⁶

The Kpelle reportedly met two groups in the area: ancestors of the Bassa to south and the Dan to the east. Northeast of the Kpelle were the Bobo and Senufo, two groups that now live much further east.⁶⁷

From around 1200 AD, when the southwest Mande speakers probably arrived, they aligned with groups already living along the forest edge in Southern Guinea and Northern Côte d'Ivoire to form four clusters, each linked to a major trade town: Kissidugu, Beyla, Musadu and Man.⁶⁸ These trade towns and others were located conveniently at the head of rivers and within 200 miles of the Atlantic.⁶⁹

According to an estimate by historian Fernand Braudel, a town of 3,000 residents during this period needed at least 5 square miles to survive. Each of the four major trade towns apparently supported by an area of much wider than 5 square miles, giving some indication of their size.⁷⁰

These towns were significant beyond the shelter they provided; they were the centers of regional networks. As noted by historian Allen M. Howard, networks are significant because "they provide a context for action and practice. ... Secondly, towns, roads, and other regional features of commerce and politics become patterned over time. ... Thirdly, networks were repositories of identity, history and meaning."⁷¹

From east to west, there was Kissidugu, inhabited by the Bandi, Mende, Loma and some Kissi.

Another key town in the area, Beyla, was an ethnic melting pot. As early as the 1200s, it was a trading station visited by Dyula merchants traveling from the Niger to buy kola and slaves.⁷² It was likely founded by Kru speakers or ancestors of the Ma. They were joined by the Loma and Kpelle, who respectively settled in the western and eastern sections of the town.

Some Loma also put down roots in the southern part of Kankan and the eastern half of Kissidugu, two Kissi towns. Oral traditions describe both the Loma and the Kono in Guinea as cousins of the Kissi, suggesting an initial landlord-stranger relationship.⁷³

For a time, Musadu was the most legendary town in the region. According to many groups throughout Liberia, at least some of their ancestors lived in the town before moving to their current locations. These groups include the Gola, Loma, Kpelle, Kono, Bassa, Bandi, Dan and Ma.⁷⁴

The name "Musadu" was given by the Mandinké, but the town existed long before they arrived around 1500.

The town was probably founded by ancestors of the Bassa as a trading post that attracted Mande speaking traders. In oral traditions, it is linked most closely to the Kpelle and Loma. The town was a well known stop on a trade route linking the forest to the Sahel as early as 1200 AD.

Because many groups have occupied the town over the years, its history is highly contested. Loma oral traditions credit the town's founding to Musa, a herbalist. He reportedly abandoned his previous residence in a predominantly Muslim Malinké town because he refused to convert to Islam, the majority religion.

In Malinké oral history, Musa was a Kpelle "slave" who bore a Malinké last name, Kromah. If Musa was born a slave, it seems unlikely he could have founded a successful trading town. Instead, the story implies that Musa's wealth and renown attracted the Malinké, who then "enslaved" the founder and residents of the town.

The story further identifies Musa as a rich fisherman and linked his wealth to a nearby creek.[75] But, fishing alone is not likely to have produced great wealth. Instead, Musa's wealth probably derived from gold deposits that existed in Kpelle territory.

Further east of Musadu, around the town of Man, were the Ma, Dan and Wee.

Many groups in Liberia, including the Gola, the Loma, the Kpelle, the Ma, the Dan, as well as Kru-speakers, recognize mountains as the dwelling place of the ancestors. For this reason, many of these groups engaged in regular pilgrimages to whichever mountain originally sheltered them, where rituals of propitiation and thanksgiving were performed.

These traditions have been mislabeled as "mountain worship." But they are not very different from the practices of the Israelites in the Old Testament, who went to Mount Sinai to be closer to God and whose psalmist and king, David, wrote, "I lift up my eyes onto the mountain. From where shall my strength come? My strength comes from the Lord."[76]

People of the Poro and Sande

In this context, two pan-ethnic regional power associations arose that cut across language, ethnic and cultural differences. These two associations were Poro for men and Sande for women. They are distinctive in their "extreme secrecy" in relations to non-members and because their "rituals and sanctions supersede those of any other association or institution."

Although often labeled "secret societies," these organizations were not the private sectarian entities suggested by that name. Instead, they were "power associations,"[77] the equivalent of church and state in all but name. They addressed the distribution of power — both earthly and spiritual.

In multiethnic communities, these ritual institutions countered the often centrifugal processes of competing lineages in several ways:

First, they organized rites of passage that varied in length from months to years. During these rites, childish attachments to nuclear families died and youths emerged reborn with ties to peers and elders drawn from across lineages.

Second, the policy and judicial decisions of institutional authorities were binding on the entire society, but their identities were hidden, insulating them from lineage rivalries.

Third, authorities were masked when performing rituals and pronouncing sentences for crimes, giving them the cloak of "impersonal manifestations of the collective will."[78]

Gola, Vai and Dei oral traditions all point to the Gola as founders of the Poro and Sande, which then spread to neighboring groups.[79] The Kissi reportedly inducted the Loma.[80] As the first groups in the area, the Gola and Kissi apparently had first place in both Poro and Sande, in keeping with ritual deference show to groups that first worked the land.[81]

Poro eventually spread along a chain that ran from the Gola, Dei and Vai through the Kissi, Bandi, Kuwaa, Loma, Bassa, Kpelle and some Dan in the middle, to the Lobi, Birifo, Dya and Senofu[82] at the northern-most tip.

These were groups that traded and intermarried within a shared environment. But, they also needed to defend their trade interests and traditional religious practices from encroachment by Sahelian empires.

The Dark Side of Trade

Along with the many benefits of trade, there is a dark side. It creates winner and losers.[83] At the international level, Africa was losing. It was supplying raw materials and slaves to the Mediterranean world and elsewhere for finished goods.

Within West Africa, the forest belt was losing because Mande traders were taking a profit both on the goods they sold and those they bought. Plus, the rulers of Sahelian empires were seizing captives from societies near the forest.

Wealth from trading also bred inequality on several levels: Within the region, wealth flowed from the forest to the home base of Dyula merchants, present-day Mali.

As wealth increased there, so did the population. After all, merchants required servants. And artisans, entertainers and other creative professionals moved closer to the money. By 300, several cities like Jenne and Gao emerged along the Niger, as formerly scattered villages melded into one large mass.[84]

Whereas earlier trade had been conducted mainly for the benefit of rulers and their clients, this revolution saw control of trading shift to a class of merchants who sought profits from an ever-expanding circle of products, not just showy exotic goods.[85]

Relations between the core groups of Sahelian empires and neighboring societies were dynamic. Initially, local rulers would maintain autonomy, as long as they paid the imposed tribute in the form of slaves or natural resources. Some stateless societies capitulated. They adopted Islam or Malinké culture and language, to lessen their chance of being enslaved.

Others would resist due to local pressures from specialist guilds or traditional religious leaders. Sometimes resistance worked. In 1326 AD, Mansa Musa described one such case where gold miners had forced concessions from his zealous predecessors:

> as soon as one of them conquers one of the gold towns and Islam spreads and the muezzin calls to prayer there the gold there begins to decrease and then disappears, while it increases in the neighboring heathen countries. When they had learnt the truth of this by experience they left the gold countries under the control of the heathen people and were content with their vassalage and the tribute imposed on them.[86]

For non-gold producers, however, resistance often resulted in them being crushed or having to migrate beyond the reach of the empire.[87]

As inequality increased, rulers along the Niger continued to use kinship language to justify their power, but the system lost its original meaning. Kinship terms were stretched to make new arrangements seem "normal."[88]

Among traders, wealth stayed within family networks. Young merchants were launched with credit or funds from relatives that were unavailable to outsiders. But, families were extended beyond "blood" relatives to include in-laws and close peers.[89]

In a similar way, warlords who seized power would use the kinship system to justify passing power to their sons or nephews. A common "ancestor," including divine ones, could be assigned to rulers who were actually unrelated.[90]

Wealth replaced seniority as the basis of authority and respect. Young men with wealth now outranked elders in reality, although they may have continued showing superficial deference. The "father" labels would now be applied to warlords who were not elders.[91]

Over the course of over 1400 years, West Africa had been knitted together into one vast network of trading and political ties. But, the societies of the region had become polarized into two contrasting types: The Sahel was dominated by Islam, and its rulers were profiting from slaves and resources extracted from the forest belt. Meanwhile, forest societies had become strongholds of older Niger-Congo customs and ideas, including the belief in a distant Sky God who had no book.

But, information about the malagueta, salt, gold and other resources of this region had fired the imagination of powerful people in Europe. They were now determined to enter this trade directly, cutting out their longtime suppliers — and religious enemies – in North Africa and the Sahel.

[1]. For definitions of a social system, as employed in this study, see Immanuel Wallerstein, *The Capitalist World-Economy* (New York: Cambridge University Press, 1979), p. 5; and Wallerstein, Vol. 1, 1974, pp. 301-302.

[2]. Niane, 1997, pp. 124-125.

[3]. Jansen, 1995, p. 15. For state building and "royal" families, see Brooks, 1989, p. 33.

[4]. Wolf, 1982, pp. 81, 98.

[5]. Bureau of Folkways, 1955, p. 58.

[6]. Dirk Hoerder, "Migrations" (pp. 269-287), in Jerry H. Bentley, ed., *The Oxford Handbook of World History* (Oxford: Oxford University Press, 2013), p. 270.

[7]. Andah, 1992, p. 261.

[8]. Brooks, 1985, pp. 20-21, 24.

[9]. J. Devisse, "Trade and trade routes in West Africa" (pp. 190-214) in I. Hrbek, ed., *General History of Africa: Africa from the Seventh to the Eleventh Century*, Vol. III. Berkeley: University of California Press, 1992), especially p. 193.

[10]. Willi O. Schulze, "Early iron industry in the Putu range in Liberia," *University of Liberia Journal*, 4, 2 (1964): 29-35. As explained by Dr. Dougbeh Nyan, the Putu people are a part of the Killipo group that is positioned between the Krahn and the Grebo. The Putu/Killipo practiced iron smelting.

11. Medeiros, 1992, p. 69; Levtzion, 1972, p. 131; Brooks, 1993, p. 106; Brooks, 1985, pp. 97, 110, 119; Muhammad El Fasi and Ivan Hrbek, "Steps in the development of Islam and its dissemination in Africa" (pp. 56-91) in *General History of Africa: Africa from the Seventh to the Eleventh Century, Vol. III*. Berkeley: University of California Press, 1992), pp. 190-214, especially p. 75.
12. Niane, 1992, pp. 50-69, especially p. 50-52; Levtzion, 1972, p. 131; Cornevin. 1960, pp. 268, 274, 348-349.
13. Christian Kordt Højbjerg, *Resisting State Iconoclasm Among the Loma of Guinea* (Durham, NC: Carolina Academic Press, 2007), p. 83; Person, 1968, p. 558.
14. Højbjerg, 2007, p. 81.
15. Akyeampong, Gates and Niven, 2012, p. 291; Howard, 2000, p. 13.
16. Rashid, 2006, p. 121; Tal Tamari, "The development of caste systems in West Africa," *Journal of African History* 32 (2), pp. 221-250.
17. Niane, 1992, pp. 50-69, especially p. 50-52; Levtzion, 1972, p. 131; Cornevin. 1960, pp. 268, 274, 348-349.
18. Howard, 2000, pp. 13-15.
19. Howard, 2000, p. 13.
20. Howard, 2000, p. 15.
21. Massing, 1985, pp. 36-37, 41; George E. Brooks, *Kola Trade and State Building: Upper Guinea Coast and Senegambia, 15th and 17th Centuries* (Boston, MA: Boston University, African Studies Center, 1980), p. 268; Person, 1968, p. 558; Beávogui, 2001, p. 54.
22. Massing, 1985, pp. 36-37, 41; Brooks, 1980, p. 268.
23. Massing, 1985, pp. 36-37, 41; Brooks, 1980, p. 268.
24. Massing, 1985, pp. 36-37, 41; Brooks, 1980, p. 268.
25. William E. Welmers, "Niger–Congo, Mande" (pp. 113-140), in Thomas A. Sebeok, Jade Berry, Joseph H. Greenberg et al., eds., *Linguistics in Sub-Saharan Africa: Current Trends in Linguistics*, 7 (The Hague: Mouton, 1971).
26. Vydrin, 2009, pp. 108, 112.
27. For spread of Mandikan, see Eric Charry, *Mande Music: Traditional and Modern Music of the Maninka and Mandink* (pp. 16-17). For spread of Dyula along trade route in West Africa, see René A. Bravmanm, *Islam and Tribal Art in Africa* (p. 60). The Dyula was a long-distance trading caste called "Marka" on the Niger Bend; cited in Elizabeth Allo Isichei, *A History of African Societies to 1870* (Cambridge: Cambridge University Press, 1997), p. 223. Dyula called themselves *Dyulanke*, but the Guro called them *Va*; see Diedrich Westermann, Margaret A. Bryan, and D. W. Arnott, *The Languages of West Africa* (London: Dawsons, 1970), (for names of various groups and what their neighbors called them. For the spread of Dyula in particular, see: Louis Tauxier, *Le noir de Bondoukou* (Paris: E. Leroiux, 1921); Maurice Delafosse, "Un etat négre: la république de Liberia," *Bulletin du comité de d'Afrique Française*, Supplément (1900), p. 191; Maurice Delafosse, "Les Vai, leur langue et léur systême d'ecriture," *l'Anthropologie*, 10 (1899), p. 132.
28. Sylvester Corker and Samuel Massaquoi, *Lofa County in Historical Perspective* (Monrovia: W. V. S. Tubman High School, 1972), pp. 39-59; Adam Jones, "Who are the Vai?" *Journal of African History* 22 (1981): 159-178, pp. 169-171; Brooks, 1989, p. 32.
29. Corker and Massaquoi, 1972, pp. 39-59; Jones, 1981, pp. 169-171.
30. Valentin Vydrine, "Who Speaks 'Mandekan'?: A note on current use of Manding and Mande ethnonyms and linguonyms," *MANSA Newsletter*, 29 (Winter 1995-96) : 6-9.
31. Andah, 1992, p. 262; Bravmann, 2009, p. 63; Conrad and Frank, 1995, p. 140.
32. Westermann, Bryan and Arnott, 1970, p. 35.

33. Bureau of Folkways, 1955, p. 58.
34. Bureau of Folkways, 1955, p. 58.
35. Andah, 1992, p. 268.
36. Massing, 1985, pp. 37-38; George W. Ellis, *Negro Culture in West Africa: A Social Study of the Negro Group of Vai-Speaking People* (New York: Neale, 1914), pp. 27-28; James Fairhead, "Kouankan and the Guinea-Liberia Border," in Jacquieline Knör and Wilson Trajano (ed.), *The Powerful Presence of the Past: Integration and Conflict along the Upper Guinea Coast* (Leiden, the Netherlands: Koninklijke Brill NV, 2008; Yves Person, *Samori: Une Révolution Dyula* (Dakar: l'Institute fondamental d'Afrique noire, 1968), p. 242; Person, 1987, p. 249; Tim Geysbeek, History from the Musadu epic: The formation of Manding power on the southern frontier of the Mali empire. Ph. D. dissertation, Michigan State University, 2002; Paul M. Korvah, "Notes on the traditional history of the tribes in the Voinjama District of Lofa County," *Rural Africana*, 1 (1960): 30-36, especially pp. 31, 33; Paul Degein Korvah, *The History of the Loma People* (Oakland, Ca.: O Books, 1995); Adam Jones, *Raw, Medium, Well Done: A Critical Review of Editorial and Quasi-Editorial Work on Pre-1885 European Sources for Sub-Saharan Africa, 1960-1986* (Madison: Studies in African Sources, 1. African Studies Program, University of Wisconsin, 1987; Massing, 1985, p. 36; James Fairhead, Tim Geysbeek, Sven E. Holsoe and Melissa Leach, eds., *African-American Exploration in West Africa: Four Nineteenth-Century Diaries* (Bloomington: Indiana University, 2003), p. 136.
37. Cited in Massing, 1985, pp. 37-38.
38. This tradition was collected by historian Adam Jones from a man of Massaquoi and Kuruma (Kromah) descent; it is cited in Massing, 1985, pp. 37-38.
39. Ellis, 1914, pp. 27-28.
40. Fairhead, 2008; Person, 1968, p. 242; Person, 1987, p. 249; Geysbeek, 2002; Korvah, 1960, pp. 31, 33; Korvah, 1995; Jones, 1987; Massing, 1985, p. 36; Fairhead, Geysbeek, Holsoe and Leach, 2003, p. 136.
41. Massing, 1985, pp. 35-36, citing A. Klingenheben, "Die entstehung des Vai volkes: Vai texte," *Zeitshrift fur Eingeboremen Sprachen*, XVI, 1-2 (1926), pp. 126-127.
42. Massing, 1985, pp. 35-36, citing Klingenheben, 1926, p. 131.
43. The year 1678 was when Barbot visited Cape Mount and learned of this custom. Barbot, 1732, pp. 117, 120, 133; Little, 1951, p. 37. Compare with Medeiros, 1992, p. 71; Budge, 1861, pp. xii-xxiii; Muḥammad Abū'l-Qāsim Ibn Ḥawqal, Ṣurat al-'Arḍ (الأرض صورة; "The face of the Earth") (pp. 44-52), in Levtzion and Hokpins, 2011, especially p. 52 (on burial of slaves with rulers in Ghana); Abu 'Ubayd 'Abd Allah b. Abd al-Aziz al-Bakri, *Kitāb al-Masālik w'al- Mamālik* (كتاب والممالك المسالك, "Books of Roads and Kingdoms") (pp. 63-86), in Levtzion and Hokpins, 2011, especially pp. 80-81 (on burial of slaves with rulers in Ghana); Abū 'Abd al-Lāh Muḥammad ibn 'Abd al-Lāh l-Lawātī ṭ-Ṭangī ibn Baṭūṭah, *Rihla* (الرحلة, "Journey"), in Levtzion and Hokpins, 2011, especially p. 28 (on burial of slaves among non-believers, implying the practice had ended in Mali proper).
44. Jack Goody, "The Mande and the Akan heartland" (pp. 192-218), in Jan Vansina, Raymond Mauny and L. V. Thomas, *The Historian in Tropical Africa* (London: Oxford University Press, 1964), p. 175.
45. Kirill Babaev, "On the origins of southwest Mande ethnonyms," Institute of Linguistics for the Russian Academy of Sciences, pp. 1-3, http://llacan.vjf.cnrs.fr/fichiers/mande2011/bublio/babaev.pdf, accessed August 18, 2013.

46. Babaev, 2013. The practice of naming settlements based on the characteristics of their location existed among other ethnic groups in Liberia, although it is possible to say how frequently. For example, the town Suehn is said to have derived its name from the Dei word soiwoin (meaning "on the banks of the soi), Kpokon from Dei (meaning on the hill), and Bocomu (meaning "beneath the Bo Mountain) from Kpelle (Ballah, 1955, pp. 46, 60, 35).
47. David Dwyer, "The Mende problem" (pp. 29-42), in Koen A. G. Bostoen and Jacky Maniacky, eds., *Studies in African Comparative Linguistics With Special Focus on Bantu and Mende* (Tervuren, Belgium: Royal Museum for Central Africa, 2005), pp. 29-42, citing W. Welmers, "The Mande languages," *Georgetown University Series on Languages and Linguistics* 11 (1958): 1-7.
48. Dwyer, 2005, p. 29-42.
49. Korvah, 1960, pp. 31, 33; also Korvah, 1995.
50. Béavogui, 2001, p. 27.
51. Jacques Germain, *Guinée: Peuples de la Forêt* (Paris: Académie des Sciences d'Outre-Mer, 1984), pp. 87, 47; R. P. Casthelain. *La langue Guerzé*. Mémoire *l'Institute francais d'Afrique noire*, no. 20, Dakar, 1952; (le Capitaine) Duffner "Croyances et coutumes religieuses chez les Guerzé et les Manon, Guinée française," *Bulletin du Comité d'Etudes Historiques et Scientifiques de l'Afrique Occidentale française*, T. XVII, no. 4, Larose, Paris (October-December 1934): 525-563, especially p. 528. The tradition claims that Niama came down from the moon onto the mountain, but references to a celestial origin are merely a literary device for addressing time beyond memory.
52. Germain, 1984, pp. 47-48.
53. Germain, 1984, p. 87.
54. Lovejoy, 1980, pp. 101-102, 104, 109.
55. Andah, 1992, p. 258-260.
56. The tradition claims that Dané came down from heaven onto the mountain, but references to a celestial origin are merely a literary device for addressing time beyond memory.
57. Germain, 1984, p. 48.
58. Germain, 1984, p. 63; Yves Person, "Les Kissi et leurs statuettes de pierre dans le cadre de l'histoire ouest-africaine," *Bulletin de l'Institute francais d'Afrique noire*, Série B, t, XXIII, no. 1-2, (1961), Annexes, pp. 47, 50.
59. Germain, 1984, p. 48. As noted by Dr. Dougbeh Nyan, similar sounding names (like Nyan and Nya) among the Klao, Grebo, Ma and Dan suggest longstanding ties among them.
60. Germain, 1984, p. 48; André Arcin, *Histoire de la Guinée française* (Paris: A. Challamel, 1911), p. 6, note 6.
61. Højbjerg, 2007, pp. 80, 82.
62. Højbjerg, 2007, p. 82.
63. Højbjerg, 2007, p. 82.
64. Højbjerg, 2007, p. 82.
65. Corker and Massaquoi, 1972, pp. 59; The oral tradition on Loma-Kissi relations is from former Liberian county commissioner and teacher Paul M. Korvah; see Korvah, 1960, p. 31.
66. Béavogui, 2001, p. 25.
67. Germain, 1984, p. 63; John M. O'Sullivan, "Slavery in the Malinké kingdom of Kabadougou (Ivory Coast)," *The International Journal of African Historical Studies*, Vol. 13, No. 4 (1980): 633-650, especially p. 639. O'Sullivan dates the Malinké military displacement of the Senofu to around 1760.

68. Historian Fernand Braudel provides two numbers from his study of population dynamics in Europe that can be used to estimate the area and number of people served by each town. First he notes (Vol. 2, 1982, pp. 42-43) that market towns in England, Wales and Bavaria serve an area with at least 7,000 people. He also estimated (Vol. 3, 1984, p. 282) that a town of 3,000 residents would require 106 miles including woods, cultivated lands and pastures. Assuming those general rules applied to the West African forest belt, then Kissidugu, Beyla, Musadu, Man and other trade towns would have served an area of at least 212 miles.
69. Brooks, 1989, p. 34.
70. Braudel, Vol. 1, 1981, p, 486.
71. Howard, 2000, p. 16; his framework is based on an analysis of places derived from John Agnew, "Representing space: Space, scale, and culture in social science" (pp. 251-271), in James Duncan and David Ley, eds., *Place/Culture/Representation* (London: Routledge, 1993).
72. Germain, 1984, p. 87.
73. Germain, 1984, p. 56; Person, 1961, pp. 1, 58, 15, 17, 45.
74. Béavogui, 2001, p. 26; Fairhead, 2008; Person, 1968, p. 242; Person, 1987, p. 249; Geysbeek, 2002; Geysbeek, 1995, p. 3; Korvah, 1960, p. 7; Korvah, 1995; Jones, 1987; Massing, 1985, p. 36; Fairhead, Geysbeek, Holsoe and Leach, 2003, p. 136; Højbjerg, 2007, p. 80, n. 19.
75. Brooks, 1985, p. 109.
76. Psalm, 121: 1; also Germain, 1984, p. 49; Ph. Bouys, "Sur le Tonkoui," *Notes africaines*, no. 19 (juillet 1943), IFAN, Dakar.
77. Brooks, 1985, pp. 132-139.
78. Horton, 1972, pp. 102-103, 113; G. W. Harley, *Masks as Agents of Social Control in North-east Liberia* (Cambridge: Peabody Museum, Harvard University, 1950); Schwab, 1947; Hans Himmelheber, "Sculptors and sculptures of the Dan" (pp. 243-255), in Langley J. Brown and Michael Crowder, eds., *Proceedings of the First International Congress of Africanists* (Evanston: Northwestern University Press, 1964); Kenneth Little, "The political function of the Poro: Part II," *Africa* 36, 1 (1966): 62-72; Kenneth Little, "The Mende chiefdoms of Sierra Leone" (pp. 239-259), in Cyrille Daryll Forde and Phyllis Mary Kaberry, *West African Kingdoms in the Nineteenth Century* (London: Oxford University Press, 1967).
79. d'Azevedo, 1959, p. 67-70, especially 67, citing Schwab, 1947 and Johnson, 1957.
80. Korvah, 1995, p. 19.
81. The association of the Poro with claims to the land is evident in the name. According to Harley (1941, p. 7), "Poro" means the earth or the ground.
82. M. Izard, "The people and kingdoms of the Niger Bend and the Volta basin from the twelfth to the sixteenth century," *General History of Africa: Africa from the Twelfth to the Sixteenth Century*, Vol. IV. Berkeley: University of California Press, 1992), pp. 94-96.
83. Meillassoux, 1978, p. 167; Wolf, 1982, p. 84; Posnansky, 1992, pp. 726-727. As explained by Posnasky, trading has a centralizing effect because it "leads to increased wealth, and that increased wealth is eventually manifest in social stratification. Wealth leads to power of patronage and the ability to control other activities, such as the exploitation of minerals, the manufacture of consumer goods and the production of food."
84. MacDonald 1998b; McIntosh and McIntosh 1988, 1993; Reid, 2003, p. 82.
85. Ehret, 2002, pp. 164-167, p. 327.
86. Ibn Fadl Allah al-'Umari, *Masalik al-absar fi mamalik al-ansar*, in N. Levtzion and J. F. P. Hopkins, eds., *Corpus of Early Arabic Sources for West African History* (Princeton: Markus Wiener Publishers, 2011), p. 262.

[87]. Wolf, 1982, pp. 80-81.
[88]. Meillassoux, 1978, p. 167; Wolf, 1982, p. 97.
[89]. Azumah, 2001, p. 29; Stewart, 1979, pp. 286-287.
[90]. Meillassoux, 1978, p. 167.
[91]. Meillassoux, 1978, p. 166.

Chapter 7
The World Turned Upside Down

> Things fall apart; the centre cannot hold;
>
> Mere anarchy is loosed upon the world,
>
> The blood-dimmed tide is loosed, and everywhere
>
> The ceremony of innocence is drowned;
>
> The best lack all conviction, while the worst
>
> Are full of passionate intensity.
>
> — *"The Second Coming" by William Butler Yates*

The two ships came to anchor near the Junk River along the coast of present-day Liberia in 1462, perhaps to take aboard firewood and fresh water. Each was 65 feet long, powered by sails and weighing nearly 50 tons. They made the largest dugout canoes used by local mariners look like dwarfs.

But, it wasn't just their size that inspired awe: They had eyes painted on their prow, as was the custom in their country of origin. They probably had the square cross of the Order of Christ on their sails, a sign that they were on a religious mission.

Captain Pedro de Sintra and his crew had travelled 2,000 miles from Portugal. The men on board had skin as pale as albinos,[1] regarded locally with superstition.

Their ships had hugged the African coast. A few of their compatriots had visited some places further north on the West African coast. Their maps and notes had guided this crew. Now, de Sintra and his men were stopping at previously unknown locations to record useful navigational details as aids to later travelers.[2]

The Portuguese arrived in the mid-1400s as West Africa was imploding. A drought was beginning that led to one failed harvest after another.[3] Soon, natural disaster and famine were followed by political unrest in the Sahelian heartland. The Portuguese presence along the coast would destabilize the region further by drawing people and power from the Niger toward the Atlantic. But, those changes were still decades away.

On August 15, de Sintra and his men arrived at the site of what is today Monrovia. The next night they saw "many fires among the trees and along the shore, made by the blacks on sighting the first Christian vessels which had ever been seen by them."

It was the peak of the rainy season, so local farmers would not have been burning their farms to prepare them for planting. Instead, the flames were probably set to signal to strangers that goods were available for trading, a common signal in this region.[4]

Sailing 16 miles toward the Junk River, de Sintra noted "a great forest of very green trees which grow right down to the water's edge." He and his men had reached 6° 10' N. latitude. Their location was calculated by the height of the Pole Star above the horizon as seen with the naked eye.[5]

They arrived on the day Catholics celebrate Jesus' mother's ascension to heaven, to they named this place St. Mary's Grove ("Arvoredo de Santa Maria").[6]

The Portuguese ships then came to anchor beyond this grove. They were soon approached by several canoes, each with two or three Africans aboard.[7]

Three of the local men boarded one of the mysterious vessels. They were armed with only small knives, sharpened poles that looked like darts, two leather shields and three bows between them.[8]

Figure 31. Portuguese caravel, based on the Arab dhow

To the amusement of the fully clothed Christians, their visitors were naked, decorated only with what looked like human teeth inserted into their pierced ears and noses. But, the actions of de Sintra and his men were probably more shocking to their visitors.[9]

The Portuguese had ventured further south than any Europeans. In keeping with the *regimentos* ("detailed orders") given by the King of Portugal, they kidnapped one of the Africans. The King's hope was that "some of the many Negros, who were in Portugal, would understand his Language; or that, by learning Portugueze Tongue, he might be able to give an Account of his Country."[10]

Random kidnappings were then common in Europe and Africa, as a means of securing slaves. The Portuguese in particular had used it against the Moors in the Iberian peninsula.[11]

Western authorities presented slavery as approved by the Bible as punishment for sin.[12] By the 1400s, European rulers and thinkers disapproved of Christians enslaving other Christians. Instead, they advocated the enslavement of "infidels" and "pagans" as a way of bringing them into the true religion.[13]

Their stance was shaped by the ongoing rivalry between Christianity and Islam along the Mediterranean, especially in Spain. This gave European slavery a religious and semi-racial cast since the "heathens" in this context were mainly non-European.

The Persistent Presence of Portuguese

A description of de Sintra's travels was first published in 1507. It was part of a collection of exotic travelogues, *Paesi novamente retrovati*. That book included narratives of voyages made to the Americas by Christopher Columbus. A Genoese who previously lived in Lisbon, the author had earlier visited West Africa on a Portuguese caravel.

The account of de Sintra's travel was written by Alvise da Cá da Mosto based on oral and written sources. A native of Venice, he had reportedly moved to Portugal to recover from his family's economic ruin back home. For him, the exciting new West African trade presented a path to quick profits. He had previously explored the region of Senegal and the Cape Verde islands in 1456.[14]

Writing four decades after de Sintra's voyage, da Mosto was not able to verify if it occurred in 1461 or 1462. In copying notes from de Sintra's voyage, the Venetian gave an Italian name to one of the first points visited in present-day Liberia: *Capo del Monte* (for "chief mountain"). This came to be rendered as Cape Mount in English.

Cá da Mosto also named the river now known as Mesurado. The word he used, "Misurato" was Italian.[15] That name has been the subject of controversy for centuries. What did it mean? What is archaic Portuguese or French? The mystery was created in part because the rest of his account was written in Portuguese.

Writing in 1700, for example, a British author known only as "R. B." speculated that the river was named "Miserado" by the Portuguese "because it is incompassed with Rocks that lye under water, and inevitably destroy any Vessel which should come nearer than half a League." Or, he speculated, by the French "who were Massacred here, cryed out Misericorde, Misericorde, Mercy, Mercy."

In truth, the name had a much more prosaic meaning. In the original Italian it simply meant "a passage performed in measured time."[16]

De Sintra's visit was momentous. It marked the first European contact with the area now known as Liberia.

Other voyagers from Portugal would follow de Sintra. They would map this coast and gave names to many of its features. They named geographical features like "Cape Palmas" and such rivers as "St. Paul's" and "St. John's."

They also named countless towns, including "Grand Cess" and "New Sestros" (from the Portuguese "cesta" for the wicker baskets widely used for transporting produce in this region).

Since then, all maps of the region have carried those names or translations in other European languages.

So, what became of the African kidnapped at Junk River? In Portugal, the King "caused diverse negroes to speak with him. Finally, a negress, the slave of a Lisbon citizen, who had also come from a far off country, understood him, not through his own language but through another known to both." This suggests preexisting links between this coast and people living further west in Sierra Leone or Gambia.

After being given "some clothes" by the King, the man seized from the Junk River was returned home within a year, according to Cá da Mosto.[17] Millions of others would not be so lucky.

Grains, God and Gold

The voyages of de Sintra and Cá da Mosto were conceived and funded by Prince Henry (properly the Infante Dom Henrique). He was the fourth son of King João I of Portugal.

Henry had fought in Morocco as a knight some fifty years earlier, along side his father and brother Duarte. In 1415, they captured Ceuta from Morocco, a country of six million people. That gave them a two-fold victory: They seized control of trade that had previously been held by a Genoa agency. More important, they captured a town that had been a center of gold trading and coin minting for 500 years.[18]

Figure 32. Portuguese words in Liberia

Mandinka *coolear* from "colher" (spoon) • Mende *fanye* from "farinha" (flour) • Gola *patá* from "prata" (silver) • Vai *páwa* from "paga" (wages) • Names of rivers including **St. Paul's** and **St. John's** • Geographical features like **Cape Palmas** • Town names like **Grand Cess** and **River Cess** from "cesta" for wicker baskets • **Palava** from "palaver" (idle chatter, talk intended to flatter) • **Dash** from "dasme" (gratuity, will you give me) • **Pikin** from "picaninny" (small child)

Better still, they had unlocked closely guarded secrets regarding the sources of Ceuta's gold. They heard tales there of gold and slaves being traded for beads and other trinkets in Timbuktu. Their intelligence pointed to sources along the coast of West Africa. Those stories inspired Henry to seize this African prize "by way of the sea."[19]

Henry left court life at Lisbon and took up residence at Sagres, a center of navigation, shipbuilding and cartography. The town attracted mariners from across the Mediterranean world (including Cá da Mosto's home in Venice) and as far away as Scandinavia.

While Henry was living there, Sagres led the way in shipping innovations. These included the quadrant, new mathematical tables used to calculate latitude and a new type of ship.

The economic development of Europe was initially inhibited by various large bodies of water. Several mighty rivers dissect the continent. In addition, the ocean isolated the British Isle and threatened to drown the Netherlands.

But, Europeans turned that potential limitation to their advantage by developing larger watercraft. By the mid-1400s, Europe's shipbuilding industry gave its merchants a decided advantage over competitors in many parts of the world.[20] As a result, they could move goods faster and more cheaply.[21]

But, even this advantage did not stem solely from independent innovation. It resulted from borrowings: The Chinese were using rudders on ships and compasses by the 1000s, and some of their ships had four decks. The Arabs had developed the triangular sails adopted by the Portuguese.[22]

The caravel was based on Arab naval design. It had been developed expressly for exploring the West African coast.

It was ships of this new design that carried de Sintra and his men to what is now the central coast of Liberia. Those vessels must have seemed strange to Africans. They would have been equally unusual in Europe, where ships used in long-distance trade were heavier, wider, and slower.[23]

Prince Henry had three stated goals: First, foster Christianity in West Africa. Second, cultivate trade. By achieving the first two, he also hoped to check the expansion in that region of the Moors, his North African Muslim enemies.

But, Prince Henry's Christianity had little in common with the early version promoted by St. Mark and St. Augustine. His was a crusading religion, absolutely convinced that it alone was true and right. It was to serve as the handmaiden of crusaders intent on remaking the world in their own image. In those ways, it was indistinguishable from Arab Islam, which Prince Henry loathed. In short, the Christianity of early Egyptians and other Africans was a lamb, while this European version would prove to be a devouring lion.

Another factor driving European exploration during this period, although often left unmentioned, was an internal threat. Men who had fought and plundered in North Africa were now jobless. Decision makers hoped to diffuse this danger by shipping jobless men overseas.[24]

To some extent, early Portuguese voyagers were motivated to reach West Africa by the search for malagueta spice. This spice had been available as early as 700 years before on the markets of southern Europe, where it was called "guinea grain" or "grain of paradise." It was thought to be a good stomach medicine when pickled in vinegar or lime-juice.[25]

Tropical spices first entered European markets in large amounts when Crusaders shipped them from the Middle East in the 1100s. As elsewhere in the world, they helped to enliven boring meals.[26] Demand increased in 1300s as Europeans began eating more meat.[27] After trade ties were developed with West Africa, malagueta sales quickly exceeded those of Asian peppers and ginger combined.[28]

Pepper was "the most notable speculative commodity of the [sixteenth and seventeenth centuries], attracting the attention of the greatest merchants and capitalists of the age." The divisibility and durability of pepper, as well as its profit market, "rendered it an excellent object of speculation."[29]

In the 1500s and 1600s, pepper made up 70 percent of the spice trade.[30] As noted by historian Fernand Braudel, "a kilo of pepper, worth one or two grammes of silver at the point of production in the Indies, would fetch 10 to 14 grammes in Alexandria, 14 to 18 in Venice, and 20 to 30 in the consumer countries of Europe."[31]

Of the forest-margin crops, the most commercially important was malagueta spice (*Aframomum melequeta*), a perennial shrub that grows to about 5 feet high.

The records of early European explorers and traders made it clear that Malaguetta was cultivated rather than simply being gathered from the wild.

One of the first Europeans to leave a record of his visit to this area, Duarte Pacheco Pereira, reported buying large quantities of this spice near Sestros River in the late 1400s. All of this spice could not have been consumed locally, so production was probably being done expressly for sale to the savannah. The presence of Europeans on the coast would have simply served to redirect the trade in spice toward the south.

Between 1498 and 1514, about 77 tons of West African spice was exported to Antwerp alone. Most probably came from the "Malagueta Coast."

By 1687 Barbot, in reference to the area of Liberia, said, "The Dutch used formerly to export a great quantity of melegueta yearly, loading whole ships; but it is now less sought after."

Of coastal residents, from Sestros River to Growa, it was said in the early 1700s, "They are also very good husbandmen to improve their lands, for rice, millet, and maneguetta; which is their chief dependence both for food and trade."[32]

During the 1800s, long after Europe had established reliable deliveries of a more desirable spice from Asia and importation of malagueta had declined significantly, pre-Liberia was said to be still exporting about 100 tons of spice annually.[33]

In addition to spice, the Portuguese had come seeking ivory and – most consequentially – slaves, many of whom were initially acquired through kidnapping.[34] But, mainly they were driven by the quest for gold.

In the early 1400s, Europe was facing an acute gold shortage due to two factors: First, significant gold reserves had been used in minting coins. Second, gold was being exchanged by Europeans for Indian and other Asian goods, leading to a drain. This shortage was one of the main factors that fueled Portuguese (and later Spanish) explorations.[35]

In the metal trade, scarcity bred demand and high value. European governments and companies would make their greatest profits from control of the worldwide trade in precious metals. That trade included metals of all forms — ore, semi-processed metals and coins.

In that trade, European merchants enjoyed an advantage as middlemen: Each major continent valued different metals. Asian currencies were based on silver and copper, which was plentiful in South America. Copper, which was not found in West Africa, fetched a higher price in local markets than gold. And Europe had an insatiable appetite for gold, which poured in from around the world.[36]

A Napoleon Complex

Portugal was a small country with a Napoleonic complex. In 1400, it consisted of one million people in 35,000 square miles. But, it held a strategic position at the gateway of the Mediterranean to the Atlantic and as a transit point between Africa and Northern Europe.[37]

By 1460, Portuguese voyagers had reached as far south as present-day Freetown, Sierra Leone. Of all the points they visited along the coast, this yielded the most high-quality gold. Nine years later, a Lisbon capitalist Fernão Gomes received exclusive rights to buy gold from Freetown. In exchange, he promised to explore at least 300 nautical miles a year eastward along the coast.[38]

By 1471, Gomes had hit the jackpot. His hired captain, Alvaro de Esteres, reached what came to be known as the Gold Coast, present-day Ghana. As a consequence, Gomes won a seat on the Royal council and a title. He adopted a coat of arms with three blacks wearing gold collars.

Gold exports from West Africa shot from 20,000 doubloons a year in 1469 to 170,000 in 1505. Each doubloon (a Spanish gold coin) contained 26.66 grams of gold and was worth $16 then. The gold in each doubloon would fetch $400 today. At that rate, West African gold shipments to Spain in 1505 alone would be worth $68 million![39]

Giving Fernão Gomes a contract to explore the coast was the European way. In other parts of the world, the rulers of tributary states gathered wealth directly and closely controlled trade. In West Africa, for example, all gold ore belonged to the emperor and only gold dust could be privately traded. But, European rulers derived significant wealth from partnerships with traders, who were given a lot of freedom.[40]

Thanks to African gold, Portugal began minting the *cruzado*, a coin with 3.54 grams of fine 24 carat gold in 1457, and England launched a coin appropriately called the *guinea*. The *cruzado* quickly rose to dominate Mediterranean currencies.[41]

Columbus, Spain and the New World

But, several factors in the 1500s challenged Portugal's grip on the world's gold market: First, Portugal's self-awarded royal monopoly was regularly ignored by private European buyers. Second the caravan trade to North Africa was revived, due to the conquest of Songhai by the Sultan of Morocco. Third, Portugal's success in Africa had inspired its neighbor, Spain, to launch its own hunt for spices and gold.[42]

A major catalyst for Spain's effort was navigator Christopher Columbus from Genoa. He had gained experience in Atlantic sailing under the Portuguese along the West African coast. As a result, he developed the idea of sailing across the ocean to the Indies in search of gold and spices. After the Portuguese responded coldly, he turned to the elites of Spain, who backed his expedition.[43]

In 1492, Columbus sailed west from Spain across the Atlantic. About 181 years before, Mansa Abu Bakr the Second, an emperor of Mali, had sailed that route but had not returned. Columbus did, after reaching the Caribbean.

Columbus did not reach India as planned. But, he and his backers gained more than they ever imagined. They accessed the Americas, a world Europeans did not know existed. Like Prince Henry of Portugal, Columbus and his Spanish backers quickly put aside all religious pretensions to pursue gold.

Europeans also began competing to establish trading posts along the West African coast. The Portuguese and Spaniards seized a series of Atlantic islands near West Africa. These included the Azores and Madeira, as well as the Canary Islands and Cape Verde, all the way south to Sao Tomé and Principe.

By 1500, the Portuguese had transferred sugar plantation model from the Mediterranean to the Atlantic. They implanted a plantation on Sao Tomé that used enslaved Africans from the mainland Kongo and Benin empires.[44]

Early European Accounts

Within decades of Portugal's breakthrough to West Africa, Spain, too, was taking captured blacks as slaves. By 1582, black slaves were so common in Seville, one visitor claimed (with some exaggeration) they made up half the city's residents.[45]

To counteract these "interlopers," Portugal completed the first of several fortresses along the West Africa coast some 19 years after de Sintra's visit. Not surprisingly, it laid at the terminus of a route that led to the gold mines in the Akan forest in present-day Ghana and came to be called Elmina ("the mine") in Spanish or Mina in English. The chapel at Elmina was symbolically named after St. James, the so-called killer of Moors.[46]

By 1682, about 20,000 people lived around the fort. This community was, in the words of historian Ira Berlin, "meeting place for African and European commercial ambitions."[47]

From 1550, other small fishing villages in West Africa were similarly transformed by the trans-Atlantic trade: Mouri (site where the Dutch built Fort Nassaw) went from 200 to 1,500 people; Cape Coast from 20 houses to over 500; and Axim from 500 residents to about 3,000.[48] Along the estuary of the Niger River, villages like Bonny, New Calabar and Wari grew into city-states, fattened by profits from the traffick in slaves.[49]

Given the growing economic significance of the slave trade, Elmina and all other European fortresses along this coast came to serve primarily as holding cells for enslaved Africans.[50]

Gold from Coya

Early European visitors to the area of Liberia were interested mainly in trading. As a result, their writings focused on trade while ignoring living conditions. In addition, these visitors stayed mainly on the coast, so they wrote nothing beyond speculations about the interior.

What is more, they wrote about some parts of the coast more than others. Their attention focused especially on Cape Mount, Cape Mesurado and the Sestros River.[51]

Duarte Pacheco Pereira, writing c. 1505, left the earliest surviving detailed European account of the Upper Guinea coast. He reported that 23-carat gold was for sale at the Sierra Leone peninsula. All of it came from a territory called Coya. Located 104 miles up the Rio dos Monos (probably the Mano River), it was inhabited by people called Cobales.[52]

Coya's distance from the coast sounds precise, but it was just a guess. Pareira had no way of measuring the distance, especially since he did not visit the town.

The Cobales reportedly gave gold in exchange for coastal salt. Such a high value for salt suggests Coya was a trading town involved in supplying salt to the Sahel. This site was probably Coyah in Guinea, which was a major trading town.[53]

Pereira described Cape Mesurado, but mentioned no inhabitants or trade. He then identified the coast beginning two leagues east and continuing for 120 miles as the location of the malagueta trade. That area — between River Cess and Cape Palmas — came to be known to European traders as the

Figure 33. Kola plant & seeds

"Malagueta Coast."

Another early visitor who left a record on the area was captain André Álvares de Almada, the son of a Portuguese father and Cape Verdean mother. He actually observed events in the Sierra Leone peninsula around 1560.

Almada described the area as once "peaceful and its inhabitants were happy, since if there was a fine country [along the Upper Guinea coast], this was it, for it had everything in abundance. Those who went to Guinea thought they had seen nothing if they did not go to this place. ... For apart from being productive in everything and having many fine products, it was a shelter and refuge for many persons, who going there with nothing raised themselves (in the world)."

Among regular visitors to the area now called Freetown were Soso traders who travelled in caravans of up to 2,000 men.[54] The groups living on the coast of this region at the time included the Sape (who consisted of the Baga and Landuma), Temne, Bullom, Limba and Yalunka (the eastern section of the Soso).[55]

There was a widespread custom of filing their teeth among Atlantic-language groups, specifically the Temne, Bullom, Buramo, Kissi and Papel.[56]

Writing in 1616, Almada characterized the forest region of Liberia and Sierra Leone as the only source of kola. This might have been an exaggeration, but it indicated just how important the kola trade was to the area (and vice versa). He stated that iron was smelted by the Loko and sold to the Portuguese in "great quantity" before an invasion disrupted the trade.[57]

The Portuguese arrived along the coast just as Mali was fraying. Their presence only hastened the old empire's collapse by overturning regional patterns of trade and relations of power that were centuries old. Suddenly, Niger traders and empires were no longer able to dictate choices to people living along the West African coast.[58]

This shift was almost immediately noticeable in the gold trade. By 1500s, the Portuguese were exporting over half a ton from the Gold Coast. This caused a drop in gold going to the Niger. In addition, the Ashanti, who straddled the gold fields, gained increased wealth and access to weapons from direct trade with Europeans. With these, they were able to establish a strong state that stopped paying tribute to the Niger.[59]

Until the late 1600s, Gold Coast sellers enjoyed tremendous profits. And Niger buyers had to compete against multiple European rivals.[60]

More Slaves for More Weapons and Horses

By 1450 AD, Sahelian grandees were richer than ever because an out-of-control world gold market had driven prices sky high. With more wealth, they wanted more servants. Furthermore, the Middle East and Mediterranean world had acquired an appetite for African slaves.[61]

Sahelian empires went through at least two phases in their dealings with enslaved persons from outside. At first, slaves were permitted to join the dominant ethnic group. They did so by adopting the culture and language of their captors and by proving their loyalty. Some trusted slaves rose to high positions, including governors of provinces.[62]

But, Mali expanded its slave hunting around 1450 for several reasons. Thanks to imported horses and weapons, the empire possessed unrivaled military superiority over its neighbors. Once people were captured, the same weapons and massive army used to seize them would now prevent them from escaping.[63]

Because it was religiously forbidden (haram) for one Muslim to enslave another, some commoners began converting to Islam as a preventive measure against enslavement.[64] In contrast, non-believers were fair game. In Sunni law, Muslims could seize them, take their property, smash their shrines.[65]

Black slaves were carried to the Arab world via several routes: One went from West Africa through the Sahara to Morocco and Tunisia. Another started in Chad and ended in Libya. An East African route followed the Nile into Egypt. Still another crossed the Red Sea to Arabia and Persia.[66]

In Arab societies, blacks were stripped of power legally and sexually. Most black women performed housekeeping chores in the homes of rich families. But, many were forced to serve as concubines or sexual pets. Often, they were kept together in harems to satisfy the sexual whims of their male owners.[67]

The fate of many black men was often worse: They had their testicles chopped off — and sometimes their penises, too — to prevent them from having children.

Because Arabs castrated so many black men and overworked others, fresh slaves were constantly brought from Africa to replace those who died without having children.[68]

This toxic mix bred a vicious, self-destructive cycle. More slaves to the Mediterranean and Arabia brought more horses and weapons. A need for more and more slaves kept the army growing. And, a larger, better-equipped army brought more slaves from the edge of the empire. On and on and on.

The Songhai Empire and Expansion of Islam

Just as Mali had risen from a province to an empire, one of its former provinces, Songhai, now dominated the Sahel. The Malian province of Songhai emerged as a separate state in the 1430s, under the leadership of Sonni Ali.[69] Although nominally Muslim, Ali and his descendants preserved traditional religion and opposed proselytizing by Muslim clerics.[70]

In 1492, the Sonni clan were overthrown by Mohamed Torodo, the governor of Hombori province. He took the title *askiya*, which was also used by his successors.

Askiya Mohammed Toure, as he came to be known, was a devote Muslim, his pilgrimage to Mecca cost 300,000 dinars and included 800 horsemen.[71]

At Songhai's peak around 1582, its capitol, Gao, reportedly had about 45,000 residents. Timbuktu reached the apex of its reputation as a center of learning, with some private libraries of over 1,600 volumes. Local scholars were churning out works of biography, poetry, sharia, grammar, syntax, and local history.[72]

In 1447, a letter sent from a Sahara oasis to Genoa by merchant Antonio Malfante accurately described the West African interior. By the late 1400s, Italian cloth was being sold in Timbuktu, and Italian traders were familiar with the city.[73]

The African tradition of hospitality had obligated land-holding families to host visiting Muslims as "strangers." Muslim clerics or traders who first settled in non-Muslim communities would often marry local women and start families. In turn, they would serve as hosts for subsequent Muslim visitors.[74]

In areas dominated by the way of the ancestors, people were identified first by ethnicity, then by profession. People were rarely identified by their religion, except for clerics. An outsider would be identified as a Malinké trader, for instance.[75]

In these communities, each culture worshipped in its own way. Local people saw a person's religion and ethnicity as inseparable. For this reason, many could not conceive of "converting" to Islam or any other religion.[76]

Religion here was less about God-talk and more about behavior: where you lived, how you dressed, which rituals you observed.[77]

In this context, Islam advanced in three phases:

First, Muslims were accorded freedom of religion, but were confined to a separate section of the main towns or their own villages. Next, Muslim men married non-Muslim women, as people of the two religions freely socialized. Finally, Muslim jurists would launch a campaign of internal Islamic reform linked to external conversions.

Through this process, Islam expanded from coastal North Africa cities through the Sahara into the grasslands.[78]

Adherents to traditional religion were probably impressed by the way Muslims cared for each other: They gave alms to the poor, aid to orphans and widows, and descent burials to their dead.[79]

The introduction of Islam reshaped the culture of the Sahelian region.[80] In extreme cases, knowledge was no longer derived from the study of the life-force in nature. Instead, it rested on claims of foreign blood. In Muslim societies, for example, powers previously exercised by herbalists and diviners now shifted to people who claimed descent from the *Quraysh*, the ethnic group of the Prophet Muhammad. These *shurafa* (from the Arabic *sharif* — "noble") were thought to possess special powers of healing and fortune telling, among other skills.[81]

Despite centuries of Islamic proselytization, some among the northern Mande, especially in the rural areas, continued to practice forms of Islam mixed with traditional religion. Often this involved ritualized communication with the life force associated with sacred formations.[82]

Relations between Muslim "strangers" and their hosts were fraught with tension over two key issues: land and women. Muslims resented land being held by a family with a role in traditional religion. On the other hand, local men resented not being able to marry Muslim women when Muslim men freely married local women.[83]

An exchange of women between the men of different ethnic groups was seen as a sign of equality. But, intermarriage was not often possible because the Muslim pioneers were usually men. Unequal exchanges continued because Islamic law bars Muslim women from marrying non-Muslim men but permits Muslim men to marry women of other religions.[84] Tensions over land and women continue.

Due to such tensions, the initial warm stranger-host relation between Muslims and traditionalists turned icy. It would turn scorching hot, as Songhai Muslim leaders unleashed a holy war against the region's non-Manlinké traditionalists.[85]

From 1464, the rulers of Songhai led unrelenting military campaigns against people living in the region of the Niger Bend and the Volta Basin. That region was originally home to many small-scale societies with distinct cultures and different languages, including the Mossi, Gur and Southeast Mande.[86] But, cultural and linguistic lines had blurred; the Bwa, for example, spoke a Gur language but shared cultural practices with the Mande-speaking Bobo.[87]

In this *jihadi* policy, Songhai leaders were influenced by Abd al-Karim al-Maghill (d. 1505), a Tunisian jurist. He pushed for sexual segregation and "proper" dressing by women. He also urged an end to divination, astrology and the making of amulets. More notoriously, Al-Maghili led a massacre of Jews in Tuwat and Gurara.[88]

When the end came for Songhai, it was doubly ironic. First, it was at the hands of a Muslim.[89] The Sultan of Morocco had ordered an invasion in 1591 to gain better access to the gold mines. Second, his army consisted mostly of foreign slaves and Spanish renegades.

But, the invasion was ill-timed. The Sultan seized the mines just as the Portuguese was upending the gold market. After decades of effort, one of his most bitter enemies had found new sources of gold. Morocco was about to begin a slow decline, along with its North African and Arabian allies.[90]

The spread of Islam into the forest was almost a thousand years away. It would be led by indigenous African Sufis, adherent to a mystical branch of Islam.[91] Meanwhile, the woodlands and forest societies remained bastions of traditional religion, clan organization, matrilineal transmission of power and property, and egalitarian power relations.[92]

1. For local belief that albinos resulted from the breach of a sexual taboo, see A. T. von S. Bradshaw, "Vestiges of Portuguese in the languages of Sierra Leone," *Sierra Leone Language Review*, Vol. 4 (1965), pp. 5-37, especially p. 5.
2. For evidence that the Portuguese voyages to West Africa were guided by previously collected intelligence, see Masonen, 2000, p. 63, n. 1.
3. Karen Ordahl Kupperman, *The Atlantic in World History* (New York: Oxford University Press, 2012), pp. 32-33.
4. Gerald Roe Crone, ed. and trans., *The Voyages of Cadamosto and Other Documents on Western Africa* (London: Hakluyt Society, 1937), pp. xxvii, 83; Peter Russell, *Prince Henry 'the Navigator': A Life* (New Haven, Conn.: Yale University Press, 2000), pp. 226-227, 233, 339, 342; Also see C. Raymond Beazley, *Prince Henry the Navigator: The Hero of Portugal and of Modern Discovery, 1394-1460 A. D.* (New York: Burt Franklin, 1895); Edward Gaylord Bourne, "Prince Henry the Navigator" (pp. 173-189), in *Essays in Historical Criticism* (Freeport, New York: Books for Libraries, 1967, reprint of 1901 edition); C. R. Boxer, *The Portuguese Seaborne Empire, 1415-1825* (New York: Alfred A. Knopf, 1969); Bailey Diffie and George D. Winius, *Foundations of the Portuguese Empire, 1415-1580* (Minneapolis: University of Minnesota Press, 1977); Ivana Elbl, "Man of his time (and peers): A new look at Henry the Navigator," *Luso-Brazilian Review*. Vol. XXVIII, No. 2 (1991), pp. 73-89; Malyn Newitt, *A History of Portuguese Overseas Expansion, 1400-1668* (London: Routledge, 2005); Elaine Sanceau, *Henry the Navigator: The Story of a Great Prince and His Times* (New York: W. W. Norton, 1947); John Ure, *Prince Henry the Navigator* (London: Constable, 1977).
5. Crone, 1937, p. 83; Diffie and Winius, 1977, pp. 125, 133, 141; Russell, 2000, p. 334,
6. Russell, 2000, p. 340.
7. Piedro De Cintra, "Voyages to the coasts and islands of Africa, in John Green, *A New General Collection of Voyages and Travels*, Vol. 1 (London: Thomas Astley, 1745-1747), p. 598; Russell, 2000, p. 230.
8. De Cintra, 1745-1747, p. 598; Russell, 2000, p. 230.
9. De Cintra, 1745-1747, p. 598; Russell, 2000, p. 230.
10. De Cintra, 1745-1747, p. 598; Russell, 2000, p. 230.
11. Hugh Thomas, *The Slave Trade: The Story of the Atlantic Slave Trade, 1440-1870* (New York: Simon & Schuster, 1997), pp. 23, 56.
12. David Brion Davis, "The response to slavery in Medieval and Early Modern thought" (pp. 91-121), in David Brion Davis, *The Problem of Slavery in Western Culture* (Ithaca: Cornell University Press, 1966), p. 91.
13. Davis, 1966, p. 100.
14. Thomas, 1997, p. 60; Ure, 1977, pp. 159-160; Crone, 1937, pp. xxx-xxxvi, xliii, 78; Newitt, 2005, pp. 48-49; Boxer, 1969, p. 27. For Cá da Mosto and his impact on the writing of African history, see Masonen, 2000, pp. 124, 129-136.
15. Crone, 1937, pp. xxx-xxxvi, 83-84; Robin Hallett, *The Penetration of Africa* (London: Routledge and K. Paul, 1965), pp. 60-66; Russell, 2000, p. 333-335.

16. R. B., "Dickeys Cove," in The English acquisitions in Guinea & East-India containing first, the several forts and castles of the Royal African Company, from Salley in South Barbary, to the Cape of Good Hope in Africa ... secondly, the fort and factories of the Honourable East-India Company in Persia, India, Sumatra, China, &c. ... : an account of the inhabitants of all these countries ... : likewise, a description of the Isle of St. Helena, where the English refresh in their Indian voyages by R. B. (London: Nathaniel Crouch, 1700), pp. 24-30; Crone, 1937, pp. 83-84; also see Barbot, 1732, p. 109, where the story of this massacre is repeated, but the nationality of the victims is changed from French to Portuguese. An alternative name given to Mesurado by Cá da Mosto was "Capo Cortese" (for well-mannered, fine or courteous chief).
17. Crone, 1937, p. 84.
18. Vilar, 1984, pp. 48-49; Eric Williams, *From Columbus to Castro: The History of the Caribbean* (New York: Vintage, 1984), p. 13; David Brion Davis, *Inhuman Bondage: The Rise and Fall of Slavery in the New World* (Oxford: Oxford University Press, 2006), p. 84.
19. Thomas, 1997, pp. 51, 69; also see Boxer, 1969, pp. 18-38, especially p. 18; Elbl, 1991, pp. 73-89.
20. Braudel, Vol. 2, 1982, pp. 361-369.
21. Wolf, 1982, p. 85.
22. Braudel, Vol. 1, 1981, pp. 385, 393, 403, 407.
23. Thomas, 1997; Crone, 1937, pp. xvii-xxi; Diffie and Winius, 1977, pp. 24-29, 121-143, 146-147. For examples of recent scholarship that ascribed a lesser role to Prince Henry in fostering Portuguese navigation in West Africa, see P. E. Russell, *Prince Henry the Navigator: the Rice and Fall of a Culture Hero* (Oxford: Clarendon Press, 1984); Newitt, 2005, pp. 20-29; Elbl, 1991, pp. 73-89.
24. Wallerstein, Vol. 1, 1974, pp. 46-51.
25. John Green, *A New General Collection of Voyages and Travels*, Vol. 2 (London: Thomas Astley, 1745-47), p. 552.
26. Wallerstein, Vol. 1, 1974, p. 333.
27. Wallerstein, Vol. 1, 1974, p. 333.
28. Wallerstein, Vol. 1, 1974, p. 333.
29. Wallerstein, Vol. 1, 1974, p. 334.
30. Felipe Fernández-Armesto and Benjamin Sacks, "The global exchange of food and drugs" (pp. 127-144), in Frank Trentmann, ed., *The Oxford Handbook of the History of Consumption* (Oxford: Oxford University Press, 2013), p. 132.
31. Braudel, Vol, 2, 1982, p 405.
32. Kassam, 1976, pp. 85-87, 105, 190; Purseglove, 1974, p. 527; Barbot, 1732, p. 138.
33. Bovill, 2008, pp. 105, 190; Kassam,1976, pp. 85-87; Purseglove, 1974, p. 527; Periera,1937, pp. 103-104; John W. Blake, (ed.), *Europeans in West Africa, 1450-1560*, Second Series, LXXXVI (London: The Hakluyt Society, 1941-42), pp. 84-85; Barbot, 1732, p. 132; J. Corry, *Observations upon the Windward Coast of Africa: The Religion, Character, Customs, etc.* (London: Frank Cass, 1968; first published 1807), pp. 53-54.
34. Newitt, 2005, pp. 2-10, especially p. 10, and pp. 30-31; Boxer, 1969, pp. 18-38, especially p. 29.
35. Wilks, 1961, p. 28.
36. Braudel, Vol. 2, 1982, pp. 194-204, 221; Masonen, 2000, p. 85.
37. Pierre Vilar, *A History of Gold and Money, 1450-1920* (London: Verso, 1984), p. 49.
38. Vilar, 1984, p. 52.
39. Vilar, 1984, p. 53. Also see Moseley, 1992, p. 536 and "Gold doubloon worth $16 more than two centuries ago expected to fetch at least 45 million at auction," *Daily Mail Online*, July 16, 2014.
40. Wolf, 1982, p. 85.

41. Vilar, 1984, p. 56; James A. Rawley, *The Transatlantic Slave Trade* (New York: W. W. Norton, 1981), p. 10.
42. Vilar, 1984, pp. 57-58.
43. Vilar, 1984, pp.61-68; Williams, 1984, pp. 14-17.
44. Curtin, 1990, pp. 17-25; Davis, 2006, p. 84; McNeil, 2013, p. 332; Mintz, 1985, p. 31. From this point onward, my presentation of the Liberia region's history follows the recommendation of historian Alan L. Karras (2013, p. 532), who argued, "It is probably best to consider the Atlantic world as a single entity from the time that the four continents bordering the Atlantic Ocean became linked through exploration, migration, and commerce.
45. Defourneaux, 1970, p. 84; Antonio Domínguez Ortíz, "Le esclavistud en Castilla en la edad moderna," *Estudios de historia social de Espana*, 1952, pp. 9-10, quoting Damasio Friás, "Dialogo en alabanza de Valladad," 1582.
46. King, 1986, p. 90.
47. Berlin, 1998, p. 19, also p. 18; also Newitt, 2005, p. 46.
48. Berlin, 1998, p. 19, also p. 18; also Newitt, 2005, p. 46.
49. Thomas, 1997, p. 145.
50. Thomas, 1997, pp. 74, 77.
51. P. E. H. Hair, "Guinea" (pp. 197-207), in D. B. Quinn, ed., *The Hakluyt Handbook*, Vol. I (London: The Hakluyt Society, 1974), especially pp. 204-205; Blake, 1942, pp. 251, 253, 257, 286, 289.
52. Periera, 1937, pp. 108; J. D. Fage, "A commentary on Duarte Pacheco Pereira's account of the Lower Guinea coastlands in his *Esmeralda de Situ Orbis* and on some other early accounts," *History in Africa*, 7 (1980), p. 50. On Duarte Pacheco Pereira, see Masonen, 2000, pp. 148-152.
53. Periera, 1937, pp. 108; Fage, 1980, p. 50.
54. Almada, 1984, p. 24, Chapter 13, p. 13 ("caravan trade").
55. Almada, 2010, p. 108-118; Hair, 1984, Chapter 15, n. 6.
56. Almada, Chapter 15 n. 18; Pacheco Periera, liv. 1, cap. 33, p. 84?; 'Ali b. Musa Ibn Sa'id al-Maghribi, *Kitab Bast al-ard fi 'l-tul wa-l-'ard*, in Levtzion and Hopkins, 2011, p. 187. 'Ali b. Musa Ibn Sa'id al-Maghribi, writing c. 1269, described a people called the Jabi who filed their teeth and lived at the southern end of the Niger.
57. Almada, Chapter 15 n. 8, who referred to the Loko as "Logos."
58. Ivor Wilks, "The Mossi and Akan states" (pp. 344-386), in J. F. Ade Ajayi and Michael Crowder, *History of West Africa*, Vol. 1 (New York: Columbia University Press, 1972), pp. 361-362.
59. Wilks, 1972, pp. 361-362.
60. Wilks, 1972, pp. 361-362.
61. Lewis, 1990, p. 11; Moseley, 1992, pp. 530-532.
62. Levtzion, 1972, p. 147.
63. Patrick Manning, "Slavery & slave trade in West Africa" (pp. 94-117), in Emmanuel Kwame Akeyampong (ed.), *Themes in West Africa's History* (London: James Currey, 2006), especially p. 99.
64. Hunwick, 2006, p. 55, 75-77; Lewis, 1990, pp. 5-6.
65. Azumah, 2001, pp. 65-66.
66. Lewis, 1990, p. 11. Lewis used the term "Islamic," but I think "Arab" is more accurate; he does not include non-Arab areas of the Islamic world on his list, such as Spain and India.
67. Lewis, 1990, pp. 14, 56; Azumah, 2001, p. 157.
68. Lewis, 1990, p. 10.

69. M. Ly-Tall, "The decline of the empire of Mali: the fifteenth to sixteenth centuries," *General History of Africa: Africa from the Seventh to the Eleventh Century, Vol. IV.* Berkeley: University of California Press, 1992), pp. 70-76; Levtzion, 1972, p. 145.
70. Azumah, 2001, p. 69.
71. Azumah, 2001, p. 69; John C. DeGraft-Johnson, *African Glory: The Story of Vanished Negro Civilizations* (Baltimore: Black Classics Press, 1986), pp. 104-106; Christopher Wise, ed., *Ta'rikh al Fattash: The Timbuktu Chronicles, 1493-1599* (Trenton: Africa World Press, 2011).
72. Hunwick, 2006, pp. 26, 32, 40, 56; Mahmoûd Kâti ben el-Hâdj el-Motaouakkel, *Tarikh el-fettach ou Chronique du chercheur, pour servir à l'histoire des villes, des armées et des principaux personnages du Tekrour* (in French), O. Houdas and M. Delafosse, eds. and trans. (Paris: Ernest Leroux, 1913), p. 262. According to Kâti, a housing survey ordered by Askiya Al-Hajj (1582–1586) reported 7,626 houses in Gao. An average of six persons per house yields 45,000 residents. Masonen (2000, p. 135) cites a population of 50,000.
73. Masonen, 2000, p. 117, 119-122; Stephen A. Epstein, *Genoa & the Genoese, 958-1528* (Chapel Hill: University of North Carolina, 1996), p. 286.
74. King, 1986, p. 84.
75. Azumah, 2001, p. 48.
76. Azumah, 2001, p. 48.
77. Azumah, 2001, p. 55, citing L. Sanneh, *The Crown and the Turban: Muslims and West African Pluralism* (Boulder: Westview, 1997), p. 27.
78. King, 1986, pp. 85-86.
79. King, 1986, p. 88.
80. Webb, 2006, p. 44.
81. Azumah, 2001, p. 27.
82. David C. Conrad, "Oral tradition & perceptions of history from the Manding peoples of West Africa" (pp. 73-96), in Emmanuel Kwame Akeyampong (ed.), *Themes in West Africa's History* (London: James Currey, 2006), especially p. 84; Pashington Obeng, "Religious interactions in pre-twentieth-century West Africa" (pp. 141-162), in Emmanuel Kwame Akeyampong (ed.), *Themes in West Africa's History* (London: James Currey, 2006), especially pp. 148-154; Eric Charry (ed.), *Mande Music: Traditional and Modern Music of the Maninka and Mandinka of Western Africa* (Chicago: University of Chicago, 1999); David C. Conrad and Barbara E. Frank (eds.), *Status and Identity in West Africa: Nyamakalaw of Munde* (Bloomington, IN: Indiana University Press, 1995).
83. Azumah, 2001, p. 56.
84. Azumah, 2001, pp. 39-41, 136-137.
85. Webb, 2006, p. 45.
86. M. Izard, "The people and kingdoms of the Niger Bend and the Volta basin from the twelfth to the sixteenth century," *General History of Africa: Africa from the Twelfth to the Sixteenth Century, Vol. IV.* Berkeley: University of California Press, 1992), pp. 87-96
87. Izard, 1992, pp. 94-96.
88. Azumah, 2001, pp. 70, 72.
89. S. M. Cissoko, "The Songhay from the twelfth to the sixteenth century," *General History of Africa: Africa from the Twelfth to the Sixteenth Century, Vol. IV.* Berkeley: University of California Press, 1992), pp. 77-86, especially pp. 79-80, 85; Levtzion, 1972, p. 145, 157.
90. King, 1986, p. 86; Masonen, p. 233.
91. Azamah, 2001, p. 29.

[92]. Ehret, 2002, pp. 164-167, 327; Levtzion, 1972, p. 154-157.

Chapter 8
Dispersal of the Malinké

> "The rope that you ignore will be used to tie you"
> — *Vai proverb*

The death in 1360 of Malian Mansa Sulayman created a vacuum at the heart of the empire. The Tuareg seized Timbuktu and other principal towns in the north, interrupting Mali's trade with the western Mediterranean world around 1433. By the 1450s, the Djolof were controlling the former Malinké-led units on the northern bank of the Gambia.

In the 1460s, Malinké and other residents of the Futa Jallon came under the control of Fula leader Tengella. After his death in 1512, his son Koli shifted the locus of control to the Futa Toro in present-day Guinea. The Fula would control that region for 250 years.[1]

Mali petered out between 1590 and 1600 during the reign of Mansa Mahmud IV. The empire had already been reduced to a small core. Its end came after Mahmud's defeat by Moroccans near Jenne. Its death knoll was sounded with the loss to the Fula empire of the Bambuk gold field. After Mahmud's death in 1610, the core was split between his three sons.[2]

Mali's all-important trade with the outside world was cut off by three military and economic superiors: Songhai in the east, Morocco in the northwest and Portugal in the south.

The wheel of history had come full cycle. After centuries of seizing forest dwellers and selling them to Arabia as slaves, the rulers of Mali were being pushed toward the forest themselves. They were about to taste the kind of bitter exile away from the Niger that Sumaoro, the Soso ruler, and his followers had faced at the hands of Sundiata, Mali's founder.

Northern Mande speakers, at the core of Mali, had the best intelligence on conditions from all points of the compass. The northern trade routes were blocked by their old enemies, the nomadic Tuaregs, who seized the northern section of Mali, including Timbuktu. The west was controlled by the powerful Wolof. Trade to the Volta region had fallen to the non-Muslim Mossi, whom they had harassed since the early 1300s.

Their best option was to head southward into lands rich in gold, iron and kola and occupied by people who were neither Muslim nor capable of mounting an effective defense, given their localized governments.[3]

The in-coming Malinké followed trade routes previously plied by Mande traders and artisans; they targeted mainly trade and artisan towns.[4] Centuries-old long-distance trade routes and the integrated economy they engendered set the platform for the next exciting stage in the history of West Africa.[5] It laid the foundation of what would become the Liberian people.

Those Malinké who fled to the area of Liberia were led by five formerly aristocratic families in Mali: the Keitas (Sundiata's lineage), the Kamaras, Kourankos, Konionkés and Diomandés. The descendants of those who brought the fight to the forest are known in Malinké as *sonangui*, meaning "warrior bands" or "war houses."[6]

Three of these incursions overturned life along the forest edge of present-day Sierra Leone, Guinea and Liberia. These expansions were more militaristic and desperate than earlier incursion by the Dyula merchants who were ancestors of the Vai.[7] As a result, many of these incursions would violate longstanding customary law regarding the obligations of "strangers" to "landlords."

When Mali was at its peak in 1300, the Malinké were confined between Siguiri on the Upper Niger River and Bougouni on the Balue River. By 1800, they had spread to the source of the Niger and as far south as present-day Liberia.

The Kouranko clan invaded territory south of the Niger. They first settled between the Niger and Niadan, especially around Koinadougou. They later penetrated all the way to Macenta, deep in Loma territory.

The Kamara clan emerged from the area around Lake Debo in the 1000s and settled towns like Sibi, Tabou and Kangaba in the heart of Mali.[8] A member of this clan, Faran Kamara, was a close ally of Sundiata in his battle with Sumanguru. After Sundiata consolidated control over Mali, the clan undertook an aggressive expansion in areas around Selegongou and Niani.[9]

By the late 1400s, the Kamara clan settled in Musadu,[10] and it is possible that their expansion might have extended further south.

Foningama, a descendent of a well-known Kamara, came to rule Musadu sometime in the late 1550s.[11] This historic town is now regarded by 12 Kamara lineages as their religious center. It would remain a key stop along a trade route linking coastal Liberia to the heart of West Africa well into the late 1800s.

Around the 1550s, the northern end of Kissidugu was occupied by the Keita lineage, scions of Mali royalty. Today, people who speak Lele, a Malinké dialect, sit like an island ringed by Kissi speakers.[12]

Further east, another northern Mande clan, the Kone, plunged south from the Niger, between the Kpelle and Loma on the one hand and the Senufo and Guro on the other. In the process, they pushed the Senufo north and the Guro to the southeast, among the Kru-speaking Mwa (also known as Mona), Nwa (also called Wan) and Ngan (labeled in some cases as Nguin).[13] Squeezed by northern Mande groups, the Kpelle pushed the Ma toward the east before settling among them and intermarrying.

According to a Kpelle oral tradition, they were able to repeal the Konionké from Konodougou, with a gun brought from the coast by the Gou clan of the Dan who settled among them under the direction of Zougoussogoli.[14] The mention of a gun in story memorializes the arrival of Western arms and suggest the Kpelle still did not have direct access to the coast at the time of this incident.

Like the Loma and Kpelle, Ma and Dan oral traditions suggest their group identities emerged after they settled along the rim of the forest, not earlier. Because the Kpelle and Ma converged on Nzerekore around the same time, it is possible to date the arrival of the southeast Mande roughly to sometime after 1235 AD, when ancestors of the Kpelle left Mali.

The Mane Conquest of the Sierra Leone Peninsula

Several European sources from the 1500s documented invaders along the coast of western Liberia and eastern Sierra Leone. Some referred to invaders called Mane.[15] Other documents cited a group called Quoia.[16]

In a groundbreaking history of the Upper Guinea Coast, historian Walter Rodney suggested that the various documents actually employed different names for what was essentially one invasion. That conclusion has since been overturned, but many of his other significant findings have endured. More importantly, his work served to draw the attention of other scholars, not only to those documents as valuable sources of historical data, but also to this region in the 1500s as a neglected field for historical research.[17]

A key source on the Mane was captain André Álvares de Almada, who actually observed events in the Sierra Leone peninsula around 1560. The Mane first appeared in the region at Sherbro Island, where they subdued the Bullom.[18] Members of the invading party terrorized the local populations: First, by desecrating graves in search of gold. Then, by cooking and eating some of their victims.[19]

In the view of Almada, local groups were crushed because of their lack of organization, inexperience in warfare and refusal to assist each other.[20]

The Sape found themselves facing certain defeat and possibly being consumed by the invader. Instead, their ruler surrendered himself, his wives and many of his people to the Portuguese, who sold them into slavery.[21]

The Mane began at Sherbro Island and travelled about 240 miles north-northwest. They transversed hills, swamps and rivers to reach the Iles de Los, their northernmost point of conquest.[22]

Facing little resistance, the Mane subjugated various communities along Sherbro Island and the Sierra Leone peninsula. They then set their sights on what was the most prosperous and powerful group in the region: the Soso.

Prior to the attack, the Mane did to the Soso what they had done to other groups. They sent an ultimatum in the form of cloths and arms, representing a choice between surrender or war.

The Soso indicated a willingness to live in peace. But, they sent copies of their own weapons, signaling a readiness, if their challengers chose war.

Taking offense, the Mane assembled the largest collection of weapons this region had ever seen. Their unusually large army included a Portuguese marksman and many of the people they had conquered.

The Soso, on the other hand, were aligned with the equally powerful Fula.

In preparing for battle, the Soso ruler gave a speech to his troops. He reportedly said, "If there is one man among us whose heart has said that he should not fight, I here give him permission to go back and join the company of the women."[23]

As the Mane approached, the Soso sent a patrol ahead with several cows, which they killed and cooked in large pots. They left the food behind, as if in flight from the enemy.

The Mane fell for the trick and devoured the meal. They died in large numbers because the food was laced with poison.

The Soso were led by seven men riding short Fula horses, decked with breast plates and great bells. Their army featured archers in the center with shield-bearers in front and on the sides.

The Mane fled across a river, pursued by the Soso and their allies who knew the area better. Only the fastest and bravest Mane forces were able to escape. The Soso killed or captured the rest.

According to Almada, the Mane-Soso battle lasted about three days.[24] After this decisive defeat, the Mane settled down to governing the previously conquered region and avoided provoking the Soso.[25]

Making Sense of the Invasion

Anthropologist Andreas W. Massing analyzed the dates given in five European sources from the 1500s. He estimated that the Mane left the Niger sometime between 1495 and 1505, arrived on the coast between 1545 and 1556, and were firmly in control by 1560. Given this span of time, he argued, the conquest was the result, less of a single invasion, and more of "a gradual infiltration and colonization."[26]

The Mane invasion was apparently a grasp by groups based inland for control of the growing coastal trade. It consisted mainly of male warriors whose offsprings were absorbed into the language communities of their mothers.[27] So, it did not alter the language map.

Almada noted similarities in attire and weapons between the Mane and a trading party from the West African interior that he had seen near the Gambia River.

The weapons of both groups consisted of short bows and short poison arrows. Like the Mane, some members of Gambia party wore "smocks of cotton cloth which they commonly call shirts, these stop above the knees, and the wide sleeves go to the elbows. Their trousers almost reach the ground, with the bottoms more than a span below the knees; the trousers are wide and the smocks large. They wear many plumes of birds' feathers in their shirts and caps."[28]

Almada conjectured that the Mane originated in the Mali empire. His informants claimed that the people involved in the Mane incursion had been involved in invasions going back to ancient times; scholars have interpreted this as pointing to a northern Mande connection, especially the Kamara clan.

Among the Kamara clan of the Beyla Prefecture in Guinea, oral traditions recall military movements to the sea.[29] The leaders of the Mane invasion, who came via the coast, seem to have used alternative names for Kamara, including *shere* or *sere*. In contrast, the Kamara variant is widely used in the rest of southern Sierra Leone and western Liberia that were affected by the later Quoja invasion.[30]

The identity of the invaders has been obscured, in part, by the mystery surrounding their colorful foot soldiers, called "Sumba" by Portuguese explorer André Dornelas and "Kumba" by Dutch geographer Olfert Dapper. Both authors described them as cannibals, who acted under the direction of leaders who were not.[31]

This has led many scholars to assume the two groups belonged to different ethnic groups, one being more "civilized" than the other. In keeping with prevailing stereotypes, various ethnic groups with longer-standing roots in the region have been cast as the "cannibals," from the Kru to the Loma.[32]

Historians now broadly agree that the Mane, or at least their leadership, consisted of Northern Mande speakers.[33]

Anthropologist Andrea W. Massing pointed to the Mane use of *Falma* and the surname *Shere*. The first term was apparently derived from *faama/farma/falma*, designating a governor in Mandinka territorial-military organization. The second is an alternative name for the Kamara clan, which was used as a Mandinka title in the Gambia region.[34]

But the case for a Northern Mande origin of the Mane has been built without equal consideration being given to alternative explantations.

According to André Donelha, for example, the Mane were led by a female leader called *Macarico*.[35] That does not fit with what is known about the patriarchal structure of northern Mande groups at that time.

In addition, northern Mande farmers and merchants did not typically bedeck themselves in feathers, as was worn by some members of the group at the Gambia cited by Almada.

As for the style of weapons carried by the two groups observed by Almada, there is an account by a pre-1170 AD Arab chronicler of West African life who linked that style to the Ququ, people who were neither Mande nor Muslim. "They shoot arrows poisoned with the blood of a yellow snake ... Their bows ... are short and so are their arrows ... The other [people of West Africa] are useful as slaves and laborers, but not the *Ququ*, who have no good qualities except in war."[36]

The Quoia Invasion

A second invasion near Cape Mount — and the political unit it created — were recorded by Dutch geographer Olfert Dapper. They were included in a book he published in 1668. It was the fullest description of Africa to that date.

An English translation was published in 1669-70 by John Oglivy with the title *Africa: Being an Accurate Description of the Regions of Egypt, Barbary, Lybia, and Billedulgerid, the Land of Negroes, Guinee, Ethiopia, and the Abyssines.*

Dapper himself never visited Africa, but he drew upon many Dutch works available only in manuscript form. Especially important was the writing of Samuel Bloomeasrt, a Dutch trader who lived in the area of Sierra Leone and Cape Mount sometime between 1614 and 1651.[37] Dapper also used the published work of Pierre d'Avity (also Davity), a French soldier.[38]

Dapper began his description of societies in present-day Liberia with a "Kingdom" called Quoia. He said it was conquered "antiently" by the Karou who were assisted by the Folgia.

The origin of the "Quoia" name is not explicitly addressed by Dapper's informant. Linguist P. E. H. Hair has suggested it meant "place by the sea." In contrast, linguist David Dwyer has proposed "the descendants of Ko." However, it is worth noting how similar it is to *Quoja*, the Vai word for "bushcow," suggesting an oblique reference to the invaders' origin in the direction of the forest.[39]

Dapper claimed that the Karou and Folgia previously lived by a river (which he identified as the Junk), where they engaged in continuous quarrels.[40]

Their eastern neighbor entered into a conflict with the Folgia, who subdued them. This group, called Quabe, was located at another river (identified by historian Andreas W. Massing as River Scarcies). To the west of Folgia was a group that Dapper's informant called "Manou" (which simply means "the people" in contemporary Vai).[41]

A final straw in the Karou-Folgia feud came when the Folgia threw boiled fish with scales into a Karou pond. This act violated two of the group's well known taboos. First, the Karou regarded the pond as the point where their first ancestor had descended from heaven to earth. And second, the Karou observed a strict prohibition against eating fish with scales. The Karou took up arms to avenge this wrong, but the Folgia people prevailed.[42]

Soon after this victory, the Folgia leader, Mendino, died. His brother Manimassah was subjected to trial-by-ordeal on suspicion of being responsible.[43] He survived the ordeal, but left home in outrage.

Manimassah went to live among the Gola, who inexplicably appointed him as their ruler. But, his subjects failed to pay proper homage, so he appealed to the Folgia ruler (his brother-in-law) for support. Folgia troops were sent, and they reportedly imposed Manimassah as the undisputed ruler of the Gola.[44]

Living among the Folgia was a man named Fesiach who pursued them to attack the Vai. He had lived among the Vai and his uncle Flonikerry had led the conquest of the Gola. The present-day Mende and Bandi name for the Vai, *Karou*, echoes the name of one set of warriors who invaded Cape Mount.[45]

With help from their former enemies, the Karou, Folgia warriors conquered the Vai, using poisoned arrows.

But, the conquerors were then attacked by the Gola, led by Minimique, Manimassa's son.[46] During the battle, the leading Folgia fighter, Flonikerry, was slain. With help from the Vai, the Folgia were able to rally, defeat the Gola and subdue (without a fight) the Puy, who lived next to the Vai.

The conquerors were savoring this victory when word came of rebellions by the Bullom and Dogo, two previously conquered groups. Folgia fighters returned and crushed them, before marching off to Cape Mesurado to subdue the Gebbe.[47]

European sources did not document exactly how the invaders got to Cape Mount, but they likely took the well-travelled route from Musadu to Bopolu, then down to the coast.

If that was the case, the group probably emerged from Coyah, Guinea, which was along that route and, according to Pereira, had been conducting a vigorous exchange of gold for salt with the coast. The Northern Mande group in the area at the time was the Konianke, which traces its origin to the Mali empire in the 1200s.[48]

Interpreting the Quoja Invasion

A challenge for scholars tackling the Quoia text has been the confusing web of labels applied to various groups. But, the movements described in the Quoia manuscript can best be understood, not as wholesale migrations of ethnic groups. Instead, they were military maneuvers by warlords and their fighters.

The type of movement implied in the Quoia text conforms to the "migrant band," one of four political organizations that existed historically in what is now western Liberia. According to anthropologist Warren L. d'Azevedo, each band consisted of "a leader accompanied by a group of his kinsmen together with any number of unrelated followers and slaves.

Bands of this kind varied in size from less than a score of persons to hundreds. They were landless groups moving from place to place, forming temporary attachments with permanently established units, then continuing on in search of advantageous situations."

As noted by d'Azevedo, many of the encounters described in oral traditions did not involve "confrontations between massive and unitary entities," but rather "interrelations among small independent human groups spreading out and merging with other groups to form new units in which any one of a number of 'ethnic' traditions might predominate, depending on the historical circumstances. In such a context the term 'tribe' in its standard definition can scarcely comprehend the realities of cultural pluralism, multiculturalism and multiple local traditions of origin and 'ethnicity' which obtain within situations that are only superficially — and fre-

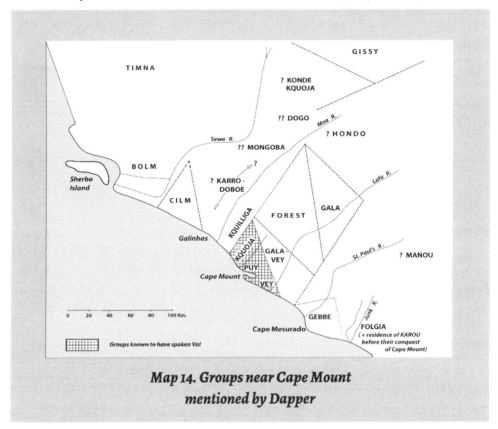

Map 14. Groups near Cape Mount mentioned by Dapper

quently only temporarily — characterized by a predominant 'tribal' orientation."[49]

Adding to the confusion are the many different groups mentioned by Dapper. These apparently ranged from clans through various language groups and political units. Dapper's informant referred to one group simply as "the people." He apparently belonged to this group, which was central to the story. He added the "people" suffix to all other ethnic groups (e.g., "Puy-Manou").

The present-day identity of this group is revealed later in the text when it is noted that the Folgia referred to "the people" as Mendi (meaning "lord'). It was also the name given to the Quoia by the Folgia, the Bolum and the Temne.[50]

In light of these details, the Quoia narrative clearly offers a history of the Mende ("the people") told by someone rooted in that community.

The language of the Folgia was called Mendi-co ("lordly tongue") by neighboring groups because it was considered "courtly and eloquent." This similarity in names suggests a close affinity between the two groups, at least in the ears of their coastal subjects. It is worth noting that the present-day Manya on the Liberia-Guinea border are known as Komendi.[51] It is likely that the Quoia, Folgia, and Karou were mere clans of the Mende, and the details given on its composition resulted from the narrator's perspective as an insider.

Of the groups mentioned, the most culturally diverse was the "Kingdom or Countrey" of Quoia. Within it were the Quoia (among whom the narrator apparently lived), the Vai, the Gola-Vai, the Pui, and, to a lesser extent, the Karou.[52]

Several scholars assumed these subunits were different ethnic groups with discrete languages. But, they appear to have been clans who spoke the same language, a language which Dapper labeled as "Quoia." Linguist P. E. H. Hair has established their vocabulary as similar to contemporary Vai.[53]

Dapper's informant thought the Vai were dying out, but he was obviously wrong. As is generally the case, a small group of male invaders were successful in usurping political power in the short-term. But, in the long-term, the culture and language ("mother-tongue") of local women prevailed, given their role in the early socialization of children.[54]

These ancestors of the Vai had enjoyed centuries of contact with the Arabs of North Africa. This interaction influenced the style of Vai clothes and left Arabic words embedded in the Vai language. For example, all of the Vai words for weekdays are derived from Arabic.[55] (See "Vai Words for Weekdays" above.) Such borrowing occurred in many other languages, such as the English use of Arabic words like "assassin" and "algebra."

According to Dapper's informant, Quoia territory was nursed by several bodies of water, including (from west to east): Magwibba (Magowi), Mavah (Mafa), Plizoge (Lake Piso, which he mislabeled as a river), and Menoch.

The groups listed as living in Quoia included the Vai, the Puy (who had intermarried with the Karou to such an extent as to be indistinguishable), the Quoia, and Gola-Vai, a mixture of Gola (who were driven from their home by the Hondo) and the Vai (among whom they settled).[56]

North of Quoia territory were the Hondo, among whom some of the Mende also lived. The group labeled as the Hondo by Dapper is identified in oral traditions as the Bandi, who are described as having displaced some elements of the Gola.

Farther north were the Upcountry Mende and the proper Gola. Beyond them was a territory which Dapper labeled "Kingdom of Folgia and Manou." From the name, it seems this was a political unit composed of two clans of one group, the

Mende-co and the Mende. It was said to be located between two rivers identified as the Anverado [Mesurado?] and the Junk.⁵⁷

Dapper's informant identified the Karro-doboe, who lived 32 miles up the Gallinas River as the only group in the area that used canoes.

Quabbe was one of several groups said to be living along the Cestos River. This was possible the Kuwaa, who would be pushed west when the Kpelle and Ma entered from the north.

The Quea is undoubtedly the Kwea, a Bassa group in present-day Liberia. According to Dapper's informant, the Quoia, the Karou, the Folgia, the Manou, the Hondo, the Gola and the Gebbe all shared the Poro association and practiced circumcision.⁵⁸

Anthropologist Sven E. Holsoe argued, "There is little alternative but to accept the Folgia as the present-day Kpelle — they are the only Mande-speaking people living in the central section of Liberia, and there are no other small clusters of [Mande speakers] who might have preceded them."

Regarding the Karou, he averred, "it is likely that they were Kru-speaking people" (although he doesn't say why) and it seems that most likely, from the location given in the account and the knowledge we have of present-day tribal locations, that they are the ancestors of the Bassa people."

He concluded "one has to assume that the Gebbe were [Dei] whose descendants were still living in that area ... in the early nineteenth century."⁵⁹ These arguments assume that culture has stood still since the Quoia incursion and do not take into account the malleability of group identities.

Two other aspects of the Quoia manuscript have proven challenging for understanding the events it purports to recount, namely the narrator's treatment of time and space.

Descriptions of the power structures and relations given in the section titled "The Kingdom or Countrey of Quoia" are presented as existing in Dapper's day, unless specifically labeled as "antient."

However, other events are told mainly in chronological order, but seem to

Figure 34. Arabic influences on Vai words for weekdays

Vai	Arabic	English
Lahadi	Al-Ahadu	Sunday
Tanee	Al-Thalahau	Monday
Talata	Al-Thalath	Tuesday
Alaba	Al-Rabau	Wednesday
Aikamisa, Aimisa	Al-Khamisu	Thursday
Aljuma, Aijima	Al-Jumatu	Friday
Simbiti	Al-Sabtu	Saturday

Dispersal of the Malinké

fall vaguely between "antient" times and the time of the narration. They are described in the section titled "A Relation, in What Manner the Karou's Subdued by force of Arms, by the assistance of the Folgians, the Countreys of Vey, Puy, and Quoia-Berkoma,"[60]

Dapper's informant gives rich details within Quoia territory, including the names of towns, islands, and even various types of trees. But, when discussing events outside Quoia, he shifts to citing broad coastal landmarks that were likely to be known to European audiences, especially rivers.

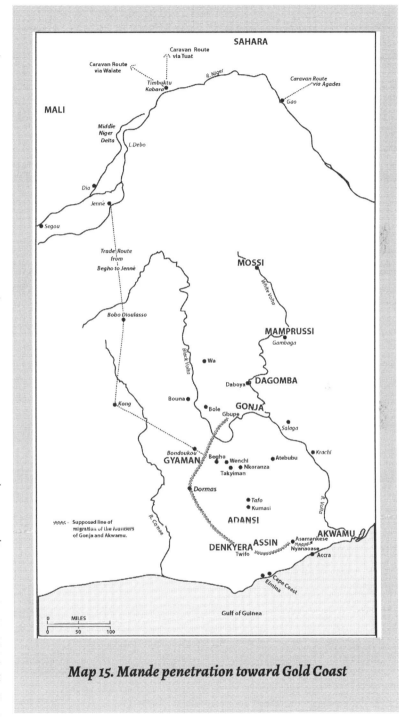

Map 15. Mande penetration toward Gold Coast

Emergence of Mende, Disappearance of Dama

Many scholars have assumed that the events recounted in this section of the Quoia document occurred near the *mouths* of the named rivers in the same timeframe as those in Quoia. But, that was apparently not the case.

They more likely occurred higher up along these rivers. For example, the Mende and their allies the Mende-co apparently descended south from somewhere between the headwaters of the Mesurado and the Junk rivers.

This relocation must have occurred far enough in the past that an entirely new Gola-Vai hybrid clan was living in Cape Mount when the Mende arrived. In that case, the Gola would have arrived at least a generation or two earlier.[61]

The Mende fighters probably passed through Gola territory to reach Cape Mount. The narrator does not explicitly say this, but it is likely since some Folgia fighters had earlier subdued the Gola.[62]

As noted by linguist David Dwyer, the language terrain in Sierra Leone is highly unusual, even for a region with language fragmentation. It has three "dialect archipelagos," meaning "a situation in which two closely related languages or dialects (the islands) are separated by a third less closely related languages (the sea)."

These paired dialects are Kissi/Bullom, Vai/Kono and Loko/Bandi. All three are wedged apart by a sea of Mende-speakers flowing between them. Kissi and Bullom are close to being mutually intelligible but different enough to be considered separate languages. Vai and Kono are so closely related that they are considered dialects of one Mande language. Loko and Bandi are dialects of another, and they are both closely related to Mende.[63]

The direction of the Mane and Quoia invasions can be detected in the layout of the Bullom languages (a subgroup of Atlantic). Shading in population from heavy to light, these languages are Kissi (at the border of northern Liberia and southern Guinea), Sherbro, Klim, Blom and Mani, with a few hundred remaining speakers at the western Sierra Leone and coastal Guinea border.[64]

Historian Walter Rodney argued that Mende culture and language arose from a mixing of the conquerors and the conquered, mainly the Bullom and the Temne. Linguist David Dwyer rejects the implication of a 50-50 mixture of languages. Instead, he argues that Mende developed as a lingua franca, characterized by "linguistic simplification" resulting from the loss of some morphological complexities.[65]

The Mende settled in an area occupied by the Dama. That group lived midway between the Kono and Vai and spoke a language closely related to its two neighbors. Dama has disappeared, but in the 1960s traces of its vocabulary were known to older Mende people.[66]

As noted by Dwyer, this configuration of languages could only have resulted from population movements.[67]

From the Quoia text, it is not clear if the Mende had moved *en masse* to their current location. That is because the narrative lacks time markers and focuses narrowly on the actions of fighters. But, the manuscript helps to establish several important aspects of the region's history:

First, some Mende, if not all, settled between the northern edge of the forest and the coast. Second, the Bandi moved southward and some Gola settled among the Vai at least one generation before the narrative was collected. Third, several institutions transcended the limits of individual ethnic groups, including the Quoia "kingdom" and the Poro association.[68]

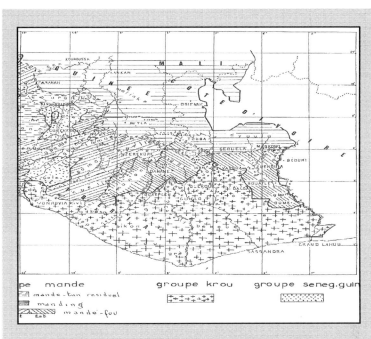

Map 16. Languages in Mano River Region

A Movement that Shook the Entire Region

As noted by historian Allen M. Howard, "Mande migrants came from many places, generation after generation, trekked along cross-cutting paths, and settled widely throughout the north-west. Mande movements and settlements were in response to historical 'push' and 'pull' factors in the interior, in the northwest, and on the coast, particularly commercial factors."[69]

During this period, the northern Mande pursued two distinct approaches to people living in the forest: one pacifist, the other militarist.

The development of trading diasporas closer to the forest and coast was indirectly encouraged by the teachings of Al-Hajj Salim Suwari. He taught that nonbelievers weren't evil and their ignorance of Islam was to be accepted as the will of God. The influence of this Soninké cleric rose as Mali was collapsing.

As noted by historian Ivor Wilks, Suwari "formulated a praxis of co-existence" that enable Muslim traders "to operate within lands of unbelief without prejudice to their distinctive Muslim identity, allowing them access to the material resources of this world without foregoing salvation in the next."[70]

As early as the 1450s, Malinke warriors led by Tiramakhan Traore had established a political unit at the mouth of the Gambia, under the authority of Mali.[71] Between the Gambia and Casamance Rivers, two types of political units emerged, both ruled by Malinké tied to Mali: One was settled by Malinké farmers and traders. In the others, the only Malinké presence were the rulers and their retinues.[72]

Those soft incursions were followed by more violent ones: Around 1500, large numbers of northern Mande groups repeatedly dispersed southward often led by horse warriors who conquered vast territories inhabited by speakers of Atlantic, Gur and Southern Mande languages.

The horsemen and other warriors who descended onto the forest belt of present-day Guinea were mainly Maninka speakers.[73] The interests of Malinké griots and blacksmiths were tied to the warrior class. Blacksmiths supplied their weapons and griots their heroic stories.[74]

Historian Ivor Wilks dated the consolidation of Dyula communities in modern-day Ghana to the early-1400s, just as European demand for gold was increasing.[75] In the mid-1500s, Muslim Dyula founded the core of Gonja, a state north of the Black Volta River.[76] According to a Gonja tradition recorded in Arabic, the state was founded by Malian troops. They were reportedly sent south by the Mansa to assist Begho (an earlier Malinké community) in restoring the flow of gold toward the empire.[77]

From Begho and Gonja, leading Mande families disbursed westward into present-day Côte d'Ivoire, where they displaced or imposed control over other groups. The Ouattara clan from Kong, along with the Kamarte and Diabagarate, had a presence in Gonja, Koulango and Abron.[78] Some Kamara settled in Larbanga. Members of the Ligbi clan from Begho also built a presence in Kintampa, Fougoula and Boundoukou.[79]

Before 1642, the gold from Begho in present-day Ghana flowed northward to the Sahel and beyond. But, that year, the Dutch ousted the Portuguese trading monopoly from the Gold Coast. They were followed by the Danish, English and other Europeans.[80]

As competition for gold increased along the coast, supplies from Begho were diverted south, especially after the 1670s.[81] Mande emigrants from Begho went on to settle in Salaga in present-day Ghana and Kong, Bonduku, Bouna and Bole in Côte d'Ivoire.[82]

Between 1500 and 1630 AD, rainfall increased in West Africa. As a result, the "Tsetse fly line" moved about 124 miles north. This improved grazing grounds in the Sahara and Sahel, to the advantage of Fula and other herders.[83]

Dispersal of the Malinké

Over time, differences between Malinké and Fula would blur, leading to a new Mande-Fulbe mix of Hal Pular speakers.[84]

After 1630, increased dry weather caused the Tsetse flies to retreat further south, by several hundred miles. Maninke horsemen seized the chance to conduct slaving raids on communities close to the forest.[85]

As noted by historian George E. Brooks, Malinké movement set off a chain reaction that involved Soso (also called Susu), Baga and Nalu moving south from the Futa Jallon, followed by some Southwest Mande and Kru language groups moving into what is now eastern Sierra Leone and northern Liberia.

The Malians were now hell-bent on seizing the coastal trade. Their invasions turned the settled life of communities along the forest rim upside down. Societies bound by Poro, committed to traditional religion and democratic rules were suddenly overrun by Muslim horsemen claiming loyalty to "royal" families. They did not clear virgin land, as other groups had done. Instead, they seized control of key trading districts that were already occupied.

Historian Yves Person characterized this Northern Mande expansion south as "one of those movements of peoples that have shaken whole regions of the continent," like the Zulu would centuries later.[86]

---

[1]. Levtzion, 1973, pp. 96-98; Levtzion, 1972, p. 145; Ly-Tall, 1992, pp. 70-76.
[2]. Levtzion, 1973, p. 99.
[3]. d'Azevedo, 1959, pp. 53-55.
[4]. Brooks, 1993, p. 106.
[5]. Horton, 1972, p. 116.
[6]. Ivor Wilkes, "The Juula and the expansion of Islam into the forest" (pp. 93-115), in Nehemia Levtzion and Rudall L. Pouwels, eds., *The History of Islam in Africa* (Athens: Ohio University Press, 2000), pp. 94-95.
[7]. G. Tucker Childs, *An Introduction to African Language* (Philadelphia: John Benjamins Publishing Co., 2003), pp. 21-22, citing Brooks, 1993, pp. 59, 67.
[8]. Massing, 1985, p. 35, n. 29.
[9]. E. Leynaud and Y. Cissé, *Paysans Malinké du Haut Niger: Tradition et développement rural en Afrique Soudanaise* (Bamako: Imprimerie populaire du Mali, 1978), pp. 28, 31, 151-152; D. T. Niane, *Recherches sur l'empire du Mali au Moyen Age* (Paris: Présence africaine, 1975), pp. 95, 78.
[10]. Fairhead, 2008, p. 81.

[11]. Fairhead, 2008; Person, 1968, p. 242; Person, 1987, p. 249; Geysbeek, 2002; Korvah, 1960, p. 7; Korvah, 1995; Jones, 1987; Massing, 1985, p. 36; Fairhead, Geysbeek, Holsoe and Leach, 2003, p. 136.

[12]. Childs, 1995, p. 1.

[13]. Germain, 1984, p. 70.

[14]. Germain, 1984, p. 80.

[15]. Andrea Alvares d'Almada, *Brief Treatise on the Rivers of Guinea*, translated by P. E. G. Hair (Liverpool: University of Liverpool, 1984); 'Alvares, 1990.

[16]. G. Dabien, M. Delafosse and G. Thilmans, "Barbot's Description of the African Coasts," *Bulletin de l'Institute francais d'Afrique noire*, Série B, 40 (1979): 235-395.

[17]. Rodney, 1980; Person, 1971, pp. 669-689; Massing, 1985, pp. 21-55.

[18]. The place names used here are from Massing, 1985, p. 26 n. 13; they were given in Almada, 1964, pp. 125-127, as ilha de Toto and Tausente.

[19]. Almada, 2010, p. 124.

[20]. Almada, 2010, pp. 125-127.

[21]. Almada, 2010, pp. 127-128.

[22]. Almada, 1984, Chapter 17 n. 6.

[23]. Almada, 2010, pp. 130-134, especially pp. 131-132.

[24]. Hair, 1984, Chapter 18 n. 5.

[25]. Almada, 2010, p. 133.

[26]. Massing, 1985, p. 27.

[27]. Wondji, 1992, pp. 187-203, especially pp. 189-191; Yves Person, "The coastal people from Casamance to the Côte d'Ivoire lagoons: First Contacts with the Portuguese" (pp. 118-127), in Djibril Tamsir Niane, *Africa from the Twelfth to the Sixteenth Century* (Berkeley: University of California Press, 1997), especially pp. 119, 123, 125.

[28]. Almada, 2010, p. 124.

[29]. Almada, 1964, pp. 131, 138; Almada, 2010, p. 127; Person, 1971, p. 675.

[30]. Dwyer, 2005, p. 31.

[31]. André Dornelas, *An Account of Sierra Leone and the Rivers of Guinea of Cape Verde*, with notes and English translation by P. E. H. Hair (Lisboa: Junta de Investigaçöes Cientificas do Ultramar, 1977), p. 107. For Joao Bermudes' erroneous linking of the Mane to the Jaga of Angola, see Andrew Battel, Samuel Purchas and Anthony Knivet, *The Strange Adventures of Andrew Battell of Leigh, in Angola and the Adjoining Regions* (London: The Hakluyt Society, 1901), pp. 149-153. He seems to have conflated the Mane invasion with events in Angola, which has a town called Sumba

[32]. For the Loma as cannibals, see Person, 1971, p. 685; Holsoe, 1967, p. 8, citing W. Volz, "Reisedurch das Hinterland von Liberia," *Jahresbericht der Geographischen Gesselchaft von Bern*, 22 (1908-1910): 213-218 For the Kru, see Rodney, 1980, pp. 51-56.

[33]. Massing, 1985; Person, 1971, pp. 675-679; Rodney, 1971, pp. 43-51; Avelino Teixeira da Mota, "Introduction," in André Donelha, *An Account of Sierra Leone and Rivers of Guinea of Cape Verde (1625)*, with notes and English translation by P. E. H. Hair (Lisboa: Junta de Investigaçoes Cientificas do Ultramar, 1977), p. 47.

[34]. Massing, 1985, pp. 25; Rodney, 1970, p. 47.

[35]. Dornelas, 1977, p. 107; Almada, 1984, Chapter 17 n. 2.

[36]. Abu Hamid al-Ghanati, *Tuhfat al-albab*, in Levtzion and Hopkins, 2011, p. 133.

37. John D. Fage, *A Guide to Original Sources in Precolonial Western Africa Published in European Languages, for the Most Part in Book Form* (Madison: African Studies Program, University of Wisconsin-Madison,1994), pp. xi.
38. Hallett, 1965, p. 67; P. E. H. Hair, "Barbot, Dapper, Davity: A Critique of Sources of Sierra Leone and Cape Mount," *History of Africa*. 1 (1974): 25-54, especially pp. 33-39; P. E. H. Hair, "An early seventeenth-century vocabulary of Vai," *African Studies*, 23, 3-4 (1964): 129-139. The Quoia manuscript was published in 1668 by Dutch writer, translator, geographer and historian Olfert Dapper in a book with the title *Naukeurige Beschrijvinge der Afrikaensche Gewesten*. Dapper, who never visited Africa, relied on the records of the Dutch West India Company, especially the papers of one of its officials, Samuel Bloomeasrt. An English translation of Dapper's book was published in 1670 with the title *Africa: Being an Accurate Description of the Regions of Egypt, Barbary, Lybia, and Billedulgerid, the Land of Negroes, Guinee, Ethiopia, and the Abyssines* and attributed to John Oglivy. I have used the Oglivy translation but have credited it to Dapper.
39. Hair, 1968, p. 50 n. 25; Dwyer, 2005, p. 34; Oglivy, 1670, p. 385.
40. Oglivy, 1670, pp. 407-408.
41. Oglivy, 1670, p. 408; Massing, 1985, p. 26, n. 15.
42. Oglivy, 1670, p. 407. Many communities among the Bandi, Loma, Kpelle, Ma and Dan maintained pools with protected catfish (*Siluridae*); see Schwab, 1947, pp. 338-339.
43. Oglivy, 1670, p. 408.
44. Oglivy, 1670, pp. 408-409.
45. Hair, 1968, p. 64; also Migeod, 1972, p. 162; Dwyer, 2005, p. 30 n. 2.
46. Oglivy, 1670, pp. 409-410.
47. Oglivy, 1670, pp. 410-411.
48. The Konianke are also known as Coniagui, Konagi, Koniagui and Konyanke. Despite roots in Mali, they are now highly concentrated in Guinea, Côte d'Ivoire and Sierra Leone. They are related to the Diamande, the Gyomande, the Mahu and the Old Diula; see James Stuart Olson, *The Peoples of Africa: An Ethnohistorical Dictionary* (Westport, Conn.: Greenwood Press, 1996), p. 296; Christian K. Hyjbjerg, *Resisting State Iconoclasm: Among the Loma of Guinea* (Durham, NC: Carolina Academic Press, 2007), p. 80; Person, 1997, p. 312.
49. d'Azevedo, 1989, pp. 103, 99.
50. Oglivy, 1670, pp 379, 407-412. For the linking of *monou* from the Quoia text to the Vai word *moenu* (meaning "people"), see Hair, 1964, p. 132 n. 11b.
51. Dwyer, 2005, p. 34.
52. Oglivy, 1670, pp. 381, 409-411.
53. Hair, 1964, 129-139.
54. Oglivy, 1670, p. 379.
55. H. Boikai Freeman, "The Vai and their kinfolk," *Negro History Bulletin*, 16, 3 (Dec. 1, 1952): 51-64, especially p. 59.
56. Oglivy, 1670, p. 379-381.
57. Oglivy, 1670, p. 381. The text refers to the people beyond the Hondo as the "Konde-Quoia's, that differ in Speech from the Maritime Quoia's." I have substituted Upcountry for *Konde* based on a translation from Hair, 1964, p. 132 n. 12.
58. Oglivy, 1670, pp. 402-405; Susan Bailey, "Circumcision and male initiation" (pp. 88-91), in Theodore Celenko, ed., *Egypt in Africa* (Indianapolis: Indiana University Press, 1996.
59. Holsoe, 1967, p. 13.

60. Oglivy, 1670, pp. 379-407.
61. Oglivy, 1670, p. 381; for oral traditions, see Germain, 1984, p. 67; Bureau of Folkways, 1955; Johnson, 1961; d'Azevedo, 1959; Person, 1961.
62. Oglivy, 1670, pp. 408-409.
63. Dwyer, 2005, p. 33.
64. G. Tucker Childs, "What happens to class when a language dies? Language change vs. language death," *Studies in African Linguistics* 38, 2 (2009): 113-130.
65. Rodney, 1967, p. 237; Dwyer, 2005, p. 37.
66. T. D. P. Dalby, "The extinct language of Dama," *Sierra Leone Language Review*, No. 2 (1963): 50-54.
67. Dwyer, 2005, p. 33-34. The argument of population movement was suggested by Rodney and supported by Person, but initially disputed by Hair. While accepting Dwyer's explanation of language displacements, I would argue that the population movements and subsequent group interactions he assigned to the Mane invasion fit more closely with the Quoia incursion.
68. Hair, 1968, p. 50 n. 25; Dwyer, 2005, p. 34; Oglivy, 1670, p. 385.
69. Howard, 2000, p. 18.
70. Wilks, 2000, pp. 98; Doudou Diene, *The Routes of al-Andalus: Spiritual Convergence and Intercultural Dialogue* (Paris: UNESCO, 2001).
71. Nehemia Levtzion, *Ancient Ghana and Mali* (London: Methuen, 1973), p. 95.
72. Levtzion, 1973, pp. 95-96. The Portuguese named one of the rivers Casamanse because there was a political unit known as Kasa that was governed by a Mansa — Malinké for "ruler."
73. Brooks, 1989, p. 36.
74. Brooks, 1989, pp. 36-37.
75. Ivor Wilks, "The northern factor in Ashanti history: Begho and the Mande," *Journal of African History*, 11, 1 (1961): 25-34, especially p. 28.
76. Wilks, 1961, p. 30; Levtzion, 1973, p. 102.
77. Wilks, 1961, p. 30; Wilks, 1972, p. 362; Stewart, 1979, pp. 293-295.
78. Parinbam, 1973, p. 425.
79. Parinbam, 1973, p. 425.
80. Wilks, 1961, p. 32.
81. Wilks, 1961, pp. 28, 32.
82. Wilks, 1961, pp. 25, 29-30; Parinbam, 1973, p. 425.
83. Brooks, 1989, p. 37.
84. Howard, 2000, p. 13, n. 1
85. Brooks, 1989, p. 37.
86. Person, 1988, p. 125.

Chapter 9
Into the Forest

> Pull rope, and rope will pull bush
>
> — *Liberian proverb*

Oral traditions confirm the accounts in the Quoia document of people moving into the forest of present-day Liberia. A careful comparison of traditions from different ethnic groups provides an outline of the basic order in which various groups moved. Fortunately, several early European documents provide rough dates for when these movements occurred. They would have been sometime between the Mane invasion around 1560 and well before 1651, when the principal source on the Quoia invasion, Samuel Bloomeasrt, ended his engagement with the area around Sierra Leone and Cape Mount.[1]

Prior to the Malinké incursions, the ancestors of most Liberians were congregated in the north along the edge of the savannah and in the south along the coast near a few river banks. The other 90 percent of the territory, covered by forests, was practically uninhabited.

This is suggested by the large number of leopards and other destructive animals that inhabited the region until around 1700. For example, Europeans named the nearby territory "Côte d'Ivoire" based on the large number of elephants and tusks. Generally, the number of wild animals decreased as the number of people went up.[2]

Oral traditions make it clear that the forest-rim in present-day Guinea was already occupied by southwest Mande, southeast Mande and Kru groups when ancestors of most Malinké arrived. Also in the area were several offshoots of the Dyalanke, including the Vai, Kono and Dama.

From east to west, there were ancestors of the Ma, Dan and Wee near Man, Côte d'Ivoire. Around Musadu were the Gola, Loma, Kpelle, Kono, Bassa, Bandi, Dan and Ma.[3] They formed four clusters, each linked to a major trade town: Kissidugu, Beyla, Musadu and Man.

The major trading town of Kankan was occupied by some Loma and some Kissi, the town's original settlers.[4] Another key town in the area was Beyla, an ethnic melting pot. Further west was Kissidugu, inhabited by the Bandi, Mende, Loma and some Kissi.

According to historian Allen M. Howard, Northern Mande identity in Sierra Leone formed first "around people, practices, institutions, and values associated with nodal places. Secondly, identity was also form through the working of economic, social, and political networks that linked nodes and with ideas flowing in such networks. Thirdly, identity was given content by meaningful events that happened in particular places and in places connected by networks and by the contested historical memories of events. Thus, Mande identities were shaped through interactions, and so-called ethnic identities often grew out of confrontations that involved the mobilization of people and the production of meanings and symbols."[5]

Howard's insights probably applied to other groups in the area.

Movement from Man

As Malinké speakers pushed south, the distribution of ethnic groups and languages in the region was radically rearranged in two majors waves. The first incursion occurred in the east, probably around the time of the Mane invasion of 1560. It moved the Ma, some Dan and some Kru-speakers, including the Wee, from northern Côte d'Ivoire to the northern edge of the Liberian forest.[6]

Historian Yves Person[7] suggests that a southward invasion of Northern Mande-speakers into northern Côte d'Ivoire around 1600 AD dislodged the Siamon toward Burkina Faso and left the Aizi isolated.

The Touba were pushed south of Seguela Ouobé to the Man Mountain. The Dan moved to the right bank of Bafing, leaving two isolated Dan groups, Santa and Silakoro, on two hills.

Historian George E. Brooks suggest, "The siting of Ma, Dan, Kwene/Gur, and Mwa and Nwa remnant groups along the upper reaches and tributaries of the St. Paul, Cavalla, Sassandra, and Bandama Rivers suggests trade links with Kwa groups using these waterways to transport malagueta, kola, and salt."[8]

One block of Kru speakers migrated from Njaja (Nyaya) northeast of the Sassandra River in Côte d'Ivoire to Mt. Gedeh. This group included some ancestors of the Glebo, Klao, Kuwaa, and Krahn (specifically the Palipo, Kelipo, Chelepo, Jidepo, Forpo and Blepo lineages).[9]

According to art historian Han Himmelheber, the Dan began moving from the mountainous savannah of northern Côte d'Ivoire, about the same time as the Ma, who lived further east.[10]

From this point on, the histories of the Ma and Dan become interwoven. They later spread together to what is now called Mossorodougou and Saouro to Nzérékoré (which is called *Nehenkoheba* in Ma).

In the course of migrating from Kong in Côte d'Ivoire,[11] the Ma came into association with the Kono (who now live north of them in Guinea) and the Dan (whom they regard as their "small brothers" and whose language is closest to theirs). According to one Ma oral tradition, some of their first ancestors spoke a language which sounded like Kono in Guinea, which is a Southwestern Mande language.

According to oral traditions of the Ma and Dan, their ancestors knew the art of forging iron weapons and casting brass ornaments before coming to Liberia. They brought with them the *cire-perdue* method of forging brass, a bronze-like alloy used in the famous Benin works of art. This process was used for making metal weapons, brass ornaments and figures.[12]

The significance of metal working to their self-identity is evident in their origin stories. According to the Ma, the first family, *Nea Mia*, made by *Wala*, the Creator, descended from heaven by a chain. The Dan creation story holds that the first people descended from heaven in a brass bucket.[13]

According to linguists, the Kru groups immediately to the south and southeast of the Dan speak one language, Wee, with Sapo, Kran, Guéré and Wobé being dialects. In the process of disbursing southward, the Wee divided into the Western Wee (Kran), Eastern Wee (Guéré in Côte d'Ivoire), and Northern Wee (Wobe).[14]

Mt. Gedeh (also called Mt. Niété) was the focal point of several Kru migrations from the north and east, including ancestors of the Krahn, the Glebo, and the Klao.[15] The rich iron-ore deposits in the hills apparently gave rise to the area's name "Pahn" (meaning, "rich country").[16]

Migration into Western Liberia

The second dispersion occurred in the western region and was linked to the Quoja invasion of 1651. It moved ancestors of the Mende, Bandi, Kissi, some Loma, Kpelle, Ma, Dan and related groups from Guinea into what is now Liberia. In turn, those groups pressed Kru speakers around Mt. Gedeh toward the coast.[17]

Oral traditions of many different groups living in northwestern Liberia all point to the Gola as the first inhabitants of the territory. The Gola were then living in the mountains of northeastern Liberia, a region known as Komgba, in what is now Bopolu-Siehn District. They had previously been blocked from access to salt-making villages on the coast by the Dei and Vai, who closely guarded their valuable salt-making process.[18]

The first people pushed south by the Malinké in the region of Guinea above northwestern Liberia was the block of southwest Mande from Kissidugu that later splintered into the Bandi, Loko and Mende. This movement probably dates to sometime around 1600 AD.[19]

Long before southwest Mande groups arrived in the area of Liberia, they shared a common language and perhaps a common name. According to linguist Kirill Babaev, that collective name was "Bandi" (or a word close to it). He has identified remnants of that name in various forms among many of the offshoot groups.

Babaev points to the following facts: First, there is the name Bandi, which is applied to one Liberian ethnic group. Second, the Limba in Sierra Leone call the neighboring Loko *Wu-bandi* and their language *Hu-bandi*. Third, several Loma dialects have names with echoes of the word, such as *Bandi, Gbunde, Bunde* and *Bode*.

In addition, the northern most dialect of Kpelle is called *Gbanli-woo* (meaning, "language of the Gbali). According to Babaev, the difference in final consonant stems from the widespread use of a soft "l" in Kpelle, where a strong "d" is used in Bandi.[20]

When the Southwest Mande splintered, the southern-most segment became known as the Loko, the central block as the Mende and the rearguard as the Bandi.

According to Babeav, the current names of other southwest Mande ethnic groups and their dialects were assigned based on where each settled. Examples include *Loko* (meaning "river mouth land") and *Hasa-la* (a subgroup of the Bandi whose name means "the rocky place").

Mende oral traditions claim their ancestors came into Liberia seeking a piece of the growing coastal trade and fleeing forced conversion by Islamists pushing down from the north.[21] They settled among the Dama, a northern Mande group, whose language eventually disappeared.[22]

One Bandi oral tradition claims the group migrated into present-day Liberia from a town called Korblima in Guinea. Their move is said to have been motivated by a search for fertile farm land, which they found in Liberia in abundance with no previous inhabitants.[23]

Loko and Bandi oral traditions cited by historian Yves Person claim the Loko originated in Bandi territory but went west to fight a war. The Limba, who were among the earliest inhabitants of Sierra Leone, call the Loko *Gandimbe*, in recognition of their Bandi ancestry.[24] In migrating, the Bandi pushed the Kono south.[25]

Among the Bandi, blacksmiths and professional entertainers were generally exempt from public works required of other adult males. Their oral history credits Malinké salt and slave traders with introducing country cloth weaving. Later, Malinké settlers came from Musadu in Guinea and built a town called Masaubolahun, one mile from Bolahun.[26]

As ancestors of the Mende and Bandi were moving south, they pushed some Kissi from near the Niger headwaters in Sierra Leone, about 93 miles south, into territory previously occupied by the Gola. Some Kissi now occupy the northeast side of the Makona River in Guinea, but place names in their area indicate some Loma once lived in that territory.[27]

According to Liberian Kissi oral history, they migrated to western Liberia by crossing the Makona River from their previous home. This move was reportedly spurred by a hunter's search for wild game. In the process, they pushed the Kono into present-day Sierra Leone.[28]

Gola oral traditions credit the Mende with pushing some Kissi into the territory formerly held by the Gola, their long-time neighbors.[29] Those Kissi were later

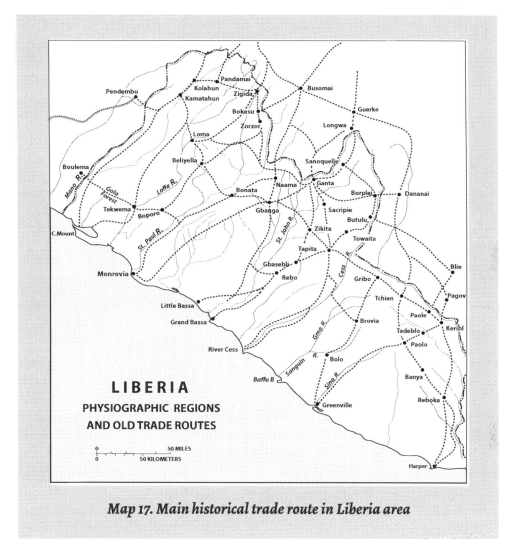

Map 17. Main historical trade route in Liberia area

joined by some Bandi.

This later encounter initially led to conflicts between the two groups, but the Kissi assimilated with the Bandi overtime.[30] Several towns in Liberia now occupied by the Kissi were originally Bandi, including Kaemblahuu, Kelema, Koblama, Kpandelo and Vabalahuu.[31]

The Kissi living in Liberia are regarded as more "authentic" than their compatriots living in Guinea. This view stems from the fact that those in the Kissi homeland have assimilated more closely with the Malinké.[32]

Under pressure from the Mende and Kissi, the Gola began a southwestern migration into the area they now occupy closer to the coast. That area was then dense forest.[33] The Gola regard the Mende, Loma, Kissi and Bandi as having powerful

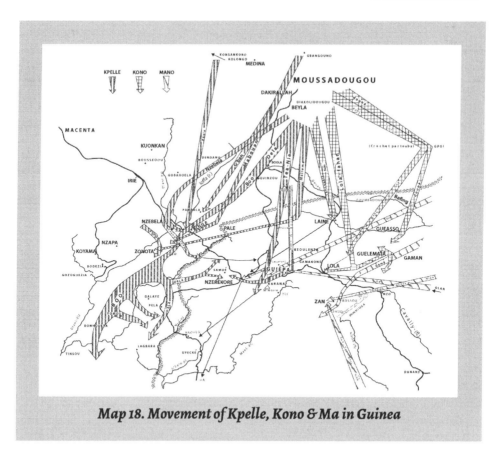

Map 18. Movement of Kpelle, Kono & Ma in Guinea

"medicine" for warfare. That probably stems from the role played by those groups in displacing the Gola from their original home in Komgba.[34]

The Gola remember a shortage of food and wild game during this period. It was also a time of overpopulation, due to an influx of diverse ethnic groups.[35]

According to Gola oral traditions collected by anthropologist Warren d'Azevedo, most migrants placed themselves under the protecting care of diverse established communities. In addition, many remote villages were founded in the sheltering forest between the Mano and St. Paul Rivers.

These "landlords" were generally eager to accept the "strangers" because of the labor they contributed and the security-in-numbers they provided. Migrations from original territories to current locations occurred in small groups over the course of generations.[36]

That process of migration probably applied to non-Gola refugees, too.

When the Gola arrived near the coast, they encountered the Kuwaa, Dei and Bassa.[37] The Dei gave them permission to establish the towns that came to be known as Zoodi, Todien and Sugbulum (on the current Bomi Hills road).[38] Some Gola moved further south, where they placed themselves under the protection of their old trading partners, the Vai and Dei in Kone, Cape Mount.[39]

The Loma and the Kokologi Agreement

Of the forced migrations of this period, the movement of the Loma and Kpelle from around Musadu was probably the most disruptive. First, Musadu had served as a trading center for many groups in the area, including the Gola, Loma, Kpelle, Kono, Bassa, Bandi, Dan and Ma.[40] Second, the number of people displaced must have been massive since the Kpelle form the largest ethnic group in Liberia today.

According to Kpelle oral traditions, their ancestors came into Liberia seeking a piece of the growing coastal trade and fleeing forced conversion by Islamists pushing down from the north.[41] Four Kpelle brothers are said to have left Missadougou, one going southwest into Liberia and the other three going southeast. The one who went on his own is remembered as Missa Coma Zoho. He was such a Poro *zo*, according to legend, he initiated others before he was initiated![42]

Liberian Loma oral traditions cite three reasons for their initial migration from Musadu into Liberia: a search for wild game, the need for fertile land, and harassment by Malinké in Guinea.[43] The Loma left towns called Yusumoundu and Tworluazaasu.[44]

For both the Loma and Kpelle, the Malinké occupation of the Musadu region was the result of a deep betrayal.

Throughout Loma territory, oral traditions refer to an agreement, *kokologi*, sealed by sacred pledge to "avoid warfare and to respect the traditions and customs of the original inhabitants, in particular their sacred sites." Malinké oral traditions also refer to "laws" in the Konyan region of Guinea that protected trading and traditional religious practices.[45]

Those stories often link the *kolokogi* to Musadu. They are also linked to Feren (also known as Fali Kama, Fonigama and Fanggama), a non-Muslim leader of the Kamara clan who arrived around 1550.

According to a Kpelle narrative, Feren was given vast farm lands in the region after accepting initiation into the Poro. One of his sons, Fala Wubo, is credited as the founder of Wubomai Chiefdom in Lofa Country, Liberia.

The Loma reportedly established the town of Macenta in Guinea before crossing the Makonna River into Liberia, with the three-peaked Whonsava Mountains as their landmark. In Liberia, they then founded Zigida in Zorzor district, Woniguomai, Gissimai (meaning "on the hill"), Wubormai, Wulorballah and Zieyema.[46]

The Loma now straddle the border with Guinea at the northern edge of the forest between the 9° and 7° latitude north and the 9° and 10° longitude west. They live primarily within the Macenta prefecture in Guinea and Lofa County, Liberia.[47] The St. John's River in Liberia marks their southeastern border.[48]

In the northern-most region, above the Makona, dominance is divided between four Loma clans: the Guilavogui, Onivogui, Zumanigui and Beavogui. In the southern-most region, Loma speakers are bounded by Kpelle speakers to the south and Koniyanke to the northeast. In this area, Loma districts are held by the following clans: Guilavogui, Onivogui (also known as Pivi), Bilivogui, Grovogui, and Beavogui.

The Guilavogui and Zumanigui clans first settled two district: Weybhalaga and Manzama. But, they were later joined by large numbers of the Kamara clan.

The situation is very different in districts between the Makona River to the northwest and the Ziama mountains to the southeast. Those districts are dominated mainly by two clans. This arrangement suggests a homogenous migration by people belonging to the Kamara and Koivogui clans. The Kamaras arrived sometime in the 1500s and 1600s, setting out from around Krouane and passing through Diomandou.[49]

Of the 14 chiefdoms between Ziama mountains and the Makona River, the Koivoguis dominate four: Ugbéme/Wubomai, Yala, Famoila and Famoila-Kpetea. Similarly, the Kamaras control four: Mandugu, Muidu, Kunukoro and Oniguame. Koivoguis share control with another clan in three "chiefdoms": Fasalo, Koeme and Ninbu.

The concentration of control by a few clans in the middle belt is especially great, historian Mike McGovern argues, because Koivogui is merely the Loma version of Kamara. Both clans share the leopard as their protective animal.[50] The Kamara-Koivogui merger probably stemmed from Northern Mande-speakers having adopted Loma identities after settling among them.[51]

Two-thirds of Woniguimai, originally a Loma town, was later seized and occupied by some Mandinké from Guinea.[52] Given this background, tensions between the Loma and the Malinké can be traced, in part, to later Northern Mande "strangers" violating the original *kokologi* pledge to respect local customs and sites related to traditional religion.

The resulting large-scale relocation probably boosted the population of the area now known as Liberia since Mande-speakers today make up at least 50 percent of Liberia's people.[53]

Kpelle and Ma Interactions

A mix of northern Mande groups, consisting of Konaianké, Malinké and Diomandé, pushed some Kpelle from Konyan into territory previously occupied by the Gola. The Kpelle and their neighbors in Guinea, the Kono, consider themselves to be "cousins" and their languages share a 52-67 percent lexical similarity.

Many Kpelle fled Missadougou, one of their important and ancient towns, due to religious strife between northern Mande-speakers (who were Muslims) and

Kpelle adherents of traditional religious practices. One Kpelle emigré from Missadougou named Mouon is credited with founding the town of *Guiéta* (*Guiépa* in Ma), which became the epicenter of the Nzérékoré region. Some went on to settle in the Guinean towns of GPaï, Koulé, Bélégneouon, N'Zebela, Kelezala and Boma.[54] As a consequence, they straddle the border with Guinea at the northern edge of the forest.[55]

As the Kpelle moved south, they pressed the Dan, Ma and Kono toward the forest but later settled among them.[56] Pressured from the savannah into a much narrow band of territory against the edge of the forest, Southeast Mande groups, with the Ma as the vanguard, began migrating into the forest.[57]

Oral traditions recall two Ma brothers who stopped over in the town called Guiéta while traveling from the Touba region of Côte d'Ivoire. One of them, Mahou Yagbara, used a gun to kill a leopard that had been menacing the area. After marrying a daughter of the local ruler, he settled among the Kpelle.[58] One of Mahou Yagbara's descendants reportedly migrated to Liberia through Gbélé.

Yagbara's story presents in simple form a larger truth: Guiéta was a point of transit used by many other groups migrating to Liberia.

A number of Ma originally from Gbenson went on to found the towns of Gonon (Manansèlé), Gbeibola, G'bélé, Gbélépie, Gboa Davoi and Gboa Yila.[59] A smaller group of Ma ancestors reportedly took a different route.

A difference in migration times might account for sharp distinctions that linger between two sections of the Ma. The northern Ma culture is heterogenous and language is heavily influenced by Malinké.

Tensions generated in what must have been a fractious process of relocation between the Ma, on the one hand, and the Kpelle and Malinke, on the other, still linger.[60]

The Ma and Dan migrations into Liberia were reportedly led by women chiefs (a possible allusion to an earlier matrilineal tradition). Many secret societies existed among the Ma and Dan, but only some Ma belonged to the Poro. Those who had Poro distinguished themselves proudly from those who did not (and vice versa).[61]

As the Ma and Dan moved south, Kru-speakers who lived south of them move into what is now Grand Gedeh County and down along the Cavalla River.[62]

The Kuwaa, the Gbeta and the Kabor all share traditions that their ancestors once lived in close association with Mande-speakers.[63]

Long-term, sustained contacts between the Dan, the Ma and Kru-speakers led to the development of a shared style of carved wooden masks. The most widespread was an idealized style featuring human figures showing no emotions, elongated noses, slit mouths and geometrically shaped eyes. A small subset of masks with frightening expressions were used for exorcism of evil forces.

Some local carvings reflected a naturalistic style resembling portraits. Still other carvings were done in an abstract style, usually featuring rhythmically repeated geometric shapes and exaggerated attention to certain features of animals considered to be ritualistically important.

Many of those animals were highly valued for having provided the ancestors knowledge, protection or direction in their quest for land. For that reason, those animals were not to be killed or eaten.[64]

Regarding Dan and Krahn wooden carvings, ethnogrpaher Etta Becker-Donna noted, "in none of the figures is any stress laid on likeness to the original [human model]; but it is essential that the pattern of the cicatrization works on the body and face should be followed exactly. The mode of dressing the hair must also be reproduced accurately. Any ornaments worn must be copied, and the very common umbilical hernias are faithfully reproduced also. In the case of women, stress is also laid on a faithful representation of the breast."[65]

Figure 35. Impact of Kru Cultures

From towns along the southeastern coast of Liberia, maritime Klao-speakers established communities along the West African coast from Sierra Leone to Nigeria. In the process, their language formed the basis for what is called Kru pidgin in Ghana, and their style of guitar playing and drumming laid the foundation for a popular musical style called Highlife.

Dispersal from Mt. Gedeh

Kpelle, Dan, Ma and Guro moved into their present locations sometime around 1651, the time of the Quoja invasion. In the process, they dislocated southward some Kru-speakers,[66] who flowed into southeastern Liberia from Mt. Gedeh and the forest rim.

Through this process, other Kru speakers from diverse points of origin joined the ancestors of the Dei, the Kabor and parts of the Gbeta clans who were already living in the territory of what is now Liberia.

The Wee in Liberia reflect the apparent merger of at least three separate migrations. The earliest group are the ancestors of Gbo, Kweon and some Sapo. They claim to have traveled along the St. John River.

A second stream of Wee ancestors originated in an area called Nyaya, located northeast of the Sassandra River in Côte d'Ivoire. It was part of a large block of Kru speakers that included some ancestors of the Kuwaa, Sapo, Grebo, and Eastern Krahn (specifically clans now known as Gbarzon, Gbarbo, Nyezon, Marbo, Gborbo, Borbo, Niabo, Konebo, Glio and Twabo).[67]

Several developments in the Niger region might have caused these movements. In the early 1600s, the Bambara left their Nioro homeland for the middle Niger valley near Segou and San. By 1650, Bobo and other former residents had moved south towards Wasoulous and northern Côte d'Ivoire. At that time, northern Mande speakers were moving from Dioma, Hama and Sankaran toward the Mahou and Touba mountains. They were led by the Diomanden clan.[68]

These migrations seem to have converged around Kong in present-day Côte d'Ivoire sometime between 1615 and the late 1700s. Some residents trace their roots to Bambara clans from the Segou-San area. Others claim Mande ancestors who migrated through Guinea and northwestern Côte d'Ivoire, some settling in Korodougou, Boron and Korhogo.[69]

Anthropologist Schwartz attributed the exodus of the Eastern Krahn and the Glebo from the area now known as Côte d'Ivoire to expansion of the Akan across the Bandama River in the mid-1600s.[70] Anthropologists Gunter Schröder and Hans Dieter Seiber date the split of Sapo from the Krahn and Glebo to 1650-1680 (assuming the genealogies given in the oral histories are correct).[71]

A third group — the nucleus of the Northern Krahn — reportedly originated near the town of Man in northern Côte d'Ivoire. They moved west in search of wild game, as well as encroachments on their territory by populations from further north. After entering the Cavalla Valley, they overcame a timid group that was already living in the area.

Schwartz credits the collapse of the Songhai empire and subsequent southward movement of Mande-speakers with pushing the northern Krahn into the Cestro River Valley sometime around 1750-1770.[72]

The origin stories of Kru-speaking groups often recount migrations from the interior, with groups dividing before traveling to the coast along parallel rivers. Settlements along each river were linked in structured relationships. Those near the coast were regarded as "junior" to those higher up.

Those disbursals probably followed the pattern of pastoralists, with groups of young adults colonizing uninhabited resource-rich areas, but within traveling distance to parent communities.[73]

When the original block of Kru-speakers reached a hill (probably Mt. Gedeh), the Kuwaa migrated west reportedly in pursuit of wild game, while the Klao and Glebo went south.[74] This is confirmed by Glebo oral traditions, which hold that some of their ancestors, then known as Gbobo, once lived further north in an area now occupied by the Krahn.[75]

From Mt. Gedeh, some ancestors of Kru-speaking groups traveled south together along the St. John River before disbursing to their current scattered locations.[76] Both Krahn and Glebo oral traditions claim their ancestors met a "fearful"

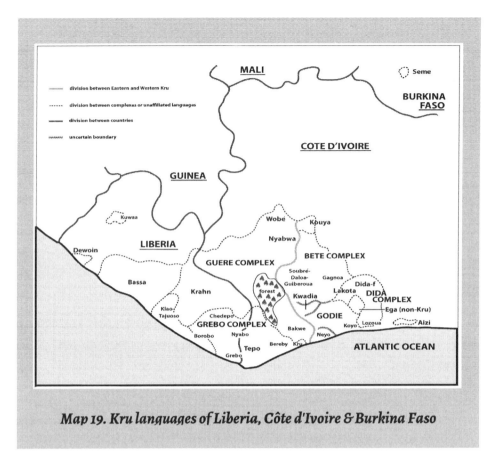
Map 19. Kru languages of Liberia, Côte d'Ivoire & Burkina Faso

people when they entered the area now called Grand Gedeh. Those timid inhabitants, who relocated south, were probably ancestors of the Bassa.

According to Bassa oral traditions, some of their ancestors originally lived at the northern margin of the forest belt, where the Krahn and Sikon now live.[77] They cite Mount Niété in Grand Gedeh as their ancestral home, the summit of which is said to be the site of a village of the dead.[78] Oral traditions suggest the ancestors of the Bassa engaged in metal smelting in Grand Gedeh, probably to make iron tools.[79]

According to one Krahn oral tradition, some of their ancestors and those of the Kuwaa were part of a major migration that followed the St. John River, but they split after encountering the Bassa. Some ancestors of the Klao went east where they became known as the Gbeta-Kru and the Mama Klao.[80]

The location of the Kuwaa suggests an incursion of Mande-speakers, notably the Kpelle, pushed them west, where they encountered the Gola.[81]

Due to conflicts with in-coming groups around Mt. Gedeh, ancestors of the Glebo moved south to the area around Bereby in present-day Côte d'Ivoire. From there, they journeyed west to Cape Palmas in canoes. Those who made it to Cape

Palmas were called Glebo (derived from "gle-" for "monkey" because they navigated the waves "like monkeys swinging through trees"). Others who fell behind came to be called Wlebo (meaning "the capsizers").[82]

Some Glebo ancestors were already living near Cape Palmas around 1505-1508. They were undoubtedly the "Egrogeboes" identified at that time by Pacheco Pareira Duarte, a Portuguese sea captain and cartographer. Swiss physician Samuel Braun, who visited the area in 1614, reported people called the "Gruvo."[83]

They apparently absorbed other immigrants who came later. Some Glebo oral traditions claim the journey to the Cape Palmas area was made around 1700.[84] Their time frame fits with another Glebo origin story, which points to a European presence at the time of their arrival — in the form of a building and slave traders.[85]

The earliest Glebo settlements were Nyomowe (from the River Nyamo, now called Hoffman) west of Cape Palmas and Kudemowe (from Lake Kude, near Rocktown). From those two towns all other Glebo settlements reportedly "received their fire."[86]

The Glebo also credit some of their ancestors with founding Grand Cess, Picininny Cess and Sasstown.[87]

From Mt. Gedeh, ancestors of the Bassa migrated south along the St. John River to the coast. Some kept moving west until they encountered the Dei near Cape Montserrado. The area was home to a large number of cats, so the Dei called it *Blisue* and the Bassa *Sogila* or *Soila* — all three terms meaning "cat mountain." Ancestors of the Bassa and Dei came to share another level of the Poro, *Ndoge*, not present among neighboring ethnic groups.[88]

One Bassa tradition claims that their ancestors encountered Europeans when they first reached the Atlantic Ocean.[89] They claim to have learned canoe building from the Klao only after relocating near the coast.[90] After moving to their present location, they continued smelting iron using ore from Mt. Finley.[91]

According to Klao oral tradition, their ancestors came from the north, and they established their earliest residence at Pisiyo Sigli. They later moved south to the coast where they established the towns called Kankiya, Matiye (south of the Nonbwa River), Tuglo and Siglipo (Klao for "pass through town").

Kankiya was later swept away by the Nonbwa River, and Siglipo came to be known as Grand Cess. Of these villages, the people of Matiye alone kept fields and canoe landing station separate from the others, suggesting it might have been settled by people of different origin.[92]

Some Klao ancestors had apparently engaged in rice cultivation in their previous location along the forest rim. That facilitated its transfer to their current location, where the soil is especially favorable.

Klao ancestors later established Pakyo to the east of Siglipo, Papuklo to the north and Tubwegh to the west on the coast. According to a Klao oral tradition, the towns of Little Kro, Sestra Kroo, Kroo-bar, Nana-Kroo and King Wills Town were all founded by sea-farers from present-day Ghana. These oral claims are buttressed by other cultural affinities between people in the two regions.

Well into the nineteenth-century, for example, the Klao were said to value "as highly as gold" small blue pipe beads imported from the Gold Coast that were 3/16 inch in diameter and 3/4 inch in length. This taste for what were known as Aggrey or Popo beads was not shared by non-Kru speakers in the Liberia area.[93]

Several Kru lineages probably converged on the coast. They were still forging terms of coexistence in the early 1800s as European visits to the coast were increasing in frequency.[94]

Early accounts of the Kru Coast often described three groups that were codependent and culturally related. Yet these groups were distinct in terms of their residence and source of livelihood: One group was the Sapo, who lived away from the coast and controlled trade with the interior. Outsiders called them "Bushmen" because of their location.[95]

Two groups on the coast controlled the Atlantic trade and often sent young men to labor aboard foreign ships. There were those who fished, called *Kle-po* or *Swa-po*, and those who farmed, known as *Nana-kru*. English speakers called them "Fishmen" and "Krumen."

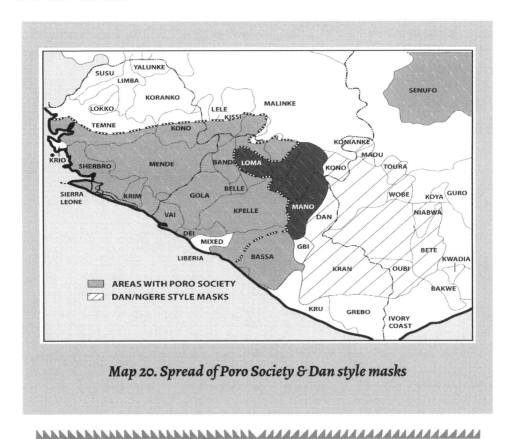

Map 20. *Spread of Poro Society & Dan style masks*

"Fishmen" were mainly members of the Kabor and parts of the Gbeta clans. They lived among the Klao, the Bassa, the Dei and the Vai further west. They were very likely the men in canoes who bravely rowed out to Pedro de Sintra's ship in 1462.

"Krumen" referred initially to residents of the Five Towns (Little Kroo, Setra Kroo, Kroo-Bar, Nana Kroo and King Will's Town). But, this label later came to be applied to all coastal Kru-speakers along the Sinoe coast. All Klao towns were located on the sea coast mainly between 4° 54' and 5° 7' north latitude. By the 1850s, the "Krumen" label was also applied to the Glebo.[96]

Very little evidence is available by which to date the arrival of the first major influx of Klao people. Massing said sometime in the 1500s is "conceivable." He based this conclusion mainly on Olfert Dapper, who published a description of the Liberian coast in 1668, citing a group called Quaabe-Monou approximately where the Klao are located today.[97]

The many accounts of migrations by Kru-speaking groups are not mutually exclusive. Instead, they point to multiple ancestral streams and paths that flowed into the current groups.

Unique Features of the Southeast Region

The southeast region of what is now Liberia differs in several ways from the western and central parts. These differences include the size of political units, patterns of settlement, religious rituals and language development.

To begin with, political structures in the southeast were flatter, generally consisting of only three levels. From lowest to highest, these were the household, a hamlet (with several households) and the ethnic group (composed of patrilineages and characterized by sharing a common territory, common traditions of origin and migration, set of political positions beyond lineage elders).

Regarding how communities were laid out in the forest, three patterns predominated, according to historian Robin Horton.[98]

The rarest was the segmentary lineage system, which organized society on the basis of an all-encompassing genealogy. The settlement pattern consisted of scattered villages. This pattern was typical of communities that were expanding into new, uninhabited lands. It was common among the Kissi, Gola and Kru groups.

In the second type, community is linked to a clearly defined, shared territory. Although the role of genealogy is muted, these communities distinguished between the landowning lineages, who supplied the earth priests, and the newcomers, who gained membership by aiding the landowners in cultivating and defending the land.

The third settlement type consisted of the large compact village, which developed, Horton theorized, as a refuge from "formidable" attackers. In this context, various institutions that transcend lineages are most pronounced, including associations for enculturating children, artisans and artists. These institutions distributed political and ritual offices among various lineages on a more or less complimentary basis. This third pattern came to predominate among the Loma and Kpelle.

In addition, overall population in southeastern Liberia is 25 inhabitants per square miles, compared to 50 per square mile among Mande groups. Consequently, Kru political units are small, ranging in size from 50 along the coast to 13,000 at most further inland.[99]

In the southeast region "a great proliferation of small medicine societies based upon oaths of secrecy and a set of ritual rules. Others are more general and non-secret ancestral associations to which both men and women belong." The emphasis was "more on private kin-based ancestral ... associations formed around specific ritual objects."[100]

This is in contrast to the northeast and central regions, with their Poro association, which spanned many language and ethnic groups.[101]

Ethnic groups in Liberia also show different patterns in sickle-cell frequencies, which suggests something of their history.

Writing in 1958, biological anthropologist Frank B. Livingston proposed a link between sickle-cell spread and rice farming. In other words, groups that were involved in rice-farming for a longtime would show a high frequency of the sickle-cell gene.

Livingston's theory was supported by sickle-cell frequencies among several rice-growing groups: the Kissi (with a 19.46 percent frequency) and southwest Mande groups like the Kpelle (13.03 percent), Loma (12.72 percent), Vai (13.98 percent) and Mende (16.88 percent).

Among southeast Mande speakers, there was wide divergence: the Bobofing in Burkina Faso is high (25 percent), while in Liberia the Ma (2.72 percent) and Dan (2.10 percent) show low frequencies. This suggests the gene was introduced to the latter group *after* the Southeastern Mande languages separated.

Most Kru-speakers were not rice farmers, including the Glebo (1.45 percent) and Krahn (0.65 percent). The frequencies of those groups offer support for Livingston's thesis.

Running counter to Livingstone's hypothesis was the relatively high sickle-cell gene distribution among the Gola (12.02 percent), who were not historically rice growers.

There were also anomalies among Kru-speaking groups: On the one hand, both the Kuwaa (10.34 percent) and Bassa (7.15 percent) had higher frequencies. That could be explained by their having intermarried over a long period with rice-farming Mande neighbors.

On the other hand, the Klao, who were longtime rice growers, showed a low frequency (0.68 percent).

Into the Forest

All of these anomalies suggest a different theory from the one proposed by Livingston. Instead of rice-growing, low population density links more consistently with low sickle-cell frequency. That connection is logical because low population densities would have inhibited the spread of malaria, resulting in a low infection rate.[102]

In southeastern Liberia, a combination of dispersed small settlements and small polities apparently contributed to the development of many dialects that shade gradually from one to next. That situation helps to explain the multiplicity of confusing ethnic labels often applied to Kru-speaking groups.

Regardless of ethnic labels and language difference, the ancestors of most Liberians shared deep connections. They lived together on the forest's edge for centuries — trading and intermarrying. Those in the west shared the Poro and Sande associations, those in the east a highly developed style of art. Their common ties and share motivations are echoed again and again in various oral traditions, drawn from speakers of Atlantic, Mande and Kru languages.

Many of the migrations reported in oral traditions match details of the Mande and Quoja incursions recorded by Europeans. For that reason, it is possible to state with a high degree of certainty that most Liberian ethnic groups occupied their current territories between 1560 (the time of the Mane invasion) and 1651 (when facts were gathered regarding the Quoja invasion).

Given these longstanding connections, it is only logical that the ancestors of diverse groups would have entered the formidable forest together. According to oral traditions, they did so mainly to escape persecution, to shelter sacred traditions and to seize new economic opportunities. In short, for rights. For rites. And for rice.

---

[1]. Bloomeasrt's contact with Sierra Leone area is from Fage, 1994, pp. xi.

[2]. Braudel, Vol. 1, 1981, pp. 65-66.

[3]. Béavogui, 2001, p. 26; James Fairhead, "Kouankan and the Guinea-Liberia Border," in Jacqueline Knör and Wilson Trajano (ed.), *The Powerful Presence of the Past: Integration and Conflict along the Upper Guinea Coast* (Leiden, the Netherlands: Koninklijke Brill NV, 2008; Person, 1968, p. 242; Person, 1987, p. 249; Geysbeek, 2002; Korvah, 1960, p. 7; Korvah, 1995; Jones, 1987; Massing, 1985, p. 36; Fairhead, Geysbeek, Holsoe and Leach, 2003, p. 136.

[4]. Germain, 1984, p. 56; Person, 1961, pp. 1, 58, 15, 17, 45.

[5]. Howard, 2000, p. 14.

[6]. Lovejoy, 1980, pp. 101-102, 104, 109.

[7]. Yyes Person, "Des Kru en Haute-Volta," *Bulletin de l'Institute francais d'Afrique noire*, Série B, t. 28 (1967): 485-492, especially p. 491.

[8]. Brooks, 1985, p. 16.

[9]. Massing, 1970-1971, p. 177; also Schröder and Seiber, 1974, p. 23.

10. Hans Himmelheber, "Gelbgussringe der Guere (Elfenbeingkuste)," Linden-Museum für Völkerfunde, Stuttgart, *Tribus*, No. 13 (December 1964), dated this migration to 1700, but Person has proposed 1500 instead by correlating oral traditions with the scant available written sources. Becker-Donner, 1939, p. 2. For a discussion of similarities between the Dogon, on the one hand, and the Kpelle and Dan, on the other, see: Ronald James Harrison Church, *West Africa: A Study of the Environment and Man's Use of It* (pp. 26, 1-24). For similarities of Dan and Dogon, see Conrad and Frank, 1995, pp. 68-69.
11. Massing, 1980-1981, pp. 1-2.
12. For metal smelting traditions in modern Liberia, see Schwab, 1947, pp. 136-146 (Ma, D, Sapo, Loma, Bandi, Kpelle); Becker-Donner, 1939, pp. 43, 48-49; Harley, 1941, p. 24.
13. Donner-Becker, 1939, p. 43.
14. Massing, 1977, p. 27; Holsoe and Lauer, 1976, pp. 143, 145. To capture the linguistic gradation of the region, anthropologist Andreas W. Massing proposed using Western Wee in place of Kran, Eastern Wee for Guéré in Côte d'Ivoire, and Northern Wee instead of Wobe. Similarly, he suggested Western Kru for Krou in Côte d'Ivoire, Central Kru in place of Grebo in Liberia and Eastern Kru for Klao.
15. Martin, 1968, p. 48; "Tour two hundred miles interior," *African Repository*, 1869, pp. 153-154; "Missionary exploration," *African Repository*, 1869, pp. 308-313.
16. Schröder and Seibel, 1974, pp. 27-28.
17. Person, 1961. Among the Kpelle of Liberia, for example, three oral traditions exist regarding their origin: One holds that they came from Guinea; a second claims they dispursed from the area around Gbarnga; a third traces their origin to the Gbaaleng-Vavala district, but it is found mainly in the Bocomu-Goe area. These differ on details but may be referring to migrations that took place in different time periods. In all likelihood, the first Kpelle in Liberia came from Guinea and settled in the Gbarnga area. From there, most Kpelle would have subsequently dispersed, following significant population growth. The movement from Bocomy-Goe to Gbaaleng-Vavala probably described a small-scale, third-wave migration. See Ballah, 1955, p. 34.
18. d'Azevedo, 1959, pp. 53-55.
19. This date is midway between between the Mane invasion of around 1560 and 1651 AD, the approximate departure date from the Sierra Leone area of Samuel Bloomeasrt, who provided the fullest account of the Quoja invasion that was used by author Olfert Dapper.
20. Kirill Babaev, "On the origins of southwest Mande ethnonyms," Institute of Linguistics for the Russian Academy of Sciences, pp. 1-3, http://llacan.vjf.cnrs.fr/fichiers/mande2011/bublio/babaev.pdf, accessed August 18, 2013.
21. Andah, 1992, p. 267.
22. Jones, 1981, pp. 169-171.
23. Corker and Massaquoi, 1972, pp. 11-12.
24. A. Abraham, A rise of traditional leadership among the Mende: A study in the acquisition of political power. Master's thesis, Fourah Bay College, University of Sierra Leone, 1971, pp. 24-25.
25. Corker and Massaquoi, 1972, pp. 39-59.
26. Corker and Massaquoi, 1972, pp. 11, 19, 24, 27.
27. Mike McGovern, *Unmasking the State: Making Guinea Modern* (Chicago: University of Chicago Press, 2013), p. 43-46.
28. Corker and Massaquoi, 1972, pp. 39-59.

29. Warren C. d'Azevedo, "Uses of the Past in Gola Discourse," *Journal of African History*, III, 1 (1962), pp. 11-34, especially pp. 12-13; Bureau of Folkways, 1955, p. 2.
30. Corker and Massaquoi, 1972, pp. 11-12.
31. Corker and Massaquoi, 1972, pp. 1-2; G. Tucker Childs, *A Grammar of Kisi: A Southern Atlantic Language* (Berlin: Mouton de Gruyer, 1995), p. 4; also see d'Azevedo, 1959, p. 50; Kup, 1961; Person, 1961, pp. 1-59. Linguist G. Tucker Childs is exceptional in suggesting that Kissi pushed *north* to settle in their current position straddling the border of Liberia, Sierra Leone and Guinea sometime around 1850 split off from the Bullom, Sherbro, Krim and Mani.
32. Andreas W. Massing, "A Segmentary Society Between Colonial Frontiers: The Kissi of Liberia, Sierra Leone and Guinea, 1892-1913," *Liberian Studies Journal*, IX, 1 (1980-1981), pp. 1-12, especially p. 1-2.
33. d'Azevedo, 1962, pp. 12-13; Bureau of Folkways, 1955, p. 2.
34. d'Azevedo, 1959, pp. 58, 73.
35. d'Azevedo, 1959, pp. 58, 73.
36. d'Azevedo, 1959, pp. 58, 73.
37. d'Azevedo, 1959, pp. 53-55.
38. Bureau of Folkways, 1955, p. 53.
39. d'Azevedo, 1959, pp. 53-54, 57, 63.
40. Béavogui, 2001, p. 26; Fairhead, 2008; Person, 1968, p. 242; Person, 1987, p. 249; Geysbeek, 2002; Korvah, 1960, p. 7; Korvah, 1995; Jones, 1987; Massing, 1985, p. 36; Fairhead, Geysbeek, Holsoe and Leach, 2003, p. 136.
41. Andah, 1992, p. 267.
42. Germain, 1984, pp. 90-91, 94.
43. Béavogui, 2001, p. 27; Andah, 1992, p. 267.
44. Béavogui, 2001, p. 27.
45. Geysbeek, 1994, pp. 74, 81, n. 445; Karin Weisswange, Feindshaft und Verwandtshaft: Konflikt und Kooperation in Zusammenleben von Loma und Mandingo in dem Ort Bobrkeza in Liberie, M. A. thesis, Johan Wolfgang Goethe-Universität, Frankfurt, 1969, pp. 75.
46. Corker and Massaquoi, 1972, pp. 60-61; Andah, 1992, p. 267.
47. Béavogui, 2001, p. 28.
48. McGovern, 2013, p. 43-46.
49. McGovern, 2013, pp. 39, 46.
50. McGovern, 2013, pp. 43-44. For taboos, totems and familiars in Liberian cultures, see Schwab, 1947, pp. 345-357.
51. Massing 1985, p. 44; McGovern, 2013, pp. 41-46.
52. Corker and Massaquoi, 1972, pp. 60-61.
53. Person, 1971; Willi O. Schulze, *A New Geography of Liberia* (London: Longman, 1973), p. 47; S. E. Holsoe, "Economic Activities in the Liberian Area: The Pre-European Period to 1900," in V. R. Dorjahn and B. L. Isaac (eds.), *Essays on the Economic Anthropology of Liberia and Sierrra Leone* (Philadelphia: Institute for Liberian Studies, 1979), pp. 65-68; Atherlon, 1970-71, pp. 83-111; Gabel, 1976, pp. 21-35; Gabel, Borden, and White, 1972-74, pp. 87-105; Johnson, 1961; Massing, 1980, p. 66.
54. Germain, 1984, p. 89.
55. Andah, 1992, p. 267.
56. Germain, 1984, p. 75.
57. Germain, 1984, p. 80.

[58]. Germain, 1984, pp. 75-76.
[59]. Germain, 1984, pp. 80, 84.
[60]. Zetterström, 1976, pp. 14-17; Bauman, 1940, p. 315; Fage, 1981, p. 37; Himmelheber, 1964, pp. 2, 17; Harley, 1941, p. 6; Person, 1961, pp. 29-32; Westermann, 1970, p. 39.
[61]. James C. Riddell, Kjell Zetterström, Peter G. Dorliae and Michael J. Hohl, "Clan and Chiefdom Maps for the Mã (Mano) and Dã (Gio)," *Liberian Studies Journal*, IV, 2 (1971-72), pp. 157-162, especially p. 158.
[62]. Germain, 1984, p. 80.
[63]. Schröder and Seibel, 1974, p. 22.
[64]. Segy, 1969, pp. 44-45.
[65]. Becker-Donner, 1939, p. 150.
[66]. Person, 1961, pp. 47-55.
[67]. Schröder and Seibel, 1974, p. 23.
[68]. Massing, 2000, pp. 297-298.
[69]. Massing, 2000, pp. 298-299. The Bambara *dyamou* (clans) include Baro, Daou, Balo, Cissé and Touré, while the Mande *dyamou* consist of Kanté, Konaté and Kone.
[70]. Martin, 1968, p. 50; Innis, 1966, p. 142. Historian Jane J. Martin cites the Mane invasion to explain movements toward the coast, including ancestors of the Glebo. However, that seems implausible in light of recent findings on the Mane invasion that are presented in Chapter 8 of this book.
[71]. Alfred Schwartz, *Ziombli: L'organization sociale d'un village Guéré-Nidrou* (Paris: O. R. S. T. O. M., 1965), p. 13; Schröder and Seiber, 1974, pp. 24-26; Martin, 1968, p. 42. Schröder and Seiber calculate that the Glebo crossed into what is now Liberian territory around 1760-1770, the Sapo in the 1790s, and the Eastern Krahn in the early 1800s, but the Glebo arrival was earlier, as indicated in the records of Duarte and Braun.
[72]. Martin, 1968, p. 50; Innis, 1966, p. 142.
[73]. Massing 1977, p. 32; Schröder and Seibel, 1974, p. 21.
[74]. Massing, 1970-1971, pp. 173-205, especially p. 177; also Schröder and Seiber, 1974, p. 23.
[75]. Martin, 1968, p. 39.
[76]. Schröder and Seibel, 1974, p. 22.
[77]. Martin, 1968, p. 42; Person, 1966, p. 491.
[78]. Martin, 1968, p. 48; "Tour two hundred miles interior," *African Repository*, Vol. 45, Vol. 5 (May 1869), pp. 153-154; "Missionary exploration by a native, *African Repository*, Vol. 45, Vol. 10 (October 1869), pp. 308-313.
[79]. Siegmann, 1969, p. 8; Martin, 1968, p. 48; "Tour two hundred miles interior," *AR*, 1869, pp. 153-154; "Missionary exploration," *AR*, 1869, pp. 308-313.
[80]. Massing, 1970-71, p. 177, citing J. Nma, History of the Gbeta-Tribe," unpublished ms.; also Johnson, "Traditions," p. 46. The *Mama Klao* is the earliest confederation of sake (meaning "section") among the Klao of Monrovia. It is also known as the Five Tribes.
[81]. Massing, 1970-71, pp. 180-181.
[82]. Martin, 1968, pp. 41, 43.
[83]. Martin, 1968, pp. 41, 43.
[84]. Martin, 1964, p. 40; Innes, 1966, p. 142.
[85]. Martin, 1964, p. 40.
[86]. Martin, 1968, p. 50; Innis, 1966, p. 142.
[87]. Martin, 1968, p. 50; Innis, 1966, p. 142.
[88]. Bureau of Folkways, 1955, p. 39, 4; Martin, 1968, p. 42; Person, 1966, p. 491.

89. Siegmann, 1969, p. 4.
90. Siegmann, 1969, p. 7.
91. Siegmann, 1969, p. 8; Martin, 1968, p. 48; "Tour two hundred miles interior," *African Repository*, 1869, pp. 153-154; "Missionary exploration," *African Repository*, 1869, pp. 308-313.
92. Thomas Ludlam, "An account of the Kroomen, on the coast of Africa," *African Repository*, April 1825, pp. 43-55; H. Scudder Mekeel, "Social administration of the Kru: A preliminary survey," *Africa* 10 (1937): 75-96.
93. Brooks, 1972, pp. 105-106.
94. Conneau, 1976, p. 336; Captain William Allen and T. R. H. Thompson, *A Narrative of an Expedition (sent by Her Majesty's Government) to the River Niger in 1841* (London: Richard Bentley, 1841), pp. 114-115; Francis Bacon, "Cape Palmas and the Mena, or Krooman," *Journal of the Royal Geographical Society*, 12 (1842): 196-206; Great Britain, "Report from the Select Committee on the West Coast of Africa," *British Parliamentary Papers* XI, 551 (1842): 435-436; Horatio Bridge, *Journal of an African Cruiser* (London: Dawsons of Pall Mall, 1968, reprint of 1845 edition), p. 76; James W. Lugenbeel, "Native Africans in Liberia — Their customs and superstitions," *African Repository*, January 1852, pp. 13-17; February 1852, pp. 53-55; June 1852, pp. 171-174; July 1852, pp. 212-214; October 1852, pp. 310-315.
95. Massing, 1977, pp. 36, 62; Brooks, 1971, pp. 108-112.
96. Martin, 1968, p. 14.
97. Massing, 1970-71, p. 179; Olfert Dapper, *Naukeurige Beschryvinghe der Afrikaensche gewesten* (Utrecht, 1668), pp. 384-430.
98. Horton, 1972, pp. 84-85, 94-95, 97, 100-101.
99. Frederick D. McEvoy, "Levels of ethnic reality." Paper read at Annual Conference on Social Science Research in Liberia, 1973; Massing, 1977, pp. 29-31.
100. d'Azevedo, 1959, p. 67-70, especially 67; Schwab, 1947; Johnson, 1957.
101. d'Azevedo, 1959, p. 67-70, especially 67; Schwab, 1947; Johnson, 1957.
102. Frank B. Livingston, "Sickle cell gene in West Africa," *American Anthropologist* 60 (1958): 533-562, especially 546; Etta Becker-Donner, *Hinterland Liberia* (London: Blackie & Son, 1939); Vendeiz, 1924; Louis Tauxier, *Nouvelles notes sure le Mossi et le Gourounsi* (Paris: E. Larose, 1924); Massing, 1977, p. 49. Livingstone offered two theories to account for low sickle-cell gene frequencies among some language groups: 1. low population densities, and 2. their recent conversion from hunting-and-gathering to adoption of intensive agriculture. The second explanation was adopted by d'Azevedo (1962, pp. 512, 538), but, with Massing, I am inclined toward the first theory as more acceptable because it is less complicated and more elegant.

Chapter 10
"They work excellent well in Iron"

> Speaking of blacksmiths at Grand Cess, "They work excellent well in Iron, they mended our shears for us, with which we cut out our barrs of Iron, and gave them such a temper as made them incomparably better than they were at first."
>
> – *Nicolas Villault c. 1666*

Histories of European expansion often focus on the explorers and the governments that sent them. Only by digging beneath the surface can one understand how money and power really worked in the past — and, perhaps, continue to work in the present.

For example, Portugal was never at the center of European *economic* power, despite its dazzling accomplishments. Behind the colorful captains and kings laid the bankers who financed their voyages. Its economy remained under the control of bankers and merchants based in Italian cities, mainly Venice and Genoa.[1]

According to historian Fernand Braudel, European capitalism began in 1200s, centered in one Italian city after another.[2]

Key sources of credit for European governments were mainly in Florence around 1300, Genoa in the late 1500s and early 1600s, and Amsterdam in the 1700s.[3] Their hidden but dazzling power determined the rise and fall of governments and national economics.

The power of Italian cities was distinct from the Greek and Roman empires whose powers derived mainly from military might. Those cities began as subordinated partners in the same trade network as West Africa with its center in the Middle East. Africa's trade with Italian cities was not just in luxury items. It included necessities like salt, fish and wheat.[4]

Venice, Genoa and Florence eventually separated and became the nexus of a competing European system.[5]

The rise of Italian cities was made possible by improved farming, trade and intensified craft production. One of the first, Venice, emerged around 1200 when Byzantium's control of imports to Europe was ended by the Crusades. Similar to what Phoenicians had done in North Africa, Venician merchants created trading posts strung along a route to the Middle East. The city remained Europe's dominant city until the late 1400s.[6]

The city's economic position was consolidated in the early 1440s when wealth from trading was invested heavily in farming. It remained one of Europe's busiest ports at least until the 1600s.[7]

A close second was Genoa, the hub of a trading network that ran from Egypt to England. At the center of the city's power was the *Casa San Giorgio*, a quasi-public bank and mint of currency. In 1372, the Genoa banned imports that competed with local products. A key Mediterranean slave mart, the city supplied mostly women to both Muslim and Christian buyers.[8]

Given this history, Genoese abroad were often predisposed toward expanding slavery in their host societies. A key example is Christopher Columbus. After returning from the Americas, he quickly made two recommendations to his Spanish sponsors: First, rely on slave labor to exploit the New World. Second, introduce enslaved Africans.[9]

As Venice was declining, a northern rival arose. It was the trading city of Bruges, Belgium. It grew from 35,000 residents in 1340 to about 100,000 in 1500. During the 1300s, a rival was Lübeck in the Hanseatic League in which is now Germany.[10]

From at least the 800s AD, Europe was divided into two distinct regions, each pulling in a different direction. On the one hand, the southern Mediterranean region was fattened by trade through the Levant with the Middle East, Africa and Asia. On the other hand, the northern portion was leaner, more isolated but more self-reliant.[11]

Northern Europe became the core of the economy around 1590 because the cost of doing business there was cheap: Wages were lower, workshops were more efficient, ships cost less to build and sail.[12]

After 1517, many northern Christians broke away from the Catholic Church. From then on, the rivalry between the two regions was reinforced by their religious differences.[13]

Within three years of reaching the Caribbean, the Spaniards had plundered all of the gold jewelry accumulated by the local people over 1,000 years. Next, they organized a forced search for more. Local people, mostly women, worked from dawn to dusk. Between 1503 and 1530, they extracted 41,870 lbs. of gold (or 20 US tons) from the Caribbean islands alone.[14]

During this period, ore mining depended on people not machines. Large numbers of workers were required to mine, tunnel and carry precious metals.[15] Unrelenting forced labor nearly wiped out the people of the islands, first Hispaniola (now Haiti and the Dominican Republic), next Puerto Rico and finally Cuba.[16]

In the early 1500s, Europeans — mainly the Portuguese — were taking away about £100,000 worth of gold per year from West Africa. By the beginning of the 1700s, gold exports were up to £250,000 per year.[17] Between 1675 and 1731, the Dutch West Indies Company alone was exporting a half a ton of pure gold annually from the Gold Coast.[18]

From 1528, the quest for precious metals turned to the mainlands of South and Central America. The Spanish began by plundering the treasures of the Inca empire of Peru, which the people had gathered over centuries. As in the Caribbean, they next organized forced mining of gold. Between 1531 and 1535, 25,873 lbs. of gold (or 12 US tons) were extracted from Peru.[19]

By the 1620s, the residents of the Mexico area dropped from 25 million to 750,000, and those of the Andes from 60 million to 600,000.[20] The biggest factor were epidemics smallpox, typhus, measles and other diseases imported from Europe that Native Americans had no immunity against. Also important was forced labor.[21]

The riches Portugal derived from West Africa was like a stream compared to the rivers of wealth that flowed to Spain from the Americas and to Holland from the Asian spice trade. By 1651, pepper was woven into European cuisine, and it was the number one import of the Dutch East India Company (or *Verrnigde Oost-Indische Compagnie*).[22] What was called the "spice trade" included more than seasonings. It included sugar, medicines, dyes and salt, which was also used as a preservative.[23]

Portugal's fall was as dramatic as its rise 160 years before. Portugal's eclipse was finalized in 1578 when its king was killed while fighting in Morocco. Two years later, while the Portuguese were quarreling over who would succeed King Sabastian, Spain seized control of its neighbor.[24]

Not only did Portugal lose most of its overseas trading posts, its economy was taken over by British investors. They used northern vineyards to produce port wines for export and imported goods, ranging from wheat to codfish.[25]

Taking advantage of this crisis, the Dutch and the English moved into trading areas previously held by the Portuguese. By 1640, they had lost all of their forts and trading posts in West Africa, including the renown El Mina on the Gold Coast.[26]

European countries received two benefits from American colonies: First, those territories produced tobacco, sugar, cotton, and other tropical crops. Second, colonies bought finished products from their European metropole.[27]

Overseas trade was too expensive and complex to be accomplished by individuals. To overcome those barriers, Europeans formed companies that were given exclusive control over trade in certain places or over certain goods.[28]

As noted by historian Fernand Braudel,[29] "A company monopoly depended on the coming together of three things: first the state, which might or might not be effective, but which was never absent; then the world of trade, that is capital, banking, credit and customers — a world which might be hostile or cooperative — or both at once; lastly there was the trading zone to the exploited in some distant land and this could itself be a decisive factor in many ways."[30]

In all major European powers, trading was spearheaded by monopolies.

England had the Muscovy Company (1555), the Levant Company (1581), the Royal Africa Company (1750), the English East India Company (1599). In Holland, there was the Dutch East India Compan. French monopolies included French East India Company (1602), French Levant Company (1670), the West India Company (1674).[31]

Between 1450 and 1640, a new world order emerged. Europe shifted from an economy based on tribute to a system of capitalism. As noted by Immanuel Wallerstein, this new economy relied on "the appropriation of a surplus which was based on more efficient and expanded productivity (first in agriculture and later in industry) by means of a world market mechanism with the 'artificial' (that is, nonmarket) assist of state machineries."[32]

This shift was made possible, Wallerstein argued, through long-distance trading, "the development of variegated methods of labor control for different products and different zones of the world-economy, and the creation of relatively strong state machineries in what would become the core-states of this capitalist world-economy."[33]

Politics continued as usual; it remained focused at the level of the city, province or country. But, the thinking of merchants, bankers and financiers broke beyond those narrow channels; their focus was the world-economy.[34]

Decision makers in Portugal and Spain remained trapped in the old way of thinking. But, their counterparts in Amsterdam and London were less guided by political considerations, more by global supply and demand.[35]

After Burges and Lübeck, a third northern trading and banking power, the city of Antwerp, Belgium, emerged between 1501 and 1521. This was the first of three expansions. It was sparked when Portugal began bringing tropical pepper to the city for sale throughout northern Europe. Its golden era ran from 1535 to 1557. This boom resulted from Spain bringing in silver from the Americas to exchange for timber, wheat, ships and other products of northern countries.[36]

Figure 36. Coat of Arms of John Hawkins

Shows a lion for Sierra Leone and a bound enslaved African

Antwerp's third growth spurt occurred between 1559 and 1568. This one was due to the increased production of goods around the city and in Holland, including ships.[37]

From Antwerp, the baton passed southward briefly to Genoa, specifically its bankers. Their climb to power began with profits from the Spanish trade with America, which they financed. Genoa's dominance of European finance lasted from 1550 to 1620. Genoese merchants and financiers were not merely financing Spain from a distance. Many married Spaniards and were integral members of the local aristocracy.[38]

Over centuries, England, Holland, Germany and Scandinavia slowly developed their crafts and farming. In turn, those countries attracted merchants and financiers. Around 1600, the center of European power decisively shifted north.[39]

Losers were Spain, Portugal, Flanders, parts of Germany and Northern Italy. Winners included Sweden, Brandenburg, Prussia, New England and the Middle Atlantic colonies of North America.[40]

Brandy and rum quickly became key items in trade with Africa for several reasons: They travelled well without losing flavor. They also fetched higher prices and profits than beer or wine because they had more alcohol.[41] Historian Fernand Braudel called brandy and rum "Europe's poisoned gifts" to the rest of the world.[42]

The French and English Enter the West African Trade

After a century-long monopoly by the Portuguese (with challenges from the Spanish), the African trade began attracting the attention of French captains in the 1530s.[43] The two Iberian rivals controlled key African trading locations, like the fort at Elmina. As a result, the French and other interlopers were initially confined mainly to less profitable stretches of the coast, like that of present-day of Liberia.[44]

One of the first French vessels to reach this region was piloted by a Portuguese renegade João Afonso (also known as Jean Alfonce), who traded for gold and ivory at Cape Mount and the Junk River in 1533.[45] While on a voyage to West Africa some 12 years later, a Bordeaux captain recorded what he termed "le langaige de Guynee," which twentieth-century linguists have identified as a vocabulary of the Klao, inhabitants of the Malagueta Coast.[46]

Around this time, English adventurers arrived. Notable among them was William Hawkins, whose ships bartered for ivory at the mouth of the River Sestros between 1530 and 1532. Because the Portuguese controlled trading along the West African coast down to Cape Mount, British traders in West Africa focused on points further east, especially Sestros and Mina on the Gold Coast.

Most of these early English traders recorded few details, if any, on the cultures they encountered. One of the most detailed early English accounts was written by John Lok. He led a convoy of three vessels that departed for West Africa from Dartmouth, England, on Nov. 1, 1554.

In an account published in 1814, he was poetic when describing geographical and navigational features. About Cape Mesurado, he said, it "rises into a hummock like the head of a porpoise" with one tree resembling a hay-stack and another to the southward like a gibbet. River Sesto, where he bought a ton of malagueta spice, was "easily known by a ledge of rocks" to the southeast and "five or six trees without leaves" at the mouth.

Lok was the first to record the names of several towns between River Sestro and Cape Palmas, including *Cakeado, Shawgro, Shyawe* or *Shavo* ("where fresh water may be had"), and *Croke*. Cape Palmas was described as "a fair high land, some low parts of which by the waterside seem red red cliffs, with white streaks like highways."

Seeking to further future English expeditions, he warned those traveling home from Mina that from Cape Palmas "the current sets always to the eastwards."[47]

The only major description of West Africans in Lok's account was a glib assertion added by his publisher, Richard Eden, that they are "a beastly living people, without God, law, religion, or government, and so scorched by the heat of the sun, that in many place they curse it when it rises." He claimed, quoting some "credible persons," that Lok's crew had "felt a sensible heat in the night from the beams of the

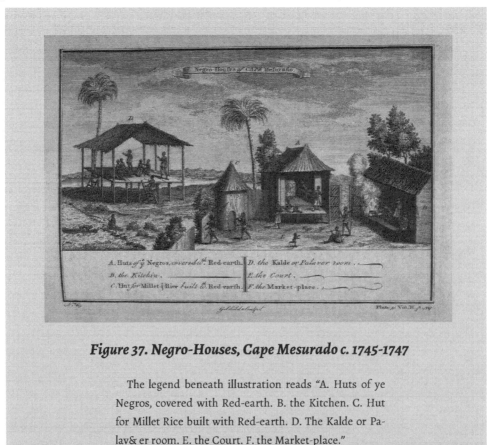

Figure 37. Negro-Houses, Cape Mesurado c. 1745-1747

The legend beneath illustration reads "A. Huts of ye Negros, covered with Red-earth. B. the Kitchen. C. Hut for Millet Rice built with Red-earth. D. The Kalde or Palav& er room. E. the Court. F. the Market-place."

moon," an assertion that would likely have furthered the exotic image of Africa among his readers.

Eden provided accurate details about elephants — the number of joints in their legs, tusk length, average lifespan and apparently emotional sensitivity.

But, then he added information that can best be described as fantastic: "They have continual war with dragons, which desire their blood because it is very cold; wherefore the dragon lies in wait for the passing of an elephant, winding its tail of vast length round the hind legs of the elephant, then thrusts his head into his trunk and sucks our his breath, or bites him in the ears where he cannot reach with his trunk." He asserted authoritatively that a mixture of elephant blood mingled with dragon blood was the source of cinnabar or vermillion!⁴⁸

Two Portuguese documents from that period survived. André 'Alvares de Almada in 1594 recorded the first extant description of a female initiation association in the region called *Cabondos*. It resembled the modern Temne Bundu society and Sande associations of other groups.

An account by Manuel 'Alvares, written in 1616, was more detailed and apparently more accurate. According to him, girls between ages 10 and 12 were secluded for three to four months in "a secret place in the forest," where they were taught a secret language.

Both Almada and 'Alvares agreed that the girls were instructed by an old man, sequestered even from their parents, given a new name and returned to their parents at a ceremony, where the girls danced for the

Figure 38. Popular foreign goods from Sierra Leone to the Gold Coast, 1558

Clothing: cloaks or overcoats, gowns, hats, cheap groves, leather bags

Containers: basins of various sorts, but mainly brass or bronze, pots of course tin that hold a quart or more, Dutch kettles with brass handles, large engraved brass basins, large engraved pewter basins and pitchers, large basins used for bathing, Dutch basins, red cans

Fabrics: linen cloth, cheap red cloth, coarse French coverlet, packing sheets, Spanish blankets

Furniture: small Flemish locked boxes, cheap chests

Implements: cheap knives, large pins, wedges of iron, horse nails, axe heads hammers, short pieces of iron

Jewelry: brass bracelets, lead bracelets, cheap beads, blue corals, small bells

Weapons: swords, daggers

Plus "any other trifling articles you will"

public.

Both writers noted the custom of male infant circumcision among the Temne. Neither mentioned clitoridectomy in the context of female initiation, suggesting the practice had not been instituted.[49]

Much more revealing of local cultures was London merchant William Towerson, who first visited the area with Lok. On Oct. 21, 1555, he led two ships from Dartmouth, England, arriving at Sestros River on December 15.

By Towerson's reckoning, the "greatest abundance" of malaguetta was to be found between River Cess and Cape Palmas. In one day at Sestros, he exchanged basins, bracelets and beads for 1,100 pounds of spice and two ivories.

Towerson described the town as consisting of 20 "small hovels, covered over with large leaves." The houses were open on all sides with floors raised almost a yard off the ground. The only animals were two goats, a few small dogs and some hens.

Inhabitants, both men and women, were engaged in carving "many ingenious things of the barks of trees" and working in "iron, making very pretty heads for javelins, tools for making their boats and various other things."[50]

Unlike many European visitors, Towerson made an effort to record some vocabulary of the residents. Included in his account were 11 phrases written (with translations) as *Bezow! bezow!* (meaning, "hello"), *manegete afoye* ("spice plentiful"), *crocow afoye* ("hens plentiful"), *zeramme afoye* ("Do you have enough?"), *begge sacke* ("give me a knife"), *beggy come* ("give me bread"), *borke* ("silence!"), *contrecke* ("you lie!"), *veede* ("put forth" or "empty"), *brekeke* ("row!"), and *diago* or *dabo* ("captain" or "chief").

Of the local language, he said, "they speak very thick, often repeating one word three times successively, and always the last time longer than the two former." For the amusement of the English visitors, several women danced, clapped and sang repeatedly what sounded to Towerson like "*Sakere, sakere, ho! ho! Sakere, sakere, ho! ho!*"[51]

Next to enter the fray were the Dutch, who sent a fleet to Sierra Leone in 1626. As a consequence of their presence, Cape Mount in particular was devastated by an unintended import: cholera or the "bloody flux," blamed for killing "multitudes" after "they have lost all their blood." This outbreak was followed soon after by the measles, which "swept away the best part of the people" (due probably to a lack of immunity).[52]

Samuel Brun of Basel, Switzerland, left one of the earliest descriptions of local culture and people in 1611 and 1620.[53] Living among the Vai in 1620 were several Dutch sailors, survivors of a ship wreck one year before.

In addition to a few locals who spoke a little Portuguese, Brun XE "trade:few goods reported at Cape Mount" noted that "Flamore," the *thaba* or monarch, spoke French. In 1620, the *thaba* and his people had "nothing to sell except ivory, rice and a little gold."[54]

The *thaba*'s wife (whom the Dutch called Maria) was a native of Cameroon, spoke "good Dutch." She had come to Cape Mount with a Dutch trader, who had taught her his native tongue. Six years before Brun's visit, the Dutchman died fighting on behalf of "Flamore," who promptly married Marie.[55]

Throughout the 1600s, Cape Mount is said to have been ruled by men with similar names. Their names were written as "Faramborey," "Faran Bure," "Frambore," "Flambourre,"[56] and "Falam Bûrre."[57] All of these suggest the family whose name is now spelled "Fahnbulleh."

Local Farming and Foods

After Towerson and Brun, Europeans began leaving more detailed accounts of local cultures. In the area now known as Liberia, three types of vegetation were important to local economies.

The first, forest plants, consisted of trees and plants that were indigenous to the West African forest. Forest vegetation provided the basis for important specializations. Herbalists, for example, discovered the medicinal properties of countless plants including "fever bush" used to treat malaria.[58]

Of the forest plants, the kola nut was without doubt the most economically important. The kola trade encouraged related activities like the weaving of baskets (used for transportation) and pottery (used for storage).

Another set of plants, the forest-margin tradition, centered around the production of tubers. These roots did not require extensive land-clearing and intensive cultivation. Probably because of their easy adaptability to the forest, these plants are most widely distributed over the area that would come to be known as Liberia.

Although a firm date of arrival is not known, they were locally available by the time of de Sintra's voyage.[59]

Within local societies, the African oil palm (Elaeis guineensis Jacq.) was the most useful and widely distributed forest-margin crop. It is neither a wild plant nor a domesticated forest crop. Although rarely cultivated before the 1800s, the oil palm spread to the forest due to selective encouragement, dissemination and utilization.

By 1687, two types of palm could be found all along the Windward Coast. One genotype of this plant yielded wine, wood for fences and floors, and flax for bags, cloths and fine mats. The true oil palm grows nuts in bunches of two to three hundred, about five to six feet off the ground.[60]

> … each tree commonly produces five or six such cluster. The oil drawn from the nuts is of the saffron-colour, smelling strong; at first extracting, it looks like oil of olives, as to its consistence, which, growing old, turns thick and lumpy like butter, and may be transported everywhere, and kept twenty years in some

proper vessel. This oil is much recommended throughout all Europe for obstructions, fractures, windy and cold humours. The natives use it much, with almost every thing they eat, as we do butter; and most days rub and anoint their bodies with it, to render the skin softer and shining, and the body stronger.[61]

Other widely distributed forest-margin crops were beans, eddoes, peas, nuts, yams, okra and several fruit.

Two forest-margin root crops served as staples: yams and eddoes. Yams can reach maturity in five months. Yams grow to three feet long and thirty pounds in weight. They usually cooked by boiling and were mainly staples in cultures east of the Mesurado.[62]

Savannah agriculture emphasized the production of rice, millet and other cereals. The main staple, rice, was eaten throughout the territory. But, it was grown mainly along the coast and in the northwestern and central regions.

Another crop of considerable economic importance was cotton (*Gossypium herbaceum*). The origin of cotton in West Africa remains unclear. But, it seems to have spread along with crops of the savannah complex. It was typically planted in the same field with rice. The cotton bolls were picked after the rice harvest in November.

Dutch merchant William Bosman described the inhabitants of Cape Mount in the early 1700s as "industrious to the last degree," mainly in growing rice and extracting salt from sea water. At River Sestre, he found the people "very Industrious, especially in the Planting of Rice, which is their chief Employment." The rice harvest here was so prodigious that "in a very short time we easily get enough to load a Ship." Those "above the common Rank," he noted, were engaged in a "perpetual trade" in rice, malaguetta and a small quantity of ivory.[63]

In 1678, Jean Barbot, a French supercargo on a English vessel, commended residents of the Malagueta Coast for their hard work in cultivating rice and millet.[64]

One item from the Americas would become a staple: cassava.

The staple food was boiled rice, which residents rolled in their hands into a ball that they ate with mutton, fish, chicken, goat, and fresh or dried monkey meat, a favorite around Sestros. Chickens were plentiful and so cheap, Barbot bought several for a penny worth of trifling commodities.[65]

Only a few economic activities and products were common to all of the Liberia area. These included black-smithing, the use of herbs as medicines, forest-margin crops and animal husbandry.[66]

Cloth was usually made by mixing cotton from the *Gossypium herbaceum* plant with that of the silk-cotton trees. Those same wild and gigantic trees also provided wood for canoes.

Cotton was the basis for a complex industry that involved weaving, dyeing and other auxiliary activities. These were especially developed among the precursors of the Vai, Bandi, Loma and Kpelle.

Most dyeing was done with indigo, obtained from the leaf of a tree. This dye rendered cloth various shades of blue. Natural brown and yellow dyes were also used.

Cloth-making through West Africa was characterized by a peculiar division of labor by sex. Typically, cotton was picked and spun by women. Using a vertical loom, each woman would weave enough cloth for her family's use. Women used fixed-frame treadles which produced cloth up to twenty inches wide and seventy-two long. Cloth produced by women was rarely tailored.

The production of cloth for trade and tailoring was generally done by men. They used a horizontal treadle loom, which produced extremely long strips of between six and fourteen inches in width.[67]

Cotton-cloth weaving was least developed east of River Cess. Instead, people made cloths from grass, raffia and tree bark. Cotton tended to replace those alternatives wherever it became available because those fabrics were less sturdy.[68]

Like many European visitors, Nicolas Villault in 1666 was struck by the relative lack of body covering by common people. "They go all naked both women and men, only a little cloth before them, but the women wear theirs from their stomack, to their mid-legg."[69]

In 1666, clothing along the Malagueta Coast consisted of "only a little piece of linnen before," with nothing on the head.[70]

At Cape Mount around 1701, the men's attire was "like a Surplice," which was a knee-length overgarment with full sleeves worn by European clergy or choirs. Women, on the other hand, wore a narrow cloth around their waist, "tucked in at their sides to fasten it," but without the girdles worn by women on the Gold Coast. "Sometimes they shamelessly go around naked," he added, "as if they wear proud of what Nature bestows on them in common with the rest of their Sex."[71]

According to Barbot, women at Sestros dressed simply, with a cloth tied "round their loin."[72]

Nicolas Villault and the Voyage of the Europa

One of the first detailed accounts was left by French nobleman Nicolas Villault de Bellefond. He sailed as comptroller of the 400-ton frigate Europa in 1666-1667, sponsored by the French West Indian Company.

The voyage was intended to secretly investigate prospects for a more vigorous French engagement in West Africa. For that reason, the ship was outfitted with goods and crew in Amsterdam, and at least once on the Windward Coast Villault misrepresented his sponsors as Dutch.

Three years after returning to France, the nobleman published a 280-page account of his voyage in English, titled *A Relation of the Coasts of Africk called Guinee*. It was, according to the front page, "Written in French, and faithfully Englished."[73]

If Villault's sponsors were expecting objective information on how West Africans viewed various European powers, he was the wrong choice for fact-finder. An ardent nationalist, he dedicated his book to Jean-Baptiste Colbert, the French naval minister. He included this chauvinistic claim: "If you approve the account I give of Guinea, is there any Frenchman, who will fail to support your intentions, who will not give his assistance towards re-establishing us in these countries which we possessed in the past?"

Villault asserted early in the book that sailors from the French port of Dieppe had preceded the Portuguese in West Africa. He interjected throughout the text questionable claims about people speaking French and favoring the French over other Europeans. He also sprinkled in stirring calls for vigorous French engagement in West Africa.[74]

In two passage that were probably embellishments, he claimed the ruler of Cape Mount, Falam Boure, had "with tears (as it were) of joy assured me, that the *French* should be always welcome to him."[75] Later, he averred the man's daughter-in-law had answered him in French, *Monsieur vous remercie*, and told him that her father-in-law "had lived always amongst the French when they were in those parts."[76]

On January 8, 1666, the *Europa* came off the coast of Cape Mount. No settlements or buildings were visible from aboard the ship, but Villault and some crew members went ashore. There they came upon about five huts where people were engaged in boiling seawater to make salt. The residents promised to send word of his arrival to their ruler, whose residence was three-days' journey inland.

The next morning the crew fired two guns to signal a desire to trade, as had been agreed. In response, the people lit fires onshore as a sign that goods were available. The next two days were spent bartering aboard the ship, mainly for ivory.

On the 12th, Villault ventured ashore. He was carried on the backs of crew members part of the way because rough waves prevented their small boat from landing. On shore, he found that the residents had built a large thatched structure "to keep our commodities dry, and shelter us from the violence of the sun."

Within two days, people who came from distant places had built a large number of houses for trading. According to Villault, this temporary market filled a plain about three miles in circumference.[77]

In the midst of trade negotiations, however, the local people began running "Pell-mell" from their houses and abandoned their merchandise. It turned out, that they were rushing to welcome their ruler, Falam Boure, and his entourage. Villault's description of the scene is one of the earliest accounts of the political culture of Cape Mount [See box labelled "Welcoming Falam Boure"].

Falam Boure wore a blue robe while the men of his entourage were dressed in blue-and-white striped gowns, obviously made from what is known in Liberia as "country cloth."[78] Villault estimated the local ruler's age to be above 60 years and described him as "grave and venerable" at one point and "sensible and majestick" at another. Falam Boure told his guest in Portuguese it had been four years since any "Whites" had visited.[79]

Villault resorted to hyperbolic descriptions of some locations. These were apparently intended to spur his sponsors to move into those areas before rival European powers.

Regarding Cape Mount, he said, "were all the rest of *Africk* like this point of it, it was indubitably to be preferred to any part of *Europe*. No sooner is your foot upon the ground, but you are presented with a fine plaine, planted on this side and that, with curious groves, perpetually green, and in their leaves not unlike to our Laurel."

Glancing inland from the Cape, he added, "there is no stop nor termination of the eye, it may delight and lose itself, in vast meadows and playnes, beautifi'd and perfum'd with excellent verdures, and water'd with several pritty Rivers, which open and expan'd themselves to the [Blacks,] and seem to invite them to a communication with those that live higher up in the Countrey."

Later, he added, "in this place (if any where) a man live happily, all things contributing to make his life pleasant; the beauty and bounty of the

Figure 39. Welcoming Falam Boure

"Before him marched his Drum, and his Trumpet, 8 to 10 of his kindred and friends, and the rest were his Officers: his Wives, and his Daughters, marched on his side, behind him his Slaves followed, and a certain number of women carrying his dinner in bowls of Wood, and of Tyn, which they held up as high as they could possible:

By him he had four Slaves marching, two of them covering him with two large Bucklers, and the other carrying his bow and arrows, and javelin. As he approached, the [Blacks] divided themselves, the Men on one side, the Women on the other, singing, and dancing, and leaping up and down, and testifying their joy in a thousand different pastures. [Falam Boure] took a dart, and pretended to throw it at them, upon the ground, and at the same time they which came along with his Majesty took their turn, both to dance and sing.

Presently the [ruler] took an arrow, which he shot up into the aire, and presently all ran to the place where it fell, and happy was he that could take it up first, and bring it to him; after this he made a show of shooting directly amongst them, & they throwing themselves down again, with great acclamation, continued this past time for a quarter of an hour: In this triumph and grandour, he was conducted to us; we received him as honorably as we could, saluting him with volleys of small shots."

Countrey, the humour and disposition of the people, the aboundance of all necessaries, the considerableness of the gain [from trade], and the aptness and convenience for building in all places wherever *you come*.[80]

Regarding foodstuff at Cape Mount, Villaut noted citrons, oranges, berries, melons, gourds and "a sort of plums, not much unlike our Brugnons," but not as tasty.[81] He noted the presence of rice and millet and said maize was "more plentifull, and grows in greater quantity, than in any other part of *Guinee* whatsoever."

At Cape Mount, Villault said residents used corn to make bread. If true, this culinary feature disappeared overtime.

A wide variety of fowl was available and cheap, including hens, pidgeons, ducks and mallards. In addition to tortoises that yielded "excellent meat" but worthless shells, there was a "great store" of both saltwater and freshwater fish. He also noted a good supply of goats, hogs and apes, "but ugly ones."[82]

Like many European visitors, Villault was struck by the relative lack of body covering by common people. "They go all naked both women and men, only a little cloth before them, but the women wear theirs from their stomack, to their mid-legg."

In contrast to some other writers, however, he was not uniformly condescending toward the residents and their practices. Overall, he thought the people at Cape Mount to be "handsome," "goodnatured" and "tractible."

Villault was struck by how careful the local people were in roasting meat over wooden spits, "turning them with great care, and observing very curiously least one side be more roasted then the other. He also pronounced them "very neat in their feeding."[83]

Regarding gender conventions, Villault "could perceive" that many of the men were circumcised. Many husbands spent hours "with their heads in their Wives lapps" having their hair combed and platted. He judged husbands to be "commonly more jealous" and the women to be "more chast then the rest." But it was not clear if he was comparing the chastity of women to local men or to women elsewhere on the coast.[84]

Although Villault tried to learn as much as possible about the local religion, he came away knowing only that "all of them have their Fetishes." In response to his enquiries, a local person reportedly told him that "the Whites pray'd to God, and the Blacks to the Devil." This comment, if true, revealed the extent to which Africans had already internalized a negative image of themselves after two centuries of contact with Europeans.[85]

Social status apparently defined, not only differences in dress, but also in housing. In contrast to the nondescript huts of salt-makers, the "houses of their Nobility" contained "a distinct appartment where their beds are made either upon plancks, or mat; about a yeard from the ground, about which they hang a cloth (instead of curtains and valence) and so sleep all night upon them.

Over the course of four days, the *Europa* crew bought mainly mats, rice and ivory, which were "plentiful and excellently good." Concluding that the store of ivory was exhausted at Cape Mount, Villault and company sailed on January 13. They arrived the following day amidst a "thick fog" off the coast of Cape Mesurado. They fired off two guns to signal their interest in trading.

On the 15th, two local men came aboard from a canoe. They informed Villault it had been "a full year since they had seen any Whites" and promised to bring "some great store of ivory to the Sea side" the next day.[86]

But, Villault's impression of Cape Mesurado was clouded by apprehensions borne either from hearsay or his own misguided attempt at etymology. First, he dubbed the cape *"Miserado"* rather than the original Italian *"Misurato."* Then, based on that false label, he speculated that the name was given by the Portuguese because underwater rocks "inevitably destroy any Vessel, which should come nearer than one-and-a-half miles. Or by the French, some of whose sailors cried *"Misericorde, Misericorde"* as they were being massacred by local people.[87]

Another sign of the "Natives of this place being very cruel," in his view, was the name of the river, Duro, which he deduced meant "hard and fatal to the White."

Based on these apprehensions, Villault and company made sure, when going onshore to trade on January 16, that they "fortified" their little boat with "a great Gun, to fright them and keep them in order." His fear of the Mesurado people fueled suspicions on their part leading them to ask why he had brought a canon in his little boat if he had come in peace.[88]

Upon landing, Villault found the local ruler with about 60 associates sitting under a tree, some equipped with darts, bows, arrows and swords. The few women among them were immediately sent to the woods, where they remained for most of the day.

The peoplehere were described as merely "clothed," but the leader was dressed in a red robe and red "bonnet." Villault described him as "a very lusty man of a severe aspect."[89] He and his associates "freely" consumed the two bottles of brandy that were given as presents before leading their visitors to the trading house.

Villault learned that the local trade was mainly in ivory and rice "in great abundance." He also concluded that the local people showed "great deference and respect" to their priests, "believing every word they spake an Oracle," but "above all things, their greatest superstition is of their *Fetishes*."

At dinner, Villault observed one of the leading men offer a libation of palm wine, so that "if his dead Father should be dry, he would come thither to drink."[90]

Intimacy and a Unique Handshake

After the meal, the leader of the community reportedly gave one of his daughters to Villault "for my Wife, after which we grew very intimate and great." In the aftermath of this "intimacy," the rest of the residents hailed him as their "kinsmen and friend," offered him palm wine and promised him slaves.

Although Villault was shown some "excellent" ivory, he did not buy because he felt the prices were too high. Upon learning that the English had a warehouse beyond the Cape, he developed a "suspicion" that those archenemies of France were baiting him with the ivory while planning an attack. So, despite a promise to return the next day and leaving a gold ring as surety, Villault and his men left early the next morning for River Cess.[91]

Figure 40. "Bridge in the Quoja's Country" c. 1745-1747

Items in the illustration are labeled "Coco trees [meaning coconut], porcupine, jackal, tiger [meaning leopard], trap.

While anchored off the coast of River Cess, the *Europa* was approached by local fishermen who enticed the Europeans to come ashore with the promise of many ivories. Taking some commodities in a boat, some crew members sailed more than nine miles up the river to meet the ruler of the area and present him with gifts "according to the Custome."

Upon returning to the ship, one crew member described the local leader as "a very lusty man, with a stern and supercilious aspect." He professed "a great friendship for the English," who once had a store house nine miles up river that was now in ruins.

Although there was a large quantity of ivory, the price was high, driven up – – the ship's comptroller assumed — by two vessels that had stopped here two weeks before on their way to the Gold Coast.[92]

While the crew was ashore, the ship was approached by about 12 canoes with a variety of fish, including a sea pike, which Villault declared "an excellent good fish." Perhaps based on the fishermen who visited the ship, he concluded that the local people "are generally well proportioned."[93]

Regarding their "manner of salutation" at River Cess, he noted, "they take our fore finger and thumb, into their hands, they pull them hard, and make them snap." This is the earliest documented description of the unique handshake among men for which Liberians have come to be known. The local greeting was "Aquio," which "is as much as *your servant* with us."[94]

Regarding foodstuff, Villault thought River Cess was "very fertile, well furnish'd" with fowl, rice and millet, "which they carry with them in their *Canoes*, when they go fishing." As for trade goods in particular, rice, malaguetta and ivory would likely yield a profit for "He that would stay upon the place." He insisted that the kindness of the local people "has been always more conspicuous to the French, then either to the Hollander or Portugal, neither of which they would ever suffer to cohabit with them."[95]

At dawn on January 23, as the *Europa* was sailing for Sanguin River, Villault observed a "little fleet" of fishing canoes that dispersed in every direction. He was impressed by how "very neat and axact" fishermen were in keeping their boats clean. Although the ship's destination, Sanguin, laid only 36 miles away, it had to sail south to avoid the many rocks in its path before shifting northward, taking four hours in all.[96]

By Villault's estimation, the Malagueta Coast began at the Sanguin River and ran for 150 miles to Cape Palmas. Along this stretch of coast laid Cestro-Crou, Brova, Battou, Zino, Crou, Crou Sestre, Wapo, Batou, Grand-Sester, Petit-Sester and Goiane, all of which the *Europa* visited over the course of 19 days. Villault noted that each town on this coast was located on the bank of a river, the main ones being the Sanguin River and the Grand Sestra River.[97]

Based on what Villault had read or heard from sailors before embarking on this voyage, he opined that "few of the Whites can stay long [on the Malaguetta Coast] without being sick." This illness, which he attributed to the many small waterways, was apparently malaria.[98]

"Salutation" along the Malagueta Coast consisted of grasping each other by the upper arm, then stretched them out while saying what sounded to him like *Toma*. Then clasping the elbow hard, people would say *Toma* again. After snapping fingers, people greeted each other with *Enfa Nemate*, which he was told meant, "all that I have is at your service." Given this explanation, he concluded, "The language is more elegant than we imagine, to one that understands it."[99]

Clothing here consisted of "only a little piece of linnen before," with nothing on the head.[100]

The local staples were rice and millet, which was "bountiful." The area also produced beans, citrons, oranges, peas ("very tender and good, boyled"), plums ("which are so pleasant"), and nuts ("without any skin over the kernel, but all round like your Almonds or *Pistaccios* of *Spain*"). As for meats, there was a "store" of cows, goats, hogs, chickens and other fowls. Villault declared the local palm wine "very good."[101]

Villault apparently did not go onshore at Sanguin, but he estimated the town contained about 100 huts. While anchored near the town, the *Europa* was visited by the local ruler, dressed in a blue robe like his counterpart at Cape Mount. Villault described him as "an ancient man, very grave, and venerable, his hair very white, yet his person large and lusty." He drank "neither Wine nor Strong-water nor Palme-Wine," which the French visitor found "most remarkable."

Another visitor to the ship was the ruler's brother, who spoke "very good Dutch, having spent three years in Holland. While spending the night aboard the *Europa*, he informed the mainly Dutch crew that a small vessel had recently kidnapped about 12 people from Crou Sester and carried them off.[102]

Because the first man reportedly had 50 wives and the second claimed 15, Villault surmised that men here could "have as many Wives as they can keep."[103]

Of the French author's many comments about the people of the Liberian coast, one of his most positive was offered at Grand Cess. "They work excellent well in Iron," he said, because "they mended our shears for us, with which we cut out our barrs of Iron, and gave them such a temper as made them incomparably better than they were at first."[104]

From Villault's book, it is clear that European ship-traffic along the Malagueta Coast was, not only frequent, but riddled with tension. About a month before his visit to Sanguin, a Flemish vessel had reportedly been chased off by an English ship. Two weeks later, two Flemish ships visited River Cess on their way to Mina.

While at Wapo on February 3, Villault and his crew spent all night at their weapons preparing to seize a vessel they thought was English, but by morning it had vanished.

Two days later, they resolved to capture an approaching ship that was as large as the *Europa*. However, it turned out to be the 400-ton frigate *Amsterdam* with 36 pieces of ordnance. With the anticipated fight averted, Villault and the *Amsterdam* captain — each standing on the deck of his ship – toasted each other glasses of wine.[105]

1. Braudel, Vol. 3, 1984, pp. 140-141; Smith and Kelly, 2013, p. 495.
2. Braudel, Vol. 3, 1984, pp. 57, 89; also Epstein, 1996, p. xiv; Bonnie G. Smith and Donald R. Kelley, "Europe and Russia in world history" (pp. 475-493), in Jerry H. Bentley, ed., *The Oxford Handbook of World History* (Oxford: Oxford University Press, 2013), p. 481.
3. Braudel, Vol. 2, 1982, pp. 392-395.
4. Smith and Kelly, 2013, p. 497; Abulafia, 2013, p. 505.
5. Braudel, Vol. 2, 1982, pp. 284-287, 559; Smith and Kelley, 2013, p. 479.
6. Braudel, Vol. 3, 1984, pp. 110-111, 118-136.
7. Braudel, Vol. 3, 1984, p. 96; Braudel, Vol. 2, 1982, pp. 284-287, 559.
8. Epstein, 1996, pp. xvii, 229, 232.
9. Epstein, 1996, pp. 283, 310-311.
10. Braudel, Vol. 3, 1984, pp. 99, 102-106.
11. Braudel, Vol. 2, 1982, p. 569.
12. Braudel, Vol. 2, 1982, p. 569.
13. Braudel, Vol. 2, 1982, p. 570; Smith and Kelley, 2013, p. 480.
14. Vilar, 1984, pp. 66-67; Williams, 1984, pp. 18-25; Davis, 2006, p. 97; Eduardo Galeano, *Open Veins of Latin America* (New York: Monthly Review Press, 1997), pp. 11-58.
15. Rawley, 1981, p. 10.
16. Vilar, 1984, pp. 66-67; Williams, 1984, pp. 30-45.
17. Richard Bean, "A note on the relative importance of slaves and gold in West African exports," *Journal of African History*, XV, 3 (1974): 351-356, especially pp. 351-352.
18. Curtin, 1993, pp. 133-134.
19. Vilar, 1984, pp. 109-111.
20. Rawley, 1981, p. 56; Galeano, 1997, pp. 11-58.
21. Blaut, 1992, pp. 32-35; Edward J. Davies II, "The Americas, 1450-2000" (pp. 508-528), in Jerry H. Bentley, ed., *The Oxford Handbook of World History* (Oxford: Oxford University Press, 2013), p. 510.
22. Braudel, Vol. 1, 1981, pp. 220-223.
23. Braudel, Vol. 2, 1982, pp. 190-191; Fernández-Armesto and Sacks, 2013, p. 131; Mintz, 1985, p. 79.
24. Braudel, Vol. 2, 1982, pp. 160; Masonen, 2000, p. 165; Russell-Wood, 1998.
25. Braudel, Vol. 2, 1982, pp. 212-213.
26. Masonen, 2000, p. 166.
27. Wallerstein, Vol. 2, 1980, p. 103; Davis II, 2013, p. 511.
28. Mintz, 1985, p. 34; Braudel, Vol. 2, 1982, p. 449-451; Norton, 2010, p. 155 (tobacco monopoly in Spain).
29. Braudel, Vol. 2, 1982, p. 444.
30. Braudel, Vol. 2, 1982, p. 449-451; Mintz, 1985, pp. 34, 41.
31. Braudel, Vol. 2, 1982, p. 449-451.
32. Wallerstein, Vol. 1, 1974, p. 38; also Wolf, 1982, pp. 77-79; Mintz, 1985, p. 55; Braudel, Vol. 3, 1984, p. 57. These authors offer different dates for when capitalism arose. Braudel suggests the 1200s, Mintz says the late 1700s.
33. Wallerstein, Vol. 1, 1974, p. 38; also Braudel, Vol. 2, 1982, p. 408; Maurice Dobb, *Studies in the Development of Capitalism* (New York: International Publisher, 1950), pp. 190-191.
34. Wallerstein, Vol. 1, 1974, pp. 67-68.

35. Wallerstein, Vol. 1, 1974, pp. 67-68, 266-281; Mintz, 1985, p. 35.
36. Braudel, Vol. 3, 1984, pp. 143-154; Davis II, 2013, p. 511.
37. Braudel, Vol. 3, 1984, pp. 143-154.
38. Braudel, Vol. 3, 1984, pp. 154-174; Defourneaux, 1970, p. 79.
39. Braudel, Vol. 3, 1984, pp. 97-99; Wallerstein, Vol. 1, 1974, pp. 36-37, 225-226.
40. Wallerstein, Vol. 1, 1974, p. 179.
41. Braudel, Vol. 1, 1981, pp. 241-246.
42. Braudel, Vol. 1, 1981, p. 248.
43. Thomas, 1997, pp. 157, 183, 199, 201-203.
44. Villault, 1745-47, p. 381.
45. P. E. H. Hair, "Some minor sources for Guinea, 1519-1559: Enciso and Alfonce/Fonteneau," *History in Africa*, Vol. 3 (1976), pp. 19-46, especially pp. 30-31; P. E. H. Hair, "Some French sources on Upper Guinea, 1540-1575," *Bulletin de l'Institute francais d'Afrique noire*, Série B, t, 31, no. 4 (1969): 1030-1034.
46. David Dalby and P. E. H. Hair, "'Le langaige de Guynee': A sixteenth century vocabulary from the Pepper Coast," *African Language Studies*, 5 (1964), pp. 174-191.
47. Captain John Lok, "Voyage to Guinea in 1554," in Robert Kerr, *A General History and Collection of Voyages and Travels*, Vol. VII (London: T. Cabell, 1824), pp. 229-246.
48. Lok, 1824, pp. 236-242, especially 237-238, 241-242.
49. André 'Alvares de Almada, *Brief Treatise on the Rivers of Guinea, Part I: Translated Text*. Translated with annotations by Paul E. H. Hair ([S. I.]: Andreas Heuijerjans, 2010), pp. 117-118; 'Manuel 'Alvares, S. J., *Ethiopia Menor e descricao geográfica da Provincia da Serra Lioa*. Translated with annotations by Paul E. H. Hair (Liverpool: Department of History University of Liverpool, 1990, reprint of 1616 edition), Chapter 8, p. 1; also Ogilby, 1670, pp. 402-405. For the historical depth and widespread practice of circumcision in Africa, see Baily, 1996, pp. 88-91.
50. William Towerson, Merchant of London, "Voyage to Guinea in 1555," in Robert Kerr, *A General History and Collection of Voyages and Travels*, Vol. VII (London: T. Cabell, 1824), pp. 246-257. Towerson purchased one hogshead and 100 pounds, which I have converted to 1,100 pounds.
51. Towerson, 1824, pp. 246-257, especially pp. 252-254.
52. Barbot, 1732, p. 118; Hair, 1974, pp. 25-54.
53. Brun, 1983, pp. 74-75, n. 185.
54. Brun, 1983, pp. 74-75, n. 185.
55. Brun, 1983, pp. 74-75, n. 185; Sieur de Bellefond Nicolas Villault, "A relation of the coast of Africa called Guinea," in John Green, *A New General Collection of Voyages and Travels*, Vol. 2 (London: Thomas Astley, 1745-47), pp. 382-383. For the claim that Portugese was spoken by Falam Bûrre and French by one of his daughters-in-law, see Villault, 1745-47, p. 379.
56. Barbot, 1732, p. 108.
57. Villault, 1745-47, p. 379.
58. C. S. Finch, "The African background to medical science," in I. Van Sertima (ed.), *Blacks in Science* (New Brunswick, NJ: Transaction Books, 1984); Barbot, 1732, pp. 119, 135.
59. Gabel, 1976, p. 31; D. G. Coursey, "The origins and domestication of yams in Africa," in B. K. Swartz and R. E. Dumett (eds.), *West African Culture Dynamics: Archeological and Historical Perspectives* (New York: Mouton, 1980).
60. J. Harlan, "The origins of indigenous African agriculture," J. D. Fage and R. Oliver (eds.), *The Cambridge History of Africa*, Vol. 1 (New York: Cambridge University Press, 1982), p. 631; Barbot, 1732, pp. 106, 110, 112, 113, 137; Villault, 1745-47, p. 380; John Green, *A New General Collection of Voyages and Travels*, Vol. 2 (London: Thomas Astley, 1745-47), p. 523.

61. Barbot, 1732, pp. 112-113.
62. Lugenbeel, 1853, p. 14.
63. Bosman, 1967, pp. 480-481.
64. Hair, Jones and Law, 1992, Letter 30, pp. 288, 292.
65. Hair, Jones and Law, 1992, Letter 29, pp. 269, 276-277.
66. Carl Patrick Burrowes, "Economic activities of pre-Liberian societies: Production for use and exchange," *Liberia Forum*, Vol. 2, No. 2 (1996): 25-44.
67. Dennis, 1972, pp. 27, 54-55, 192; C. Wrigley, "Speculations on the economic prehistory of Africa," in J. D. Fage and R. A. Oliver (eds.), *Papers in African Prehistory* (Cambridge: Cambridge University Press, 1974), pp. 62-63; d'Azevedo, 1962, pp. 520-521; Warren L. d'Azevedo, "Sources of Gola artistry," in Warren L. d'Azevedo, *The Traditional Artist in African Societies* (Bloomington, Ind.: Indiana University Press, 1975), p. 326; Roy Sieber, *African Textiles and Decorative Arts* (New York: Museum of Modern Art, 1972); Lars Sundstrom, *The Exchange Economy of Pre-Colonial Tropical Africa* (New York: St. Martin's Press, 1974), pp. 151-152.
68. Lars Sundstrom, *The Exchange Economy of Pre-Colonial Tropical Africa* (New York: St. Martin's Press, 1974), pp. 153-154.
69. Nicolas Villault, *A Relation of the Coasts of Africa called Guinea* (London, 1670), p. 62.
70. Villault, 1670, p. 94.
71. Bosman, 1967, pp. 474, 472.
72. Hair, Jones and Law, 1992, Letter 29, pp. 275, 272, 273.
73. F. Swanzy, "A French voyage to West Africa in 1666-1667," *Journal of the Royal African Society*, Vol. 7, No. 26 (Jan. 1908): 190-204, especially p. 193 and Villault, 1670 pp. 66-67.
74. Swanzy, 1908, p. 193; Villault, 1670, p. 62-63, 65, 76-77.
75. Villault, 1670, pp. 58-59.
76. Villault, 1670, pp. 60-61.
77. Villault, 1670, p. 56.
78. Villault, 1670, p. 57.
79. Villault, 1670, pp. 58-59.
80. Villault, 1670, pp. 60-61, 65, emphasis added.
81. Villault, 1670, p. 61.
82. Villault, 1670, pp. 61-62.
83. Villault, 1670, p. 62.
84. Villault, 1670, pp. 63, 65. Villault said wives "spend much of their time in combing and ordering their Husbands hair," but I have substituted "platting" for "ordering."
85. Villault, 1670, p. 64.
86. Villault, 1670, p. 64.
87. Villault, 1670, pp. 67-68.
88. Villault, 1670, pp. 68, 70-72.
89. Villault, 1670, pp. 69-70.
90. Villault, 1670, pp. 69, 72-73.
91. Villault, 1670, pp. 71-77. I have omitted Villault's insubstantial and brief descriptions of the Junk River and "Petit Dieppe."
92. Villault, 1670, pp. 77-80.
93. Villault, 1670, pp. 77-80.
94. Villault, 1670, pp. 81-82.
95. Villault, 1670, p. 82.

96. Villault, 1670, pp. 82-83.
97. Villault, 1670, pp. 87, 93.
98. Villault, 1670, p. 84.
99. Villault, 1670, p. 98.
100. Villault, 1670, p. 94.
101. Villault, 1670, p. 96.
102. Villault, 1670, pp. 89-90.
103. Villault, 1670, p. 96.
104. Villault, 1670, p. 95.
105. Villault, 1670, pp. 88, 78, 90-92.

Chapter 11
Two-Story Huts & Sugar-Loaf Baskets

Tensions in West Africa between ships of different countries reflected growing economic and political conflicts in Europe. In the shadow of Spain, Amsterdam had quietly emerged as Europe's third banking capital. Its rise stemmed from the city's role as a central market. It traded beef from Denmark, cowrie shells from Ceylon, herring from the North Sea, silver from the Americas and white cloth from England.

Amsterdam soon became the glue that bound seven tiny Dutch states, known as the United Provinces. They later united to form Holland.[1]

Like Portugal before, Holland was an unlikely candidate for world domination. Half of its land was underwater and another quarter was unfit for farming. Its people imported about 75 percent of their food. Most of what they initially produced consisted of cheese, butter and clay for making pottery.[2]

Long-distance trading helped boost Amsterdam's role as a ship-building and ship-servicing center. The eventual ascent of the Dutch came through banking and superior navigation. It was consolidated in the early 1600s when Amsterdam merchants won control of the Asia spice and textile trade from the Portuguese. In 1652, the Dutch established a post at the Cape of Good Hope, South Africa, which ensured control of the Asian trade.[3]

But, European powers were not content simply with buying cheap and selling dear. They decided to seize control of production with force. An early victim was Ceylon (now Sri Lanka), the world's main source of cinnamon. In the early 1600s, the Portuguese placed troops along the edge of the island. They then forced residents increase production and to sell only to them.[4]

The Dutch took this approach even further. When they arrived in Bantam in the 1600s, the island was supplying pepper to China and Europe. To drive prices up, the Dutch fought for almost ten years until they reduced the pepper crop. Further east, they overthrew the sultanate on Sulawesi, to end supplied of spices to the Portuguese.[5]

After 1621, the Dutch made a concerted push into the Atlantic trade. From the Portuguese, they seized northeast Brazil, Elmina in West Africa and Luanda in Angola. In the 1600s, the Dutch were importing Caribbean salt into Europe.[6] By 1669, they had more ships than all other European countries combined.[7]

Immanuel Wallerstein credits Amsterdam's dominance of the world economy to three factors: a significant share of world trade, "sound public finances," and profits from Dutch foreign capital investments.[8]

Dutch economic dominance was by no means limited to Asian islands and African forts. In the 1600s, control of the French economy rested in the hands of Dutch wholesalers based in Bordeaux and Nantes. At that time, Dutch shippers also controlled England's trade with the outside world.[9]

The Dutch significantly escalated the trade in African slaves. While they were challenging the Portuguese and Spanish, the English and French used the opportunity to seize territories in the Caribbean and the Americas.[10] Amsterdam grew from 50,000 residents in 1600 to 200,000 in 1700. Its dominance of Europe lasted roughly from 1620 to 1680.[11]

William Bosman on the Sexual Habits of Local Women

As the Dutch tightened their control of world trade, their presence increased in the area now known as Liberia. In the early 1700s, a detailed account of West African life was published by William Bosman, a Dutch merchant. From the age of 16, he spent 14 years in West Africa. He served as chief factor mainly at the Elmina fort on the Gold Coast and was the second highest ranking Dutch official on what was then called the Guinea Coast.[12]

Bosman's manuscript was structured in the form of 22 letters to his uncle in Holland, who had visited West Africa himself. It was written between early 1701 and September 1702, during a period when Dutch supremacy in West Africa was being eclipsed by the British and French.[13]

While sailing along the coast of what is now Liberia, from Nov. 28, to Dec. 25, 1701, Bosman repeatedly inquired about local wars. He was apparently trying to assess the prospective availability of slaves. He also remarked time and again on the sexual proclivities of local women, unintentionally revealing his own prurient fascination. In addition, he often noted how reticent local people were to approach his ship, a consequence of at least one recent massive kidnapping sweep by two European vessels.[14]

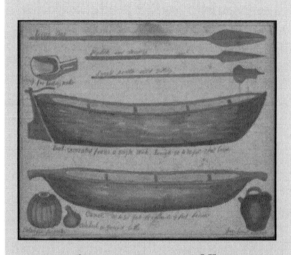

Figure 41. Canoes, paddles & other objects from Kru Coast

As with many sixteenth-century writers, Bosman engaged in very little critical thinking about himself or his culture, reserving criticism for others instead. If he was unable to communicate with locals, for example, this was due to their "Barbarous" speech, not to the impenetrability of Dutch. If people in coastal communities were materialistic, this was assumed to be a reflection of traditional values, rather than having been influenced by over a century of Atlantic trading.

Bosman came ashore at Cape Mount on Nov. 29, hoping to buy ivory. Mistaking Lake Piso for a "very fine river," he noted, it flows into the sea but once a year during the heavy rains. The surrounding country, he observed, was "very pleasant, and also seems very fertile."[15]

Bosman was "very civilly welcomed" with several pots of palm wine. However, his assessment of the number of residents seemed contradictory. On the one hand, he claimed the "Whole shoar" was filled with local people upon his arrival, but later noted only "three small Villages, the whole amount of which was not full thirty houses."[16]

After an hour's wait, the ruler of the area, known as "Jan Capo Monte," arrived from three miles inland with an entourage of men. On the one hand, Bosman "rose up in order to meet him before he entered the Village, and to salute him with a profound Reverence." On the other hand, his private written comments were disparaging — a deceitful engagement that would be employed by countless other visitors over the centuries.

Jan was "an elderly Man, as appeared by his grey Head and Beard." According to local informants, the ruler had over 400 wives "who all live with him in one village." And yet, somewhat incongruously, he had only 12 sons. Upon each of them, Bosman noted with apparent sarcasm, "he hath bestowed the Government of a village containing eight huts."

Of Jan's four daughters, he added disparagingly, "they did their best to pass honestly thro' the World; their principal Trade lay in relieving the Travelers Necessities at a very reasonable Price," an apparent allusion to prostitution.[17]

Bosman described the inhabitants of Cape Mount as "industrious to the last degree," mainly in growing rice and extracting salt from sea water. Both activities, he claimed, "all of the Negroes are oblig'd to do for the King, whose Slaves they are accounted." It is not clear if those characterized as "slaves" of Jan were a segment of the population along the shore or, less likely, all of his subjects.

As on the Gold Coast, where Bosman lived, he noted the presence here of pineapples, bananas and "Paquovers."[18] All other foodstuff were in short supply, including "great Milhio," yams and potatoes.[19]

The lake, in contrast, was said to be filled with fish, which were caught with large nets.

One indirect sign of the area's relative underpopulation was the large number of predatory animals, including elephants and leopards.[20] Bosman was told that the bows and arrows worn by local men were more ornamental than functional because wars were rare.[21]

Describing the attire of Jan, Bosman noted dismissively, he was "clothed, or rather hung with a brown Cloak, and a woolen cap on his Head, so that his whole Equipage, if sold to the Brokers, would not yield forty shillings."[22]

Asked about the local religion, residents allegedly told Bosman that "it principally consisted in Reverencing and obeying" their government and "without troubling themselves with what was above" it.

Rather than accurately reflecting local beliefs, this account depicts the difficulty of translating abstract concepts from one language (Dutch) to another (Vai) through a third (Portuguese), which neither of the communicating parties probably spoke very well.

Had the question been put by residents of Cape Mount to the common seamen aboard Bosman's ship, the response would probably not have corresponded with the views of Dutch clergy.

As for the relationship between the sexes, Bosman noted, each man was allowed as many wives as he could maintain, which wasn't very difficult since women maintained themselves through their own hard work! "They seem also to live very contentedly with their Wives." The husbands, he added condescendingly, were not "much concerned if they venture on unlawful Pleasures with other Men."[23] This alleged willingness to overlook adultery might have selectively applied to European visitors, but Bosman wasn't in a position to know that.

Finding only two tusks available, Bosman left Cape Mount, and arrived at Cape Mesurado on Nov. 25. Upon landing, he asked why none of the local people had ventured out to his ship. He was told that two months before "the English had been there with two large Vessels, and had Ravaged the Country, destroyed all their Canoas, Plundered their Houses, and carried off some of their People for Slaves; upon which the remainder fled to the Inland-Country, where most of them were at present."

Two miles west of Mesurado (probably on what is now known as Bushrod Island) stood three villages with 20 houses each. These houses, Bosman reported, were the finest seen on his entire voyage, "covered at the top much like our Hayreaks in Holland." Each unit contained three apartments, which together housed 50 to 60 "Men, Women and Children, all of which confusedly intermix in their lodging." He paid seven pounds of copper as "dash" to two old men, who "pretended to be Captains," or rulers.[24]

As at Cape Mount, Bosman asked probing questions about the sexual availability of women and described what struck him as a strange gender-based division of labor. "The women are handsome," he noted, "and as the Men informed me, are permitted to earn what Money they please with their Bodies."[25]

As for the men, they "do not trouble themselves with working, but rather leave that to their wives; as believing they have sufficiently fatigued themselves with trading a little, mostly in Palm Wine, which is very plenty and good here." In two days, he bought 300 lbs. of ivory, which he regarded as meager. Despite the alleged laziness of local men, he noted a daily traffic of canoes to trade at River Cess because that town attracted more European vessels.[26]

Bosman had less to say about the produce and livestock here, only noting in passing their similarity to those at Cape Mount. Mesurado residents, too, reported having no enemies — except the English, whom they were determined to capture in numbers equal to those of their compatriots who had been carried off in two large vessels.[27]

Wild Men, Fruitful Women and a Funeral

Sailing from Cape Mesurado, Bosman saw only a handful of villages, which he presumed were linked to salt boiling, rather than being settled, diversified communities. No one ventured out to his ship until he was three miles from River Cess. At that point, a canoe full of locals came aboard from a village they called *Corra*, which was not previously known to European seamen. Bosman was determined to explore this newly discovered site. Told there were plenty ivories, he braved the "fierce" ocean waves in a canoe.

Upon landing, he was led a quarter mile into the woods to "two miserably Built Salt Villages, one of twelve, and the other of six Houses, whose inhabitants Seemed to be Wild Men." None of them, he surmised, had seen a white person before, so all communication was conducted through hand signs.

If accurate, the crudeness of the dwellings and inhabitants' lack of familiarity with Europeans suggest this stretch of coast was just being settled by people who were drawn to the ocean by the prospect primarily of making salt for inland markets and by the Atlantic trade.

Despite the "Wild and Strange" appearance of the residents, Bosman concluded they were "very Civil and Courteous." He reached this conclusion because "an old Man that looked like their Governour" insisted that he eat and drink before returning to his ship.

Bosman recorded little about the natural or cultivated environment. But, after seeing a mother of quadruplets, he concluded that local women were "very Fruitful." Not finding any ivory or other trade goods on shore, he sailed further east.[28]

Arriving at Rio Sestre on Dec. 3, Bosman was impressed by several imposing aspects of the landscape: in the background were two high hills, "one of which appears like a Semicircle or Rainbow" and to the east a distinctive peninsula extended into the ocean.

These attractive features were counterweighted by a more menacing aspect: the entrance to the river was lined with rocks hidden six feet beneath the surface.[29]

Close to the shore was a village of "very neatly built" multistory houses that were so high they could be seen from three miles at sea. Adding to the "charm" of the river was the multitude of villages that lined its banks.

Bosman characterized the inhabitants as "very Industrious, especially in the Planting of Rice, which is their chief Employment." The rice harvest here was so prodigious that "in a very short itme we easily get enough to load a Ship." Those "above the common Rank," he noted, were engaged in a "perpetual trade" in rice, malaguetta and a small quantity of ivory.[30]

Three miles up the river was the village of the local ruler, Peter, who, like "The Great or Principal Men hereabouts," had assumed European names. Bosman described him as a "Silver Haired very old Man," who was "very agreeable, obliging." Peter claimed all the inhabitants of his village were his descendants, "Which is very probable, they not being very numerous."

The Dutch visitor could learn of no local conflicts, except for a few "Skirmishes," which supposedly began when people from the interior burned a local village in a surprise attack. Hostilities ended, however, after local residents seized many of their inland attackers and sold them into slavery.

Of the local people's "Habit, Fruits of the Earth, Cattle and Fish," he noted little except their similarity to those at Cape Mount. Bosman was prevented from exploring the country more fully, he wrote, because the English ships generally "come so thick upon this coast."[31]

One significant local rite, a funeral, was recorded by Bosman because he thought it was "strange;" it was probably the first written description of a local death ceremony.

Immediately after an old woman died, her body was covered with a cloth and surrounded by villagers – young and old – holding banana leaves to shade it from the sun.

The men began running about her house in what he described as a "Desparate and Distracted manner." Had she been half dead, he added sarcastically, their continual and dismal howling would have been "sufficient to have accelerated her Departure."

The women, who sat around the body, began crying loudly. "This jarring Discord continued incessant" for a day. The next day an empty canoe was brought, into which was placed the corpse, one pot of rice, another of palm wine and a variety of green plants, all intended to sustain her on her journey in the afterlife.[32] Several aspects of this funeral scene echo the rituals of ancient Egypt, including the offerings of food and drink, as well as conveying the body by boat.

After another half hour of weeping by villagers, the loaded canoe was carried to the river by "ten young vigorous Fellows." The deceased was taken to her birthplace for burial, in keeping with local custom. Three days after, those relatives and friends who had accompanied the body returned with a sheep and a good supply of palm wine for a commemorative feast.[33]

Bosman was famished after a day spent trading for rice, so he joined in eating and drinking "heartily" for "as long as either Wine or Edibles lasted." The next morning, to his surprise, the mourners insisted that he help defray the cost of the feast. This experience, he noted sarcastically, "obliged me to clap down as a Memorandum in my Note-Book never again to venture to an old Woman's funeral."[34]

After eight days of trading at River Cess, Bosman sailed east on Dec. 11. He recorded descriptions of interesting geographical features but spent little time in most locations.

Three miles east laid Little Sestre, characterized by a "great Mountainous Rock, on which grows a very high Tree." About a mile and a half farther along was Sanguin, which could be distinguished by a nearby point jutting into the sea and a large rock that was "white at the Top, and at Sea looks like a Ship under Sail." Of the residents, he warned, "They readily buy whatever Commodities they see, but are sure never to pay for them."[35]

While anchored off Bossoe, about a mile east of Sanguin, Bosman's ship was visited by the local ruler, James, who spoke a "confused sort of Language, being a mixed Jargon of English and Portuguese," and talked incessantly about women and sex. James reportedly told Bosman, without being asked, that he had ten wives, some of whom he occasional allowed to sleep with his son. When told by the Dutch visitor that *"no place in the World allowed it*, James laughed aloud and said, *That they were then Fools to insist on such a Trifle; and that as his People were better informed, they acted accordingly."*[36]

About three miles east laid Bottewa, which was framed by two large rocks in the sea – one about half a mile to the west, the other a mile to the east. Without anchoring, he traded for malagueta with locals who ventured out to his ship.[37]

At Sino (about a mile and a half beyond Bottewa), Bosman had difficulty understanding what he called the "Barborous Language" of the residents. As a result, he gathered little information, except that the river extended far into the interior.

On Dec. 20, he reached Settre Crou, which laid on low land and had two large rocks on the shore, about half a mile apart. Bosman described the village as "beautiful," as well as "rather larger and more extensive than Elmina." Although the language was "utterly unintelligible," he deemed the residents "a good sort of People, honest in their Dealings." The place was well furnished with cattle and fruits similar to those at Cape Mount. Meanwhile the "Fishery and the Fish are not at all different from those on the Gold Coast."

Trading concluded, Bosman sailed three miles east to Wappo, marked by a large rock on the shore and a high hill beset with several straggly trees whose tops looked red from a distance. From Wappo, the land was flat until about three miles west of Cape Palmas, where a point of land jutted into the Sea that from a distance "looks like a Dolphin." Not attracting any traders from shore, he sailed on Christmas night pass Cape Palmas, where he saw no villages or people.[38]

Amsterdam's Decline, England's Rise

Between 1600 and 1750, England and France were competing to replace Amsterdam as the dominant power. While the great powers contended, sea traffic was plagued by pirates engaged in private plunder, especially along the sea lanes of the Caribbean and the Mediterranean.[39] Those pirates created what historian Alan L. Karras called a "criminal political economy."[40] They were pioneers of today's drug cartels and money-laundering banks.

The rivalry took the form of apparently "unending wars over the issues of land, allies, and markets in Europe and over supplies (of slaves, of tropical and semitropical products such as sugar, and of furs and naval stores) in the periphery and the external arena."[41]

While the "elephants" fought, sea traffic was plagued by plundering pirates, especially in the Caribbean and the Mediterranean.[42] In an ironic turn, governments that had plundered entire continents and killed hundreds of thousands were denouncing with straight faces the crimes of these vagabonds. It was a classic case of what Liberians call "steal from steal makes God laugh."

In the competition for dominance of the world economy, France was hampered in an important respect. It came late to the plunder of Asia, Africa and the Americas, after Portugal, Spain, the Dutch and England had seized the choicest portions.[43]

In the 1600s, European countries created 28 colonies in the Americas. The Dutch held three, France eight and England 17. Englishmen living in the Caribbean islands were twice the number of Frenchmen. In North America, the French colonies of Quebec and Louisiana were a sliver of English North America in both size and number of residents.[44]

In 1700, as noted by world-systems analyst Immanuel Wallerstein, "the English had 350,000-400,000 subjects (including slaves) as against 70,000 for the French."[45]

From 1648 to 1689, the Dutch joined England in an alliance against France. But, the Dutch were slowly reduced to junior partners. In 1701, England acquired a monopoly to supply slaves to Spanish America. Its power was strengthened six years later when Scotland was annexed.[46]

Amsterdam's slow decline between 1680 and 1720 was partly self-inflicted. On the one hand, the previously successful Dutch East India Company was bled dry by its corrupt agents in various posts around the world. On the other hand, its merchants were willing to sell anything to anyone living anywhere. As a result, they sold arms to the Portuguese that were used to drive the Dutch from Brazil![47]

In addition, Amsterdam's economy was rooted in making money from money, not from directly making things. As a result, the Dutch willingly taught English planters in the Caribbean to grow cane and supplied them with enslaved African. Dutch merchants eagerly sold English sugar, too.[48] That policy proved short-sighted.

As noted by economic historian Fernand Braudel, "*production* was never the section in which fortunes were made."[49] That was true for West African producers of malagueta, gold or slaves. It was even true for masters of sugar and tobacco plantations in the Americas. The real money went to the middlemen who traded between Africa, the Americas and Europe.[50]

The greatest profits went to companies like Dutch East India Company of Holland and England's Africa Company. Profits were kept even higher by placing artificial controls in place. For example, sugar-producing islands were not allowed to produce white sugar. They were required to send raw sugar to Europe to be refined.[51]

After Amsterdam's decline, nations would play the role once confined to cities. National markets did not emerge spontaneously. Unity was strenuously resisted from every angle: cities with their own policies, the self-sufficient countryside, as well as producers and merchants, with their separate interests. It had to be imposed from above by the state.[52]

England emerged as the dominant world power between 1763 and 1783. Immanuel Wallerstein dates the "definitive triumph" of England to 1763.[53]

Before that, it had been an inferior partner with France in an economic bloc controlled from Amsterdam. During that period, resources were poured into reclaiming marshes and forest for farming.[54] By 1600, England had subjugated Ireland's economy, making it a colony in all but name. Between 1660 to 1700, most exports from the Americas to Europe were passing through English ports.[55]

As an island, England enjoyed more clearly defined boundaries and internal cohesion than many European rivals. It also developed a stronger government, especially after 1530.[56] A key factor in England's success was its stable currency. Other countries' money climbed and fell wildly in value, but the pound sterling kept its worth.[57]

Fueling England's rise was the exploitation of India and its colonies in Americas, worked by enslaved Africans. But West Indian merchants and planters were indebted to English merchants.[58] They focused on producing one or two crops while importing everything else. No less an authority than Thomas Jefferson described the Virginia plantations as "a species of property annexed to certain mercantile houses of London."[59]

England also seized control of the textile business by means both fair and foul. It grew its textile business by putting production in rural areas, where wages were lower. Thus, it could sell cheaper than European competitors.[60]

As cotton cloth became popular, a local industry emerged. But, what passed for English cotton until 1773 was mixed with linen. In 1699, England banned the importation of Irish wool, which destroyed a key rival. This was followed one year later by a ban on calico imports, mainly from India.[61]

In 1789, France emerged as the first European nation. The nation was something new. In the past, the people in a state were considered "subjects" of their ruler, who was the ultimate judge and lawgiver. A nation reversed the power dynamic, with "citizens" imposing their will on elected officials.

More than any recent scholar, historian Perry Anderson transformed the study of nations. They emerged, he argues, because people developed feelings of being bound to their homeland, to each other and to a common purpose. Those passions were only possible thanks to the use of vernacular languages by the printing press. Especially important were maps and censuses that, for the first time, gave former "subjects" a sense of shared identify. In addition, books, newspapers and pamphlets widely circulated a common stock of ideas, images and information. Working together with newly created museums, various print media generated a kind of collective mindset.[62]

However, its economy was still not integrated. In addition to an "extensive road network," people and goods traveled along the country's many waterways. Two cities vied for dominance — Paris (linked to Amsterdam) and Lyon (which was still tied to Italy and the Mediterranean).[63]

The French turned increasingly toward Africa during the late 1700s, after losing territories in India and North America to the British.[64] But, they were somewhat late to the trade.

British exports to Africa grew from £130,000 in 1720 to £866,000 in 1772.[65]

England's eclipse of Amsterdam was sealed by the Anglo-Dutch war of 1780-1784.[66] The Dutch retained control of global finance, with most investments going to England.[67]

Jean Barbot Visits Cape Mount and the Malagueta Coast

England's growing global empire was reflected in an increased presence in West Africa. Few English visitors to the area of Liberia during this period recorded their impressions. An exception was Jean Barbot (1655-1712).

A French Protestant, he was living in exile in England when he undertook two voyages to West Africa (1678-79 and 1681-82) as a commercial agent on slave ships. He wrote a lengthy description of West Africa that was published in English after his death.

Barbot drew on his own observations, as well as a mixture of previously published sources that he sometimes did not credit. One appeal of his work were the masterful illustrations prepared by the author himself, 120 of which were included in the French version of his manuscript.

During Barbot's visits, he merely viewed Cape Mount from aboard a ship. As a result, his description of that region was derived from other writers, mainly Dapper and, to a lesser extent, Bosman.[68] In contrast, his accounts of the Kru coast were informed by firsthand observation. He is known to have spent eight days in December 1678 on land there while regularly returning to sleep aboard the ship at night.[69]

In 1678, Barbot claimed the Malagueta Coast extended approximately 168 miles from River Sestros to Cape Palmas, "according to the general view," and was rich in spice and ivory. He commended the residents for their handicrafts, "especially in adorning their cannoes very handsomely," and for their hard work in cultivating rice and millet.[70]

Going from west to east, the distances between villages along this coast were: Rio Sestro to Little Sestros (14-and-a-half miles), Little Sestro to Cap das Baixos Svino (one-and-a-half miles), Sanguin (at a river by the same name), then four-and-a-half miles to a town called variously Baffa, Befoe or Bofou; from Baffa to S'eterna or Serres (six miles).

Serres was followed immediately by Dassa, then Buttouwa, followed by Souweraboe or Sabrebou to Crou Setter (15 miles), with Sino between; from Crou Sestro to Wappen or Wappo (15 miles) with the village of Badoe between, followed by Droe and Niffa, then from Droe to Grand Cess (seven-and-a-half leagues).[71]

Cap das Baixos Svino was distinguished by several small rocks to the south and one large one with a tree to the north. Bottou was located on "a large bluff by the sea." Wappo was recognizable by a large island and three rocks in the sea, one turned white by bird droppings. Cape Palmas gained its name from the palm trees that shaded the town from all sides along the seaside.

According to Barbot, Wappo was "at least as large and fine as that of Mina on the Gold Coast." By 1682, about 20,000 people lived around the fort.[72]

Along the stretch of coast including Wappo, Crou and Bottouwas, commodities were carried in woven baskets shaped like sugar loafs. Grand Cess stood out because some residents reportedly spoke French, Barbot claimed, due to their long relationship with traders from the port of Dieppe.[73]

Sea-going along the Malagueta Coast, often by a single man in a small canoe, was noted in 1471-75, 1600, and 1623.[74] Until the late 1700s, the name Junk was originially applied to what is now the St. John River.[75]

Speaking of the coast east of the Junk River, Barbot noted, "Here is where they begin to demand the ceremony of taking sea water and putting a handful on the head thrice, as a promise taken at sea not to cheat them in anything, for the sea is their fetish and god."[76]

Using phrasing that suggested sea-going at Sestros was a specialized activity, Barbot noted, "*Those among them* who venture to sea have little canoes in which they come out to ships passing along their coasts." He also referred to fishermen as "others" who paddle six to nine miles out to sea in the morning and return at noon.[77] According to Barbot, there were only fishermen living at both Little Sestros and Cap das Baisox Svino.[78]

A village at the mouth of the Sestros River reportedly had about 30 huts in 1670, but had grown to about 150 by 1701.[79]

According to Barbot, who travelled inland on the Sestros River, it was lined with large trees on the western bank and mangroves on the opposite side. He noted two villages there in 1688: One near the ocean had 100 huts situated between a field of malagueta shrubs on the sea side and, on the river bank, a collection of banana trees that shielded the village from the glare of the sun. The other about six miles inland contained 25-30 huts, which were enclosed by a clay wall of about six feet in height.[80]

Houses in this area were apparently built of bamboo or what Barbot called "rushes or reeds." This material made them susceptible to being destroyed by the fires that were kept burning continuously in each one. Ladders were required to enter them because they were on pillars with flooring about three feet above the ground due to the predatory leopards that prowled at night.[81]

The lower portions of some interior walls were painted black or red. All of the huts had two stories, each about three-and-a half feet tall, which made standing in them impossible.[82]

One exception was "the Whiteman's Hut," which laid outside the wall of the inland village. It was circular and 60 feet in circumference, with a pointed roof. At the center was a large wooden icon of a woman and child, where food and drink offerings were made and oaths were administered.[83]

The first published uses of a name like "Bassa" in reference to this coast appear at two points in Barbot's book.

At one point, he refers to a river called "Little Barsay," which marked the boundary between the Monou people to the west and the Quabee people of Sestro to the east.[84] Later he refers to the ruler of the Sestro River region as a man named Barsaw, who was known as "Pieter" to foreigners. His territory extended from the St. John river to "Croe," in a straight line covering 35 leagues. Various European visitors to River Cess noted the presence of a ruler named Peter, Pieter or Pedro in 1682, 1693, 1701 and 1727.[85]

During Barbot's visit, Barsaw lived at the inland village while the coastal town was led by an underling named Jacob. He was dressed in a white gown with embroidery of various colors. His hair was braided to two points on the side that looked like "the horns of some animal." He wore a conical straw cap decorated with small porcupine tails, goat horns and "other trifles, which are they *grigri*." Attached to a necklace, two young goat's horn hung near his stomach.

Other than his attire, "Almost nothing clearly distinguished him from what is common among the other blacks." Hunched on his heels, he was smoking a pipe with the bowl resting on the ground. In front of him were two large pots of palm-wine.[86]

Scarification and Traditional Religion at Sestros

Sitting with Barsaw in a palava hut when Barbot arrived were about 20 grandees, also dressed in "Moorish [Arab] style." These leading men adorned themselves with little bells around their arms, legs, shoulders and waists, as well as glass beads in various colors. A few wore iron rings of more than 3 lbs. on their legs.

Men at Sestros were allowed as many wives as they could maintain, Barbot noted. Although Barsaw reportedly had 30 wives, his visitor saw only six, including the first wife, who led the others "like a Sultana."

Like many women in the region, this head wife was decorated with scarification that had been applied with hot irons. Hers was confined to her arms, legs and middle, but some women were covered from head to feet.[87] Scarification of both men and women was noted south of River Cess in the 1550s.[88]

According to Barbot, women dressed simply, with a cloth tied "round their loin." Mothers with infants carried them in "a kind of leather box" tied to their backs "to prevent accidents." He regarded mothers here as "outstanding in their tender care for their infants."

Men were circumcised, Barbot added, "like Arabs and Moors" and wore their hair like those at Cape Mount, probably meaning platted.[89]

Regarding the traditional religion at Sestros, Barbot offered the earliest published account. He reportedly witnessed two manifestations.

One was a shrine with rocks around it that was located "about a musket-shot beyond the village." It contained a two-foot high image of a man made from dark brown soil. Every evening while there, he saw Barsaw and others wash themselves before visiting the shelter to offer chickens as sacrificial offerings.

The other was a ritual of dancing and sacrificial offerings to ensure a good harvest that was performed one day before rice planting. Participants included "an excessive number of blacks," including some non-residents," some with faces smeared in blood and then covered with flour." He met a priest named Jacob who also served as doctor based on his knowledge of medicinal plants[90]

Barbot made a number of observations about social arrangements among the people he visited. They were often (but not always) based on unflattering comparison with his own society.

He presumed that the interior was teeming with elephants and only an "indifference to amassing wealth" kept Sestos residents from collecting tusks "with diligence." The local people were "good," but he attributed their virtue to them living in "great simplicity, without wars, without ambition, without suspicion."

Barbot found the women "submissive" and the men so "wildly jealous" of their wives that "they make them go within the house when they see that a white man wishes to speak to them." To show the degree of male dominance, he noted, "The father takes his meal first, then the mother follows the father, and the children come after each of them."

Such criticisms notwithstanding, he cited the kindness of Sestros residents, or, as he put it, their "much human feeling." To illustrate this, he recounted a night when a storm forced him and about 34 crew members to shelter on land at 10 p.m. It was "delightful to see these good people coming from all sides, some with salt, others with rice, one with wood, another with water; after which they withdrew without the least signs of suspicions. They also gave a thousand embraces to a little black boy, a Jaloff, I had with me – the women mainly."[91]

An essential prerequisite of doing business on this coast was an exchange of gifts or, at the very least, a *dash* awarded by European visitors to local rulers. At Sestros, Barbot initiated business by presenting Barsaw with two iron bars, a bundle of glass beads, two flasks of brandy and a few knives. In return, he was given a large baskets of rice and two hens.[92]

From Sestros River through the Malagueta Coast, the preferred trade goods included "iron bars, brandy, basins, kettles, cooper mugs, anabas [cloths], royal waist-cloths, white and blue glass beads, red and blue Fusian cloths, Flemmish knives, cowries, white and blue margiette beads, billhooks from Dieppe, low price knives, pewter mugs and dishes."[93]

Barbot noted the presence of a disease that soon "put the strongest constitution out of order." Without using the term "malaria," he gave an evocative description of its symptoms. It begins, he noted, with "violent head-aches, attended with vomiting and pains in the bones, which turn to violent fevers, with distraction in the brain, and in a few days prove mortal."

Of 40 of his men sent to work on shore, several fell ill, took a long time to recover and a few even died. He recommended, rather perceptively, keeping the crew aboard the ship at night, especially during the rainy season. He attributed the disease to the "intemperate air of the woody and swampy ground." That was a common explanation at the time because people did not know that mosquitos were the vector responsible for spreading malaria.[94]

Barbot took notes – and even drew illustrations – of some of the creatures be observed. They included fireflies, caterpillars (some are "hideous"), large green flies ("whose sting draws blood"), large ants in the woods (whose sting raises "painful blisters"), pigs ("sometimes found here"), dogs ("not handsome") and sheep ("the size of ours, but without wool").

Of the birds, he observed, "Nature has surpassed itself in colouring" their plumage.

Barbot was especially impressed by the weaver birds that filled just one tree

Two-Story Huts & Sugar-Loaf Baskets

at the coastal Sestos village with 1,000 nests. "The nests contain a thousand twists to and fro, and the completed work is so solid that when the birds are in it they are sheltered from weather of all kinds. I could not but admire how creatures so feeble could arrange, so artistically, rushes so large and thick as the ones with which they make their lodging."[95]

Regarding foodstuff, Barbot noted beans, "abundant" kola, "some" pineapples, bananas, "figs," oranges, lemons and "many" yams. From the yams, residents made "a boiled pap," like porridge, that was fed to their children.[96]

Although the list of available foods included several that had been brought from the New World, conspicuously absent was one item from the Americas that would become a staple: cassava.

The staple food was boiled rice, which residents rolled in their hands into a ball that they ate with mutton, fish, chicken, goat, and fresh or dried monkey meat, a favorite around Sestros. Chickens were plentiful and so cheap, Barbot bought several for a penny worth of trifling commodities.[97]

Although Barbot arrived at Sestros during rice-planting season (which is often a time of food shortage), he was able to buy about 600 lbs. of rice and 200 chicken. He later wrote, "the Sestros rice is not as large or as white as that of the Levant (the area of Lebanon), and the hens are not as large, but they are better tasting."[98]

Surveyor William Smith and the Soundings of the Rivers

Another major record of what is now the Liberian coast was produced by William Smith. He was a surveyor sent in 1726 by the Royal African Company of England to "take exact Plans, Draughts, and Prospects of all [the Company's] Forts and Settlements ... from Gambia to Whyday." He was also charged with surveying the major rivers and collecting information on soundings, bearings and other details on the waterways of the region.

Smith left England for Africa in August 1726 and returned in September 1727. About 17 years after his return, he published his account of the voyage. As historian H. M. Feinberg noted, however, a large section on the Gold Coast was copied from Bosman.[99]

On Dec. 29, 1729, Smith's ship anchored off Cape Mount and remained for four days, but he apparently did not venture onshore. From his vantage point aboard, he reached two conclusions about local people. First, they seemed "very industrious" because "they all go clad with their own manufactures." This implied a contrast to other Africans he had seen previously at other points on the West African coast. Second, those who came aboard to trade "were mighty timorous," especially if any weapons were visible, "for fear of being panyar'd" or kidnapped.[100]

On Jan. 4, 1727, his ship arrived off Cape Mesurado and laid offshore for a day, but "none of the Natives would presume to come off to us,"[101] due probably to a similar fear of being kidnapped. At River Junk one day later, Smith went ashore to take its soundings and bearings. But he returned aboard at 6 p.m. "without having any discourse with the Natives, tho' we saw many of them on the Shoar."[102]

Sailing east, Smith spent January 9-14 measuring the entrance to the Sestros River. He declared the Village at the mouth "large and handsome," and the residents "courteous enough to Strangers, tho' somewhat shy of the English." The ship took on water and wood, but provisions were scarce, except for rice and fowls.

Within an hour of arriving off "Cetra-Crue" on January 20, a canoe approached, suggesting less reticence by residents towards the English. During a visit to the town the next day, Smith observed that the local dinner consisted of "boil'd Rice and Palm Oil" but provisions were scarce, except for malagueta and "a few Pine Apples, the most delicious Fruit in the whole World.[103]

From Sestra Kru, Smith's ship sailed pass Cape Palmas to the coast of present-day Côte d'Ivoire, then moving on to his main destination on the Gold Coast.[104]

Smith and Barbot. Two Englishmen. Two very different portraits of life along the coast of what is now Liberia. Conditions seem to have changed drastically between 1678 and 1727. And not for the better.

Food was scarce. The West African drought that began around 1462 — the time of de Sintra's arrival — lingered until 1700. Especially in the drier, hotter Sahel, farmers had eaten their reserve seeds and turned to gathering wild plants.[105] Food shortages had driven some south toward the coast.

And local people were more fearful of Europeans, especially the English. For good reason.

Residents were disappearing, never to be seen again. Some were enticed onto ships with false promises of gifts. Others were seized by midnight raiders from neighboring towns and sold. The kidnapping that began with de Sintra's taking of one man had escalated to a torrent.

---

[1]. Braudel, Vol. 3, 1984, pp.
[2]. Braudel, Vol. 3, 1984, pp. 177.
[3]. Braudel, Vol. 3, 1984, pp. 174-266, especially pp. 211-220; Wallerstein, Vol. 2, 1980, pp. 46, 52, 54-55, 77

4. Fernández-Armesto and Sacks, 2013, p. 136; André Wink, "South Asia and Southeast Asia" (pp. 418-436), in Jerry H. Bentley, ed., *The Oxford Handbook of World History* (Oxford: Oxford University Press, 2013), p. 434.
5. Fernández-Armesto and Sacks, 2013, pp. 137-138.
6. Fernández-Armesto and Sacks, 2013, p. 132.
7. Braudel, Vol. 3, 1984, pp. 174-266, especially pp. 211-220; Wallerstein, Vol. 2, 1980, pp. 46, 52, 54-55.
8. Wallerstein, Vol. 2, 1980, p. 57.
9. Braudel, Vol. 3, 1984, pp. 256, 261. For the role of Dutch merchants in England, see Wallerstein, Vol. 2, 1980, p. 53.
10. Wallerstein, Vol. 2, 1980, p. 52.
11. Wallerstein, Vol. 2, 1980, p. 52.
12. John Ralph Willis, "Introduction, in William Bosman, *A New and Accurate Description of the Coast of Guinea* (New York: Barnes & Nobles, 1967), pp. xvii; vii, xviii, viii-ix; William Bosman, *A New and Accurate Description of the Coast of Guinea* (New York: Barnes & Nobles, 1967),, p. 471; Jones, 1990, pp. 171-209.
13. Willis, 1967, p. 471; Adam Jones, "Decompiling Dapper: A preliminary search for evidence," *History in Africa* XVII (1990), pp. 171-209.
14. Bosman, 1967, pp. 471, 475, 477-478, 538-540, 544.
15. Bosman, 1967, pp. 473, 475.
16. Bosman, 1967, pp. 472-473.
17. Bosman, 1967, pp. 472-473.
18. Bosman, 1967, p. 473. "Paquovas" likely refer either to papayas or quavas.
19. Bosman, 1967, pp. 473-474. "Great milhio" could refer to corn or, more likely, millet.
20. Bosman, 1967, pp. 473-474.
21. Bosman, 1967, p. 474.
22. Bosman, 1967, pp. 474, 472.
23. Bosman, 1967, p. 474.
24. Bosman, 1967, pp. 475-476.
25. Bosman, 1967, pp. 476-477.
26. Bosman, 1967, pp. 476-477.
27. Bosman, 1967, pp. 475-476.
28. Bosman, 1967, pp. 478-479.
29. Bosman, 1967, p. 479.
30. Bosman, 1967, pp. 480-481.
31. Bosman, 1967, pp. 480-483.
32. Bosman, 1967, pp. 481-483.
33. Bosman, 1967, pp. 481-483.
34. Bosman, 1967, pp. 481-483.
35. Bosman, 1967, p. 483.
36. Bosman, 1967, p. 484, italics in the original document.
37. Bosman, 1967, p. 485.
38. Bosman, 1967, pp. 485-486.
39. Wallerstein, Vol. 2, 1980, pp. 151, 158-163; Dunn, 1972, pp. 22, 149; Abulafia, 2013, p. 505.
40. Karras, 2013, p. 535.
41. Wallerstein, Vol. 1, 1974, p. 241, 248.

42. Peter Linebaugh and Marcus Rediker, *The Many-Headed Hydra: Sailors, Slaves, Commoners, and the Hidden History of the Revolutionary Atlantic* (Boston: Beacon Press, 2000, pp. 143-173; Marcus Rediker, *Villains of All Nations: Atlantic Pirates in the Golden Age* (Boston: Beacon Press, 2004).
43. Wallerstein, Vol. 1, 1974, p. 290; also Richard S. Dunn, *Sugar & Slaves: The Rise of the Planter Class in the English West Indies: 1624-1713* (Chapel Hill: University of North Carolina Press, 1972), p. 19.
44. Wallerstein, Vol. 1, 1974, p. 290; Mintz, 1985, p. 38.
45. Wallerstein, Vol. 2, 1980, p. 103.
46. Wallerstein, Vol. 1, 1974, pp. 250-255.
47. Braudel, Vol. 3, 1984, pp. 174-277, especially 187, 228-234; Wallerstein, Vol. 2, 1980, p. 46.
48. Dunn, 1972, pp. 62, 65-66, 72; Mintz, 1985, p. 53.
49. Braudel, Vol. 2, 1982, p. 192.
50. Braudel, Vol. 2, 1982, p. 194.
51. Braudel, Vol. 2, 1982, p. 194.
52. Braudel, Vol. 3, 1984, pp. 277, 287; Wallerstein, Vol. 1, 1974, p. 265-266.
53. Wallerstein, Vol. 1, 1974, p. 245.
54. Braudel, Vol. 3, 1984, pp. 352-354.
55. Wallerstein, Vol. 2, 1980, p. 96; Wallerstein, Vol. 1, 1974, pp. 269, 281.
56. Wallerstein, Vol. 1, 1974, pp. 230-235.
57. Braudel, Vol. 3, 1984, p. 356. From 1560 to 1931, the value of the pound sterling remained close to four ounces of sterling silver.
58. Wallerstein, Vol. 2, 1980, p. 171; Mintz, 1985, pp. 42, 55.
59. Braudel, Vol. 3, 1984, p. 401, aslo pp. 387-412, 429, 401; Dunn, 1972, pp. 25, 67, 197; Eric Williams, *Capitalism and Slavery* (Chapel Hill: University of North Carolina Press, 1994), pp. 34, 98-105.
60. Wallerstein, Vol. 1, 1974, pp. 228-229.
61. Wallerstein, Vol. 1, 1974, pp. 264-265.
62. Perry Anderson, *Imagined Communities: Reflections on the Origin and Spread of Nationalism* (London: Verso, 1983), pp. 6. 43, 25, 19, 35-36, 163-185.
63. Braudel, Vol. 3, 1984, pp. 312, 315, 335.
64. Masonen, 2000, p. 246.
65. Masonen, 2000, p. 251.
66. Braudel, Vol. 3, 1984, p. 379.
67. Wallerstein, Vol. 1, 1974, pp. 275, 280.
68. Hair, Jones and Law, 1992, pp. 257-263.
69. Hair, Jones and Law, 1992, pp. xlii, xcii, xlvi-xlvii. Hair, Jones and Law established that Barbot, sometimes without giving credit, borrowed from several works, notably: Dapper, 1668; Villault, 1669; Thomas Phillips, "A Journal of a Voyage Made in the Hannibal of London, Ann. in 1693 from England to Cape Monseradoe, Africa" (pp. 173-239) in Awnsham and John Campbell, eds., *A Collection of Voyages and Travels*, Vol. 6 (London: Awnsham and John Campbell, 1732); Pieter de Marees, "Description and Historicall declaration of the golden Kingdom of Guinea" (pp. 247-352) in Samuel Purchas, *Purchas his pilgrimage: or Relations of the world and the religions observed in all ages and places discovered, from the creation unto this present. In foure parts. This first containeth a theologicall and geographical historie of Asia, Africa, and America, with the ilands adiacent. Declaring the ancient religions before the floud ... With briefe descriptions of the countries, nations, states, discoveries*, Vol. 6 (1625; translation of original Dutch edition published in 1602).

70. Hair, Jones and Law, 1992, Letter 30, pp. 288, 292.
71. Hair, Jones and Law, 1992, Letter 30, pp. 288-292.
72. Berlin, 1998, p. 19, also p. 18; also Newitt, 2005, p. 46.
73. For a 1694 account of the Malagueta Coast, see Phillips, 1732, p. 195, where reed baskets are reported in use at River Cess. The information on Sino, Sabrabon and Croe are from Dapper, pp.1668, 57/11-12. The description of Wappo is from Dapper, 1668, p. 581. The alleged Dieppe discovery and French greeting at Grand Cess is from Villault, 1670, pp. 155, 159-160. Garwai corresponds to modern Garraway. Barbot's description of Cape Palmas is from Dapper, 1668, p. 814. Baffa was first noted in 1602 by Marees (1625) and corresponds to current town of Baffar Point; the villages named Butu and Tassu exist today; Sabrabon is now Bluebarra or Blubar; and Crou Setter became Settra Kru in the late 1700s, according to Hair, Jones and Law (1992, Letter 30, pp. 289-291, p. 294 n. 4, 294 n. 4, 294-295 n. 6, 295 n. 7, 296 n. 9, 296 n. 10).
74. Duarte Pacheco Periera, *Esmeraldo de Situ Orbis*, translated by George H. T. Kimble (London: The Hakluyt Society, 1937; written c. 1505-1508), p. 104; Marees, 1625; Ruiters, 1623, p. 302/69; Villault, 1670, p. 86.
75. Hair, Jones and Law, 1992, p. 253 n. 25.
76. Hair, Jones and Law, 1992, p. 241.
77. Hair, Jones and Law, 1992, Letter 19, p. 273.
78. Hair, Jones and Law, 1992, Letter 30, p. 289.
79. Anonymous, "Relation du voyage fait sur les costes d'Afrique aux mois de novembre & décembre de l'année 1670, janvier & février 1671, commençant au Cap-Vert," in H. Justel, ed., *Recueil de divers voyages faits en Afrique et en l'Amérique, qui n'ont point esté encore publiez* (Paris: Louis Billaine, 1674), pp. 10-12; Gérard Chouin, "Minor Sources? Two Accounts of a 1670-1671 French voyage to Guinea: Description, authorship and context," *History in Africa*, Vol. 31 (2004): 133-155; Nathaniel Uring, *A History of the Voyages and Travels of Capt. Nathaniel Uring* (London: John Clarke, 1727), p. 24.
80. Hair, Jones and Law, 1992, Letter 29, pp. 265, 271.
81. Hair, Jones and Law, 1992, Letter 29, pp. 265, 271-272. Barbot erroneously identified the predatory animals as "tigers," which did exist in this region.
82. Hair, Jones and Law, 1992, Letter 29, pp. 272, 265.
83. Hair, Jones and Law, 1992, Letter 29, p. 265.
84. Hair, Jones and Law, 1992, Letter 19, p. 242. According to Hair, Jones and Law (1992, p. 254 n. 31), the term "Barsay" was very likely derived from the Portuguese *baixa* (meaning "shoal" or "shallow'), but, given the shallowness of other rivers along this coast, it's not clear why it would have been applied specifically to this one. More likely, the name was linked to the ruler at River Cess, who Barbot later mentions.
85. Bosman, 1967, p. 480; Phillips, 1732, p. 195; Atkins, 1735, p. 64; Jones, 1985, p. 33.
86. Hair, Jones and Law, 1992, Letter 29, pp. 266, 271, 273.
87. Hair, Jones and Law, 1992, Letter 29, pp. 270-273.
88. Hakluyt, 1589, p. 101.
89. Hair, Jones and Law, 1992, Letter 29, pp. 275, 272, 273.
90. Hair, Jones and Law, 1992, Letter 29, pp. 274-275, 281 n. 9, 286 n. 31.
91. Hair, Jones and Law, 1992, Letter 29, pp. 270, 272.
92. Hair, Jones and Law, 1992, Letter 29, p. 266.
93. Hair, Jones and Law, 1992, Letter 29, p. 270.

94. Hair, Jones and Law, 1992, Letter 29, pp. 277-278.
95. Hair, Jones and Law, 1992, Letter 29, pp. 268-269.
96. Hair, Jones and Law, 1992, Letter 29, pp. 268-269.
97. Hair, Jones and Law, 1992, Letter 29, pp. 269, 276-277.
98. Hair, Jones and Law, 1992, Letter 29, p. 268.
99. H. M. Feinberg, "An eighteenth-century case of plagiarism: William Smith's *A New Voyage to Guinea*," *History in Africa* 6 (1979): 45-50, especially p. 46; William Smith, *Voyage to Guinea*, Second Edition (London: John Nourse 1744).
100. Smith, 1744, p. 104.
101. Smith, 1744, p. 105.
102. Smith, 1744, pp. 105-106.
103. Smith, 1744, p. 109.
104. Smith, 1744, pp. 109-110.
105. Ordahl Kupperman, 2012, p. 33.

Chapter 12
Lamentations and Chants of Grief

> "Do you remember the days of slavery?
>
> And how they beat us
>
> And how they worked us so hard
>
> And they used us
>
> 'Til they refuse us
>
> Do you remember the days of slavery?"
>
> – *Winston Rodney, pan-Africanist griot*

Two decades before de Sintra's voyage, other Portuguese caravels had brought back a large cargo of kidnapped Africans to the port of Lagos. There, they were distributed to Prince Henry and other grandees of the city.

An official chronicler described the scene after they were disbursed. "Some held their heads low," he said, "their faces bathed in tears as they looked at each other." Another group "groaned very piteously, looking towards the heavens fixedly and crying out aloud, as if they were calling on the father of the universe to help them.

As African mourners at funerals often do, others "struck their faces with their hands and threw themselves full length on the ground." Still others "lamented in the form of a chant, according to the custom of their native land, and though the words of the language in which they sang could not be understood by our people, the chant revealed clearly enough the degree of their grief."

"But what heart," he asked, "however hardened it might be, could not be pierced by a feeling of pity at the sight of that company?"[1]

By the time of Henry's death in 1460, over 15,000 Africans had been brought to Portugal against their will under license from the Navigator Prince. Most were kidnapped. A mix of Arabs, Berber, Canary Islanders and Africans, they were a visible presence in Lisbon.[2]

Partly in response to Portugal's sea trade with Africa, Spain sponsored the voyage of Christopher Columbus to the Americas in 1492. The two Iberian neighbors became rivals for control of trans-Atlantic sea lanes and commerce.

After Europeans gained access to the Americas, Spain practically abandoned the West African trade to its rivals in pursuit of the richer trade with the New World.

This shift would be reversed when the need for labor in the mines and sugar plantations of the New World led to a sharp increase in the capture and sale of Africans.[3]

In 1449, a Sicilian had invented a three-roller vertical press for squeezing more juice from sugar cane. That device was transferred first to Atlantic islands held by the Portuguese off the coast of Africa.[4]

The European appetite for sugar expanded, so production spread to Brazil around 1580. The Dutch introduced sugar growing to Barbados in 1637, using cane grown by enslaved Africans on large plantations. The three-roller mill remained in use there until the 1700s.[5]

Sugar cane farming was back-breaking work. It began with the digging of trenches for planting of old stalks. This was done from October to December, during the early rains. About 16 months later, the young sprouting cane had to be weeded and fertilized with manure or cane trash. To get manure, planters kept large numbers of sheep and cows.[6]

A major threat to the growing of cane was rats. For that reason, large gangs of slaves were employed in catching rats.[7]

For field slaves, the toughest work came at harvest time. Working in groups, they cut the ripe cane, stripped the outer leaves and tied the stalks into bundles. Precision had to be balanced against speed. After all, razor-sharp cutlasses could slice through human flesh as easily as cane.[8]

Figure 42. African slave merchant

With the know-how available at that time, sugar cane lost flavor soon after harvest. For that reason, it needed to be milled quickly. Milling involved two major steps: grinding and boiling.[9]

In the interest of speed, planters did their own milling right on their plantations. For this reason, sugar production closely combined farming and industry to a degree not required by other crops.[10]

Even more dangerous was the work of squeezing juice from the cane. Some mills were turned by water, others by cows. One observer noted, "If a Mill-feeder be catch'd by the finger, his whole body is drawn in, and he is squeezed to pieces."[11]

Finally, the juice was boiled to produce sugar. The syrup was transformed through a series of five copper pots, each smaller and hotter than the one before.[12]

Despite suffocating heat, the slaves responsible for boiling had to keep stirring and adding lime juice as a thickener. Boiling, too, came with risks. "If a Boyler get any part with the scalding sugar," an observer noted, "it sticks like Glow, or Birdlime, and 'tis hard to save either limb or life."[13]

Boiling yielded two products: brown sugar and molasses. Both could be sold as they were or further refined. By baking brown sugar in clay pots, the color would be bleached away. The resulting white sugar fetched a higher price. Molasses could also be distilled to produce rum.[14]

As noted by historian Richard S. Dunn, "The story of sugar was not all sweetness. ... Sugar and slavery developed had in hand in the English islands, two faces of a single phenomenon."[15]

As late as 1572, sugar was considered a medicine in Europe, distributed only through drug stores. It gained wider acceptance around 1680, after the explosion of sugar plantations in the Americans. But, sugar was still unknown in half of Europe as late as 1783.[16]

African slave-sellers and their European buyers shared few, if any, norms and little trust. As a result, miscommunication and suspicion often disrupted the order and routine of the trade. This was unlike the earlier trans-Saharan trade, wherein African sellers shared with their Arab buyers fealty to Islam.[17]

Figure 43. Slave deck, "Wildfire," Key West, Florida, 1860

It is widely held, with some justification, that land in pre-Liberia was community property. But while there was no individual ownership of land in Western terms, its control was often unevenly dispersed among households and lineages.

In many local languages, a community's land, along with all other forms of property, was known as "that which has come by virtue of the hand." In other words, this was "manufactured" land. One gained access to such land mainly by membership in a lineage which had invested several generations of labor in it.[18]

Inequality was also evident in the degree of control people had over their own labor, as well as the labor of others. Of the ruler of Cape Mount it was said, "His slaves follow, with several women carrying his dinner in wooden and tin bowls which they held as high as they could."[19]

Among the three commodities that a bridegroom presented to his bride's family during this period, two did not vary: jewelry and cloths. For the third item, the range of choices included a trunk, a brass kettle or a slave. Both at Cape Mount and Sestros, slaves were sacrificed at the death of their owners and their bodies placed in the grave along with other possessions.[20]

Initially, it seems local slaves were used mainly as luxury possessions from which local rulers derived some prestige and pleasure. According to Kru oral accounts, male war captives were originally considered unassimilable and, therefore, had to be ransomed, sold or killed.[21]

However, with the expansion of the trans-Atlantic slave trade, these conditions changed. By the late 1700s, the pool of local slaves had expanded and they were increasingly being used in agriculture and other production processes. But these changes developed unevenly, more pronounced in the northwest, especially along the coast.[22]

Local suppliers of slaves usually obtained captives through kidnapping, especially nighttime marauding in villages further inland. People were kidnapped while away from their homes or captured in skirmishes with neighboring societies. In most such cases, slave hunters were not condemned or punished by their own communities because the victims were "outsiders." In this context, members of each ethnic group protected only the "rights" and interests of their kin.

This system of one-sided justice proved self-destructive over time. It encouraged each group to extract revenge for wrongs done *to* its members, while turning a blind eye to wrongs done *by* its own. Over time, speakers of the same language turned on each other as opportunistic slave hunters raided neighboring towns. As a result, the boundaries of groups grew narrower, as loyalties became more and more localized.

In a more destructive process, some rulers sold members of their own communities into slavery. This was justified by convicting individuals as anti-social "witches" or adulterers.

Over time, the hunt for "witches" reached epic levels, fueled by three factors: More slave raids brought more rips in the social fabric which led to hysterical attempts at repairing them. In addition, the standards used for convicting "witches" were nebulous. Finally, slave raiders, brandy sellers and others fueling a breakdown in society were too powerful to challenge, so vulnerable women and poor men were blamed instead.[23]

At first, European seeking to mine precious metals in the Americas tried many types of workers. Some were paid to work, others were forced. Some were poor Europeans, others Native Americans. But, mine operators increasingly turned to African slaves. The discovery of gold in Brazil in the late 1690s, dramatically boosted the demand for African slaves.[24]

By 1550, South America and the Caribbean had replaced Europe as the principal destination of enslaved Africans carried on European vessels. By 1699, a direct trade in slaves had begun between Africa and the eastern coast of what is now known as the United States of America.[25]

By the 1600s, European thought was marked by a stark dualism: On the one hand, they were demanding more liberty for themselves. On the other hand, they were enslaving more and more non-Europeans and crafting elaborate justifications for the oppression of non-whites.[26]

An image of non-whites emerged that was inextricably linked to the anxieties of Europeans. They judged other societies to be inferior if they lacked Christian-

Figure 44. West African slave market
From oil painting by Francois Auguste Baird

ity, writing and a Western approach to thinking. The belief systems of non-Europeans were being labeled "superstition" and "sorcery." At the same time, Europeans and Americans were engaged in efforts to root out "witches" in their midst. In the process, thousands of people were killed for being involved in "witchcraft," mostly women. at the cost of thousands of lives.[27]

Over time, European opinions of "others" became split. Some condemned India and China as being oppressive, but others promoted those societies as models for Africans and Native Americans. In a similar vein, Native Americans came to be presented as either proud and peaceful children of nature by some whites or naturally warlike and cruel by others. Likewise, both slave masters and evangelists cite the "inferiority" of Africans to justify paternalism.[28]

Initially, the main export to Europe from the Liberian coast was malagueta,

Figure 45. Slave exports by regions

Years	Senegambia and offshore Atlantic	Sierra Leone	Windward Coast	Gold Coast	Bight of Benin	Bight of Biafra and Gulf of Guinea islands	Total
1514-1525						300	300
1526-1550	11,157					1,393	12,550
1551-1575	2,087	300				812	2,899
1576-1600	21,843					3,070	24,913
1601-1625	23,706				3,948	3,946	27,652
1626-1650	12,893	90		1,087	5,550	14,968	27,861
1651-1675	13,562	793	316	15,309	32,031	30,485	44,047
1676-1700	29,498	1920	379	40,988	143,075	42,013	71,511
1701-1725	28,609	2,654	5,298	121,352	281,225	40,334	68,943
1726-1750	50,877	6,723	14,716	135,045	290,887	93,766	144,643
1751-1775	111,834	71,557	106,526	186,185	248,942	267,436	379,270
1776-1800	72,716	70,452	49,428	185,650	243,377	303,719	376,435
1801-1825	64,675	46,668	19,733	54,933	162,134	187,154	251,829
1826-1850	9,825	36,224	3,779	2,983	105,368	101,163	110,988
1851-1865		1,640			14,144	675	16,459
Totals	453,282	239,021	200,175	743,532	1,530,681	1,090,934	1,560,300

but exports fell sharply as Europeans incorporated new Asian spices into their cuisines and medicine chests.

A shift in trading priorities along the Windward Coast was evident even by the late 1550s: In 1530, English sea captain William Hawkins was pleased to buy ivories and spices at Sestros. But, his younger son, John, sailed to the region seven years later with a single-minded mission of capturing slaves to sell in the New World. Upon being knighted, the younger Hawkins took as his crest an African woman, bejeweled but bound.

Figure 46. Trans-Atlantic Slave Trade, 1514-1865

Years	Spain/Uruguay	Portugal/Spain	Great Britain	Netherlands	USA	France	Total
1514-1525		924					924
1526-1550	217	1,905					2,122
1551-1575		2,144	1,666			60	3,870
1576-1600	3,418	37,691		1,031			42,140
1601-1625	18,263	76,123		1,829			96,215
1626-1650	2,307	49,934	10,902	31,738	447	1,645	96,973
1651-1675	6,782	17,088	58,720	91,608	181	6,414	180,793
1676-1700	6,058	85,381	230,957	85,126	3,011	26,535	437,068
1701-1725		246,433	400,622	72,999	2,480	112,333	834,867
1726-1750		450,136	539,995	83,133	30,510	246,051	1,349,825
1751-1775	4,158	379,157	822,126	133,118	76,441	308,976	1,723,976
1776-1800	7,433	486,525	747,593	40,865	54,509	411,087	1,748,012
1801-1825	171,040	1,101,382	283,293	2,675	86,707	124,367	1,769,464
1826-1850	224,321	885,967	572	356	36,545	73,688	1,221,449
1851-1865	31,630	11,686			75,966	1,805	121,087
Totals	475,627	3,832,476	3,096,446	544,478	366,797	1,312,961	9,628,785

England's interest in the West African trade was initially weak. Things changed around 1650, driven mainly by the desire for slaves to work plantations in Jamaica and other Caribbean islands.[29]

By 1700, traders documented an emergent trade in ivory and trickles of gold, but both commodities would be overtaken fifty years later by the traffick in Africans.[30] As European interest in slaves grew, they stopped buying African products, like cotton cloth, for sale to Europe and other regions.[31] Soon all European naval powers were scrambling for lands in the Americas, including the Swedes and Danes. And for enslaved Africans to work them.[32]

In creating New World plantations, Europeans moved decisively beyond just trading. They formed factory farms that were worked by imported African laborers. Through this system, they now controlled every step in the supply chain of key crops. This was a major step in seizing control of world trade.[33]

Stimulated by the profits to be made from this traffick, the Royal African Company was formed in London in 1672 and within 17 years had exported 90,000 Africans.[34] By the 1770s, some English ship captains reported paying gold for slaves at the Gold Coast. This was due to at least two factors: Competition from gold mines in the Americas. And, the rise in slave exports from West Africa.[35]

As noted by historian Hugh Thomas, "five times as many Africans went to the New World as did white Europeans" between 1492 and 1820. "Most of the great enterprises of the first four hundred years of colonization owed much to African slaves: sugar in Brazil and later the Caribbean; rice and indigo in South Carolina and Virginia; gold in Brazil and, to a lesser extent, silver in Mexico; cotton in the Guyanas and later in North America; cocoa in what is now Venezuela; and, above all, in clearing land ready for agriculture."[36]

Between 1630 and 1700, England's colonies in the America took in five Africans for every two Europeans. The number increased four to one between 1700 and 1780.[37]

Other societies in the past may have used slaves, but in such "societies with slaves," as noted by Berlin, "slaves were marginal to the central productive processes." In contrast, the plantation systems that developed in the Americas placed slavery "at the center of economic production, and the master-slave relationship provided the model for all social relations."[38]

Between 1514 and 1866, an estimated 12.5 million captives were removed from Africa. The major carriers were Portugal (including Brazil), 3.8 million; Great Britain, 3 million; France (including the West Indies), 1.3 million; the Netherlands, 544,478; Spain, 475,6 27; United States, 366,797; and Denmark and the Baltic countries, 102,889.[39]

Approximately 1.8 million died during the Atlantic crossing and another 2 to 3 million died in Africa *en route* to the coast.[40]

Working painstakingly through records held in research collections around the world, scholars have assembled data from 34,948 trans-Atlantic voyages by slave ships which have been made available in an online searchable database.[41]

Based on these data, it is estimated that approximately 40,380 voyages each removed an average of 265 persons. The average voyage took about 60 days. About

64.6 percent of shipped Africans were male and 20.9 percent were children, defined as "ten years or younger based on casual inspection by Europeans," in addition to "infants at the breast."

The data (Chart 1) also show that the trade grew geometric over time: the period 1514-1525: 924 persons; 1601-1625: 96,215; 1701-1725: 842,062; and 1801-1825: 1,782,857. [42]

Three factors influenced the number of persons exported from each region within Africa: the military capacity of local polities which enabled them to hold people against their will; the population density in the catchment areas; and the existence of natural harbors that allowed large ships to be loaded directly from shore (or as close to it as possible). The top nine supplying regions were West Central Africa and St. Helena, 3.3 million; Bight of Biafra and Gulf of Guinea Island, 1.1 million; Gold Coast, 743,523; Senegambia and offshore Atlantic, 453,420; Southeast Africa and Indian Ocean Island, 402,609; Other Africa, 336,937; Sierra Leone, 200,175; and the Windward Coast, 200,175.[43]

Figure 47. Windward Coast slave trade, 1659-1840

Years	Spain/ Uruguay	Portugal/ Brazil	Great Britain	Netherlands	USA	France	Total
1659-1675						316	316
1676-1700			199				199
1701-1725			711			760	1471
1726-1750			4,856	1,132	293	3,253	9534
1751-1775			92,871	1,298	987	3,202	98358
1776-1800			31,325	1,211	941	2,412	35889
1801-1825	1,734	382	7,002	150	3,698	3,000	16956
1826-1840	703	1,457				1,619	3779
Totals	2437	1839	137954	3791	5919	14562	166502

The term "Windward Coast" was originally applied by the Royal African Company to the coast west of its forts on the Gold Coast in present-day Ghana. When the Company abandoned its fort at Sherbro Island two years later, British captains and merchants began using the phrase in reference to the stretch of the coast from Rio Nunez in Guinea and Cape Palmas (and sometimes further east).[44]

In a massive census of the trans-Atlantic slave trade published in 1964, historian Philip D. Curtin defined the Windward Coast as extending from Cape Mount to Assini in Côte d'Ivoire. His definition has come to be widely employed in studies of the West African slave trade.[45]

There have been relatively few studies of the slave trade along the Windward Coast in particular. In one of the earliest, historians Adam Jones and Marion Johnson argued that the number of Windward slaves suggested in Curtin's global census of the trans-Atlantic trade was too high.

Based on Curtin's definition, the Windward Coast consisted of a sliver of Sierra Leone, the coast of what is now Liberia and the western coast of Côte d'Ivoire. Compared to other regions, it lacked military capacity, population density and natural harbors.

The ability of African suppliers to participate in the slave trade was conditioned in part by geography. On that score, the Windward Coast was severely "disadvantaged."

About the Windward Coast, Barbot wrote, "All views seem the same, everywhere forest and hardly anywhere distinguishable, this being the case from Cape Mount to Cape Lahou!"

The dense, virtually impenetrable forest along the Windward, which extended close to within miles of the ocean shore, in the view of historian Yves Person, "made commerce unattractive up to the colonial era."

In addition, the rivers that dissect the coast between the Mano and Bandama were navigable only near the ocean, thus inhibiting the large-scale movement of slaves from inland. Furthermore, the Windward shoreline was characterized by steep beaches, heavy surf, a lack of river inlets and a shortage of natural harbors.

"For want of natural harbors," historian Philip D. Curtin noted, "trade along this coast was fragmented, divided among many small ports or shipping points."[46]

Just east of the Junk river, Barbot warned mariners to anchor at least three miles out from shore in windless conditions because the opposing currents tend to drive ships ashore.

Conditions at Rio Sestro were especially treacherous. "The anchorage is half a league out from the bar, in eight fathoms of waters, black mud bottom. The bar is full of rocks, some of them show ing at high tide and others hidden."[47]

Ships stopping off Sestos often anchored about three miles from shore in water that was eight to ten fathom deep in an area that was rocky and filled with hard sand.

This presented crews with two difficult choices, Barbot noted: Either pull up anchor everyday, which was tiring, or risk the anchor cable being cut in a few days from continually rubbing against rocks. He recommended instead that ships anchor about one-and-a-half miles from the bar where the water was eight to nine fathoms deep and the ground "ouzy," providing a good hold for anchors.[48]

Geographic conditions on the Windward Coast gave the slave trade here an unusual cast. Rather than having their African partners force-marching captives over long distances to a major embarkation point, European buyers had to stop near some 54 small towns along the coast.

Using smoke, sellers would signal the availability of captives or other commodities. Slave ships sometimes had to sail back and forth in order to fill a vessel, an especially dangerous method given the powerful ocean currents and rocky shoals along this stretch of coast. Vessels of the Dutch Middelburgse Company, for example, spent an average 222 days plying the Windward Coast for slaves.[49]

This coast was the last region in West Africa to be significantly exploited by European slave buyers also because it was apparently underpopulated. In 1694, English captain Thomas Philllips documented a village of 40 huts near the St. Paul River and one with 30 to 40 huts at River Sestos. Seven years later, Jan Snoek noted "three separate small villages, the whole amount of which is not full thirty houses" at Cape Mount and "three villages containing about twenty houses" at Cape Mesurado. Another village at River Sesters contained approximately 60 huts, and "a multitude of villages" up the river held a total of 30 huts.[50]

Given a scarcity of commodities and captives, the Windward Coast served the trans-Atlantic trade mainly as a provisioning area, where ships obtained water, firewood, salt, rice, yams and fowl.

Of the embarkation points along the Windward, two fell in what is now Sierra Leone (Mano River and River Kissey).

Thirteen were in Liberia (Bassa, Cape Mount, Cess, Grand Bassa, Little Bassa, Grand Junk, Little Junk, Grand Mesurado, Petit Mesurado, Grand Sestos, Rock Sestos, St. Paul and Trade Town).

There were eight in Côte d'Ivoire (Cape Lahou, Dembia, Drouin, Grand Bassam, Rio Assini, Sassandra, Tabou and Ivory Coast, now known as Abidjan).

Figure 48. Windward Coast slave disembarkation by region

Years	Mainland North America	Caribbean	Spanish American Mainland	Africa	Total
1710-1725	158	997			1,155
1726-1750	546	6,648			7,194
1751-1775	12,141	80,154		196	92,491
1776-1800	751	32,517	120		33,388
1801-1825	2,832	9,886		1,740	14,458
1826-1840		1,744		555	2,299
Totals	16,428	131,946	120	2,491	150,985

The number of slaves sent from each section of the Windward corresponded roughly to its proportion of ports. Sierra Leone supplied 1,649 slaves, Côte d'Ivoire 17,927, Liberia 80,357 and unspecified ports 86,145. Sierra Leone accounted for 1.7 percent of persons taken from known towns, Côte d'Ivoire 17.9 percent and Liberia 80.4 percent.

When the slaves from unknown ports are divided among the three sections of the coast based on the percentage each supplied, that adds 1,464 persons to Sierra Leone, 15,420 to Côte d'Ivoire and 69,261 to Liberia for totals of 3,113, 33,347 and 155,406 respectively.[51]

Already underpopulated to begin with, the area now known as Liberia supplied between 80,357 and 155,406 enslaved persons to the Americas. Within Liberia, Cape Mount supplied the largest number of enslaved persons, 41,319. Next were the towns around what is now the city of Buchanan (Little Junk, Grand Junk, Bassa, Grand Bassa and Little Bassa28,457. Then towns around present-day Monrovia (Grand Mesurado, Petite Mesurado and St. Paul), 6,238. Last were towns near Grand Cess (Trade Town, Grand Sestras, Rock Sestos, Cess), 4,333.

When the slaves from unknown ports are divided among the four coastal sections of Liberia based on the percentage each supplied, that adds 7,926 persons to Cape Mount, 1,203 to Monrovia, 5,458 to Buchanan, and 833 to Grand Cess, for totals of 33,910, 7,441, 33,915 and 5,166 respectively.[52]

Figure 49. Enslaved Africans being loaded into hold of slave ship

The Windward traffick mirrored the overall slave trade in terms of the length in days of the average voyage and the death rate, but it differed in one respect: 29.3 percent of enslaved persons were children, compared to 20.9 for the trade in general.[53]

British Interpolers and French Adventurers

By Dec. 25, 1701, the devastating impact of human seizures along this coast was evident, as reported by Bosman on a visit to Cape Mesurado. He reported, "about two Months before, the English had been there with two large Vessels, and had Ravaged the Country, destroyed all their canoa's, Plundered their Houses, and carried off some of their People for Slaves, upon which the remainder fled to the Inland-Country, where most of them were at present."

Barbot did not come ashore at Cape Mesurado during his visits to the Windward in 1688. Yet, he blamed local people for tensions with Europeans. "Their uncivil behaviour towards strangers has, from time to time, put some Europeans, upon ravaging the country, destroying their canoos, and carrying off some of their people into captivity, which has occasioned ill blood in them; and instead of changing their rough manners, does rather render them more peevish and ill-natur'd."

Then, adding insult to injury, he went on to include a claim that seemed to contradict his own portrayal of Cape Mesurado residents as uncivil. He claimed, "these Blacks are civil enough to strangers, especially the women, who are here handsome, very complaisant, and ready to prostitute themselves for a very slender gain."[54]

Over the course of four centuries, the overall trans-Atlantic slave trade increased every 100 years until its end. In contrast, the Windward trade peaked and then fell, going from 316 in the period 1659-1675 to 106,072 in 1751-1775 then dropping to 3,779 in 1826-1840.

The ranking of slave-transporting nations was also different along the Windward: Great Britain led with 142,738, followed by France, 17,450; the Netherlands, 12,844; United States, 5,967; Portugal/Brazil, 4,642; and Spain/Uruguay, 2,437.

Dutch slave merchants turned to the Windward around 1740. They had been pushed out of the more lucrative Bight of Biafra and Bight of Benin by British, French and Portuguese traders.

Over time, the Dutch would remove 16 percent of all their slaves from this coast, more than from any other region. They usually began buying slaves near Cape Mesurado and continued at towns all along the Windward.[55]

The Windward Coast supplied as much as 70 percent of the slaves obtained by Dutch free traders (buyers who were not working for the large companies). It also produced 40 percent of all slaves sent to Dutch colonies in the New World.

Historian Jelmer Vos examined trade relations between Dutch buyers and African suppliers on the Windward in the late 1700s. He used the ship records of the Middelburgse Commercie Compagnie (MCC), the largest private Dutch slave trading firm of that period. He found that the Windward supplied 89,000 slaves to the Dutch, approximately 11,000 more than contained in the *Voyages* database.[56]

In 1750, spearheaded by Liverpool merchants, the British joined the Dutch in slave purchasing here and quickly outpaced them. British participation peaked in the last quarter of the 1700s.

British buyers usually bought most of their slaves along the Sierra Leone coast (sometimes as far west as Rio Nunez), then filled up their vessels with slaves from the Windward Coast, mainly from Bassa, followed by Cape Mount.[57]

Most Windward slaves went to the Caribbean, 146,096; Brazil received 2,795; other regions of Africa, 2,595; and the Spanish American mainland, 120. Within the Caribbean, the biggest recipients of Windward captives were Jamaica, 34,162; Barbados, 15,180; Grenada, 14,545; Antigua, 12,175; and Dominica, 10,963.

Although the United States ranked fifth among shippers, it received the second highest number of slaves from this region, 16,658, the bulk of whom, 11,276, went to the rice fields of South Carolina.

According to South Carolina slave cargo data collected by historian Elizabeth Donnan, slave-buyers showed a strong preference for captives from rice-growing regions. They especially sought those from the Windward Coast.[58]

South Carolina, along with Georgia and Surinam, turned to growing rice using grains from West Africa. Although the state did not cultivate significant quantities of rice until the late 1600s, it had become economically dependent on rice exports by 1761.[59]

In 1614-1616 or 1620, rice was one of the few goods available for sale at Cape Mount.[60] At Cape Mesurado in 1666, the local trade was mainly in ivory and rice "in great abundance."[61] River Cess, too, was "very fertile, well furnish'd" with fowl, rice and millet, "which they carry with them in their *Canoes*, when they go fishing." Trade goods in particular were rice, malaguetta and ivory.[62] Around River Cess in 1701, William Bosman spent a day trading for rice.[63]

By 1729, however, William Smith reported that provisions were scarce at Sestra Kru, except for malagueta and "a few Pine Apples."[64] As a result of the slave trade, societies along the Windward Coast of West Africa went from supplying rice to European vessels to experiencing food shortages. By the late twentieth century, they were net importers of rice, much of which came from the United States. The forced transfer of labor and know-how caused by the slave trade may well help to explain this important shift in rice-growing in the two regions.[65]

Guns, Rum and Rebellion

The trade in African slaves was primarily triangular: Goods flowed from Europe to buy black captives. Enslaved people were then taken to South America, the Caribbean and the southern United States, where they produced sugar, cotton and other products. Those goods were then sold to Europe, which yielded more goods to buy slaves.[66]

In the late 1700s, New England joined the so-called triangular trade: From the West Indies, it imported molasses, which it refined into rum. In Rhode Island alone, some 24 Newport distilleries churned out a prime commodity used in buying

Africans: rum. Just before the American Revolution, the city was exporting 200,000 gallons a year to Africa.[67] Its rum and trinkets were sent to Africa to buy slaves, which were shipped to the West Indies.[68]

Adding to the havoc of the slave trade itself were the products that were used to buy captives: liquor, guns, gunpowder and gunshots.

Around the time of de Sintra's voyage, Europe was creating a new spirit from distilled wine: brandy. A distillation device had been used by the ancient Egyptians and Greeks. Around 1100, it was refined in Italy and later further improved in France. By the mid-1500s, brandy was popular in France and Germany.[69]

By 1666, brandy had been introduced to the Windward Coast. Nicolas Villault described the local ruler and his associates at Cape Mesurado sitting under a tree "freely" consuming the two bottles of brandy that were given as presents before leading their visitors to the trading house.[70]

The distillation process for making liquors was further improved. This led to cheaper prices and worldwide distribution. Soon, liquids from other crops were being

Figure 50. Slaves embarked from Grand Bassa in 1830 on the Nueva Isabel

Aboysi, 11; Ahpinge, 27; Ajouco, 23

Bahee, 24; Bahtoway, 5; Baiday, 17; Banyahbah, 23; Baproo, 30; Bawah, 24; Beahtoo, 20; Beer, 40; Beyah, 30; Bihyah, 30; Biyah, 27; Bobo, 6; Bomyah, 6; Boolah, 26; Booyah, 8; Bosenna, 21; Boy, 7; Boy, 11; Bragnuo, 24

Camoo, 28; Cokoo, 15; Cokoo, 12

Dagoo, 7; Dagoo, 5; Dandy, 30; Dayou, 4; Dong, 23

Etobahdeiah, 40

Fahbree, 6; Fahkeye, 9; Fahray, 6; Famoh, 26; Fanguannah, 27; Feiamah, 24; Fennay, 13

Gahpoh, 30; Geeah, 27; Geeay, 10; Geer, 28; Gong, 8; Guloo, 28; Guy, 29; Gwonah, 30

Iabroo, 10

Iayboo, 30; Iuah, ??; Iuah, 24; Jibbah, 8; Jibbah, 12; Joloo, 6

Kangibby, 13; Keelay, 4; Kekay, 6; Kekay, 4; Kekee, 8; Kong, 9

Madday, 9; Magee, 7; Maguay, 25; Mahdee, 8; Mahooloh, 27; Mahpoo, 8; Mahtie, 29; Maihlee, 28; Maylee, 6

(continued on next page)

Figure 51. Slaves embarked from Grand Bassa on the Neuva Isabel, 1830

(Continued from last page)

Mazeo, 27; Meah, 27; Menee, 24; Minee, 11; Minnay, 8; Mobah, 29; Mobohwe, 26; Moddee, 25; Modooway, 26; Mofrow, 30; Mogoo, 28; Mojoroe, 27; Monblay, 7; Mono, 27; Mosowah, 24; Mowirrah, 28; Moza, 24

Nahgowah, 15; Nahgrobiah, 40; Nahguloo, 28; Nahpopoh, 18; Nahquarry, 50; Napah, 20; Napyah, 24; Nemageah, 28; Nenoguah, 28; Neyah, 6; Neye, 6; Nighyamba, 38; Nokah, 22

Obouyah, 24; Omadoo, 3; Owah, 27

Pay, 9; Paymi, 25; Peshetwa, 7; Poah, 30; Poh, 24; Pooyai, 9

Quai, 4; Quanoo, 20; Quayh, 28; Quol, 2

Sahwah, 27; Sahyow, 24; Sainwie, 8; Samwah, 7; San, 9; Saybroo, 6; Sayee, 6; See, 28; Seeoh, 5; Seirragee, 25; Sesera, 28; Shuray, 28; Shuray, 6; Shuray, ; Sooke, 20

Tah, 28; Tayoh, 20; Tayoh, 20; Tie, 6; Toopah, 30

Wennow, 28; Whyoo, 23; Womah, 9; Woolay, 8; Worajoo, 7; Wordnoo, 20; Wouma, 23, Zuy, 29

---

distilled to produce other strong liquors. In Europe, especially in the north, grains were distilled to produce gin, whiskey and vodka. In the West Indies, sugar cane juice was being turned into rum.[71]

Rum was first distilled in the Caribbean in the early 1600s. The drink was called "kill devil," a testament to its potency. Another, equally color name was *rumbullion*, which meant "a great tumult." The word captured the volatile behavior of *rumbullion* drinkers. The name was was shortened to rum by the early 1650s.[72]

Key conduits in the early spread of rum were sailors. Many received it as part of their food and drink ration. They gradually spread it to societies on the other side of the Atlantic Ocean. It was cheap to store and ship, plus it improved with age.[73]

By the late 1600s, rum was an international currency. Caribbean planters exchanged it for European and North American goods. Merchants in Boston, London, Amsterdam and other major port cities then sold some to local buyers. Some was sent on to Africa to buy captives.[74]

During that period, rum was selling in West Africa. It was spread in part as "dash" mainly from Dutch traders to rulers and other power men.[75]

In the early 1700s, rum was caught in a crossfire of conflicting national interests. On the one hand, it was banned from Spain and France in an effort to protect wine and brandy producers.[76]

On the other hand, England embraced it as an alternative to currency-draining wine and brandy.[77] In 1719, rum surprised brandy imports to Britain. Two major customers were the Royal Navy and the Army.[78]

By the late 1700s, about 300,000 gallons of rum from New England and Brazil were being sent *each year* to buy captives from West and Central Africa. The appetite for rum was so entrenched that Sierra Leone alone is reported to have absorbed 80,000 gallons in 1791.[79]

Of course, Africa's dependence on American rum did not end with the slave trade. As with any addiction, it grew exponentially: In the 1780s, it was 750,000 gallons. Eighty years later, it was up to 6.1 million gallons![80]

Historian J. E. Inikori has estimated that an annual average of 338,500 guns, 847,075 lb. of gunpowder, and 200,000 lb. of lead and shot were imported into West African from England alone between 1750 and 1807. Based on the surviving records of a small group of Liverpool slave traders linked to the firm of William Davenport, he showed that just 13 voyages carried 12,896 guns to the Sierra Leone and the Windward Coast during that period, for an average of 992 guns per voyage.

One study of the British trade with West Africa showed that between 1757 and 1806 five ships alone exchanged 5,366 guns on the Windward Coast for slaves, yielding about four guns per captive. [81]

In 1787, one ship trading along the Windward Coast, the *Fly*, exchanged 245 guns for 53 captives, an average of 4.6 guns per slave.

Of 33 types of firearms exported to West Africa, the five most popular with traders at Sierra Leone and Windward Coast (in number of units traded) were Danish guns (3,603), round muskets (1,965), trading guns (1,437), tower guns (1,165) and riononas (1,030). Not so popular were weapon for personal defense like pistols (221) or collective defense, such as cannon (0).[82]

Data on the Windward slave trade from the *Voyages* database shatters two often-repeated myths in Liberia: (1) that few, if any, Kru people were ever enslaved; and (2) that slaves were mainly, if not always, criminals or war captives.

In fact, coastal Kru-speaking people accounted for nearly a quarter of all West Africa slaves carried by the Dutch to Surinam, as well as Demerara and Essequibo (both in present-day Guyana).

In addition, more adult women than men were exported from this region, and 40 percent of all slaves were children under 10 years of age, hardly the profile of hardened criminals. Reflecting a sexual bias in the dispensation of justice, women "convicted" of adultery were usually sold to European buyers, but male adulterers could satisfy a judgment by supplying a slave to take his place as a forced laborer in the New World.[83]

Further details on the Windward trade can be gleaned from examining the records of slave ships seized along the coast by the British navy after 1800. [See two boxes above with names and ages of recaptured Africans.] For example, the captives from St. Paul's River that were aboard an unidentified ship taken in 1813 consisted of 46 percent children and eight percent women.

First names that appeared more than once included Bala (4), Balo (2), Banda (3), Bessy (3), Bomboo (2), Boy (2), Cai (3), Corree (2), Coru (2), Dua (2), Era (3), Fahngha (4), Farra (2), Gray (2), Kaingrie (2), Manah (3), Miah (2), Moree (2), Nacoi (8), Pay (3), Sa (2), Saree (4), Sarie (2), Sessay (4), Tafui (2), Tamba (3), Whyewo (2), Wossay (2) and Yarra (2).

Names like Cai, Fahngha, Nacoi and Tamba suggest origins among local ethnic groups in western and northwestern Liberia like the Vai, Loma and Kissi.

Among captives loaded at Grand Bassa aboard the *Nueva Isabel* that was seized in 1830, there were 39 percent children and 15 percent women.

Many of the names on this ship, like Bahtoway, Fanguannah, Feiamah, Gahpoh, Juah, Jibbah, Mahpoo, Quanoo, Sayee, Tah, Tayoh, Toopah and Wardnoo, suggest origins among ethnic groups like the Bassa, Klao and Kpelle in central and southeastern Liberia.

The repeated names aboard the *Nueva Isabel* included Boy (2), Cokoo (2), Dagoo (2), Juah (2), Jibbah (2) Shuray (3) and Tayoh (2).

A Fisher of Men

Among the men who prowled this coast abroad European vessels to haggle over the price of African captives was John Newton (1725-1807). A native of London and son of a sea captain, Newton went into the African slave trade at age 19 in hopes of making a fortune.

In 1747, he lived in Sierra Leone, working for two slave traders, a European man and his African concubine. He made four trans-Atlantic voyages aboard slave ships between 1748 and 1754, the first as mate and three as captain. His employer was Joseph Manesty, a Liverpool merchant deeply invested in the slave trade who was a friend of his father.

While on various voyages, Newton wrote 127 letters to his wife and filled a large 336-page leather-bound journal with detailed entries in a graceful script.[84]

Placed in charge of slave vessels, Newton would often begin his purchases in Sierra Leone, where he had lived. A favorite stop was Bance Island, an outpost of the London-based Grant, Oswald & Co. located 18 miles up the Sierra Leone River. Its fortified pens could hold up to 700 captives, which provided buyers an opportunity to obtain a significant portion of their human cargo from one location. Bance Island also offered mariners many rare luxuries, including Africa's only golf course during that period.

But amidst the amenities for some were the ever-present and wrenching sights, sounds and smells of human suffering, as recorded by a visitor to the island.

Lamentations and Chants of Grief

"What a scene of misery and distress is a full slave ship in the rains. The clanging of chains, the groans of the sick and the stench of the whole. ... Two or three slaves thrown overboard every day dying of fever, flux, measles, worms all together. All the day the chains Rattling or the sounds of the armour riveting some poor devil just arrived in galling heavy irons."[85]

Newton's first voyage as captain took him on Aug. 11, 1750, from Liverpool to the Windward Coast. He travelled aboard the *Duke of Arygle*, a relatively small ship of 100-tons, with two masts and ten mounted cannon. Commissioned to buy 250 slaves, he outfitted the ship with a crew of 30. That provided a ratio of nearly one crew to eight slaves.

Figure 52. Slaves embarked from St. Paul's River on an unidentified ship, 1813

Bai, 8; Bakee, 15; Bala, 25; Bala, 25; Bala, 22; Bala, ?; Balla, 14; Balo, 29; Balo, 25; Balo, 14; Bamboo, 10; Banda, 14; Banda, 9; Banda, 16; Bango 14; Banna, 23; Basso, 7; Battay, 10; Ben, 21; Bendoa, 9; Bessay, 8; Bessy, 25; Bessy, 14; Bessy, infant; Bethay, 14; Blaman, 27; Blamgo, 27; Bobo, 9; Bombajarra, 23; Bomboo, 29; Bomboo, 9; Bono, 7; Botto, 25; Boy, 10; Boy, 9; Boye, 40; Brima, 9

Cai, 11; Cai, 8; Cai, 9; Canaba, 23; Candacai, 20; Canday, 7; Cangarra, 29; Cauley, 30; Cofang, 9; Coi, 27; Comay, 12; Coona, 8; Coree, 15; Corree, 11; Corree, 8; Coru, 6; Coru, 5; Coseree, 21; Cura, 8

Damba, 10; Dawollo, 35; Dee, 8; Dogbo, 14; Dogbua, 9; Dogua, 40; Doray, 10; Dua, 7; Dua, 7; Duaro, 26

Ea, 9; Era, 49; Era, 11; Era Goomba, 8

Facoree, 27; Fallee, 21; Fallo, 14; Famai, 9; Fangha, 40; Fangha, 26; Fangha, 26; Fangha, 8; Farra, 9; Farra, 11; Farra, 9; Farree, 8; Fauree, 29; Fingbacuree, 14; Firrah, 14; Fogea, 20; Fongha, 35; Fouree, 35; Fro, 20

Gai, 21; Gamba, 14; Gamboo, 26; Gay, 9; Gaywo, 9; Ghee, 14; Ghema, 8; Goi Albicoie, 11; Gola, 11; Gombo, 8; Gomboo, 28; Gombyarra, 28; Gongue, 11; Goomba, 8; Goong, 9; Gracoi, 8; Gray, 29; Gray, 26; Gurie, 10; Gurra, 10

Jaen bajuro, 28; Jenny, 11; Jerra, 9; Jongo, 8; Juma, 9

Kaingrie, 25; Kaingrie, 33; Kaman, 9; Kayang, 16; Konbah, 22; Kong, 10

Along with 14 seamen, a boatswain and three mates, the crew included a surgeon, carpenter, stewart, cook, cooper, tailor, gunner, three young apprentices and a fiddler, for entertainment.

Newton began buying captives on Banana Island, Sierra Leone, on October 23, but slaves were few and prices were high. Among the Africans from whom he bought captives were African men named Samuel Skinner, "Yellow Will," and Henry Tucker.

Complicating Newton's mission, the few slaves he purchased began to die on January 9. Despite having the rooms scraped, the deck washed with vinegar and the ship smoked for two hours, the deaths continued until May.[86]

In early March 1751, however, the misfortune of another captain presented Newton with an opportunity. Captives aboard a French vessel at Sherbro had rebelled, killed six crew members and driven three overboard. However, the rebels were subsequently overpowered by local slave dealers who were offering to resell them to Newton.[87]

Despite the grave risk, Newton bought two lots, including those who had led the insurrection. The *Duke of Argyle* then sailed along the Windward Coast buying other slaves before sailing for the Caribbean on May 22, 1751.

Five days later, however, an insurrection among the captives was discovered. A young enslaved man had been allowed to roam freely on deck out of irons due to a large ulcer. He slipped a tool through the gratings to the male slaves below. Twenty of them managed to break their irons quietly before the plot was foiled and they were punished. It was Newton's view that he and his men had been saved by a "Favour of Providence."

The *Duke of Argyle* arrived in Antigua on July 3, 1751, with 146 slaves, far less than the 250 Africans it had set out to transport. In the course of the voyage, seven crew members and 28 captives had died.[88]

After two more slave-buying voyages, Newton was in Liverpool in 1754 when, two days before a scheduled tip to Africa, he had a mysterious seizure. He took this as a divine sign that he was to pursue a calling away from the libertine world of cursing and carousing sailors.

Ten years later, he was ordained as an Anglican priest and assigned a parish northwest of London. Over the course of the next 30 years, Newton wrote six books, preached thousand of well received sermons and penned 280 hymns, including the world-renown "Amazing Grace."

During this period, however, he continued to fraternize with slave-ship captains and to invest in slave voyages. It wasn't until January 1788, that Newton publicly expressed a prix of conscience regarding the trade in enslaved Africans, from

> **Figure 53. Slaves embarked from St. Paul's River on an unidentified ship, 1813**
> (Continued from last page)
>
> Maining, 24; Mamoroo, 16; Manay, 27; Manay, 18; Manay, 19; Manee, 11; Manjai, 18; Mano, 7; Matindey, 22; Mattay, 19; Mayonna, 16; Messay, 29; Mia, 8; Miah, 22; Miah, 25; Moree, 14; Moree, 12; Moru, 29; Mousa, 25
>
> Nacoi, 22; Nacoi, 21; Nacoi, 26; Nacoi, 23; Nacoi, 9; Nacoi, 8; Nacoi, 7; Nacoi, 8; Napay, 9; Nazang, 32; Nibea, 30; Ninge, 9; No, 10; Nocai, 9
>
> Ohawy, 11
>
> Panda, 24; Panday, 25; Paway, 11; Pawine, 14; Pay, 35; Pay, 8; Pay, 6; Pheena, 21; Pissay, 9; Prince, 8; Pungher, 15
>
> Quay, 17; Queebo, 16
>
> Sa, 8; Sa, 9; Sagro, 19; Sambee, 19; Sangaree, 26; Sangolu, 21; Sara, 9; Saree, 10; Saree, 8; Saree, 8; Saree, 9; Sarie, 20; Sarie, 19; Sessay, 7; Sessay, 10; Sessay, 10; Sessay, 7; Sessy, 19; Sewa, 8; So, 9; Soirundoo, 18; Somasee, 9; Son, 22; Soo, 9; Sungbo, 22
>
> Tabanna, 30; Tafui, 27; Tafui, 28; Tamba, 23; Tamba, 14; Tamba, 14; Tambo, 14; Tamiay, 22; Tandu, 27; Taway, 7; Taylay, 10; Tendoa, 26; Tong, 9
>
> Verekai, 15
>
> Warrug, 10; Werree, 8; Werricure, 19; Whyewo, 23; Whyewo, 16; Wojoe, 28; Wona, 8; Woorie, 19; Wossay, 27; Wossay, 8; Wunga, 12
>
> Yanta, 7; Yarra, 29; Yarra, 10; Yaseera, 26; Yaseera, 20; Yattee, 12; Yembo, 14; Yowo, 8
>
> Zangbo, 10; Zeena, 20; Zenee, 7; Zo, 8; Zon, 8; Zong, 25

which he had profited. He did so in a pamphlet, *Thoughts Upon the African Slave Trade*. By then, the British abolitionist movement was well underway.[89]

African Resistance to Slavery

Like the insurrectionists aboard the *Duke of Argyle*, many enslaved Africans took extraordinary steps to gain their freedom. They often did so against more numerous, better armed and well organized foes.

At least 45 other incidents of resistance to enslavement aboard ships from the Windward Coast were recorded in the Voyages database. These included four attacks by Africans on land that prevented slave ships from reaching the Americas.

Between 1755 and 1761, just one ship, *Philadelphia*, captained by Jan Menkenveld faced three antislavery actions, ranging from several captives jumping overboard to two insurrections.

Undoubtedly, many more anti-slavery actions occurred among groups now living in Liberia. One of the few that survives in legend is the heroic story of Vanja-Vanja.[90]

Born in the Dowo Mountains of the Komgba region, Vanja-Vanja was reputedly a man of "gigantic size and extraordinary physical strength." On a visit to Gahulong on the coast, he became indignant at the sight of a large number of Gola youth being loaded onto a slave ship. Determined to counteract this, he persuaded an acquaintance to tie him up and sell him to the slaver on the pretext that he wanted to visit the country of the whites.[91]

Figure 54. Enslaved Africans in hold of slave ship, 1827

Once aboard the slave ship, Vanja-Vanja took note of "a very huge and ferocious dog" used to keep the captives terrorized. Once the ship had cleared land, he unleashed his plan: Seizing the dog first, he threw it overboard, followed by every crew member but one. He spared the pilot, who he compelled to steer the ship to shore, where he freed all the captives.[92]

Vanja-Vanja eventually returned to Komgba, where his grave in the Dowo Mountains was preserved at least until the 1950s.[93]

The quest for black freedom and repatriation reached a major turning point in 1772 with the case of James Sommerset, "a Negro," on a writ of Habeas Corpus before the King's Bench in London.[94]

Figure 55. Antislavery actions on the Windward Coast

Ship Name	Year	Disembarkation	Action
Dichosa Estrella	1822	Sierra Leone	Vessel attacked from shore
Africa	1765	Dutch Caribbean	slave insurrection
Enigheid	1764	Dutch Guianas	slave insurrection
Granadier	1752	Dutch Guianas	slave insurrection
Haast U Langzaam	1765	Dutch Guianas	slave insurrection
Jonge Rombout	1741	Dutch Guianas	slave insurrection
Nieuwe Hoop	1771	Dutch Guianas	slave insurrection planned but thwarted
Philadelphia	1755	Dutch Guianas	slave insurrection
Philadelphia	1757	Dutch Guianas	slave insurrection
Philadelphia	1761	Dutch Guianas	Three or more slaves escaped overboard
Prins Willem de Vijfde	1762	Dutch Caribbean	slave insurrection planned but thwarted
Vrouw Johanna Cores	1765	Dutch Guianas	slave insurrection
Pink	1764	Dutch Guianas	slave insurrection
Vine	1747	[unknown]	slave insurrection
Jolly Prince	1764	[unknown]	slave insurrection
[unknown]	1772	[unknown]	Cut off by Africans from shore, ship did not reach the Americas
Restoration	1728	[unknown]	slave insurrection
Fox	1775	[unknown]	Vessel's boats attacked from shore
Galathée	1738	[unknown]	slave insurrection
Nécessaire	1771	Windward Coast	slave insurrection
Sally	1765	Antigua	slave insurrection
Ruby	1731	[unknown]	Vessel's boats attacked from shore
Dolphin	1731	[unknown]	Vessel attacked from shore
Sally	1773	[unknown]	Vessel attacked from Shore

Three years earlier, white Virginia resident Charles Seuart had brought Sommerset as "his slave and property" from the United States to London. As described by historian Steven M. Wise, the world's largest city was "800,000 souls, chaotic, compact, crowded, cruel, dangerous, dark, dirty, diseased, squalid, stinking, and violent, a twisting maze of alleyways and courtyards."[95]

In October 1771, the black man vanished among the 14,000 or 15,000 people of his complexion then living in England, most of whom were slaves brought from overseas.[96]

Before rendering the landmark ruling, Lord Chief Justice Mansfield had "worried aloud" about the "very disagreeable" potential effects of declaring all these people free. But he opted to render judgment "ruat cœlum" – though the heavens may fall![97]

Although Mansfield's handwritten ruling did not survive, one third-party version contained the line, "The air of England has long been too pure for a slave, and every man is free who breathes it."[98]

The heavens did not fall, but the ruling led to an upsurge in the number of poor blacks in England. Some were slaves abandoned without compensation by their masters. Others were laid-over African seamen. Still others were African-Americans who sought refuge from plantation slavery. Many were reduced to begging on the crowded streets of London and Liverpool.

To improve the condition of these descendants of Africa, abolitionist Granville Sharp spearheaded an initiative in 1786 to establish a colony in Africa. A site near Sierra Leone was selected. It was suggested by Henry Smeathman, an amateur botanist who had visited the area to gather specimens 15 years earlier.

In highly exaggerated fashion, Smeathman described a land "of immense fertility perfectly healthy for those who lived temperately, where the soil need only be scratched with a hoe to yield grain in abundance, where livestock propagated themselves with a rapidity unknown in cold climates, where a hut provided adequate shelter at all seasons."[99]

In 1787, 300-plus black men, women and children sailed for the Province of Freedom (the colony's official name). They were accompanied by 100 white male clergy, artisans and officials and indigent white women. Within two and a half years, their settlement was decimated first by disease, then by a war between slave traders and members of the neighboring Temne ethnic community.[100]

Despite this initial setback, the back-to-Africa desires of New World blacks in the 1800s came to be fixated upon the province at Sierra Leone.

The repatriation of free blacks to Africa was the goal of the first black self-governing organization in the United States. Founded in 1780, the Free African Union Society of Newport, Rhode Island, met once every three months "to consider what can be done for our good and the good of all Africans, and in the meantime we still wait on the Lord, and are ready to do all the good we can, whether we are called to go there, or stay here."[101]

Rhode Island then was more deeply implicated in the triangular trade in Africans than many states with large enslaved populations, including South Carolina. In addition to building ships used by slavers elsewhere, Rhode Island residents owned vessels that carried at least 100,000 Africans across the Atlantic before 1808.

Rum, together with the shipping of captives, provided the mainstay of wealth of the state's most prominent families, including John and Moses Brown (founders of Brown University). Another family, the DeWolfs, operated an integrated and extensive multinational slaving enterprise. It included sugar plantations in Cuba, distilleries in Bristol, along with finance and insurance offices in Rhode Island.[102]

For the Union's founders and other blacks in Newport, Africa was not some faintly remembered place. It was a source of stunning wealth to which ships ventured and returned regularly bearing news as well as commodities.

Figure 56. Antislavery actions on the Windward Coast

(Continued)

Ship Name	Year	Landed	Action
Race Horse	1753	[unknown]	Cut off by Africans from shore, ship did not reach the Americas
Diana	1798	Barbados	slave insurrection
Adlington	1753	Jamaica	slave insurrection
Thomas & Ellinor	1748	[unknown]	slave insurrection
Floramell	1750	Barbados	Vessel's boats attacked from shore
Duke of Argyle	1751	Antigua	Insurrection planned, but thwarted
African	1753	St. Kitts	slave insurrection
Racehorse	1759	Antigua	Vessel's boats attacked from shore
Perfect	1759	Windward	slave insurrection
Ann and Betty	1758	Virginia	Cut off by Africans from shore but recaptured
Sisters	1765	Dominica	slave insurrection
Trimmer	1765	[unknown]	slave insurrection
Delight	1770	Dominica	slave insurrection
Duke of Bridgewater	1770	[unknown]	slave insurrection
African Queen	1771	Antigua	slave insurrection
Carrick	1771	Barbados	Cut off by Africans from shore but recaptured
Matty	1772	Barbados	slave insurrection
Burrowes	1775	Barbados	Cut off by Africans from shore but recaptured
Industry	1729	Barbados	slave insurrection
[unknown]	1770	[unknown]	Cut off by Africans from shore, ship did not reach The Americas
[unknown]	1770	[unknown]	Vessel attacked from shore
[unknown]	1786	[unknown]	Cut off by Africans from shore, ship did not reach the Americas

Seven years after the Union was formed, 75 blacks in Massachusetts seeking repatriation to Africa petitioned the General Court for aid. Significantly, the petitioners included Prince Hall, founder and leader of the first African-American fraternal order of Masons.[103]

In 1794, France became the first European power to abolish slavery. The motives were not all pure. One goal was to undermine British troops, who were occupying territories in the Caribbean formerly held by France. Eight years later, France restored slavery.[104]

Black demands for freedom were intensified and quickened by the American War of Independence and the French Revolution. As the leaders of those upheavals had done, blacks, too, began insisting, "Give me liberty, or give me death," and demanding "liberty, fraternity and equality." This was most evident in the Haitian Revolution of 1794.[105] Events in Haiti reverberated in various parts of the United States, in the form of rumblings among blacks and fits of panic among whites.[106]

In 1804, the people of Haiti defeated a 5,000-man army sent by Napoleon to crush them. They then established a republican government in the western end of Hispaniola — the first black state in the modern world. This was followed by the freeing of all slaves and the killing of many whites who did not leave. Some former masters fled to Louisiana and the Chesapeake region of the United States (consisting of Virginia and Maryland), accompanied in some cases by their slaves.

The Haitian revolution quickened political changes around the world. On 1 January 1808 – thanks to pressure from the British, the United States Congress passed a law that banned both the importation of slaves and the outfitting of ships for that purpose.[107]

The Windward slave trade declined sharply after 1800 when the Dutch withdrew. It dropped more drastically seven years later when Britain outlawed purchases by its citizens.[108]

In 1818, the British Anti-Slavery Squadron began putting pressure on major slave trading areas like Rio Pongo, the Gallinas and Dahomey. As a result, the traffic moved to previously minor ports like Cape Mount and Cape Mesurado. The area around Cape Mount alone is said to have shipped around 3,000 persons in 1823 and about 15,000 per year between 1840 and 1850.

But, even as the Atlantic slave trade declined, West Africans were still being captured and sold to Arabia. By the 1700s, the number of black slaves in North Africa was massive. Moroccan Sultan Mawlay Isma'il (1672-1727) alone reportedly had an army of 250,000 enslaved black men. He systematically used a large number of black women to breed future black servants and soldiers.[109]

By the early 1700s, significant changes crystalized that undermined Maninké dominance in Guinea. Fula groups in the Fula Jallon highlands mastered the use of horses for cavalry. In addition, a militant Muslim clergy spearheaded the unification of the Fula. They then seized control of the region in the 1720s and held it for about 100 years.[110]

After 1746, Europeans for the first time began penetrating beyond the West African coast into the interior. They focused mainly on charting the Niger River and finding the fabled empires that reportedly lined it.[111]

These explorations were funded by people with a motley mix of motivations: hard-nosed traders, curious scholars, idealists wanting to end the slave trade, and romantic adventurers.[112] However, the interior of West Africa would remain a mystery to Europeans until 1859. That year the German explorer Heinrich Barth (1821-1865) published the first detailed descriptions of Timbuktu and the course of the Niger.[113]

---

[1]. Gomes Eannes de Azurara, *The Chronicle of the Discovery and Conquest of Guinea*, Eng. Tr. ed. C. R. Beazley and Edgar Prestage, 1st ser., vols. 95 and 100 (London: Hakluyt Society, 1896 and 1899), vol. 95, pp. 81-83; Russell, 2000, p. 242.

[2]. Russell, 2000, pp. 258-259.

[3]. Masonen, 2000, p. 124, n. 7.

[4]. Dunn, 1972, p. 60.

[5]. Braudel, Vol. 1, 1981, pp. 224-225; Frederick H. Smith, *Caribbean Rum: A Social and Economic History* (Gainesville: University Press of Florida, 2005), especially pp. 13-14; Dunn, 1972, p. 60; Mintz, 1985, p. 27; Mintz, 1985, p. 37.

[6]. Dunn, 1972, p. 191.

[7]. Dunn, 1972, p. 191.

[8]. Dunn, 1972, p. 192.

[9]. Dunn, 1972, p. 192; Mintz, 1985, pp. 47, 49.

[10]. Dunn, 1972, p. 192; Mintz, 1985, pp. 49, 51.

[11]. Dunn, 1972, p. 192; Mintz, 1985, p. 49.

[12]. Dunn, 1972, p. 194.

[13]. Dunn, 1972, p. 194.

[14]. Dunn, 1972, p. 194-197; Mintz, 1985, p. 22.

[15]. Dunn, 1972, p. 189.

[16]. Braudel, Vol. 1, 1981, pp. 224-225; Smith, 2005, especially pp. 13-14; Mintz, 1985, p. 45.

[17]. Dunn, 2012, p. 293.

[18]. Schulze, 1973; Schwab, 1947, p. 417; Butt-Thompson, 1929, p. 141; G. E. Currens, "Land, labor and capital in Loma agriculture," in V. R. Dorjahn and B. L. Isaac (eds.), *Essays on the Economic Anthropology of Liberia and Sierra Leone* (Philadelphia: Institute for Liberian Studies, 1979), pp. 79-102; for a discussion of "manufactured land," see Samir Amin, *Class and Nation: Historically and In the Current Crisis* (New York: Monthly Review Press, 1980), pp. 36-45.

[19]. Villault, 1745-47, p. 379; Barbot, 1732, p. 133.

20. Barbot, 1732, pp. 117, 120, 133; Little, 1951, p. 37. Compare with Medeiros, 1992, p. 71; Budge, 1861, pp. xii-xxiii; Muḥammad Abū'l-Qāsim Ibn Ḥawqal, Ṣūrat al-'Arḍ (الارض صورة; "The face of the Earth") (pp. 44-52), in Levtzion and Hokpins, 2011, especially p. 52 (on burial of slaves with rulers in Ghana); Abu 'Ubayd 'Abd Allah b. Abd al-Aziz al-Bakri, Kitāb al-Masālik w'al-Mamālik (كتاب المسالك والممالك, "Books of Roads and Kingdoms") (pp. 63-86), in Levtzion and Hokpins, 2011, especially pp. 80-81 (on burial of slaves with rulers in Ghana); Abū 'Abd al-Lāh Muḥammad ibn 'Abd al-Lāh l-Lawātī ṭ-Ṭanǧī ibn Baṭūṭah, Rihla (الرحلة, "Journey"), in Levtzion and Hokpins, 2011, especially p. 28 (on burial of slaves among non-believers, implying the practice had ended in Mali proper).
21. Brooks, 1972, p. 108.
22. Bureau of Folkways, 1955, pp. 14, 80; Anderson, 1971, p. 41; d'Azevedo, 1972, p. 423.
23. Bourdillon, 2011, p. 190; King, 1986, p. 70.
24. Rawley, 1981, pp. 37, 56.
25. Thomas, 1997, pp. 115, 133, 209; Davis II, 2013, p. 511; Dunn, 1972, p. 73.
26. Davis, 1966, p. 108.
27. M. Adas, Machines as the Measure of Men: Science, Technology, and Ideologies of Western Dominance (Ithaca, New York: Cornell University Press, (1989), pp. 53, 40, 70-71; also Umaru Bah (2008). Rereading The Passing of Traditional Society: Empathy, orthodoxy and the Americanization of the Middle East. Cultural Studies, 22 (6), 1-25; Edward W. Said, Orientalism (New York: Vintage Books, 1979); T. Todorov, The Conquest of America (R. Howard, Trans.) (Norman: University of Oklahoma Press, 1999); Mudimbé, 1988; on hunt for witches in Europe, P. Zagorin, How the Idea of Religious Tolerance Came to the West (Princeton: Princeton University Press, 2003), pp. 82-83; J. Demos, The Enemy Within: 2,000 Years of Witch-Hunting in the Western World (New York: Viking, 2008).
28. Ada, 1989, pp. 33, 171, 8; J. M. Coward, The Newspaper Indian: Native American Identity in the Press, 1820-1890 (Urbana, Ill.: University of Illinois Press, 1999), p. 7.
29. Masonen, 2000, p. 124, p. 7.
30. Vos, 2010, p. 32; Vos, 2012, p. 3.
31. Ehret, 2013, p. 469.
32. Thomas, 1997, pp. 157, 183, 199, 201-203.
33. Fernández-Armesto and Sacks, 2013, p. 139.
34. Thomas, 1997, pp. 157, 183, 199, 201-203.
35. Bean, 1974, pp. 352-353.
36. Thomas, 1997, p. 793.
37. Michelle Craig McDonald, "Transatlantic consumption" (pp. 111-126), in Frank Trentmann, ed., The Oxford Handbook of the History of Consumption (Oxford: Oxford University Press, 2013), p. 115.
38. Berlin, 1998, p. 8.
39. Thomas, 1997, pp. 804-805 and pp. 861-862, for a discussion of various estimates from which the total number is derived.
40. J. E. Inikori, "The import of firearms into West Africa, 1750-1807: A quantitative analysis," Journal of African History, Vol. 18, No. 3 (1977): 339-368; Philip D. Curtin, The Atlantic Slave Trade: A Census (Madison: University of Wisconsin, 1969), p. 118, Table 6; Jones & Johnson, 1980, pp. 17-34, especially p. 34; Lovejoy, 1983, pp. 47-48; Nathaniel R. Richardson, Liberia's Past and Present (London: The Diplomatic Press, 1979), especially p. 325.
41. http://www.slavevoyages.org/tast/index.faces.
42. http://www.slavevoyages.org/tast/index.faces.

43. http://www.slavevoyages.org/tast/index.faces.
44. Adam Jones and Marion Johnson, "Slaves from the Windward Coast," *Journal of African History* 21 (1980): 17-34, especially p. 21; William Smith, *A New Voyage to Guinea* (London: John Nourse, 1745), p. 102; K. G. Davies, *The Royal African Company* (London: Longmans, 1957), p. 200.
45. Curtin, 1969, pp. 128, also pp. 122-123; e.g., Vos, 2010, p. 32.
46. Hair, Jones and Law, 1992, pp. 240-241; Yves Person, "Le Soudan nigérien et la Guinée occidentale," in Hubert Deschamps, ed., *Histoire général de l'Afrique noire, de Madagascar, et des archipels*, Vol. I (Paris: Presses Universitaires de France, 1970), p. 292; Philip D. Curtin, *African History: From the Earliest Times to Independence* (London: Longman, 1995), pp. 198-199; also Vos, 2010, pp. 38, 45.
47. Hair, Jones and Law, 1992, Letter 27, p. 264.
48. Hair, Jones and Law, 1992, Letter 29, p. 275.
49. Vos, 2010, pp. 38-39.
50. Vos, 2010, p. 45; Jones and Johnson, 1980, p. 17; for contemporaneous accounts of underpopulation, see Thomas Phillips, "Journal of a Voyage ... to Cape Monseradoe ... (1693-94)," in Awnsham and John Churchill, *A Collection of Voyages and Travels*, 6 vols. (London: Awnsham and John Churchill, 1704-32), VI, pp. 387-395; Snoek, 1806-14, p. 540; Bosman, 1705, Letters XIV and XII.
51. http://www.slavevoyages.org/tast/index.faces.
52. http://www.slavevoyages.org/tast/index.faces.
53. http://www.slavevoyages.org/tast/index.faces.
54. Hair, Jones and Law, 1992, Letter 22, p. 475, Letter 19, p. 239, 253, n. 24. The year of Bosman's visit is not given in his account, but it is said to have occurred on his way back from Elmina, which he left in 1701. Although he copied from Bosman's account, Barbot dropped the Dutchman's reference to the English role in plundering (perhaps to shield the role of his adopted countrymen).
55. Vos, 2010, pp. 34-35; Vos, 2012, p. 6.
56. Jones and Johnson, 1980, pp. 17-34; Johannes M. Postma, *The Dutch Atlantic Slave Trade, 1600-1815* (Cambridge: Cambridge University Press, 2009), pp. 122-123; Vos, 2010, pp. 29, 37; Jelmer Vos, David Eltis and David Richardson, "The Dutch in the Atlantic World: New Perspectives from the Slave Trade with particular reference to the origins of the traffic," in David Eltis and David Richardson, eds., *Extending the Frontiers: Essays on the New Transatlantic Slave Trade Database* (New Haven: Yale University Press, 2008), Table 8.2. In a broad study of the Dutch Atlantic slave trade, historian Johannes Postma noted the Windward supplied a higher than average number of slaves. His estimates have largely been borne out by more recent and comprehensive data from the *Voyages* database.
57. Vos, 2010, p. 33; Vos, 2012, pp. 1-2.
58. Elizabeth Donnan, "The slave trade into South Carolina before the revolution," *American Historical Review*, 33 (1927-28): 804-828, especially pp. 816-817, 825-827, and Elizabeth Donnan, *Documents Illustrative of the History of the Slave Trade to America*, Vol. 4 (New York: Octagon Books, 1969), pp. 237-570. On slavery and rice growing in South Carolina, also see Peter H. Wood, *Black Majority: Negroes in Colonial South Carolina* (New York: Knopf, 1974), pp. 35-62; Peter H. Wood, "'More like a Negro country': Demographic patterns in colonial South Carolina, 1700-1740 (pp. 131-172)" in Stanley L. Engerman and Eugene D. Genovese, *Race and Slavery in the Western Hemisphere: Quantitative Studies* (Princeton: Princeton University Press, 1975).

59. Donnan, 1927-28, pp. 816-817, 825-827; Donnan, 1969, pp. 237-570; Wood, 1974, pp. 35-62; Wood, 1975; MacNeill, 2013, p. 338.
60. Brun, 1983, pp. 74-75, n. 185.
61. Villault, 1670, pp. 69, 72-73.
62. Villault, 1670, p. 82.
63. Bosman, 1967, pp. 481-483.
64. Smith, 1744, p. 109.
65. For late twentieth-century rice exports from the United States and imports into Sierra Leone and Liberia, see Dan Morgan, *Merchants of Grain* (New York: Penguin, 1980), pp. 454-455, and Vernon R. Dorjahn and Barry L. Isaac, *Essays on the Economic Anthropology of Liberia and Sierra Leone* (Philadelphia: Institute for Liberian Studies, 1979), p. 21.
66. Mintz, 1985, p. 43.
67. Anne Farrow, Joel Lang and Jenifer Frank, *Complicity: How the North Promoted, Prolonged, and Profited from Slavery* (New York: Ballantine Books, 2005), pp. 95-119; Mintz, 1985, p. 43.
68. Wallerstein, Vol. 1, 1974, p. 232.
69. Braudel, Vol. 1, 1981, pp. 241-246.
70. Villault, 1670, pp. 69, 72-73.
71. Braudel, Vol. 1, 1981, pp. 241-247.
72. Smith, 2005, especially pp. 1, 16-17.
73. Smith, 2005, p. 27.
74. Smith, 2005, pp. 29-31.
75. Smith, 2005, p. 95.
76. Smith, 2005, pp. 56-57, 71.
77. Smith, 2005, pp. 56-57, 71.
78. Smith, 2005, pp. 73, 75.
79. Farrow, Lang and Frank, 2005, pp. 95-119.
80. Smith, 2005, pp. 97, 220.
81. Inikori, 1982, pp. 126-153; also Curtin, 1969, p. 118, Table 6; Jones and Johnson, 1980, pp. 17-34, especially p. 34; Lovejoy, 1983, pp. 47-48; Richardson, 1979, p. 325.
82. Inikori, 1977, pp. 345, 349, 353-354, 356-357.
83. Hair, Jones and Law, 1992, p. 301; Vos, 2010, pp. 46-47; Vos, 2012, pp. 1, 12. Rodney (1982, p. 71) refuted the widely repeated canard that even before the trans-Atlantic slave trade adultery was punishable with enslavement. That claim, he showed, confused cause with effect.
84. Adam Hochschild, *Bury the Chains: Prophets and Rebels in the Fight to Free an Empire's Slaves* (New York: Houghton Mifflin Company, 2005, pp. 11-18, 20, 24; Marcus Rediker, *The Slave Ship: A Human History* (New York: Viking, 2007), pp. 158-159; John Newton, *The Works of the Rev. John Newton*, 2 vols. (New York: Robert Carter, 1847).
85. Hochschild, 2005, pp. 24-26; Smeathman journal, 10 July 1773, in Christopher Fyfe, ed., *Sierra Leone Inheritance* (London: Oxford University Press, 1965), pp. 76-77.
86. Rediker, 2007, pp. 164, 167-168, 172.
87. Rediker, 2007, pp. 168, 172-174.
88. Rediker, 2007, pp. 168, 172-174.
89. Hochschild, 2005, pp. 75-76, 130-131.
90. Johnson, 1961, pp. 142-144.
91. Johnson, 1961, pp. 142-144.
92. Johnson, 1961, pp. 142-144.
93. Johnson, 1961, pp. 142-144.

94. Steven M. Wise, *"Though the Heavens May Fall:" The Landmark Trial that Led to the End of Human Slavery* (Cambridge, Mass.: DaCapo Books, 2005), pp. 129, 5-7, 209, 173, 189.
95. Wise, 2005, pp. 129, 5-7, 209, 173, 189.
96. Wise, 2005, pp. 129, 5-7, 209, 173, 189.
97. Wise, 2005, pp. 129, 5-7, 209, 173, 189.
98. Wise, 2005, pp. 129, 5-7, 209, 173, 189.
99. Johnson U. J. Asiegbu, *Slavery and the Politics of Liberation, 1787-1861: A Study of Liberated African Emigration and British Anti-Slavery Policy* (New York: Africana Publishing Corporation, 1972), pp. 3-4.
100. George E. Brooks, Jr., "The Providence African Society's Sierra Leone Emigration Scheme, 1794-1795," *International Journal of African Historical Studies*. Vol. 7, No. 2 (1974), 187-188; Nemata Amelia Blyden, *West Indians in West Africa, 1808-1880: The African Diaspora in Reverse* (Rochester, New York: University of Rochester Press, 2000), pp. 1-2; Sylvia R. Frey, *Water from the Rock: Black Resistance in a Revolutionary Age* (Princeton, N.J.: Princeton University Press, 1991), p. 195; Wise, 2005, pp. 217-225.
101. Robert J. Cottrol, *The Afro-Yankees: Providence's Black Community in the Antebellum Era* (Westport, Conn.: Greenwood Press, 1982), p. 45; Brooks, 1974, 187; Henry N. Sherwood, "Early Negro Deportation Projects." *Mississippi Valley Historical Review* 2, No. 4 (1916), pp. 484-508, especially pp. 502-506.
102. Farrow, Lang and Frank, 2005, pp. 95-119.
103. "Negro Petitions for Freedom," Collections of the Massachusetts Historical Society, 5th Series (1877), pp. 436-437, cited in Elizabeth Raub Bethel, "Images of Hayti: The construction of an Afro-American lieu de memoire," *Callaloo*, Vol. 15, No. 3 (Summer 1992), pp. 827-841, especially p. 829; Lorenzo J. Greene, "Prince Hall: Massachusetts Leader in crisis," *Freedomways* I (Fall, 1961), pp. 238-258.
104. Masonen, 2000, p. 258.
105. The work with which to begin any study of the Haitian Revolution remains C. L. R. James, *The Black Jacobins* (New York: Vintage, 1963); also see Davis II, 2013, p. 514.

[106] For the international consequences of the Revolution and the response of the America government to it, see Gordon S. Brown, *Toussaint's Clause: The Founding Fathers and the Haitian Revolution* (Jackson: University Press of Mississippi, 2005); Richard S. Dunn, "Society in the Chesapeake, 1776-1810," in Ira Berlin and Ronald Hoffman, eds., *Slavery and Freedom in the Age of the American Revolution*, pp. 49-82. Urbana, Ill.: University of Illinois Press, 1986), pp. 80-81; Theodore S. Babcock, "Manumission in Virginia, 1782-1806." M. A. thesis, University of Virginia. 1974, pp. 7-19; Virginius Dabney, *Richmond: The Story of a City* (Garden City, New York: Doubleday and Co., 1990), pp. 50-51; Allan Kulikoff, "Uprooted peoples: Black migrants in the age of the American Revolution." in Ira Berlin and Ronald Hoffman, eds., *Slavery and Freedom in the Age of the American Revolution* (Urbana, Ill.: University of Illinois Press, 1986b), pp. 416-420; Franklin W. Knight, "The American Revolution and the Caribbean," in Ira Berlin and Ronald Hoffman, eds., *Slavery and Freedom in the Age of the American Revolution*, pp. 237-261. (Urbana, Ill.: University of Illinois Press, 1983), 237-261; David Brion Davis, *The Problem of Slavery in the Age of Revolution, 1770-1823* (Ithaca: Cornell University Press, 1975), pp. 557-564; David Brion Davis, "American Slavery and the American Revolution," in Ira Berlin and Ronald Hoffman, eds., *Slavery and Freedom in the Age of the American Revolution* (Urbana, Ill.: University of Illinois Press, 1983), pp. 262-280; Benjamin Quarles, "The Revolutionary War as a Black Declaration of Independence," in Ira Berlin and Ronald Hoffman, eds., *Slavery and Freedom in the Age of the American Revolution* (Urbana, Ill.: University of Illinois Press, 1986), pp. 283-301; John C. Miller, *The Wolf by the Ear* (New York: The Free Press, 1977), pp. 133-141. The War also served to expand the horizons of those slaves who were forced to travel with their master in the Continent Army.

[107] John T. Noonan, Jr. *The Antelope: The Ordeal of the Recaptured Africans in the Administrations of James Monroe and John Quincy Adams* (Los Angeles: University of California Press, 1977), p. 17; "An Act to prohibit the importation of slaves into any port or place within the jurisdiction of the United States," 2 March 1807, 9th Cong., 2nd Sess., Public Statutes at Large II, pp. 426-430. From the founding of the American republic, the federal government had lacked the power to limit the slave trade, thanks to Article II of the Constitution which prevented it from interfering with "the Migration or Importation of Such Persons as any of the States now existing shall think proper to admit." For political reasons, the Constitution's authors mentioned neither "slaves" nor "Africans," but they and their contemporary readers fully understood their intended meaning.

[108] Vos, 2010, p. 33.

[109] Lewis, 1990, p. 69.

[110] Brooks, 1989, p. 38.

[111] Masonen, 2000, pp. 246-247.

[112] Masonen, 2000, pp. 250-251.

[113] Masonen, 2000, pp. 271-275.

Chapter 13
Crawling Ahead, Falling Behind

> We are never as steeped in history as when we pretend not to be, but if we stop pretending we may gain in understanding what we lose in false innocence. Naiveté is often an excuse for those who exercise power. For those upon whom that power is exercised, naiveté is always a mistake.
>
> – historian Michel-Roph Troullot

Living conditions in Africa lag so far behind Europe today it leads many people to assume things were always as they are. That false conclusion is reinforced by history books and films that repeatedly contrast the lavish lifestyles of European royalty against images of impoverished Africans.

To reach valid conclusions, it is essential that like items be compared. To do so, conditions from different parts of the world must be drawn from the same period in the past. More important, evidence should be drawn from similar sectors of each society.

Take the English Caribbean, for example. In those societies, heaven and hell existed side by side. Presenting the living conditions of an "average" person would merely mask the staggering inequalities.

On the one hand, enslaved Africans faced some of the most wretched living conditions anywhere in the world. They died earlier than most people because they were brutalized, over worked, and ill fed. Day in and day out, they were fed small servings of corn, plantains, sweet potatoes, peas or beans, mixed with a little dried salt fish. They received meat, if a sick cow or horse died.[1]

Slave families usually slept on the ground together. Neither enslaved men nor women had shoes or hats. Clothing for women were loin cloths, smocks or skirts. Men wore loin cloths or drawers, with shirts on Sundays. Their children wore no clothes until puberty.[2]

In close proximity were slaveholders, who lived in opulence. In the words of historian Richard S. Dunn, they "dined richly, drank copiously, and entertained lavishly." When hosting visitors, they spent four to five hours on dinner and after dinner drinking.[3]

To avoid mixing mangoes and butterpears ("avacadoes"), it is best to ignore enslaved persons and the superrich to focus instead on the living conditions of poor farmers around the world. After all, they were the majority. Fortunately, the basis for such comparisons was laid by historian Fernand Braudel, a pioneer of global history. In a three-volume study, he compared living conditions around the world between 1400 and 1800.

Brudel's findings are summarized here in 11 key areas (together with extra evidence from elsewhere): Cities; Famine and Illness; Sources of Energy; Farming and Foods; Meat and Other Sources of Proteins; Clothes, Furniture and Dishes; Mud and Wood Dwellings; Civility and Sexual Mores; Transportation; Making Things; and Markets, Money and Monopolies. In each section, living conditions in the Liberia area are described first, followed by evidence from elsewhere.

Until the early 1700s, West Africa shared with Europe and the rest of the world certain basic life patterns: People died early, including many infants, from widespread malnutrition, epidemics and famines. As a result, the number of deaths roughly equaled the number of births. Due to poor diets, many of the rural poor had weak immune systems and stunned growth.[4]

During this period, common tools throughout the world consisted of a knife, an axe and a spade. Ordinary ploughs were rare.[5]

Europe was no exception. It, too, had subsistence economies until the 1700s.[6] As late as 1820, people in Germany and England lived on average until age 40.[7]

In this period, Europe was *not* the most advanced region of the world. As early as 4000 BC, Southwest Asia was the site of many key discoveries. Animals domesticated there were cows, pigs, sheep, goats and horses. Crops included peas, lentils, broad beans and chick peas. All of these were later imported into Europe and Africa.[8]

Arabia had developed algebra and a system of numerals. The Abbasid caliphate (750-1258) helped spread sugar, rice, cotton and citrus fruits from India across the Mediterranean world.[9]

Regarding Africa in particular, linguist Christopher Ehret argued that its "notable developments" followed "similar pathways and proceeded at similar paces as comparable changes elsewhere in the world."[10]

One of the world's foremost economic historians, Fernand Braudel, noted, "One thing seems clear to me: the gap between the West and the other continents appeared late in time."[11]

Encounters with other cultures sparked in Europe a number of innovations. Italy began making silk fabrics and England printed and dyed calicoes, both adopted from Asia.[12] From the Native Americans of Peru, Europeans learned the use of quinine to suppress the symptoms of malaria.[13]

In the early 1700s, enslaved blacks introduced to North America a process of immunizing people to smallpox by introducing pus from a diseased person into the skin of those who had not been infected. This process had been practiced in Asia, Arabia and Africa for centuries before.[14]

Cities: Seats of the Good Life?

Between 1400 and 1820, West Africa differed from other parts of the world in one obvious way: a lack of cities. Land was abundant here, so rising densities generally led to migration.

The largest cities in the region were along the Niger: Timbuktu with between 100,000 and 400,000 residents in the 1300s and Jenne, 100,000.[15] The largest town along the Windward Coast was Wappo; according to Jean Barbot, it was "at least as large and fine as that of Mina on the Gold Coast," a town with 20,000 residents by 1682.[16]

When de Sintra sailed to West Africa, some of the world's largest cities were Bejing, with 672,000 residents; Vijayanagar, India, 500,000; and Cairo, 450,000. But the Mediterranean had the most cities. They included Alexandria, Antioch, Athens, Florence, Genoa, Pisa and Venice, to mention a few. They were small (with between 60,000 and 150,000 residents) but among the most densely packed cities in the world.[17]

The Islamic world supported an unusually large number of cities because it was the hub of a dazzlingly wealthy world-economy. These extended like a necklace of pearls along the nape of the Mediterranean. Andalus (in present-day Spain) had Cordoba, Seville and Granada (with 70,000 residents). Morocco had Fez and Marrakech (with 150,000 residents). Tunisia supported Qayrawan and later Tunis. Egypt had Fustat and the mother-of-all Mediterranean cities, Cairo.[18]

In what is now called the Middle East, Syria boasted Damascus and Aleppo. Iraq had Baghdad, Mosul and Basra. Western Arabia was home to Medina and Mecca (with 60,000 residents), host of the annual pilgrimage of Muslim's worldwide.[19]

In the 1300s, the three largest Muslim-majority cities were Cordoba, Cairo and Baghdad. With at least 250,000 residents each, they had no equal in Europe then. The second tier of Arab cities were Aleppo, Damascus and Tunis. Each had about 75,000 residents.[20]

In the 1400s, the largest cities in Europe were Florence, Venice, Milan and Paris, with about 100,000 residents each. They had no equal in England, Belgium, Holland, Germany or Central Europe.[21]

After 1500, Europe began to develop larger cities, thanks to international trade. London, a port town, grew from 93,000 residents in 1563 to 317,000 in 1632 to 860,000 in 1790. The next closest European city in size was Paris, which went from 225,000 residents in 1500 to 560,000 in 1750.[22]

Given the centrality of cities to Mediterranean life, it is not surprising that early writers from the region, like Greek philosopher Aristotle, saw cities as seats of the good life.[23] That elevated view of urban areas remains entrenched among Western scholars.[24]

For example, some scholars have argued that economic development is possible only in societies with a high density of people. They order societies into three groups based on density: pioneer zones (with 14 people per square kilometers or less); middle zones (with 15 to 20 people per square kilometers); and high density zones (with densities over 20 per square kilometers).[25]

According to this argument, people in some parts of Europe and China developed key labor-saving techniques because population climbed beyond 19 people to the square mile in areas where land and resources were scarce.[26]

This model is open to question for several reasons. First, some country towns were vibrant and worldly because they laid along heavily travelled trade routes. Second, cities differed from each other. Some, like Madrid, grew mainly because they were the seat of royal power. Meanwhile, others were port cities, like Seville. Through the 1600s at least, the pace of life in port cities was set by the comings and goings of ships trading with the tropics.[27]

City residents were a diverse lot. They ranged from long-distance traders, through small shopkeepers and craftsmen, to a vast group of semi-employed people.[28]

Cities also had significant disadvantages. They were filled with "filth and rubbish." They were home to crime and large numbers of people who were extremely poor. These included beggars, pickpockets, ruffians, adventurers and even killers for hire. As late as 1637, the quartered corpses of executed convicts were displayed along various streets of Madrid.[29]

People moved to cities for a variety of reasons. One was unbearably high taxes, which sometimes cost poor farmers their few and meager possessions. In Spain, tax collectors would seize land and homes. If not sellable, homes would be stripped of timber and tiles. As a result, up to a third of rural Spaniards fled to cites or even to foreign countries.[30]

Given congestion in cities, death often came as dramatic tidal waves of epidemics that swept away thousands of people. But, rural West Africa was no elysium. Residents commonly faced a different threat: the slow draining away of life by malaria.

"Hungry Times," Smallpox and the Plague

Hunger and famines were an ever-present threat around the world. Hard numbers are not available for West Africa, but famines or "hungry times" are a frequent theme in folk tales.[31]

In Europe, Florence only had 16 good harvest between 1371 and 1791. France experienced seven famines in the 1400s, 13 in the 1500s, 11 in the 1600s and 16 in the 1700s.[32] In Scotland, there were four between 1695 and 1699. A famine in Finland around 1696-97 wiped out about a third of its people.[33]

Food shortages and malnutrition often opened the door for diseases to spread widely. To make matters worse, people weakened by one disease became more vulnerable to others.

In Europe, a recurring threat was the plague. It struck Paris six times between 1612 and 1668, and London five times between 1612 and 1668. Between 1622 and 1628, Amsterdam lost 35,000 residents to the plague and London 156,463 between 1593 and 1665. In 1656-57, the plague killed a quarter of Genoa's 80,000 residents.[34] Smaller cities and towns were all impacted.[35]

The plague only subsided in Europe after 1720, which coincided with a widespread shift in home-building materials from wood to stone.[36]

In 1775, smallpox affected an estimated 95 out of every 100 inhabitants of France. Other common ailments in France were diphtheria, whooping cough, typhoid, jaundice, consumption, epilepsy and rheumatism, to name a few.[37]

Many diseases had long circulated through Asia, Europe and Africa. These included influenza, measles, mumps and whopping cough. Many adult survivors in those places were resistant.[38]

Often by accident, European mariners took those illnesses to the Americas, where people had no immunity to them. They also carried malaria and yellow fever from Africa. Those diseases together reduced the number of Native Americans by 50 to 90 percent.[39]

War was a crucial contributor to the spread of both famines and illnesses. Between 1648 and 1989, people fought an estimated 171 major wars. Europeans were involved in 133 of these. Before 1918, non-Europeans fought only five major wars without European involvement![40]

Human Labor and Other Sources of Energy

Before the 1800s, people around the world used a few simple and similar sources of energy: human labor, wood, charcoal, animals, wind, running water and coal.[41] The most commonly used everywhere were humans and work animals.[42]

Widely used work animals included horses, camels, cows and mules. According to one estimate, a horse could carry as much as seven men. Horses were fast and versatile, which fueled their use by armies.[43]

For daily farm work, however, horses were less valuable than the lowly mule.[44] In the late 1700s, there were 250,000 mules in Spain and 500,000 in Peru.[45]

In the region of Liberia, people mainly relied on human labor, charcoal and wood. West Africans in areas free of the Tsetse fly used horses, cows and camels.[46]

Throughout the world, wood was used extensively for cooking, for building and for smelting ore. Europe was no exception. As late as 1789, France alone was using 20 million tons of firewood and charcoal.[47]

Perhaps the biggest change in British homes in the 1600s was the shift from firewood to coal. This shift brought about changes in fireplaces, chimneys and cookware. Round-bottom cast-iron pots that hug over fires were replaced with flat-bottom brass cookware that sat on stoves.[48]

One versatile labor-saving source of energy had major consequences: the watermill. It originated in China, and it was spread by Arabs to Europe in the Roman era. Its use expanded across Europe around 1000 AD.[49]

The waterwheel used the power of a running river or stream to turn a wheel. Power from the turning wheel was converted to turn a saw or grind grain or perform other chores. Each waterwheel produced five times as much as two men using hand mills.[50]

Waterwheels gained greater popularity after 1500s especially in Holland, where they were used to remove water from the drenched lands.[51]

But, the energy source that provided the greatest bang for the buck was coal. It was successfully used in large-scale metal smelting around 1780. Its widespread adoption came in the 1800s. Cheap and efficient, it helped spur what came to be known as the Industrial Revolution, first in England.[52]

Farming and Foods

Before the 1700s, farming remained largely unchanged in most parts of the world.[53] Until the late 1800s, about 85 percent of people in all regions ate little more than a single starch.[54]

In each major culture area, one grain initially dominated: wheat in Europe, North Africa and Egypt; rice in China, India and West Africa; and corn in the Americas. After the early 1500s, corn was adopted by societies in Southern and East Africa.[55]

Farming in each region was shaped in part by the special demands of the dominant grain. Wheat, for example, required lots of animal manure, which was the main form of fertilizer. This encouraged a close relationship between farmers and herders.

Compared to wheat, rice had several advantages. It produced a higher yield — 26 quintals per hectare compared to 16.6 for wheat. And wheat provided only 50 to 70 percent of what each European ate. In contrast, rice supplied 80 to 90 percent of people's diet in areas where it was grown. Rice lasted longer, too, if kept in the husk. Moreover, it was possible to grow two harvests in one year.[56]

But rice was harder to grow and to process. Its roots need oxygen, which is best supplied by moving water. For that reason, rice fields work best if irrigated. In

China, this gave rise to extensive terracing of hills and sophisticated hydraulics.

After harvest, rice requires more hard work to remove the husk. In West Africa, this was done by pounding in mortars, followed by fanning to separate grains from husk.[57]

Compared to other grains, the yield of wheat was low — only about four grains for every one planted.[58] For this reason, wheat was rarely grown alone. It was usually farmed alongside millet, rye, oats and barley. Of these secondary grains, some barley went to feed horses, and rye was eaten mainly by the poor.[59]

In the wheat-growing regions of Europe, most people ate gruel and cheap bread made from secondary grains — over and over again. Until at least 1750, white bread made from wheat was reserved for the rich.[60]

Maize had an even higher yield than rice. According to one estimate, early American growers of this almost magical grain could feed their families by working only 50 days a year. Their time away from farming was not idle, however. Their rulers put them to work building large pyramids and other massive public projects.[61]

Meat and Other Sources of Protein

Between the 1400s and the 1700s, the amount of meat eaten was low in Africa, Asia, the Middle East and Europe: Only rich people routinely ate meat. The poor made do with a monotonous diet of grain and vegetable.[62]

In the West African forest belt, the presence of the Tsetse fly inhibited the development of animal husbandry. So, people hunted or fished to provide necessary protein. Hunting predominated in the northern forest where wild game was plentiful, while a system of fishing and sea-faring developed along the coast.[63]

In Asia, meat was not widely available. In Turkey, the main form of meat in 1693 was said to be dried beef. In China, it was the household pig, along with chickens, dogs and wild meat. In Japan, wild game was almost the only source of meat as late as 1609. In Spain, the main meat was mutton.[64]

In Arabia, poor people mainly ate the flat unleavened bread known as *pita*. They ate meat rarely, mainly on special occasions.[65]

In Europe, meat-eating among poor people increased as the economy grew during the 1400s and 1500s. According to one estimate, Madrid's 100,000 residents in the late 1500s annually ate 50,000 sheep, 12,000 oxen, 60,000 goats, 10,000 calves and 13,000 pigs. That works out to less than one animal annually per year person. These figures were unusually high because the city was home to the king, the nobles and their hanger-ons.[66]

Commoners faced very different choices. The quantity of meat available to them fell after 1550 as poverty increased.[67] In Spain, the cooked meat sold at various city stalls was of "dubious quality." One rumor held that the meat pies (*empanadillas*) was filled with the flesh of executed convicts![68]

In France, Germany and Denmark, to take three examples, each poor person between 1751 and 1854 ate between 44 and 144 lbs. of meat mixed with bones annually. That translates to between four to 12 hamburgers of one lb. each per year. Most of that meat was stale, salted and smoked, especially during the winter.[69]

In the absence of meat, major sources of protein in Northern Europe were cheese, eggs, milk and butter. But, dairy products sold to the poor were often diluted with water. In Southern Europe, people substituted bacon fat, lard and olive oil.[70]

Areas of the world with work animals enjoyed a potential protein advantage. After being used as sources of energy, horses and mules could be eaten. But, in societies with unequal social groups, even the carcasses of work animals went primarily to the rich.

Around the world, seafood was an important source of protein, at least in coastal communities. Both in Japan and southern China, diets included a variety of seafood.[71]

In Southern Europe, seafood consisted mainly of tiny sardines and anchovies. From the late 1400s, larger herring and cod were caught mainly along the coast of England and Scotland.[72]

In order to supply distant markets, catches had to be preserved quickly. This was often done immediately aboard the ships that caught them. The preferred methods for cod was drying and salting. Herring was smoked and salted.[73]

Clothes, Furniture and Dishes

As late as 1750, most poor people made their own cloth for everyday clothes. Available descriptions of the clothes people wore along the Windward Coast highlighted their lack of clothing compared to Europeans.

From Cape Mount to the area around Sestros, the rulers and other powerful men dressed similarly in robes. Several were apparently made of blue-and-white "country cloth" and at least one gown was embroidered.

In contrast, few details were offered on the attire of commoners. In 1666, Nicolas Villault noted, "They go all naked both women and men, only a little cloth before them, but the women wear theirs from their stomack, to their mid-legg."[74] Clothing along the Malagueta Coast consisted of "only a little piece of linnen before," with nothing on the head.[75]

At Cape Mount around 1701, more typical men's attire was "like a Surplice," which was a knee-length overgarment with full sleeves worn by European clergy or choirs. Women, on the other hand, wore a narrow cloth around their waist, "tucked in at their sides to fasten it," but without the girdles worn by women on the Gold Coast.[76]

In the 1600s, English commoners wore clothes that were "crudely made, shapeless, baggy, and ill fitting." No women — rich or poor — wore underwear. Poor rural women typically wore head covering and coarse linen smocks with ground-length skirts. In the summer, small farmers wore pants, shirts and caps. They added drawers, coats, stocking and boots in cold weather or when not working.[77]

Until the 1700s, working people in the French countryside wore clothes mainly made of rough broadcloth and hemp in black, grey or brown. Women's wardrobes consisted of coarse shirts, skits, stockings and clogs. Each woman typically owned a few of each. Working men typically owned about 13 hemp shirts, one or two suits, a hat, and one pair of shoes.[78]

In China there were few differences in the shape and styles of men and women clothes. Both commonly wore pants and underclothes. Clothes were made of wool, linen, cotton and a lot of silk. The rich wore a rich variety of vibrant colors, but the poor mainly wore black.[79]

Early European visitors to the area of Liberia, spent very little time in the homes of local people. For that reason, they left no descriptions of interior furnishings.

According to historian Fernand Braudel, homes in India, Arabia and Africa were similarly furnished during this period. Few, if any, had chairs or high tables. A common item was a wooden chest that held clothes and other valuables.[80]

In Arabia, wood furniture consisted of little more than chests and cupboards. Most other items were textiles, such as drapes, stuffed pillows and carpets. Often those were woven by the women of the family.[81]

Instead of eating utensils, Arabs mainly used pieces of bread to pick up their stews. Dishes consisted of clay bowls and cups, as well as large copper or silver trays for serving food. Metalworks were often supplied by traveling smiths.[82]

Everywhere, lighting at night was provided by candles and oil lumps. In Arabia, night light was usually supplied by copper oil lamps.[83]

At the time of de Sintra's voyage, Chinese homes had the best furnishings. These typically included low tables, chairs, curtains and shelves. Some even had cup boards and cabinets.[84]

Before the 1700s, plates and bowls for individual diners were common only in China. During the Ming dynasty (1368-1644), the Middle Kingdom had built large porcelain factories in Jingdoghen. They produced vast quantities of blue-and-white porcelain that were sold in many parts of the world.[85]

Art historian Craig Clunas described that distinctive looking porcelain as the "first global 'brand'."[86] People began calling porcelain dishes "china" because of where they originated, and the name stuck to this day.

In contrast, the insides of commoners' homes in Europe were bleak. Furniture typically consisted of a table, a bench, some barrels, wooden or earthenware plates, one cast iron pot for cooking, a cauldron for boiling water, a pail and some tubs. Most people slept on the floor.[87]

As late as 1660, even some European royals were described as eating with their fingers. These conditions prevailed until the 1800s, when the poor could finally afford "luxury" items like chairs and mattresses.[88]

In the 1700s, fireplaces and glass window panes were added to houses of the rich. Only the rich had curtains and screens to block the cold.[89] But, even *their* homes were infected with the fleas and bugs that plagued towns and cities.[90]

Mud and Wood Dwellings

Early European visitors to the Windward Coast left few descriptions of local buildings. They often described aspects of local societies that were strikingly different from their societies, especially if the African features were exotic or "inferior." For that reason, their silence on the dwellings of commoners suggests local ones were not very different from contemporary buildings in Europe.

One description was left by Dutch merchant Willem Bosman in 1688. He noted houses two miles west of Mesurado as the finest seen on his entire voyage, "covered at the top much like our Hay-reaks in Holland."[91]

Along the Sestros River, houses were apparently built of bamboo or what Bosman called "rushes or reeds."[92] These were probably recent or temporary housing, built to capitalize on trade. Until 1747 at least, most houses east of Cape Mesurado were built on stilts due to continued threats from man-eating animals.[93]

In South Asia and Southeast Asia, buildings were made of mud, bamboo, thatch and wood, even in cities. Stone and brick were reserved for palaces, fortresses and religious shrines.[94]

Housing for the poor in Arabia consisted of mud brick huts in the cities and tents in most of the countryside. As in many other regions of the world, only the rich lived in stone buildings.[95]

Chinese homes, even in cities, were typically one story. They were usually made of wood or, in the north, of mud.[96]

In Europe, wood was still the main building material. Poor Europeans, especially in towns and villages, still lived in log cabins or huts with thatched roofs and compacted earth floors. Their dwellings often housed people together with their domesticated animals, especially in winter.[97]

Most Spaniards lived in squat one-story homes made of mud or brick. Even some homes of the rich were built of mud, with stone facades.[98]

European cities began slowly shifting to stone and brick after huge fires nearly devoured Paris in 1547 and London in 1666.[99]

In the 1600s, about a quarter of all dwellings in Paris consisted of one room. Half had two to three rooms. But in the French countryside, most homes had one room, one chimney, thatched roofs, very little outside light, and one bed shared by the whole family.[100]

In Worcestershire, England, one-room homes fell to less than 50 percent only around 1700.[101]

Arabian workshops were small, providing barely enough room for an artisan, along with a few apprentices and workers.[102]

In Europe, urban artisans and shopkeepers typically conducted business from a section of their homes. Until the 1700s, the idea of "privacy" was limited to the rich and powerful. It spread to other groups in Europe as homes were built larger and with more rooms.[103]

Civility and Sexual Mores

A Dutch merchant who sojourned to the coast of what is now Liberia noted that the people were "not ashamed to shew their naked bodies." However, they all bath often and take care "not to let a Fart, if any bodie be by them," unlike the "Netherlanders."[104] This comment highlighted difference in what various cultures defined as acceptable behavior.

French nobleman Nicholas Villaut was not uniformly condescending toward the residents of the Windward Coast and their practices. Writing in 1666, he described the people at Cape Mount as "handsome," "goodnatured" and "tractible."

Villault noted how careful the local people were in roasting meat over wooden spits, "turning them with great care, and observing very curiously least one side be more roasted then the other. He also pronounced them "very neat in their feeding."[105]

Around 1701, William Bosman described some villagers near River Cess as "very Civil and Courteous." He reached this conclusion because "an old Man that looked like their Governour" insisted that Bosman eat and drink before returning to his ship.[106] He deemed the residents of Settre Crou "a good sort of People, honest in their Dealings."[107]

Jean Barbot regarded mothers at Sestros as "outstanding in their tender care for their infants." He cited the kindness of Sestros residents, or, as he put it, their "much human feeling."[108]

Several early European voyagers suggested that women along the Windward Coast were promiscuous or sexually available. An example is Bosman's disparaging comment about some local women, whose "principal Trade lay in relieving the Travelers Necessities at a very reasonable Price.[109] At Cape Mount, he claimed, women "are permitted to earn what Money they please with their Bodies."[110] Even husbands were not "much concerned" if their wives "venture on unlawful Pleasures with other Men."[111]

Those comments reveal as much about Bosman as about the people he was describing. After all, male sailors were notorious for seeking sexual partners in various ports, especially at the end of months-long voyages.[112]

The home countries of these sailors, especially port cities, maintained multiple sexual standards. In 1459, for example, the city of Genoa operated official brothels, staffed by women previously convicted of prostitution. Shiploads of those women were periodically taken to the docks to service sailors and visitors.[113]

In the late 1500s, Spain regulated sex workers. Each city had a section where prostitutes worked the streets freely. Their services were said to be cheaper than most goods.[114]

Until the late 1700s, getting water to drink, cook and bathe was a challenge throughout the world. In most places, people had to bring fresh water in containers over great distances on a daily basis.

During this period, Islamic societies placed the greatest stress on personal cleanliness of all the major regions of the world. This stemmed from a religious requirement that Muslims wash before praying. To accommodate the faithful, public baths were created early in predominantly Muslim cities. In Europe, they first appeared in Rome, then spread to other cities and large towns.[115]

Only a few exceptional cities in Turkey, Italy and Portugal had installed clay pipes to bring water from rivers to where people lived.[116]

In England, the rural poor rarely bath or washed their clothes. The rich rarely bathe, either. Under their layers of clothes, they were as smelly as their servants. But, wealth bought privileges: The rich covered their rank odor with fragrances![117]

From the 1400s to the 1600s, however, there was a decline in "bodily cleanliness" in Europe. After 1600, most Europeans stopped using public baths for fear of contracting syphilis or some infection.[118]

Transportation

Whether in Asia, Africa, Arabia or Europe, most people walked barefoot on narrow paths. Only the rich and powerful were carried by people or rode domesticated animals.[119]

In West Africa, goods were carried on the backs and heads of people because the Tsetse fly limited the use of pack animals. Porters not only carried less than horses and camels, they were also slower. And slow-moving goods were more likely to spoil.[120]

A daily traffic of canoes plied the coast from Sestro to Cape Mesurado.[121] Trading canoes also linked Cape Mesurado to Sestro. There was probably a regular traffic of canoes along the rest of the coast, although on a less frequent basis.

The advantage of access to the ocean which the Malagueta Coast enjoyed was exploited in the form of trade with communities in what are present-day Côte d'Ivoire. Because trading was important, neighboring villages competed with each other.

The Indian Ocean was originally controlled by Muslim navies. They were destroyed within fifteen years after the European arrival by Portuguese gunships.[122]

By the mid-1400s, Europe's shipbuilding industry gave its merchants a decided advantage over competitors in many parts of the world.[123] As a result, they could move goods faster and more cheaply.[124]

The rich in European cities had horse-drawn carriages. But, the roads they travelled on were usually unpaved, potted with holes, filled with water and too narrow for two carriages to pass at one time. Coaches first appeared in Europe in the late 1500s, but they did not have glass windows until the 1600s.[125]

Making Things

Another key sector of the economy involved the making of things. In that context, dramatic growth in productivity and the economy as a whole usually stemmed from improvements in industry not farming.[126]

Workshops took four forms. The smallest were family shops. They were plentiful and grouped together. On a slightly larger scale were workshops with artisans from different households. They often shared business connections although some were far apart. A third type brought several related but not competing products under one roof. This clustering helped artisans produce more and better goods. The most productive workshops used machines and non-human energy sources, like waterwheels. Those fit the label of "factories."[127]

Obviously, family workshops existed all over West Africa. It is possible, too, that some slightly larger non-family workshops produced iron, salt, mats, soap, canoes, and cloth for sale.[128] However, there is no evidence from this region of workshops that fitted into the third or fourth type.

Along the Windward Coast, the main engines of growth were apparently cloth making and iron smelting. As early as the 1100s, West African cotton cloth was being sold in Europe. This textile was called *harinkan* (from the Mande word for "garment"). It came to be known as *barrakan* in Arabic, as well as *barra cana, bucaranum* and *boqueranus* in Europe.[129]

These cloths were among items imported from West Africa to Europe by the Portuguese. The market for "country cloth" was so large, the Portuguese set up workshops on Cape Verde to produce the textile. Some cloths were exported from the area of Liberia.[130]

Hardening and sharpening iron were skills at which local blacksmiths excelled. Kissi and Loma blacksmiths were especially renown. They produced the twisted iron bars called Kissi money that functioned as currency throughout what is now northwestern Liberia.[131] West African smelters could cast metal and produce steel, but they lacked access to coal.[132]

A key engine of economic progress worldwide was iron smelting. It provided sturdy tools, as well as weapons.

At the time of de Sintra's voyage, China was most advanced in this field. From about 400 BC, it was able to cast iron, make steel, and use coal-fired smelting.[133]

In China, the Song dynasty (960-1279) also fostered the making of high quality salt, silk and paper in large quantities. Chinese pottery was the world's most advanced and desirable. Its potters had developed glazes that were thin, attractive, durable and waterproof.[134]

Europeans acquired all three iron smelting techniques relatively late: iron casting in the 1300s and smelting with coal in the 1600s. In 1525, it is estimated that Europe was producing 100,000 tons of iron per year while the rest of the world contributed 300,000 tons.[135]

Between 1500 to 1700, European blast furnaces doubled their capacity. This was done by harnessing power from watermills and the high-temperature burn of coal. Their improvement was mainly in quantity of output. Production went from 180,000 in 1700 to 600,000 in 1790.[136]

In Europe, additional engines of growth were textile, shipbuilding and sugar refining.[137]

Markets, Money and Monopolies

The absence of natural harbors made the Windward Coast one of the areas of West Africa least frequented by European ships. But, it was nonetheless integrated into the trans-Atlantic trade. It served as a supplier of cargo, provisioning area for ships, and hiring station for ship-hands.[138]

When European merchants first began trading along the Windward Coast in the 1400s, they mainly sought ivory, hides and malagueta. Those were exchanged mostly for European alloys, jewelry and cloths.[139]

The malagueta trade was so wide-spread and important that it fostered basket-weaving on a large-scale. Moreover, the wicker baskets used locally to carry dried malagueta and other produce became entrenched as units of measure.[140]

As a result, the Portuguese word for a pannier or large basket, "cesto," came to form a part of many place-names along this coast – *Sestros* River, Grand *Cess*, Little *Cestos* and others. Similarly, the name "Kru," by which an ethnic group of this coast is known, may have been derived from the local word for such units – "kroo."[141]

By 1650, it was reported that along this coast, "Those above the common rank drive a perpetual trade in rice, malaget (spice) and elephants teeth."[142] For the rulers at Cape Mount, the trans-Atlantic trade was so important they did not "permit any of those of the north countries to travel to the east, thro' their lands, nor those in the east to pass thro' to the westward: by which means they also have much greater share in the trade, from one part to another."[143]

Over the course of several centuries, local people developed discriminating tastes. They sought specific goods offered by European traders, as well as products from particular places. Popular foreign goods included Venetian glass beads, French brandy, Indian calico, Danish flintlock guns, Dutch manila basins, New England rum, Brazilian tobacco, and cowries from the Maldives Islands.[144]

Trade with Europe and the Americas, rather than being superficial, was woven into local economies. It also wrought significant cultural changes.

Until the 1700s, the main method of trading throughout the world was barter or exchange of goods. Money operated on the margins of society, circulating mainly among merchants and the nobility.[145]

Beyond the level of barter, the value of items to be traded was estimated in terms of a common unit of value. This was done especially for goods traded in large quantities and over long-distances. Along the Kru Coast, for example, the standard of value in trade was the "kroo," approximately 6 imp. Gal. of 3 kg.

As production developed expressly for exchange, cloth, salt and iron functioned as currencies or commodity moneys. These were used to measure the value of trade items but could be consumed, if necessary.[146] The idea that money is consumable lies behind the common reference today to corrupt officials "eating the people's money."

Around the world, highly valued commodities also served as currencies. In Japan, it was rice; in the Americas, tobacco, sugar and cocoa; in West Africa, salt and cowries.[147]

Until the 1400s, Arab money — *dinars* (gold) and *dirhems* (silver) — was considered the safest and most stable throughout the Mediterranean world, North Africa, West Africa, the Middle East and parts of Asia. Over the next century, it was displaced by European currencies that were modeled on the *dinar* and *dirhem*.[148]

China had its own stable currency from 200 BC until at least the late 1600s. Called the *caixas*, it was a mixture of copper and lead. But, some of the economic features of Europe, like fairs, were not common in China.[149]

West Africa's economic history is not well known, but its features probably resembled the economies of Arabia to which it was linked.

The earliest descriptions of markets in the area now know as Liberia date to the mid-1800s. They were recorded by a Liberian surveyor and explorer, Benjamin Anderson, who traveled in the northwest region. The features he portrayed probably existed prior to 1800.[150]

Anderson noted daily markets in Bopolu, Borkeza, Zolowo, Zigita, Zorzor and perhaps Fisabu. In addition, there were weekly markets in Zorzor (Thursday), Borkeza (Saturday), Zigita (Sunday), Popalahun (Monday?), Ziggah Porrah Zue (Sunday) and Kabawena (Monday). Other markets existed in "Comma's town, Kpandemai, Mbaloma and Belle Mbaloma, but Anderson did not note how often they met.[151]

Trade was mainly done by women. Farmers' wives sold most foodstuff, while the wives of other specialists traded palm oil, rice and smoked fish. Cotton cloth was sold only by men.[152]

According to Anderson, the Zorzor market was attended by about 6,000 people dressed in their finest. The women wore "blue and colored country clothes girded tastefully around their waists, their heads bound round with a large three-cornered handkerchief of the same material." Around their necks were strings of blue beads intermixed with brass buttons.[153]

"The hum of voices," Anderson noted, "could be heard in the distance like the noise of a waterfall." He described the markets as having "the character of holiday or pleasure-days."[154]

From earliest days, North Africa was known for its *souks*, narrow streets linked with shops. Cairo alone had 35 different markets, some specializing in silk, seafood or sour milk.[155]

In Arabia, *mausim* meant markets, as well as seasonal festivals. The largest fair in the Islamic world coincided with the annual hajj to Mecca.[156] Other periodic markets were held in neutral areas somewhere between districts that produced different goods. Some met as often as weekly, others as infrequently as once a year, often on the day set aside to honor a local saint[157]

Some cities grew up around markets. Those usually attracted a diverse range of goods in large quantities. Often, they were located at the crossroads of major trading routes.[158]

In Europe between 1400 and 1800, goods traveled from sellers to buyers along several well traded paths: At a basic level were markets for common goods, which were held often but not necessarily daily.[159]

Markets arose only when there were a large number of full-time artisans who no longer grew their own food.[160]

At another level were shops that opened daily. The first shops were operated by artisans who sold their own handicrafts out of a space in their workshops. Single-purpose shops developed later when traders began operating as middlemen between all kinds of sellers and buyers.[161]

These were the seeds of capitalism. As noted by historian Fernand Braudel, "the principal reason for the development of shops was credit."[162]

Filling the gap between markets and shops were peddlers. They carried goods from larger population centers to outlying villages. Their migrations followed the seasons. Many were "Jacks of all trade," but some specialized, such as book peddlers.

During times of peace and stability, peddlers often served as agents of shopkeepers. During times of war and crisis, they operated in league with smugglers.[163]

At the highest level of the economy were regional fairs. They were held seasonally, often once a year. These featured the rarest, most exotic goods, along with a sideshow of professional performers. As a result, fairs disrupted the settled rhythm of traditional societies and served as conduits for new ideas.[164]

Between 1500 and 1640, each market in England, Wales and Bavaria served about 7,000 persons. This number is a rough guide, not a law.[165]

In Asia, the Dutch inserted themselves into an extensive, existing trade network.[166] After 1713, British merchants were doing well enough they could afford to extend credit to foreign representatives. By this means, they were able to swamp South American markets with British cloth in return for silver.[167]

At the highest level of world trade, Europeans served largely as conduits for precious metal from territories in West Africa and the Americas to areas where they were most valued.[168]

How Europe Crawled Ahead of Africa

Evidence from around the world makes it clear that Europe remained roughly on par with the rest of world until at least the late 1700s. China was the one region with slightly better living standards.

In the judgment of at least one historian, China had the world's most advanced technology during this period.[169] For example, the Ming dynasty (1369-1644) had built the world's longest canal running from Beijing to southern China.[170]

China had invented the magnetic compass to guide travelers, but it was preoccupied with reclaiming vast tracks of frontier lands for rice farming. So, the Middle Kingdom was expanding inward as Europe was expanding beyond its borders.[171]

China had invented gunpowder, guns and canons, but it lacked incentives for improvements due to long periods of internal peace. In Europe, by contrast, constant wars between various countries led to steady advancements in armaments.[172]

Many factors contributed to Europe's rise. First, slightly better ships enabled Europeans to grab control of ocean travel and global trade. Second, better guns allowed them to seize key resources directly in the Americas and parts of Asia. They did so indirectly in Africa by supplying arms to slave catchers.[173]

Moreover, Europe repeatedly banned foreign imports to protect local producers. Time and time again, its governments provided subsidies, formed partnerships with businessmen, and passed laws to protect local economies.[174]

In addition, two hidden factors helped: fixed capital goods and the use of money to make money. Examples of fixed capital goods include roads, bridges and machines. These are durable items that can be inherited. They facilitate production and distribution of goods. Because such goods deteriorate, they must be repaired and even rebuilt from time to time.[175]

Between 1400 and 1820, fixed capital goods in West Africa consisted of footpaths, minimally cultivated kola trees, as well as workshops built from wood and clay and with palm-thatch roofs.

In addition, bridge-builders wove vines and fibers to create elaborate bridges. These structures eased the flow of goods through areas which, otherwise, would have been inaccessible.[176] But, these bridges, workshops and footpaths were short-lived.

Even farm land in the West African forest belt was fragile. Thus, it required frequent investments of labor in clearing new farms.

Clearing paths, building workshops and building bridges required less initial labor than the Great Wall of China or the dikes of Holland. But, they were made from less durable material, so labor had to be mobilized more frequently to repair and rebuild them. Such conditions allowed for little capital accumulation.

In addition, West Africa's weak system for moving goods blocked its economic growth. One exception was the fleet of fishing and trading canoes along the Malagueta Coast. The limited means of transportation was a hindrance to West Africa's prosperity, especially in the forest belt. Efficient transportation was important for more than the movement of goods. It was essential for learning quickly about prices. For merchants, knowledge of prices was a key source of power. It determined where goods were sent and when they were hoarded.[177]

Unfortunately, people in the forest belt had to perform a range of chores that were left to animals elsewhere. In contrast, Europe used 50 million workers (equal to 900,000 horse-power), wood (5 million horse-power), 14 million horses and 24 million oxen (10 horse-power), and waterwheels (two horse-power).[178]

Another factor contributed to Europe's rise: It systematically collected and centralized information and intelligence on all parts of the world. As noted by historian Jerry H. Bentley, "Europeans enjoyed asymmetric advantages in that they were able to compile a much more comprehensive body of global cultural knowledge than any other people."[179]

When Europe first encountered the rest of the world, commoners in West Africa actually had two clear advantages over their peers elsewhere: They had access to land and control over their own labor. This was the case even in the area now known as Ethiopia, where commoners differed sharply in power and wealth from the *Negus* (king) and the aristocracy. But, there, too, farmers retained rights to their lands.[180]

These advantages were rooted in local realities: Land was plentiful and labor was scarce. As a result, the most valued economic asset was human labor. In this context, a wealthy person was someone who controlled a large network of kin or clients. This wealth-in-people system favored patrons who could offer protection and material goods to a large number of clients.[181]

In many other parts of the world, however, poor farmers were serfs paying the rich for access to land and wild game.[182]

By the early 1800s, the table had turned: The poor in Europe were gaining both access to land and political freedom. On the other hand, commoners in Africa and descendants of Africa throughout the world had lost political and economic ground.[183]

Important, too, was control of trade. For centuries, trading was organized along two poles: the small-scale local markets (where profits were measured in pennies) and the wholesale international networks (that soaked profits from countless markets).

African traders have long operated at the level of markets while networks are controlled by non-Africans. Control of wholesale trade has shifted from Phoenicians, to Arabs, to Portuguese, to transnational corporations in North America and Europe.[184]

Furthermore, money in West Africa was hoarded or used mainly in ostentatious displays. Either way it was idle and stagnant.

In contrast, merchants in Europe and parts of Asia were reinvesting money to make more money.[185] They nurtured a network of money lenders who advanced funds in exchange for interest. According to historian Fernand Braudel,[186] these money markets fueled both economic growth in Europe and the rise of capitalism.

According to world-system analyst Immanuel Wallerstein, the factory system was unknown in Europe up to 1700.[187] Until then, European weapons were still mainly made in craft shops, not factories.[188] The scythe was not widely adopted for harvesting grain until the early 1800s.[189]

The face of Europe changed dramatically in the 1800s. Gas lighting came into use around 1808. In the 1800s, piped water became common in major cities and the number of waterwheels increased to about 550,000. European diets only began to improve significantly after 1850.[190]

European iron quality did not begin to rival China's or West Africa's until Europeans finally unravelled the secret of steelmaking in the 1800s. By 1840, Europe was producing up to 28,0000 tons and flooding markets around the world.[191]

In the 1830s, a fifth of British manufacturing (measured in value) was made up of cotton textiles. Using machines, English industrialists made cheap calicos in such quantities, they put Indian weavers out of business.[192]

In the 1800s, European merchants also began selling mostly their own products to the rest of the world for the first time. Before then, they acted mainly as middlemen — buying items from one region to sell in others.[193]

Over several centuries, Africans watched the terms of trade shift steadily, then dramatically in favor of Europeans. As a result, some assumed — in keeping with local beliefs — that the focus of this shifting power laid in "the white man's witch."[194]

In short, Europe's industrial takeoff dates to the 1800s.[195] That's when it crawled ahead of Africa in the 1800s. Its ascent was not the result of "witch," or racial superiority, or God's will. It resulted from seizing one opportunity, consolidating it and then building upon that to acquire others.

1. Gary B. Nash, "Foreward," in Richard S. Dunn, *Sugar & Slaves: The Rise of the Planter Class in the English West Indies: 1624-1713* (Chapel Hill: University of North Carolina Press, 1972), p. xix; Dunn, 1972, p. 278.
2. Dunn, 1972, pp. 283-284.
3. Dunn, 1972, p. 279.
4. Braudel, Vol. 1, 1981, p. 91; Margairaz, 2013, p. 208; Carole Shammas, "Standard of living, consumption, and political economy over the past 500 years" (pp. 211-228), in Frank Trentmann, ed., *The Oxford Handbook of the History of Consumption* (Oxford: Oxford University Press, 2013), especially p. 218.
5. Defourneaux, 1970, p. 100; Braudel, Vol. 1, 1981, p. 335.
6. Smith and Kelly, 2013, p. 483.
7. Margairaz, 2013, p. 208; Shammas, 2013, especially p. 218.
8. J. R. McNeil, "Biological exchanges in world history" (pp. 325-344), in Jerry H. Bentley, ed., *The Oxford Handbook of World History* (Oxford: Oxford University Press, 2013), p. 328.
9. McNeil, 2013, p. 330.
10. Ehret, 2013, p. 471.
11. Braudel, Vol. 2, 1982, pp. 134. Based on a comparison of China to Europe, Wallerstein (Vol. 1, 1974, pp. 62-63) concludes there was little difference between the two regions.
12. Braudel, Vol. 2, 1982, pp. 312-313.
13. Fernández-Armesto and Sacks, 2013, p. 139.
14. A. M. Behbehani, "The smallpox story: Life and death of an old disease," *Microbiology Review*, 1983, 47 (4): 455-507, especially pp. 464-465; Robin Walker, *West African Contributions to Science and Technology* (Reklaw Education, 2013), Locs. 62, 473-475, 598.
15. Niane, 1985, p. 64.
16. The description of Wappo is from Dapper, 1668, p. 581. Also see Berlin, 1998, pp. 18-19; Newitt, 2005, p. 46; Tertius Chandler and Gerald Fox, *Four Thousand Years of Urban Growth* (New York: Academic Press, 1974), p. 357.
17. Defourneaux, 1970, p. 82; Chandler and Fox, 1974, p. 357.
18. Hourani, 1991, p. 110; Chandler and Fox, 1974, p. 357.
19. Hourani, 1991, p. 110; Chandler and Fox, 1974, p. 357.
20. Hourani, 1991, p. 111; Chandler and Fox, 1974, p. 357.
21. Hourani, 1991, p. 111.
22. Braudel, Vol. 1, 1981, p. 548; Chandler and Fox, 1974, p. 358.
23. André Wink, "South Asia and Southeast Asia" (pp. 418-436), in Jerry H. Bentley, ed., *The Oxford Handbook of World History* (Oxford: Oxford University Press, 2013), p. 422.
24. Simon Parker, *Urban Theory and the Urban Experience: Encountering the City* (New York: Routledge, 2004).
25. Braudel, Vol. 1, 1981, pp. 60-61, 174-175.
26. Braudel, Vol. 1, 1981, pp. 60-61, 174-175.

27. Dominique Margairaz, "City and country: Home, possessions, and diet, Western Europe 1600-1800" (pp. 192-210), in Frank Trentmann, ed., *The Oxford Handbook of the History of Consumption* (Oxford: Oxford University Press, 2013), pp. 194; Defourneaux, 1970, p. 75.
28. Hourani, 1991, pp. 112-113.
29. Defourneaux, 1970, pp. 68, 87, 88, 103.
30. Defourneaux, 1970, p. 99.
31. "Hungry times" or famines are common in West African folktales. See Bascom, 1976, pp. 206-207; Dayrell, 1910, pp. 86-90; Frobenius, 1926, pp. 294-296. In one set of famine tales, Spider and an animal agree to sacrifice one family member each for the other to eat. The dupe fulfills his part of the contract only to find that Spider had reneged.
32. Braudel, Vol. 1, 1981, p. 74; Wallerstein, Vol. 1, 1974, pp. 258, 292.
33. Braudel, Vol. 3, 1984, p. 370; Braudel, Vol. 1, 1981, pp. 73-78.
34. Epstein, 1996, p. 320.
35. Braudel, Vol. 1, 1981, pp. 83-88.
36. Braudel, Vol. 1, 1981, pp. 83-88.
37. Braudel, Vol. 1, 1981, pp. 79-81.
38. McNeil, 2013, p. 333.
39. McNeil, 2013, p. 334.
40. Charles Tilly "States, state transformation, and war" (pp. 176-194), in Jerry H. Bentley, ed., *The Oxford Handbook of World History* (Oxford: Oxford University Press, 2013), p. 190.
41. Braudel, Vol. 1, 1981, pp. 334-337.
42. David E. Nye, "Consumption of energy" (pp. 307-325), in Frank Trentmann, ed., *The Oxford Handbook of the History of Consumption* (Oxford: Oxford University Press, 2013), especially p. 309.
43. Braudel, Vol. 1, 1981, pp. 336-337.
44. Braudel, Vol. 1, 1981, pp. 336-337.
45. Braudel, Vol. 1, 1981, pp. 336-337; Wallerstein, Vol. 1, 1974, p. 56.
46. Braudel, Vol. 1, 1981, pp. 336-337; Wallerstein, Vol. 1, 1974, p. 56.
47. Braudel, Vol. 1, 1981, pp. 334-337.
48. Clunas, 2013, pp. 71-72.
49. Braudel, Vol. 1, 1981, pp. 353-358; Mintz, 1985, p. 26.
50. Braudel, Vol. 1, 1981, pp. 353-355, 371.
51. Braudel, Vol. 1, 1981, pp. 358-359; Wallerstein, Vol. 2, 1980, p. 40.
52. Braudel, Vol. 1, 1981, pp. 368-371.
53. Braudel, Vol. 2, 1982, pp. 180-181.
54. Mintz, 1985, pp. 3, 13, 77.
55. Braudel, Vol. 1, 1981, pp. 104-109, 166-167; S. A. M. Adshead, *Material Culture in Europe and China, 1400-1800* (New York: St. Martin's Press, 1997). Adshead (p. 42) noted the importance of sorghum in China and Ethiopia, where it was first domesticated. But compared to the other grains, it was less widespread.
56. Braudel, Vol. 1, 1981, pp. 145-146, 152.
57. Braudel, Vol. 1, 1981, pp. 145-146, 154.
58. Braudel, Vol. 1, 1981, pp. 108-117, 120.
59. Braudel, Vol. 1, 1981, pp. 108-117, 120.
60. Braudel, Vol. 1, 1981, pp. 130, 137; Margairaz, 2013, p. 207.
61. Braudel, Vol. 1, 1981, p. 161.

62. Braudel, Vol. 1, 1981, pp. 104-109, 166-167. According to Wallerstein (Vol. 1, 1974, p. 56), meat consumption declined in Europe between 1500 and 1800.
63. Atkins, 1735, p. 68; Barbot, 1732, p. 109, 113, 132, 138; Villault, 1745-47, p. 383; Bosman, 1705.
64. Braudel, Vol. 1, 1981, pp. 104-109, 166-167; Marcelin Defourneaux, *Daily Life in Spain in the Golden Age* (New York: Praeger, 1970), pp. 64, 82.
65. Hourani, 1991, p. 127.
66. Defourneaux, 1970, pp. 64, 82.
67. Braudel, Vol. 1, 1981, pp. 190, 194-198, 201; Margairaz, 2013, p. 208. For the impoverishment of poor Europeans between 1660 to 1750, see Wallerstein, Vol. 2, 1980, pp. 88-90.
68. Defourneaux, 1970, p. 65; Mintz, 1985, p. 81. A claim made by some sources that pepper was used to disguise the taste of tainted meat is disputed by Fernández-Armesto and Sacks, 2013, p. 134.
69. Braudel, Vol. 1, 1981, pp. 190, 194-198, 201. For the impoverishment of poor Europeans betweenn 1660 to 1750, see Wallerstein, Vol. 2, 1980, pp. 88-90.
70. Braudel, Vol. 1, 1981, pp. 190, 194-198, 201-202, 210, 211-212; Margairaz, 2013, p. 208.
71. Braudel, Vol. 1, 1981, pp. 199, 201, 214.
72. Braudel, Vol. 1, 1981, pp. 215-220.
73. Braudel, Vol. 1, 1981, pp. 215-220. According to Margairaz (2013, p. 208), fish was rare away from the coast.
74. Villault, 1670, p. 62.
75. Villault, 1670, p. 94.
76. Bosman, 1967, pp. 474, 472.
77. Dunn, 1972, pp. 282-283.
78. Margairaz, 2013, pp. 205-206.
79. Adshead, 1997, p. 74.
80. Braudel, Vol. 1, 1981, pp. 285-288, 290-293.
81. Hourani, 1991, pp. 109, 127.
82. Hourani, 1991, p. 127.
83. Hourani, 1991, p. 127.
84. Braudel, Vol. 1, 1981, p. 288.
85. Craig Clunas, "Things in between: Splendor and excess in Ming China" (pp. 47-63), in Frank Trentmann, ed., *The Oxford Handbook of the History of Consumption* (Oxford: Oxford University Press, 2013), especially p. 50; Hourani, 1991, p. 111.
86. Clunas, 2013, p. 50.
87. Braudel, Vol. 1, 1981, pp. 183-187, 206, 208; Defourneaux, 1970, pp. 96, 103; Margairaz, 2013, p. 199. Many items now common were rare luxuries. These include china dishes, tea sets, coffee pots, umbrellas, dining forks and spoons, as well as glass window panes.
88. Braudel, Vol. 1, 1981, pp. 266-282.
89. Margairaz, 2013, pp. 195-196.
90. Braudel, Vol. 1, 1981, pp. 266-278, 297-299, 305.
91. Bosman, 1967, pp. 475-476.
92. Hair, Jones and Law, 1992, Letter 29, pp. 265, 271-272. Barbot erroneously identified the predatory animals as "tigers," which did exist in this region.
93. Brooks, 1985, p. 5.
94. Wink, 2013, p. 423.
95. Hourani, 1991, pp. 109, 126-127.
96. Adshead, 1997, p. 121.

97. Braudel, Vol. 1, 1981, pp. 266-282.
98. Defourneaux, 1970, p. 46.
99. Braudel, Vol. 1, 1981, p. 268.
100. Margairaz, 2013, pp. 195-196.
101. Margairaz, 2013, p. 195.
102. Hounari, 1991, p. 113.
103. Braudel, Vol. 1, 1981, pp. 280, 308.
104. Richard Jobson, "A description of Guinea," in Samuel Purchas, *Puchas His Pilgrimes*, 5 Vols. (London: Henrie Fetherstone, 1625), p. 265.
105. Villault, 1670, p. 62.
106. Bosman, 1967, pp. 478-479.
107. Bosman, 1967, pp. 485-486.
108. Hair, Jones and Law, 1992, Letter 29, pp. 270, 272.
109. Bosman, 1967, pp. 472-473.
110. Bosman, 1967, pp. 476-477.
111. Bosman, 1967, p. 474.
112. Defourneaux, 1970, p. 77. For example, voyages to Caribbean usually took three to six months.
113. Esptein, 1996, p. 283.
114. Defourneaux, 1970, pp. 223-225.
115. Braudel, Vol. 1, 1981, p. 329; Hourani, 1991, p. 120; Virginia Smith, *Clean: A History of Personal Hygiene and Purity* (New York: Oxford University Press, 2007), pp. 102-124, especially p. 124.
116. Braudel, Vol. 1, 1981, pp. 228-229.
117. Dunn, 1972, pp. 282-293.
118. Braudel, Vol. 1, 1981, p. 329; Smith, 2007, p. 199.
119. Braudel, Vol. 1, 1981, pp. 415, 425.
120. Atkins, 1735, p. 59.
121. Green, 1745-47, p. 179-180, 382; Barbot, 1732, p. 131.
122. Wink, 2013, pp. 430-431.
123. Braudel, Vol. 2, 1982, pp. 361-369.
124. Wolf, 1982, p. 85.
125. Braudel, Vol. 1, 1981, pp. 415, 425.
126. Braudel, Vol. 2, 1982, pp. 180-181.
127. Braudel, Vol. 2, 1982, pp. 297-300.
128. Towerson, 1824, pp. 246-257 (iron); Villault, 1670, p. 64 (canoes); Hair, Jones and Law, 1992, Letter 30, pp. 288, 292 (handicrafts); Barbot, 1732, pp. 106, 138 (canoes);. Adams, 1823, p. 90 (canoes); Bosman, 1705, pp. 469-493 (salt-making); Green, 1745-47, pp. 380, 523 (soaps); Periera, 1937, pp. 97-114; Blake, 1941-42, pp. 270, 316, 330, 367, 372, 393-95 (soaps).
129. Dunn, 2012, p. 291; Wallerstein, Vol. 1, 1974, p. 39; Masonen, 2000, p. 123, n. 1.
130. Rodney, 1980, pp. 152, 168, 170, 181-183.
131. For the role of Loma blacksmiths in making "Kissi money," see White, April 1974, p. 12. d'Azevedo (1959, p. 59) dates the spread of Kissi money to the period of slave trading.
132. Walker, 2013, locs. 416-417.
133. Braudel, Vol. 1, 1981, pp. 373-375; Headrick, 2013, p. 236.
134. Headrick, 2013, p. 236.
135. Braudel, Vol. 1, 1981, p. 381.
136. Braudel, Vol. 1, 1981, p. 379.

137. Wallerstein, Vol. 2, 1980, pp. 40-46.
138. Curtin, 1995, pp. 198-199; also Vos, 2010, pp. 32, 38, 45.
139. Burrowes, 1986, pp. 25-44, especially p. 37.
140. Burrowes, 1986, pp. 25-44.
141. Rodney, 1980, p. 193; Davis, 1976, p. 2.
142. Bosman, 1967, pp. 480-481.
143. Barbot, 1732, p. 122.
144. Stanley B. Alpern, "What Africans got for their slaves: A master list of European trade goods, *History in Africa*, Vol. 22 (1995), pp. 5-43; Marion Johnson, "The Atlantic slave trade and the economy of West Africa," in Roger Anstey and P. E. H. Hair, *Liverpool, the African Slave Trade, and Abolition* (Bristol: Historical Society of Lancashire and Cheshire, 1976), pp. 14-38.
145. Braudel, Vol. 1, 1981, p. 393.
146. Atkins, 1735, p. 67; also Barbot, 1732, p. 122; Sundstrom, 1974, pp. 66-116.
147. Braudel, Vol. 1, 1981, pp. 393, 442; Marcy Norton, *Sacred Gifts, Profane Pleasures: A History of Tobacco and Chocolate in the Atlantic World* (Ithaca: Cornell University Press, 2010), pp. 1, 64.
148. Braudel, Vol. 1, 1981, pp. 440-442, 450.
149. Braudel, Vol. 1, 1981, pp. 440-442, 450.
150. Benjamin J. K. Anderson, *A Journey to Musardu* (New York, 1870; reprint London: Frank Cass and Co., 1971); W. Penn Handwerker, "Market places, traveling traders, and shops: Commercial structural variation in the Liberian interior prior to 1940," *African Economic History*, No. 9 (1980): 3-26.
151. Anderson, 1870, pp. 7, 53, 64-67, 77-79.
152. Anderson, 1870, pp. 44, 54-55.
153. Anderson, 1870, pp. 54-55.
154. Anderson, 1870, pp. 54-55.
155. Braudel, Vol. 2, 1982, pp. 114-115.
156. Braudel, Vol. 2, 1982, pp. 127-127.
157. Hourani, 1991, p. 109.
158. Hourani, 1991, p. 110.
159. Braudel, Vol. 2, 1981, pp. 54-94.
160. Braudel, Vol. 2, 1981, pp. 54-94.
161. Braudel, Vol. 2, 1981, pp. 54-94, especially p. 73.
162. Braudel, Vol. 2, 1981, pp. 54-94, especially p. 73.
163. Braudel, Vol. 2, 1981, pp. 54-94.
164. Braudel, Vol. 2, 1982, pp. 54-94.
165. Braudel, Vol. 2, 1982, pp. 42-43. The Bopolu market in the Liberia area in mid-1800s fit Braudel's parameter. According to Anderson (1870, p. 39), it served a region with about 10,000 people.
166. Braudel, Vol. 2, 1982, p. 121.
167. Braudel, Vol. 2, 1982, p. 175.
168. Braudel, Vol. 1, 1981, pp. 458-463; Wallerstein, Vol. 2, 1980, pp. 106, 114.
169. Headrick, 2013, p. 236.
170. Headrick, 2013, p. 236.
171. Wallerstein, Vol. 1, 1974, p. 57; Headrick, 2013, p. 236.
172. Wallerstein, Vol. 1, 1974, p. 60-61; Daniel R. Headrick, "Technology, engineering, and science" (pp. 229-245), in Jerry H. Bentley, ed., *The Oxford Handbook of World History* (Oxford: Oxford University Press, 2013), p. 236.

[173]. Moseley, 1992, p. 538.
[174]. Braudel, Vol. 2, 1982, p. 449-451; Vilar, 1984, pp. 57-58; Mintz, 1985, pp. 34, 41; Wilks, 1961, p. 32; Wallerstein, Vol. 1, 1974, pp. 250-255; Norton, 2010, p. 155 (tobacco monopoly in Spain).
[175]. Braudel, Vol. 2, 1982, pp. 242-243. According to Braudel (p. 242), "the industrial revolution was above all a transformation of fixed capital."
[176]. C. S. Finch, "The African background to medical science," in I. Van Sertima, ed., *Blacks in Science* (New Brunswick, NJ: Transaction Books, 1984); Barbot, 1732, pp. 119, 135.
[177]. Braudel, Vol. 2, 1982, pp. 349-357, 412-416.
[178]. Braudel, Vol. 1, 1981, p. 371.
[179]. Jerry H. Bentley, "Cultural exchanges in world history" (pp. 343-360), in Jerry H. Bentley, ed., *The Oxford Handbook of World History* (Oxford: Oxford University Press, 2013), p. 355.
[180]. Ehret, 2013, p. 465.
[181]. Jeremy Prestholdt, "Africa and the global life of things" (pp. 85-110), in Frank Trentmann, ed., *The Oxford Handbook of the History of Consumption* (Oxford: Oxford University Press, 2013), pp. 86-87; Ballah, 1955, p. 14.
[182]. Defourneaux, 1970, p. 103.
[183]. Meillassoux, 1982, pp. 98-99.
[184]. Braudel, Vol. 2, 1982, pp. 228-230.
[185]. Braudel, Vol. 2, 1982, pp. 248-249.
[186]. Braudel, Vol. 2, 1982, p. 51.
[187]. Wallerstein, Vol. 1, 1974, p. 225.
[188]. Braudel, Vol. 1, 1981, p. 393.
[189]. Defourneaux, 1970, p. 100; Braudel, Vol. 1, 1981, p. 335.
[190]. Braudel, Vol. 1, 1981, pp.190, 194-198, 201-202, 210, 211-212, 228-229, 310-311, 313, 315, 353-358.
[191]. Braudel, Vol. 1, 1981, pp. 381-382, 386.
[192]. Parthasarathi and Riello, 2013, p. 146; Braudel, Vol. 1, 1981, p. 327.
[193]. Smith and Kelly, 2013, p. 484.
[194]. Daniel Coker, *Journal of Daniel Coker, A Descendant of Africa* (Baltimore: Edward J. Coale, 1820); Mary Antoinette (Grimes) Brown, Education and National Development in Liberia, 1800-1900. Ph. D. dissertation, Cornell University, 1967, pp. 107, 119; John d'Amico, Spiritual and secular activities of the Methodist Episcopal Church in Liberia, 1873-1933. Ph. D. dissertation, St. John's University, 1977, p. 120; Mecal Sobel, *Trabelin' On: The Slave Journey to an Afro-Baptist Faith* (Princeton: Princeton University Press, 1988), pp. 58-75, especially p. 67.
[195]. Wallerstein, Vol. 1, 1974, p. 225.

Chapter 14
A New World Order

> Fundamentalism "in its different transformations — ethnic, cultural, or religious — is one of the most dangerous phenomena of our age"
> — Anthropologist Jean-Loup Amselle

Liberians today often divide themselves from each other on the basis of "cultural differences." In doing so, they usually assume that each culture is unique, shares little in common with others, and never changes.

In truth, culture is like water, it freezes in times of cold, melts in heat, and shifts course as it flows from one generation to the next. Creeks and streams often are only temporarily separate before merging into a mighty river.

But, changes in traditions only become visible when viewed overtime. The light of history shows that many cultures embraced by Liberians today emerged in the 1600s or even later. From "African" fabrics commonly called "Fanti cloth" to our beloved *domboy*, many key features are not "indigenous." They emerged from the encounter of West Africa with Europe and the rest of the world.

By 1600, for example, many of the rulers and leading traders along the coast of what is now Liberia bore European names and spoke a smattering of European languages. Based on the influence of Portuguese Jesuit missionaries based in Sierra Leone, a local ruler named *Ferabure* converted to Catholicism and took the name Philip. Those changes are not surprising given European-African interactions dating back to the mid-1400s.

During a visit in 1667, French nobleman Nicolas Villault claimed that everyone he encountered bore a European saint's name. To learn why, he offered one of the local men an alcoholic drink, which he added, "they love better then their Wives." His informant explained, "when any Vessels passed that way, and did the Natives any kindness, it was usual to begg their Names at their departure. They gave those names afterwards to their children, in memory of the courtesie they had received." The man then requested Villault's name to bestow on his next child, in case his very pregnant wife had a son.[1]

By the late 1600s, according to Jean Barbot, some Cape Mesurado residents could "explain themselves in Dutch and some in Portuguese, mixed with French." At Sestros, some residents reportedly spoke "a little Dutch or English."[2]

Barbot also noted two traders near the St. Paul River who adopted the names Philips and Shirley from two English captains with whom they traded. Around this time, a broker at Cestos River bore the name Jacob. He was succeeded by another called Captain Richard Lumley, a name adopted from an English trader. The ruler of a town several miles up river came to be known as King Peter, a name given by Dutch traders.

English slave trader John Newton noted several leaders with English names along the Liberian coast in the early 1750s: At Cape Mount, there were four: Peter Williams, King Cole, Peter and George. Between the St. Paul and Junk rivers, the main broker was Peter Freeman. At Junk, there was Andrew Ross.

Living in Liverpool, a village at the mouth of the St. Paul, were William Grey, William Purcell, Tom Bristol and John Will. Between Grand Bassa and Tabocaney, there were Yellow Will, Jonathan Gray and William Freeman. Little Bassa had Will Adams. And at Little Sestos there was Ben Johnson.[3]

As Dutch slave buying increased along the coast in the late 1700s, so did the use of Dutch names by some of their African partners: There were Claesz and Pietersz, two leading men at River Cess in December 1678. Jan Vrijman (John Freeman) was the name of one local man at Grand Bassa in 1791.[4]

At Sestros in 1688, Barbot noted that a number of children bore European names, "At least the names of those whites who visit there and treat them best. Hence some are called Pieter, some Claes, some Jan, Domingo, Antonio, Jacomo, etc."[5]

From the Sanguin River to Cape Palmas, however, the use of European pidgin was apparently not yet common in 1667. At that time, French nobleman Nicolas Villault reported that he and his men had to communicate through hand gestures. Nonetheless, the author went on to claim — in the interest obviously of exciting French engagement — that inhabitants spoke French more "intelligibly" than any other European language.[6]

By the early 1700s, Portuguese seems to have functioned as a *lingua franca* (meaning, a trade language). It was the basis through which African and European traders conducted transactions.[7]

Over time, local languages even incorporated words from Portuguese. These include Mandinka *coolear* from "colher" (spoon), Mende *fanye* from "farinha" (meal, flour), and Gola *patâ* from "prata" (silver). Vai also has traces of Portuguese (such as *páwa* from "paga" for wages) and French (for example, *koto* from "le couteau" for knife).[8]

Elephants and Leopards

A local creature that had been the subject of mystery and romance since the days of Pedro de Sintra was the elephant. The beast had once been so plentiful that an entire region of West Africa was named the "Ivory Coast."[9]

Until the early 1600s, people at Cape Mount and Cape Mesurado conducted a brisk trade in ivory.[10]

By 1687, only the Malagueta Coast was rich in tusks. French trader Jean Barbot, who had made repeated visits to West Africa, noted that the supply of ivory had dried up at River Sestro and Sanguin to the west. At Cape Mount, too, it was "so much exhausted, that very often there are few or none at all." He credited this to the "concourse of Europeans to traffick here."[11]

The elephant stock had been significantly reduced due to foreign demand for elephant tusks. During that period, ivory was used for tool handles, billiard balls, ornate drinking cups, and other luxury items. Another factor was local access to increasingly more powerful European and American weapons.

Leopards had also been more numerous. Locally, their skin and claws were reserved for traditional rulers. Their meat was not widely consumed locally (probably because these animals sometimes ate human flesh). Leopards, too, were decimated due to such external factors as imported firepower and a foreign market for exotic hides.

From Calicos and Batiks to "African" Fabrics

Europeans brought about local changes not only with goods they made but also with items they imported to West Africa from elsewhere in the world.

For example, a key item of world trade was cotton cloth. European merchants bought cotton textiles from producers throughout the world, including West Africa and Egypt, but especially India. When dyed deep blue with indigo, cotton fabrics had a "particular smell and feel that appealed to buyers around the world."[12]

In West Africa, cotton cloth was more than functional. It was so woven into Mande culture, it played a role in diplomacy. Before a military offensive, the attacker would send two items to the people being targeted: a strip of cotton cloth and a weapon. If the textile was returned, it symbolized a desire for peace.[13]

In Europe, Indian cotton cloth came to be called "calico." Some calicos were sold in Europe, which did not grow cotton. These imports were superior to locally made cloths. The colors were more vibrant and long-lasting; the material was also softer on the skin than linen and wool.[14]

The cloth trade drastically changed in the 1600s when the Dutch seized control of the Java section of Indonesia. They then began exporting Javanese *batik* fabric with symbolic images, which proved more popular with Africans than European textiles.[15]

The patterns printed on Asian cloths were multicultural like the societies that produced them. There were crowned snakes for female fertility from Hindu mythology, a dagger point or broken blade design called *parang rusak* worn by Djakarta royal men, the Chinese mythical snail, and Islamic-influenced geometric shapes.[16]

Although West Africans produced cotton "country cloth," they still bought

Asian cottons from European merchants. Those fabrics had been popular with Africans from as early perhaps as the 1100s based on their bright colors, low prices and high quality. But, Europeans increased the *quantity* of those textiles in local markets, thanks to their large ships.[17]

The African market for calico was critical to producers both in England and France. Imported cottons were key items exchanged for enslaved Africans. This exchange doubly undermined African self-sufficiency: First, it removed productive laborers, including (very likely) some growers and weavers of cotton. Second, it undercut the sale of local cloths.[18]

In Europe, cotton was quickly adopted for beddings and under clothes. It grew wildly popular, especially around the 1690s. But, it had to be replaced often because it was short-lived.[19]

Overtime, the "calico craze" provoked a backlash from European producers of silks, linens and wools.[20]

In the late 1600s, London businessmen began making and printing cheap imitation calicos locally. In 1720, one calico-printing factory alone employed over 200 workers. But, Indian calicos were still being imported in large quantities from India.[21]

Not content with serving as middle-men in the trade between Java and Africa, the Dutch began manufacturing imitation *batiks* with designs for the African market, in place of the handcrafted originals. In this context, the so-called African print fabrics emerged that are now used as *lappas* or *rappas* in West and Central Africa.[22]

"Fanti cloths" (as they are known in Liberia) are manufactured today by multinational companies headquartered mainly in Holland and Britain. As explained by Tunde M. Akinwumi, these fabrics are "machine-printed using wax resins and dyes in order to achieve batik effect on both sides of the cloth." They are marketed under names like Real English wax, Veritable Java Print and Guaranteed Dutch Java Hollandis.[23]

Brazil's Gifts of Domboy and Gbassajamba

What we eat is often a key marker of whether we "belong" to a group.[24] For this reason, it is remarkable that many ingredients of local cuisines were adopted from thousands of miles away.

Plantains, bananas and oranges – all originally from Asia – were among the non-indigenous plants widely adopted in West Africa by the early 1600s.[25]

In addition, European merchants introduced other crops from far-flung corners of the globe. In the process, they created new markets and new appetites. That process is best illustrated by looking a few foods, drinks and spices.

Many New World crops reached the rest of the world for the first time, thanks to European voyages. These included maize (corn), potato, cassava, tomatoes, cacao, peanut, sweet potato, pumpkin, squash and pineapple.[26]

In exchange, the Americas received millet, okra, watermelon and yam from Africa. The New World also received barley, rye wheat and rice, both Asian and African.[27]

By the late 1600s, several New World crops were growing freely in the area of Liberia, including pineapples.[28] But, in some cases, the adopted items were less nutritious than locally available ones.

In 1666, maize was said to be "plentiful" at Cape Mount. It had apparently been present for sometime because it already had a local name, *magzi-jonglo*.[29] According to French nobleman Nicolas Villault, residents made bread from maize.[30] If true, this culinary feature disappeared overtime.

Although the list of available foods included several that had been brought from the New World, conspicuously absent during this period was cassava. That root crop from Brazil is now deeply embedded in coastal cuisines in the area of Liberia.[31]

The stem of this shrub is multiple jointed and grows to eight feet in height. The numerous branches are lined with leaves that divide into three, five or seven lobes.

The roots grow to eighteen inches long and eight inches wide. They are ready to be harvested in nine months. They are sometimes roasted in the coarse rough skin or boiled after peeling.[32]

Cassava made possible two key ingredients of local cuisines: One is *gbassajamba*, the Vai name for a sauce made from the leaves of the plant. The leaves are eaten after being pounded in a mortar and cooked in palm oil with meats, fish and seasonings. The other is *domboy*, the Bassa name for a glutinous entreé made from the pounded root.[33]

Cassava entered West African diets in the 1700s. Together with maize, it enabled a "veritable agricultural revolution." The addition of these two plants fueled a population boom. That meant more captives for the trans-Atlantic slave trade.[34]

Maize in particular allowed rulers to "maximize their power by centralizing the storage and distribution of food." This was possible because maize kept its value when dried better than yam, millets and sorghums.[35]

Also imported into coastal Liberian cuisines as a result of the European trade were dried cod and smoked herring (commonly called "smoked fish" in Liberia). European sailors were the main missionaries of codfish and other foreign foods that became entrenched in local diets. During that period, they subsisted on dried meat, salt fish, hardtack biscuits, oil and wine.[36]

Because people everywhere resist changing their diets, these new foods were adopted usually during emergencies, like famines. For example, sweet potato was adopted in China and Japan in the 1500s after a period of famine. White potato (sometimes called "Irish" potato) was adopted in Europe as a ration for armies during times of war. Soldiers then spread it unintentionally across that continent.[37]

From Palmwine to Brandy and Rum

When Europeans first arrived along the Windward Coast, the common alcoholic drink was palm wine.[38] In the 1600s, Europeans cultivated local markets for strong liquors by offering them first as "dash" (meaning, a present or bribe) to local rulers. By the 1700s, large quantities of both French brandy and rum from the New World were being exchanged for local captives.

In Arabia, drinking alcohol is forbidden by the Qu'ran, but many Muslims drank wine and strong liquors imported from Europe.[39]

In Europe until the 1700s, poor people mainly drank one of two weak alcoholic drinks. If they lived in the northern region, it was beer, made mainly from wheat, oats, barley, rye or millet. Brewers began adding hops as a preservative from the 1300s.[40]

Wine, on the other hand, was consumed mostly along the Mediterranean, where grapes were grown. At first, it could not be safely carried far due to a lack of air-tight containers. Until the 1700s, wine was commonly transported in wooden barrels. But, air often seeped in, turning the precious drink into vinegar. Whatever little wine survived the journey to England and northern Europe was drunk by the wealthy.[41]

Wine only became widely exported in the 1700s, after glass bottles became commonplace. Improved storage techniques led for the first time to vintage wines, like champagne. They also led to more local public drunkenness[42] and more exports.

By the 1500s, Europeans began distilling strong liquors from various crops. France specialized in turning grapes into brandy. In northern Europe, grains were distilled to produce gin, whiskey and vodka. In the West Indies, sugar cane juice was turned into rum. All of these were heavily exported to Africa and other regions.[43]

In return for brandy, rum and other liquors, Europe received three stimulants from abroad: tea, coffee and tobacco. Their use was first adopted in places where people gathered. In Europe, common sites were barbershops, taverns and, later, coffee shops.[44] In West Africa, smokers often sat together in palava huts.

When Europeans arrived in the New World, cocoa seeds served as currency in the "Chocolate Zone," from present-day Mexico through Nicaragua and Costa Rica. Chocolate (made from cocoa seeds) was the first stimulant drink adopted by Europeans from the wider world.[45]

The use of chocolate and tobacco seeped into Europe's bloodstream in the 1600s, through Madrid, the beating heart of the Spanish empire. From there, they easily pulsed through the veins of the global trade network to the far corners of the world. They were spread mainly by sailors, merchants, missionaries and colonial officials who had lived in the Americas.[46]

Tea had been enjoyed in China since 600 BC. Some had trickled into Southern Europe over time. But, the first major shipment arrived in Holland in 1610. By 1710, Canton alone was exporting 15 million pounds to Europe.[47]

Coffee was discovered in Ethiopia, where a daily coffee ritual is embedded in the culture. It reached Europe around 1615 through Arabia. Consumption spread so rapidly, Europeans began growing coffee on plantations they controlled: Java in 1712; Martinique, 1723; Jamaica, 1730; and Santo Domingo, 1731.[48]

Even more successful worldwide than tea and coffee was tobacco because it is addictive. It was used in three forms — smoke, snuff and chew.[49] First brought to Europe's attention by Columbus, it was being cultivated in Spain by 1558. As with coffee, Europeans quickly began growing tobacco on their own plantations: Virginia in 1588; Macao after 1600; Java in 1601; then India and Ceylon after 1605.[50]

New tobacco smokers, whether in Europe or elsewhere, adopted more than the leaf of the plant. They acquired pipes and other items related to its use.[51] Tobacco-smokers in West Africa initially used cheap clay pipes that were imported from England, Wales, Scotland, North America and the Caribbean.[52]

Tobacco already had a presence along the Windward Coast by 1678, when the ruler of River Cess was described as hunched on his heels, smoking a pipe with the bowl resting on the ground.[53]

As Europeans began drinking tea, coffee, chocolate and sugar, they drank less beer and wine. They also worked longer and produced more.[54]

In today's world, *caffeine* (found in coffee) is the most widely used psychoactive substance, and *nicotine* from tobacco is third. Chocolate is rich in *theobromine*, a relative of the drug *caffeine*.[55]

Local Impact of the Slave Trade

The trade in rum, tobacco and arms was driven by an expanding reliance on forced labor in the New World – with violent fallout for local societies.[56]

The routines of everyday life were disrupted, replaced by generalized suspicion, distrust of each other, and obsessive precautions against kidnappers and slave raiders.

At the height of the slave trade, each principle town had three to eight satellite villages within a five-mile radius. These were usually manned by slaves, some awaiting sale to trans-Atlantic buyers. Those villages served as defensive outposts as well as sources of supplementary food. The forest trees surrounding each cluster of villages were usually felled for about a quarter mile all around to make it difficult for invaders.[57]

By the early 1800s, the Windward Coast was dotted with "war towns." These were settlements rigged by hard-wood stockades and encircled by stake-filled ditches. A few such stockades remained standing well into the 1900s. They were called *Gono* in Vai, *Nwo Gohn* in Gola and *Gbohn* in Dei.[58]

Within Africa, there developed a traffick in women and girls, probably measuring in millions. They had been seized in raids but were not as desired in the slave marts of the Americas as boys and men. Most captured women were sold to African buyers who took them far from their homes. They ended up living among people whose language and culture differed from their own.[59]

Involvement in slave-trading enriched some groups, like the Asante along the Gold Coast. Expansion of the Asante Empire caused a series of migrations in waves: The Brong were pushed west, causing the Anyi and Baule to move west. In turn, they squeezed other, small communities from Cote d'Ivoire into present-day Liberia.

As this trade mounted over the course of centuries, rival claims to political offices came to be settled on the basis of imported prestige goods and superior weapons. Disadvantaged in this process were low-status individuals and land-locked ethnic groups that did not have access to European and American suppliers.[60]

Within the area known as Liberia the traffick in humans deepened divisions *between* various communities. Interior ethnic groups were preyed upon from two directions at the same time. Both kidnappers on the coast as well as raiders in the north had access to foreign arms.

Communities that suffered big losses were the Gola, Dei, Mende, Bandi, Loma, Kpelle, Ma and Dan. As a result, the Dan continue to be called "Gio" (slaves) by their neighbors and viewed as social inferiors by some. So many Gola-speakers were taken to South Carolina and Mende to Jamaica that words from their languages remain in use in those two areas.[61]

Within communities, the slave trade widened the gulf between free and unfree persons. It expanded the local pool of servile laborers.[62]

Gola customary law, for example, allowed men to be sold into slavery, if accused of adultery by the wives of rich and influential compatriots.[63] Given polygyny, however, most pubescent women were married to rich and influential men. So, the letter of the law was quite easy to satisfy.

Even the Sande school did not remain untainted. According to Gola traditional history, a local ruler, Zolu Duma, once enticed an entire graduating class of girls onto a slave ship to dance for the crew. Unknown to the girls and their parents, he had pre-sold the entire shipload of adolescents to the captain.[64]

Some coastal Kru and Grebo were willing to enslave their kinsmen living inland, whom they referred to disparagingly as "bushmen."

For over three centuries, the widespread and injurious trade deeply scarred the societies along this coast. On the one hand, the common people (especially in the interior) were victimized by the trade. On the other hand, rulers (particularly on the coast) grew dependent on it for the guns and jewelry that ensured their prestige.

A French cartographer and navigator who visited the region several times between 1704 and 1727 noted that people all along the coast of what is now Liberia had "learnt of the Europeans to be fond of what comes from aboard, and to slight what they have at home."[65]

In the 300 years since then, the taste of local people for all things foreign has deepened, not lessened. It extends from a mass market for imported used clothes – known locally as *dokafleh* – to the replacement of local civil society groups by Western non-governmental organizations. That appetite continues to fuel a system of growth (defined as rising spending on consumer goods and services) without development (meaning, technological advancement tied to agricultural self-sufficiency).

1. Alvares, 1990, p. 2; Villault, 1670, pp. 80-81.
2. Hair, Jones and Law, 1992, pp. 240, 273.
3. Vos, 2012, pp. 13-14; Atkins, 1735, pp. 58-59; Phillips, 1746, pp. 210-211; Hair, Jones and Law, 1992, pp. 270, 273-274; Bernard Martin and Mark Spurrell, *Journal of a Slave Trader* London: Epworth Press, 1962], pp. 28-92.
4. Hair, Jones and Law, 1992, p. 278 n. 1; Vos, 2012, p. 14.
5. Hair, Jones and Law, 1992, Letter 29, p. 275.
6. Villault, 1670, pp. 94, 97.
7. Willis, 1967, pp. xvii-xviii.
8. Bradshaw, 1965, pp. 5-37.
9. e.g., Lok, 1824, pp. 236-242.
10. Brun, 1983, pp. 74-75, n. 185; Bosman, 1967, pp. 476-477.
11. Hair, Jones and Law, 1992, Letter 30, pp. 288, 292; Bosman, 1967, pp. 478-479. Around 1701, Willem Bosman found no ivory around River Cess.
12. Prasannan Parthasarathi and Giorgio Riello, "From India to the world: Cotton and fashionability" (pp. 145-172), in Frank Trentmann, ed., *The Oxford Handbook of the History of Consumption* (Oxford: Oxford University Press, 2013), pp. 147, 157, 159.
13. Almada, 2010, pp. 130-134.
14. Parthasarathi and Riello, 2013, pp. 157-159.
15. Tunde M. Akinwumi, "The 'African Print' hoax: Machine produced textiles jeopardize African print authenticity," *The Journal of Pan-African Studies*, Vol. 2, No. 5 (July 2008): 179-192; Parthasarathi and Riello, 2013, p. 155.
16. Akinwumi, 2008, pp. 179-192; Parthasarathi and Riello, 2013, p. 155.
17. Parthasarathi and Riello, 2013, p. 150; Christopher B. Steiner, "Another image of Africa: Toward an ethnohistory of European cloth marketed in West Africa, 1873-1960," *Ethnohistory*, Vol. 32, No. 2 (1985): 91-110.
18. Parthasarathi and Riello, 2013, pp. 161-162.
19. Parthasarathi and Riello, 2013, pp. 157-159.
20. Defourneaux, 1970, pp. 76, 92; Parthasarathi and Riello, 2013, p. 158.
21. Clunas, 2013, p. 82.

22. Parthasarathi and Riello, 2013, p. 145-172; Clunas, 2013, p. 82; Akinwumi, 2008, pp. 179-192; Steiner, 1985, pp. 91-92.
23. Akinwumi, 2008, pp. 179-192; Steiner, 1985, pp. 91-110.
24. Mintz, 1985, pp. 3, 13.
25. McNeil, 2013, p. 332; also Villault, 1670, pp. 61-62, 96; Barbot, 1732, pp. 109, 113; Smith, 1744, p. 109; Bosman, 1967, p. 473.
26. McNeill, 2013, pp. 335-336.
27. McNeill, 2013, pp. 335-336.
28. McNeill, 2013, p. 334; e.g., Bosman, 1967, p. 473
29. Hair, 1964, p. 134. The word *magzi-jonglo* was apparently a combination of "maize" and *jonglo* (the Vai word for "grain").
30. Villault, 1670, pp. 61-62.
31. Lugenbeel, 1853, p. 14; McNeill, 2013, pp. 331, 337.
32. In the 1800s, the name was sometimes spelled "cassada;" see for example, Lugenbeel, 1853, p. 14.
33. Bradshaw, 1965, pp. 33-34; W. O. Jones, *Manioc in Africa* (Stanford: Stanford University Press, 1959).
34. Thomas, 1997, pp. 115, 133, 209.
35. McNeill, 2013, p. 337.
36. Defourneaux, 1970, p. 77.
37. Braudel, Vol. 1, 1981, pp. 146, 167-167, 177; Fernández-Armesto and Sacks, 2013, p. 128.
38. Villault, 1670, p. 96; Hair, Jones and Law, 1992, Letter 29, pp. 266, 271, 273; Bosman, 1967, pp. 472-473, 476-477, 481-483.
39. Hourani, 1991, p. 128.
40. Braudel, Vol. 1, 1981, pp. 238-240.
41. Braudel, Vol. 1, 1981, pp. 230-237.
42. Braudel, Vol. 1, 1981, pp. 230-237.
43. Braudel, Vol. 1, 1981, pp. 241-247.
44. Clunas, 2013, p. 74; Norton, 2010, pp. 159, 164-165.
45. Norton, 2010, pp. 1, 3, 64; Clunas, 2013, p. 74.
46. Clunas, 2013, p. 74; Norton, 2010, pp. 3, 11, 102, 146, 161.
47. Braudel, Vol. 1, 1981, pp. 249-251; Fernández-Armesto and Sacks, 2013, p. 139.
48. Braudel, Vol. 1, 1981, pp. 256-260.
49. Norton, 2010, p. 171.
50. Braudel, Vol. 1, 1981, pp. 260-262; Mintz, 1985, p. 36.
51. Norton, 2008, pp. 3-4.
52. Clunas, 2013, p. 75.
53. Hair, Jones and Law, 1992, Letter 29, pp. 266, 271, 273.
54. Smith and Kelly, 2013, p. 483.
55. Norton, 2008, p. 3.

56. Henry A. Gemery and Jan S. Hogendorn, "The economic costs of West African participation in the Atlantic slave trade: A preliminary sampling for the Eighteenth Century," in Henry Gemery and Jan Hogendorn, *The Uncommon Market: Essays in the Economic History of the Atlantic Slave Trade* (New York: Academic Press, 1979), pp. 143-142; J. E. Inikori, "Introduction," in J. E. Inikori, *Forced Migration: The Impact of the Export Slave Trade on African Societies* (New York: Africana Publishing Co., 1982), pp. 13-60; Albert van Dantzig, "Effects of the Atlantic slave trade on some West African societies," in Inikori, 1982, pp. 187-241.
57. Bureau of Folkways, 1955, p. 8; G. T. Stride and C. Ifeka, *Peoples and Empires of West Africa: West Africa in History, 1000-1800* (New York: Africana Publishing Company, 1971), pp. 230-31.
58. Bureau of Folkways, 1955, p. 8; Stride and Ifeka, 1971, pp. 230-31; Rodney, 1982, pp. 66-67.
59. Rosalyn Terborg-Penn, "Women and slavery in the African diaspora: A Cross-cultural approach to historical analysis," *Sage*, Vol. III, No. 2 (Fall 1986), pp. 11-14, especially p. 11.
60. Johnson, 1961; Rodney, 1982, p. 65; Walter Rodney, *West Africa and the Atlantic Slave Trade* (Cambridge, Mass.: Africa Research Group, 1972).
61. George E. Brooks, Jr., *The Kru Mariner in the Nineteenth Century* (Newark, Del.: Liberian Studies Association, 1972); Jones and Johnson, 1980, pp. 17-34; Adam Jones, *From Slaves to Palm Kernels* (Wiesbaden: Franz Steiner Verlag GmBH, 1983), pp. 35-36; Siegmann, 1969, p. 30; Rodney, 1972.
62. Rodney, 1985, p. 69
63. Rodney (1982, p. 71) argues persuasively that customary laws punishing adultery with enslavement did not precede the trans-Atlantic slave trade. Rather, the trade brought those laws into existence.
64. Johnson, 1961, pp. 142-144.
65. Chevalier des Marchais, "A Voyage to Guinea, and the adjacent Islands, in 1725," in T. Astley, *A New General Collection of Voyages and Travels*, Vol 2 (London, 1745), p. 459.

Conclusion

> "Those who cannot remember the past are condemned to repeat it"
>
> — *George Santayana, philosopher*

> My people self dey fear too much
> We fear for the thing we no see
> We fear for the air around us
> We fear to fight for freedom
> We fear to fight for liberty
> We fear to fight for justice
> We fear to fight for happiness
> We always get reason to fear
>
> — *Fela Anikulapo Kuti, "Sorrows, Tears and Blood"*

In some villages deep in Lofa and Bong counties lives a breed of hunting dogs called Basenji that does not bark. Africans brought the Basenji into existence through selective breeding, as they did with several yams, African rice, and cotton. Hunters wanted dogs that would not scare away their prey, so they mated quiet dogs with other quiet dogs until they produced one that is nearly silent.

These unique dogs were once prized by the pharaohs of Ancient Egypt, who attached bells around their necks in order to know where they were.

In many ways, the story of the Basenji is similar to the history of the Liberian people: We generally know next to nothing about the regal past and the torturous journey of the dog and the people who brought it here. As the dog was bred to be barkless, Liberians have been inculcated to glorify the past of others and to dismiss our own.

Overtime, the local past fell silent. Today, Liberians typically show little regard either for the ways of their ancestors or for the dog, which we often look down upon for being barkless.

To give voice to the past, *Between the Kola Forest and the Salty Sea* summarizes what is known about the past of the people now living in Liberia.

For example, it shows that early West African societies had acquired important insights into the workings of natural forces. Those insights were linked to religious rituals that today would be labeled as "science." During that period, cultures around the world viewed knowledge as integrated. People sought connections between farming, iron smelting and worship.

Regarding kola, Western chemists and pharmacologists have recently confirmed what West Africans discerned thousands of years before: the "energy" in this seed stimulates the nervous system and suppresses thirst.

Similarly, the close resemblance of a child to a grandparent or other ancestors was attributed to a "force" that was transmitted from one generation to another. Today, Western geneticists attribute such occurrences to DNA, an equally mysterious and invisible factor.

In addition, the profile of a typical "witch" closely matches what is now known in the Western world as a "sociopath." Such people were said to be controlling of others, manipulative and conning, and lacking shame, guilt or remorse. They were impulsive, parasitic, egocentric, pathological liars, sexually promiscuous, and given to criminal behavior. The process used to identify "witches" may seem esoteric to outsiders, but so too is that used by psychiatrists and criminologists to identify "sociopaths."

Oral traditions from throughout western Liberia identify the Dei as both the earliest producers of salt from boiling sea water and as the earliest known residents of the Po River region. Those facts make it highly likely that ancient salt-boiling tools found at the Po River were left by ancestors of the Dei.

By 1214 AD both malagueta spice and kola were known to Europeans, which could only mean they already were widely traded in West Africa through Niger River empires like Ghana and Mali. Linguistic evidence ties the Gola to the early kola trade. The presence of the Klao at the center of the area where malagueta grew most heavily suggest their longterm trading of that commodity.

The ancestors of all Mande-speaking Liberians originally lived in the region of the Niger River that formed the core of West African empires. In 1326, the Mali Empire achieved notoriety in the Mediterranean world when Mansa Musa undertook his first hajj. He crossed the Sahara with 100 camels loaded with gold ore. The entourage spent so freely in the bazaars of Cairo, the value of gold fell in Egypt.

The emperor was behaving like many African rulers a thousand years later: buying trinkets in foreign bazaars rather than spending money at home to foster development.

Migration from the Niger

After a seven-year drought around 1100, Mande speakers from the Niger River began migrating into the forest region around what is now Liberia. They were attracted by the presence of salt, kola, iron ore and other resources.

The first group consisted of traders from the Dyula (also Juula) caste. They formed the core of what became the Vai, Dama and Kono ethnic groups on the Sierra Leone-Liberia border.

Between 1200 and 1235, the collapse of the Ghana Empire led to major power struggles and additional migrations. A defeated contender for power, Dankaran Tuman, fled to Kissidugu in present-day Guinea, with his Mande troops, dependents and loyalists. They likely included some ancestors of the Kpelle and Loma.

A third set of Mande immigrants came after Sumaoro Kanté of the Soso Kingdom was defeat in 1235 by Sundita Keita of Mali. It included a large number of Soso and allied groups who fled *en masse* from the Beledougou region of Mali (near Segou) into the Futa Jallon. Among them were likely some ancestors of the Bande, Mende and Loko.

Mande-speakers would likely have followed several routes from the Niger. All of them passed through Kankan, which was the main transit point for the flow of goods between the Buré gold-working region and forest societies on the one hand and the Sahel on the other.

The Dyula apparently took a route to the Sierra Leone peninsula before slowly gravitating toward Cape Mount. Southwest Mande speakers apparently took a route from Kankan to Musadu. The Soso and ancestors of the Bandi, Loko and Mende apparently traveled from Kankan down to the Milo River then to Makona.

As those southwest Mande speakers were moving south, some southeast Mande speakers were approaching from the east, following the Sassandra River. They eventually met around Nzerekore, Guinea.

Living in the Guinea highlands were the Kissi and Gola, along the western rim of the Liberian forest. Along the eastern edge of the forest were Kru speakers.

Many details from this time of upheaval are lost because they were not written down, but this much is known: The first block of people forced to abandon their longstanding home area were in the east, around Man, Côte d'Ivoire. They were ancestors of the Ma and Dan, as well as the Wee and other Kru speakers. They went west. The Ma and Dan settled near Nzérékoré in Guinea and Kru speakers around Mt. Gedeh.

The next group pushed southward by Malinké invaders were longtime residents of the Kissidougou area. These ancestors of the Loko, Mende and Bandi, along with the Kissi, were pressed into western Liberia and eastern Sierra Leone.

The third area to be destabilized was Nzérékoré. This led Kru speakers along the forest rim to move into the forest area of Liberia, with ancestors of the Ma and Dan pressing in behind them.

Finally, the Loma and Kpelle around Musadu were pushed south into Liberia. In the process, the Bassa were pressed to the coast. The Kuwaa pushed into the northeast corner of the territory and cut off from other Kru speakers.

How do we know this?

First, there are the oral traditions. In the east, the Ma, Dan and several Kru-speaking groups, including the Wee, acknowledge being dispersed west from around Man, Côte d'Ivoire.

In the western region of Liberia and eastern Sierra Leone, all groups say the Loko, Mende and Bandi were the first to push south. In the process, they overran the Dama and displaced some Kissi and Gola. The Kissi, in turn, pressed the Kono lower than they had been. Some Gola joined the Vai and Dei nearer the Coast.

The third block to disperse southward consisted of the Loma and Kpelle. They were preceded by the Ma, Dan and Kru speakers because the Kpelle say they met the Ma, Dan and Wee in Nzérékoré when they arrived.

By the time the Kpelle settled in the area of Liberia, Kru speakers had already spread westward from Mt. Gedeh. That placed ancestors of the Bassa and Kuwaa below the Kpelle, as can be seen from their relative positions on the map.

Oral traditions from all groups in the region also overlap to a certain extent with evidence from the Quoja text. That document also makes it clear that as of 1600 many of the ethnic identities existing in Liberia today were either not formed or not known. Exceptions include the Mende, which was a product of that displacement, as well as the Vai and Gola, whose identities predated that invasion.

Similar to West Africans uprooted in violent conflicts of the late twentieth century, those earlier refugees did not arrive *en masse*. Instead, they came in trickles of families that bit-by-bit built into a stream of many thousands.

As new groups moved south, they reshaped the environment mainly through farmers clearing land by slashing and burning bush, as well as blacksmiths cutting timber to make charcoal. These activities transformed former savannah-woodlands and forests to savannah, allowing for more planting and greater population growth.

The Problem of "Purity"

One of the main problems of Liberian studies — one that has blocked the writing of the region's history — is the assumption of cultural and ethnic "purity."

As shown in this book, however, purity never existed. African religious ideas impacted Judaism, and through it, Islam and Christianity. Likewise, African culture was impacted by imported elements, such as the use of Indian Ocean cowries in traditional religious rituals.

Similarly, the Wee, Glebo and Klao resulted from the blending of various Kru-speaking groups. The Mende emerged from the mixing of southwest Mande and northern Mande. The Loma acknowledge that they are a blend of southwest Mande and some Kissi ancestry. The Kpelle and Ma are a fusion of Mande and Kru speakers, with some Kono as well.

The evidence shows that ethnic identities did *not* exist along the coast from time immemorial. Neither were they brought intact from someplace else. Instead, each was woven like a fabric, out of many threads.

Early European visitors to the area now known as Liberia recorded several customs that have endured over time. According to Jean Barbot, men at Sestros were circumcised "like Arabs and Moors." In 1666, Nicolas Villault observed one of the leading men offer a libation of palm wine before dinner.

In addition, two Portuguese documents recorded the earliest description of a female initiation association in the region called *Cabondos*. It resembles the modern Sande association. Both writers agreed that the girls were instructed by an old man, sequestered even from their parents, given new names and returned to their parents at a ceremony, where the girls danced for the public. But, neither mentioned clitoridectomy in the context of female initiation, suggesting the practice had *not* been instituted.

Regarding the traditional religion at Sestros, Barbot recorded two manifestations. One was a shrine with rocks that contained a two-foot high image of a man made from dark brown soil. Every evening people would wash themselves before visiting the shelter to offer chickens as sacrificial offerings.

The other was a ritual of dancing and sacrificial offerings to ensure a good harvest that was performed one day before rice planting. Participants smeared their faces in blood and then covered them with flour.

One significant local rite, a funeral, was recorded around 1701 by Willem Bosman because he thought it was "strange." It is probably the first written description of a local death ceremony. Several aspects of the ceremony, including the repast after the burial, echo in today's practices.

One aspect of the culture did not endure: Men wore their hair platted both at Cape Mount and Sestros.

Because many specifics remain to be clarified, the details of Liberia's early history presented here are likely to be revised in light of new archeological findings, linguistic research and other evidence.

Likely to endure, however, are four broad conclusions: That the people living in the area now called Liberia were integrated into the earliest known trade networks of West Africa, as suppliers certainly of kola, malagueta and salt. That long before large-scale in-migrations by savannah groups, iron-working was an integral feature of local cultures. That the Poro, rather than being a creation of northern Mande-speakers, was a defense of local religious and cultural identities.

Above all, that a quest for political and religious asylum led the ancestors of many, if not most, Liberians to shelter in this territory between the forest and the sea.

The Lingering Legacy of de Sintra

The arrival of de Sintra and other European explorers from the mid-1400s onward reordered political and economic arrangements throughout the world. But one would not be evident for sometime. West Africa was about to end its second-class partnership with Mediterranean and Arab societies that had lasted for centuries. It was beginning a new second-class partnership with Europe and America that continues.

The worst aspect of the trans-Atlantic encounter was the trade in enslaved Africans, which lasted over 300 years. But, it wasn't just Arab and European slave traders who undermined local institutions and values. Major contributors were local warlords who would seize power from landholding families and, with help from praise singers, declare themselves the rightful heirs.

Soon, an essential prerequisite of doing business on this coast was an exchange of gifts or, at the very least, a *dash* or bribe awarded by European visitors to local rulers.

Within West Africa, the traffick deepened divisions between various communities. It also widened the gulf within societies between free and servile people. As rich and powerful men acquired more wives, women were locked into an increasingly unequal status and young poor men were locked out of marriages.

The legacy of the African slave trade is especially evident to West Africans during World Cup soccer matches. From the Reggae Boys of Jamaica to the teams of Brazil and other countries of the Americas, the black and beige faces are stark reminders of the bodies and talents that were robbed from the region.

As shown repeatedly, European and North American societies gained economic power by relying on strong states and state-backed monopolies. Western policy-makers have learned these essential lessons of history. But, to retain their hold, they routinely recommend *opposite* lessons to Africans. They urge decentralization of states in Africa and no state involvement in markets.

First from Arabs, then from Europeans, the way of the ancestors came under multiple assaults. Long-distance trade, especially the slave trade, benefited the allies on non-Africans at the expense of traditional religious authorities. Over time, merchants and war chiefs displaced priests and those rulers whose authority derived from their families claims on the land.

In this context, Western stereotypes of Africans took root. As Africans learned European languages, they began using words like "witch" and "fetish" to describe their own reality.

An over-reliance on the labor of servile dependents served to impede economic development in West Africa. As long as human labor remained cheap, there was little incentive for inventing labor-saving techniques and devices because labor was cheap, disposable and replaceable. As a result, a vicious cycle ensued.

Worse still was the region's no-win position as supplier of slaves — first to the Arab world, then to European colonies in the Americas.

Conclusion

As Africa fell behind Europe and America in wealth and technology, local people ascribed this to religious superiority, not the devastating events of the slave trade. That perspective is reflected in a popular saying, "white people eat witch."

At that point, European control went from merely economic and technological to include the mental. Control was complete.

Europe retained control of African economic life for centuries. It was only around 1950 that relations began shifting — symbolically at least, as African nations emerged from centuries of colonial rule.

The last European power to withdraw was the one that had led the way: Portugal. In 1975, African liberation movements in Angola, Cape Verde, Guinea Bissau and Mozambique defeated the Portuguese army and its Western allies — ending more than 500 years of occupation.

Still, both black lives and African culture continue to be devalued. African traditional beliefs are routinely dismissed as "superstitions," Dutch-made "African" prints are preferred over locally woven cotton cloths, and conveyor-belt media constantly deliver a daily diet of Disney in cinema and dysfunctional ditties on the radio.

As in the worse days of the slave trade, hundreds of thousands of Africans continue to die year in and year out at the hands of Africans acting hand in glove with overseas allies. The most obvious are blood-soaked "war lords" turning children into soldiers and exchanging diamonds for arms.

But, many impeccably dressed and eloquent officials contribute to wars. They do so by failing to forge national ties that bind. And, also by routinely fanning ethnic divisions for political gain.

What is more, they studiously follow Western policies that quietly kill many through a variety of means. Their schools produce graduates lacking skills, alienated from their heritage, and devoid of creativity or dreams. Their failed food policies leave rural residents famished and forced to eat bats. Their lopsided budgets gut health systems leaving many to die needlessly from preventable illnesses, including malaria, diabetes and Ebola.

Toward the Future

As this books makes clear, life conditions for most Liberians remain frozen as they are in the 1700s. Sadly, that is true for many other Africans today.

For example, African traditional beliefs continue to be demonized. As best, they are treated with contempt and condescension by educated city dwellers. As worst, they are cynically exploited by sociopaths for political reasons in the form of ritualistic killings.

As shown by the spread of Ebola in 2014, however, the beliefs of the majority must inform public health decisions and all aspects of public policy. Officials do not have to embrace them, but they must seek to understand them. If not, policies will continue to fail.

But, there is an even more urgent reason for an understanding of traditional beliefs. Without it, there can be no empathy between social groups. And without empathy, the "nation" exists in name only. A skeleton without a beating heart and feeling skin.

Local farming, too, remains frozen. To produce more and better crops, farmers need basic inputs. For example, work animals would help perform routine tasks and to supply manure. For that to happen, the scourge of the Tsetse fly must be tackled.

Also frozen are relations with non-African businesses and governments. They continue to hold African economies hostage. They continue to set artificially high prices for what Africans buy from their factories, including life-saving drugs. At the same time, they pay starvation-level prices for the products of African farms and mines.

Through this process, coffee, tea and other products from around the world are taken to Europe and America to be branded and sold back to the producer countries at exorbitant markup in prices.

As a result, many people today accept without question Switzerland as the world's capital of chocolate and Antwerp as the center of diamond grading.

But, those arrangements are not natural. Instead, they are the outcome of human decisions. Without an understanding of history, these unfair, illogical and unequal relations are likely to continue.

Before more areas of West Africa are opened up to mineral mining and timber harvesting, there is an urgent need for archaeological surveys. Those would help to identify and preserve historically significant remains, especially in mountains and at Bopolu and other trade towns.

The oldest human-made items found so far date to between 410 BC and 1085 AD. The fact that many of these items were in rock shelters suggests one of two conclusions: Perhaps items hidden in cave-like areas were preserved because they were better protected from the rains and other elements.

Or, the people who left these were among the first to reach the area. They may have been advanced scouting parties, perhaps of hunters. In that case, they may have temporarily sheltered in caverns until towns were built. The only way to know which of these options is right is to search for more items left by early people in areas of Liberia besides mountains.

Although the Liberian government's Bureau of Folklore initiated an admirable program of collecting oral traditions in the 1950s, there is an urgent need to undertake a wider, more systematic preservation process. Many societies in the forest region of West Africa, including Liberia, lack a specialist group entrusted with accurately memorizing and recalling historical knowledge.

As a result, traditions were haphazardly preserved. More importantly, many elders, who acted as custodians of collective memory dating back three generations or more, were killed in recent regional wars or suffered losses to memory and recall due to trauma.

In addition, a national historical society is needed that will place markers at important sites. Key among those is the grave of antislavery hero Vanja-Vanja in Komgba, which was preserved at least until the 1950s.

Now that you have journeyed to the end of this book, I hope three insights linger with you: That many ties bind Liberians — from common patterns of culture to overlapping journeys. That the trials and triumphs of the West African past can only be understood when we transcend narrow boundaries of ethnicity and language. That the ancestors of the Liberian people, whose stories I have tried to tell without favoring some over others, deserve a new and profound respect.

As the African ancestors always insisted, the path to a better future lies in knowledge of the past.

Index

'Alvares, Manuel
    claimed female initiates were instructed by old man, 223
    noted custom of male infant circumcision among the Temne, 224
    recorded detailed and accurate account of female initiation in Liberia region in 1616 AD, 223

'Amr ibn al-'As
    descendant of Ethiopian was Muslim conqueror of Egypt, 108

Abbasid caliphate (750-1258)
    helped spread sugar, rice, cotton and citrus from India, 292

Abrahamic religions
    nurtured in Africa, 98

absolutism
    as basis of Sahelian empires, 123

Abu Bakr the Second
    Mansa of Malian empire who sailed for Americas almost 200 years before Christopher Columbus, 166
    ruler of Mali empire who reportedly sent fleet to cross the Atlantic, 132

Adagh (also Adrar des Ifoghas)
    terminus of important trade route seized by Sundiata, 131

Adams, Will
    local man at Little Bassa, 318

Afonso, João (also known as Jean Alfonce)
    Portuguese renegade pilot of early French vessel to Cape Mount and Junk River, 221

Afrasiatic language family
    also called "Afrasian", 36

Africa
    historic loser in unfair global trade, 151
    locked into exchanging raw materials for finished products, 151
    supplier of raw materials and slaves to other regions, 151

African groundnuts
    first cultivated in West Africa, 39

African independence movements
    impact on the writing of African history, 11

African philosophy
    rooted in a materialist view of life, 87

African slaves
    carried via three routes to Arabia, 169
    common in Spanish city of Seville by 1582 AD, 166
    destination shifted from Europe to New World after 1550 AD, 263
    estimated deaths en route to human markets, 266
    estimated number of days en route to New World, 266
    estimated number of trans-Atlantic slave ship voyages, 266
    estimated number removed by Europeans, 266
    females as concubines and sexual pets in Arabia, 169
    females seized in raids and often sold to distant buyers in Africa, 324
    imported to North Africa after Roman conquest, 118
    introduced smallpox immunization to U.S., 292
    males often castrated in Arabia, 169
    nine million from West Africa sold to Mediterranean region, 118
    percentage of men and children, 267
    present in Lagos, Portugal, 259
    shift in treatment by Sahelian empires, 169
    stripped of legal and sexual power in Arabia, 169
    used on large sugar cane plantations along

Mediterranean, 118
used to drain marshes and dig mines in Arabia, 118
war captives originally ransomed, sold or killed, 262
African slave-sellers
initially shared few norms with white buyers, 261
African sleeping sickness
confined use of camels to desert, 116
African traditional religion
also see "Way of the Ancestors", 15
denigrated by early Arab and European visitors, 15
dismissive reference to by William Bosman at Cape Mount, 242
duality with Islam noted in Sahel by Ibn Battuta in 1352 AD, 126
duality with Islam practiced by Sahelian rulers, 126
holy days, 79
local priests deeply respected by residents of Cape Mesurado in mid-1600s, 231
major authorities and their roles, 80
not animist, 71
resistance by forest belt residents to forced conversion and increased work load, 152
African-American civil rights movement
impact on the writing of African history, 11
Africanist history
involved in a constant conversation between the perspective and the evidence, 19
Africanist perspective
definition, 11
Africanus, Leo (Arab historian)
report on Jews in West Africa, 105
afterlife
Ancient Egyptian ideas about, 96
central focus of Ancient Egyptian cosmology, 100
viewed in African religion as moving slowly and free of violence, 76
age groupings, 80

Aggrey beads (also Popo beads)
highly valued along Kru Coast, 208
agricultural revolution
indigenous to West Africa, 37
Ahaggar mountains
origin of now-depleted Saharan river, 121
Akan (ethnic group)
expansion from Ghana to Côte d'Ivoire caused migration of Eastern Krahn and Glebo to Liberia, 205
al Hakam (d. 871), Ibn Abd (Egyptian historian), 28
al-Bushi, Muhammad
Sijilmasa resident with relatives in China, 132
Alexander the Greek
his empire's extension into North Africa, 104
Alexandria, Egypt
seat of early Christianity for 400 years, 107
Ali, Sonni
founder of Songhai empire, 169
preserved traditional religion, 169
al-Kahina
mysterious woman who resisted Arab conquest of North Africa, 109
al-Maghill, Abd al-Karim (d. 1505)
Tunisian jurist who pushed Songhai rulers toward jihadi policy, 171
Almoravids
attack on Ghana empire, 140
importation of West African gold, 119
invasion was death blow to Ghana empire, 128
meaning "men of the ribat (monastery)", 125
plundered the Sahel and imposed Islam, 125
weakened the Ghana empire, 125
West Africans among troops that conquered Spain, 125
al-Sahili, Abu Ishaq
Andalusian who reportedly built the Great Mosque of Timbuktu, 131
Amenhotep IV
Ancient Egyptian pharoah who imposed monothesism, 97

American colonies
    produced tobacco, sugar and cotton for Europe, 219
American War of Independence
    quickened New World black demands for freedom, 284
Amharic
    example of dominant language, 124
Amsterdam
    as central global market for beef, cowrie shells, herring, silver and cloth, 239
    center of ship-building and ship servicing, 239
    decline self-inflicted in part, 246
    dominance of Europe from 1620 to 1680 AD, 240
    economy rooted in making money from money, 247
    Europe's third banking capital, 239
    glue that bound seven tidy Dutch states, 239
    growth in population, 240
    key source of credit for European governments in the 1700s, 217
    once controlled economic bloc that included England and France, 247
    politics guided by global supply and demand, 220
Amsterdam (ship)
    40-ton frigate off Malagueta Coast in mid-1600s, 234
ancestors
    communicating through insights, creativity and dreams, 77
    definition, 76
    honored by passing their names to their descendants, 77
    honored by preserving their memory, 77
    honored for the moral foundation they had laid, 77
    intermediaries between their descendants and God, 76
    viewed as living in slower time, 88
    wellspring of vital energy, 77

Ancient Egypt
    called Kmt by its residents, meaning "the black land", 36
    Coffin texts, 96
    cultural traits traced to African roots, 95
    Pyramid texts, 96
    religious counter-revolution, 98
    religious parallels to ideas and practices in West Africa, 95
    Spells for Going Forth by Day (so-called Book of the Dead), 96
    system of government, 37
Ancient Greece
    misconception of Ancient Egyptian religion, 95
Ancient Rome
    its control of trade in North Africa, 104
    misconception of Ancient Egyptian religion, 95
Andah, Basseh W. (Nigerian archeologist)
    notes stylistic differences between nomoli and pomtan sculptures, 61
Anderson, Perry (British historian)
    emergence of nations, 248
Andes
    drastic population decline due to epidemics and forced labor, 219
animal sacrifice
    three phases of, 78
animals
    as energy source, 295
    used as energy sources before being eaten, 298
anthropologists
    usefulness of their works for recovering African history, 2
Antwerp, Belgium
    center of European economic power from 1501 to 1568 AD, 220
    displaced by Genoa as center of European economic power, 220
    invested in regional production of goods and ships, 220

aquatic culture
   apparently linked to ancestors of Kru, 35
   developed in flooded West African savannah, 33
   likely roots of Kru speakers, 34
   linked to wavy-line and dotted-line pottery, 33
Aquio
   local greeting at River Cess in mid-1600s, 233
Arabia
   homes featured drapes, pillows and carpets, 299
   initially more advanced than Europe, 292
   meat eaten on special occasions, 297
   mud bricks used for homes of poor, 300
   traffic in African slaves continued as Atlantic traffick declined, 284
   unleavened bread main food for the poor, 297
   wood furniture limited to chest and cupboard, 299
Arabic
   adopted for writing by Sahelian traders and rulers, 126
   example of dominant language, 124
   knowledge of conferred advantage to Sahelian traders and rulers, 125
   used for divining and preparing amulets, 125
Arabs
   conquest of North Africa, 109
   depictions of Africans as primitives, 110
   early racist accounts of Africans, 7
   importation of Asian crops into North Africa, 109
   introduced standardized currencies to West Africa, 125
   invasion greatly expanded slavery in West Africa, 118
   invasion of North Africa in 639 AD, 9
   stabilized rates of exchange, 125
   their money as model for later European currencies, 305
   their money considered the safest and most stable for centuries, 305
   traders in Africa followed by Muslim clerics and scholars, 116
   traders kept away from West African gold mines, 119
Aristotle
   cities as seats of the goodlife, 294
Ark of the Covenant
   reportedly housed in Ethiopian Highlands, 99
artisans
   as perceived in African religion, 82
   responsibility for specific rituals, 82
artists
   as perceived in African religion, 82
Arvoredo de Santa Maria
   name given to grove near Junk River by Pedro de Sintra and his men, 160
Asante Empire
   expansion caused western population movements, 324
Asian currencies
   based on silver and copper, 165
Atlantic
   language group formerly labeled as Mel, 3
Axum
   eastern neighbor of Ancient Egypt, later called Abyssinia, 36
Baba, Ahmad (1556-1627)
   Malian jurist who pioneered an Africanist perspective in construction of knowledge, 11
Babaev, Kirill (linguist)
   identified "Bandi" as root collective name among southwest Mande groups, 146
   suggests "Bandi" as original name of southwest Mande group around Kissidugu, 197
   suggests names of southwest Mande ethnic groups assigned based on location, 198
badenya ("mother-childness")
   a spirit of affectionateness, 83
Badoe
   town along Malagueta Coast in late 1600s, 249
Baffa (also Befoe or Bofou)
   town along Malagueta Coast in late 1600s, 249
Bamako

Index

position on Niger River, 121
Bambara (ethnic group)
  migration from Nioro to Segou in early 1600s, 205
  northern Mande-speakers who live in the east, 120
  people call themselves "Bamana", 120
  pushed Bobo and other groups south towards Wasoulous, 205
Bambuk gold field
  seized from Mali by Fula empire, 177
bananas
  among foodstuff at Sestros, 253
  Asian plant adopted in West Africa by early 1600s, 320
  present at Cape Mount in early 1700s, 241
Bance Island, Sierra Leone
  sights, sounds and smells of human suffering, 276
  site of Africa's only golf course, 276
Bandi
  Loma dialect, 198
Bandi (ethnic group)
  assimilated with Kissi over time, 199
  blacksmiths and professional entertainers exempt from public works, 198
  close historical affinity to Soso, 142
  credit Malinké with introducing country-cloth weaving, 198
  dispersion caused by Malinké invasion around 1600 AD, 197
  displaced some Kissi, 142
  joined Kissi who had moved into Gola territory, 199
  matched description of group known as "Hondo" in Quoia text, 185
  oral tradition claim Loko originated in Bandi territory, 198
  outgrowth of migration south from Sahel, 141
  previous home was reportedly Korblima in Guinea, 198
  preyed upon by slave kidnappers, 324
  pushed Kono south, 198
  pushed some Gola south, 185, 189
  pushed some Kissi south, 198
  rearguard of splintered Southwest Mande block, 198
  reportedly came into Liberia seeking fertile land, 198
  supported cotton weaving and auxiliary activities, 227
  with Loko and Mende, considered dialect of one language, 147
Bandi (or similar sounding word)
  once common name of southwest Mande groups, 146
  original name of southwest Mande speakers centered around Kissidugu, 197
Bandi language
  closely related to Loko, 188
  uses strong "d" where Kpelle language uses soft "l", 146
Bantu
  example of dominant language, 124
Bantu speakers
  migration into southern Africa, 49
baqt (meaning contract)
  required delivery of Nubian slaves to Arab overlords for five centuries, 118
Barbot, Jean (1655-1712)
  assumed Sestos interior was teeming with elephants but people were too lazy to hunt, 251
  claimed Sestos residents displayed "much human feeling", 252
  commended residents of Malagueta Coast for handicrafts as well as rice and millet farming, 249
  described affection shown by Sestros women to Wolof boy in his company, 252

described canoes along Malagueta Coast as adorned "handsomely", 249

described River Cess mothers as "tender" in their care for infants, 251

described Sestros women as "submissive" and men as "wildly jealous", 252

description of birds at Sestros, 252

description of Sestros River banks, 250

Franco-English commercial agent on slave ships, 248

included 120 masterful illustrations in his book, 248

list of local insects and animals he illustrated, 252

list of local traders and rulers with European names, 317

noted use of Dutch, Portuguese, French and English along Windward Coast, 317

observed Kru Coast first hand, 249

only viewed Cape Mount from aboard ship, 249

published description of West Africa based on own observation and published sources, 248

published first account of traditional religion at Sestros, 251

repeated claim made by Nicholas Villault of early French ties to Grand Cess, 249

said rice at Sestros was smaller but tastier than those of the Levant, 253

several of his men stricken by malaria and a few died, 252

unflattering comparisons of local societies to his society, 251

barinkan
Mande word for "garment", 118

Barsaw
ruler of Sestro River region, 250
described by Jean Barbot, 250
reportedly had 30 wives, 251

barter
main method of trading worldwide until 1700s, 305

Barth, Heinrich (1821-1865)
first European to publish detailed description of West African interior, 285

Basenji
African dog bred for huting, 34

Bassa
name was first recorded by Jean Barbot, 250

Bassa (ethnic group)
ancestors reportedly lived in area now inhabited by Krahn and Sikon, 206

belief in Neegee, humans born beneath bodies of water, 99

identified with Karou group in Quoia text by anthropologist Sven E. Holsoe, 186

met by Gola when moving south, 200

migrated west until encounter with Dei, 207

preceded Kpelle in Liberian territory, 149

probably founded town in Guinea known as Musadu, 150

probably the group displaced from Grand Gedeh by Krahn and Glebo, 205

relatively high sickle-cell frequency, 210

reportedly learned canoe building from Klao, 207

reportedly met Europeans upon arrival on Atlantic coast, 207

reportedly once engaged in iron smelting in Grand Gedeh, 206

share with Dei a unique level of Poro called "Ndoge", 207

Bassa language
common first names among Windward slaves, 276

batiks
export trade from Java seized by Dutch in the 1600s, 319

imitations produced by Dutch for West African markets, 320

Javanese fabric exported by Dutch to West Africa, 319

multicultural designs, 319

symbolic imagery proved popular with Africans, 319

Index

bays
    as natural habors, 59
beans
    among foodstuff at Sestros, 253
    example of forest-margin crop important to local diets, 226
Beavogui
    a leading Loma clan, 202
Becker-Donna, Etta (Austrian ethnographer)
    importance of reproducing hair, ornaments and cicatrization on Dan and Ma carvings, 204
beer
    common to northern Europe prior to 1700s, 322
    hops added as preservative in 1300s, 322
    made mainly from wheat, oats, barley, rye or millet, 322
Begho
    early Malinké community in Gold Coast region, 190
    gold redirected southward after Dutch arrival, 190
    initially gold flowed northward to Sahel, 190
Beledougou, Mali
    area abandoned by Soso who settled in Futa Jallon, 140
bells
    worn by River Cess men on arms, legs, shoulders and waists, 251
Bentley, Jerry H. (American historian)
    asymmetric advantages enjoyed by Europeans, 308
Benue River
    as tributary of Niger, 121
Berber (ethnic group)
    agents and hosts in Sahel for other Muslim traders, 126
    as "lost tribe of Israel", 105
    joined Malinké in far-reaching Muslim trade network, 126
    major traders in Ghana by 700 AD, 128

Berette, Tasuma
    mother of Dankaran Tuman, 130
Berlin, Ira (historian)
    master-slave relationship provided model for all social relations in U. S., 266
    slaves at center of New World economic production, 266
    West African towns as creole communities, 166
Beyla, Guinea
    likely founded by Kru-speakers or Ma, 149
    one of four early regional trade centers, 149
    trade hub for Kru-speakers, Ma, Loma, Kpelle, 149
    visited by Dyula merchants, 149
Bilal ibn Rabah
    African descendant who served as Islam's first muezzin, 108
Bilivogui
    a leading Loma clan, 202
black-eye peas
    first cultivated in West Africa, 39
blacksmith's workshop
    akin to shrine, 78
    argument-free zone, 78
blacksmiths
    as perceived in African religion, 82
    lower caste and permanent "outsiders" among Mande, 123
    most respected artisans in context of African religion, 82
    their bellows as sites for swearing oaths, 82
    their wives as potters and weavers, 82
Blisue
    Dei name for Cape Montserrado, meaning "cat mountain", 207
Bloomeasrt, Samuel
    Dutch trader whose manuscript was used by Olfert Dapper, 182
    ended engagement with Cape Mount around 1651 AD, 195

Blyden, Edward Wilmot (pan-Africanist intellectual), xxviii
  advanced idea that Islam was better suited to African culture than Christianity, 17
  advanced myth of Mandingo and Islamic superiority in Liberian studies, 16
  his Africanist perspective, 13
Bobo (ethnic group)
  previously lived near Kpelle, 149
Bobofing
  Burkino Faso language related to Ma and Dan, 147
Bode
  Loma dialect, 146, 198
body as sinful
  view common to Islam and Christianity, but not to traditional African religion, 126
Bolahun
  site of rock shelter with early evidence of human habitation, 45
Bonaparte, Napoleon (French autocrat)
  his army defeated by Haitians, 284
  his invasion and looting of Egypt, 8
Bongo, Fasouma
  father of Woko Soroqui, 148
Bonny
  Nigerian town that grew into city-state based on profits from slave trade, 167
Book of Job
  allusions to Ancient Egyptian civilization, 99
Bopolu
  founded as trade town by ancestors of Dei, 59
  origin of name, 60
  site where coastal salt was exchanged for commodities from Sahel, 60
Bosman, William
  allusion to prostitution at Cape Mesurado, 242
  allusion to prostitution at Cape Mount, 241
  asked about local wars along Liberian coast to assess prospect of slaves, 240
  assumed villagers east of Cape Mesurado in early 1700s had never seen a white person before, 243
  characterized Sanguin residents as rogues in early 1700s, 245
  cited houses near Cape Mesurado as most beautiful he had seen on voyage, 242
  claimed husbands at Cape Mount not concerned if wives slept with other men, 242
  commented repeatedly on sexual proclivities of local women, 240
  considered all inhabitants of Cape Mount to be "slaves" of their ruler, 241
  credited reticence of local people to Europeans to recent massive kidnappings, 240
  deceitful interaction with Cape Mount ruler, 241
  described language at Sinoe as "barbarous", 245
  description of Cape Mount, 241
  description of funeral at River Cess in early 1700s, 244
  description of geographical features along Malagueta Coast, 245
  description of Jan Capo Monte, 241, 242
  description of Sanguin ruler, James, 245
  dismissive reference to local religion at Cape Mount, 242
  Dutch merchant and chief factor at Elmina fort, 240
  little critical thinking about himself or his culture, 240
  noted daily traffic of trading canoes between Cape Mesurado and River Cess, 243
  noted polygyny at Cape Mount, 242
  published detailed account of West African life in early 1700s, 240
Bottou
  geographic feature, 249
Boure, Falam
  Cape Mount ruler who was described as "grave and venerable", 229
bows and arrows
  worn by men at Cape Mount in early 1700s but

Index

said to be more ornamental than functional, 242

Bozos
Niger fishing folk who reportedly migrated from Nile River, 121

brandy
consumed by leading men at Cape Mesurado, 231
introduced to Windward Coast by 1666, 273
key item in Europe's trade with Africa, 221
large quantities exchanged for local captives, 322
liquor based on distilled wine, 322
popular from mid-1500s, 273

Braudel, Fernand (French historian)
called brandy and rum "Europe's poisoned gifts" to rest of world, 221
Europe's lead over other regions came late, 292
ideal ratio of population to land, 149
Italian roots of European capitalism, 217
laid basis for comparative analysis of living conditions, 292
on European trade monopolies, 219
on spice trade, 164
production secondary to trading in generating wealth, 247
rise of capitalism fueled by money markets, 309
rules that govern behavior of a world economy, 109
shops linked to growth of credit, 306
similarity of furniture in India, Arabia and Africa, 299

brick buildings
initially reserved for palaces, fortresses and shrines in Asia, 300

brideprice
commodities presented by groom to bride's family, 262

bridge-builders
as perceived in African religion, 82

Bristol, Tom
local man near St. Paul River, 318

Britain
abolition of slave purchases, 284
Anti-Slavery Squadron sent to West Africa in 1818, 284
gun trade with Windward Coast, 275
investors used northern Spain to produce port wine for export, 219
its merchants extended credit to foreign partners who then bought British goods, 307
Liberia-area slaves removed mainly from Bassa and Cape Mount, 271
main exporter of slaves from Windward Coast, 271
naval records on Windward slave ships, 275
turned to Windward Coast for slaves after 1750 AD, 271
use of firewood in homes until 1600s, 296

Brooks, George E. (American historian)
chain reaction produced by Malinké movement south, 191
linked Kru migration to trade in malagueta spice and other commodities, 54
position of Kru-speakers and southeast Mande groups along upper reaches of rivers suggest trade involvement, 196
showed impact of rainfall patterns and ecological conditions on historical developments, 18

Brown, John and Moses
founders of Brown University whose wealth derived from slave trade, 283

Brown-Sherman, Mary Antoinette
leading Liberian scholar, xxix

Bruges, Belgium
key European economic power from 1300 to 1500 AD, 218

Brun, Samuel (Swiss merchant)
cited several locals who spoke Portuguese, 224
left description of local culture and people from early 1600s, 224

reported few trade goods at Cape Mount, 224
Budge, E. A. Wallis (Egyptologist)
  traced roots of Ancient Egyptian religion to black Africa, 95
Bühnen, Stephen (German historian)
  link of Soso and Jalonke, 130
Bullom (ethnic group)
  rebellion against Folgia, 183
  southern vanguard of Atlantic languages, 46
  subdued by Mane invaders, 179
Bullom language
  layout reveals direction of Mane and Quoia invasions, 188
Bulu-ye-ma
  Loma dialect whose name means "on the salt water", 146
Bunde
  Loma dialect, 146, 198
Buré
  major gold producing region of early West Africa, 141
  miners work slowdown as protest against direct state control of mining, 145
Busa
  southeast Mande language in Nigeria, 148
Bushmen
  name used by outsiders for Sapo, 208
Buttouwa
  town along Malagueta Coast in late 1600s, 249
Cabondos
  name of female initiation association recorded by André Álvares de Almada in 1594 AD, 223
cacao
  New World crop adopted by West Africans, 321
caffeine
  psychoactive substance in coffee, 323
Cairo
  site of 35 different markets, 306
caixas
  copper and lead money of China, 305
  stable Chinese currency from 200 BC to late 1600s, 305
calico
  cheap imitations produced by London businessmen by late 1600s, 320
  imports provoked backlash from European textile producers, 320
  Indian cotton cloth known for durability and vibrant colors, 319
Caliph 'Umar
  grandson of an Ethiopian, 108
camels
  advantages for desert trade, 116
  brought to North Africa by Assyrian invaders, 116
  conferred advantages over societies reliant on porters, 124
Camoe River
  route apparently taken by Kru language groups, 47
canoes
  local production process, 58
  mode of transportation along Malagueta Coast, 302
  reportedly used in daily trading between Cape Mesurado and River Cess, 243
  small fleet observed between River Cess and Sanguin, 233
  types of, 58
  used for trading from Cape Mesurado to Sestro, 302
Cap das Baisox Svino
  all residents involved in fishing according to Jean Barbot, 250
  geographic features, 249
  town along Malagueta Coast in late 1600s, 249
Cape Mesurado
  brisk trade in ivory until 1600s, 318
  daily traffic of trade canoes to River Cess, 243
  English said to have inland warehouse in mid-1600s, 232
  leading men promised slaves to French visitor in mid-1600s, 232

Index

local ruler described as wearing red robe and red "bonnet", 231

local weapons consisted of darts, bows, arrows and swords, 231

location popular with early European visitors due to available trade goods, 167

men engaged mainly in trading, 242

no inhabitants or trade mentioned by Duarte Pacheco Periera, 167

produce and livestock similar to Cape Mount in early 1700s, 243

residents called "uncivil" by Jean Barbot, 271

residents claim English were their only enemies in early 1700s, 243

ruler reportedly offered his daughter as sexual partner to visiting Frenchman, 231

site of plundering and kidnapping by English in early 1700s, 242

slave exports grew as pressure increased on former major slave marts, 284

some roofs of dwellings compared to Dutch "Hay-reaks", 300

use of Dutch, French and Portuguese by some residents, 317

women charaterized by Jean Barbot as sexually pliant, 271

Cape Mount

brisk trade in ivory until 1600s, 318

described by Nicholas Villoult in effusive terms to encourage French engagement, 229

foodstuff consisted of citrons, oranges, berries, melons, gourds and "a sort of plums" in mid-1600s, 230

inhabitants described as "industrious" in early 1700s, 241

ivory trade exhausted by 1687 AD, 319

location popular with early European visitors due to available trade goods, 167

many men described as circumcised in mid-1600s, 230

men's attire compared to "surplice,, 227

residents described as "neat" eaters, 230

residents said to be careful in roasting meat, 230

slave exports grew as pressure increased on former major slave marts, 284

supplied highest number of slaves from Liberia region, 270

women wore cloth wrapped around waist, 227

Cape of Good Hope, South Africa

post established by Dutch, 239

Cape Palmas

described as resembling a dolphin, 245

distinguishing feature, 249

name given by Portuguese, 161

capital

flow impeded by kinship relations in West Africa, 124

Capo del Monte

meaning "chief mountain", 161

name given by Alvise da Cá da Mosto to place now known as Cape Mount, 161

caravans

precise and rigid patterns of travel, 116

caravel (ship)

developed expressly for exploring West African coast, 163

lighter and faster than other long-distance European vessels, 163

Portuguese vessel based on Arab naval design, 163

type of vessels used by Pedro de Sintra and his men, 163

Caribbean

its merchants and planters indebted to English merchants, 247

slaveholders obulent living conditions, 291

slaves living conditions among most wretched anywhere, 291

carriages

confined to rich in Europe until 1500s, 303

Carthage
    dominated trading to the Sahara, 102
Casa San Giorgio
    quasi public bank at center of Genoese power, 218
cassava
    absent from list of foodstuff at Sestros in late 1600s, 253
    apparently adopted in Liberia area after 1600s, 321
    Brazilian root crop adopted by West Africans, 321
    description of plant, 321
    entered West African diets in 1700s, 321
    helped fuel a population boom in West Africa, 321
    now deeply embedded in coastal cuisines of Liberia, 321
    tuber from the Americas incorporated into local cuisines, 226
    with maize spurred a "veritable agricultural revolution" in West Africa, 321
castes
    definition, 122
    intergenerational transmission of skills, 122
    rise of among Mande, Wolof and Soninké, 122
cesta
    Portuguese word for a pannier or large basket, 304
    Portuguese word meaning "wicker baskets", 161
    Portuguese word that became entrenched as a place name along Malagueta Coast, 304
Cestos River
    presence of local broker named Jacob, 318
chickens
    plentiful and cheap at Sestros in late 1600s, 253
    said to be plentiful and cheap in early 1700s, 226
chief
    term indiscriminately used by early Europeans for any African and Native American ruler, 19
children
    forty percent of slaves from Windward Coast, 275
China
    clothes made of wool, linen, cotton and silk, 299
    homes furnished best, 299
    individual bowls and plates for dining, 299
    invented gunpowder, guns and canons, 307
    invented the magnetic compass, 307
    living standards slightly better than rest of world, 307
    men and women wore similar clothes, 299
    Ming dynasty (1368-1644) built large porcelain factories, 299
    Ming dynasty (1369-1644) built world's longest canal, 307
    most advanced iron industry in 1400s, 304
    name given to porcelain dishes based on original place of origin, 299
    possessed most advanced tehnology in the world, 307
    produced large quantities of blue-and-white porcelain, 299
    rich wore vibrant colors, 299
    Song dynasty (960-1279) fostered large-scale salt, silk and paper industries, 304
    underclothes commonly worn, 299
    visited by natives of Sijilmasa, West Africa, 132
    was expanding inward as Europe was expanding globally, 307
    world's most advanced pottery industry, 304
chocolate
    spread worldwide by European sailors and others who had lived in New World, 323
    stimulant drink adopted from New World by Europeans and exported worldwide, 322
Christianity
    implanted in the Sahara before reaching Greece or Rome, 106
    its early spread to Axum, 108
    its early spread to Nubia, 108
    its special appeal to Eyptians, 105

Index

rivalry with Islam along the Mediterranean, 161
shift from passive version of St. Mark to
   crusading religion of Prince Henry's time, 163
spread to North African coutryside, not just
   cities, 107

circumcision
   at River Cess, 251
   common to Quoia, Karou, Folgia, Manou, Hondo,
      Gola and Gebbe according to Quoia text, 186
   marker in life cycle, 80

cire-perdue
   brass-forging method used in Benin and known
      to Ma and Dan ancestors, 197

cities
   disadvantages, 294
   diversity of residents, 294
   long valorized in Western scholarship, 294
   powers eclipsed by nations after Amsterdam's
      decline, 247
   scenes of epidemics, 294

Claesz
   Dutch name of local man at River Cess in 1678,
      318

clans
   basic units of kinship groups, 53
   family grouping that formed the outer limit of
      social and political structuring in Niger-Congo
      cultures, 51

cloth
   functioned as currency in many societies, 305

clothes
   Cape Mount and Sanguin rulers dressed in similar
      blue robes, 234
   Chinese commonly wore undergarments, 299
   defined by social status at Cape Mount, 230
   made of wool, linen, cotton and silk in China, 299
   Mane's consisted of cotton smocks and wide-
      bottom trousers, 181
   men and women dressed similarly in China, 299
   men's attire at Cape Mount compared to
      "surplice," European choir robe, 227
   of Malagueta Coast people, 227
   poor people throughout the world made their
      own, 298
   raffia and tree bark originally used east of River
      Cess, 227
   reflected social status along Windward Coast,
      298
   relative skimpiness along Windward Coast, 298
   said to be minimal along Malagueta Coast, 234
   those of English commoners "crudely made", 298
   those of French commoners made from rough
      broadcloth, 299

clothing
   Cape Mesurado ruler described as wearing red
      robe and red "bonnet", 231
   grandees at River Cess in "Moorish [Arab] style",
      251
   River Cess women wore loin cloth in late 1600s,
      251
   women at Cape Mount wore cloth wrapped
      around waist, 227

Clunas, Craig (British art historian)
   Chinese porcelain as "first global brand", 299

coal
   absence from West Africa inhibited iron industry,
      303
   cheap and efficient source of energy, 296
   energy source that provided biggest bang for the
      buck, 296
   helped spur the Industrial Revolution, 296
   used in large-scale metal smelting, 296

cocoa
   seeds served as currency in parts of Central and
      South America, 322
   source of chocolate, 322
   used as currency in New World, 305

codfish
   imported from Europe in dried and salted form,
      321

introduced to West Africa by European sailors, 321
now entrenched in local diets, 321
preserved by drying and salting, 298
coffee
African drink adopted by Europeans and exported worldwide, 322
large plantations established by Europeans in early 1700s, 323
reached Europe via Arabia around 1615 AD, 323
use as stimulant drink discovered in Ethiopia, 323
Colbert, Jean Baptiste
French ultra nationalist and naval minister to whom Nicholas Villault dedicated his book, 228
Cole, King
Cape Mount ruler in early 1750s, 318
Columbus, Christopher
Genoese navigator who sailed to America with backing of Spanish elites, 166
his pro-slavery worldview shaped by slavery's centrality in his native Genoa, 218
recommended to his backers reliance on Native American slave labor and introduction of African slaves to New World, 218
religious motivation for exploration superseded by pursuit of gold, 166
roundtrip voyage to Caribbean, 166
Spain's sponsorship of his American voyage prompted by Portugal's African exploration, 259
Venetian who visited West Africa aboard Portuguese vessel, 161
commodity moneys
resulted from production expressly for exchange, 305
commoners
gained access to land and political freedom in Europe by early 1800s, 308
lost political and economic ground in Africa by 1800s, 308
once paid the rich for access to land and wild game in many places outside Africa, 308
communal rites
designed to harness the power inherent in universal energy, 79
compact village system
characterized by institutions that transcend lineages, 209
common among Loma and Kpelle, 210
comparative analysis
clothes, furniture and dishes, 298
dwellings of commoners in Europe and Windward Coast, 300
eating utensils, 299
farming and foods, 296
fixed capital goods, 307
furniture throughout the world, 299
modes of transportation, 302
nighttime lighting, 299
protein sources, 297
trading methods, 305
workshops, 303
contact studies
definition, 4
copper
not found in West Africa, 165
plentiful in early South America, 165
used as currency, 119
Coptic churches of Africa
marginalized by Roman Christianity, 108
Corra
village east of Cape Mesurado, 243
villagers described as "civil and courteous", 243
Côte d'Ivoire
embarkation points in trans-Atlantic slave trade, 269
stone tools in use by 3,500 BC, 39
cotton (properly gossypium herbaceum)
basis for a complex local industry, 226
cloth weaving from fiber important to local economies, 226

Index

plant important to local economies, 226
planted in same fields as rice, 226
weaving developed among Vai, Bandi, Loma and Kpelle, 226
cotton cloth
African sales of declined as Europeans sought more slaves, 266
Asian imports popular in West Africa from 1100s AD, 319
imports undermined West African production, 320
imports wildly popular in Europe around 1690s, 320
Indian version known as "calico" in Europe, 319
industry emerged in England, 248
key item exchanged for enslaved Africans, 320
made in West African and sold in Europe, 118
narrow horizontal loom spread throughout West Africa, 115
once imported by Europe from Egypt, West Afria and India, 319
products of West Africa sold in Europe, 303
sold mainly by men in West Africa, 306
symbol of desire for peace in local conflicts, 319
tended to replace grass, raffia and tree bark fabric because it was sturdier, 227
usually made from mix of fibers from regular plant and giant silk-cotton tree, 226
weaving as major engine of growth along Windward Coast, 303
workshops established by Portuguese on Cape Verde, 303
woven into Mande culture, 319
cotton gown
as payment for access to land, 53
cotton tree (Ceiba pentandra), 78
cotton weaving
characterized by peculiar division of labor by sex, 227
least developed east of River Cess, 227
women produced cloth for daily use, 227
country devil
demeaning phrase used for ritual masquerade dancers, 19
Courlander, Harold (American folklorist), 14
cowries
interpretation by diviners, 81
used as currency, 119
used as currency in West Africa, 117, 305
used for decoration and divination, 117
Coya (also Coyah)
inland territory cited by Europeans as source of gold, 167
likely place of Folgia origin, 183
resident reportedly exchanged gold for salt from the coast, 167
creation
period that stood outside time, 88
Creator
Ancient Egyptian conception of, 96
distant from human affairs in African religion, 72
criminals
myth that they supplied most New World slaves, 275
cruzado
Portuguese coins minted mainly with West African gold, 165
cultural pluralism
commonplace in early Mano River region, 184
culture
as basis of divisions among Liberians, 317
changed by global trade, 319
changes visible when traditions are viewed over time, 317
fundamentalist view of common among Liberians, 317
its fluidity, 317
currencies
main ones in West Africa, 119
curtains

in Europe, confined to homes of rich, 300
Curtin, Philip D. (American historian)
   contrasting of empires to stateless societies in West African, 10
   fragmented trade along Windward Coast, 268
   his definition of Windward Coast, 267
d'Avity, Pierre
   French soldier whose manuscript was used by Olfert Dapper, 182
d'Azevedo, Warren L. (American anthropologist), xxix
   fluidity of ethnic identity, 184
   historical types of political units in western Liberia, 183
da Mosto, Alvise da Cá
   compiler of Pedro de Sintra travelogue, 161
   explored Senegal and Cape Verde aboard Portuguese vessel, 161
   gave Italian names to places described in Pedro de Sintra's notes, 161
dairy products
   major protein source in Northern Europe, 298
Dalon
   town near Millsburg significant in history of Dei, 59
Dama (ethnic group)
   disappeared from area now occupied by Mende, 188
Dan (ethnic group), 196
   ancestors migrated from direction of Burkino Faso, 147
   ancestors reportedly knew iron forging and brass casting before entering Liberia, 197
   called "Gio" (meaning "slaves") because they were preyed upon during slave trade, 324
   came into association with Ma, 196
   dispersion caused by Malinké invasion around 1600 AD, 197
   first ancestor named Dio or Guio, 148
   first ancestors descended from heaven in a brass bucket, 197
   history interwoven with Ma, 196
   identity formed in the forest belt, 179
   labeled "Gio" or slave by Malinké, 17
   low sickle-cell frequency, 210
   masked ritual performers on stills, 74
   migration into Liberia reportedly led by women, 203
   moved to the right bank of Bafing, 196
   movement of some ancestors from northern Côte d'Ivoire to area of Liberia, 196
   only some belonged to Poro association, 203
   oral traditions help identify movements, 148
   preceded Kpelle in Liberian territory, 149
   pressed south by Kpelle, 203
   pressured Kru-speakers south into Grand Gedeh, 203
   preyed upon by slave kidnappers, 324
   proportedly living in area when Ma ancestors arrived, 148
   regarded as "small brothers" of Ma, 196
   related to languages in Burkino Faso, Benin and Nigeria, 147
   reportedly helped Kpelle expel Konionké from Konodougou, 179
   rules for engagement of strangers, 53
   Santa and Silakoro subgroups left on two hills, 196
   spread to Nehenkoheba (town) with Ma, 196
   style of carved wooden masks shared with Ma and Kru-speakers, 203
Dané
   oral tradition cites as first ancestor of Ma, 148
Dapper, Olfert
   description of Quoia power structures, 186
   Dutch geographer who described Quoia invasion, 182
   his informant identified Karro-doboe as only canoe users in Quoia area, 186
   his informant thought Vai were dying out, 185
   his informant's use of "Manou", 184
   informant's rich details on Quoia territory, 187

Quoia account drawn from Dutch manuscripts, 182
dash
　in form of iron bars, glass beads, brandy and knives, 252
　in form of rice and hens given by Barsaw to Jean Barbot, 252
　paid by Dutch merchant to grandees near Cape Mesurado, 242
　presented to Barsaw by Jean Barbot, 252
Dassa
　town along Malagueta Coast in late 1600s, 249
Davidson, Basil (British Africanist historian)
　Black Africa as homeland of Ancient Egyptians, 95
de Almada, André Álvares
　cited Sierra Leone/Liberia forest as only source of kola, 168
　claimed female initiates were instructed by old man, 223
　described Upper Guinea region as productive and peaceful, 168
　key eye-witness source on Mane invasion, 179
　noted custom of male infant circumcision among the Temne, 223
　Portuguese sea captain who left record of life in Mano River region, 168
　recorded first known description of a female initiation association in Liberia region in 1594 AD, 223
　similarity of Mane attire and weapons to group near Gambia, 180
　son of a Portuguese father and Cape Verdean mother, 168
　supposed Mane originated in Mali, 181
de Esteres, Alvaro
　Portuguese sea captain employed by Fernáo Gomes, 165
　reached Gold Coast, 165
de Sintra, Pedro
　description of Cape Mesurado area by his scribe, 159
　description of Junk River area by his scribe, 160
　Genoese captain of Portuguese vessel, 159
　kidnapping of local man from Junk River area, 160
　led first successful European expedition to pre-Liberia, 159
　voyage conceived and funded by Prince Henry, 162
death
　viewed as change in status in African religion, 76
Dei (ethnic group), 49
　ancestors as founders of Bopolu, 59
　ancestors likely left salt-making artifacts, 47
　ancestors probably living in Liberia area by 990 AD, 47
　apparently reached coast via St. Paul River, 47
　clues regarding origin, 59
　founding legend, 59
　gave protection to Gola fleeing fighting in homeland, 201
　linked in oral traditions to salt trade, 57
　linked to salt trade, 59
　met by Gola when moving south, 200
　oral traditions, 59
　oral traditions cite Gola and Vai as earliest neighbors, 143
　oral traditions cite intermarriage with Vai and Gola, 143
　oral traditions claim salt trade attracted other groups to Liberia area, 59
　oral traditions say Gola pushed Vai ancestors toward them, 143
　origin stories, 47
　pattern of small, scattered villages, 53
　present near Cape Montserrado when Bassa arrived, 207
　previously blocked Gola from access to salt-making villages, 197

preyed upon by slave kidnappers, 324
reportedly gave Gola permission to built Zoodi, Todien and Sugbulum, 200
share with Bassa a unique level of Poro called "Ndoge", 207
southern vanguard of Kru speaking groups, 47

Dei (ethnic group)
ignored for study at Liberia College by Edward W. Blyden, 17

destructive animals
plentiful in Liberia before 1700 AD, 195

DeWolf family, Rhode Island
operators of multinational slaving enterprise, 283

Dewulo
legendary founding mother of Dei ethnic group, 59

Diabé, Manga
daughter of Ghana's last ruler and wife of Sundiata, 131

dialects
high number linked to small settlements and small polities, 211

diaspora
definition, 128

Diata, Sogolon
ruler of Mali empire commonly known as "Sundiata" or "Sunjata", 130

dinars
gold money of Arabia, 305

Dio (or Guio)
first ancestor of Dan, 148

Diomanden
Malinké clan led migration south toward Mahou and Touba mountains, 205

Diop, Chekh Anta (Senegalese Africanist historian)
contribution to the decolonization of African scholarship, 14

dirhems
silver money of Arabia, 305

discourse
definition, 15

diseases
common ones in France, 295
Dutch brought to Cape Mount cholera and measles that killed many, 224
several of Jean Barbot men stricken by malaria and a few died, 252
smallpox in France in 1775, 295
some shared by Asia, Europe and Africa, 295

distance
measured in time, as in "Town A is one day's walk from Town B", 88

diviners
displaced in Muslim societies by people who claimed descent from the Prophet Muhammed, 170
their role in African religion, 80

Djolof
seized Mali territories on banks of Gambia River, 177

Do
political unit of Soso/Jalonke, 130

dog totem
shared by Traore clan (Bamana and Malinké) and Guilavoqui clan (Loma), 148

Dogo
rebellion against Folgia, 183

domboy
Bassa name for a glutinous entrée made from pounded cassava root, 321
resulted from fusion of cultures, 317

dominant language
expands at the expense of others, 124
wider access to knowledge and privileged communication, 124

Donelha, André
claimed Mane invaders were led by a woman, 181

Donnan, Elizabeth (American historian)
preference for Windward slaves in South Carolina, 272

Index

dotted-line pottery
    linked to aquatic culture in flooded West African savannah, 33

Drake, St. Clair (African-American sociologist and pan-Africanist scholar), 7

dried fish
    trade linked to Klao ethnic group, 57

Droe
    town along Malagueta Coast in late 1600s, 249

drought
    as cause of Soninké dispursal, 140
    began in 1400s and led to natural disaster, famine and political unrest in West Africa, 159
    caused scattering of West Africans in search of water, 120
    effects of from 1462 to 1700, 254

dry season
    extent and impact, 50

Duke of Arygle
    slave ship on which John Newton travelled, 277

Dunn, Richard S. (American historian)
    living conditions of English Caribbean slaveholders, 291
    sugar and slavery as two sides of a coin, 261

Duro
    another name for river at Cape Mesurado, 231

Dutch
    also see Holland, 239
    brought cholera and measles to Cape Mount that killed many, 224
    Cape of Good Hope post gave control of Asian trade, 239
    established post at the Cape of Good Hope, South Africa, 239
    increased presence in Liberia area, 240
    kidnapped 12 people from Kru Cess in mid-1600s, 234
    more ships in 1669 than all other European countries combined, 239
    overthrew the sultanate of Sulawesi, 239
    push into Atlantic trade after 1621 AD, 239
    reduced pepper crop in Bantam to drive up prices, 239
    seized key territories from Portuguese in 1600s, including Brazil, Elmina and Luana, 239
    shipwreck survivors were living among the Vai, 224
    significantly escalated African slave trade, 240

Dutch East India Company
    also Verrnigde Oost-Indische Compagnie, 219
    bled dry by corrupt agents, 246
    Dutch trading monopoly, 220
    number one import was pepper, 219
    trading company that benefited from artificial barriers, 247

Dutch West India Company
    exporting half a ton of gold from Gold Coast annually, 218

Duwan
    Dei ruler who reportedly made Gola pay to taste salt water although his mother was Gola, 60

dwellings
    built on stilts along Malagueta Coast, 300
    comparative analysis, 300
    made of "rushes or reeds" at Sestros, 300
    made of bamboo or reed along Sestros River in late 1600s, 250
    multistory structures at River Cess, 244
    three feet off ground near Sestros River due to prowling leopards, 250
    traditional design in Niger-Congo cultures, 51
    two stories high along Sestros River, 250

Dwyer, David J. (American linguist)
    noted three "dialect archipelagos" in Mano River region, 188
    southwest Mande language relationships, 146
    suggests Mende arose as lingua franca, 188

Dyula (ethnic group)
    diasporas established near gold fields in forest belt, 128

first Mande speakers encountered by many non-Mande groups, 140
name incorrectly applied to all Mande traders by many non-Mande groups, 140
possible ancestors of Kono, Dama and Vai, 143
trading caste that dispersed through West Africa after fall of Ghana, 128

Dyula traders
active in forest belt, 121

Eastern Krahn
ancestors originated near Nyaya, Côte d'Ivoire, 204
migration from Côte d'Ivoire to Liberia linked to Akan expansion, 205

eating utensils
comparative analysis, 299

economic development
linked to high population density by some scholars, 294

eddoes
example of forest-margin crop important to local diets, 226
staple of local diets, 226

Egrogeboes
identified by Paheco Pareira Duarte, 207

Egypt
Arab conquest of, 108
as place of refuge for Jesus and his parents, 106
contributions to early Christianity, 108
derived from the Greek word "Aigyptios", 36
first country to adopt Christianity en masse, 108

Ehret, Christopher (linguist)
definition of "uncivilized", 15
developments in Africa similar to elsewhere, 292

elders
control over allocation of resources, 53

elephants
also ivory, 241
many reported at Cape Mount in early 1700s, 241
numbers reduced due to foreign demand for ivory, 319
numbers reduced due to use of powerful imported weapons, 319
once plentiful along "Ivory Coast", 318
subject of mystery and romance since mid 1400s, 318

Elmina
Portuguese fort near gold mines of Gold Coast, 166

energy sources
common ones in region of Liberia, 295
extent of reliance on mules, 295
humans and animals most common, 295
importance of wood, 296
most common work animals, 295
spread of watermills from China to Europe, 296
superiority of horses to humans, 295
use of firewood in British homes until 1600s, 296

Enfa Nemate
said after snap-finger handshake along Malagueta Coast, 233

England
adventurers reportedly plundered and kidnapped at Cape Mesurado in early 1700s, 242
adventurers' arrival along Liberian coast, 221
banned Indian calico to protect its own textile industry, 248
banned Irish wool to protect its textile industry, 248
benefited from clearly defined borders, 247
commoners wore "crudely made" clothes, 298
competing with France to replace Amsterdam as dominant power after 1600 AD, 246
eclispe of Amsterdam sealed by Anglo-Dutch war of 1780-1784, 248
emergence as dominant world power after 1763 AD, 247
exclusive supplier of slaves to Spanish America, 246
formed alliance with Holland against France, 246

Index

held 17 American colonies in 1600s, 246
increased presence in West Africa, 248
influence of Arabic on language, 185
interest in West African trade fueled after 1650 by need for Caribbean plantation slaves, 265
its adventurers ravished Cape Mesurado region, 270
its success due in part to stable currency, 247
its trade with outside world controlled by Dutch shippers, 240
living conditions of its Caribbean slaves contrasted to masters', 291
merchants held sway over Amerian and Caribbean merchants and planters, 247
most homes in Worcestershire consisted of one room until 1700, 301
power increased by annexing Scotland, 246
rich covered their rank odor with fragrances, 302
rise fueled by African slave trade and exploitation of non-European lands, 247
rural poor rarely bath or washed clothes, 302
seized Caribbean territory while Holland was challenging Portugal and Spain for world dominance, 240
seized control of global textile industry, 247
strong central government aided its rise, 247
subjugation of Ireland's economy, 247
twice as many of its people in Caribbean as French in 1600s, 246

English East India Company
  trading monopoly, 220
English Royal Africa Company
  its export of African slaves, 266
  trading monopoly, 220, 247
ethical system
  inherent in African religion, 84
Ethiopia
  home to large number of Jews, 104
  second country to adopt Christianity en masse, 108
ethnic chauvinists
  so-called "tribalists", 17
ethnic group
  definition, 53
Eurocentrism
  assumed non-white societies to be inferior, 263
  contradictory views of India, China and Native Americans, 263
  copied by uneducated Africans who copied it from Western missionaries and "scholars", 19
  definition, 6
Europa
  ship that brought Nicholas Villault to Windward Coast, 228
  visited by local fishermen at River Cess, 232
Europe
  arrival in West Africa shifted locus of regional trade and power from Sahel to coast, 168
  began selling more of its own manufacture than global goods in 1800s, 309
  commoners lived in log cabins, 300
  commoners lived with their domestic animals, 300
  commoners' homes described as bleak, 299
  competition for West African trading posts, 166
  constant wars led to steady advances in arms, 307
  decline in bodily cleanliness after 1600 AD due to epidemics, 302
  demand for African slaves to work New World lands, 266
  encounters with other regions sparked innovations, 292
  expansion initially funded by Venician and Genoese bankers, 217
  first penetrated West African interior after 1746, 285
  gold removal from West Africa, 218
  histories of global expansion focus on explorers and their governments, 217

homes of rich infected with fleas and bugs, 300
industrial takeoff dates to 1800s, 309
initially not the most advanced region, 292
involved in most major wars, 295
its governments repeatedly provided subsidies to local businesses, 307
its rise fueled by collection and centralization of information, 308
key engines of growth, 304
key factors in its advancement above other regions, 307
largest cities initially along Mediterranean, 293
late in acquiring key iron-smelting techniques, 304
living standards improved dramatically in 1800s, 309
Mediterranean section fattened by global trade, 218
merchants as middlemen in global precious-metal trade, 307
merchant-state partnerships encouraged in contrast to West Africa, 165
money and power behind expansion, 217
most artisans worked in their homes, 301
most people ate gruel and cheap bread, 297
most people slept on floors, 299
northern countries more isolated and self-reliant than Mediterranean region, 218
northern section as core of world economy from 1590 AD, 218
people of southern cities held longstanding interest in West Africa, 119
politics focused on city, province and country while merchants operated globally, 220
power shifted to northern region around 1600 AD, 221
rapid growth of iron industry, 304
regional distinctions reinforced by Catholic-Protestant rivalry, 218
repeatedly banned foreign imports to protect local producers, 307
rise of northern section due to lower business costs, 218
role of companies in trade monopolies, 219
roughly on par with rest of world until 1700s, 307
royals ate with their fingers up to 1660 AD, 300
sailors' diet of dried meat, salt fish, hardtack biscuits, oil and wine, 321
scramble for lands in New World by naval powers, 266
shift from tributary economy to capitalism after 1450 AD, 220
shift from wood buildings to stone due to city fires, 300
shipbuilding industry gave its merchants important advantages, 303
trade spearheaded by monopolies, 219
traders kept away from West African gold mines, 119
turned waterways from limitation to advantage, 163
two distinct regions from 800 AD, 218
unravelled secret of steelmaking in 1800s, 309
urban growth due to internatonal trade, 293
West African forts as holding cells for slaves, 167
Windward Coast people apprehensive of ship traffic due to kidnappings, 234
European names
common among local rulers and traders along Windward Coast, 318
commonly used by local rulers along Liberian coast in early 1700s, 244
used by children at Sestros in 1688 AD, 318
evergreens
forest trees that keep leaves year round, 49
evil
seen in African religion as originating in unclean hearts of antisocial people, 85
evil people
driven by unbridled passions, 86
sociopaths or so-called "witches", 86
threats to the moral order, 86

Index

viewed in African religion as allies of bats and
  other loathed creatures, 87
viewed in African religion as egocentric and
  egotistical, 86
viewed in African religion as knowledgable but
  selfish, 86
extinction
  constant danger to early societies, 51
faama (also farma/falma)
  Mandinka title for military leader, 181
factory farms
  controlled every step in the supply chain of key
    crops, 266
  crucial to European seizure of world trade, 266
fadenya ("father-childness" or
  a spirit of competitiveness), 83
fairs
  common in Europe but not in China, 305
  conduits for new ideas, 307
Falasha
  Ethiopian Jews, 104
famines
  caused by periodic expansion of Sahara, 35
  European cases, 295
  once common everywhere, including Europe,
    292
  period when new foods are most likely to be
    adopted, 321
Famolla
  district dominated by Loma Koivoguis clan, 202
Famoila-Kpetea
  district dominated by Loma Koivoguis clan, 202
Fanti (ethnic group)
  known for early expert fishing traditions, 57
Fanti cloths
  Liberian name for European imitations of
    Javanese batiks, 320
  resulted from fusion of cultures, 317
farming
  largely the same throughout the world until
    1700s, 296
fasciparum malaria
  replaced vivax variety, 49
Ferabure
  ruler at Sierra Leone converted to Catholicism
    and took name "Philip", 317
Feren (also known as Fali Kama, Fonigama and
    Fanggama)
  non-Muslim leader of Kamara clan linked to
    kokologi in Loma oral tradition, 201
ferruginous laterite
  reddish pebbles formed when iron-laced soil is
    exposed to rain, 49
Fesiach
  nephew of Flonikerry who persuaded Folgia to
    attack Vai, 183
fetish
  label applied by Portuguese to African carvings,
    which they dismissed as "false gods", 16
figs
  among foodstuff at Sestros, 253
finger-snap handshake
  standard at River Cess in mid-1600s, 233
fireplaces
  confined to homes of rich Europeans up to
    1700s, 300
fish
  at Settre Crou said to be similar to Gold Coast,
    245
  caught with large nets at Cape Mount in early
    1700s, 241
  similar at River Cess, Cape Mesurado and Cape
    Mesurado, 244
fishing communities
  location of towns, 59
  specialized knowledge, 58
Fishmen
  name applied by English-speakers to Kle-po, 208
Five Towns
  towns purportedly founded by Gold Coast

immigrants, namely Little Kroo, Setra Koo,
Kroo-Bar, Nana Kroo and King Will's Town,
209
fixed capital goods
    stark contrast between Europe and West Africa,
307
Flamore
    thaba or ruler of Cape Mount spoke French, 224
Flonikerry
    Folgia leader slain during attack by Gola, 183
    led Folgia conquest of Gola, 183
Florence
    key source of credit for European governments
around 1300 AD, 217
    later competitor to Middle Eastern trade
network, 217
foivo
    chief musical instrument in Poro ceremonies of
Dei ethnic group, 59
Folgia
    cited in Quoia text as north of Hondo, 185
    crushed rebellions by Bullom and Dogo, 183
    defeated Gola attackers with help from Vai, 183
    likely route taken to the coast, 183
    located between Anverado (Mesurado?) and
Junk rivers, 186
    origin traced to Junk River by Olfert Dapper, 182
    possibly a clan of Mende, 185
    violated Karou taboo by dumping fish with scales
in their sacred pool, 182
    warriors used poisoned arrows in attack on Vai,
183
Foningama
    member of Kamara clan who ruled Musdadu in
late 1550s, 178
forced labor
    killed off local people from Hispaniola, Puerto
Rico and Cuba, 218
    relied on by Spain for gold extraction from
Caribbean, 218
    relied on by Spain for gold extraction from Peru,
219
forces
    used in context of African religion in place of
"spirits" or "supernatural beings", 71
foreign goods
    list of popular items, 305
forest belt
    geographic expanse of West African
communities, 49
forest belt communities
    blacksmiths excelled as hardening and
sharpening iron, 303
    lack of pack animals inhibited growth, 308
    overrun by Sahelian, 191
forest-margin plants
    importance of tubers and oil palm, 225
    importance to local economies, 225
fowls
    plentiful at River Cess in mid-1600s, 233
    plentiful at Sestros River in 1727 AD, 254
    said to be plentiful and cheap at Cape Mount in
mid-1600s, 230
France
    commoners worn clothes made from rough
broadcloth, 299
    competing with England to replace Amsterdam
as dominant power after 1600 AD, 246
    first European "nation", 248
    first European power to abolish slavery, 284
    held eight American colonies in 1600s, 246
    its economy in 1600s controled by Dutch
wholesalers, 240
    its people in Caribbean in 1600s half of English,
246
    latecomer to plunder of non-European lands, 246
    most rural homes consisted of one room, 300
    restored slavery eight years after original
abolition, 284
    second-ranked exporter of slaves from
Windward Coast, 271
    seized Caribbean territory while Holland was

Index

challenging Portugual and Spain for world
dominance, 240
turned to Africa in late 1700s after losing trade
elsewhere, 248
West Africa trade initially confined to less
profitably areas like Liberia, 221
Free African Union Society of Newport, Rhode Island
back-to-African movement, 282
Freeman, Peter
broker between St. Paul and Junk rivers in early
1750s, 318
Freeman, William
local man between Grand Bassa and Tabocaney,
318
Freetown, Sierra Leone
establishment of free black colony, 282
focal point of New World black emigrationist
impulse, 282
officially known as "Province of Freedom", 282
place where early Europeans bought high-quality
gold, 165
French East India Company
trading monopoly, 220
French Levant Company
trading monopoly, 220
French Revolution
quickened New World black demands for
freedom, 284
French West India Company
trading monopoly, 220
Fula (ethnic group)
allies of Soso in defense against Mane, 180
also Fulani, 16
calvary skills led to capture of Guinea from
Maninké, 284
herders originated in Mauritania, 40
knowledge of metal smelting and herding, 35
present in Futa Toro, Guinea by 1,300 BC, 40
split from Wolof, 46
unification by militant Muslim clergy, 284

Fula empire
seizure of Bambuk gold field from Mali, 177
Fula herders
included in Mali empire, 132
Fula horses, 180
Fulfunde
example of domiant language, 124
language of the Fulani, 9
previous classification as "Hamitic", 9
fundamentalism
main perspective on culture among Liberians,
317
funeral
description of at River Cess in early 1700s, 244
earliest recorded description of one along
Liberian coast, 244
functions, 79
furniture
chest and cupboard common in Arabia, 299
comparative analysis, 299
drapes, pillows and carpets common in Arabia,
299
featured tables, chairs, curtains, shelves,
cupboards and cabinets in China, 299
wooden chest common in many regions, 299
Futa Jalon
Fulfunde word for "Jalo land", 130
Futa Toro
region in Guinea controlled by Fula for 250 years,
177
Gabriel, Richard A. (Canadian historian)
Ten Commandments not a code of ethics, 100
Gandimbe
Limba name for Loko implying Bandi ancestry,
198
Gao
capitol of Songhai empire and renown center of
learning, 170
position on Niger River, 121
Sahelian city formed as formerly scattered

villages melded into one mass, 151
Garamantes
    dominant traders across eastern half of Sahara, 102
    mysterious group of unknown origin that created watering system in Sahara, 102
Garvey, Marcus (Jamaican pan-Africanist), xxvii
Gbanli-woo
    meaning "language of the Gbali", 146
    northern-most dialect of Kpelle, 198
gbassajamba
    Vai name for a sauce made from cassava leaves, 321
Gbenson
    hometown in Guinea of many Liberian Ma, 203
Gbeta (Kru sub-group)
    oral tradition cites early association with Mande-speakers, 203
    southern vanguard of Kru speaking groups, 47
Gbetu
    masked performer on ritual occasions, 74
Gbohn
    Dei word for war town, 324
Gbunde
    Loma dialect, 146, 198
Gebbe
    group near Cape Mesurado subdued by Gebbe, 183
General Court of Massachusetts
    petitioned by free blacks for funds to return to Africa, 284
Genoa
    center of European finance, 221
    early cradle of capitalism, 217
    key Mediterranean slave mart, 218
    key source of credit for European governments beginning in late 1500s AD, 217
    later competitor to Middle Eastern trade network, 217
    merchants intergral to Spain's rise, 221
    resident produced oldest map of West Africa, 119
    rise fueled by ban on competitive imports, 218
    trading network ran from Egypt to England, 218
George
    Cape Mount ruler in early 1750s, 318
Georgia
    preference for Windward slaves, 272
geze
    small hoe-shaped implements that functioned as currency in kola-producing region, 63
Ghana (c. 830-c. 1235 AD)
    center of West African salt trade, 128
    factors leading to decline, 128
    first mention in European sources, 118
    first significant West African empire, 128
    its collapse as spur of conflicts and migrations, 140
    its fall led to major political realignments in the Sahel, 128
Gissimai
    one of first Loma towns in Liberia, 201
Gizi-ma
    Loma dialect whose name means "on the Mountain", 146
Gjuilavogui, Joseph (historian)
    on name of Loma ethnic group, 147
glass beads
    worn by River Cess men in various colors, 251
glass windows
    confined to homes of rich Europeans up to 1700s, 300
Glebo (ethnic group)
    ancestors known as Gbobo reportedly lived in area now occupied by Krahn, 205
    ancestors moved from Grand Gedeh to Bereby, 206
    ancestors originated near Nyaya, Côte d'Ivoire, 204
    low sickle-cell frequency, 210
    migration from Côte d'Ivoire to Liberia linked to Akan expansion, 205

Index 365

migration of some ancestors from northeast of the Sassandra River to Mt. Gedeh, 196
migration toward Mt. Gedeh, 197
oral tradition claim their ancestors founded Grand Cess, Picininny Cess and Sasstown, 207
oral tradition claim they met Europeans upon first arrival at Cape Palmas, 207
probably group identified as "Egrogeboes" in 1505-1508 AD, 207
probably group identified as "Gruvo" in 1614 AD, 207
purported origin of group's name, 206
glottochronology
  definition, 4
God
  all good but not all powerful in both Ancient Egyptian and African religions, 96
  discussed poeticallly using nicknames in context of African religion, 72
  source of all life forces in African religion, 74
Gola (ethnic group), xxviii
  ancestors probably linked to early human remains at Kolahun, 47
  attacked Karou and Folgia conquerors of Vai, 183
  Bandi and Mende pushed some Kissi into their territory, 198
  cited in oral tradition as founder of Poro, 151
  cited in Quoia text as located north of Hondo, 185
  credit war "medicine" to Mende, Loma, Kissi and Bandi, 199
  customary law allowed men to be sold as slaves if accused of adultery by richmen's wives, 324
  defeated by Folgia, 183
  displaced by Kpelle, 202
  early link to northern kola trade, 55
  encountered Kuwaa, Dei and Bassa during southward migration, 200
  established remote villages in forest to escape fighting, 200
  first Atlantic group in Liberia area, 46
  high sickle-cell frequency, 210
  identified in many oral traditions as first inhabitants of northern forest rim, 197
  identity as outcome of choice and validation, 54
  ignored for study at Liberia College by Edward W. Blyden, 17
  labeled as hunters and gatherers by some anthropologists, 16
  living along forest belt when Mande speakers arrived, 142
  long dismissed by Eurocentric scholars as "primitive", 61
  many captives were taken to South Carolina during slave trade, 324
  markedly different from Kissi, 46
  moved southwest into dense forest under pressure from Mende and Kissi, 199
  name for "January", 28
  name for "November", 50
  oral traditions, 46
  oral traditions cite Dei and Vai as earliest neighbors, 143
  oral traditions cite intermarriage with Dei and Vai, 143
  oral traditions credit Mende with pushing some Kissi into their territory, 198
  oral traditions say they expelled Vai ancestors toward Dei, 143
  originally confined to Komgba Mountain, 142
  originally inhabited northeastern mountains in Liberia, 197
  pattern of small, scattered villages, 53
  previously blocked from Dei salt-making villages, 197
  preyed upon by slave kidnappers, 324
  recall food shortage when other ethnic groups moved into territory, 200
  reportedly punished by Folgia for disrespecting Manimassah, 183

rites of passage, 79
ruler reportedly sold entire Sande society class of girls to slave buyer, 324
settlement pattern conforms to segmentary lineage system, 209
shared Poro with Quoia, Karou, Folgia, Manou and Hondo, 186
some placed themselves under protection of Vai and Dei, 200
some preceeded Mende in Cape Mount by two generations, 188
some settled among Vai, 189
southern vanguard of Atlantic languages, 46
standing in Poro probably derived from status as early settlers of area, 151
territory produced most desirable kola, 56
their salt trade allegedly attracted Vai ancestors to region, 143

Gola language
example of loan word from Portuguese, 318

Gola-Vai
as inhabitants of Quoia country, 185
group resulting from mixture of Vai hosts and Gola driven south from home in "Hondo", 185

gold
acute shortage facing Europe in early 1400s, 164
arrival of Europeans shifted trade and profits within West Africa from Sahel to coast, 168
discovery in Brazil boosted demand for African slaves after 1690s, 262
drained away from Europe by early Asian trade, 164
early West African exports, 165
Fernáo Gomes given exclusive rights to buy from Freetown, 165
major motivating factor for early Portuguese explorations, 164
Morocco invaded Songhai Empire to seize mines, 171
Portugal's grip on world market challenged, 165
Portuguese direct access to West African mines fueled decline of rival Morocco, 171
revival of caravan trade from West Africa to North Africa, 166
Sahelian empires as major supplier to Europe and Muslim world, 119
scarcity bred demand and high value, 165
spending by Mansa Kanka Musa's entourage in Cairo led to worldwide devaluation, 132
used as currency, 119
used to buy slaves as demand increased, 266
West Africa's at the base of early European currency systems, 119

Gold Coast
historical and cultural ties with Kru Coast, 208

Gomes, Fernáo
exploration of Gold Coast led to seat on Portuguese royal council, 165
funded initial voyage to Gold Coast, 165
Lisbon capitalist given exclusive rights to buy gold from Freetown, 165

Gonja
state north of the Black Volta founded by Dyula, 190

Gono
Vai word for war town, 324

goro
alternative name for "kola" possibly derived from the word "Gola", 56

Gouin Mountain
location near Touba, Côte d'Ivoire where Dan reportedly originated, 148

Govero, Niger
location of the Sahara's largest and oldest graveyard found to date, 31

Grand Cess
name given to town by Portuguese, 161
originally called "Siglipo", 207
some residents spoke French, 249
town along Malagueta Coast in late 1600s, 249

Grand Gedeh
site of early iron smelting sites, 45

Grant, Oswald & Co.
   slave factory on Sierra Leone River, 276
grass fiber
   used for clothing east of River Cess, 227
Gray, Jonathan
   local man between Grand Bassa and Tabocaney, 318
Great Mosque of Timbuktu
   commissioned by Mansa Kanka Musa, 131
   reportedly built by Andalusian architect Abu Ishaq al-Sahili, 131
Grey, William
   local man near St. Paul River, 318
griots
   purveyors of official history among Mande, 123
Grovogui
   a leading Loma clan, 202
Gruvo
   group identified by Samuel Braun in 1614 AD, 207
Guéré (also N'Guéré)
   adopted from Malinké by French, 18
   applied to the Krahn and Sapo in Côte d'Ivoire, 18
   Malinké term meaning "uncivilized", 18
Guéré (ethnic group)
   also called "Eastern Wee" by linguists, 197
Guiépa (Guiéta in Kpelle)
   Ma town where Kpelle ancestors settled, 147
Guiéta (Guiépa in Ma)
   epicenter of Nzérékoré region, 203
   town founded by Kpelle emigré from Missadougou, 203
   town in Guinea used as transit point by many groups migrated into Liberia, 203
Guilavogui
   a leading Loma clan, 148, 202
Guinea
   British coin minted mainly with West African gold, 165
   derived from Arabic word "Janawa", 119
Guinea current
   strong continuous flow of Atlantic Ocean parallel to the Liberian coast, 58
guinea fowl
   domesticated in West Africa, 39
Guio (or Dio)
   first ancestor of Dan, 148
gunpowder
   major commodity used to buy slaves, 273
guns
   major commodity used to buy slaves, 273
   popular types on Windward Coast, 275
gunshots
   major commodity used to buy slaves, 273
Guro (ethnic group)
   ancestors migrated from direction of Burkino Faso, 147
Habash
   one label applied to Africans by Arabs, 109
Habashat
   section of Ethiopia that gave refuge to followers of Prophet Muhammad, 109
Hair, P. E. H. (British linguist)
   Quoia vocabulary similar to contemporary Vai, 185
Haiti
   creation of republican government, 284
   defeated army sent by Napoleon Bonaparte, 284
   first black state in modern world, 284
   its revolution drove white former masters to seek refuge in U. S., 284
   its revolution quickened political changes around the world, 284
   its revolution spread panic among whites and hope among blacks in U.S., 284
hajj
   requirement that every able adult Muslim visit holy sites in Saudi Arabia, 109
Hal Pular speakers

mixture of Malinké and Fula, 191
Hall, Prince
    among blacks seeking repatriation to Africa, 284
    founder of black order of Free Masons, 284
Ham, Biblical story of
    basis for racist stereotyping of Africans as cursed, 7
Hamitic myth
    cites Malinké and Fula as superior to other West Africans, 9
    devastating impact on the writing of African history, 8
Han (China)
    example of dominant language, 124
hardtack biscuits
    introduced to West Africa by European sailors, 321
hardwoods
    needed for ironsmelting, 140
Harmattan
    warm, dry and dusty air mass that blows south from the Sahara in January, 27
Hasa-la
    Bandi subgroup whose name means "the rocky place", 146, 198
Hausa
    Afrasiatic language of Nigeria, 36
    example of dominant langauge, 124
Hawkins, John
    included on his crest a bound and bejeweled African woman, 265
    sought slaves exclusively while his father had been content with ivories and spices, 265
Hawkins, William
    content to buy ivories and spices but his son sought slaves, 265
    English adventurer who bartered for ivory near River Sestros between 1530 and 1532 AD, 221
healers-diviners
    derisively labeled "medicine men" by Europeans, 81
    skillful readers of people and the properties of organic materials, 81
herbalists
    displaced in Muslim societies by people who claimed descent from the Prophet Muhammed, 170
herders
    beneficiaries of hospitality shown to "strangers", 116
herring
    preserved by smoking and salting, 298
Himmelheber, Han (historian)
    movement of Dan ancestors, 196
historical comparative linguistics
    definition, 4
historical knowledge
    rules for organizing and ensuring reliability, 5
Hoerder, Dirk (historian
    migrations as constant in history, 139
Hoggar
    terminus of important trade route seized by Sundiata, 131
Højbjorg, Christian Kondt (Daninsh anthropologist)
    linked origin of Loma ethnic group to Konianké, 140
Holland
    country that encompassed seven formerly separate Dutch states, 239
    also see Dutch, 239
    global ascent came through banking and navigation, 239
    half its land was underwater and a quarter unfit for farming, 239
    held three American colonies in 1600s, 246
    imported about 75 percent of food, 239
    its merchants inserted themselves into an extensive, existing Asian network, 307
    its shippers controlled England's trade with outside world, 240
    its wholesalers controlled French economy in 1600s, 240

Index

reduced to junior parner of England, 246
removed more slaves from Windward Coast from than any region, 271
rivers of wealth from Asian spices, 219
third-ranked exporter of slaves from Windward Coast, 271
turned to Windward Coast for slaves after 1740, 271
unlikely candidate for world domination, 239

Holsoe, Sven E. (American anthropologist)
identification of Bassa with Karou group in Quoia text, 186
identification of Kpelle with Folgia group in Quoia text, 186

holy days
liturgical calendar of African religion, 79

Hondo
group north of Quoia among whom some Mende lived, 185
name given to Bandi ancestors by Olfert Dapper, 185
previous home of Gola who settled among Vai, 185

horses
once used to cross the desert, 116
provided Sahelian calvaries psychological superiority over other West Africans, 124

Horton, Robin (English anthropologist)
three patterns of settlements in forest belt, 209

hospitality
African standard of obligated land-holding families to host "strangers", 170
African standards of, 108, 115

housing
defined by social status at Cape Mount, 230

Howard, Allen M. (American historian)
borders of West African states shaped by shifting spheres of authority, 124
fluidity of ethnic identity, 54
Northern Mande identity and nodal places, 195

on Mande movements and settlements, 189
regional ties of leading traders, 122
significance of regional trade centers, 149

Hu-bandi
Limba name for Loko language, 146, 198

human labor
once was most valued economic asset in Africa, 308

hungry times (also famines)
common theme in Liberian folktales suggesting prevalence of famines, 51
frequent theme in folk tales, 294

hunters, 336
as perceived in African religion, 82
beneficiaries of hospitality shown to "strangers", 116
characterized in Mande cultures as possessing fadenya, "father-childness" or competitiveness, 83
combined personality of explorer with advanced knowledge of nature, 83
credited by Vai oral tradition with discovering ocean and Gola salt trade, 144
essential to smooth functioning of society, 83
heroic role in founding tales, 49
physical skills and unseen powers, 83
status in Mande societies, 83
viewed by others with respect and fear, 83

hunters and gatherers
"primitive" label erroneously applied to Kru, Kissi and Gola by Eurocentric scholars, 61
label applied dismissively by some anthropologists to Gola, Kissi and Kru-speaking people, 16

hunters' shirts
embodied the disorder and life-force of the bush, 83

Ibn Battuta, Muhammad (1304-1369 AD)
Tangiers-born world traveller and author, 125
viewed enslavement of non-Arabs as ordained by

God, 118
Ibn Hawqal (Mesopotamian visitor to the Sahel)
    salt prices, 56
Ibn Khaldun, Rahman (1332-1406 AD)
    Arab geographer who described blacks as closer to dumb animals than to humans, 110
    Tunis-born geographer, economist and historian, 125
incest
    thought to produce infertility, 77
Indian Ocean
    once controlled by Muslim navies, 303
indigo
    blue dye obtained from the leaf of a tree, 227
    blue dye used on cotton cloth, 227
industry
    important source of economic productivity, 303
inequality
    rise of among Mande, 123
Inikori, J. E. (historian)
    importance of guns, gunpowder and shots in slave trade, 275
interlopers
    term applied by Portuguese to European competitors for West African trade, 166
intermarriage
    between Kru-speakers and Mande groups, 148
    between Ma and Kpelle, 179
    between Puy and Karou, 185
    between Vai, Gola and Dei, 143
    Kpelle as fusion of Mande and Wee, 147
iron
    functioned as currency in many societies, 305
    historic significance of commodity in West Africa, 54
    large quantities smelted by Loko and sold to Portuguese, 168
    Mande root of word for this item was not shared by other local languages, 63
    probably did not diffuse from Mande-speakers to forest, 63
iron bars
    used as currency, 119
iron rings
    weighing 3 lbs. worn by a few River Cess men, 251
iron smelting
    African origin near Central African Republic, 39
    diffusion along the Atlantic coast, 39
    key engine of economic progress worldwide, 303
    major engine of growth along Windward Coast, 303
Isis
    cult of in southern Europe, 105
    her statutes as basis for Black Madonna cult, 106
    wife of Osiris in religion of Ancient Egypt, 105
Islam
    African conversions impeded by traditional local religion, 126
    forbidden (haram) for one Muslim to enslave another, 169
    found refuge in Africa from attacks by Arab non-believers, 108
    idea that it was better suited to African culture than Christianity advanced by Edward Wilmot Blyden, 17
    increased imposition over time by Sahelian empires on forest belt neighbors, 152
    initially offered protection to Christians in North Africa, 109
    its conquests created a world economy, 109
    its conquests created first caliph or world government, 109
    Muslim men permitted to marry non-Muslim women, 171
    Muslim women prohibited from marrying non-Muslim men, 171
    phases of its advance in West Africa, 170
    projected by Arabs as inseparable from their culture, 109
    spread from Gaza Strip to Egypt, 108
    spread to forest led by African Sufis, 171

Index

spread to North Africa, 108
Islamic societies
   placed greatest stress on personal cleanliness, 302
Isma'il, Mawlay (1672-1727)
   Moroccan sultan who reportedly operated army with 250,000 enslaved black men, 284
Italian cities
   power distinct from Greek and Roman empires, 217
   rise funded by improved farming, trade and crafts, 217
   subordinate partners in Middle Eastern trade network, 217
itinerant artists
   beneficiaries of hospitality shown to "strangers", 116
ivory
   brisk trade at Cape Mount and Cape Mesurado until 1600s, 319
   Cape Mount trade exhausted by 1687 AD, 319
   Jean Barbot assumed Sestos interior was teeming with elephants but people were too lazy to hunt, 251
   major trade item at Cape Mesurado in mid-1600s, 231
   meager supply at Cape Mesurado in early 1700s, 243
   motivating factor for early Portuguese explorations, 164
   plentiful along Malagueta Coast until 1687 AD, 319
   plentiful at Cape Mount in mid-1600s, 231
   plentiful at River Cess in mid-1600s but expensive, 233
   prices at Cape Mesurado said to be too high in mid-1600s, 232
   scarce along Windward Coast by 1687 except for Malagueta Coast, 319
   trade dried up at Cape Mount, River Sestro and Sangwin by 1687, 319
   used in Europe for tool handles, billiard balls, ornate cups and other luxury items, 319
Jacob
   assistant to River Cess ruler named Barsaw, 250
   local broker at Cestos River, 318
Jalo/Concho
   political unit of Soso/Jalonke, 130
Jalonke
   northern Mande word for "people from Jalon", 130
   with Soso, as center of longstanding polity, 130
James
   ruler of Bossoe town in early 1700s, 245
   said to talk incessantly of women and sex, 245
Jan Capo Monte
   Cape Mount ruler in early 1700s, 241
   said to have 400 wives, 241
Janawa
   Arabic word for section of West Africa, 119
Jara
   remnant unit of Ghana absorbed by Mali, 131
Jefferson, Thomas (U. S. president and slaveholder)
   his racism attacked by Joseph Jenkins Roberts, 12
   on economic power of English merchants over American planters, 247
   racist ideas of, 8
Jenne
   leading town of Mali empire, 132
   Sahelian city formed as formerly scattered villages melded into one mass, 151
Jenne-Jeno, Mali Empire
   site of industrial-scale iron production, 39
Jews (ethnic group)
   left Hebrew inscriptions in western Sahara, 105
   showed little interest in converting Africans to Judiaism, 105
   smattering of merchants and artisans in early West Africa, 104
Johnson, Ben

local man between Grand Bassa and Tabocaney, 318
Johnston, Harry (British colonial official and historian)
    presented Fula as the embodiment of the mythical Hamitic race, 16
Jomani, Kamala Ba
    Malian credited by Vai oral tradition with expedition to coast, 144
Jones, Adam and Marion Johnson (British historians)
    their estimate of Windward Coast slave exports, 268
Judaism
    differs from African religion because it lacks a conception of afterlife, 100
    impact of Akenaten's religious revolution, 102
    ties to Ancient Egypt, 99
junior brothers
    tensions with senior brothers inherent in kinship system, 53
junior wives
    tensions with senior wives inherent in kinship system, 53
Junk River
    apparent links between people here and Sierra Leone or Gambia, 162
    area explored by Pedro de Sintra, first European visitor to region, 159
    entrance measured by William Smith for Royal African Company, 254
    name was applied to what is now St. John River until late 1700s, 249
Kabor (Kru sub-group)
    oral tradition cites early association with Mande-speakers, 203
    southern vanguard of Kru-speaking groups, 47
Kaemblahuu
    previously held by Bandi, 199
Kamabai, Sierra Leone
    site of rock shelter with early evidence of human habitation, 45

Kamara
    Malinké clan linked to Mane invasion by scholars, 181
    Malinké clan that expanded after Sundiata's victory over Sumanguru, 178
    Malinké clan that originated near Lake Debo in Mali, 178
    Malinké clan that settled in Musadu after collapse of Mali, 178
    names used by Mane invaders, 181
    oral traditions recall military movements to the sea, 181
Kamara, Faran
    close ally of Sundiata in his battle with Sumanguru, 178
Kambai Bli
    historically significant town in history of Dei, 59
Kambo Mountains
    location temporarily settled by Vai founders, 144
Kangaba
    sub-unit of Mali empire, 131
Kankaba
    Soninké town that supplied most Dyula traders to forest belt, 140
Kankan, Guinea
    main transit point for Buré gold and forest products, 141
    originally a Kissi town, 149
Kankiya
    among earliest Klao towns, 207
    swept away by Nonbwa River, 207
Kanté, Kémoko
    forged political unit rooted in Soso (also "Susu" or "Soosoo") ethnic group, 129
Kanté, Sumaoro (also Sumanguro)
    son of Kémoko Kanté, 129
Karana
    town founded by Dané, first ancestor of Ma, 148
Karou
    allied with Folgia in conquest of Vai, 183
    as inhabitants of Quoia country, 185

enemies of Folgia before alliance against Quoia, 182
Mende and Bandi name for the Vai, 183
origin traced to Junk River by Olfert Dapper, 182
possibly a clan of Mende, 185
reportedly conquered Quoia with assistance of Folgia, 182
taboo against eating fish with scales, 182

Karras, Alan L. (American historian)
pirates created "criminal political economy", 246

Kebra Nagast
book chronicling the history of Ethiopian rulers, 104

Keita
Malinké clan that occupied Kissidugu after fall of Mali, 178

Kejugu, Sogolon
mother of Sundiata, 130

Kelema
previously held by Bandi, 199

kidnapping
common in Europe and Africa as means of securing slaves, 160

kin relations
hierarchical arrangement of, 53

King Solomon of Israel
his link to Queen Makeda in Ethiopian traditions, 99

King Wills Town
one of five towns reportedly founded by seafarers from the Gold Coast, 208

kinship labels
application to many non-kinship domains, 52
used by contenders for power to mobilize support, 139
used by Sahelian rulers to justify their power, 152

kinship system
function of, 52
tensions between the rulers and the ruled, 53
undermined by reliance on trading, 122

Kissi (ethnic group)
ancestors probably linked to early human remains at Kolahun, 47
assimilated with Bandi over time, 199
dispersion caused by Malinké invasion around 1600 AD, 197
high sickle-cell frequency, 210
known as "the rice people" because they grew so much, 60
labeled as hunters and gatherers by some anthropologists, 16
Liberian branch regarded as more authentic than Guinean, 199
link to early iron-working tradition, 62
living along forest belt when Mande speakers arrived, 142
long dismissed by Eurocentric scholars as "primitive", 61
longterm symbiotic relationship with Loma, 149
markedly different from Gola, 46
oral traditions credit their ancestors for stone sculptures found buried in areas of Mano River region, 61
originally in territory now held by Kono, Loma, Bandi and Mende, 142
pattern of small, scattered villages, 53
produced twisted iron bars that functioned as currency in forest belt, 303
renown for blacksmiths, 303
reportedly crossed into Liberia seeking wild game, 198
settlement pattern conforms to segmentary lineage system, 209
some live in territory previously help by Bandi, 199
some now live in areas with Loma place names, 198
some were pushed south by Mende and Bandi, 198

southern vanguard of Atlantic languages, 46
standing in Poro probably derived from status as
  early settlers of area, 151
those in Guinea assimilated with Malinké, 199
town with names in its language now held by
  groups that arrived later, 143

Kissi language
  closely related to Bullom, 188
  common first names among Windward slaves,
    276

Kissidugu, Guinea
  occupied by Keita clan after fall of Mali, 178
  one of four early regional trade centers, 149
  originally a Kissi town, 149
  previous residents displaced by Malinké
    splintered into Bandi, Loko and Mende, 197
  refuge of Dankaran Tuman and his loyalists who
    fled Mali empire, 130, 140
  trade hub for Bandi, Mende, Loma and some
    Kissi, 149

Ki-Zerbo, Joseph (Burkinabé historian)
  called for a new total African history, 19

Klao (ethnic group)
  affinity for Aggrey beads suggest early link to
    Gold Coast, 57
  ancestors probably living in Liberia area by 990
    AD, 47
  ancestors reportedly came from north, 207
  apparently reached coast via Cestros River, 47
  arrival in present location tentatively dated to
    1500 AD, 209
  canoes important for transportation of goods
    and people, 57
  iron ring as insignia of high priest, 82
  likely early exporters of malagueta spice, 57
  linked in oral traditions to salt trade, 57
  longstanding fishing tradition, 57
  low sickle-cell frequency, 210
  migration of some ancestors from northeast of
    the Sassandra River to Mt. Gedeh, 196
  migration toward Mt. Gedeh, 197
  myth that members were not enslaved, 275
  now located where Quaabe-Monou lived in 1668
    AD, 209
  reportedly taught canoe building to Bassa, 207
  sample words recorded by Bordeaux captain in
    1545 AD, 221
  some ancestors had apparently engaged in rice
    farming along forest rim, 207
  some ancestors reportedly went east after
    encounter with Bassa, 206

Klao language
  common first names among Windward slaves,
    276

Kle-po (or Swa-po)
  composed of Kabor and Gbeta clans, 209
  lived among Klao, Bassa, Dei and Vai group, 209
  name of group on Kru Coast who fished, 208

knowledge
  as ultimate force or power, 85

Koblama
  previously held by Bandi, 199

Koelle, Sigismund (German missionary and linguist),
  3

Kohiré (also Sango)
  mountain from which first ancestor of Ma
    descended, 148

Koivogui
  Loma clan that shares leopard as protective
    animal with Kamara, 202

kokologi
  agreement credited to Feren in Loma oral
    tradition, 201
  agreement entered into by strangers in Loma
    territory to respect sacred sites, 201
  agreement linked to Musadu in Loma oral
    tradition, 201

kola, xxxi, 80
  abundant at Sestros, 253
  apparent availability in early Mediterranean
    markets, 55
  as social lubricant, 55

c. nitida variety as most valuable, 55
care and protection of trees by Loma and Kpelle, 147
characteristics of plant, 55
example of forest plant important to local economies, 225
geographic spread of plants, 55
historic significance of commodity in West Africa, 54
interpretation by diviners, 81
local words for linked to two ethnic groups, 55
loses flavor quickly, 115
ritual offering to ancestors, 77
source of caffine and other stimuli, 55
trade as factor attracting migrants from Sahel, 141
trade centered in Mali Empire, 55
trade involving Kru-speakers and southwest Mande groups, 196
traded from Liberia region to Niger River, 115
used as currency, 119

Kolahun
site of rock shelter with early evidence of human habitation, 45

Koli
son of Tengella who shifted Fula control to Futa Toro, 177

Komendi
another name for Manya ethnic group living along Liberia-Guinea border, 185

Komgba
ancestral home of Gola, 197

Kone
Malinké clan that pushed Kpelle south, 178

Konianké
displaced Loma from Beyla region of Guinea, 148
Malinké clan dominant in Coyah region, 183

Kono (ethnic group of Guinea)
reportedly descended from Ma, 148
similar language once reputedly spoken by some ancestors of Ma, 196

Kono (ethnic group of Sierra Leone)
name reputedly derived from phrase meaning "those left behind", 144
pushed to present location by Kissi, 198

Konodougou (town)
reportedly liberated from Konoinké by Kpelle with help from Dan, 179

Korblima, Guinea
previous reputed home of Bandi, 198

Kouranko
Malinké clan that invaded terrritory south of Niger after fall of Mali, 178
Malinké clan that seized Macenta after fall of Mali, 178

Kpandelo
previously held by Bandi, 199

Kpelle (ethnic group), 147
ancestors departure from Mali, 179
ancestors met Wee people in area, 147
ancestors reportedly met Bassa and Dan in area, 149
ancestors settled in Guiépa among the Ma, 147
betrayed by Malinké occupation of Musadu, 201
came into Liberia reportedly seeking to engage in coastal trade, 201
care and protection of kola trees, 147
claim to have expelled Konionké from Konodougou with helped from Dan, 179
consider Kono of Guinea to be their cousins, 202
dispersion caused by Malinké invasion around 1600 AD, 197
first encountered Ma near Nzerekore, 179
fled Missadougou due to strife with northern Mande groups, 202
high sickle-cell frequency, 210
identified with Folgia group in Quoia text by anthropologist Sven E. Holsoe, 186
identity as outcome of choice and validation, 54
identity formed in the forest belt, 179

largest and probably most disruptive migration into Liberia, 201
linked to Basenji dog, 34
mixture of Mande and Wee, according to oral tradition, 147
northern most dialect called Gbanli-woo, 146
oral traditions claim land given to Feren was linked to his Poro membership, 201
oral traditions help identify movements, 148
origin along Mali-Guinea border, 147
origin along route taken by Dankaran Tuman after his defeat, 147
origin stories similar to those of Ma, 148
origin traced by oral traditions to Mahana, Mali, 147
outgrowth of migration south from Sahel, 141
pressed Dan south before settling among them, 203
preyed upon by slave kidnappers, 324
pushed Ma eastward before intermarrying with them, 179
pushed south by Konaianké, Malinké and Diomandé, 202
rites of passage, 79
rules for engagement of strangers, 53
separated from Loma by Kone invaders, 178
separated from Senofu and Guro by Kone invaders, 178
some moved south and displaced Kuwaa west, 186
some of towns they founded in Guinea have been renamed by Malinké, 17
supported cotton weaving and auxiliary activities, 227

Kpelle language
common first names among Windward slaves, 276
uses soft "l" where Bandi use strong "d", 146, 198

Krahn (ethnic group)
also called "Western Wee" by linguists, 197
current home previously occupied by Bassa, 206
low sickle-cell frequency, 210
migration of some ancestors from northeast of the Sassandra River to Mt. Gedeh, 196
migration toward Mt. Gedeh, 197
reportedly split from Kuwaa after encounter with Bassa, 206

Krim (ethnic group)
southern vanguard of Atlantic languages, 46

kroo
equal to about 6 imp. gal. of 3 kg., 305
unit of measure along Malagueta Coast, 304

Kroo-bar
one of five towns reportedly founded by seafarers from the Gold Coast, 208

Kru (ethnic group)
assumed by some scholars to be foot soldiers of Mane invaders, 181

Kru Coast
historical and cultural ties with Gold Coast, 208
three culturally related and codependent groups, 208

Kru language groups
a quarter of all slaves to Guyana and Surinam, 275
ancestors probably linked to early human remains at Sanniquellie, Grand Gedeh and Po River, 47
distinct from Kwa languages, 3
labeled as hunters and gatherers by some anthropologists, 16
living along wetern rim of Liberian forest when Mande speakers arrived, 142
long dismissed by Eurocentric scholars as "primitive", 61
mainly confined to forest rim before 1651 AD, 195
migration from northeast of the Sassandra River to Mt. Gedeh, 196
pattern of small, scattered villages, 53
preceded Mande groups in forest region, 148

Index

separation from Niger-Congo family, 47
settlement pattern conforms to segmentary lineage system, 209
style of carved wooden masks shared with Ma and Dan, 203

Krumen
label for Five Town residents later broadened to all Klao and Glebo, 209
name applied by English-speakers to Nana-kru, 208

Kudemowe
one of first Glebo towns near Rocktown, 207

Kumba
female Kissi ancestor of Loma, 148

Kumba (or Sumba)
foot soliders of Mane invaders, 181

Kunkenyi, Farako Makan
father of Dankaran Tuman and Sundiata, 130

Kunukoro
Loma district dominated by Kamara clan, 202

Kuraan
Dan name for the Wee ethnic group, 17

Kurukanfuga
town where leading Malinké families united to back Sundiata, 131

Kuwaa (ethnic group)
apparently pushed west by Mande-speakers incursion, 206
encounter with Gola, 206
met by Gola when moving south, 200
migration of some ancestors from northeast of the Sassandra River to Mt. Gedeh, 196
oral tradition cites early association with Mande-speakers, 203
relatively high sickle-cell frequency, 210
reportedly moved west in pursuit of wild game, 205
reportedly split from Krahn after encounter with Bassa, 206
split from Northern Krahn and Glebo, 205

Kwea (Bassa sub-group)
cited in the Quoia text as "Quea", 186

labor
rules for allocation in early societies, 51
unequal control over in West Africa, 261

labor-saving techniques
linked to high population density by some scholars, 294

lagoons
as sources of freshwater fish, 59

Lagos, Portugal
presence of black slaves, 259

Lake Chad
drying down, 34
reed boats, 57
refuge for people fleeing Sahara, 35

Lamp, Frederick J. (Art historian)
credits stone sculptures to itinerant carvers, 61

land
claimed by virtue of community labor and known as "manufactured land", 261
control unevenly dispersed among West African households and lineages, 261
major source of tension between Muslim "strangers" and non-Muslim hosts, 171
ownership linked to earliest lineages, 209
rules for allocation in early societies, 51
value undermined by reliance on trading, 122

landholding lineage
significance of, 52

lappas (also rappas)
European imitations of Javanese batiks, 320

Latin
example of once dominant language, 124

lausing
Kpelle word for "forest spirits", 49

le langaige de Guynee
Klao vocabulary recorded by Bordeaux captain in 1545 AD, 221

leatherworkers

as perceived in African religion, 82
Lele (ethnic group)
  Malinké speakers near Kissidugu who are ringed by Kissi, 178
lemons
  among foodstuff at Sestros, 253
Leopard Society
  evidence of society in crisis, 80
leopards
  many reported at Cape Mount in early 1700s, 241
  numbers reduced due to foreign market for exotic hides, 319
  numbers reduced due to imported weapons, 319
  once locally numerous, 319
  skin and claws once reserved for rulers, 319
Levant Company
  English trading monopoly, 220
libations
  consisted of palm wine at Cape Mesurado in mid-1600s, 231
  drink offering to the ancestors, 77
  traditionally in form of fresh water, millet beer or palm wine, 77
Liberian territory
  embarkation points for trans-Atlantic slave trade, 269
  migration into driven by search for land, 48
  practically empty before Malinké incursions, 195
Libya
  homeland of some Ancient Egyptians, 37
life force
  water bodies as sources of good fortune if properly satiated, 75
life-force
  embodied and channeled by masquerades, 75
  forest as one of most powerful in West Africa, 75
  forest's viewed as combining powers of constituent elements, 74
  midwives envisioned in African religion as repositories, 73
  mountain's viewed as combining the powers of constituent elements, 74
  vital energy envisioned in African religion as dwelling in all matter, 73
  water bodies' among most powerful in West Africa, 75
lingua franca
  trade language, 318
linguists
  their contribution to recovering African history, 4
liquors
  consumption forbidden by the Qu'ran, 322
  distillation process improved in 1500s, 322
  heavily exported to Africa, 322
  local market cultivated by Europeans through "dash" to local rulers, 322
  major commodity used to buy slaves, 273
Little Barsay
  between Monou and Quabee people near Sestros River, 250
Little Kro
  one of five towns reportedly founded by seafarers from the Gold Coast, 208
Little Sestros
  all residents involved in fishing according to Jean Barbot, 250
  town along Malagueta Coast in late 1600s, 249
Liverpool
  village at mouth of St. Paul, 318
livestock
  grazing improved due to increased rainfall between 1500 and 1630 AD, 190
  list of available ones at Sestros, 253
  similar at Cape Mount and Cape Mesurado in early 1700s, 243
  similar at River Cess, Cape Mesurado and Cape Mesurado, 244
  similar at Settre Crou, Cape Mesurado, River Cess and Cape Mount, 245
living conditions
  Africa compared to Europe, 291

Index 379

    Caribbean slaves, 291
    comparisons must be made using similar items, 291
    false comparisons between Africa and Europe made by media, 291
    key areas for comparative analysis, 292
    local ones ignored in early European writings on West Africa, 167
Livingston, Frank B. (American biological anthropologist)
    linked sickle-cell spread to rice farming, 210
Lok, John
    bought ton of malagueta spice from River Sesto, 222
    captain of three English vessels to Liberia area in 1554, 221
    first to record names of several towns on Liberian coast, 222
    his publisher added claim of elephants fighting "dragons", 223
    his publisher added claim of hot moon beams in West Africa, 222
    his publisher called West Africans "beastly", 222
    his publisher included accurate details on elephants, 223
    poetic descriptions of geographical and navigational features, 221
Loko
    meaning "river mouth land", 146, 198
Loko (ethnic group)
    called Wu-bandi in Limba, 146
    close historical affinity to Soso, 142
    oral tradition claim they originated in Bandi territory, 198
    southern-most segment of splintered Southwest Mande block, 198
    with Bandi and Mende, considered dialect of one language, 147
Loma (ethnic group)
    also known as Toma, Twaan, Kénia, Gbalawi, Bouse and Gboande, 149
    area with their place names now occupied by some Kissi, 198
    assumed by some scholars to be foot soldiers of Mane invaders, 181
    betrayed by Malinké occupation of Musadu, 201
    bounded by Kpelle in Liberia and Koniyanke in Guinea, 202
    call Toma by Malinké, 17
    care and protection of kola trees, 147
    dispersion caused by Malinké invasion around 1600 AD, 197
    displaced some Kissi, 142
    group identity likely emerged after 1235 AD, 147
    high sickle-cell frequency, 210
    identity formed in the forest belt, 179
    left Musadu for Liberia to find land and wild game and to flee Malinké harassment, 201
    linked to Basenji dog, 34
    longterm symbiotic relationship with Kissi, 149
    longtime neighbors and sometime allies of Manya, 140
    mainly found in Macenta, Guinea, and Lofa, Liberia, 201
    masked ritual performers on stills, 74
    name proportedly derived from location where ancestors first settled, 147
    name reputedly derived from "joiner" based on membership in Poro, 147
    names of several dialects sound like "Bandi", 146
    oral tradition claim Konian as former residence, 148
    oral traditions help identify movements, 148
    origin tied to Konianké sub-group of the Malinké, 140
    outgrowth of migration south from Sahel, 141
    preyed upon by slave kidnappers, 324
    renown for blacksmiths, 303
    rites of passage, 79
    separated from Kpelle by Kone invaders, 178

some of towns they founded in Guinea have been renamed by Malinké, 17
supported cotton weaving and auxiliary activities, 227
tensions with Malinké over violation of kokologi, 202

Loma language
common first names among Windward slaves, 276
most distinct of southwest Mande group, 147

London
destroyed by huge fire in 1666 AD, 300
politics guided by global supply and demand, 220

Long, Edward (English historian of the Caribbean)
racist ideas of, 8

low population density
apparent link to low sickle-cell frequency, 211

Löwöma Vhéati
headwaters of St. Paul River where Loma ancestors first settled, 147

Lübeck, Hanseatic League
key center of European economic power in 1300s, 218

Lulama, Guinea
area with the fewest non-Loma speakers, 148

Lumley, Captain Richard
local broker at Cestros River, 318

Ma (ethnic group)
ancestors met Wee in area, 148
ancestors migrated from direction of Burkino Faso, 147
ancestors mixed with Kru-speaking inhabitants of area, 148
ancestors reportedly knew iron forging and brass casting before entering Liberia, 197
came into association with Dan and Kono of Guinea, 196
dispersion caused by Malinké invasion around 1600 AD, 197
history interwoven with Dan, 196
low sickle-cell frequency, 210
migration of ancestors from Kong, 196
movement of some ancestors from further east to area of Liberia, 196
northern section heavily influenced by Malinké, 203
oral traditions help identify movements, 148
origin stories similar to those of Kpelle, 148
preyed upon by slave kidnappers, 324
related to languages in Burkino Faso, Benin and Nigeria, 147
some ancestors reputedly spoke a language like Kono in Guinea, 196
some moved south and displaced Kuwaa west, 186
some of towns they founded in Guinea have been renamed by Malinké, 17
spread to Nehenkoheba (town) with Dan, 196
style of carved wooden masks shared with Dan and Kru-speakers, 203
vanguard of southeast Mande migration into forest, 203

Maat
Ancient Egyptian code of ethics, 97
world's first written code placing limits on behavior, 97

Macarico
reputed female leader of Mane invaders, 181

Macenta
town in Guinea reportedly founded by Loma, 201

Madrid
beating heart of Spanish empire, 322
entrepoint through which chocolate and tobacco entered Europe, 322

Magwibba (Magowi)
river in Quoia territory, 185

magzi-jonglo
Vai name for maize, 321

Mahmud IV
last mansa (ruler) of Mali, 177

maize (also corn)
Cape Mount said to grow greatest quantity in

Index

West Africa in mid-1600s, 230
helped fuel a population boom in West Africa, 321
helped West African ruler to centralize power, 321
higher yield than rice, 297
New World crop adopted by West Africans, 321
plentiful at Cape Mount in 1666, 321
reportedly used by Cape Mount residents to make bread, 321
required only 50 days of work per year to feed a family, 297
with cassava spurred a "veritable agricultural revolution" in West Africa, 321

Majorca
several residents produced detailed maps of West Africa, 119

Malagueta Coast
attire of local people, 227
cited as roughly between River Cess and Cape Palmas, 168
distances between towns as given by Jean Barbot, 249
dwellings built on stilts, 300
few whites stayed long without getting sick, 233
interesting geographical features, 245
limits of according to Jean Barbot, 249
parameters as described in mid-1600s, 233
preferred trade goods listed, 252
rich in ivory until 1687 AD, 319
rich in spice and ivory in late 1600s, 249
single rower in small canoes noted here from 1471 to 1623 AD, 249

malagueta spice
a major crop from Sestros River to Growa, 164
average annual yield, 56
characteristics of plant, 56
distribution, 56
Dutch formerly bought ship-loads along Liberian coast, 164
exports from Liberia area fell sharply in 1600s due to new supplies of Asian spices, 264
historic significance of commodity in West Africa, 54
known in early southern Europe as "grain of paradise", 163
Liberia-area reportedly still exporting 100 tons in 1800s, 164
loses flavor quickly, 115
perennial shrub known as Aframomum melequeta, 164
sales in Europe exceeded those of Asian peppers and ginger, 164
search for as factor motivating Portuguese exploration, 163
sought in early southern Europe, 56
trade fostered basket-weaving on large scale, 304
traded from Liberia region to Niger River, 115
trading at Bottewa, 245
volume of trade to Antwerp, 164

Malal
another name for Mali empire, 130

malaria
apparently kept whites from staying long along Malagueta Coast, 233
attributed to "intemperate air of the woody and swampy ground" by Jean Barbot, 252
decimated Native Americans, 295
described by Jean Barbot during visit to Malagueta Coast, 252
mosquito-borne illness, 49
role of mosquitos as vectors unknown in late 1600s, 252
spread probably inhibited by low-population density, 211

Malfante, Antonio
Genoa merchant who visited Timbuktu, 170

Mali Empire
also known as "Mande" and "Malal", 130

center of early kola trade, 55
decline hastened by diversion of trade from Sahel to coast, 168
expansion of slave hunting around 1450 AD, 169
former rulers as refugees in the forest belt, 177
former rulers hell-bent of seizing coastal trade, 191
horses and weapons gave unrivaled military superiority over its neighbors, 169
increasingly drew salt supplies from Atlantic coast, 131
its size, 132
more prosperous than Ghana, 131
peak of its power, 132
refugees followed trade routes into forest, 178
refugees into forest led by five families, 178
rulers pushed toward forest belt, 177
split between three sons of Mahmud IV, 177
supplied two-thirds of world's gold, 132

Malikite
main school (madh'hab) of Islamic law imposed by Almoravids, 126
school of Islamic law that influenced West African jurists, 125

Malinké (ethnic group)
also Mandingo, 130
at center of large political unit called Mande, Malal or Mali, 130
core of northern Mande language family, 120
credited by Eurocentric scholars with bringing iron smelting and rice farming to forest belt, 61
incursions led to redistribution of ethnic groups and languages, 196
myth of their superiority advanced by Edward Wilmot Blyden, 16
presented by some scholars as embodiment of mythical Hamitic race, 17
second dispersion of ethnic groups and languages around 1600 AD, 197
spread southward between 1300 and 1800 AD, 178
warriors patronized blacksmiths who supplied them weapons, 190
warriors patronized griots who supplied their heroic stories, 190
western dispursal from Begho and Gonja to Côte d'Ivoire, 190

Malinké language
example of loan word from Portuguese, 318

Malinké traders began converting to Islam around 1000 AD, 126

Mami Watta
best known West African water power, 75
female Indian divinity Lakshmi as model for her image, 75
mermaid as model for her image, 75

Man
one of four early regional trade centers, 149

Mande
another name for Mali empire, 130
developed farming along the Niger, 120
dominant Liberian language family, 3
dominated West African trade, 119
drawn to iron-smelting resources of forest belt, 140
example of dominant language, 124
initial organization by kinship, 122
northern branch split on basis of religion and region, 120
political hierarchy featured ruler and traders at top, farmers in middle and "outsider" castes at bottom, 123
three stages of southward migration, 139
traders drawn mainly from Malinké castes of Dyula, Jakhanke and Soninké, 121

Mande languages
Eastern branch of, 120
homeland in Southern Sahara, 120
Mandekan branch centered around Bambuk and Bouré goldfields, 120
separation into Southwestern and Southeastern

Index

branches, 120
southern branch of, 120
Southwest branch of, 120

Mandugu
Loma district dominated by Kamara clan, 202

Mane
assembled the region's largest collection of weapons, 180
attempted invasion of Soso, 179
attire consisted of cotton smocks and wide-bottom trousers, 181
conquered from Sherbro Island to Iles de Los, 179
invaders led by Northern Mande speakers, 181
invaders linked to Kamara clan by scholars, 181
invaders of western Liberia and eastern Sierra Leone, 179
invaders used alternative names for Kamara, 181
invaders wore plumes of bird feathers, 181
invasion as grasp by in-land groups for control of coastal trade, 180
invasion did not alter area languages, 180
invasion helps to date movement of people into forest region of present-day Liberia, 195
their army included Portuguese marksman, 180
ultimatum to choose between surrender or war, 180

Manimassah
brother of Mendino, 183
moved to live among Gola, 183
tried for his brother's death, 183

Mannheim, Karl (Hungarian sociologist)
his theory of partial perspectives in the construction of knowledge, 11

Manou
cited in Quoia text as north of Hondo, 185
located between Anverado (Mesurado?) and Junk rivers, 186
Vai word for "the people", 182
western neighbors of Folgia, 182

Mansa
title given to head of Mali empire, meaning "ruler", 132

Mansfield, Lord Chief Justice
his Sommerset case decision led to upsurge in number of free blacks in England, 282
rendered antislavery decision in James Sommerset's case, 282

Manya (ethnic group)
group along Liberia-Guinea border known as "Komendi", 185
likely descendants of Dankaran Tuman loyalists, 140
so-called "bush Mandingo", 140

Manzama
district settled by Guilavogui and Zumanigui clans, 202

Maquet, Jacques (Belgian sociologist)
coined the word "Africanity", 14

Maria
Cameroon-born companion of Dutch trader who brought her to Cape Mount, 225
wife of Thaba Flamore, 225

Mark (also John Mark)
Christian apostle who was born in North Africa, 106
his mother's home as site of Pentacostal visitation, 106
laid foundation of Christianity in North Africa, 106

markets
arose only in presence of large numbers of non-farming full-time artisans, 306
description of in Liberia from mid-1800s, 305
each typically served about 7,000 persons, 307
embryos of cities, 306
held daily or weekly in alternating towns of Liberia area, 305
often emerged at crossroads of major trade routes, 306

Masaubolahun
    town near Bolahun proportedly built by Malinké from Musadu, 198
masks
    idealized carving style, 203
    naturalistic portrait sytle, 204
Massaquoi
    name reputedly derived from mansa goi, meaning "you are indeed a king", 145
Massing, Andreas W. (German agricultural economist and anthropologist)
    dates associated with Mane invasion, 180
    his theory of Wakoré/Wangara dispursal, 128
maternal uncle
    significance in early West African societies, 52
Matiye
    among earliest Klao towns, 207
    original residents kept separate fields and canoe landing station from other early Klao ancestors, 207
    south of the Nonbwa River, 207
matrilineal order
    original structure of Niger-Congo societies, 122
mats
    plentiful at Cape Mount in mid-1600s, 231
Mauritania
    homeland of Atlantic languages, 39
mausim
    markets or seasonal festivals in Arabia, 306
Mavah (Mafa)
    river in Quoia territory, 185
Mazuri, Ali Al'amin (Kenyan political scientist), 14
McGovern, Mike (American political anthropologist)
    argues Koivogue clan is Loma version of Kamara, 202
McNaughton, Patrick R. (American art historian)
    status of hunters in Mande societies, 83
meat
    "dubious quality" sold to European commoners, 297
    consumption among poor increased in Europe from 1400s, 297
    consumption low throughout the world, 297
    eaten on special occasions in Arabia, 297
    estimate of consumption in Madrid, Spain, 297
    European commoners ate stale, salted and smoked, 298
    European commoners ate with bones mixed in, 298
    only rich people routinely ate, 297
    roasting method along Windward Coast, 301
    supplied by cows, goats, hogs, chickens and other fowls along Malagueta Coast in mid-1600s, 234
Mecca
    site of largest fair in Arabia coinciding with annual hajj, 306
medicine societies
    great proliferation in southeastern Liberia, 210
Mediterranean
    intelligence gathering on West Africa by residents, 119
    location of most of world's largest cities in mid-1400s, 293
Meinhof, Carl (German linguist)
    proponent of the Hamitic myth in African history, 9
Mema
    remnant unit of Ghana absorbed by Mali, 131
Memphis
    capital of Ancient Egypt, 96
Mende (ethnic group), 188
    central segment of splintered Southwest Mande block, 198
    cited in Quoia text as residents of Folgia and Manou territory, 186
    close historical affinity to Soso, 142
    deny historical link to stone sculptures found buried throughout their region, 61
    dispersion caused by Malinké invasion around 1600 AD, 197
    displaced some Kissi, 142

fighters probably crossed through Gola territory
to reach Cape Mount, 188
high sickle-cell frequency, 210
identity as outcome of choice and validation, 54
language as lingua franca, 188
many captives taken to Jamaica during slave
trade, 324
met Gola-Vai hybrid in Cape Mount, 188
movement of, 189
name derived from man-da, meaning "lord" or
"lordship", 146
outgrowth of migration south from Sahel, 141
overran Vai-related Dama group, 188
possibly once consisted of Quoia, Folgia and
Karou clans, 185
preyed upon by slave kidnappers, 324
probably descended south from headwaters of
the Mesurado, 188
pushed some Kissi south, 198
reportedly came into Liberia seeking to join
coastal trade, 198
reportedly left previous location fleeing forced
conversion to Islam, 198
separates Kissi from Bollum, Vai from Kono and
Bandi from Loko, 188
some moved south between northern edge of
forest and coast, 189
some reportedly lived north of Quoia among
"Hondo", 185
with Bandi and Loko, considered dialect of one
language, 147
Mende language
example of loan word from French, 318
example of loan word from Portuguese, 318
Mendi
Folgia, Bollum and Temne name for Quoia, 184
language considered to be "courtly and
eloquent", 185
meaning "lord", 184
Mendi-co

allies of the Mende, 188
cited in Quoia text as residents of Folgia and
Manou territory, 186
meaning "lordly tongue", 185
name given to Folgia language by their
neighbors, 185
Mendino
leader of the Folgia, 182
Menelik of Ethiopia
son of Queen Makeda and King Solomon,
according to Ethiopian traditions, 99
Menkenveld, Jan
captain of slave ship Philadelphia, 280
Menoch
river in Quoia territory, 185
mercenaries
Castilians as sources of information on West
Africa, 119
Catalonians as sources of information on West
Africa, 119
Mesufa nomads
included in Mali empire, 132
metal-smelting revolution
indigenous to West Africa, 38
Mexico
drastic population decline due to epidemics and
forced labor, 219
Middelburgse Company (Dutch)
its slave trade along Windward Coast, 269
Middle East
an unusually large number of cities due to trade,
293
Middle Niger floodplain
innovation center for pottery making and cereal
processing, 39
midwives
envisioned in African religion as repositories of
life-force, 73
Migeod, Frederick W. H. (British coloonial officer)
claimed personal knowledge of "dwarfs" in

Liberia area, 47
migrant band
    definition, 183
milhio
    millet or corn in short supply at Cape Mount in early 1700s, 241
military force
    basis of power in Sahel, Greece and Rome, 123
    capacity of local polity directly related to number of slaves exported, 267
millet
    African crop adopted by people in the Americas, 321
    bountiful along Malagueta Coast, 234
    farming developed along Malagueta Coast in late 1600s, 249
    grown at Cape Mount in mid-1600s, 230
    plentiful at River Cess in mid-1600s, 233
    reportedly grown along Malagueta Coast in 1678 AD, 226
Mininique
    leader of Gola attack against Karou and Folgia, 183
    son of Manimassa, 183
Missadougou
    ancient town of Kpelle, 202
Misurato
    confusion, 161
    meaning "passage performed in measured time", 161
    name, 161
modernization theory
    sought to make Africans "civilized", 10
money
    hoarded or used for ostentatious displays in West Africa, 309
    initially confined to merchants and nobility worldwide, 305
    reinvested to make more money by merchants in Arabia, Europe and Asia, 309
monkey meat
    a favorite around Sestros, 253
moon calendar and festivals
    ancient West African tradition spread throughout the region, 33
Moor
    derived from Greek word for "black", 132
    used as derogatory word for Africans, 132
Morocco
    conquest of Songhai empire, 166
    invaded Songhai Empire to gain access to gold mines, 171
    its Songhai invaders consisted of foreign slaves and Spanish renegades, 171
    seized trade from Mali, 177
Moses
    his link to Ancient Egypt, 99
    link to monotheism of Akenaten, 100
    linked to Ethiopia by the Talmud, 99
Mossi (ethnic group)
    persecuted by Mali rulers for being non-Muslim, 177
    seized Volta-region trade from Mali, 177
mountains
    cited as ancestral home by Gola, Loma, Kpelle, Ma, Dan and Kru-speakers, 150
Mouon
    Kpelle emigré from Missadougou who reportedly founded Guiéta, 203
Mt. Finley
    site of Bassa iron smelting, 207
Mt. Gedeh (also called Mt. Niété)
    evidence of early iron smelting, 47
    focal point of several Kru-speakers' migrations, 47, 197
mud bricks
    used for homes of poor in Arabia, Asia and other regions, 300
Muidu
    Loma district dominated by Kamara clan, 202
multistory dwellings
    reported at River Cess by William Bosman in

Index

early 1700s, 244
Musa
  rich fisherman and reputed founder of Musadu, 150
Musa, Mansa Kanka
  ruler of Mali empire, 131
  spending by his entourage in Cairo led to worldwide devaluation of gold, 132
  Sundiata's nephew, 132
Musadu
  its history highly contested by various claimants, 150
  likely founded by ancestors of Bassa but name was given by Malinké, 150
  Loma oral tradition credit town's founding to Musa, a herbalist who rejected Islam, 150
  Malinké oral traditions credit town's founding to a Kpelle slave named Kromah, 150
  most closely linked to Kpelle and Loma, 150
  one of four early regional trade centers, 149
  regarded as religious center of Kamara clan, 178
  trade hub for Gola, Loma, Kpelle, Kono, Bassa, Bandi, Dan and Ma, 149
Muscovy Company
  English trading monopoly, 220
Muslims
  naval control of Indian Ocean overthrown by Europeans, 303
  North Africans as major contributors to Islamic thought, 125
  North Africans developed Sahf'ite and Malikite schools of Islamic law, 125
  showed impressive charity, 170
naming
  as means of revealing inherent characteristic or force, 85
Nana-Kru (also Nana-Kroo)
  name of group on Kru Coast who farmed, 208
  one of five towns reportedly founded by seafarers from the Gold Coast, 208

nations
  definition, 248
  displaced cities as power centers after Amsterdam's decline, 247
  unity imposed from above by European governments, 247
natural harbors
  importance for the export of slaves, 267
Nea Mia
  first family of Ma, 197
neck rings
  symbolic meaning of, 85
New Calabar
  Nigerian town that grew into city-state based on profits from slave trade, 167
New England
  supplied rum and ships used in slave trade, 272
New Sestros
  name given to town by Portuguese, 161
New World colonies
  initially settled by far more Africans than Europeans, 266
New Year celebration
  echoes in Mardi Gras, Carnival and Carnaval, 79
Newton, John (1725-1807)
  author of "Amazing Grace" and hundreds of other hymns, 278
  author of antislavery Thoughts Upon the African Slave Trade, 279
  employed by Liverpool merchant Joseph Manesty, 276
  English slave buyer and sea captain, 276
  kept extensive journal, 276
  lived in Sierra Leone, 276
  noted several local rulers with English names in early 1750s, 318
Niama
  cited as first ancestor of Kpelle by oral tradition, 147
Niani

capital of Mali empire established by Sundiata, 131
close to sources of gold, ivory, palm oil and salt, 131
leading town of Mali empire, 132
nicotine
psychoactive substance in tobacco, 323
Niffa
town along Malagueta Coast in late 1600s, 249
Niger River
heartland of the Mande language group, 39
history and description, 121
location of West Africa's largest cities, 293
refuge for people fleeing Sahara, 35
Niger-Congo cultures
earlier matrilineal transmission of office and property, 122
earliest art forms, 31
music characterized by patterned, rhythmical arrangement, 75
polyrhythmic dance and music, 32
role of healers-diviners, 81
similar institutions for keeping society in proper moral balance, 80
similarities in rituals, aesthetics and beliefs, 71
Niger-Congo languages
dominant West African language family, 3, 34
similar despite their diversity, 33, 34
splintering of, 38
nighttime lighting
comparative analysis, 299
Nile River
cultural similarities to Niger societies, 32
flooding as marker of time, 101
links to the Atlantic world, 32
normal flow and flooding, 37
papyrus boats, 57
refuge for people fleeing Sahara, 35
shift from herding to farming, 36
Nini-bu
Loma dialect whose name means "under the shade", 146
Nok, Nigeria
site of industrial-scale iron production, 39
nomoli
characteristics, 61
Mende name for stone sculptures found buried in their territory, 61
non-Muslims
conversion to Islam as means to escape enslavement, 169
Northern Krahn
migrated into Liberia in search of wild game and to escape encroachments by northern Mande speakers, 205
originated near Ma in Côte d'Ivoire, 205
pushed into Liberia area by Mande-speakers fleeing collapse of Songhai, 205
northern Mande
groups adopted two approaches to people living in forest belt, 189
groups employed soft incursions to forest belt followed by violent ones, 190
language group formerly known as Mande tan, 3
Northern Nigeria
apparent dispursal point of Kwa speakers, 39
Nubia
forced to export slaves after Muslim conquest, 118
homeland of some Ancient Egyptians, 37
southern neighbor of Ancient Egypt, 13, 36
Nugent, Paul (South African historian)
fluidity of ethnic identity, 54
numbers
symbolic association with genders, 73
nuts
example of forest-margin crop important to local diets, 226
Nwo Gohn
Gola word for war town, 324
Nyomowe
one of first Glebo towns near Hoffman River, 207

Index

Nzerekore
  town settled by early Ma ancestors, 148
Obenga, Théophile J. (Congolese (Brazzaville) Africanist historian), 2
objects of veneration
  awe-inspiring natural formations, 78
offering to the dead
  consisted of rice, palm wine and greens, 244
Oglivy, John
  published Olfert Dapper's account of Quoia in English, 182
okra
  African crop adopted by people in the Americas, 321
  example of forest-margin crop important to local diets, 226
  first cultivated in West Africa, 39
Oniguame
  Loma district dominated by Kamara clan, 202
Onivogui (also known as Pivi)
  a leading Loma clan, 202
oral traditions
  their limitations, 4
  usefulness in recovering African history, 4
oranges
  among foodstuff at Sestros, 253
  Asian plant adopted in West Africa by early 1600s, 320
Oromo
  Afrasiatic language of Ethiopia, 36
Osiris
  God symbolized by the moon in Ancient Egyptian religion, 97
  his rise accompanied by an end to blood sacrifices, 97
  similar in appearance to many African rulers, 97
Ouroboros
  image of a snake swallowing its own tail as Egyptian symbol of infinity, 102
oxen
  once used to cross the desert, 116
Paesi novamente retrovati
  book of exotic travelogues that contained narrative of Pedro de Sintra's voyage, 161
Pahn
  another name for Mt. Gedeh area, meaning "rich country", 197
Pakyo
  early Klao town established east of Siglipo, 207
palava huts
  gathering place for early West African tobacco smokers, 322
palm
  raffia used for clothing east of River Cess, 227
  two types significant to local economies, 225
  West Africans begin harvesting oil, 39
  West Africans begin harvesting raffia, 39
palm wine
  "very good" along Malagueta Coast, 234
  common alcoholic drink when Europeans first arrived, 322
  plenty and good at Cape Mesurado in early 1700s, 243
Papuklo
  early Klao town established north of Siglipo, 207
paquovers
  papayas or quavas present at Cape Mount in early 1700s, 241
Paris
  destroyed by huge fire in 1547 AD, 300
  one-fourth of homes had only one room, 300
Parrinder, Edward Geoffry (British comparative religion scholar), 73
patriliny
  shift in Niger-Congo societies resulting from Arab influence and reliance on warriors, 122
peanut
  New World crop adopted by West Africans, 321
peas
  example of forest-margin crop important to local

diets, 226
peddlers
  filled gap between markets and shops, 306
  migration followed seasonal patterns, 306
  operated in league with smugglers in times of war and crisis, 306
  some specialized in specific commodities, 306
  took goods from trading centers to outlying areas, 306
pepper
  object of financial speculation by European capitalists, 164
  woven into European cuisine by 1651 AD, 219
Pereira, Duarte Pacheco
  earliest detailed European account of Upper Guinea, 167
  early Portuguese visitor to Liberian coast, 164
  reported buying malagueta spice near Sestros River, 164
Persian Muslims
  early racist accounts of Africans, 7
person
  non-physical aspects conceived similarly in Ancient Egyptian and African religion, 100
Person, Yves (historian)
  adverse impact of ocean shore on Windward Coast commerce, 268
  northern Mande movement south shook entire region, 191
  southward invasion of Northern Mande speakers around 1600 AD, 196
personal hygiene
  comparison of Holland and Liberia region, 301
  public baths created early in predominantly Muslim cities, 302
Peter (also Pieter or Pedro)
  Cape Mount ruler in early 1750s, 318
  local ruler near Cestros River, 318
  River Cess ruler described by William Bosman in early 1700s, 244
  River Cess ruler from 1682 to 1727, 250

Pharaoh Necho II
  Ancient Egyptian ruler who commissioned mariners to sail around Africa, 37
Philadelphia
  ship that faced three slave rebellions, 280
Philips
  local trader at St. Paul River, 317
Phoenicians (ancestors of Lebanese and Syrians)
  dominated Mediterranean trade and shipping, 102
  trading colonies along North African coast, 102
  trading networks similar to today multinational corporations, 102
pidgin language
  not common between Sanguin River and Cape Palmas in 1667, 318
  spoken at Cape Mesurado and Sestros by late 1600s, 317
Pietersz
  local man at River Cess in 1678, 318
pineapples
  among foodstuff at Sestros, 253
  growing freely in Liberia area by late 1600s, 321
  New World crop adopted by West Africans, 321
  present at Cape Mount in early 1700s, 241
pipe
  smoked by Barsaw with bowl resting on the ground, 251
pirates
  especially active in Caribbean and Mediterranean seas, 246
  plagued ship traffic while great powers contended for control over seas, 246
Pisiyo Sigli
  earliest residence of Klao ancestors in Liberia area, 207
plague
  recurring threat in Europe, 295
  subsided after 1720 AD due to shift from wood to stone buildings, 295
plantains

Index

Asian plant adopted in West African by early 1600s, 320
Plizoge (Lake Piso)
  body of water in Quoia territory, 185
  filled with fish in early 1700s, 241
Po River mouth
  site of early pottery and other signs of human habitation, 45
poetry
  as means of transmitting wisdom, 84
political structures
  flatter in southeastern Liberia than in other parts of territory, 209
  smaller in southeastern Liberia, 210
pomtan
  characteristics, 62
  Kissi name for stone sculptures found buried in their territory, 61
  stone sculptures still found in areas held by Bandi, Kono, Loma and Mende, 143
population density
  influence on slave exports, 267
  lower in southeastern Liberia, 210
Poro
  absent from southeastern Liberia, 210
  addressed distribution of earthly and spiritual powers, 151
  common to Quoia, Karou, Folgia, Manou, Hondo, Gola and Gebbe according to Quoia text, 186
  Dei and Bassa share a unique level called "Ndoge", 207
  encompassed Gola, Dei, Vai, Kissi, Bandi, Bassa, Kuwaa, Loma, Kpelle, some Dan, Lobi, Birifo, Dya and Senofo, 151
  its policy and judicial decisions were binding on society, 151
  its rituals and sanctions superseded other local groups, 150
  Kamara clan leader, Feren, given land upon initiation, 201
  Kissi reportedly inducted the Loma, 151
  known for extreme secrecy, 150
  Loma reportedly inducted by Kissi, 151
  masked authorities viewed as above lineage rivalries, 151
  multiple oral traditions cite Gola as founders, 151
  organized rites of passage for boys, 151
  power association for men, xxix, 10, 52, 59, 147, 150
porters
  disadvantages, 302
  used extensively in West Africa given lack of pack animals, 302
Portugal
  access to West African gold fueled decline of rival Morocco, 171
  completion of first West African fortress, 166
  displaced from West Africa by Dutch and English, 219
  eclipse sealed by king's death while fighting in Morocco, 219
  economy taken over by British investors, 219
  explorers arrived in West Africa as Mali empire was fraying, 168
  its dramatic decline, 219
  its grip on world's gold market challenged, 165
  lost West African trading posts by 1640 AD, 219
  navigators instructed by king to kidnap Africans, 160
  seized trade from Mali, 177
  seizure of Atlantic islands near West Africa, 166
  strategic position at the gateway to Atlantic, 165
  transferred sugar plantation model from Mediterranean to the Atlantic, 166
  unlikely candidate for world domination, 239
Portuguese
  arrived in the mid-1400s as West Africa was imploding, 159
  enslaved many Sape to whom they had offered "protection", 179

gave names to many geographic features of area, 161
local joblessness as motivation for exploration, 163
presence along West African coast would destabilize the region, 159
seized cinnamon production in Ceylon by force, 239
Portuguese language
original basis of lingua franca along Windward Coast, 318
words from incorporated into local languages, 318
possession
freedom from expected behavior, 81
frequent in highly rigid societies, 81
interpretation by religious authorities, 81
more common in sub-Saharan African than elsewhere, 81
typical patterns, 81
potato (also Irish potato)
adopted in Europe as a ration for armies, 321
in short supply at Cape Mount in early 1700s, 241
New World crop adopted by West Africans, 321
pottery
world's most advanced industry in China, 304
power associations
definition, 151
powers
used in context of African religion in place of "spirits" or "supernatural beings", 71
precious metal
mining in New World fueled trans-Atlantic slave trade, 262
precious metals
greatest source of profits for Europeans, 165
price-gorging
source of tensions within Sahelian empires, 139
Prince Henry of Portugal (properly the Infante Dom Henrique)
author of policy authorizing kidnapping of Africans, 259
called "the Navigator" because he conceived and funded first European voayages to West Africa, 162
fought alongside his father in Morocco, 162
fourth son of King Joåo I, 162
helped capture gold-trading town of Ceuta from Morocco, 162
motivations for West African exploration, 163
religious motivation for exploration superseded by pursuit of gold, 166
privacy
limited to the rich in Europe until 1700s, 301
produce
at Cape Mont in mid-1600s, 230
consisted of beans, citrons, oranges, peas, plums and nuts along Malagueta Coast, 234
similar at Cape Mount and Cape Mesurado in early 1700s, 243
similar at River Cess, Cape Mesurado and Cape Mesurado, 244
similar at Settre Crou, Cape Mesurado, River Cess and Cape Mount, 245
production of food and tools
key priority of early societies, 51
Prophet Muhammad
advised followers to seek haven in Ethiopia, 108
regarded Ethiopia as friendly, 108
prophets
their role in African religion, 81
protein sources
comparative analysis throughout the world, 297
wild game and fish in forest belt, 297
proverbs
as means of transmitting wisdom, 84
pumpkin
New World crop adopted by West Africans, 321
Punt
ancient name for region of Somalia and Eritrea, 36

Index

homeland of some Ancient Egyptians, 37
Purcell, William
    local man near St. Paul River, 318
Puy
    as inhabitants of Quoia country, 185
    indistinquishable from Karou due to intermarriage, 185
    Vai neighbors subdued by Folgia, 183
Pygmies
    possible presence in early Liberia, 47
pygmy animal species
    presence of several in Liberia area, 48
Quaabe-Monou
    group located by Olfert Dapper in 1668 AD in area now inhabited by Klao, 209
Quabbe
    cited in Quoia text as near Cestros River, 186
    eastern neighbors of Folgia, 182
    origin traced to River Scarcies by Andreas W. Massing, 182
    possibly Kuwaa who were pushed west by Kpelle and Ma, 186
Quea
    probably the Bassa sub-group known as Kwea, 186
Queen Makeda of Ethiopia
    widely known as Queen of Sheba, 99
quinine
    use against malaria discovered by Native Americans of Peru, 292
Quoia
    country also inhabited by, Vai-Gola, Pui and Karou, 185
    invaders of western Liberia and eastern Sierra Leone, 179
    labeled "kingdom" by Olfert Dapper, 182
    possibly a clan of Mende, 185
    several scholars assumed subunits were distinct ethnic groups, 185
    subgroups all spoke "Quoia" language, 185
    vocabulary similar to contemporary Vai, 185
Quoia text
    as narrative of Mende history, 185
    confirms oral accounts of people moving into forest region of present-day Liberia, 195
    described movement of warlords and their fighters, 183
    described political units at many levels, 184
    groups described conform to "migrant bands", 183
    helps to date movement of people into forest region of present-day Liberia, 195
Quoja
    Vai word for "bushcow", 182
Ququ
    non-Muslim group whose weapons resembled Mane invaders', 182
Quraysh
    ethnic group of the Prophet Muhammad, 170
Ra
    God symbolized by the sun in Ancient Egyptian religion, 97
racist self-image
    already evident at Cape Mount in mid-1600s, 230
rainfall
    dramatic increase fueled expansion of forest, 117
    dramatic increase in West Africa, 116
    increased in West Africa between 1500 and 1630 AD, 190
rainy season
    extent and impact, 50
red
    ritually significant color in African religion, 76
refugees
    beneficiaries of hospitality shown to "strangers", 116
regional fairs
    featured most exotic goods, 306
    operated at highest level of an economy, 306
religion

difficulty of translating abstract concepts from one language to another, 242
reproduction of people
    key priority of early societies, 51
Rhode Island
    deeply implicated in African slave trade, 283
    major supplier of rum used to buy slaves, 272
rice
    swamp cultivation, 35
rice, 336
    African and Asian varieties adopted by people in the Americas, 321
    buying by Dutch merchant at River Cess in early 1700s, 245
    common names in Atlantic languages, 61
    cooked and rolled into ball for eating at Sestros, 253
    disadvantages compared to wheat, 296
    example of savannah plant important to local diets and economies, 226
    gave rise to extensive terracing in China, 297
    greater labor requirement than tuber farming, 60
    growing area in West Africa inhabited mainly by Atlantic-language groups, 60
    grown at Cape Mount in mid-1600s, 230
    grown mainly in northwest and central regions of Liberia, 226
    harder to grow and process than wheat, 296
    longer shelflife than tubers, 60
    major trade item at Cape Mesurado in mid-1600s, 231
    plentiful at Cape Mount in mid-1600s, 231
    plentiful at River Cess in mid-1600s, 233
    plentiful at Sestros even during planting season, 253
    plentiful at Sestros River in 1727 AD, 254
    prodigious harvest reported at River Cess in early 1700s, 244
    production requirements as basis for large-scale collaborations, 61
    removal of husk required hard work, 297
    reportedly grown along Malagueta Coast in 1678 AD, 226
    seasonal and geographic limitations, 60
    staple along Malagueta Coast, 234
    supplied up to 90 percent of people's diet, 296
    typical production process, 60
    used as commodity in Japan, 305
rice (oryza glaberima), 40
rice farming
    along Malagueta Coast in late 1600s, 249
    major activity at Cape Mount, 241
    major activity at River Cess in early 1700s, 244
    preceeded one day before by religious ritual at Sestros, 251
    preference for Windward slaves in New World growing regions, 272
    probably brought to Liberia area by Atlantic language groups, 60
riding animals
    mode of transportation used mainly by the rich, 302
Rihla or Book of Travels
    account of travels by Muhammad Ibn Battuta, 125
Rio Sestro (also River Cess and Rio Sestre)
    imposing aspects of landscape, 243
    town along Malagueta Coast in late 1600s, 249
    treacherous nature of shoreline, 268
rites of passage
    purposes, 79
    types and phases, 78
ritual
    performed one day before rice planting in late 1600s, 251
ritual objects
    composed of objects with rare and significant life-force, 75
    effectiveness determines faith in, 75
    sacred and metaphorically radioactive during ritual performance, 75
    their powers remain latent until unlocked by

Index

people, 76
River Cess (also Rio Sestro and Rio Sestre)
   abandoned English warehouse reported nine miles up the river, 232
   civility of inhabitants, 301
   daily traffic of trade canoes to River Cess, 243
   description of funeral in early 1700s, 244
   entrance to river lined with hidden rocks, 243
   local fishermen described as "generally proportioned", 233
   men circumcised and wore platted hair, 251
   ruler in mid-1600s described as "lusty," "stern" and "supercilious", 232
   ruler said to live nine miles up the river, 232
   site of multistory dwellings, 244
   trade in rice, malaguetta and ivory characterized as perpetual, 244
   variety of fish reported in mid-1600s, 233
Roberts, Joseph Jenkins (Liberia's first president)
   his Africanist perspective, 12
rock paintings
   portray life from 12,000 BC, 32
   representations of masked dancers, 74
   showed early cattle herding, 39
Rodney, Walter A. (Guyanese historian and pan-Africanist scholar), xxix
   groundbreaking study of Upper Guinea coast, 179
   proposed Mende as fusion of conquered and conquerors, 188
Ross, Andrew
   local leader at Junk River in early 1750s, 318
rum
   a global currency by late 1600s, 274
   also called "kill devil" or "rumbullion", 274
   annual exports to Africa by late 1700s, 275
   banned in Spain and France to protect wine and brandy, 274
   distilled from sugar cane juice or molasses, 274
   embraced by England as alternative to wine and brandy, 275
   first distilled in Caribbean in early 1600s, 274
   key item in Europe's trade with Africa, 221
   large quantities exchanged for local captives, 322
   offered as "dash" to African rulers and grandees, 274
Russwurm, John B. (founder of the *Liberia Herald* newspaper)
   his Africanist perspective, 12
sacraments in African religion
   animal sacrifices and rites of passage, 78
Sagres
   Portuguese town known as center of navigation and cartography, 162
Sahara
   area contains several deserts, 28
   arrival of camels, 116
   barrier to incursions by Mediterranean empires, 102
   before 1,000 BC, 39
   continues to expand and contract, 35
   crossed by Arab traders in pursuit of slaves, 7
   disappearance of large animals, 32
   disappearance of shade trees, 35
   eastern section, 36
   final stage of turning into desert, 34
   hidden wealth, 35
   home to 30,000 rock paintings and drawings, 31
   its drying and retreat of Niger-Congo speakers to wetter regions, 35
   largest and oldest graveyard found at Govero, 31
   Africa's largest desert, 28
   oceans of pure water lie beneath, 29
   once home to four rivers, 121
   origin of Mande languages, 34
   origin of the Harmattan, 27
   original home of West Africans, 27
   original people saved by Nile and Niger rivers, 37
   southern section as homeland of Mande languages, 120

southward movement of Mande speakers, 34
two groups of inhabitants about 4,000 BC, 32
Sahel
  meaning the desert "shore", 28
  once infested with tsetse flies, 34
Sahelian empires
  attracted creative professionals from beyond borders, 151
  combined many cultures and political units in one economy, 124
  conflicts over transfers of power, 139
  controlled gold mining but left trading to merchants, 119
  drawn to forest belt as source of valuable commodities, 139
  factors that gave them advantages over neighbors, 125
  fueled by long-distance trading, 118
  increased imposition on forest belt neighbors over time, 152
  major supplier of gold to Europe and Muslim world, 119
  population grew with increased wealth, 151
  profited from slaves seized from forest region, 151
  reliance on armies to acquire slaves and wealth from beyond borders, 124
  reliance on fulltime armies, 124
  shift in treatment of enslaved outsiders, 169
  slave sellers shared fealty to Islam with Arab buyers, 261
  traders profited both on goods they bought and sold to forest region, 151
Sahf'ite
  school of Islamic law that influenced West African jurists, 125
sailors
  major conduit for global spread of rum, 274
  partially paid in rum and other liquors, 274
salt, 56, 183
  as factor motivating migration of Vai ancestors, 145
  boilers said to be living in nondescript huts, 230
  boiling of sea water as major activity at Cape Mount, 241
  chronic shortage in Sahel region as basis for trade, 56
  derived from sea water of Atlantic Ocean, 56
  essential for human survival, 56
  functioned as currency in many societies, 305
  historic significance of commodity in West Africa, 54
  important sea-water boiling towns, 59
  Mali Empire increasingly drew supplies from Atlantic coast, 131
  production and trade by Dei attracted other groups to Liberia area, 59
  production from sea water linked in oral traditions to Dei, 57
  production from sea water linked in oral traditions to Klao, 57
  sea water boiling villages sighted east of Cape Mesurado, 243
  trade involving Kru-speakers and southwest Mande groups, 196
  trade linked to Klao ethnic group, 57
  traded from Liberia region to Niger River, 115
  used as currency, 119
  used as currrency in West Africa, 305
salutation
  along Malagueta Coast consisted of grasping upper arm, snapping fingers and saying "Toma", 233
  customary approach at River Cess in mid-1600s, 233
sand
  interpretation by diviners, 81
Sande
  known for extreme secrecy, 150
  multiple oral traditions cite Gola as founders, 151
  organized rites of passage for girls, 151
  regional power association for women, 150

Index

Sango (also Kohiré)
    mountain from which first ancestor of Ma descended, 148
Sanguin, 234
Sanguin (also Sangwin)
    local ruler dressed in blue robe like counterpart at Cape Mount, 234
    residents characterized as rogues by William Bosman in early 1700s, 245
    ruler described as "grave," "venerable" and "lusty" man who drank no alcohol, 234
    town along Malagueta Coast in late 1600s, 249
Sanhaja Berbers
    founders of Timbuktu, 131
Sankaran
    political unit of Soso/Jalonke, 130
Sanniquellie
    site of rock shelter with early evidence of human habitation, 45
Sape (ethnic group)
    many enslaved by their Portuguese "protectors, 179
    sought protection from Portuguese to escape Mane invaders, 179
Sapo (ethnic group)
    distinction among powers of masquerades, 74
    lived inland from Kru Coast and controlled trade with interior, 208
    name originally applied to a cluster of seven Wee clans, 17
    some ancestors originated near Nyaya, Côte d'Ivoire, 204
    speak dialect of Wee language, 197
    split from Krahn and Glebo, 205
sassywood
    compared to weighing of the heart in Ancient Egyptian religion, 97
savannah agriculture
    one type of vegetation important to local economies, 226
scarification
    marker in life cycle, 80
    worn by men and women south of River Cess, 251
    worn on arms, legs and middle by River Cess women, 251
Schröder, Gunther and Hans Dieter Seiber (German anthropologists)
    tentatively date split of Sapo from Krahn and Glebo to 1650-1680 AD, 205
Schwartz, Alfred (French sociologist)
    Eastern Krahn and Glebo caused by Akan expansion, 205
science
    African religion not hostile to, 85
    previously linked to magic in Western societies, 85
seafood
    important protein source throughout the world, 298
sea-water oath
    sworn along Malagueta Coast east of Junk River, 249
segmentary lineage system
    common among Kissi, Gola and Kru-speaking groups, 209
    settlement based on all-encompassing genealogy, 209
Seimavileh
    brother of Fala Wubo, 148
    reported founder of Malinké community in Wonnegoma, 148
Seligman, Charles E. (British ethnologist)
    advanced "new" Hamitic myth, 9
semi-deciduous
    forest trees that shed leaves annually, 49
Senufo (ethnic group)
    previously lived near Kpelle, 149
    pushed north away from Kpelle by Kone invaders, 178

Serres (also S'eterna)
   town along Malagueta Coast in late 1600s, 249
Sestra Kru (also Cetra-Crue, Sestra Kroo and Settre Crou), 254
   described at larger than Elmina in early 1700s, 245
   inhabitants described as "honest", 301
   one of five towns reportedly founded by seafarers from the Gold Coast, 208
   provisions scarce in 1727 except for malagueta and pineapples, 254
   residents described as honest, 245
   town along Malagueta Coast in late 1600s, 249
Sestros
   "tender care" of mothers for infants, 301
   focal point of initial English traders, 221
   residents described as having "much human feeling", 301
   sea-going described as specialized activity in late 1600s, 249
   use of "a little" Dutch and English by some residents, 317
   women wore cloth tied around "their loin", 227
Sestros River
   entrance measured by William Smith for Royal African Company, 254
   location popular with early European visitors due to available trade goods, 167
   village near mouth, 250
Seth
   source of evil in Ancient Egyptian religion, 96
Settra Kru (ethnic group)
   origin stories, 47
Seuart, Charles
   white Virginian who brought enslaved James Sommerset to England, 282
sexual mores
   "adultery" justified sale as slave, 262
   allusion to prostitution at Cape Mesurado, 242
   allusion to prostitution at Cape Mount, 241
   Barsaw reportedly had 30 wives, 251
   Cape Mesurado ruler reportedly offered his daughter as sexual partner to visiting Frenchman, 231
   Cape Mesurado standard as interpreted by French visitor, 231
   Cape Mesurado women charaterized by Jean Barbot as sexually pliant, 271
   Cape Mount ruler said to have 400 wives, 241
   erotic dancing frowned on by Islam, 126
   gender segregation not strictly enforced in Sahel in 1351 AD, 127
   phallic and fertility symbols in art frowned on by Islam, 126
   polygyny at Cape Mount noted by William Bosman, 242
   polygyny at River Cess in late 1600s, 251
   prostitution allowed in Genoa, 302
   sailors notorious for seeking partners in various ports, 301
   Sanguin ruler reportedly had 50 wives and his brother 15, 234
   sex workers regulated in Spain, 302
   William Bosman claimed husbands at Cape Mount not concerned if wives slept with other men, 242
   William Bosman commented repeatedly on sexual proclivities of local women, 240
   Windward Coast women described as promiscuous by Europeans, 301
sharif
   Arabic word meaning "noble", 170
sharp angles
   associated in art with maleness, 85
Sharp, Granville
   English abolitionist leader, 282
Shaw, Thurston (Archeologist)
   Ancient Egyptian way of life rooted in early African customs and ideas, 95
Shere
   alternative name for Kamara clan, 181
shipbuilding

Index 399

    advantages of Europe over other regions, 303
    engine of growth in Europe, 304
Shirley
    local trader at St. Paul River, 317
shops
    single-purpose businesses operated by middlemen between all kinds of sellers and buyers, 306
    some operated by artisans out of their workshops, 306
    the seeds of capitalism, 306
shrine at Sestros
    described by Jean Barbot in late 1600s, 251
sickle-cell
    immunity to malaria, 49
sickle-cell anemia
    genetic malformation that causes illness and death, 49
sickle-cell frequencies,
    unequal distribution across ethnic groups in Liberia, 210
Siglipo (meaning "pass through town")
    among earliest Klao towns, 207
    original name for Grand Cess, 207
Sijilmasa
    northern-most town in Mali empire, 132
Sikasso, Mali
    location where Loma ancestors reportedly originated, 148
Sikon (ethnic group)
    current home previously occupied by Bassa, 206
silk-cotton trees (Ceiba pentandra)
    used in canoe production, 58, 226
silver
    plentiful in early South Africa, 165
    used as currency, 119
Simandou Mountain
    alternative homeland of Kpelle in oral tradition, 147
Sino (also Sinoe)

    town along Malagueta Coast in late 1600s, 249
Skinner, Samuel
    African slave trader on Banana Island, 278
slave hunters
    not condemned or punished because their victims were seized from outside their ethnic group, 262
    preying upon speakers of same language, 262
slave rebellions
    aboard Duke of Argyle, 278
    aboard French vessel at Sherbro, 278
    along the Windward Coast, 280
slave ships
    ratio of crew to slaves, 277
slave trade
    13 embarkation points on Liberian territory, 269
    Arab overlords required delivery of Nubian slaves for five centuries, 118
    Bassa and Cape Mount main sources along Liberia coast, 271
    Britain main exporter from Windward Coast, 271
    Britain turned to Windward Coast after 1750 AD, 271
    British naval records on Windward ships, 275
    brought weapons and horses from Arabia, 169
    Cape Mount supplied highest numbers from Liberia region, 270
    customary law allowed men to be sold if accused of adultery by rich men's wives, 324
    deepened divisions between communities, 324
    demand fueled by Europe's need for labor to work New World lands, 266
    diminished Windward Coast's rice-growing, 272
    disadvantaged low status individuals and land-locked ethnic groups, 324
    disrupted routines of everyday life, 323
    Dutch kidnapped 12 people from Kru Cess in mid-1600s, 234
    Dutch Middelburgse Company along Windward

Coast, 269

Dutch significantly escalated African slave trade, 240

England as exclusive supplier of slaves to Spanish America, 246

English adventurers reportedly plundered and kidnapped at Cape Mesurado in early 1700s, 242

English interest in West African trade fueled after 1650 by need for Caribbean plantation slaves, 265

enriched already powerful groups like Asante, 324

expansion of kidnapping in Mali Empire around 1450 AD, 169

exports from Cape Mount and Cape Mesurado grew as pressure increased on former major slave marts, 284

forced development of villages as defensive outposts, 323

France second-ranked exporter from Windward Coast, 271

fueled generalized suspicion among West Africans of each other, 323

fueled local adoption of rum, tobacco and Western arms, 323

Genoa as key Mediterranean mart, 218

Gola ruler reportedly sold entire Sande society class of girls, 324

greatly expanded in West Africa due to Arab invasion, 118

Holland removed more slaves from Windward Coast than any region, 271

Holland third-ranked exporter from Windward Coast, 271

Holland turned to Windward Coast after 1740, 271

kidnappers preyed upon Gola, Mende, Bandi, Loma, Kpelle, Ma and Dan, 324

Kru-language speakers as a quarter of all enslaved Africans to Guyana and Surinam, 275

liquor, guns, gunpowder and gunshots as major commodities, 273

local captives exchanged for large quantities of rum, 322

many Mende taken to Jamaica, 324

Portuguese enslaved many Sape to whom they had offered "protection", 179

preference for Windward slaves in South Carolina, Georgia, and Surinam, 272

role of leading Rhode Island businessmen, 283

Sahelian empires profited from forest region captives, 151

Sahelian sellers shared fealty to Islam with Arab buyers, 261

spurred violent rival claims to political offices, 324

traffic to Arabia continued as Atlantic traffick declined, 284

United States fourth ranked exporter from Windward Coast, 271

widened the gap between free and unfree persons, 324

William Bosman asked about local wars along Liberian coast to assess prospect of slaves, 240

slavery

expanded in West Africa after Arab invasion, 118

France restored eight years after original abolition, 284

fueled England's rise, 247

original justifications for, 118

presented by Western authorities as punishment for sin, 160

recommended by Western authorities for religious conversion of infidels and pagans, 160

slaves

burials with rulers abolished in ancient Egypt and Sahel but persisted among Vai, 146

initially viewed as luxury possessions locally, 262

motivating factor for early Portuguese

Index

explorations, 164
obtained through kidnapping, 262
one option for brideprice, 262
originally sacrificed at death of owners, 262
promised to French visitor by leading men at Cape Mesurado, 232
some sold by their own rulers, 262
their seizure approved by system of one-sided justice, 262

Smeathman, Henry
English botanist who suggested Sierra Leone as resettlement site for London's poor blacks, 282

Smith, Robert (historian)
canoes in West Africa, 57

Smith, William
credited Cape Mount residents with being industrious for wearing locally made clothes, 253
described Cape Mount residents as "timorous" due to recent kidnappings by Europeans, 253
described pineapples at "Cetra-Crue" as "most delicious Fruit in the whole World", 254
described Sestros River residents as "courteous" but "shy" to the English, 254
did not venture onshore at Cape Mesurado, 253
did not venture onshore at Cape Mount, 253
English surveyor sent by Royal African Company to take measurements in West Africa, 253
his book included large section copied from William Bosman, 253
his ship was not visited by Junk River residents perhaps due to recent kidnappings by Europeans, 254
measured entrance of Sestros River, 254
took soundings and bearings at Junk River, 254
visited "Cetra-Crue", 254

smoked herring
imported from Europe in dried and salted form, 321
introduced to West Africa by European sailors, 321
now entrenched in local diets, 321

Snake Society
evidence of society in crisis, 80

social system
West Africa as example of, 139

Sociéte Africaine de Culture
its contribution to the decolonization of African history, 14

sociopaths
exposed and punished in African religion as agents of moral and social decay, 87
same personality traits as so-called "witches", 87

Sogila or Soila
Bassa name for Cape Montserrado, meaning "cat mountain", 207

Sommerset, James
victorious plaintiff in major antislavery case, 280

sonangui
incursions more militaristic and desparate than earlier Dyula migrations, 178
incursions overturned life along forest belt, 178
incursions violated customary landlord/stranger relationship, 178
Malinké "warrior bands" who fought their way into forest region, 178

Songhai empire
destroyed by Moroccan invasion, 171
emerged as separate state in 1430s, 169
former province of Mali empire, 169
Muslim rulers unleashed holy war against non-Muslim neighbors, 171
seized trade from Mali, 177

Soninké (also Wagadu)
ethnic group at heart of Ghana empire, 128

sorghum
used as currency, 119

Soso (ethnic group)
close historical affinity to Bandi, Loko and

Mende, 142
  defeat of Mane in three-day battle, 180
  military leaders on short Fula horses, 180
  northern Mande speakers who initially resisted Islam, 120
  ruler's reported speech to troops before Mane attack, 180
  subjugated unit of Mali empire, 131
  traders cited by Europeans as regular visitors to Freetown, 168
  trap set for Mane invaders, 180
  with Jalonke, as center of longstanding polity, 130
souks
  narrow streets of North African cities lined with shops, 306
South Asia
  buildings made of mud, bamboo, thatch and wood, 300
South Carolina
  economically dependent on rice exports after 1761, 272
  preference for Windward slaves, 272
southeast Mande groups
  arrival around Nzerekore after 1235 AD, 179
  confined to forest rim before 1651 AD, 195
  language once labeled as part of Mande-fu, 3
  their southward migrations converged around Nzerekore, Giunea, 141
Southwest Asia
  more advanced than Europe around 4000 BC, 292
southwest Mande groups
  confined to forest rim before 1651 AD, 195
  ethnic names and dialect names based on where each settled, 146
  language formerly labeled as part of Mande-fu, 3
  main split in language family between Kpelle and all others, 146
  major split between Loma and Kpelle, on the one hand, and Bandi, Loko and Mende, on the other, 142
  pushed from Kissidugu by Malinké, then splintered into Bandi, Loko and Mende, 197
  their migrations in line with trade route from Niger to Musadu, 141
southwestern current
  strong continuous flow of Atlantic Ocean off Liberian coast, 58
Souweraboe (also Sabrebou)
  town along Malagueta Coast in late 1600s, 249
Spain
  early enslavement of West Africans, 166
  gold extracted from Caribbean using forced labor, 218
  initially abandoned West African trade to its European rivals, 259
  most homes made of mud or bricks, 300
  plundered 1,000 years of gold accumulations from Caribbean within three years, 218
  plundered treasures from Inca empire in Peru, 219
  renewed interest in West Africa as source of slaves for New World, 260
  rivers of wealth from metals in the Americas, 219
Spanish
  dominant language of Latin America, 124
spice trade
  included sugar, medicines, dyes and salt, 219
Spider the trickster, xxvii
squash
  New World crop adopted by West Africans, 321
St. Anthony
  early Christian from Egypt who isolated himself in the Sahara, 107
St. Augustine (354-430 AD)
  Algerian Berber whose ideas shaped early Christianity, 107
St. John's River
  name given by Portuguese, 161
  route traveled by Gbo, Kweon and some Sapo, 204

St. Paul's River
  name given by Portuguese, 161
  presence of local traders named Philips and Shirley in late 1600s, 317
starchy food
  corn predominated in New World and later in Southern and East Africa, 296
  most people lived off one until late 1800s, 296
  rice predominated in China, India and West Africa, 296
  wheat predominated in Europe and North Africa, 296
steelmaking
  secret first unravelled by Europeans in 1800s, 309
stone buildings
  initially reserved for palaces, fortresses and shrines in Asia, 300
stone sculptures
  designs similar to current Kissi wood carvings, 62
  feature filed front teeth, plaited hair and scarification, 62
  presence as evidence of early local iron-working tradition, 62
  probably locally carved given fabrication from heavy materials, 62
  said to embody Temne aesthetic, 62
  similar traditions existed among Esie and Ekos of Nigeria, 62
strangers
  expected to show respect for local traditions, 116
  rules of engagement with established communities, 52
strips of cloth
  used as currency, 119
succession fights
  produced massive and permanent relocations, unlike trading diasporas, 141
  spurred migrations from Sahelian empires, 139
  within "royal" families and military officers of Sahelian empires, 139
Südan
  word for black Africa applied by Arabs, 109
Sufism
  mystical branch of Islam, 171
sugar
  production as engine of growth in Europe, 304
  sent raw to Europe for refinement, 247
  used as currency in New World, 305
sugar cane
  expansion of large plantations from Lebanon throughout Mediterranean, 118
  expansion of plantations funded by Genoa merchants, 118
  intensive labor requirement, 118
  lost flavor soon after harvest, 260
  use of three-roller vertical press, 260
  worldwide expansion from New Guinea, 118
sugar cane production
  boiling process, 261
  boiling yielded brown sugar, molasses and rum, 261
  dangers of process, 260
  introduced to Barbados in 1637 AD, 260
  labor demands and conditions, 260
  spread to Brazil around 1580 AD, 260
sugar-cane plantation complex
  incubated on Atlantic islands of West Africa before being transferred to New World, 260
Sulayman
  Mansa of Mali whose death in 1360 created a vacuum, 177
Sumaoro
  his loyalists possible ancestors of Bandi, Loko, Mende and Soso, 142
  portrayed as a sorcerer and oppressor in epics glorifying Sundiata, 131
  Soso leader who opposed Islam and growing trade in enslaved Africans, 130
  supported by blacksmiths, 130

Sumba (or Kumba)
    foot soldiers of Mane invaders, 181
Sundiata
    suppressed blacksmiths for having supported Sumaoro, 131
    united Malinké against the Soso kingdom, 130
Surinam
    preference for Windward slaves, 272
Susu
    political unit of Soso/Jalonke, 130
Suwari, Al-Hajj Salim (Soniké cleric)
    encouraged peaceful co-existence of Muslims among non-Muslims, 189
swamp rice
    greater number of harvests, 60
sweet potato
    adopted in China and Japan during famine of 1500s, 321
    New World crop adopted by West Africans, 321
Taabli ("Taa's town")
    original Dei name of Bopolu, 60
table manners
    along the Windward Coast, 301
Taghaza
    salt-mining town in Mali empire and key stop on trade route, 132
    town in Mali empire with mosque built from salt, 132
Taodenni salt mines, 121
tea
    15 million pounds exported to Europe from Canton by 1710 AD, 323
    Asian drink adopted by European and exported worldwide, 322
    enjoyed in China since 600 BC, 323
    first major shipment to Europe in 1610 AD, 323
Teage, Hilary (author of Liberia's Declaration of Independence)
    his Africanist perspective, 13
Tengella
    established Fula control of Futa Jallon, 177
Tertullian (160-c. 220 AD)
    Tunisian Berber who contributed central ideas to early Christianity, 107
textile
    engine of growth in Europe, 304
thaba (meaning "ruler")
    name of officeholder written variously as "Faramborey," "Faran Bure," "Frambore," "Flabourre," and "Falam Bûrre", 224
The Thousand and One Nights
    Persian text with negative stories about black slaves, 110
theobromine
    psychoactive substance in chocolate, 323
Thomas, Hugh (historian)
    five times as many Africans as whites went to New World from 1492 to 1820 AD, 266
thumb piano
    invented in southern Africa, 32
Timbuktu
    commercial center and internationally renown seat of Islamic learning, 131
    position on Niger River, 121
    town established by Sanhaja Berbers that was taken by Mali, 131
time
    also measured by recurring tasks, such as market day and harvest time, 88
    conceived similarly in Ancient Egyptian and early West African cultures, 101
    measured by such natural markers as days, moons (months) and seasons, 88
    slowed or arrested during rituals, 88
    West African view of, 87
tobacco
    adopted along Windward Coast by 1678, 323
    even more successful worldwide than coffee and tea due to addictive quality, 323
    local use fueled importation of cheap European pipes, 323
    New World plant adopted by Europeans and

Index 405

    exported worldwide, 322
    plantations established by Europeans by late 1500s, 323
    spread wordwide by European sailors and others who had lived in New World, 323
    used as currency in New World, 305

Tohoma Téa clan
    led Kpelle migration from Beyla to forest region, 147

tomatoes
    New World crop adopted by West Africans, 321

tools
    common to all regions were knives, axes and spades, 292

Toure, Askiya Mohammed (also Mohamed Torodo)
    devote Muslim who undertook expensive pilgrimage to Mecca, 170
    governor of Hombori province who seized control of Songhai empire, 169

Towerson, William
    described Sestros residents as carving "ingenious things", 224
    described Sestros town as consisting of 20 small "hovels", 224
    English captain of two ships that visited River Sestros, 224
    recorded local vocabulary at Sestros, 224

trade
    adverse impact of ocean shore along Windward Coast, 268
    balance shifted definitively in favor of Europeans over Africans in 1800s, 309
    bred inequality, 151
    by canoe from Cape Mesurado to Sestro, 302
    Cape Mount, Cape Mesurado and Sestros River popular with early European visitors due to available trade goods, 167
    coastal access to trans-Atlantic goods reportedly drew Kpelle into Liberia, 201
    control at wholesale level in West Africa shifted from Phoenicians, to Arabs, to Europeans, to transnational corporations, 309
    daily traffic of canoes to River Cess, 243
    daily traffic of trading canoes between Cape Mesurado and River Cess, 243
    disadvantages of, 151
    dominated in West Africa by Mande-speakers, 120
    Florence, Genoa and Venice as later competitors to Middle Eastern network, 217
    focus in Sahel shifted from exotic goods to essentials, 152
    focus of early European writings on West Africa, 167
    forest-belt centers targeted by Mali Empire refugees, 178
    former rulers of Mali sought control of trans-Atlantic, 191
    fueled rise of Sahelian empires, 118
    Genoa network ran from Egypt to England, 218
    grasp for control of coastal a goal of Mane invaders, 180
    kola from Kru-speakers and southwest Mande groups, 196
    laid basis for new hierarchical order, 122
    linked to Kru migration, 54
    malagueta spice from Liberia region to Niger River, 115
    Portugal's loss of West African posts by 1640 AD, 219
    revival of gold caravan from West Africa to North Africa, 166
    rice a key export item at Cape Mesurado in mid-1600s, 231
    Sahel profited both on goods bought from and sold to forest region, 151
    Sahelian empires controlled mining but left trading to merchants, 119
    salt from Kru-speakers and southwest Mande groups, 196

salt from Liberia region to Niger River, 115
salt shortage in Sahel region as basis for, 56
Sapo controlled between Kru Coast and interior, 208
seized from Mali by Morocco, 177
seized from Mali by Portugal, 177
shattered social equality rooted in farming, 122
West Africa with distant markets, 115
trade network
  between Kru-speakers and Southeastern Mande groups, 115
  brought cowry shells from Indian Ocean, 117
  brought implements of war, 117
  brought luxury items, 117
  brought supplemental foods from Indian Ocean area, 117
  exported ivory, gold and slaves from West Africa, 117
trade profits
  up to seven times investments, 116
trade routes
  along the Atlantic to mouths of rivers, 115
  followed by Mali Empire refugees into forest, 178
  from Kankan to Musadu to Bopolu to Cape Mount, 141
  from Kwakwa to Algeria, 115
  from Lake Chad to Libya, 115
  from mouth of St. Paul's River through Bopolu to the Niger, 115
  from Niger through Kankan to Sierra Leone peninsula, 141
  from Senegal to Morocco, 115
  from the Niger through Cairo to Mecca, 115
  helped form the Liberian people, 178
  points of intersection, 121
traders
  Africans at historical disadvantage to non-Africans, 309
  beneficiaries of hospitality shown to "strangers", 116
  itenerant, 115

operated at level of markets in Africa, 309
operated at level of networks in many regions outside Africa, 309
used ethnicity against outside competitors, 124
trading methods
  comparative analysis, 305
trans-Atlantic slave trade
  factors influencing number of persons exported, 267
  geometric growth over time, 267
  top nine supplying regions, 267
trans-Atlantic trade
  fostered discriminating tastes among local people, 304
  led local societies to impose protectioinist measures against each other, 304
  preferred commodities along Windward Coast, 304
  woven into local economies, 305
  wrought significant cultural changes, 305
transporation
  riding animals confined to the rich, 302
transportation
  by camels in the Sahara, 116
  by canoe along Malagueta Coast, 302
  by canoe fleet between River Cess and Sanguin, 233
  by donkeys in the savannah, 116
  by foot in most parts of the world, 302
  by porters in the forest belt, 116
  comparative analysis, 302
Traore, Bako Massa
  reputed founder of Loma, 148
Traore, Tiramakhan
  Malinké warrior who established political unit near Gambia River, 190
tree bark
  used for clothing east of River Cess, 227
tribe
  concept ill-fitted to pre-Liberian realities, 184
  term used by early Europeans to inaccurately

Index

compare African systems of government to what existed among the people of ancient Rome, 19
tributary state
  rise along the Niger River, 124
  variety of forms in various regions, 124
tribute-taking
  source of tensions within Sahelian empires, 139
tsetse flies, 336
  inhibited animal husbandry in forest belt, 297
  inhibited the keeping of livestock, 16
  inhibited the reliance on animals in forest belt, 295
  retreat southward allowed Maninké horsemen to raid forest communities, 191
  vector for spread of African sleeping sickness, 49
Tuareg
  Afrasiatic language of the Sahara, 36
Tuareg (ethnic group)
  as "lost tribe of Israel", 105
  blocked trade routes and Timbuktu from Mali, 177
  seized Timbuktu and other principal towns of Mali, 177
Tubwegh
  early Klao town established west of Siglipo, 207
Tucker, Henry
  African slave trader on Banana Island, 278
Tuglo
  among earliest Klao towns, 207
Tuman, Dankaran (c. 1200-1235 AD)
  contender for Mali leadership who fled south after defeat, 130
  his loyalists as possible ancestors of Loma, 142
  older brother and rival of Sundiata, ruler of Mali empire, 130
  portrayed as a coward in epics glorifying Sundiata, 130
Twe, Dihdwo (Liberian opposition leader), xxvii
Tworluazzasu
  town in Guinea reportedly abandoned by Loma, 201
Ugbéme/Wubomai
  district dominated by Loma Koivoguis clan, 202
unit of value
  used to estimate value of common commodities, 305
United Provinces
  seven tiny Dutch states that became Holland, 239
United States
  fourth ranked exporter of slaves from Windward Coast, 271
Upcountry Mende
  cited in Quoia text as located north of Hondo, 185
Vabalahuu
  town previously held by Bandi, 199
Vai (ethnic group), xxviii
  ancestors probably followed pre-existing route of salt trade from Sahel to coast, 141
  ancestors reportedly migrated to coast in search of salt, 145
  centuries of contact between their ancestors and Arabs, 185
  clothing style, 185
  conquered by Karou and Folgia, 183
  first Mande group in western Liberia, 143
  first migration from Sahel likely around 1077 AD, 146
  gave protection to Gola fleeing fighting in homeland, 201
  high sickle-cell frequency, 210
  language contains archaic forms of Dyula, 143
  Massaquoi family as founding lineage in Sierra Leone, 145
  one oral tradition claims descent from expelled son of Malinké ruler, 144
  one oral tradition claims descent from Kamara family, 144

one oral tradition traces descent to Sumanguro, 143
one oral tradition traces origin to Malian expedition, 144
oral traditions cite Dei and Vai as earliest neighbors, 143
oral traditions cite intermarriage with Gola and Dei, 143
oral traditions cite men as group's founders, 143
oral traditions effaced women, 144
oral traditions emphasize heroic roles of soldiers and ruler, 144
oral traditions say their ancestors were drawn to coast by salt trade, 143
oral traditions seem contradictory, 143
outgrowth of migration south from Sahel, 141
persistence of slave burials with rulers, 146
probable outgrowth of Dyula immigrants, 143
proposed for study at Liberia College by Edward W. Blyden, 16
proximity to coast suggest early departure from Sahel, 141
reputedly derived from phrase meaning "those who forged ahead", 144
residents of Quoia country, 185
some oral traditions cite non-Dyula origins, 143
supported cotton weaving and auxiliary activities, 227
various oral traditions probably refer to different events, 144
various origin stories not mutually exclusive, 144

Vai language
as "mother tongue" of local women would have survived invasion by male outsiders, 185
closely related to Kono, 188
common first names among Windward slaves, 276
example of loan word from Portuguese, 318
influence of Arabic, 185

Vanja-Vanja
buried in the Dowo Mountains, 280
Gola antislavery hero, 280

vegetation
three types important to local economies, 225

Venice
decline of, 218
early cradle of capitalism, 217
later competitor to Middle Eastern trade network, 217
merchants created trading posts along route to Middle East, 217
one of Europe's busiest ports until 1600s, 218
rise linked to Crusades, 217

villages
traditional arrangement in Niger-Congo cultures, 50

Villault, Nicholas de Bellefond
arrival at Cape Mesurado, 231
author of A Relation of the Coasts of Africk called Guinee, 227
claimed Cape Mount residents made bread from corn in mid-1600s, 230
claimed everyone he met along Windward Coast bore a European name, 317
claimed French sailors reached West Africa before Portuguese, 228
claimed River Cess people preferred the French over other Europeans, 233
commented on "nakedness" of local people, 217, 227
comptroller on French ship to Windward Coast, 227
described Cape Mount ruler Falam Boure, 228
described relative nakedness of Cape Mount people, 230
described salt-making village near Cape Mount, 228
false claim regarding origin of "Mesurado", 231
his informant's explanation of why European names were so common on Windward Coast, 317
laced his book with French propaganda, 228

Index

landed at Cape Mesurado in canoe fortified with canon, 231
reportedly told by Cape Mount resident that whites pray to God and blacks pray to the Devil, 230
said blacksmiths at Sanguin "work excellent well in Iron", 234
sent to secretly check prospects for French trading in West Africa, 227
spent two days bartering for ivory at Cape Mount, 228

vivax malaria
mosquito-borne illness, 49

Volney (1757-1820), Count Constantin de (French orientalist),
countered racist assumptions about Africans, 12

Voltaire (Western Enlightenment leader)
racist ideas of, 8

Vos, Jelmer (historian)
Dutch slave trading on Windward Coast, 271

Vrijman, Jan
local man at Grand Bassa in 1791, 318

Waaduugbee
January in Gola, meaning "big dew month", 28

Wala
the Creator who (in Ma oral tradition) descended from heaven by a chain, 197

walking
main mode of transportation throughout the world, 302

Wallerstein, Immanuel (sociologist)
Amsterdam's dominance of world economy, 239
England's emergence as dominant power, 247
English-French rivalry in 1600s, 246
Europe's rise tied to exploitation of peripheral regions, 220
factory system unknown in Europe up to 1700, 309
role of European states in transition to capitalism, 220

Wappo
equal in size to Elmina, according to Jean Barbot, 249
geographic features, 249

Wappo (or Wappen)
geographic features, 245
town along Malagueta Coast in late 1600s, 249

war
helped spread famines and illneses, 295

war captives
myth that they supplied most New World slaves, 275

war towns
barracaded settlements spurred by slave trade, 323

Wari
Nigerian town that grew into city-state based on profits from slave trade, 167

water
fetched daily from great distances throughout the world, 302

water pipes
installed in a few cities in Turkey, Italy and Portugal, 302

watermelon
African crop adopted by people in the Americas, 321

watermills
equivalent to energy of ten men, 296
more popular in Europe after 1500s, 296
powered by running river or stream, 296
use as energy source, 296
used to turn a saw or grind grain, 296

waterways
Europeans went from being limited by to mastery of, 163

wavy-line pottery
found near Kamabai, Sierra Leone, 45
linked to aquatic culture in flooded West African savannah, 33

way of the ancestors
    also "African traditional religion", 71
    characterized by polarities, 72
    conceptualization of immaterial parts of a person, 74
    equivalent of "religion" in West Afrian cultures, 71
    ethnicity and religion viewed as inseparable, 170
    immaterial aspect of persons viewed as their "double", 74
    lacked firm distinction between physical and spiritual realms, 71
    preservation of life as highest goal, 73
    religious faithfulness measured by behavior and ritual observance, 170
    theories of the world's creation, 72
wealth
    replaced seniority as basis of authority and respect in trading societies, 152
weavers
    itenerant, 115
Wee (ethnic group), 17
    divided into subgroups in process of moving southward, 197
    emcompasses Krahn and Sapo, 17
    fusion of Gbo, Kweon and some Sapo, 204
    one language shared by Sapo, Kran, Guéré and Wobé, 197
    proportedly living in area when Ma ancestors arrived, 148
    some ancestors originated near Nyaya, Côte d'Ivoire, 204
West Africa
    arrival of Europeans shifted locus of trade and power from Sahel to coast, 168
    commoners initially had greater access to land and more control over their own labor than commoners elsewhere, 308
    distinct from other regions due to abundance of land, 293
    early trade with distant markets, 115
    economies linked to Arabia, 305
    interior remained a mystery to Europeans until 1859, 285
    loser in unfair trade with Sahel, 151
    visited regularly by traders from the Middle East, southern Europe and Asia, 102
    weak system for moving goods as block on growth, 308
West African interior
    unknown to early European writers, 167
Western libertarianism
    sought liberty for whites while justifying oppression of non-whites, 263
Weybhalaga
    district settled by Guilavogui and Zumanigui clans, 202
wheat
    encouraged collaboration of herders and farmers, 296
    required lots of animal manure, 296
    usually grown along with supplemental grains, 297
    yield low compared to other grains, 297
white
    ritually significant color in African religion, 76
white bread
    reserved for the rich in Europe, 297
Whiteman's Hut
    guest house near Sestros River, 250
Whonsava Mountains
    landmark during Loma migration, 201
wicker baskets
    also "kroo", 304
    entrenched as unit of measure along Malagueta Coast, 304
wild game
    major source of meat in in Japan, China and forest belt West Africa, 297
Wilks, Ivor (historian)
    credits Al-Hajj Salim Suwari with "praxis of co-existence", 190

dates Dyula communities in Gold Coast to early
1400s, 190
estimate of labor required for clearing forest
land, 49
Will, John
local man near St. Paul River, 318
Williams, Peter
Cape Mount ruler in early 1750s, 318
wind
conditions over Atlantic Ocean near Liberia, 58
Windward Coast
"disadvantaged" as supplier of trans-Atlantic
slaves, 268
characteristics of rivers and shoreline, 268
civility of inhabitants, 301
clothes reflected social status, 298
clothes relatively skimpy compared to
Europeans, 298
definition, 267
embarkation points in Liberia, 269
few extant despriptions of dwellings, 300
integrated into the trans-Atlantic trade, 304
label originally applied by the English Royal
African Company, 267
lack of natural habors inhibited ship traffic, 304
many rulers and leading traders bore European
names, 317
many rulers and leading traders spoke a
smattering of European languages, 317
method of roasting meat, 301
most slaves to U. S. went to South Carolina, 272
most slaves went to Caribbean, 272
percentage of slaves sent from each sub-region,
269
preferred trade commodities, 304
provisioning area for slave ships, 269
relatively few studies of slave trade, 268
residents said to be "fond of what comes from
abroad" by 1727, 325
shifted from rice producing to food shortages

due to slave trade, 272
slave trade declined after Dutch withdrawal in
1800, 284
supplied 40 percent of slaves to Dutch New
World colonies, 271
supplied 70 percent of slaves removed by Dutch
free traders, 271
table manners, 301
underpopulated, 270
unusual cast of slave trade, 268
women described by Europeans as sexually
promiscuous, 301
Windward slaves
common first names, 276
wine
common to southern Europe prior to 1700s, 322
once transported mainly in wooden barrels, 322
widely exported for the first time in 1700s, 322
wisdom
encoded in visual symbols, poetry and proverbs,
84
Wise, Steven M. (American legal historian)
account of James Somerset's case, 282
witches
applied negatively to African traditional religion,
16
hunt for fueled rips in social fabric, 262
hunt for used to justify enslavement, 262
nebulous standards for conviction, 262
Wobe (ethnic group)
also called "Northern Wee" by linguists, 197
Woko Soroqui
cited as founder of Loma town called Wotoumé,
148
Wolf, Eric (American athropologist)
explanation of kinship, 52
Wolof (ethnic group)
high regard for blacksmiths, even among
Muslims, 82
linked to fishing at mouth of the Senegal River,

57
    seized western trade from Mali, 177
    split from Fula, 46
Wolof language, 34
women
    described by Europeans as sexually promiscuous along the Windward Coast, 301
    exchange of as major source of tension between Muslim "strangers" and non-Muslim hosts, 171
    lingering power in patrilineal regimes of West Africa, 122
    main traders in West Africa, especially wives of artisans, 306
    outnumbered male slaves from Windward Coast, 275
    roles of different in early West Africa from traditional Western societies, 52
    rules in early societies for exchange of, 51
    those from land-owning lineages envisioned in African religion as repositories of life-force, 73
Woniguimai
    one of first Loma towns in Liberia, 201
    originally a Loma town, 202
wood
    as energy source for cooking, building and smelting metals, 296
    as energy source in Europe, 296
    main building material in many regions, including Europe, 300
work
    rules for allocation in early societies, 51
workshops
    comparative analysis, 303
    family type common throughout West Africa, 303
    multifamily type probably produced iron, salt, mats, soap, canoes and cloth in West Africa, 303
    various forms, 303
Wotoumé
    Loma residents claim descent from Malinké of Mani, 148
woven baskets
    sugar-loaf shaped and used for carrying commodities, 249
Wright, Donald R. (American historian)
    fluidity of ethnic identity, 54
writing
    extended capacity of Sahelian empires, 125
Wu-bandi
    Limba name for Loko, 146, 198
Wubo, Fala
    founder of Wubomai in Lofa County, 201
    reportedly joined Poro, 148
    reputed founder of Wubomai clan of Loma, 148
Wubomai (Loma clan)
    claim to be a mixture of Malinké and Kissi, 148
Wubormai
    one of first Loma towns in Liberia, 201
Wulorballah
    one of first Loma towns in Liberia, 201
xylophone
    adopted in Sahel during reign of Sumaoro Kanté, 129
    spread to Africa from Southeast Asia, 32
Yacouba
    label applied to Kpelle, Ma and Dan by Malinké, 17
    meaning "kola traders", 17
Yagbara, Mahou
    ancestor of Ma who migrated into Liberia, 203
    Ma emigré from Côte d'Ivoire who settled among Kpelle, 203
Yala
    district dominated by Loma Koivoguis clan, 202
yams, 39
    Afrian crop adopted by people in the Americas, 321
    among foodstuff at Sestros, 253
    example of forest-margin crop important to local diets, 226

Index

in short supply at Cape Mount in early 1700s, 241

linked to Kwa speakers, 35

staple of local diets, 226

used to make porridge for children at Sestros, 253

yams (genus Dioscorea), 39

Yasin, Abd Allah b. (d. 1059)

Moroccan founder of Almoravids, a movement to purify Islam, 125

yellow fever

decimation of Native Americans, 295

Yellow Will

African slave trader on Banana Island, 278

local man between Grand Bassa and Tabocaney, 318

Yoruba

example of dominant language, 124

Yusumoundu

town in Guinea reportedly abandoned by Loma, 201

Zie

legendary founding father of Dei ethnic group, 59

Zie-ma

Loma dialect whose name means "on the water", 146

Zieyema

one of first Loma towns in Liberia, 201

Zigida

one of first Loma towns in Liberia, 201

zig-zag pattern

symbolic meaning of, 85

Zoho, Missa Coma

leader of Kpelle migration from Missadougou to Liberia, 201

reportedly initiated others into Poro before he was initiated, 201

Zougoussogoli

Dan leader of Gou clan who settled among Kpelle, 179

Zuesse, Evan M. (Australian comparative religion scholar), 73

Zumanigui

a leading Loma clan, 202

Made in the USA
San Bernardino, CA
15 January 2020